CONTENTS

Maps

ON THE ROAD WITH FODOR'S

When I plan a vacation, the first thing I do is cast around among my friends and colleagues to find someone who's just been where I'm going. That's because there's no substitute for a recommendation from a good friend who knows your tastes, your budget, and your circumstances, someone who's just been there. Unfortunately, such friends are few and far between. So it's nice to know that there's *Fodor's New York City.*

In the first place, this book won't stay home when you hit the road. It will accompany you every step of the way, steering you away from wrong turns and wrong choices and never expecting a thing in return. It includes a wonderful, full-color map from Rand McNally, the world's largest commercial mapmaker. Most important of all, it's written and assiduously updated by the kind of people you *would* hit up for travel tips if you knew them. They're as choosy as your pickiest friend, except they've probably seen a lot more of New York City. In these pages, they don't send you chasing down every sight in town but have instead selected the best ones, the ones that are worthy of your time and money. To make it easy for you to put it all together in the time you have, they've created itineraries and neighborhood walks that you can mix and match in a snap. Just tear out the map at the perforation, and join us on the road in the Big Apple.

About Our Writers

Our success in helping to make your trip the best of all possible vacations is a credit to the hard work of our extraordinary writers.

Rebecca Knapp Adams, who worked on the Gold Guide, our Kids' chapter, our Festivals and Seasonal Events guide, and part of the Manhattan Exploring chapter lives in Park Slope, Brooklyn, with her husband, Chris, and their two cats. When she's not out gallivanting in the "other" four boroughs, she's happy to revisit favorite spots in "the best borough of all," Brooklyn.

Nightlife updater **Paula S. Bernstein** is a freelance journalist who writes about film, travel, religion, and anything else for which she'll be paid. She lives in the notorious East Village and stays up much too late much too often.

Barbara Blechman lives, paints, and designs gardens in Manhattan. She has worked in Central Park's Shakespeare Garden and written on gardens and nature for Fodor's *New Zealand* and *South Africa* guides. Our updater for Central Park, Chelsea, and Morningside Heights lives in the Chelsea neighborhood.

Bicycle activist **Hannah Borgeson** did most of her research for the Sports and Exploring chapters on two wheels. She rides mainly in Manhattan, commuting to her job as an editor and leading tours for the environmental group Time's Up! She looks forward to the day when New York City is a car-free paradise.

Our special dance correspondent **Karen Deaver** (☞ Dance with Me! *in* Chapter 8) discovered social dancing after a career as a modern dancer. When not dancing, she teaches, writes about dance, and shops for comfortable shoes.

John J. Donohue's career took off several years ago when he took a job as a messenger at *The New Yorker.* Delivering manuscripts around town gave him an intimate knowledge of the city's streets, which proved invaluable as he updated several of our Manhattan Exploring tours. Today he's a staff member of its Goings On About Town section.

Elizabeth Hawes, who contributed an essay about the city's waterfront renaissance (☞ A New Breeze Is Blowing, Down by the Riverside *in* Chapter 2), is the author of *New York, New York: How the Apartment House Transformed the Life of the City (1869–1930)*. She writes about the arts and culture for the *Nation*, the *New York Times* magazine, *The New Yorker,* and other publications.

Amy McConnell can often be found roaming the lobbies of New York City's world-class hotels in her tireless quest to discover the best of the lot. As Fodor's regular lodging reviewer, she's developed a passion for Frette linens and Gilchrist &

Soames collectible bath amenities. After having stayed in more than 50 hotels in New York City, she concludes that Eloise (of The Plaza fame) had the right idea.

Since moving to New York more than a decade ago, **Margaret Mittelbach** has written about all aspects of the city: animal, vegetable, and mineral. On any given day, you might find her examining the Art Deco interiors of midtown skyscrapers, ogling great blue herons at the Jamaica Bay Wildlife Refuge, or raising the ghost of Boss Tweed at Brooklyn's Green-Wood Cemetery. She is the coauthor of *Wild New York*, an acclaimed guide to the city's wildlife, wild places, and natural history.

From ostrich eggs to dusty books to satin stilettos, shopping updater and Fodor's editor **Jennifer Paull** combs the city for items grand, humble, and just plain bizarre. She has her family to thank for her exasperating consumer profile—half Yankee frugality ("I could get that for $10 in a thrift store in Vermont!"), half devil-may-care extravagance ("But it's Italian!"). If she could bring back one of the city's late, great stores, it would be Books & Company.

Arts writer **Tom Steele** was the founding editor of *TheaterWeek, Opera Monthly, Night and Day,* and *New York Native,* among other publications. He is currently the food editor of *Manhattan Spirit* and *Our Town,* and is writing a cookbook intended to enrage the food police.

Park Sloper **Rob Vickerman** likes New York plenty today, though he laments that it's no match for the days when, as a child, he visited his grandparents in Inwood, where they lived right near the elevated A train. He likes to seek out vestiges of old-time New York, especially in Greenwich Village, which he updated for our Exploring chapter. He has contributed to the *Boston Globe* and has worked on numerous books and articles.

Syndicated travel, food, and wine journalist **J. Walman,** who wrote the Dining chapter, dispenses culinary advice to the 2 million listeners of WEVD-AM, writes regularly for *Chocolatier* and *Troika Magazines,* and is president of Punch In–International Syndicate, an interactive electronic publishing company specializing in travel, restaurants, entertainment, and wine. He prefers to skip breakfast (rather than exercise), take vitamins (instead of giving up martinis), and is married to a beautiful, intelligent woman who shares his enthusiasm for travel, food, and wine—not necessarily in that order.

Editor **Matthew Lore**—culture vulture, foodie, and another devoted Park Sloper—first kept tabs on the latest happenings in New York as a teenager in suburban Essex Fells, New Jersey, from which he escaped to the City as often as possible. Mornings and evenings look for him commuting via bike across the Brooklyn Bridge, his hands-down favorite New York landmark. With his brother, Mark, he is the creator of *Rubberneckers: The Adventure Car Game,* due out in the spring of 1999.

Connections

We're pleased that the American Society of Travel Agents continues to endorse Fodor's as its guidebook of choice. ASTA is the world's largest and most influential travel trade association, operating in more than 170 countries, with 27,000 members pledged to adhere to a strict code of ethics reflecting the Society's motto, "Integrity in Travel." ASTA shares Fodor's devotion to providing smart, honest travel information and advice to travelers, and we've long recommended that our readers—even those who have guidebooks and traveling friends—consult ASTA member agents for the experience and professionalism they bring to your vacation planning.

On Fodor's Web site (www.fodors.com), check out the new Resource Center, an online companion to the Gold Guide section of this book, complete with useful hot links to related sites. In our forums, you can also get lively advice from other travelers and more great tips from Fodor's experts worldwide.

How to Use This Book

Organization

Up front is the **Gold Guide,** an easy-to-use section arranged alphabetically by topic. Under each listing you'll find tips and information that will help you accomplish what you need to in New York City. You'll also find addresses and telephone numbers of organizations and companies that offer destination-related services and detailed information and publications.

The first chapter in the guide, Destination: New York City helps get you in the mood for your trip. What's Where gets you oriented, Pleasures and Pastimes describes the activities and sights that make the Big Apple unique, Great Itineraries lays out a selection of complete trips, Fodor's Choice showcases our top picks, and Festivals and Seasonal Events alerts you to special events you'll want to seek out.

The Exploring Manhattan chapter is divided into neighborhood sections; each recommends a walking tour and lists neighborhood sights alphabetically, including sights that are off the beaten path. Immediately following is a chapter on exploring New York's four other boroughs—Brooklyn, Queens, Staten Island, and the Bronx, and a chapter that highlights best bets for visiting New York with kids. The remaining chapters are arranged in alphabetical order by subject (the arts, dining, lodging, nightlife, outdoor activities and sports, and shopping).

At the end of the book you'll find suggestions for pretrip research, with recommended reading and movies on tape with New York City as a backdrop.

Icons and Symbols

- ★ Our special recommendations
- ✕ Restaurant
- 🏨 Lodging establishment
- 🦆 Good for kids (rubber duck)
- ☞ Sends you to another section of the guide for more information
- ✉ Address
- ☎ Telephone number
- ⏲ Opening and closing times
- 🎟 Admission prices (those we give apply to adults; substantially reduced fees are almost always available for children, students, and senior citizens)

Numbers in white and black circles ③ ❸ that appear on the maps, in the margins, and within the tours correspond to one another.

Credit Cards

The following abbreviations are used: **AE,** American Express; **D,** Discover; **DC,** Diners Club; **MC,** MasterCard; and **V,** Visa.

Don't Forget to Write

You can use this book in the confidence that all prices and opening times are based on information supplied to us at press time; Fodor's cannot accept responsibility for any errors. Time inevitably brings changes, so always confirm information when it matters—especially if you're making a detour to visit a specific place.

Were the restaurants we recommended as described? Did our hotel picks exceed your expectations? Did you find a museum we recommended a waste of time? Keeping a travel guide fresh and up-to-date is a big job, and we welcome your feedback, positive *and* negative. If you have complaints, we'll look into them and revise our entries when the facts warrant it. If you've discovered a special place that we haven't included, we'll pass the information along to our correspondents and have them check it out. So send us your thoughts via e-mail at editors@fodors.com (specifying the name of the book on the subject line) or on paper in care of the New York City editor at Fodor's, 201 East 50th Street, New York, NY 10022. In the meantime, have a wonderful trip!

Karen Cure

Editorial Director

New York City Area

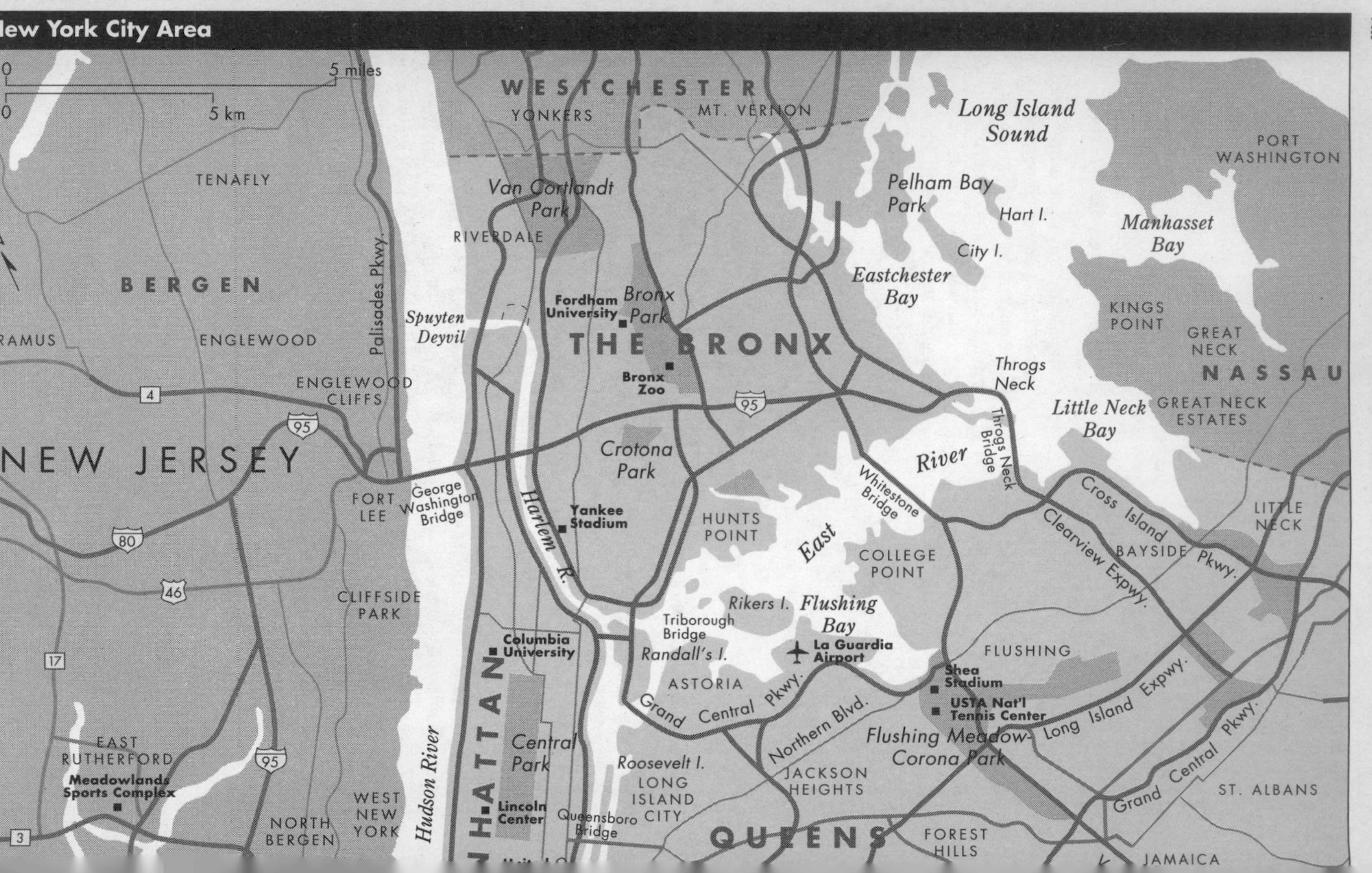

QUEENS
FOREST HILLS
JAMAICA
SPRINGFIELD GARDENS
Van Wyck Expwy.
Southern Pkwy.
J.F.K. International Airport
OZONE PARK
SOUTH OZONE PARK
Inter Boro Pkwy.
495
WEEHAWKEN
SECAUCUS
LYNDHURST
17
United Nations
Queens-Midtown Tunnel
Lincoln Tunnel
Javits Convention Center
GREENPOINT
East River
MASPETH
WILLIAMSBURG
UNION CITY
HUDSON
HOBOKEN
Holland Tunnel
Williamsburg Bridge
Manhattan Bridge
KEARNY
9
1
Brooklyn Bridge
BROOKLYN HEIGHTS
Atlantic Ave.
EAST NEW YORK
Battery Park
Eastern Pkwy.
280
Pulaski Skyway
JERSEY CITY
Ellis I.
Brooklyn-Battery Tunnel
Liberty State Park
Statue of Liberty
Governors I.
Liberty I.
PARK SLOPE
Brooklyn Museum and Botanic Gardens
Prospect Park
Brooklyn
Linden Blvd.
CANARSIE
Jamaica Bay Wildlife Refuge
NEWARK
ESSEX
78
Flatbush Ave.
Queens Expwy.
Upper Bay
BROOKLYN
Ocean Pkwy.
Newark Bay
Newark International Airport
BAYONNE
Floyd Bennett Field
Marine Park
Jacob Riis Park
BAY RIDGE
The Narrows
Kill Van Kull
BENSONHURST
Belt Pkwy
ELIZABETH
Bayonne Bridge
UNION
Rockaway Inlet
Verrazano-Narrows Bridge
CONEY ISLAND
STATEN ISLAND
Goethals Bridge
Lower Bay
ATLANTIC OCEAN

SMART TRAVEL TIPS A TO Z

Basic Information on Traveling in New York, Savvy Tips to Make Your Trip a Breeze, and Companies and Organizations to Contact

AIR TRAVEL

BOOKING YOUR FLIGHT

Price is just one factor to consider when booking a flight: frequency of service and even a carrier's safety record are often just as important. Major airlines offer the greatest number of departures. Smaller airlines—including regional and no-frills airlines—usually have a limited number of flights daily. On the other hand, so-called low-cost airlines usually are cheaper, and their fares impose fewer restrictions, such as advance-purchase requirements. Safety-wise, low-cost carriers as a group have a good history—about equal to that of major carriers.

When you book, **look for nonstop flights** and **remember that "direct" flights stop at least once.** Try to **avoid connecting flights,** which require a change of plane. Two airlines may jointly operate a connecting flight, so ask if your airline operates every segment—you may find that your preferred carrier flies only part way.

CARRIERS

➤ MAJOR AIRLINES: **America West** (☎ 800/235–9292). **American** (☎ 800/433–7300). **Continental** (☎ 800/525–0280). **Delta** (☎ 800/221–1212). **Northwest**(☎ 800/225–2525). **TWA** (☎ 800/221–2000). **United** (☎ 800/241–6522). **US Airways** (☎ 800/428–4322).

➤ SMALLER AIRLINES: **Midway** (☎ 800/446–4392). **Midwest Express** (☎ 800/452–2022).

CHECK IN & BOARDING

Airlines routinely overbook planes, assuming that not everyone with a ticket will show up, but sometimes everyone does. When that happens, airlines ask for volunteers to give up their seats. In return these volunteers usually get a certificate for a free flight and are rebooked on the next flight out. If there are not enough volunteers, the airline must choose who will be denied boarding. The first to get bumped are passengers who checked in late and those flying on discounted tickets, so **get to the gate and check in as early as possible,** especially during peak periods.

Although the trend on international flights is to drop reconfirmation requirements, many airlines still ask you to reconfirm each leg of your international itinerary. Failure to do so may result in your reservation being canceled.

Always **bring a government-issued photo ID to the airport.** You may be asked to show it before you are allowed to check in.

CONSOLIDATORS

Consolidators buy tickets for scheduled international flights at reduced rates from the airlines, then sell them at prices that beat the best fare available directly from the airlines, usually without restrictions. Sometimes you can even get your money back if you need to return the ticket. Carefully read the fine print detailing penalties for changes and cancellations, and **confirm your consolidator reservation with the airline.**

➤ CONSOLIDATORS: **Cheap Tickets** (☎ 800/377–1000). **Discount Travel Network** (☎ 800/576–1600). **Unitravel** (☎ 800/325–2222). **Up & Away Travel** (☎ 212/889–2345). **World Travel Network** (☎ 800/409–6753).

CUTTING COSTS

The least-expensive airfares to New York are priced for round-trip travel and usually must be purchased in advance. It's smart to **call a number of airlines, and when you are quoted a good price, book it on the spot**—the same fare may not be available the next day. Airlines generally allow you to change your return date for a fee. If you don't use your ticket, you can apply the cost toward the purchase of a new ticket, again for a small charge. However, most low-fare tickets are nonrefundable. To get the lowest airfare, **check different routings.** Compare prices of flights to and from different airports if your destination or home city has more than one gateway. Also price off-peak flights.

When flying within the U.S., **plan to stay over a Saturday night** and **travel during the middle of the week** to get the lowest fare. These low fares are usually priced for round-trip travel and are nonrefundable. You can, however, change your return date for a fee ($75 on most major airlines).

Travel agents, especially those who specialize in finding the lowest fares (☞ Discounts & Deals, *below*), can be especially helpful when booking a plane ticket. When you're quoted a price, **ask your agent if the price is likely to get any lower.** Good agents know the seasonal fluctuations of airfares and can usually anticipate a sale or fare war. However, waiting can be risky: The fare could go *up* as seats become scarce, and you may wait so long that your preferred flight sells out. A wait-and-see strategy works best if your plans are flexible.

FLYING TIMES

New York airports have incoming flights from all over the world. Some sample flying times are: from Chicago (3½ hours), London (7 hours), Los Angeles (6 hours), Sydney via Los Angeles (21 hours).

HOW TO COMPLAIN

If your baggage goes astray or your flight goes awry, complain right away. Most carriers require that you **file a claim immediately.**

➤ AIRLINE COMPLAINTS: U.S. Department of Transportation **Aviation Consumer Protection Division** (✉ C-75, Room 4107, Washington, DC 20590, ☎ 202/366–2220). **Federal Aviation Administration Consumer Hotline** (☎ 800/322–7873).

AIRPORTS & TRANSFERS

AIRPORTS

The major gateways to New York City are La Guardia Airport and JFK International Airport, both in the borough of Queens, and Newark International Airport in New Jersey.

➤ AIRPORT INFORMATION: **La Guardia Airport** (☎ 718/533–3400). **JFK International Airport** (☎ 718/244–4444). **Newark International Airport** (☎ 973/961–6000).

TRANSFERS FROM LA GUARDIA AIRPORT

Taxis cost $17–$29 plus tolls (which may be as high as $4) and take 20–40 minutes. Group taxi rides to Manhattan are available at taxi dispatch lines just outside the baggage-claim areas during most travel hours (except on Saturday and holidays). Group fares run $9–$10 per person (plus a share of tolls).

Carey Airport Service buses depart for Manhattan every 20–30 minutes from 6:45 AM to midnight, from all terminals. It's a 40-minute ride to 42nd Street and Park Avenue, directly opposite Grand Central Terminal. The bus continues from there to the Port Authority Bus Terminal. A short cab ride will get you anywhere else in midtown. The bus fare is $10; pay the driver.

The Gray Line Air Shuttle serves major Manhattan hotels directly to and from the airport. The fare is $12 per person; make arrangements at the airport's ground transportation center or use the courtesy phone. Shuttles operate 7 AM–11 PM.

The Delta Water Shuttle runs between La Guardia Airport's Marine Air Terminal and 34th and 62nd Streets on the East Side, including a stop at Wall Street (Pier 11). The trip lasts just under a half hour. The fare is $15, $25 round-trip.

The most economical way to reach Manhattan is to ride the M-60 public bus (there are no luggage facilities on this bus) to 116th Street and Broadway, across from Columbia University. From there, you can catch Subway 1 or 9 to midtown. Alternatively, you can take Bus Q-33 to either the Roosevelt Avenue–Jackson Heights station, where you can catch Subway E or F, or the 74th Street–Broadway station, where you can catch Subway 7. Allow 90 minutes for the entire trip to midtown; the total cost is one fare ($1.50). You can use exact change for your bus fare, but you will have to purchase a token or MetroCard to enter the subway.

➤ BUS AND SUBWAYINFORMATION: **Carey Airport Service** (☎ 718/632–0509). **Gray Line Air Shuttle** (☎ 212/315–3006 or 800/451–0455). **New York City Transit** (MTA, ☎ 718/330–1234).

➤ FERRY INFORMATION: **Delta Water Shuttle** (☎ 800/543–3779).

TRANSFERS FROM JFK INTERNATIONAL AIRPORT

Taxis charge a flat fee of $30 plus tolls (which may be as much as $4) and take 35–60 minutes.

Carey Airport Service buses depart for Manhattan every 20–30 minutes from 6 AM to midnight, from all JFK terminals. The ride to 42nd Street and Park Avenue (Grand Central Terminal) takes about one hour. The bus continues from there to the Port Authority Bus Terminal. The bus fare is $13; pay the driver.

The Gray Line Air Shuttle serves major Manhattan hotels directly from the airport; the cost is $14 per person. Make arrangements at the airport's ground transportation counter or use the courtesy phone. Shuttles operate 7 AM–11 PM.

National Helicopter flies Twinstar and Bell 206L copters to all three airports, daily 7 AM–9 PM. It departs from three city heliports, with approximately 15-minute service to JFK, La Guardia, and Newark. The fare is a flat rate of $389 per helicopter, and each helicopter carries up to five people.

The cheapest but slowest means of getting to Manhattan is to take the Port Authority's free shuttle bus, which stops at all terminals, to the Howard Beach subway station, where you can catch the A train into Manhattan. Alternatively, you can take Bus Q-10 (there are no luggage facilities on this bus) to the Union Turnpike–Kew Gardens station, where you can catch Subway E or F. Or you can take Bus B-15 to New Lots station and catch Subway 3. Allow at least two hours for the trip; the total cost is one fare ($1.50) if you use the shuttle or the Q-10 or B-15. You can use exact change for your fare on the Q-10 and B-15, but you will need to purchase a token or MetroCard to enter the subway.

➤ BUS AND SUBWAYINFORMATION: ☞ Transfers from La Guardia Airport, *above.*

➤ HELICOPTER RESERVATIONS: **National Helicopter** (☎ 516/756–9355).

TRANSFERS FROM NEWARK AIRPORT

Taxis cost $34–$38 plus tolls ($10) and take 20–45 minutes. "Share and Save" group rates are available for up to four passengers between 8 AM and midnight; make arrangements with the airport's taxi dispatcher.

New Jersey Transit Airport Express buses depart for the Port Authority Bus Terminal, at 8th Avenue and 42nd Street every 15 minutes on weekdays from 4:45 AM to 3:45 AM; on weekends, service runs nearly as frequently from 4:45 AM until 3 AM. From Port Authority, it's a short cab ride to midtown hotels. The ride takes 30–45 minutes. The fare is $7; buy your ticket inside the airport terminal.

Olympia Airport Express buses leave for Grand Central Terminal and Penn Station about every 20 minutes, and 1 World Trade Center (WTC) about every 30 minutes, from around 6 AM to midnight. The trip takes roughly 45 minutes to Grand Central and Penn Station, 20 minutes to WTC. The fare is $7. A new route runs between Port Authority and Newark. Buses will run every 30 minutes 5 AM–midnight, and less frequently in the off hours. The fare is $10.

The Gray Line Air Shuttle serves major Manhattan hotels directly to and from the airport. You pay $14 per passenger; make arrangements at the airport's ground transportation center or use the courtesy phone. Shuttles operate 7 AM–11 PM.

You can also take New Jersey Transit's Airlink buses, which leave every 20 minutes from 6:15 AM to 2 AM, to Penn Station in Newark. The ride takes about 20 minutes; the fare is $4. (Be sure to have exact change.) From there, your can catch PATH Trains, which run to Manhattan 24 hours a day. The trains run every 10 minutes on weekdays, every 15–30 minutes on weeknights, every 20–30 minutes on weekends; trains stop at the WTC and at five stops along 6th Avenue—Christopher Street, 9th Street, 14th Street, 23rd Street, and 33rd Street. The fare is $1.

➤ BUS AND TRAININFORMATION: **Gray Line Air Shuttle** (☎ 212/315–3006 or 800/451–0455). **New Jersey Transit** (☎ 973/762–5100). **Olympia Airport Express** (☎ 212/964–6233 or 718/622–7700).

TRANSFERS FROM ALL AIRPORTS

Car services are a great deal because the driver will often meet you on the concourse or in the baggage-claim area and help you with your luggage. You ride in late-model American-made cars that are comfortable, if usually a bit worn. New York City Taxi and Limousine Commission rules require that all be licensed and pick up riders only by prior arrangement. **Call 24 hours in advance for reservations,** or at least a half day before your flight's departure.

➤ CAR RESERVATIONS: **All State Car and Limousine Service** (☎ 212/741–7440, FAX 212/727–2391). **Carmel Car and Limousine Service** (☎ 212/666–6666). **Eastside Limo Service** (☎ 212/744–9700, FAX 718/937–9400). **Greenwich Limousine** (☎ 212/868–4733 or 800/385–1033). **London Towncars** (☎ 212/988–9700 or 800/221–4009, FAX 718/786–7625). **Manhattan International Limo** (☎ 718/729–4200 or 800/221–7500, FAX 718/937–6157). **Skyline** (☎ 212/741–3711 or 800/533–6325). **Tel Aviv Car and Limousine Service** (☎ 212/777–7777 or 800/222–9888).

BOAT & FERRY TRAVEL

Ferries run from Battery Park's Castle Clinton to the Statue of Liberty and Ellis Island. The fare is $7. The Staten Island Ferry departs from the tip of Manhattan and crosses New York Harbor to Staten Island. The ride is free. NY Waterway has Yankee Clipper ferries taking passengers from Manhattan ($10) and New Jersey ($15) to Yankee Stadium.

➤ FERRY INFORMATION: **Castle Clinton** (☎ 212/269–5755). **Staten Island Ferry** (☎ 718/390–5253). **NY Waterway** (☎ 201/902–8700 or 800/533–3779).

BUS TRAVEL

Long-haul and commuter bus lines feed into the Port Authority Terminal on Broadway between 40th and 42nd streets.

The George Washington Bridge Bus Station is at Fort Washington Avenue and Broadway between 178th and 179th streets in the Washington Heights section of Manhattan. Six bus lines, serving northern New Jersey and Rockland County, New York, make daily stops there from 5 AM to 1 AM. The terminal connects with the 175th Street Station on Subway A, making it slightly more convenient for travelers going to and from the West Side.

➤ BUS TERMINAL INFORMATION: **George Washington Bridge Bus Station** (☎ 212/564–1114). **Port Authority Terminal** (☎ 212/564–8484).

➤ INTERSTATE BUSES: **Greyhound Lines Inc.** (☎ 212/971–6404 or 800/231–2222). **Adirondack, Pine Hill, and New York Trailways** (☎ 800/225–6815) from upstate New York. **Bonanza Bus Lines** (☎ 800/556–3815) from New England. **Martz Trailways** (☎ 800/233–8604) from Philadelphia and northeastern Pennsylvania. **New Jersey Transit** (☎ 973/762–5100) from around New Jersey. **Peter Pan Trailways** (☎ 413/781–2900 or 800/343–9999) from New England. **Vermont Transit** (☎ 802/864–6811 or 800/451–3292) from New England.

WITHIN NEW YORK

Most buses follow easy-to-understand routes along the Manhattan grid. Routes go up or down the north–south avenues, or east and west on the major two-way crosstown streets.

Most bus routes operate 24 hours, but service is infrequent late at night. Buses are great for sightseeing, but traffic jams—a potential threat at any time or place in Manhattan—can make rides maddeningly slow. Certain bus routes now offer "Limited-Stop Service"; buses on these routes stop only at major cross streets and transfer points and can save traveling time. The "Limited-Stop" buses usually run on weekdays and during rush hours.

Actually finding the bus stop will be much easier than in the past. New bus stop signs were introduced in the fall of 1996 and completed throughout the city by 1998. **Look for a light-blue sign (or green for an express bus)** on a green pole; bus numbers and routes are listed, with the current stop's name underneath. Bus fare is the same as subway fare: $1.50 at press time, in coins (no change is given) or a subway token or MetroCard. When using a token or cash, you can **ask the driver for a free transfer coupon,** good for one change to an intersecting route. Legal transfer points are listed on the back of the slip. Transfers have time limits of at least two hours, often longer. You cannot use the transfer to enter the subway system. However, you can transfer **free from bus to subway or subway to bus with the MetroCard.** You must start with the MetroCard and use it again within two hours to complete your trip.

Route maps and schedules are posted at many bus stops in Manhattan and at major stops throughout the other boroughs. Each of the five boroughs of New York has a separate bus map, and they are scarcer than hens' teeth. They are available from some subway token booths, but never on buses. The best places to obtain them are the Convention and Visitors Bureau at Columbus Circle or the information kiosks in Grand Central Terminal and Penn Station.

➤ SCHEDULE AND ROUTE INFORMATION: **New York City Transit** (MTA, ☎ 718/330–1234), available daily 6–9. **Status information hot line** (☎ 718/243–7777), updated hourly 6–9.

DISCOUNT PASSES

Seven-day MetroCards allow you take unlimited trips during a week-long period for $17. If you will ride more than 12 times, this is the card to get.

BUSINESS HOURS

New York is very much a 24-hour city. Its subways and buses run around the clock, and plenty of services are available at all hours and on all days of the week.

Banks are open weekdays 9–3 or 9–3:30; a few branches in certain neighborhoods may stay open late on Friday or open on Saturday morning.

Post offices are open weekdays 10–5 or 10–6. The main post office on 8th Avenue between 31st and 33rd streets is open daily 24 hours.

Museum hours vary greatly, but most of the major ones are open Tuesday–Sunday and keep later hours on Tuesday or Thursday evenings.

Stores are generally open Monday–Saturday from 10 to 5 or 6, but neighborhood peculiarities do exist. Most stores on the Lower East Side and in the diamond district on 47th Street close on Friday afternoon and all day Saturday for the Jewish Sabbath while keeping normal hours on Sunday. Sunday hours, also common on the West Side and in Greenwich Village and SoHo, are the exception on the Upper East Side.

CAR RENTAL

Rates in New York City begin at $46 a day and $205 a week for an economy car with air-conditioning, automatic transmission, and unlimited mileage. This does not include tax on car rentals, which is 13¼%.

➤ MAJOR AGENCIES: **Alamo** (☎ 800/327–9633, 0800/272–2000 in the U.K.). **Avis** (☎ 800/331–1212, 800/879–2847 in Canada, 008/225–533 in Australia). **Budget** (☎ 800/527–0700, 0800/181181 in the U.K.). **Dollar** (☎ 800/800–4000; 0990/565656 in the U.K., where it is known as Eurodollar). **Hertz** (☎ 800/654–3131, 800/263–0600 in Canada, 0345/555888 in the U.K., 03/9222–2523 in Australia, 03/358–6777 in New Zealand). **National InterRent** (☎ 800/227–7368; 0345/222525 in the U.K., where it is known as Europcar InterRent).

CUTTING COSTS

To get the best deal, **book through a travel agent who is willing to shop around.** When pricing cars, **ask about the location of the rental lot.** Some off-airport locations offer lower rates, and their lots are only minutes from the terminal via complimentary shuttle.

INSURANCE

When driving a rented car you are generally responsible for any damage to or loss of the vehicle. You also are liable for any property damage or personal injury that you may cause while driving. Before you rent, **see what coverage you already have** under the terms of your personal auto-insurance policy and credit cards.

For about $15 to $20 per day, rental companies sell protection, known as a collision- or loss-damage waiver (CDW or LDW), that eliminates your liability for damage to the car; it's always optional and should never be automatically added to your bill. New York has outlawed the sale of the CDW and LDW altogether. In New York you pay only for the first $100 of damage to the rental car.

In most states you don't need a CDW if you have personal auto insurance or other liability insurance. However, **make sure you have enough coverage to pay for the car.**

REQUIREMENTS

In New York you must be 18 to rent a car. You'll pay extra for child seats (about $3 per day), which are compulsory for children under five, and for additional drivers (about $2 per day). Non-U.S. residents will need a reservation voucher, a passport, a driver's license, and a travel policy that covers each driver, in order to pick up a car.

SURCHARGES

Before you pick up a car in one city and leave it in another, **ask about drop-off charges or one-way service fees,** which can be substantial. Note, too, that some rental agencies charge extra if you return the car before the time specified in your contract. To avoid a hefty refueling fee, **fill the tank just before you turn in the car,** but be aware that gas stations near the rental outlet may overcharge.

CAR TRAVEL

If you plan to drive into Manhattan, try to time your arrival for late morning or early afternoon. That way you'll avoid the morning and evening rush hours (a problem at the crossings into Manhattan) and lunch hour.

The deterioration of the bridges linking Manhattan, especially those spanning the East River, is a serious problem, and repairs will be ongoing for the next few years. Don't be surprised if a bridge is partially or entirely closed.

Driving within Manhattan can be a nightmare of gridlocked streets and predatory motorists. Free parking is difficult to find in midtown, and violators may be towed away literally within minutes. All over town, parking lots charge exorbitant rates—as much as $15 for two hours in some neighborhoods. If you do drive, **don't plan to use your car much for traveling within Manhattan.** Instead, try to park it in a guarded parking garage for at least several hours; the sting of hourly rates lessens if a car is left for a significant amount of time. If you find a spot on the street, be sure to **check parking signs carefully,** as times differ from block to block.

GASOLINE

Fill up your tank when you have a chance—gas stations are few and far between. If you can, **fill up at stations outside of the City,** where prices will be 10 or 20¢ cheaper per gallon. The average price of a gallon of regular unleaded is $1.59, although prices can vary from station to station.

RULES OF THE ROAD

On city streets the speed limit is 30 mph. In the front and in the back, **seat belts should be worn at all times.** There is **no right turn on red** within the city limits.

CHILDREN & TRAVEL

CHILDREN IN NEW YORK

Children under six travel free on subways and buses; children over six must pay full fare.

➤ LOCAL INFORMATION: ***Where Should We Take the Kids? Northeast*** ($18), available from Fodor's Travel Publications (☎ 800/533–6478) and in bookstores.

For calendars of children's events, consult **New York** magazine, **Time Out New York,** and the weekly **Village Voice** newspaper, available free at Manhattan newsstands and bookstores. The Friday **New York Times** "Weekend" section also provides a good listing of children's activities. Other good sources of information on happenings for kids are the monthly magazines **New York Family** (✉ 141 Halstead Ave., Suite 3D, Mamaroneck, NY 10543, ☎ 914/381–7474) and the **Big Apple Parents' Paper** (✉ 36 E. 12th St., New York, NY 10003, ☎ 212/533–2277), which are available free at toy stores, children's museums and clothing stores, and other places around town where parents and children are found.

➤ BABY-SITTING: The **Baby Sitters' Guild** (✉ 60 E. 42nd St., Suite 912, ☎ 212/682–0227) can take your children on sightseeing tours. Rates start at $12 an hour for one or two children over age one, plus a $4.50 transportation charge ($7 after midnight); there are special rates for infants under one year and for foreign language (over a dozen languages are spoken among the staff). Minimum booking is for four hours.

The **Avalon Registry** (✉ Box 1362, Radio City Station, New York, NY 10101, ☎ 212/245–0250) is prepared to take very young children off your hands—at least for the day. Rates are $10 an hour for one child of any age; rates increase $2 per hour for each additional child. There is also a $3 transportation charge ($8 after 8 PM).

➤ STROLLER RENTAL: **AAA-U-Rent** (✉ 861 Eagle Ave., Bronx, NY 10456, ☎ 718/665–6633).

FLYING

If your children are two or older, **ask about children's airfares.** As a general rule, infants under two not occupying a seat fly at greatly reduced fares or even for free.

Experts agree that it's a good idea to use safety seats aloft for children weighing less than 40 pounds. Airlines, however, can set their own policies: U.S. carriers allow FAA-approved models but usually require that you buy a ticket, even if your child would otherwise ride free, since the seats must be strapped into regular seats. Airline rules vary, so it's important to **check your airline's policy about using safety seats during takeoff and landing.** Safety seats cannot obstruct the movement of other passengers in the row, so get an appropriate seat assignment as early as possible.

When making your reservation, **request children's meals or a free-standing bassinet** if you need them; the latter are available only to those seated at the bulkhead, where there's enough legroom. Remember, however, that bulkhead seats may not have their own overhead bins, and there's no storage space in front of you—a major inconvenience.

HOTELS

Most hotels in New York allow children under a certain age to stay in their parents' room at no extra charge, but others charge them as extra adults; be sure to **ask about the cutoff age for children's discounts.**

CONSULATES

➤ AUSTRALIA: The **Australian Consulate General** (✉ 150 E. 42nd St., 34th floor, New York, NY 10017–5612, ☎ 212/351–6500, FAX 212/351–6501) for other matters.

➤ CANADA: The **Canadian Consulate General** (✉ 1251 6th Ave., Concourse level, New York, NY 10020, ☎ 212/596–1628, FAX 212/596–1725).

➤ NEW ZEALAND: The **New Zealand Consulate General** (✉ 780 Third Ave., Suite 1904, New York, NY 10017–2024, ☎ 212/832–4038, FAX 212/832–7602).

➤ UNITED KINGDOM: **British Consulate General** (✉ 845 Third Ave., New York, NY 10022, ☎ 212/745–0200).

CONSUMER PROTECTION

Whenever possible, **pay with a major credit card** so you can cancel payment or get reimbursed if there's a problem, provided that you can provide documentation. This is the best way to pay, whether you're buying travel arrangements before your trip or shopping at your destination.

Finally, if you're buying a package or tour, always **consider travel insurance** that includes default coverage (☞ Insurance, *below*).

➤ LOCAL BBBS: **Council of Better Business Bureaus** (✉ 4200 Wilson Blvd., Suite 800, Arlington, VA 22203, ☎ 703/276–0100, FAX 703/525–8277).

CUSTOMS & DUTIES

When shopping, **keep receipts** for all of your purchases. Upon reentering the country, **be ready to show customs officials what you've bought.** If you feel a duty is incorrect, appeal the assessment. If you object to the way your clearance was handled, get the inspector's badge number. In either case, first ask to see a supervisor, then write to the appropriate authorities, beginning with the port director at your point of entry.

IN AUSTRALIA

Australia residents who are 18 or older may bring back $A400 worth of souvenirs and gifts (including jewelry), 250 cigarettes or 250 grams of tobacco, and 1,125 ml of alcohol (including wine, beer, and spirits). Residents under 18 may bring back $A200 worth of goods.

➤ INFORMATION: **Australian Customs Service** (Regional Director, ✉ Box 8, Sydney, NSW 2001, ☎ 02/9213–2000, FAX 02/9213–4000).

IN CANADA

Canadian residents who have been out of Canada for at least 7 days may bring in C$500 worth of goods duty-free. If you've been away less than 7 days but more than 48 hours, the duty-free allowance drops to C$200; if your trip lasts 24–48 hours, the allowance is C$50. You may not pool allowances with family members. Goods claimed under the C$500 exemption may follow you by mail; those claimed under the lesser exemptions must accompany you. Alcohol and tobacco products may be included in the 7-day and 48-hour exemptions but not in the 24-hour exemption. If you meet the age requirements of the province or territory through which you reenter Canada, you may bring in, duty-free, 1.14 liters (40 imperial ounces) of wine or liquor *or* 24 12-ounce cans or bottles of beer or ale. If you are 16 or older you may bring in, duty-free, 200 cigarettes and 50 cigars.

You may send an unlimited number of gifts worth up to C$60 each duty-free to Canada. Label the package UNSOLICITED GIFT—VALUE UNDER $60. Alcohol and tobacco are excluded.

➤ INFORMATION: **Revenue Canada** (✉ 2265 St. Laurent Blvd. S, Ottawa,Ontario K1G 4K3, ☎ 613/993–0534, 800/461–9999 in Canada).

IN NEW ZEALAND

Although greeted with a "Haere Mai" ("Welcome to New Zealand"), homeward-bound residents with goods to declare must present themselves for inspection. If you're 17 or older, you may bring back $700 worth of souvenirs and gifts. Your duty-free allowance also includes 4.5 liters of wine or beer; one 1,125-ml bottle of spirits; and either 200 cigarettes, 250 grams of tobacco, 50 cigars, or a combo of all three up to 250 grams.

➤ INFORMATION: **New Zealand Customs** (✉ Custom House, 50 Anzac Ave., Box 29, Auckland, New Zealand, ☎ 09/359–6655, 09/309–2978).

IN THE U.K.

If you are a U.K. resident and your journey was wholly within the European Union (EU), you won't have to pass through customs when you return to the United Kingdom. If you plan to bring back large quantities of alcohol or tobacco, check EU limits beforehand. From countries outside the EU, including the United States, you may import, duty-free, 200 cigarettes or 50 cigars; 1 liter of spirits or 2 liters of fortified or sparkling wine or liqueurs; 2 liters of still table wine; 60 milliliters of perfume; 250 milliliters of toilet water; plus £136 worth of other goods, including gifts and souvenirs.

➤ INFORMATION: **HM Customs and Excise** (✉ Dorset House, Stamford St., London SE1 9NG, ☎ 0171/202–4227).

IN THE U.S.

Non-U.S. residents ages 21 and older may import into the United States 200 cigarettes or 50 cigars or 2 kilograms of tobacco, 1 liter of alcohol, and gifts worth $100. Prohibited items include meat products, seeds, plants, and fruits.

➤ INFORMATION: **U.S. Customs Service** (Inquiries, ✉ Box 7407, Washington, DC 20044, ☎ 202/927–6724; complaints, Office of Regulations and Rulings, ✉ 1301 Constitution Ave. NW, Washington, DC 20229; registration of equipment, Resource Management, ✉ 1301 Constitution Ave. NW, Washington DC 20229, ☎ 202/927–0540).

DISABILITIES & ACCESSIBILITY

ACCESS IN NEW YORK

Many buildings in New York City are now wheelchair-accessible. The subway is still hard to navigate, however; people in wheelchairs do better on public buses, most of which have wheelchair lifts at the rear door and "kneel" at the front to facilitate getting on and off.

➤ LOCAL RESOURCES: The **Mayor's Office for People with Disabilities** (✉ 52 Chambers St., Office 206, New York, NY 10007, ☎ 212/788–2830, TTY 212/788–2842) has brochures and helpful information. The **Andrew Heiskell Library for the Blind and Physically Handicapped** (✉ 40 W. 20th St., New York, NY 10001, ☎ 212/206–5400) has a large collection of Braille, large-print, and recorded books, housed in a layout specially designed for easy access for people with vision impairments.

MAKING RESERVATIONS

When discussing accessibility with an operator or reservations agent, **ask hard questions.** Are there any stairs, inside *or* out? Are there grab bars next to the toilet *and* in the shower/tub? How wide is the doorway to the room? To the bathroom? For the most extensive facilities meeting the latest legal specifications, **opt for newer accommodations,** which are more likely to have been designed with access in mind. Older buildings or ships may have more limited facilities. Be sure to **discuss your needs before booking.**

TRANSPORTATION

➤ COMPLAINTS: **Disability Rights Section** (✉ U.S. Department of Justice, Civil Rights Division, Box 66738, Washington, DC 20035–6738, ☎ 202/514–0301 or 800/514–0301, TTY 202/514–0383 or 800/514–0383, FAX 202/307–1198) for general complaints. **Aviation Consumer Protection Division** (☞ Air Travel, *above*) for airline-related problems. **Civil Rights Office** (✉ U.S. Department of Transportation, Departmental Office of Civil Rights, S-30, 400 7th St. SW, Room 10215, Washington, DC, 20590, ☎ 202/366–4648, FAX 202/366–9371) for problems with surface transportation.

TRAVEL AGENCIES & TOUR OPERATORS

As a whole, the travel industry has become more aware of the needs of travelers with disabilities. In the U.S., the Americans with Disabilities Act requires that travel firms serve the needs of all travelers. Note, though, that some agencies and operators specialize in making travel arrangements for individuals and groups with disabilities.

➤ TRAVELERS WITH MOBILITY PROBLEMS: **Access Adventures** (✉ 206 Chestnut Ridge Rd., Rochester, NY 14624, ☎ 716/889–9096), run by a former physical-rehabilitation counselor. **CareVacations** (✉ 5019 49th Ave., Suite 102, Leduc, Alberta T9E 6T5, ☎ 403/986–6404, 800/648–1116 in Canada) has group tours and is especially helpful with cruise vacations. **Flying Wheels Travel** (✉ 143 W. Bridge St., Box 382, Owatonna, MN 55060, ☎ 507/451–5005 or 800/535–6790, FAX 507/451–1685), a travel agency specializing in customized tours and itineraries worldwide. **Hinsdale Travel Service** (✉ 201 E. Ogden Ave., Suite 100, Hinsdale, IL 60521, ☎ 630/325–1335), a travel agency that benefits from the advice of wheelchair traveler Janice Perkins.

➤ TRAVELERS WITH DEVELOPMENTAL DISABILITIES: **Sprout** (✉ 893 Amsterdam Ave., New York, NY 10025, ☎ 212/222–9575 or 888/222–9575, FAX 212/222–9768).

DISCOUNTS & DEALS

Be a smart shopper and **compare all your options** before making any choice. A plane ticket bought with a promotional coupon may not be cheaper than the least expensive fare from a discount ticket agency. For high-price travel purchases, such as packages or tours, keep in mind that what you get is just as important as what you save. Just because something is cheap doesn't mean it's a bargain.

CREDIT-CARD BENEFITS

When you use your credit card to make travel purchases you may get free travel-accident insurance, collision-damage insurance, and medical or legal assistance, depending on the card and the bank that issued it. American Express, MasterCard, and Visa provide one or more of these services, so **get a copy of your credit card's travel-benefits policy.** If you are a member of an auto club, always **ask hotel and car-rental reservations agents about auto-club discounts.** Some clubs offer additional discounts on tours, cruises, and admission to attractions.

DISCOUNT RESERVATIONS

To save money, **look into discount-reservations services** with toll-free numbers, which use their buying power to get a better price on hotels, airline tickets, even car rentals. When booking a room, always **call the hotel's local toll-free number** (if one is available) rather than the central reservations number—you'll often get a better price. Always ask about special packages or corporate rates.

➤ AIRLINE TICKETS: ☎ **800/FLY-4-LESS.** ☎ **800/FLY-ASAP.**

➤ HOTEL ROOMS: **Accommodations Express** (☎ 800/444–7666). **Central Reservation Service (CRS)** (☎ 800/548–3311). **Hotel Reservations Network**(☎ 800/964–6835). **Quickbook** (☎ 800/789–9887). **Room Finders USA** (☎ 800/473–7829).**RMC Travel** (☎ 800/245–5738). **Steigenberger Reservation Service** (☎ 800/223–5652).

PACKAGE DEALS

Packages and guided tours can save you money, but don't confuse the two. When you buy a package, your travel remains independent, just as though you had planned and booked the trip yourself. Fly/drive packages, which combine airfare and car rental, are often a good deal. In cities, ask the local visitor's bureau about hotel packages. These often include tickets to major museum exhibits and other special events.

EMERGENCIES

➤ DOCTORS & DENTISTS: **Doctors On Call** (☎ 212/737–2333), 24-hour house-call service. **St. Luke's-Roosevelt Hospital** (✉ 59th St. between 9th and 10th Aves., ☎ 212/523–6800) and **St. Vincent's Hospital** (✉ 7th Ave. and 12th St., ☎ 212/604–7997), both near midtown, have 24-hour emergency rooms. **Emergency Dental Service** (☎ 212/679–3966; 212/679–4172 after 8 PM) will make a referral.

➤ EMERGENCIES: Dial **911** for police, fire, or ambulance in an emergency (TTY is available for the hearing impaired).

➤ HOSPITALS: **Beekman Downtown Hospital** (✉ 170 Williams St., between Beekman and Spruce Sts., ☎ 212/312–5070). **Beth Israel Medical Center** (✉ 1st Ave. at 16th St., ☎ 212/420–2840). **Columbia Presbyterian Medical Center** (✉ 622 W. 168th St., at Ft. Washington Ave., ☎ 212/305–2255). **Lenox Hill Hospital** (✉ 100 E. 77th St., ☎ 212/434–3030). **Mount Sinai Hospital** (✉ 5th Ave. at 101st St., ☎ 212/241–7171). **New York Hospital–Cornell Medical Center** (✉ 525 E. 68th St., ☎ 212/746–5454). **St. Luke's–Roosevelt Hospital** (✉ 1000 10th Ave., at 59th St., ☎ 212/523–6800).

➤ 24-HOUR PHARMACIES: **Genovese** (✉ 2nd Ave. at 68th St., ☎ 212/772 0104) has reasonable prices. Before 10 or 11 PM look for a pharmacy in a neighborhood that keeps late hours, such as Greenwich Village or the Upper West Side, for better deals.

➤ HOT LINES: **Victims' Services** (☎ 212/577–7777). **Mental Health** (☎ 212/219–5599 or 800/527–7474 for information after 5 PM). **Sex Crimes Report Line** (☎ 212/267–7273).

GAY & LESBIAN TRAVEL

➤ LOCAL INFORMATION: The **Lesbian and Gay Community Services Center** (✉ 208 W. 13th St., New York, NY 10011, ☎ 212/620–7310).

➤ PUBLICATIONS: **Fodor's Gay Guide to New York City** ($11, ☎ 800/533–6478 and in bookstores), **Metro Source** (✉ 180 Varick St., 5th floor, New York, NY 10014, ☎ 212/691–5127; $15 for 4 issues).

➤ GAY- AND LESBIAN-FRIENDLY TRAVEL AGENCIES: **Corniche Travel** (✉ 8721 Sunset Blvd., Suite 200, West Hollywood, CA 90069, ☎ 310/854–6000 or 800/429–8747, FAX 310/659–7441). **Islanders Kennedy Travel** (✉ 183 W. 10th St., New York, NY 10014, ☎ 212/242–3222 or 800/988–1181, FAX 212/929–8530). **Now Voyager** (✉ 4406 18th St., San Francisco, CA 94114, ☎ 415/626–1169 or 800/255–6951, FAX 415/626–8626). **Yellowbrick Road** (✉ 1500 W. Balmoral Ave., Chicago, IL 60640, ☎ 773/561–1800 or 800/642–2488, FAX 773/561–4497). **Skylink Travel and Tour** (✉ 3577 Moorland Ave., Santa Rosa, CA 95407, ☎ 707/585–8355 or 800/225–5759, FAX 707/584–5637), serving lesbian travelers.

HEALTH

MEDICAL PLANS

No one plans to get sick while traveling, but it happens, so **consider signing up with a medical-assistance company.** Members get doctor referrals, emergency evacuation or repatriation, 24-hour telephone hot lines for medical consultation, cash for emergencies, and other personal and legal assistance. Coverage varies by plan, so **review the benefits of each carefully.**

➤ MEDICAL-ASSISTANCE COMPANIES: **International SOS Assistance** (✉ 8 Neshaminy Interplex, Suite 207, Trevose, PA 19053, ☎ 215/245–4707 or 800/523–6586, FAX 215/244–9617; ✉ 12 Chemin Riantbosson, 1217 Meyrin 1, Geneva, Switzerland, ☎ 4122/785–6464, FAX 4122/785–6424; ✉ 10 Anson Rd., 14-07/08 International Plaza, Singapore, 079903, ☎ 65/226–3936, FAX 65/226–3937).

HOLIDAYS

Major national holidays include: New Year's Day; Martin Luther King Jr. Day (third Mon. in Jan.); President's Day (third Mon. in Feb.); Memorial Day (last Mon. in May); Independence Day (July 4); Labor Day (first Mon. in Sept.); Thanksgiving Day (fourth Thurs. in Nov.); Christmas Eve and Day; and New Year's Eve.

INSURANCE

Travel insurance is the best way to **protect yourself against financial loss.** The most useful plan is a comprehensive policy that includes coverage for trip cancellation and interruption, default, trip delay, and medical expenses (with a waiver for preexisting conditions).

Without insurance, you will lose all or most of your money if you cancel your trip, regardless of the reason. Default insurance covers you if your tour operator, airline, or cruise line goes out of business. Trip-delay covers unforeseen expenses that you may incur due to bad weather or mechanical delays. It's important to **compare the fine print regarding trip-delay coverage when comparing policies.**

For overseas travel, one of the most important components of travel insurance is its medical coverage. Supplemental health insurance will pick up the cost of your medical bills should you get sick or injured while traveling. Residents of the United Kingdom can buy an annual travel-insurance policy valid for most vacations taken during the year in which the coverage is purchased. If you are pregnant or have a preexisting condition, make sure you're covered. British citizens should buy extra medical coverage when traveling overseas, according to the Association of British Insurers. Australian travelers should buy travel insurance, including extra medical coverage, whenever they go abroad, according to the Insurance Council of Australia.

Always **buy travel insurance directly from the insurance company**; if you buy it from a cruise line, airline, or tour operator that goes out of business you probably will not be covered for the agency or operator's default, a major risk. Before you make any purchase, **review your existing health and home-owner's policies** to find out whether they cover expenses incurred while traveling.

➤ TRAVEL INSURERS: In the U.S., **Access America** (✉ 6600 W. Broad St., Richmond, VA 23230, ☎ 804/285–3300 or 800/284–8300). **Travel Guard International** (✉ 1145 Clark St., Stevens Point, WI 54481, ☎ 715/345–0505 or 800/826–1300). In Canada, **Mutual of Omaha** (✉ Travel Division, 500 University Ave., Toronto, Ontario M5G 1V8, ☎ 416/598–4083, 800/268–8825 in Canada).

➤ INSURANCE INFORMATION: In the U.K., **Association of British Insurers** (✉ 51 Gresham St., London EC2V 7HQ, ☎ 0171/600–3333). In Australia, the **Insurance Council of Australia** (☎ 613/9614–1077, FAX 613/9614–7924).

LIMOUSINES

If you want to ride around Manhattan in style, **rent a chauffeur-driven car** from one of many limousine services. Companies usually charge by the hour or offer a flat fee for sightseeing excursions.

➤ LIMOUSINE SERVICES: **All State Car and Limousine Service** (☎ 212/741–7440). **Bermuda Limousine International** (☎ 212/249–8400). **Carey Limousines** (☎ 212/599–1122). **Carmel Car and Limousine Service** (☎ 212/666–6666). **Chris Limousines** (☎ 718/356–3232 or 800/542–1584). **Concord Limousine Inc.** (☎ 212/230–1600 or 800/255–7255). **Eastside Limo Service** (☎ 212/744–9700). **Greenwich Limousine** (☎ 212/868–4733 or 800/385–1033). **London Towncars** (☎ 212/988–9700 or 800/221–4009).

LODGING

B&BS

Most of the bed-and-breakfasts in New York City are residential apartments with some (or all) of their rooms reserved for guests. These are booked through services that don't charge a fee, but often require a deposit equal to 25% of the total cost.

➤ RESERVATION SERVICES: **Bed-and-breakfast Network of New York** (✉ 134 W. 32nd St., Suite 602, New York, NY 10001, ☎ 212/645–8134 or 800/900–8134). **Urban Ventures** (✉ 38 W. 32nd St., Suite 1412, New York, NY 10001, ☎ 212/594–5650, FAX 212/947–9320).

HOME EXCHANGES

If you would like to exchange your home for someone else's, **join a home-exchange organization**, which will send you its updated listings of available exchanges for a year and will include your own listing in at least one of them. It's up to you to make specific arrangements.

➤ EXCHANGE CLUBS: **HomeLink International** (✉ Box 650, Key West, FL 33041, ☎ 305/294–7766 or 800/638–3841, FAX 305/294–1148; $83 per year).

HOSTELS

No matter what your age, you can **save on lodging costs by staying at hostels.** In some 5,000 locations in more than 70 countries around the world, Hostelling International (HI), the umbrella group for a number of national youth hostel associations, offers single-sex, dorm-style beds and, at many hostels, "couples" rooms and family accommodations. Membership in any HI national hostel association, open to travelers of all ages, allows you to stay in HI-affiliated hostels at member rates (one-year membership is about $25 for adults; hostels run about $10–$25 per night). Members also have priority if the hostel is full; they're eligible for discounts around the world, even on rail and bus travel in some countries.

➤ HOSTEL ORGANIZATIONS: **Hostelling International—American Youth Hostels** (✉ 733 15th St. NW, Suite

840, Washington, DC 20005, ☎ 202/783–6161, FAX 202/783–6171). **Hostelling International—Canada** (✉ 400-205 Catherine St., Ottawa, Ontario K2P 1C3, ☎ 613/237–7884, FAX 613/237–7868). **Youth Hostel Association of England and Wales** (✉ Trevelyan House, 8 St. Stephen's Hill, St. Albans, Hertfordshire AL1 2DY, ☎ 01727/855215 or 01727/845047, FAX 01727/844126); membership in the U.S. $25, in Canada C$26.75, in the U.K. £9.30).

HOTELS

In addition to independently owned hotels, almost every major chain has a hotel in New York.

➤ TOLL-FREE NUMBERS: **Best Western** (☎ 800/528–1234). **Four Season** (☎ 800/332–3442). **Hilton** (☎ 800/445–8667). **Holiday Inn** (☎ 800/465–4329). **Howard Johnson** (☎ 800/654–4656). **Hyatt & Resorts** (☎ 800/233–1234). **Inter-Continental** (☎ 800/327–0200). **Marriott** (☎ 800/228–9290). **Meridien** (☎ 800/543–4300). **Quality Inn** (☎ 800/228–5151). **Ritz-Carlton** (☎ 800/241–3333). **Sheraton and ITT Sheraton** (☎ 800/325–3535). **Westin Hotels and Resorts** (☎ 800/228–3000).

MONEY

COSTS

In New York, it's easy to get swept up in a debt-inducing cyclone of $50 dinners, $80 theater tickets, $25 nightclub covers, $10 cab rides, and $150 hotel rooms. Although, one of the good things about all the boroughs is that there is such a wide variety of options that you can spend in some areas and save in others as you see fit.

ATMS

Cash machines are abundant throughout all the boroughs.

EXCHANGING MONEY

For the most favorable rates, **change money through banks.** Although fees charged for ATM transactions may be higher abroad than at home, Cirrus and Plus exchange rates are excellent, because they are based on wholesale rates offered only by major banks. You won't do as well at exchange booths in airports or rail and bus stations, in hotels, in restaurants, or in stores, although you may find their hours more convenient. To avoid lines at airport exchange booths, **get a bit of local currency before you leave home.**

➤ EXCHANGE SERVICES: **International Currency Express** (☎ 888/842–0880 on the East Coast, 888/278–6628 on the West Coast). **Thomas Cook Currency Services** (☎ 800/287–7362 for telephone orders and retail locations).

TRAVELER'S CHECKS

Do you need traveler's checks? It depends on where you're headed. If you're going to rural areas and small towns, go with cash; traveler's checks are best used in cities. Lost or stolen checks can usually be replaced within 24 hours. To ensure a speedy refund, buy your own traveler's checks—don't let someone else pay for them: irregularities like this can cause delays. The person who bought the checks should make the call to request a refund.

PACKING

LUGGAGE

How many carry-on bags you can bring with you is up to the airline. Most allow two, but the limit is often reduced to one on certain flights. Gate agents will take excess baggage—including bags they deem oversize—from you as you board and add it to checked luggage. To avoid this situation, make sure that everything you carry aboard will fit under your seat. Also, get to the gate early, and request a seat at the back of the plane; you'll board first, while the overhead bins are still empty. Since big, bulky baggage attracts the attention of gate agents and flight attendants on a busy flight, make sure your carry-on is really a carry-on.

If you are flying internationally, note that baggage allowances may be determined not by piece but by weight—generally 88 pounds (40 kilograms) in first class, 66 pounds (30 kilograms) in business class, and 44 pounds (20 kilograms) in economy.

Airline liability for baggage is limited to $1,250 per person on flights within the United States. On international flights it amounts to $9.07 per pound or $20 per kilogram for checked baggage (roughly $640 per 70-pound bag) and $400 per passenger for unchecked baggage. You can buy additional coverage at check-in for about $10 per $1,000 of coverage, but it excludes a rather extensive list of items, shown on your airline ticket.

Before departure, **itemize your bags' contents** and their worth, and label the bags with your name, address, and phone number. (If you use your home address, cover it so that potential thieves can't see it readily.) Inside each bag, **pack a copy of your itinerary.** At check-in, **make sure that each bag is correctly tagged** with the destination airport's three-letter code. If your bags arrive damaged or fail to arrive at all, file a written report with the airline before leaving the airport.

PACKING LIST

Jackets and ties are required for men in a number of restaurants—and in general, New Yorkers tend to dress a bit more formally than their west coast counterparts for special events like the theater. Jeans and sneakers are acceptable for casual dining and sightseeing just about anywhere in the city. Always **come with sneakers or other flat-heeled walking shoes** for pounding the New York pavement.

Do **pack light,** because porters and luggage trolleys can be hard to find at New York airports. And **bring a fistful of quarters to rent a trolley.**

In your carry-on luggage **bring an extra pair of eyeglasses or contact lenses** and **enough of any medication you take** to last the entire trip. You may also want your doctor to write a spare prescription using the drug's generic name, since brand names may vary from country to country. **Never put prescription drugs or valuables in luggage to be checked.** To avoid customs delays, carry medications in their original packaging. And don't forget to copy down and carry addresses of offices that handle refunds of lost traveler's checks.

PASSPORTS & VISAS

When traveling internationally, **carry a passport even if you don't need one** (it's always the best form of ID), and make **two photocopies of the data page** (one for someone at home and another for you, carried separately from your passport). If you lose your passport, promptly call the nearest embassy or consulate and the local police.

➤ U.K. CITIZENS: **U.S. Embassy Visa Information Line** (☎ 01891/200–290; calls cost 49p per minute, 39p per minute cheap rate), for U.S. visa information. **U.S. Embassy Visa Branch** (✉ 5 Upper Grosvenor St., London W1A 2JB), for U.S. visa information; send a self-addressed, stamped envelope. Write the **U.S. Consulate General** (✉ Queen's House, Queen St., Belfast BTI 6EO) if you live in Northern Ireland.

PASSPORT OFFICES

➤ AUSTRALIAN CITIZENS: **Australian Passport Office** (☎ 131–232).

➤ NEW ZEALAND CITIZENS: **New Zealand Passport Office** (☎ 04/494–0700 for information on how to apply, 0800/727–776 for information on applications already submitted).

➤ U.K. CITIZENS: **London Passport Office** (☎ 0990/21010), for fees and documentation requirements and to request an emergency passport.

REST ROOMS

Public rest rooms in New York run the gamut when it comes to cleanliness. Facilities in Penn Station and Grand Central Terminal are often quite dirty and are inhabited by homeless people. Rest rooms in subway stations have largely been sealed off because of vandalism and safety concerns.

As a rule, **head for midtown department stores, museums, or the lobbies of large hotels** to find the cleanest bathrooms. Public atriums, such as the Citicorp Center and Trump Tower, also provide good public facilities, as does the newly renovated Bryant Park and the many Barnes & Noble bookstores. Restaurants, too, have rest rooms, but usually just for patrons. If you're dressed well and look as if you belong, you can often just sail right in. Be aware that cinemas, Broadway theaters, and concert halls have limited amenities, and there are often long lines before performances, as well as during intermissions.

SAFETY

Despite New York's bad reputation in the area of crime, most people live here for years without being robbed or assaulted. Nevertheless, as in any large city, travelers make particularly easy marks for pickpockets and hustlers, so **be cautious.**

Do **ignore the panhandlers** on the streets (some aggressive, many homeless), people who offer to hail you a cab (they often appear at Penn Station, Port Authority, and Grand Central Terminal), and limousine and gypsy cab drivers who offer you a ride. Someone who appears to have had an accident at the exit door of a bus may flee with your wallet or purse if you attempt to give aid; the individual who approaches you with a complicated story is probably playing a confidence game and hopes to get something from you. Also **beware of strangers jostling you in crowds,** or someone tapping your shoulder from behind. Never play or place a bet on a sidewalk card game, shell game, or guessing game—they are all rigged to get your cash.

Keep jewelry out of sight on the street; better yet, **leave valuables at home.** Don't wear gold chains or gaudy jewelry, even if it's fake. Women should **never hang a purse on a chair in a restaurant** or on a hook in a rest-room stall. Men are advised to **carry wallets in front pants pockets** rather than in their hip pockets. Many New Yorkers **separate out some money** ($20 or so) in a separate pocket, which you won't mind relinquishing—just in case.

Be sure to **avoid deserted blocks in out-of-the-way neighborhoods.** If you end up in an empty area or a side street that feels unsafe, it probably is. A brisk, purposeful pace helps deter trouble wherever you go.

Although the subway runs round the clock, it is usually safest during the day and evening. Most residents of the city have a rough cut-off time—10 or 11 PM—past which they avoid riding the subway trains. The subway system is much safer than it once was, but to **err on the side of caution,** you may want to travel by bus or taxi after the theater or a concert. If you do take the subway at night, ride in the center car, with the conductor, and wait among the crowds on the center of the platform or right in front of the token clerk. Watch out for unsavory characters lurking around the inside or outside of stations, particularly at night. When you're waiting for a train, **stand away from the edge of the subway platform,** especially when trains are entering or leaving the station. Once the train pulls into the station, **avoid empty cars.** When disembarking from a train, **stick with the crowd** until you reach the comparative safety of the street.

Though they're slower, buses are often more pleasant than subways.

SENIOR-CITIZEN TRAVEL

To qualify for age-related discounts, **mention your senior-citizen status up front** when booking hotel reservations (not when checking out) and before you're seated in restaurants (not when paying the bill). Note that discounts may be limited to certain menus, days, or hours. When renting a car, **ask about promotional car-rental discounts,** which can be cheaper than senior-citizen rates.

➤ EDUCATIONAL PROGRAMS: Elderhostel (✉ 75 Federal St., 3rd floor, Boston, MA 02110, ☎ 617/426–8056).

SIGHTSEEING TOURS

➤ BOAT TOURS: A Circle Line Cruise (✉ Pier 83, west end of 42nd St., ☎ 212/563–3200) is one of the best ways to get a crash orientation to Manhattan. Once you've finished the three-hour, 35-mi circumnavigation of Manhattan, you'll have a good idea of where things are and what you want to see next. Narrations are as interesting and individualized as the guides who deliver them. The fare is $18. The Circle Line operates daily March–mid-December; Semi-Circle cruises, a limited tour, run mid-December–March.

Express Navigation (✉ Pier 11, 2 blocks south of South Street Seaport, ☎ 800/262–8743) has a hydroliner to show you the island of Manhattan in 75 minutes. The fare is $15. Boats depart May–September weekdays and Saturday at noon and 2 PM.

NY Waterway (✉ Pier 78, W. 38th St. and 12th Ave., ☎ 800/533–3779) also offers a harbor cruise; the 90-minute ride costs $16, $8 for children. The StarLight Cruise follows the same route (for the same price) at night, providing excellent views of the lit-up skyline. The harbor cruise runs daily April–early December, while the StarLight Cruise operates nightly from late May to late August, and on Friday and Saturday nights from early September to late October.

The Spirit of New York (✉ Pier 62, at W. 23rd St. and 12th Ave. on the Hudson River, ☎ 212/742–7278) sails on lunch ($35–$45) and dinner ($64–$78) cruises; the meal is accompanied by live music and dancing. There are also occasional moonlight cocktail ($20) cruises. All can be scheduled year-round.

World Yacht Cruises (✉ Pier 81, W. 41st St. at Hudson River, ☎ 212/630–8100) serves Sunday brunch ($39) on two-hour cruises, and dinner (Sun.–Fri. $70; Sat. $83; drinks extra) on three-hour cruises. The Continental cuisine is restaurant quality, and there's music and dancing on board. The cruises run daily year round, weather permitting.

At South Street Seaport's Pier 16 you can take hour-and-a-half- or three-hour voyages to New York's past aboard the cargo schooner **Pioneer** (☎ 212/748–8786); cruises depart daily May–September. **Seaport Liberty Cruises** (☎ 212/630–8888) also offers daily, hour-long sightseeing tours of New York Harbor and Lower Manhattan, as well as two-hour cruises with live jazz and blues on Wednesday and Thursday nights. Boats run March–December.

➤ BUS TOURS: **Gray Line New York** (✉ 900 8th Ave., ☎ 212/397–2620) offers a taste of yesteryear with its "NY Trolley Tour" on coaches replicating New York trolleys of the '30s, in addition to a number of city bus tours in various languages, plus cruises and day trips to Atlantic City. On weekdays between May and October, Gray Line's Central Park Trolley Tour tempts visitors to explore parts of the park that even native New Yorkers may never have seen.

New York Doubledecker Tours (✉ Empire State Bldg. at 34th St. and 5th Ave., Room 4503, ☎ 212/967–6008) runs authentic London double-deck buses year-round, 9–6 in summer, 9–3 in winter, making stops every 15–30 minutes at the Empire State Building, Greenwich Village, SoHo, Chinatown, the World Trade Center, Battery Park, the South Street Seaport, the United Nations, and Central Park. Tickets, which are valid for boarding and reboarding all day for three days, cost $19 and can be purchased at the Empire State Building. An uptown loop, which costs $28, makes stops at Lincoln Center, the Museum of Natural History, Harlem, Museum Mile, and Central Park. Hop on and off to visit attractions as often as you like.

➤ HELICOPTER TOURS: **Liberty Helicopter Tours** (✉ Heliport at W. 30th St. and Hudson River, ☎ 212/465–8905) has three pilot-narrated tours ranging from $49 to $155 per person.

➤ SPECIAL-INTEREST TOURS: **Art Tours of Manhattan** (☎ 609/921–2647) custom-designs walking tours of museum and gallery exhibits as well as artists' studios and lofts; most center on the SoHo area.

Backstage on Broadway (☎ 212/575–8065) is a talk about the Broadway theater held in an actual theater, given by a theater professional. Reservations are mandatory; tour groups of 25 or more only.

Bite of the Apple Central Park Bicycle Tour (☎ 212/541–8759 or 212/603–9750) organizes two-hour bicycle trips through Central Park with stops along the way, including Strawberry Fields and the Belvedere Castle.

Gracie Mansion Conservancy Tour (☎ 212/570–4751) will show you the

1799 house, official residence of New York City mayors since 1942. The mansion is open to the public on Wednesday; the tours run late March–mid-November, and reservations are mandatory. Suggested $4 donation.

Grand Central Station (☏ 212/818-1777) provides the setting for architectural tours that take you high above the crowds and into the Beaux Arts building's rafters. No charge and no reservations for individuals; group reservations are required.

Harlem Spirituals, Inc. (☏ 212/757-0425) and **Penny Sightseeing Harlem Tours** (☏ 212/410-0080) offer bus and walking tours and Sunday gospel trips to Harlem. Also in Harlem, you can trace the history of jazz backstage at the **Apollo Theater** (☏ 212/222-0992).

The **Lower East Side Tenement Museum** (☏ 212/431-0233) offers tours through former immigrant communities.

Madison Square Garden (☏ 212/465-6080) has tours of the sports mecca's inner workings.

Manhattan Tours (☏ 212/563-2570) leads customized, behind-the-scenes tours inside fashion and interior-design showrooms, theaters, restaurants, and artists' lofts.

The Metropolitan Opera House Backstage (☏ 212/769-7020) offers a tour of the scenery and costume shops, stage area, and rehearsal facilities.

Quintessential New York (☏ 212/501-0827) has over a dozen specialty tours; the trump card is the behind-the-scenes take. For example, during "The Artist Colony: SoHo" tour, guests visit an artist's studio and an antique dealer's workshop. Another plus is the chauffered car.

Radio City Music Hall Productions (☏ 212/632-4041) schedules behind-the-scenes tours of the theater.

Rock and Roll Tours of New York (☏ 212/941-9464) visits the places where rock stars hung out, recorded, lived, and died. Tours are conducted by bus and are restricted to groups of 30 or more.

Sax & Company (☏ 212/832-0350) tours include visits to museums, theaters, and artists' studios and private collections.

The **South Street Seaport Museum** (☏ 212/748-8590) has tours of historic ships and the waterfront, as well as predawn forays through the bustling Fulton Fish Market.

➤ WALKING TOURS: **Adventure on a Shoestring** (☏ 212/265-2663) is an organization dating from 1963 that explores New York neighborhoods. Weekend tours are scheduled periodically and cost $5 per person; reservations are a must. Tours run year-round, rain or shine.

Big Onion Walking Tours (☏ 212/439-1090) has theme tours on weekends throughout the year, and on selected weekdays from April to late November: try "From Naples to Bialystock to Beijing: A Multi-Ethnic Eating Tour."

Citywalks (☏ 212/989-2456) offers two-hour private walking tours exploring various neighborhoods in depth; reservations are required.

The **Municipal Art Society** (☏ 212/935-3960) operates a series of walking tours on weekdays and both bus and walking tours on weekends. Tours highlight the city's architecture and history.

The **Museum of the City of New York** (☏ 212/534-1672) sponsors primarily historical and architectural walking tours on Sunday afternoons from April to early October.

New York City Cultural Walking Tours (☏ 212/979-2388) focuses on the city's architecture, landmarks, memorials, outdoor art, and historic sites, including 5th Avenue's "Millionaires' Mile." Public tours are offered every Sunday March–December, while private tours can be scheduled throughout the week.

The **92nd Street Y** (☏ 212/996-1100) often has something special to offer on weekends and some weekdays.

River to River Downtown Walking Tours (☏ 212/321-2823) specializes in lower Manhattan for 2½-hour walking tours.

Urban Explorations (☎ 718/721–5254) runs tours with an emphasis on architecture and landscape design; Chinatown is a specialty.

The **Urban Park Rangers** (☎ 212/427–4040) offer free weekend walks and workshops in city parks.

Walks of the Town (☎ 212/222–5343) will tailor a tour to your interests; special themes include "Cops, Crooks, and the Courts." Tours are available by appointment only.

Among other knowledgeable walking-tour guides are **Joyce Gold** (☎ 212/242–5762), whose history tours include "The Vital Heart of Harlem," "The Women of Washington Square," and "When China and Italy Moved to New York," and **Arthur Marks** (☎ 212/673–0477), who creates customized tours on which he sings about the city.

➤ Self-Guided Walking Tours: A free "Walking Tour of Rockefeller Center" pamphlet is available from the information desk in the lobby of the **GE Building** (✉ 30 Rockefeller Plaza).

Heritage Trails New York (☎ 212/269–1500) is a wanderer's version of connect-the-dots. Four color-coded sidewalk trails wind through the downtown area, guiding visitors to the New York Stock Exchange, Trinity Church, and other points of interest.

Pop one of the **Talk-a-Walk** cassettes (✉ Sound Publishers, 30 Waterside Plaza, Suite 10D, New York, NY 10010, ☎ 212/686–0356, $9.95 per tape, plus $2.90 packing and shipping for up to 4 tapes) into your Walkman and start strolling to an in-your-ear history of lower Manhattan or the Brooklyn Bridge.

STUDENT TRAVEL

TRAVEL AGENCIES

To save money, **look into deals available through student-oriented travel agencies.** To qualify you'll need a bona fide student ID card. Members of international student groups are also eligible.

➤ Student IDs & Services: **Council on International Educational Exchange** (✉ CIEE, 205 E. 42nd St., 14th floor, New York, NY 10017, ☎ 212/822–2600 or 888/268–6245, FAX 212/822–2699), for mail orders only, in the United States. **Travel Cuts** (✉ 187 College St., Toronto, Ontario M5T 1P7, ☎ 416/979–2406 or 800/667–2887 in Canada).

➤ Student Tours: **ContikiHolidays** (✉ 300 Plaza Alicante, Suite 900,Garden Grove, CA 92840, ☎ 714/740–0808 or 800/266–8454, FAX 714/740–2034).

SUBWAYS

The 714-mi subway system operates 24 hours a day and, especially within Manhattan, serves most of the places you'll want to visit. It's cheaper than a cab and, during the workweek, often faster than either cabs or buses. The trains have been rid of their graffiti (some New Yorkers, of course, miss the colorful old trains), and air-conditioned cars predominate on every line. Still, the New York subway is not problem-free. Many trains are crowded and noisy. Although trains usually run frequently, especially during rush hours, you never know when some incident somewhere on the line may stall traffic. Don't write off the subway—some 3.5 million passengers ride it every day without incident—but stay alert (☞ Safety, *above*).

Subway fares are $1.50, although reduced fares are available for senior citizens and people with disabilities during nonrush hours. If you're just taking a few trips, you should pay with tokens; they are sold at token booths that are *usually* open at each station, as well as at token vending machines. It is advisable to **buy several tokens at one time** to avoid having to wait in line later. For four or more subway trips, you might find it easier to use the New York City Transit (MTA)'s MetroCard Gold, a thin, plastic card with a magnetic strip; swipe it through the reader at the turnstile, and the cost of the fare is automatically deducted. When you put $15 or more on a MetroCard you get one free fare, making the card worthwhile if you are planning on using the subway a good bit. They are sold at all subway stations and at some stores—look for an "Authorized Sales Agent" sign. You can buy a card for a minimum of $3 (two trips) and a maximum of $80, in $6 increments. You can add more money to a card, and more than one person can use the same card: Swipe it through the turnstile once for each rider. Both tokens and MetroCards permit unlimited transfers within the system. When you use the MetroCard, you can transfer free from bus to subway or subway to bus within two hours.

Most subway entrances are at street corners and are marked by lampposts with globe-shape green lights. Subway lines are named for numbers and letters, such as the 3 line or the A line. Some lines run "express" and skip lots of stops; others are "locals" and make all stops. Each station entrance has a sign indicating the lines that run through the station; some stations are also marked "uptown only" or "downtown only." Before entering subway stations, **read the signs carefully**—one of the most frequent mistakes visitors make is taking the train in the wrong direction—although this can be an adventure, it can also be frustrating if you're in a hurry. Maps of the full subway system are posted on trains near the doors and at stations. You can usually pick up free maps at token booths, too.

For route information, **ask the token clerk, a transit policeman, or a fellow rider.** Once New Yorkers realize you're harmless, most bend over backward to be helpful.

➤ SCHEDULE AND ROUTE INFORMATION: **New York City Transit** (MTA, ☎ 718/330–1234), available daily 6–9.

TAXIS

Taxis are usually easy to hail on the street or from a taxi rank in front of major hotels, though finding one at rush hour or in the rain can take some time. You can tell if a cab is available by checking its rooftop light; if the center panel is lit and the side panels dark, the driver is ready to take passengers. Taxi fares cost $2 for the first ⅕ mi, 30¢ for each ⅕ mi thereafter, and 20¢ for each minute not in motion. A 50¢ surcharge is added to rides begun between 8 PM and 6 AM. There is no charge for extra passengers, but you must pay any bridge or tunnel tolls incurred during your trip (sometimes a driver will personally pay a toll to keep moving quickly, but that amount will be added to the fare when the ride is over). Taxi drivers expect a 15% tip.

To avoid unhappy taxi experiences, **try to have a general idea of where you want to go.** A few cab drivers are dishonest; some are ignorant; some can barely understand English. If you have no idea of the proper route, you may be taken for a long and costly ride.

TELEPHONES

The area code for Manhattan is 212; for Brooklyn, Queens, the Bronx, and Staten Island, it's 718. Pay telephones cost 25¢ for the first three minutes of a local call (this includes calls between 212 and 718 area codes); an extra deposit is required for each additional minute.

DIRECTORY & OPERATOR INFORMATION

To reach an operator, dial 0. For local directory assistance, dial 411 or 555–1212.

LOCAL CALLS

Local calls require only the seven-digit telephone number.

LONG-DISTANCE CALLS

Competitive long-distance carriers make calling within the United States relatively convenient and let you avoid hotel surcharges. By dialing an 800 number, you can get connected to the long-distance company of your choice.

➤ LONG-DISTANCE CARRIERS: **AT&T** (☎ 800/225–5288). **MCI** (☎ 800/888–8000). **Sprint** (☎ 800/366–2255).

PUBLIC PHONES

Make sure that the pay phone is labeled as a Bell Atlantic telephone; the unmarked variety are notorious change-eaters. There are also public credit-card phones scattered around the city. If you want to consult a directory or make a more leisurely call, pay phones in the lobbies of office buildings or hotels (some of which take credit cards) are a better choice.

TIPPING

The customary tipping rate is 15%–20% for taxi drivers and waiters (☞ Chapter 6); bellhops are usually given $2 in luxury hotels, $1 elsewhere. Hotel maids should be tipped around $1 per day of your stay.

TOUR OPERATORS

Buying a prepackaged tour or independent vacation can make your trip to New York less expensive and more hassle-free. Because everything is prearranged, you'll spend less time planning.

Operators that handle several hundred thousand travelers per year can use their purchasing power to give you a good price. Their high volume may also indicate financial stability. But some small companies provide more personalized service; because they tend to specialize, they may also be more knowledgeable about a given area.

BOOKING WITH AN AGENT

Travel agents are excellent resources. In fact, large operators accept bookings made only through travel agents. But it's a good idea to **collect brochures from several agencies,** because some agents' suggestions may be influenced by relationships with tour and package firms that reward them for volume sales. If you have a special interest, **find an agent with expertise in that area**; ASTA (☞ Travel Agencies, *below*) has a database of specialists worldwide.

Make sure your travel agent knows the accommodations and other services. Ask about the hotel's location, room size, beds, and whether it has a pool, room service, or programs for children, if you care about these. Has your agent been there in person or sent others you can contact?

Do some homework on your own, too: Local tourism boards can provide information about lesser-known and small-niche operators, some of which may sell only direct.

BUYER BEWARE

Each year consumers are stranded or lose their money when tour operators—even very large ones with excellent reputations—go out of business. So **check out the operator.** Find out how long the company has been in business, and ask several travel agents about its reputation. If the package or tour you are considering is priced lower than in your wildest dreams, **be skeptical.** Try to **book with a company that has a consumer-protection program.** If the operator has such a program, you'll find information about it in the company's brochure. If the operator you are considering does not offer some kind of consumer protection, then ask for references from satisfied customers.

In the U.S., members of the National Tour Association and United States Tour Operators Association are required to set aside funds to cover your payments and travel arrangements in case the company defaults. It's also a good idea to choose a company that participates in the American Society of Travel Agent's Tour Operator Program (TOP). This gives you a forum if there are any disputes between you and your tour operator; ASTA will act as mediator.

➤ TOUR-OPERATOR RECOMMENDATIONS: **American Society of Travel Agents** (☞ Travel Agencies, *below*). **National Tour Association** (✉ NTA, 546 E. Main St., Lexington, KY 40508, ☎ 606/226–4444 or 800/755–8687). **United States Tour Operators Association** (✉ USTOA, 342 Madison Ave., Suite 1522, New York, NY 10173, ☎ 212/599–6599 or 800/468–7862, FAX 212/599–6744).

COSTS

The more your package or tour includes, the better you can predict the ultimate cost of your vacation. Make sure you know exactly what is covered, and **beware of hidden costs.** Are taxes, tips, and service charges included? Transfers and baggage handling? Entertainment and excursions? These can add up.

Prices for packages and tours are usually quoted per person, based on two sharing a room. If traveling solo, you may be required to pay the full double-occupancy rate. Some operators eliminate this surcharge if you agree to be matched with a roommate of the same sex, even if one is not found by departure time.

GROUP TOURS

Among companies that sell tours to New York, the following are nationally known, have a proven reputation, and offer plenty of options. The classifications used below represent different price categories, and you'll probably encounter these terms when talking to a travel agent or tour operator. The key difference is usually in accommodations, which run from budget to better, and better-yet to best.

➤ DELUXE: **Globus** (5301 S. Federal Circle, Littleton, CO 80123-2980, ☎ 303/797–2800 or 800/221–0090, FAX 303/347–2080). **Maupintour** (✉ 1515 St. Andrews Dr., Lawrence, KS 66047, ☎ 913/843–1211 or 800/255–4266, FAX 913/843–8351).

➤ FIRST CLASS: **Gadabout Tours** (700 E. Tahquitz Canyon Way, Palm Springs, CA 92262-6767, ☎ 619/325–5556 or 800/952–5068). **Trafalgar Tours** (✉ 11 E. 26th St., New York, NY 10010, ☎ 212/689–8977 or 800/854–0103, FAX 800/457–6644).

➤ BUDGET: **Cosmos** (☞ Globus, *above*).

PACKAGES

Like group tours, independent vacation packages are available from major tour operators and airlines. The companies listed below offer vacation packages in a broad price range.

➤ AIR/HOTEL: **Continental Vacations** (☎ 800/634–5555). **Delta Vacations** (☎ 800/872–7786). **United Vacations** (☎ 800/328–6877). **US Airways Vacations** (☎ 800/455–0123).

➤ CUSTOM PACKAGES: **Amtrak Vacations** (☎ 800/321–8684).

➤ HOTEL ONLY: **SuperCities** (139 Main St., Cambridge, MA 02142, ☎ 800/333–1234).

FROM THE U.K.

➤ TOUR OPERATORS: **Americana Vacations Ltd.** (11 Little Portland St., London W1 5ND, ☎ 0171/637–7853). **British Airways Holidays** (Astral Towers, Betts Way, London Rd., Crawley, West Sussex RH10 2XA, ☎ 01293/723–121). **Jetsave** (Sussex House, London Rd., East Grinstead, West Sussex RH19 1LD, ☎ 01342/327–711). **Key to America** (1–3 Station Rd., Ashford, Middlesex, TW15 2UW, ☎ 01784/248–777). **Premier Holidays** (Westbrook, Milton Rd., Cambridge CB4 1YQ, ☎ 01223/516–516). **Trailfinders** (42–50 Earls Court Rd., London W8 6EJ, ☎ 0171/937–5400; 58 Deansgate, Manchester M3 2FF, ☎ 0161/839–6969). **Travelpack** (Clarendon House, Clarendon Rd., Eccles, Manchester M30 9AL, ☎ 0990/747–101). **Virgin Holidays Ltd.** (The Galleria, Station Rd., Crawley, West Sussex RH10 1WW, ☎ 01293/617–181).

THEME TRIPS

➤ LEARNING: **Smithsonian Study Tours and Seminars** (☞ Art and Architecture, *above*).

➤ PERFORMING ARTS: **Dailey-Thorp Travel** (330 W. 58th St., #610, New York, NY 10019-1817, ☎ 212/307–1555 or 800/998–4677, FAX 212/974–1420). **Keith Prowse Tours** (234 W. 44th St., #1000, New York, NY 10036, ☎ 212/398–1430 or 800/669–8687, FAX 212/302–4251). **Sutherland Hit Show Tours** (370 Lexington Ave., #411, New York, NY 10017, ☎ 212/532–7732 or 800/221–2442, FAX 212/532–7741).

TRAIN TRAVEL

Amtrak trains from points across the United States arrive at Penn Station (✉ W. 31st to 33rd Sts., between 7th and 8th Aves.). For trains from New York City to Long Island and New Jersey, take the Long Island Railroad and New Jersey Transit respectively; both operate from Penn Station. Metro-North Commuter Railroad trains take passengers from Grand Central Terminal (✉ E. 42nd St. at Park Ave.) to points north of New York City, both in New York State and Connecticut.

➤ TRAIN SCHEDULES: **Amtrak** (☎ 800/872–7245). **Long Island Railroad** (☎ 718/217–5477). **Metro-North Commuter Railroad** (☎ 212/340–3000).

New Jersey Transit (☎ 201/762–5100). PATH (☎ 800/234–7284).

TRANSPORTATION

When it comes to getting around New York, you'll have your pick of transportation in every neighborhood. The subway and bus networks are thorough, although getting across town can take some extra maneuvering. If you're not pressed for time, **take a public bus**; they make more stops than subways, but you can also see part of the city as you travel. True to the city's reputation, you'll see as many yellow cabs as personal cars, and while just getting into a taxi costs more than a subway or bus ride, the convenience can be worth it. Depending on the time of day and your destination, walking might be the easiest and most enjoyable option. During weekday rush hours (from 7:30 to 9:30 AM and 5 to 7 PM, **avoid the jammed midtown area, both in the subways and on the streets**; travel time can easily double.

TRAVEL AGENCIES

A good travel agent puts your needs first. Look for an agency that has been in business at least five years, emphasizes customer service, and has someone on staff who specializes in your destination. In addition, **make sure the agency belongs to a professional trade organization,** such as ASTA in the United States. If your travel agency is also acting as your tour operator, *see* Buyer Beware in Tour Operators, *above*).

➤ LOCAL AGENT REFERRALS: **American Society of Travel Agents** (ASTA, ☎ 800/965–2782 24-hr hot line, FAX 703/684–8319). **Association of Canadian Travel Agents** (✉ Suite 201, 1729 Bank St., Ottawa, Ontario K1V 7Z5, ☎ 613/521–0474, FAX 613/521–0805). **Association of British Travel Agents** (✉ 55–57 Newman St., London W1P 4AH, ☎ 0171/637–2444, FAX 0171/637–0713). **Australian Federation of Travel Agents** (☎ 02/9264–3299). **Travel Agents' Association of New Zealand** (☎ 04/499–0104).

VISITOR INFORMATION

Contact the New York City visitors information offices below for brochures, subway and bus maps, a calendar of events, listings of hotels and weekend hotel packages, and discount coupons for Broadway shows. For a free "I Love New York" booklet listing New York City attractions and tour packages, contact the New York State Division of Tourism.

TOURIST INFORMATION

➤ CITY INFORMATION: **New York Convention and Visitors Bureau** (✉ 810 7th Ave., 3rd floor, between 52nd and 53rd Sts., New York, NY 10019, ☎ 212/484–1200, FAX 212/484–1280), weekdays 9–5. **New York City Visitors Information Center** (☎ 212/397–8222).

➤ STATEWIDE INFORMATION: **New York State Division of Tourism** (✉ 1 Commerce Ave., Albany, NY 12245, ☎ 518/474–4116 or 800/225–5697).

WALKING

The cheapest, sometimes the fastest, and usually the most interesting way to explore this city is by walking. Because New Yorkers by and large live in apartments rather than in houses, and travel by cab, bus, or subway rather than by private car, they end up walking quite a lot. As a result, street life is a vital part of the local culture. On crowded sidewalks, people gossip, snack, browse, cement business deals, make romantic rendezvous, encounter long-lost friends, and fly into irrational quarrels with strangers. It's a wonderfully democratic hubbub.

A typical New Yorker, if there is such an animal, walks quickly and focuses intently on dodging around cars, buses, bicycle messengers, construction sites, and other pedestrians. Although this might make natives seem hurried and rude, they will often cheerfully come to the aid of a lost pedestrian, so **don't hesitate to ask a passerby for directions.**

WEB SITES

Do **check out the World Wide Web** when you're planning. You'll find everything from up-to-date weather forecasts to virtual tours of famous cities. Fodor's Web site (www.fodors.com) is a great place to start your on-line travels. For more information specifically on New York City visit: **New York Public Library** at www.nypl.org offers wonderful historical information; **Movielink 777–FILM Online** at www.777film.com is one-stop shopping for movie previews and tickets; The **Village Voice** at www.villagevoice.com and **New York Sidewalk** at newyork.sidewalk.com offer comprehensive, searchable events listings; The **New York Subway Finder** at www.krusch.com/nysf.html provides subway directions between any two New York addresses.

WHEN TO GO

At one time, it seemed New York's cultural life was limited to the months between October and May, when new Broadway shows opened, museums mounted major exhibitions, and formal seasons for opera, ballet, and concerts held sway. Today, however, there are Broadway openings even in mid-July, and a number of touring orchestras and opera and ballet companies visit the city in summer. In late spring and summer, the streets and parks are filled with ethnic parades, impromptu sidewalk concerts, and free performances under the stars. Except for regular closing days and a few holidays (such as Christmas, New Year's Day, and Thanksgiving), the city's museums are open year-round.

CLIMATE

Although there's an occasional bone-chilling winter day, with winds blasting in off the Hudson, snow only occasionally accumulates in the city. Summer is the only unpleasant time of year, especially the humid, hot days of August, when many Manhattanites vacate the island for summer homes. Most hotels are air-conditioned, but if you're traveling in the summer and choosing budget accommodations, it's a good idea to **ask whether your room has an air conditioner.** Air-conditioned stores, restaurants, theaters, and museums provide respite from the heat; so do the many green expanses of parks. Subways and buses are usually air-conditioned, but subway stations can be as hot as saunas.

When September arrives—with its dry "champagne-like" weather—the city shakes off its summer sluggishness. Mild and comfortable, autumn shows the city off at its best, with yellow and bronze foliage displays in the parks.

The following table shows each month's average daily highs and lows:

Jan.	38F	3C	May	72F	22C	Sept.	76F	24C
	25	-4		54	12		60	16
Feb.	40F	4C	June	80F	27C	Oct.	65F	18C
	27	-3		63	17		50	10
Mar.	50F	10C	July	85F	29C	Nov.	54F	12C
	35	2		68	20		41	5
Apr.	61F	16C	Aug.	84F	29C	Dec.	43F	6C
	44	7		67	19		31	-1

➤ FORECASTS: **Weather Channel Connection** (☎ 900/932–8437), 95¢ per minute from a Touch-Tone phone.

1 Destination: New York City

DISCOVERING NEW YORK

IN 1925 the youthful songwriting team of Richard Rodgers and Larry Hart wrote "Manhattan," arguably the loveliest city anthem ever. "We'll have Manhattan, the Bronx, and Staten Island, too," it promises, drawing its images from the merry scramble that was the city more than 60 years ago: "sweet pushcarts," "bologna on a roll," a subway that "charms," Brighton Beach, Coney Island, and the popular comedy *Abie's Irish Rose*. "We'll turn Manhattan into an isle of joy," coos the refrain.

Several decades later, in 1989, an album called simply *New York*, by aging enfant terrible rocker Lou Reed, viewed the same city with glasses fogged by despair and cynicism: Drugs, crime, racism, and promiscuity reigned in what Reed considered a sinkhole of "crudity, cruelty of thought and sound." His voice brittle with weary irony, he sang, "This is no time for celebration." Manhattan's "sweet pushcarts" now apparently overflow with deadly vials of crack.

So, whom to believe—Larry or Lou?

The truth of the matter is slippery, for New York has long been a mosaic of grand contradictions, a city for which there has never been—nor ever will be—a clear consensus. Hart himself took the city to task in another song, "Give It Back to the Indians," whose lyrics count off a litany of problems that still exist: crime, dirt, high prices, traffic jams, and all-around urban chaos. Yet for all that, millions live here, grumbling but happy, and millions more visit, curious as cats to find out what the magnificent fuss is all about.

I was in eighth grade in suburban Detroit when I first really became aware of New York. A friend's Manhattan-born mother subscribed to the Sunday *New York Times*, and at their house I'd pore over the "Arts and Leisure" section, as rapt as an archaeologist with a cave painting. The details of what I read there have blurred, but I remember vividly the sensation I felt while reading: a combined anticipation and nostalgia so keen it bordered on pain. Although I had never been there, I was homesick for New York.

It's my home now, yet I can still appreciate the impulse that draws visitors here. In a city so ripe with possibilities, we are all more or less visitors.

I think of this on an uncharacteristically warm day in late March, as fellow New Yorkers and I escape from the hives of offices and homes to celebrate spring's first preview. We unbutton our jackets, leave buses a stop or two before our usual destinations, quicken our resolve to visit that new exhibit at the Met or jog around the Central Park Reservoir. A jubilant sense of renewal infects us all, and I overhear one happy fellow saying to a friend, "I felt just like a tourist yesterday."

Whenever I get the New York blues, the best tonic for me is to glimpse the city through the eyes of a visitor. One day, after subway construction had rerouted me well out of my usual path, I found myself in the grimy Times Square station—hardly the place for a spiritual conversion. As usual I had that armor of body language that we New Yorkers reflexively assume to protect ourselves from strangers bent on (1) ripping us off, (2) doing us bodily harm, (3) converting us, (4) making sexual advances, or (5) being general pains-in-the-butt just for the hell of it. But that day, tucked away in a corner, was a group of musicians—not an uncommon sight in New York—playing the guitar, organ, and accordion with gusto and good spirits behind a homemade sign that dubbed them the Argentinean Tango Company. Like many other street musicians in Manhattan, they were *good*, but I was only half listening, too intent on cursing the city. Just as I passed the band, however, I noticed four teenagers drawn to the music—visitors, surely, they were far too open and trusting to be anything else. Grinning as widely as the Argentineans, they began to perform a spontaneous imitation of flamenco dancing—clapping hands above their heads, raising their heels, laughing at themselves, and only slightly self-conscious. Passersby, myself included, broke into smiles. As I made my way to the subway platform, buoyed by the impromptu show, I once again forgave New York. This minor piece of magic was apology enough.

I wonder whether that was the moment one of those teenagers happened to fall in love with the city. It *can* happen in a single moment, to a visitor or to a longtime resident. Perhaps it hits during a stroll through Riverside Park after a blanketing snowfall, when the trees have turned to crystal and the city feels a hush it knows at no other time. Or maybe it happens when you turn a corner and spy, beyond a phalanx of RVs and a tangle of cables and high-beam lights, the filming of a new movie. That moment could also come when the house lights dim at the Metropolitan Opera, and the chandeliers make their magisterial ascent to the ceiling; or when you first glimpse the Prometheus statue in Rockefeller Center, gleaming like a giant present under the annual Christmas tree as dozens of skaters cut swirls of seasonal colors on the ice below. You may even be smitten in that instant when, walking along the streets in the haze of a summer afternoon, you look up above the sea of anonymous faces to see—and be astonished by—the lofty rows of skyscrapers, splendid in their arrogance and power. At times like these it is perfectly permissible to stop for a moment, take a breath, and think, "Wow! *This is New York!*" We who live here do it every so often ourselves.

For some, of course, that special moment comes when they spot a street or building made familiar by movies or television, from *I Love Lucy* to *On the Waterfront*. At the Empire State Building, who can help but remember King Kong's pathetically courageous swing from its pinnacle? Or at the brooding Dakota, the chilling destiny created for Rosemary's baby within those fortresslike walls? In the mind's eye, Audrey Hepburn is eternally pairing diamonds and a doughnut as she wends her swank way down 5th Avenue to have breakfast at Tiffany's. And the miniature park on Sutton Place will always be where Woody Allen and Diane Keaton began their angst-ridden *Manhattan* love affair, with the 59th Street Bridge gleaming beyond and Gershwin music swelling in the background.

THERE'S A MOMENT OF sudden magic when a New York stereotype, seen so often on screen that it seems a joke, suddenly comes to life: when a gum-cracking waitress calls you "hon" or the Empire State Building comes unexpectedly into view, its top 30 stories festively illuminated. There's also the thrill of discovering one of New York's cities-within-the-city: Mulberry Street in Little Italy; Mott Street in Chinatown; Park Avenue's enclave of wealth and privilege; SoHo and TriBeCa, with their artistic types dressed in black from head to toe; or Eighth Avenue in Chelsea, the nexus of one of the city's prominent lesbian and gay communities. The first glimpse of a landmark could excite the visitor's infatuation, too: frenetic Grand Central Station, abustle with suburban commuters; the concrete caverns of Wall Street, throbbing with power and ambition; or the Statue of Liberty, which neither cliché nor cheap souvenir can render common.

As you ready yourself to take on New York's contradictions, prepare to wonder and to exult. Here, on a single day, you might catch a glimpse of John Kennedy Jr. or Rollerena, the gloriously tacky drag-queen-cum-fairy-godmother on roller skates, who waves her magic wand to bestow blessings on select public events. Here you can eat sumptuously at a hot-dog stand or at a world-celebrated gourmet shrine.

Excess and deprivation mingle here: As a limousine crawls lazily to take its pampered passengers to their luxe destination, it rolls past a beggar seeking the warmth that steams from the city's belly through an iron grate. It's a ludicrously bright cartoon and a sobering documentary, New York—almost too much for one city to be. It's maddening and it's thrilling; monstrous, yet beautiful beyond parallel.

And I envy anyone that first taste of it.

– Michael Adams

Writer Michael Adams finally moved to his hometown, New York City, 17 years ago.

WHAT'S WHERE

Rockefeller Center and Midtown

Apart from sweeping panoramas from the Hudson River or the New York Bay, no other city scene so clearly says "New York" than this 19-building complex known as Rockefeller Center. These 22 acres of prime real estate (between 5th and 7th avenues and 47th and 52nd streets) with the Channel Gardens; the GE, Time & Life, and Associated Press buildings; Radio City Music Hall; and plazas, concourses, and street-level shops form a city within a city. St. Patrick's Cathedral, Saks Fifth Avenue, and the rest of midtown's gleaming skyscrapers are just steps away.

5th Avenue and 57th Street

One of the world's great shopping districts, 5th Avenue north of Rockefeller Center and 57th Street between Lexington Avenue and 7th Avenue is where you'll find some of the biggest names in New York retailing as well as the crème de la crème of designer boutiques. Fifty-seventh Street also is home to several theme restaurants, such as the Motown Cafe, Planet Hollywood, and the Hard Rock Cafe.

Times Square, 42nd Street, and the Theater District

The place where the ball drops on New Year's Eve, Times Square is again one of the city's principal energy centers. Long-neglected historic theaters are being brought dramatically back to life, and new construction is radically transforming the area, especially the real 42nd Street between 7th and 8th avenues. The Times Tower itself, from which the neighborhood took its name, is at the intersection of Broadway, 7th Avenue, and 42nd Street. Thirty or so major Broadway theaters are all nearby, in an area bounded roughly by 41st and 53rd streets between 6th and 9th avenues. Also just a short walk away are Theater Row, a string of intimate off-Broadway houses on the south side of 42nd Street between 9th and 10th avenues, and Restaurant Row (46th Street between 8th and 9th avenues), where critics, actors, directors, playwrights, and spectators come to dine before and after the show. Bryant Park and the New York Public Library gloriously mark 42nd Street's midpoint. Going much farther east on 42nd Street, past 5th Avenue, you'll discover the Beaux Arts beauty of Grand Central Terminal, grandly transformed, à la Washington, D.C.'s Union Station, into a destination in its own right. East of Grand Central is the United Nations headquarters on a lushly landscaped riverside tract just east of 1st Avenue between 42nd and 48th streets.

Murray Hill to Union Square

Three distinct neighborhoods east of 5th Avenue between 20th and 40th streets—Murray Hill, Madison Square, and Gramercy Park—have preserved some of the historic charm of 19th-century New York: brownstone mansions and town houses, the city's earliest "skyscrapers," shady parks, and, yes, even in New York, some quiet streets. South of Gramercy Park lies Union Square, with its restored park, wonderful Greenmarket, and trend-setting restaurants.

Museum Mile and the Upper East Side

Once called Manhattan's Millionaire's Row, the stretch of 5th Avenue between 79th and 104th streets has been renamed Museum Mile because of the startling number of world-class collections of art and artifacts scattered along its length (some housed in the former mansions of some of the Upper East Side's more illustrious industrialists and philanthropists). It's also still home to more millionaires—and billionaires—than any other street in the city. Whatever you do, don't leave New York without visiting at least a few galleries in the largest art museum in the western hemisphere, the Metropolitan Museum of Art, on the Central Park side of 5th Avenue at 82nd Street.

Central Park

This 843-acre patch of rolling countryside is where Manhattanites go to escape from the urban jungle and reconnect with nature. Named a National Historic Landmark in 1965, Central Park offers the city's most soothing vistas and opportunities for just about any activity that a city dweller might engage in outdoors. Under the care of the private, not-for-profit Central Park Conservancy, the park is in better shape than ever before—all right in the heart of the city. The park is bordered by 59th Street, on the south; 5th Avenue, on the east, 110th Street, on the north, and

Central Park West, which is what 8th Avenue becomes above 59th Street.

The Upper West Side

The ornate prewar buildings that line the boulevards of Broadway, West End Avenue, Riverside Drive, and Central Park West provide a stately backdrop for glitzy boutiques and the scads of wanna-be soap actors hustling off to their auditions at ABC-TV and hopeful performers and aficionados making the pilgrimage to Lincoln Center. A stroll up tony Columbus Avenue should stretch at least as far as the Museum of Natural History, whose lavish grounds and pink-granite corner towers occupy a four-block tract. Farther uptown, in Morningside Heights, are the ivied buildings of Columbia University and the Cathedral of St. John the Divine, a magnificent Episcopal church.

Harlem

An important influence on American culture, this once-quiet country village grew into a suburb of apartment houses and brownstones for succeeding waves of German, Irish, Jewish, and Italian immigrants. For nearly a hundred years now it has been a mecca for African-American and Hispanic-American culture and life. Harlem extends north from 110th Street to about 145th Street (the border of Manhattanville); the most interesting sights on the tourist trail fall roughly between 116th Street and 135th Street.

Chelsea

Like its London district namesake, New York's Chelsea maintains a villagelike personality, with a number of quiet streets graced by lovingly renovated town houses. The neighborhood stretches from 5th Avenue west to the Hudson River, and from 14th to 23rd streets (and above). Chelsea has always been congenial to writers and artists, and it has also embraced a multicultural population for decades; it now includes an active gay community that frequents the lively stores and restaurants on 8th Avenue. In recent years the area has witnessed an economic boost with the opening of 6th Avenue superstores and the Chelsea Piers Sports and Entertainment Complex on the Hudson. The gallery scene thrives west of 10th Avenue from 20th to 29th streets.

Greenwich Village

Extending from 14th Street south to Houston Street and from the piers of the Hudson River east to 5th Avenue, the crazy-quilt pattern of narrow, tree-lined streets known to New Yorkers simply as "the Village" remains true to its 19th-century heritage as a haven for immigrants, bohemians, students, artists, actors, carousers, and tourists. It's one of the best parts of the city to wander for hours. The Village is still home to one of the largest gay communities in the country (centered on Sheridan Square and Christopher Street).

The East Village

Many regard the East Village—an area bounded by 14th Street on the north, 4th Avenue or the Bowery on the west, Houston Street on the south, and the East River—as the island's most colorful neighborhood. Here holdouts from the 1960s coexist with a deeply entrenched Eastern European community. Artists, punks, and account executives move freely between the Polish and Ukrainian coffee shops, galleries, trendy pasta bars, offbeat shops, and St. Mark's Place—a local thoroughfare for sidewalk vendors.

SoHo and TriBeCa

SoHo (*S*outh of *Ho*uston Street) is bounded on its other three sides by Broadway, Canal Street, and 6th Avenue. TriBeCa (the *Tri*angle *Be*low *Ca*nal Street) extends roughly as far south as Murray Street and east to West Broadway. Over the past 20 years both neighborhoods have gradually been transformed into lively realms of loft dwellers, galleries, and very trendy shops and cafés.

Little Italy and Chinatown

Little Italy—a few blocks south of Houston Street between Broadway and the Bowery—is today not as Italian as it used to be. Still, Mulberry Street and its famous—and, in some cases, infamous—eateries are rife with atmosphere. If you head east along Canal Street (the southern border of Little Italy), you will run into the ever-expanding and frenetic Chinatown (the area south of Canal on the east side), which has over the years spilled over into much of the Lower East Side's Jewish neighborhood and into Little Italy as well. One of the biggest attractions in Chinatown is simply the carnival-like atmosphere on the small streets, which are packed with shoppers and purveyors of untold varieties of pungent fish and exotic vegetables.

Wall Street and the Battery

The synonymous financial nexus and thoroughfare called Wall Street, which clusters downtown around the New York and American stock exchanges, wears its wealth on its architecturally stunning sleeve. At the bottom of the island, Battery Park is one of the few Manhattan locales that bring you the waterfront that once played a vital role in the history's growth and history. You also get fabulous views of the Statue of Liberty and Ellis Island.

The Seaport and the Courts

New York's days as a great 19th-century haven for clipper ships are preserved in lower Manhattan at South Street Seaport, centered on Fulton Street at the East River and crowned by the Brooklyn Bridge. Just blocks away, you can take in another slice of New York history by walking the streets of the city hall district, with its majestic court edifices.

PLEASURES AND PASTIMES

Fine Dining

The old reliable four-star French restaurants, steak houses, delis, and diners are still doing what they've been doing best for years (and in some cases, decades), but there's plenty new afoot. For one thing, the bistro-trattoria mania that broke out a few years ago is going strong: The French are downtown, the Italians on the Upper East Side. The mix of small ethnic eating spots reflects shifting immigration patterns, and the newest national cuisines to make their mark are Austrian, Afghan, Brazilian, Thai, Turkish, and Jamaican. Chinatown, not to be outdone, is extending its borders, and noodle shops, complete with hanging ducks, heaping bowls of fried rice, and low prices, are sprouting up everywhere.

Nightlife

New York's vibrant nightlife has something to please everyone. Much of the club life is concentrated downtown—in one night you can go to a grungy East Village dance dive, a classic West Village jazz joint, a sleekly decorated TriBeCa celebrity trap, or a preppy Wall Street hangout. Uptown's the place to go to listen to a romantic singer in a sophisticated setting like the Algonquin's Oak Room or the Cafe Carlyle. If you just want a drink, you can frequent an unpretentious neighborhood saloon in jeans or a vintage hotel bar in your tux. You can also write your novel in a coffee bar or laugh yourself silly at a comedy club.

Shopping

Whether you're planning to run your credit cards up to the max or just window-shop, New York offers a veritable orgy of options. Try the South Street Seaport for its unique combination of upscale, high-tech, and kitschy retail shops (and a spectacular view of the Brooklyn Bridge); the Lower East Side for inexpensive clothing and shoes; SoHo for art and antiques, avant-garde gifts and decorative items, gourmet foods, and funky clothes; 5th and Madison avenues for haute couture; Herald Square for the biggest department stores; Chelsea for hip, superstore bargains; Columbus Avenue for some of the city's glitziest and most upscale if not top-of-the-line shops (and one of the biggest flea markets in the city); and the Upper East Side for unique and stylish items for the home, fine antiques, and designer clothing.

Summer Arts

In summer the open spaces of the city become outdoor concert halls. Lincoln Center's Out-of-Doors, Mostly Mozart, Midsummer Night Swing, and the Lincoln Center Festival transform Manhattan's performing arts centerpiece into a virtual state fair of the arts; while the theaters fill up with music, dance, and theater productions, stages set up in the plaza accommodate jazz dancers, chamber orchestras, Broadway lyricists and composers, mimes, dance bands, children's theater, and more. Metropolitan Opera in the Parks works its way throughout the five boroughs. In Central Park the New York Shakespeare Festival stages two plays every summer, while SummerStage fills the Naumburg Bandshell with free programs ranging from grand opera to polka to experimental rock. In Brooklyn's Prospect

Park, the city's longest-running free performance series, Celebrate Brooklyn, brings a huge variety of performers to the most populous borough. To escape the heat, head to an indoor concert at the World Financial Center, near Battery Park.

Walking

New York is a walker's city. It's hard to get lost, except in the Village and lower Manhattan, in general, where New York's rigid grid pattern of streets falls apart. So step into your best walking shoes, choose any avenue or street, and follow it from one end to the other or from river to river, observing how the neighborhoods shade gradually into one another. Or hike across one of the city's many bridges for a fresh look at scenery that usually speeds by in a blur. Some of our favorite walks are 5th Avenue from 40th Street to Central Park; the path through Central Park from Grand Army Plaza to Bethesda Fountain; Broadway on the Upper West Side from Lincoln Center to 86th Street; east to west on Bleecker Street in Greenwich Village; and the Brooklyn Bridge from Manhattan to Brooklyn Heights and its Promenade.

GREAT ITINERARIES

Though it's a matter of opinion about the oft-touted claim that New York City is the "capital of the world," New York truly has something for everyone. For exactly that reason, prescribing visitor itineraries is a challenge. A theater buff may be content to spend days without leaving the vicinity of Times Square, the more historic minded may be equally swept away by the impressive architecture of old buildings in lower Manhattan, and art lovers will want to spend their time darting between uptown and downtown museums and galleries. And then there are the ever-changing restaurants and shops, and the approximately 8 million characters, many of them walking the streets, that give the city its vitality. The following suggestions are merely that; when planning your own trip, be sure to consider the weather, the time of year, the day of the week, and of course your own interests. Consult Chapters 2 and 3 for more information about individual sights.

If You Have 3 Days

Begin Day 1 at **Castle Clinton** in **Battery Park** to catch the ferries to the **Statue of Liberty** and **Ellis Island.** Arrive early to minimize the wait, and if you only have the morning to spare, choose just one of these two destinations as your goal. On your return walk northeast from Battery Park on Water Street, passing the **Wall Street** area on the way toward bustling **South Street Seaport,** where you can have lunch, shop, and get a feel for New York's maritime past. For more great views, head east to the **Brooklyn Bridge** or west to the **World Trade Center** observation deck. A great way to end the day is with a feast in **Chinatown** or **Little Italy,** both in lower Manhattan.

On Day 2 work your way north to midtown's **Grand Central Terminal,** one of the busiest places around. From here it's an easy walk or bus ride east on 42nd Street to the **United Nations** (on the East River) or west to **Times Square**; on the way you'll pass the **New York Public Library** main building, with the lions out front, and **Bryant Park.** At the United Nations your best bet is a guided tour, but at Times Square you're better off just observing life buzz around you in theaters, restaurants, and shops. After lunch (you won't have any trouble finding nourishment in midtown), head over to **5th Avenue** and walk north to **Rockefeller Center.** If you're a shopper, 5th Avenue will fill your afternoon. If not, visit the **Museum of Modern Art** or the **Museum of Television and Radio,** both near Rockefeller Center. At sunset, if you missed the World Trade Center the day before, head downtown on 5th Avenue to the top of the **Empire State Building.** Otherwise, a Broadway show, preceded or followed by dinner in the theater district, will suitably end the day.

On Day 3 head out early for upper 5th Avenue's **Museum Mile,** though which museum (or group of museums) to visit can be a hard decision. Make sure you spend some time at the **Metropolitan Museum of Art,** one of the biggest and greatest art institutions in the world. The **Guggenheim Museum** and the **Whitney Museum of American Art** (technically not on Museum Mile, but close enough) offer new and different perspectives on 20th-century art; the **Museum of the City of New York** makes Gotham's history come alive; and the **Jewish Museum** and the **Cooper-Hewitt Museum,** both quartered in former private mansions right near one another, look at Jewish culture and design, respectively, as well as the lifestyles of rich, famous, and generous New Yorkers. Break up the day with a picnic lunch and a walk in **Central Park,** conveniently only steps from the museums. If you feel that you've exhausted exhibition possibilities on the Upper East Side or if they've exhausted you, walk west across the park (79th Street is a convenient place to enter the park, or take the 79th Street crosstown bus); a whole new world awaits on the Upper West Side, including the **American Museum of Natural History** and the **New-York Historical Society.** Cap your day with a musical or theatrical performance at **Carnegie Hall** or **Lincoln Center**—perhaps something outside if it's summer.

If You Have 5 to 7 Days

Start Day 1 with the city's most famous three-hour tour, a circumnavigation of Manhattan on the Circle Line. This cruise begins and ends at Pier 83 at West 42nd Street, close enough for you to eat lunch in **Times Square** and then follow the second half of Day 2 as described in If You Have 3 Days, *above.* On Day 2 spend time in Lower Manhattan visiting the **New York Stock Exchange** and taking the ferries from **Castle Clinton** in **Battery Park** to the **Statue of Liberty** and **Ellis Island.** It's a tough call, but you'll have to choose between getting to the ferries early and looking at the New York Stock Exchange first-thing. Both the Statue of Liberty and the Stock Exchange limit the number of visitors per day, and waiting times increase as the day goes on. The exhibits at Ellis Island, on the other hand, are usually wait-free once you arrive. You can eat either at the Statue of Liberty or on Ellis Island, but be sure to squeeze in time for the obligatory stop at **South Street Seaport** before the day ends.

On Day 3 follow the third-day itinerary outlined in If You Have 3 Days, *above.* Devote Day 4 to the cool and trendy—the streets of **Greenwich Village,** the **East Village,** and **SoHo.** Start at **Union Square,** preferable on a **Greenmarket** day, when you can load up on snacks. From here there's good, varied shopping if you walk south down **Broadway** all the way though SoHo—with **Grace Church** and a few museums and galleries along the way—into **Chinatown** with its ubiquitous restaurants. If you don't wish to venture down to lower Manhattan, spend time west of Broadway in Greenwich Village (from 14th to Houston streets); the area is full of curvy lanes and charming, low-rise historical buildings. The East Village (east of 4th Avenue between 14th and Houston streets) is where tomorrow's trends emerge, and it spills into the perpetually crowded and evolving Lower East Side, heart of early 20th-century immigrant New York. Bargains and tenements still define the neighborhood; for background, stop at the **Lower East Side Tenement Museum,** on Orchard Street. No matter where you go downtown, you won't want for food or diversions. Greenwich Village, the East Village, and SoHo have a number of small theaters that stage performances more innovative than those at the midtown showplaces.

Begin Day 5 with a leisurely breakfast in one of the quaint restaurants along **Irving Place** (east of Union Square), dining at an outdoor café if possible so you can watch the pedestrian traffic. From there you can work your way north through **Gramercy Park,** then up Madison Avenue and across 34th Street past the **Empire State Building,** and on over to **Herald Square** (synonymous with Macy's). Otherwise, from Irving Place head over to Union Square and continue west to explore **Chelsea,** with its numerous superstores, boutiques, restaurants, and galleries. All the way west is **Chelsea Piers** (at 23rd Street on the Hudson River), which has places to walk by the water and a number of restaurants. The sunsets over the river are often quite lovely. At night, if you haven't already made it to a Broadway show, it's time (or if you have, how about a second performance?).

On Day 6, as long as the weather cooperates, there's no better place than **Central Park.** The Loop Road will be full of bladers, bikers, and runners, so join the crowd. In summer the lawns have picnickers, sunbathers, and Frisbee players; in winter the Wollman Skating Rink is full. And there's always the zoo, the carriage rides, and the landscaped beauty of the park. Different areas of Central Park are convenient to the **Upper East Side** and **Museum**

Mile (5th Avenue), the **Upper West Side,** or to **57th Street.** If you happen to be in the park on a summer day when there is a free evening performance of Shakespeare, the Metropolitan Opera, the New York Philharmonic, or music at SummerStage (☞ Chapter 5), precede the show with a picnic dinner, which can be procured from the many gourmet delis and take-out restaurants east and west of the park.

On Day 7 there's still so much to keep you amused, but rather than planning the day ahead of time, leave it open to indulge a newfound fancy, or in case you missed something earlier. Check out a different Manhattan neighborhood, such as **Harlem** (the **Apollo Theater, Studio Museum,** and **Schomburg Center**), **Morningside Heights** (**Columbia University,** the **Cathedral of St. John the Divine,** and **Riverside Park**), or **Yorkville** (**Gracie Mansion, Carl Schurz Park,** and old German butcher shops). Or, impress your Manhattan friends by investigating an outer borough by subway. Visit, for example, the **Brooklyn Museum of Art** and **Prospect Park** in **Brooklyn,** the **Bronx Zoo** and the **New York Botanical Garden** in the **Bronx,** or the **American Museum of the Moving Image** in **Queens,** to name just a few options.

FODOR'S CHOICE

Views to Remember

★ **The lower Manhattan skyline seen from the Brooklyn Heights Promenade.** This quiet 3-mi-long sliver of park hanging over the ferry district offers both a respite from the urban din and one of the most stunning urban panoramas: the Brooklyn Bridge, South Street Seaport, and the glittering skyscrapers of lower Manhattan, which seem to float on the water.

★ **Midtown Manhattan and New York Bay from the observation deck of the World Trade Center.** Elevators glide a quarter of a mile into the sky (107 stories) to the world's highest outdoor observation platform, where on a clear day, you can see as far as 55 mi.

★ **The vista of skyscrapers ringing Central Park.** Perhaps the best spot from which to admire this picture-postcard view (midtown's jumble of high-rises looks like a surreal two-dimensional stage set rising from the trees) is the reservoir's northwest corner or the second-floor outdoor sculpture court at the Metropolitan Museum. Gapstow Bridge, by the pond in the park, is another good vantage point.

★ **A moonlit look at the harbor from the Staten Island Ferry.** This free ride is more breathtaking at night, with the seemingly billions of lights of Manhattan twinkling in the distance.

★ **The Hudson River from the tower at Riverside Church.** Just 21 stories above street level, this perch nevertheless affords a dramatic unobstructed view of the river, the George Washington Bridge, and the Palisades of New Jersey, to the west.

Architecture

★ **Woolworth Building, Flatiron Building, Empire State Building, and the World Trade Center's twin towers.** Each is noteworthy for its own individual style and architectural features, and each, in its time, was the world's tallest building.

★ **Chrysler Building.** One of the most graceful of the city's skyscrapers, this stainless-steel tower is famous for its Art Deco pinnacle, its radiator-cap ornaments and gargoyles, and its graceful African-marble lobby.

★ **Rockefeller Center.** A 22-acre city within the city, this complex is as remarkable for its smooth limestone structures as for its plazas, concourses, public spaces, and its annual Christmas tree, which stands tall over the gold-leaf statue of Prometheus.

★ **The Dakota.** The grandam of New York apartment houses, this brick-and-stone urban castle outclasses all the other residences of Central Park West.

★ **The unbroken front of cast-iron beauties along Greene Street in SoHo.** The architectural rage of the second half of the 19th century, these facades are as functional as they are attractive.

★ **The graceful town houses along St. Luke's Place in the West Village.** These brownstones from the 1850s still rank among the most successful ensembles of urban residential architecture anywhere.

★ **Cathedral of St. John the Divine.** This immense limestone-and-granite Gothic house of worship supported entirely by stonemasonry is still a work in progress.

Museums

★ **American Museum of Natural History.** There's something for everyone in this collection of more than 36 million artifacts. The lifelike dioramas and massive dinosaur collection are especially popular with children.

★ **The Cloisters.** The Metropolitan Museum's medieval collection is housed in an annex on a peaceful wooded hilltop in Washington Heights, near Manhattan's northernmost tip. Don't miss the Unicorn Tapestries.

★ **Guggenheim Museum.** Frank Lloyd Wright's New York masterwork is like no other building in the world. Recent ambitious exhibits have focused on the arts of all of Africa and China and major single-artist retrospectives, which often spill over to the Guggenheim Museum SoHo.

★ **Metropolitan Museum of Art.** This is simply one of the world's greatest museums. Select one or two galleries, but don't leave without visiting the European Sculpture Court.

★ **The Morgan Library.** Here you'll find the repository of one of the world's finest collections of rare books, prints, and incunabula. Don't miss J. P.'s own study and library within.

★ **National Museum of the American Indian.** The first national museum dedicated to Native American culture is housed in the astonishing Alexander Hamilton Custom House in lower Manhattan.

Restaurants

★ **Jean Georges.** Celebrated chef Jean-Georges Vongerichten (also of JoJo and Vong) creates ethereal food in this minimalist setting. The prices are as dazzling as the food, but lunch gives good value. *$$$$.*

★ **"21" Club.** The city's most celebrated saloon (with red-checked tablecloths and a ceiling hung with toys) now has food to cheer about as well, thanks to executive chef Erik Blauberg. *$$$$*

★ **Barbetta.** This little island of civility is in two antiques-filled town houses with an enchanting garden full of century-old trees. The wine list has bottles dating from 1880. *$$$–$$$$*

★ **Ben Benson's.** A first-rate steak house, this is the place in midtown for chops and prime rib, Maryland crab cakes, and oversize cocktails. *$$$–$$$$*

★ **Le Cirque 2000.** Perhaps the most anticipated new restaurant of the decade, Sirio Maccioni's bravura space draws the rich, the famous, and the wanna-bes—plus some surprisingly good food. *$$$–$$$$*

★ **Petrossian.** This Art Deco caviar bar and restaurant offers an outstanding prix-fixe dinner (one of New York's great bargains in luxury dining): Enjoy 30 grams of sevruga without breaking the bank. *$$$–$$$$*

★ **Windows on the World.** The Greatest Bar on Earth, the intimate 60-seat Cellar in the Sky, and the dramatic 240-seat main dining room are grand in themselves, but don't forget those million-dollar views. *$$$–$$$$*

★ **American Place.** Executive chef Larry Forgione celebrates new American cooking in this stylish dining spot with kindly service; it just may be the country's finest regional American restaurant. *$$$*

★ **Bouterin.** Chef-owner Antoine Bouterin's short menu of unpretentious dishes focuses on the cuisine of Provence. The atmosphere is undiluted country-French. *$$$*

★ **Follonico.** The unusual pasta offerings change with the seasons at this out-of-the-way Chelsea charmer. *$$$*

★ **Diwan Grill.** The ideal place to bring your vegetarian friends for the traditional *thali,* a complete dinner of small vegetable curries, condiments, breads, and desserts served on a round tray. *$$–$$$*

★ **The Park.** Baccarat chandeliers and green velvet banquettes make for a spectacular setting, and the food is some of the best in Manhattan. *$$–$$$*

★ **Turkish Kitchen.** Manhattan's best Turkish restaurant has a striking, brightly colored multilevel dining room where you can sample delicate authentic cuisine. *$–$$*

★ **Uncle Nick's.** At this inexpensive taverna, owners Tony and Mike Vanatakis prepare each fish dish with simplicity and care. Sample a variety of the exciting appetizers. $–$$

★ **Boca Chica.** Come to this East Village hot spot for a (spicy) sampling of Latin America. $

★ **Joe's Shanghai.** Chefs study years to perfect the secret of the house specialty: dumplings filled with boiling broth and pork or crab. $

Hotels

★ **The Carlyle.** One of New York's swankiest hotels, the Carlyle combines old-school elegance with a modern sense of fun—its legendary cabaret and bar stay packed until the wee hours. $$$$

★ **Hotel Elysée.** The 99 guest rooms leave the staff time for personalized service and attention at this deluxe midtowner; downstairs is the trendy Monkey Bar. $$$$

★ **The Mark.** This classy but friendly baby grand hotel is just a few steps from Central Park. $$$$

★ **St. Regis.** This 5th Avenue Beaux Arts landmark bespeaks a bygone era of wealth and luxury with its ultrachic public spaces and butler-serviced guest rooms. $$$$

★ **SoHo Grand.** Its monumental design pays homage to SoHo's 19th-century cast-iron buildings; aesthetics are everything here. $$$$

★ **Roger Williams.** Stay out late before coming back to a nightly dessert buffet and 24-hour cappuccino at this newly redone masterpiece of industrial chic in Murray Hill. $$$

★ **Warwick.** This midtown favorite, built by William Randolph Hearst in 1927, is well placed for the theater and points west. $$$

★ **Broadway Bed & Breakfast.** Friendly and comfortable, this bargain B&B is just steps from the theaters and Restaurant Row. $

★ **Hotel Beacon.** The Upper West Side's best budget buy is three blocks from Central Park and Lincoln Center, and just footsteps from Zabar's gourmet bazaar. $

FESTIVALS AND SEASONAL EVENTS

The New York Convention and Visitors' Bureau (☎ 212/484–1222, weekdays 9–5) has exact dates and times for many of the annual events listed below, and the bureau's Web site (www.nycvisit.com) has yet more information on free activities.

WINTER

EARLY DEC.➢ One of the tallest Christmas trees in the country is mounted in Rockefeller Center, just above the golden Prometheus statue. Thousands of people gather to watch the ceremonial **tree lighting** (☎ 212/632–3975).

NEW YEAR'S EVE➢ The famous **ball drop in Times Square** (☎ 212/768–1560; 212/354–0003 Nov.–Dec.) is televised all over the world. In Central Park, a festive **Midnight Run** sponsored by the New York Road Runners Club (☎ 212/860–4455) begins at Tavern on the Green.

EARLY JAN.➢ The 10-day **New York National Boat Show,** at the Jacob K. Javits Convention Center (☎ 212/216–2000), exhibits the latest in pleasure craft (power- and sailboats), yachts, and other seaworthy equipment.

LATE JAN.➢ Leading dealers in the field of so-called visionary art—also sometimes called naive art or art of the self-taught—exhibit their wares at the **Outsider Art Fair,** at the Puck Building in SoHo (☎ 212/777–5218).

EARLY FEB.➢ Yankee fans will have their day at the **New York Yankees Fan Festival** (☎ 718/293–4300), where you can meet current and former players, test your swing, and bid in a memorabilia auction. The **Chinese New Year** (☎ 212/484–1222), celebrated over two weeks, includes a barrage of fireworks, extravagant banquets, and a colorful paper-dragon dance that snakes through the narrow streets of Chinatown.

FEB. 8–9➢ Nearly 3,000 well-bred canines and their human overseers take over Madison Square Garden for the **Westminster Kennel Club Dog Show** (☎ 800/455–3647), the nation's second-longest-running animal event (after the Kentucky Derby).

FEB. 14➢ During the **Valentine's Day Marriage Marathon,** couples marry atop the Empire State Building (☎ 212/736–3100, ext. 377).

LATE FEB.➢ In the invitational **Annual Empire State Building Run-Up** (☎ 212/860–4455), 150 runners scramble up the 1,576 stairs from the lobby of the Empire State Building to the 86th-floor observation deck.

SPRING

MAR. 17➢ New York's first **St. Patrick's Day Parade** (☎ 212/484–1222) took place in 1762, making this boisterous tradition one of the city's oldest annual events. The parade heads up 5th Avenue, starting at 44th Street at 11:30 AM and finishing at 86th Street.

MAR. 25–30➢ At the **International Asian Art Fair** (☎ 212/642–8572), 60 dealers from around the world exhibit furniture, sculptures, bronzes, ceramics, carpets, jewelry, and more from the Middle East, Southeast Asia, and the Far East.

LATE MAR.–EARLY APR.➢ Every spring the world-famous three-ring **Ringling Bros. and Barnum & Bailey Circus** (☎ 212/465–6741 for tickets, 212/302–1700 for information) comes to town. Just before opening night the Animal Walk takes the show's four-legged stars from their train at Penn Station along 34th Street to the Garden; it happens around midnight but is well worth the effort. The **Triple Pier Expo** (☎ 212/255–0020) lures more than 600 antiques dealers to Piers 88, 90, and 92, offering everything from art glass to furniture. There's a reprise of the event in November, as well.

EARLY APR.–MID-APR.➢ The week before Easter, the **Macy's Flower Show** (☎ 212/494–2922) creates lush displays in its flagship emporium and sets its Broadway windows abloom. Exquisite flower arrangements are also on display in Rockefeller Center.

APR. 4➢ As in the classic Fred Astaire movie, you can don an extravagant hat and join the **Easter Parade** up 5th Avenue. The excitement centers around St. Patrick's Cathedral, at 51st Street.

APR. 15–18➢ The 39th annual **Antiquarian Book Fair** (☏ 212/777–5218 or 212/944–8291), held at the Seventh Regiment Armory, on the Upper East Side, is a book lover's jackpot of first editions, rare volumes, manuscripts, autographs, letters, atlases, drawings, prints, and maps, with prices ranging from $25 to more than $25,000.

APR.–SEPT.➢ The **Major League baseball season** sees the New York Yankees (☏ 718/293–6000) drawing huge crowds to Yankee Stadium, in the Bronx, while the Mets (☏ 718/507–8499) play at Shea Stadium, in Queens.

EARLY MAY➢ The **Cherry Blossom Festival** (☏ 718/622–4433) is held at the Brooklyn Botanic Garden. At last count, about 30,000 cyclists turn out for the annual **Bike New York: The Great Five Boro Bike Tour** (☏ 212/932–0778). The 42-mi tour begins in Battery Park and ends with a ride across the Verrazano-Narrows Bridge (which doesn't otherwise allow bikes). A free ferry brings cyclists back to Manhattan.

MAY 7–12➢ The **International Fine Art Fair** (☏ 212/642–8752) brings dealers from all over the country to the Seventh Regiment Armory, where they show off exceptional paintings, drawings, and sculptures from the Renaissance to the 20th century.

MID-MAY➢ Congregation Shearith Israel (the Spanish and Portuguese Synagogue—the landmark home of America's oldest Orthodox Jewish congregation) sponsors a one-day **Sephardic Fair** (☏ 212/873–0300), where you can watch artists making prayer shawls and crafting jewelry, potters throwing wine cups, and scribes penning marriage contracts.

LATE MAY➢ Some of the world's best hoofers join the **Tap Dance Extravaganza** (☏ 718/597–4613); events are held in varying venues in Manhattan. For more than half a century, Memorial Day has marked the start of the **Washington Square Outdoor Art Exhibit** (☏ 212/982–6255), an open-air arts-and-crafts fair with some 600 exhibitors who set up in the park and on surrounding streets. The action continues for three weekends, from noon to sundown.

SUMMER

EARLY JUNE➢ The **Belmont Stakes** (☏ 718/641–4700), New York's thoroughbred of horse races, and a jewel in the Triple Crown, comes to Long Island's Belmont Park Racetrack.

EARLY–MID-JUNE➢ The **Texaco New York Jazz Festival** (☏ 212/219–3006), which began more than 10 years ago as an alternative to the JVC Jazz Festival (☞ *below*), sponsors 350 performances of classic, acid, Latin, and avant-garde jazz at clubs and public spaces around town. The Knitting Factory (✉ 74 Leonard St.) is a main venue; performances on the Hudson River in Battery Park City began in 1998.

JUNE➢ **Lesbian and Gay Pride Week** (☏ 212/807–7433) includes the world's biggest annual gay pride parade, a film festival, and hundreds of other activities. During the **National Puerto Rican Day Parade** (☏ 212/374–5176 or 718/401–0404), dozens of energetic bands send their loud rhythms reverberating down 5th Avenue as huge crowds cheer them on.

LATE JUNE➢ **JVC Jazz Festival New York** (☏ 212/501–1390) brings giants of jazz and new faces alike to Carnegie Hall, Lincoln Center, the Beacon Theater, Bryant Park, and other theaters and clubs about town.

LATE JUNE–EARLY JULY➢ The **Washington Square Music Festival** (☏ 212/431–1088) is a series of Tuesday evening free outdoor classical, jazz, and big band concerts.

LATE JUNE–LATE JULY➢ **Midsummer Night Swing** (☏ 212/875–5766) transforms Lincoln Center's Fountain Plaza into an enormous open-air dance hall. Top big bands provide jazz, Dixieland, R&B, calypso, and Latin rhythms for dancers of all ages; dance lessons are offered each night.

JUNE–AUG.➢ Every Monday night filmgoers throng glorious Bryant Park, the backyard of the New York Public Library's Humanities Center, for the **Bryant Park Film Festival** (☏ 212/922–

9393; ☎ 212/512–5700 film hot line early May–Aug.); the lawn turns into a picnic ground as fans of classic films claim space hours before show time, which is at dusk. In Central Park **SummerStage** (☎ 212/360–2777) presents free weekday-evening and weekend-afternoon blues, Latin, pop, African, and country music; dance; opera; and readings. **Shakespeare in the Park** (☎ 212/539–8500; 212/539–8750 [seasonal phone at the Delacorte]), sponsored by the Joseph Papp Public Theater at Central Park's Delacorte Theater, tackles the Bard and other classics, often with a star performer or two from the big or small screen. The **New York Philharmonic** (☎ 212/875–5656) chips in with free concerts in various city parks. **Celebrate Brooklyn** (☎ 718/855–7882, ext. 52), New York's longest-running free performing arts festival, brings pop, jazz, rock, classical, klezmer, African, Latin, Caribbean multicultural music, as well as spoken-word and theatrical performances, to the band shell in Brooklyn's Prospect Park.

EARLY JULY–MID-AUG➢ The Museum of Modern Art's sculpture garden becomes an alfresco auditorium on Friday and Saturday evenings for **Summergarden** performances of 20th-century classical music, played by graduate students and alumni of the Juilliard School (☎ 212/708–9400).

JULY 4➢ Lower Manhattan celebrates **Independence Day** (☎ 212/484–1222) with the Great 4th of July Festival, which includes arts, crafts, ethnic food, live entertainment, and a parade from Bowling Green to City Hall. South Street Seaport also puts on a celebration. **Fireworks** (☎ 212/560–4060) fill the night sky over the East River. The best viewing points are FDR Drive from 14th to 41st streets (access via 23rd, 34th, and 48th streets) and the Brooklyn Heights Promenade. The FDR Drive is closed to traffic, but arrive early, as police sometimes restrict even pedestrian traffic.

JULY➢ **Lincoln Center Festival** (☎ 212/875–5928), under the direction of an international summer performance event lasting several weeks, includes classical music concerts, contemporary music and dance presentations, stage works, and non-Western arts.

AUG.➢ **Lincoln Center Out-of-Doors** (☎ 212/875–5108) is a series of music, dance, and family-oriented events lasting almost the entire month. **Harlem Week** (☎ 212/862–7200), the world's largest black and Hispanic festival, actually runs for about two weeks. Come for concerts, gospel events, and the concurrent Black Film Festival and Taste of Harlem Food Festival. The music of Mozart and his peers wafts through Lincoln Center during the **Mostly Mozart** (☎ 212/875–5103) festival, whose orchestra plays under the inspired baton of Gerard Schwarz; solo guest performers illuminate chamber works in recitals. Free outdoor afternoon concerts are followed by casual evening concerts at reasonable prices.

LATE AUG.➢ **Brooklyn's County Fair** (☎ 718/689–8600) goes the old-fashioned route, with watermelon-eating contests, pony rides, and the like.

LATE AUG.–EARLY SEPT.➢ The **U.S. Open Tennis Tournament** (☎ 800/524–8440), in Flushing Meadows–Corona Park, Queens, is one of the city's premiere annual sport events.

AUTUMN

LABOR DAY WEEKEND➢ A Caribbean revel modeled after the harvest carnival of Trinidad and Tobago, the **West Indian American Day Parade** (☎ 212/484–1222), in Brooklyn, is New York's largest parade and the centerpiece of a weekend's worth of festivities. Celebrations begin with a Friday-evening salsa, reggae, and calypso extravaganza at the Brooklyn Museum and end on Monday afternoon with a gigantic Mardi Gras–style parade of floats, elaborately costumed dancers, stilt walkers, and West Indian food and music.

SEPT.➢ Garlands and lights bedeck Little Italy's Mulberry Street and environs for the **Feast of San Gennaro** (☎ 212/764–6330), the city's oldest, grandest, largest, and most crowded *festa,* held in honor of the patron saint of Naples. **Broadway on Broadway** (☎ 212/563–BWAY) brings some of the best current musical theater to the streets for a free two-hour outdoor concert held in Times Square in early September.

SEPT. 19➢ Publishers of all stripes set up displays along 5th Avenue from 48th to 57th streets for **New York Is Book Country** (☎ 212/207–7242), where you can preview forthcoming books, meet authors, admire beautiful book jackets, chat with George Plimpton at the Paris Review booth, and enjoy live entertainment and bookbinding demonstrations. Bring the kids.

LATE SEPT.–EARLY OCT.➢ Begun in 1963, the **New York Film Festival** (☎ 212/875–5610) is the city's most prestigious annual film event. Cinephiles pack various Lincoln Center venues; advance tickets to afternoon and evening screenings are essential to guarantee a seat.

OCT. 14–21➢ Considered one of the world's top art fairs, the **International Fine Art and Antique Dealers Show** (☎ 212/642–8572) brings dealers from the U.S. and Europe, who show treasures from antiquity to the 20th century; 1999 is the fair's 10th year.

OCT. 31➢ Fifty thousand revelers, many in bizarre but brilliant costumes, march up 6th Avenue (from Spring to 23rd Sts.) in the **Greenwich Village Halloween Parade** (☎ 914/758–5519).

OCT.–APR.➢ **New York Rangers Hockey** (☎ 212/465–6741) attracts passionate fans at Madison Square Garden. The ever-popular **New York Knickerbockers** (☎ 212/465–5867) basketball team continues to fill up Madison Square Garden during their home games.

NOV. 7➢ The **New York City Marathon** (☎ 212/860–4455), the world's largest, begins on the Staten Island side of the Verrazano-Narrows Bridge and snakes through all five boroughs before finishing at Tavern on the Green in Central Park.

NOV. 11➢ On **Veteran's Day** an annual parade marches down 5th Avenue to the United War Veterans Council of New York County.

NOV. 18–21➢ The 21st annual **Fall Antiques Show** (212/777–5218), the foremost American antiques show in the country and a bonanza for collectors of Americana, attracts 75 dealers from all over the U.S. to the Seventh Regiment Armory.

NOV. 25➢ The **Macy's Thanksgiving Day Parade** (☎ 212/494–4495) is a New York tradition; huge balloons float down Central Park West from 77th Street to Broadway and Herald Square. The night-before inflating of the balloons has become an event in its own right.

NOV.–JAN.➢ The **Radio City Christmas Spectacular** features the famed Rockettes at Radio City Music Hall (☎ 212/247–4777).

LATE NOV.–EARLY JAN.➢ Every year the **Christmas window displays** on view at Saks Fifth Avenue (✉ 611 5th Ave., between 49th and 50th Sts.) and Lord & Taylor (✉ 424 5th Ave., between 38th and 39th Sts.) are more inventive and festive than ever.

LATE DEC.➢ A **Giant Hanukkah Menorah** is lighted at Grand Army Plaza (✉ 5th Ave. and 59th St., ☎ 718/778–6000).

2 Exploring Manhattan

Around the next corner, a visitor to New York will always find something new to discover uptown and down—world-class museums and unusual galleries, breathtaking skyscrapers, historic town houses, interesting churches and synagogues, indoor plazas, outdoor parks and gardens. From the Battery in the south to Harlem in the north, this chapter uncovers the essential places to see in each neighborhood, as well as worthwhile sights off the tourist track. Be sure to stop and rest along the way so you can observe the fabulous street life that makes this city so unique.

Updated by Rebecca Knapp Adams, Barbara Blechman, Hannah Borgeson, John J. Donohue, Margaret Mittelbach, and Robert Vickerman

MANHATTAN IS, ABOVE ALL, A WALKER'S CITY. Along its busy streets there's always something else to look at every few yards. Attractions, many of them world famous, are crowded close together on this narrow island, and because they have to grow up, not out, new layers are simply piled on top of the old. The city's character changes every few blocks, with quaint town houses shoulder to shoulder with sleek glass towers, gleaming gourmet supermarkets sitting around the corner from dusty thrift shops, and soot-smudged warehouses inhabited at street level by trendy neon-lighted bistros. Many a visitor has been beguiled into walking a little farther, then a little farther still—"Let's just see what that copper dome and steeple belong to. . . ."

Our walking tours cover a great deal of ground, yet they only scratch the surface. If you plod dutifully from point to point, nose buried in this book, you'll miss half the fun. Look up at the tops of skyscrapers, and you'll see a riot of mosaics, carvings, and ornaments. Go inside an intriguing office building and study its lobby decor; read the directory to find out what sorts of firms have their offices there. Peep around corners, even in crowded midtown, and you may find fountains, greenery, and sudden bursts of flowers. Find a bench or ledge on which to perch and take time just to watch the people passing by. New York has so many faces that every visitor can discover a different one.

Orientation

The map of Manhattan has a Jekyll-and-Hyde aspect. The rational, Dr. Jekyll part prevails above 14th Street, where the streets form a regular grid pattern, imposed in 1811. Consecutively numbered streets run east and west (crosstown), while broad avenues, most of them also numbered, run north (uptown) and south (downtown). The chief exceptions are Broadway and the thoroughfares that hug the shores of the Hudson and East rivers. Broadway runs the entire length of Manhattan. At its southernmost end it follows the city's north–south grid; at East 10th Street it turns and runs on a diagonal to West 86th Street, then at a lesser angle until 107th Street, where it merges with West End Avenue.

Fifth Avenue is the east–west dividing line for street addresses: In both directions numbers increase in regular increments from there. For example, on 55th Street, the addresses 1–99 East 55th Street run from 5th Avenue, past Madison, to Park (the equivalent of 4th) Avenue, 100–199 East 55th Street would be between Park and 3rd avenues, and so on; the addresses 1–99 West 55th Street are between 5th and 6th avenues (the latter is also known as Avenue of the Americas), 100–199 West 55th Street would be between 6th and 7th avenues, and so forth. Above 59th Street, where Central Park interrupts the grid, West Side addresses start numbering at Central Park West, an extension of 8th Avenue. Avenue addresses are much less regular, for the numbers begin wherever each avenue begins and increase at different increments. An address at 552 3rd Avenue, for example, will not necessarily be anywhere near 552 2nd Avenue. Even many New Yorkers cannot master the complexities of this system, so in their daily dealings they usually include cross streets with an address.

Below 14th Street—the area already settled before the 1811 grid was decreed—Manhattan streets reflect the disordered personality of Mr. Hyde. They may be aligned with the shoreline, or they may twist along the route of an ancient cow path. Below 14th Street you'll find West

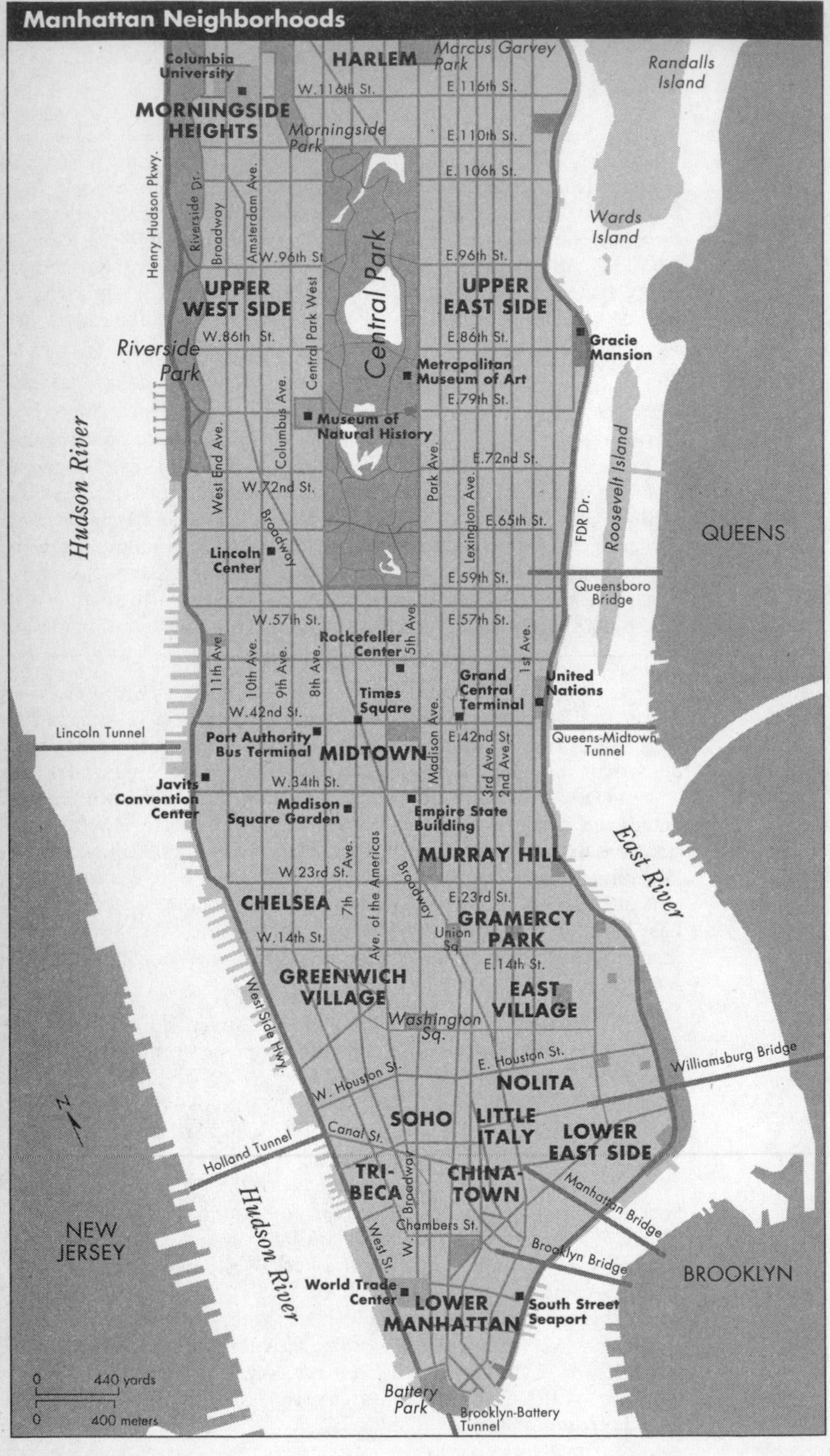
Manhattan Neighborhoods
Columbia University
HARLEM
Marcus Garvey Park
Randalls Island
W. 116th St.
E. 116th St.
MORNINGSIDE HEIGHTS
Morningside Park
E. 110th St.
E. 106h St.
Henry Hudson Pkwy.
Riverside Dr.
Broadway
Amsterdam Ave.
W. 96th St.
E. 96th St.
Wards Island
Central Park
UPPER WEST SIDE
UPPER EAST SIDE
Central Park West
W. 86th St.
E. 86th St.
Gracie Mansion
Riverside Park
Metropolitan Museum of Art
Columbus Ave.
E. 79th St.
Museum of Natural History
Hudson River
West End Ave.
Park Ave.
E. 72nd St.
Roosevelt Island
W. 72nd St.
Lexington Ave.
E. 65th St.
FDR Dr.
Broadway
QUEENS
Lincoln Center
E. 59th St.
Queensboro Bridge
W. 57th St.
E. 57th St.
Rockefeller Center
5th Ave.
1st Ave.
11th Ave.
10th Ave.
9th Ave.
8th Ave.
Grand Central Terminal
United Nations
Times Square
W. 42nd St.
Lincoln Tunnel
Port Authority Bus Terminal
MIDTOWN
Madison Ave.
E. 42nd St.
Queens-Midtown Tunnel
3rd Ave.
2nd Ave.
Javits Convention Center
W. 34th St.
Madison Square Garden
Empire State Building
MURRAY HILL
East River
7th Ave.
Ave. of the Americas
Broadway
W. 23rd St.
E. 23rd St.
CHELSEA
GRAMERCY PARK
Union Sq.
W. 14th St.
E. 14th St.
GREENWICH VILLAGE
EAST VILLAGE
West Side Hwy.
Washington Sq.
E. Houston St.
Williamsburg Bridge
W. Houston St.
NOLITA
N
SOHO
LITTLE ITALY
LOWER EAST SIDE
Canal St.
Holland Tunnel
TRI-BECA
CHINA-TOWN
Broadway
Manhattan Bridge
Hudson River
Chambers St.
NEW JERSEY
West St.
W. Broadway
Brooklyn Bridge
BROOKLYN
World Trade Center
LOWER MANHATTAN
South Street Seaport
0 440 yards
0 400 meters
Battery Park
Brooklyn-Battery Tunnel

4th Street intersecting West 11th Street, Greenwich Street running roughly parallel to Greenwich Avenue, and Leroy Street turning into St. Luke's Place for one block and then becoming Leroy again. There's an East Broadway and a West Broadway, both of which run north–south and neither of which is an extension of plain old Broadway. Logic won't help you below 14th Street; only a good street map and good directions will.

You may also be confused by the way New Yorkers use *uptown* and *downtown.* These terms refer both to locations and to directions. Uptown means north of wherever you are at the moment; downtown means to the south. But uptown and downtown are also specific parts of the city (and, some would add, two very distinct states of mind). Unfortunately, there is no consensus about where these areas are: Downtown may mean anyplace from the tip of lower Manhattan through Chelsea; it depends on the orientation of the speaker.

A similar situation exists with *East Side* and *West Side.* Someone may refer to a location as "on the east side," meaning somewhere east of 5th Avenue. A hotel described as being "on the west side" may be on West 42nd Street. But when New Yorkers speak of the East Side or the West Side, they usually mean the respective areas above 59th Street on either side of Central Park. Be prepared for misunderstandings.

ROCKEFELLER CENTER AND MIDTOWN SKYSCRAPERS

Athens has its Parthenon and Rome its Coliseum. New York's temples, which you see along this mile-long tour along six avenues and five streets, are its concrete-and-glass skyscrapers. Many of them, including the Lever House and the Seagram Building, have been pivotal in the history of modern architecture, and the 19 warm-hued limestone-and-aluminum buildings of Rockefeller Center constitute one of the world's most famous pieces of real estate.

Numbers in the text correspond to numbers in the margin and on the Midtown map.

A Good Walk

The heart of midtown Manhattan is **Rockefeller Center,** one of the greatest achievements in 20th-century urban planning. A fun way to navigate among its myriad buildings is to move from east to west following a trail punctuated by three famous statues from Greek mythology. Atlas stands sentry outside the classically inspired **International Building** ①, on 5th Avenue between 50th and 51st streets. Head one block south on 5th Avenue and turn west to walk along the **Channel Gardens** ②, a complex of rock pools and seasonally replanted flower beds. Below these are the **Lower Plaza** ③ and, towering heroically over it from an eternal ledge, the famous gold-leaf statue of Prometheus. The backdrop to this scene is the 70-story **GE Building** ④, originally known as the RCA Building, whose entrance is guarded by another striking statue of Prometheus. Straight across bustling 50th Street is America's largest indoor theater, the titanic **Radio City Music Hall** ⑤.

Two other notable Rockefeller Center buildings on the west side of 6th Avenue are the **McGraw-Hill Building** ⑥, between 48th and 50th streets, and the Time & Life Building, between 50th and 51st streets.

Continue north on 6th Avenue, leaving Rockefeller Center. On the east side of 6th Avenue between 52nd and 53rd streets, the monolithic black **CBS Building** ⑦ (also known as Black Rock) stands out from the crowd.

Midtown

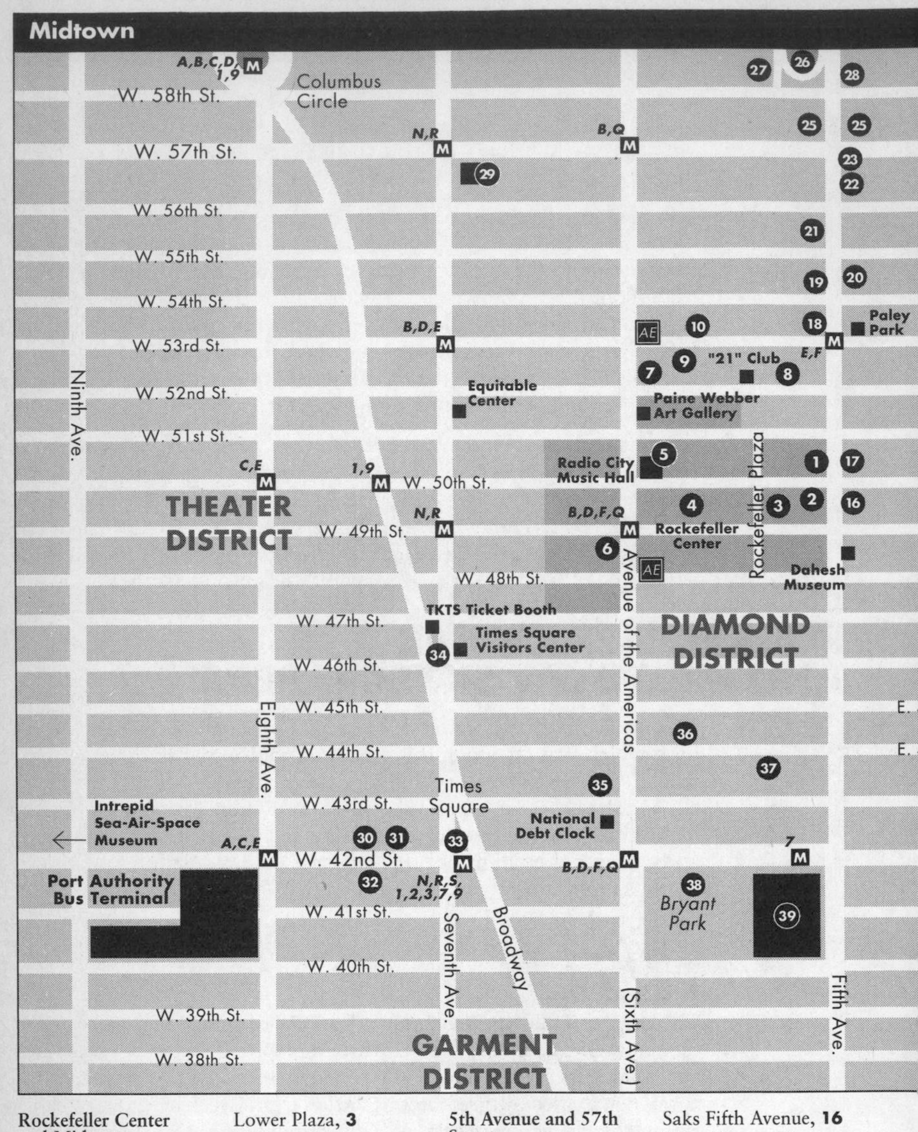

Rockefeller Center and Midtown Skyscrapers
American Craft Museum, **9**
CBS Building, **7**
Channel Gardens, **2**
Citicorp Center, **14**
GE Building, **4**
International Building, **1**
Lever House, **12**
Lower Plaza, **3**
McGraw-Hill Building, **6**
Museum of Modern Art (MoMA), **10**
Museum of Television and Radio, **8**
Radio City Music Hall, **5**
St. Bartholomew's Church, **15**
Seagram Building, **13**
Sony Building, **11**

5th Avenue and 57th Street
Bergdorf Goodman, **25**
Carnegie Hall, **29**
F.A.O. Schwarz, **28**
Grand Army Plaza, **26**
Henri Bendel, **21**
Newseum/NY, **24**
The Plaza, **27**
St. Patrick's Cathedral, **17**
St. Thomas Church, **18**
Saks Fifth Avenue, **16**
Takashimaya New York, **20**
Tiffany & Co., **23**
Trump Tower, **22**
University Club, **19**

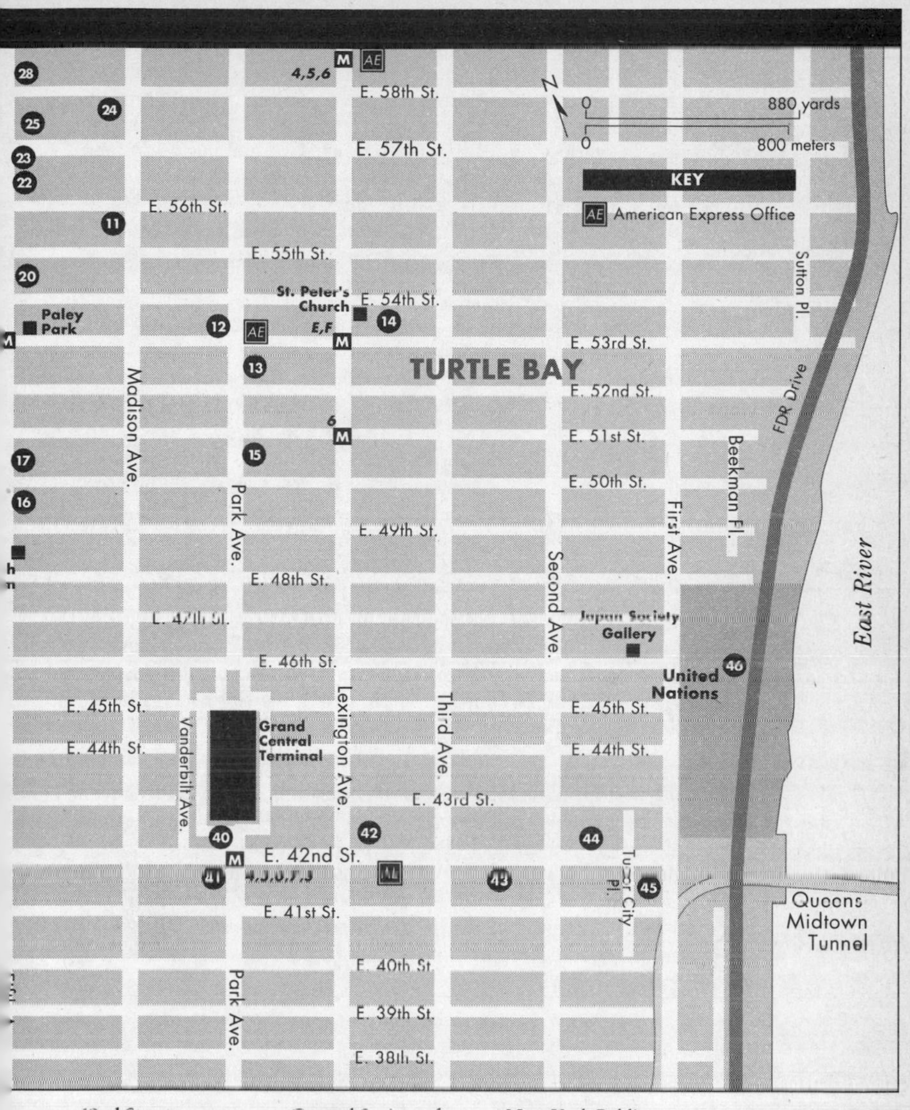

42nd Street

Algonquin Hotel, **36**
Bryant Park, **38**
Chrysler Building, **42**
Daily News Building, **43**
Duffy Square, **34**
Ford Center for the Performing Arts, **30**
Ford Foundation Building, **44**
General Society of Mechanics and Tradesmen Building, **37**
Grand Central Terminal, **40**
ICP Midtown, **35**
New Amsterdam Theater, **32**
New Victory Theater, **31**
New York Public Library (NYPL) Center for the Humanities, **39**
Times Square, **33**
Tudor City, **45**
United Nations Headquarters, **46**
Whitney Museum of American Art at Philip Morris, **41**

From here it's a short stroll to three museums enshrining contemporary culture. Go east on 52nd Street to the **Museum of Television and Radio** ⑧, devoted to the two key mediums of the modern era; here, you can screen favorite television shows from your childhood using the museum's huge library. Right next door is the landmark **"21" Club.** A shortcut through the outdoor public space close to the CBS Building or through a shopping arcade farther east, at 666 5th Avenue, takes you to 53rd Street's other museums: on the south side, the **American Craft Museum** ⑨, and on the north side, the **Museum of Modern Art (MoMA)** ⑩. A block east of MoMA, across 5th Avenue at 3 East 53rd Street, is **Paley Park,** a small vest-pocket park, with a waterfall.

The true muse of midtown is not art, however, but business, as you'll see on a brisk walk east on 53rd Street across 5th Avenue, where you'll encounter four office towers named after their corporate owners. First head north on Madison Avenue to 55th Street and the elegant rose-granite tower known as the **Sony Building** ⑪, immediately recognizable from afar by its Chippendale-style pediment. Farther east and a little south on Park Avenue stand two prime examples of the functionalist International Style: **Lever House** ⑫ and the **Seagram Building** ⑬, the only New York building designed by Ludwig Mies van der Rohe. Finally, go one block east to Lexington Avenue where, between 53rd and 54th streets, the luminous silvery shaft of the **Citicorp Center** ⑭ houses thousands more New Yorkers engaged in the daily ritual that built the city—commerce. To end your walk on a less material note, return to Park Avenue and turn south to 51st Street and **St. Bartholomew's Church** ⑮, an intricate Byzantine temple struggling to be heard in the home of the skyscraper.

TIMING

To see only the buildings, block out an hour and a half. Allow more time depending on your interest in the museums en route. At minimum you might spend 45 minutes in the American Craft Museum; the same in the Museum of Television and Radio; and 3½ hours in the Museum of Modern Art—even then you'll only dip briefly into the collections; it would be easy to pass an entire day there, ending with a movie in the museum's theater. Keep in mind that some parts of Rockefeller Center are only open during the week.

Start early in order to arrive at the Museum of Television and Radio when it opens so you won't have to wait for a TV console on which to watch your shows; break up your MoMA visit with lunch in its café.

Sights to See

9 **American Craft Museum.** Distinctions between the terms *craft* and *high art* become irrelevant at this small museum, which showcases works in clay, glass, fabric, wood, metal, paper, and even chocolate by contemporary American and international artisans. ✉ *40 W. 53rd St., at 5th Ave.,* ☎ *212/956–3535.* 🎫 *$5.* 🕓 *Tues.–Sun. 10–6, Thurs. 10–8.*

7 **CBS Building.** The only high-rise designed by Eero Saarinen, Black Rock, as this 38-story building is known, was built in 1965. Its dark-gray-granite facade bears some of the load of holding the building up and contributes to the sense of towering solidity the building conveys. ✉ *51 W. 52nd St., at 6th Ave.*

2 **Channel Gardens.** This Rockefeller Center promenade, leading from 5th Avenue to a stair connected to the ☞ **Lower Plaza,** has six pools surrounded by flower beds filled with seasonal plantings and was conceived by artists, floral designers, and sculptors—who present 10 shows a season. This area, called the Channel Gardens, separates the British building to the north from the French building to the south (above

each building's entrance is a national coat of arms). The French building contains, among other shops, the Metropolitan Museum of Art gift shop and, of course, the **Librairie de France,** which sells French-language books, periodicals, tapes, and recordings; its surprisingly large basement contains a Spanish bookstore and a foreign-language dictionary store. ✉ *5th Ave. between 49th and 50th Sts.*

⑭ **Citicorp Center.** The most striking feature of this 1977 design of the architectural firm Hugh Stubbins & Associates is the angled top. The immense solar-energy collector it was designed to carry was never installed, but the building's unique profile changed the New York City skyline. At the base of Citicorp Center is a pleasant atrium mall of restaurants and shops, where occasionally there's music at lunchtime. **St. Peter's Church,** whose angled roof is tucked under the Citicorp shadow, is known for its Sunday-afternoon jazz vespers, at 5. ✉ *Lexington Ave. between 53rd and 54th Sts.,* ☎ *212/935–2200 for St. Peter's Church.*

OFF THE BEATEN PATH

CORPORATE-SPONSORED EXHIBITS – Though it's not Museum Mile, midtown does benefit from companies that use part of their space to present free public exhibits. The **Paine Webber Art Gallery** (✉ 1285 6th Ave., between 51st and 52nd Sts., ☎ 212/713–2885), open weekdays 8–6, hosts four exhibits a year in the base of its building. The **Equitable Center** (✉ 787 7th Ave., at 51st St., ☎ 212/554–4818) has an enormous Roy Lichtenstein work in its atrium and a gallery with changing exhibits; it is open weekdays 11–6, Saturday noon–5.

DIAMOND DISTRICT – The relatively unglitzy jewelry shops at street level on 47th Street between 5th and 6th avenues are just the tip of the iceberg; upstairs, millions of dollars' worth of gems are traded, and skilled craftsmen cut precious stones. Wheeling and dealing goes on at fever pitch, all rendered strangely exotic by the presence of a host of Hasidic Jews in severe black dress, beards, and curled side locks. During the day this street becomes one of the slowest to navigate by foot in Manhattan because of all the people.

④ **GE Building.** The backdrop to the ☞ **Channel Gardens, Prometheus,** and the ☞ **Lower Plaza,** this 70 story (850 ft tall) building is the tallest tower in ☞ **Rockefeller Center.** It was known as the RCA Building until GE acquired its namesake company in 1986 (it is also known as 30 Rock): today it is also the headquarters of the NBC television network. The block-long street called Rockefeller Plaza, which runs north–south between the GE Building and the Lower Plaza, is officially a private street (to maintain that status, it closes to all traffic on one day a year); each year it is the site of the Rockefeller Christmas tree. From 30 Rock emanated some of the first TV programs ever, including the *Today* show. It's now broadcast from a ground-floor glass-enclosed studio on the southwest corner of 49th Street and Rockefeller Plaza, so if you're in the area between 7 AM and 9 AM, your face may show up on TV behind the *Today* show hosts. A one-hour tour of the NBC Studios is offered (children under 6 are not permitted). ✉ *30 Rockefeller Plaza,* ☎ *212/664–7174.* 🎫 *Tour $10.* ⏲ *Tour departs from street level of GE Bldg. every 15 mins Easter–Labor Day, weekdays 9:30–6, Sat. 9:30–7, Sun. 9:30–4:45; Thanksgiving–New Year's Day, weekdays 9:30–5, Sat. 9:30–4:30, Sun. 9:30–4:45. Other times of year, tour departs every ½ hr weekdays 9:30–4:30, every 15 mins Sat. 9:30–4:30.*

Poised above the GE Building's entrance doors on Rockefeller Plaza is a striking sculpture of Zeus, executed in limestone cast in glass by Lee Lawrie, the same artist who sculpted the big Atlas in front of the ☞ **International Building** on 5th Avenue. Inside, a dramatic mural entitled *Time,* by José María Sert, covers the ceiling of the foyer. Marble catacombs connect the various components of **Rockefeller Center.** There's a lot to see: restaurants in all price ranges, from the chic American Festival Café to McDonald's; a post office and clean public rest rooms (scarce in midtown); and just about every kind of store. To find your way around, consult the strategically placed directories or obtain the free brochure "Walking Tour of Rockefeller Center" at the GE Building information desk (☎ 212/332–6868). Before leaving the GE Building lobby, you might also take an elevator to the 65th floor to enjoy the spectacular view along with drinks or a meal in the Rainbow Room (☞ Chapters 6 and 8). When you've seen all there is to see, leave the GE Building from the 6th Avenue side to view the allegorical mosaics above that entrance. ✉ *Bounded by Rockefeller Plaza, 6th Ave., and 49th and 50th Sts.*

NEED A BREAK? **Dean & DeLuca** (✉ 1 Rockefeller Plaza, at 49th St., ☎ 212/664–1363), at the foot of the GE Building, serves coffee, tea, and hot chocolate, plus cookies, cakes, and small sandwiches. Restaurateur Pino Luongo's **Tuscan Square** (✉ 16 W. 51st St., at Rockefeller Center, ☎ 212/977–7777), simultaneously a restaurant, wine cellar, espresso bar, and housewares and accessories market, delivers an old-world Tuscan feel in the midst of Rockefeller Center.

❶ **International Building.** A huge statue of Atlas supporting the world stands sentry before this heavily visited ☞ **Rockefeller Center** structure, which houses many foreign consulates, international airlines, and a U.S. passport office. The lobby is fitted with Grecian marble. ✉ *5th Ave. between 50th and 51st Sts.*

⓬ **Lever House.** "Where the glass curtain wall began," the *AIA Guide to New York City* notes, summing up what was seminal about this 1952 skyscraper for the Lever Brothers soap company. Architect Gordon Bunshaft, of the firm Skidmore, Owings & Merrill, designed a sheer, slim glass box that rests on one end of a one-story-thick shelf, which is itself balanced on square chrome columns, making the whole building seem to float above the street. Because the tower occupies only half the space above the lower floors, a great deal of air space is left open, and the tower's side wall displays a reflection of its neighbors. ✉ *390 Park Ave., between 53rd and 54th Sts.*

❸ **Lower Plaza.** Sprawled on his ledge above this ☞ **Rockefeller Center** plaza, you will see one of the most famous sights in the complex (if not in all of New York): the great gold-leaf statue of the fire-stealing Greek hero **Prometheus.** A quotation from Aeschylus—PROMETHEUS, TEACHER IN EVERY ART, BROUGHT THE FIRE THAT HATH PROVED TO MORTALS A MEANS TO MIGHTY ENDS—is carved into the red-granite wall behind. The plaza's trademark ice-skating rink is open from October through April; the rest of the year it becomes an open-air café. In December an enormous live Christmas tree towers above this area. Most days on the Esplanade above the plaza, flags of the United Nations' members alternate with flags of the states. ✉ *Between 5th and 6th Aves. and 49th and 50th Sts.,* ☎ *212/332–7654 for the rink.*

❻ **McGraw-Hill Building.** Built in 1972 to relocate McGraw-Hill from its West 42nd Street building, this ☞ **Rockefeller Center** skyscraper is notable for its street-level plaza with a 50-ft steel sun triangle that points to the seasonal positions of the sun at noon. ✉ *6th Ave. between 48th and 49th Sts.*

★ ❿ **Museum of Modern Art (MoMA).** Home to many pivotal works of art of the modern era, MoMA is the city's—and the world's—foremost showcase of 20th-century art. Opened in 1929 on the heels of the stock market crash, the museum's first exhibition—*Cézanne, Gauguin, Seurat, van Gogh*—was revolutionary. Those now-canonized artists were at the time relatively unknown in the United States, and their Postimpressionist style had few admirers. Fortunately, Alfred Barr, the museum's first director, found an enthusiastic audience in New York City, and he continued to challenge museum goers, not only with avant-garde painting and sculpture but also by including photography, architecture, industrial arts, decorative arts, drawings, prints, illustrated books, and film under the rubric of fine art. MoMA expanded several times before moving in 1939 into its present six-story building, designed by Edward Durell Stone and Philip Goodwin. (The building has subsequently lost much of its original detailing, as well as its context—19th-century town houses and brownstones once sandwiched it on either side—so it now "appears to be the back end of a back office," as Christopher Gray has noted in the *New York Times.*) Gallery space doubled in 1984, and in 1997 the museum announced plans for a major commission, to be designed by Yoshio Taniguchi. The redesign, incorporating the former Dorset Hotel at 30 West 54th Street, will reconfigure the museum to a much greater extent than any previous revamping.

The core of MoMA's permanent collection of paintings and sculptures is on display on its **second and third floors.** Second-floor galleries begin with Postimpressionism, move onto cubism, dadaism, and surrealism, and end with Mexican art of the 1930s. The collection continues on the third floor, picking up with European art of the '40s and continuing with abstract expressionism, pop art, and contemporary works. Dozens of textbook art-history works are on display; highlights include van Gogh's *Starry Night* (1889), Rousseau's *The Sleeping Gypsy* (1897), still lifes by Cézanne, Matisse's *The Red Studio* (1911) and *Dance* (1909), and Picasso's *Les Demoiselles d'Avignon* (1907).

Rotating exhibits from MoMA's renowned photography collection are shown in second floor galleries. Drawings, prints, and illustrated books are on the third floor, architecture and design on the fourth. Included here are a Formula One race car, some extremely desirable kitchenware, and a Bell-47 helicopter suspended over the escalators. Temporary exhibits are shown throughout the museum. Also on the ground floor, the serene Abby Aldrich Rockefeller Sculpture Garden, on the site of John D. Rockefeller's first house in the city, was designed by architect Philip Johnson to be an outdoor "room," with trees, fountains, pools, and sculpture. Juilliard Music School students perform contemporary music concerts here weekend evenings in summer.

MoMA's two movie theaters are among the finest venues in the city to see foreign, independent, and classic films; several series usually run concurrently (☞ Film and Video *in* Chapter 5). ✉ *11 W. 53rd St.,* ☎ *212/708–9480; 212/708–9491 for jazz program.* 🎫 *$9.50; pay what you wish Fri. 4:30–8:30.* ⏲ *Sat.–Tues. and Thurs. 10:30–6, Fri. 10:30–8:30.*

❽ **Museum of Television and Radio.** Three galleries of photographs and artifacts document the history of broadcasting in this 1989 limestone building by Philip Johnson and John Burgee. The main attraction is consoles at which you can watch TV. The collection includes more than 60,000 television shows and radio programs, as well as several thousand commercials. ✉ *25 W. 52nd St.,* ☎ *212/621–6800 for general information and daily events; 212/621–6600 for other information.* 🎫 *$6 (suggested donation).* ⏲ *Tues.–Wed. and Fri.–Sun. noon–6, Thurs. noon–8.*

Paley Park. Named for CBS founder William S. Paley, this was the first of New York's vest-pocket parks—small open spaces squeezed between high-rise behemoths, which first sprouted in the '60s. On the site of the former society nightspot the Stork Club ("the New Yorkiest place in New York," said gossip columnist Walter Winchell), Paley Park has a waterfall, which blocks out traffic noise, and feathery honey locust trees to provide shade. A snack bar opens when weather permits. ✉ *3 E. 53rd St.*

★ 5 **Radio City Music Hall.** One of the jewels in the crown of ☞ **Rockefeller Center,** this 6,000-seat Art Deco masterpiece is America's largest indoor theater. Opened in 1932, its 60-ft-high foyer, ceiling representing a sunset, and 2-ton chandeliers astonished the hall's Depression-era patrons, who came to see first-run movies, which were shown in conjunction with live shows. The fabled Rockettes chorus line, which started out in St. Louis in 1925, has kicked up its heels on Radio City's stage since 1932. In 1979 the theater was awarded landmark status. Its year-round schedule now includes major performers, awards presentations, and special events, along with its own Christmas and Easter extravaganzas. A one-hour tour of the theater is offered most days. ✉ *1260 6th Ave., at 50th St.,* ☎ *212/247–4777 or 212/632–4041 for tour information.* 🎫 *Tour $13.75* ⏲ *Tours usually leave from main lobby every 30 mins Mon.–Sat. 10–5, Sun. 11–5. At press time renovations were scheduled Mar.–Sept.; call for opening times.*

Rockefeller Center. Begun during the Great Depression of the 1930s by John D. Rockefeller, this 19-building complex—"the greatest urban complex of the 20th century," according to the *AIA Guide to New York City*—occupies nearly 22 acres of prime real estate between 5th and 7th avenues and 47th and 52nd streets. Its central cluster of buildings consist of smooth shafts of warm-hued limestone, streamlined with glistening aluminum. The real genius of the complex's design was its intelligent use of public space: Its plazas, concourses, and street-level shops create a sense of community for the nearly quarter of a million people who use it daily. Restaurants, shoe-repair shops, doctors' offices, barbershops, banks, a post office, bookstores, clothing shops, variety stores—all are accommodated within the center, and all parts of the complex are linked by underground passageways.

Rockefeller Center helped turn midtown into New York City's second "downtown" area, which now rivals the Wall Street area in the number of its prestigious tenants. The center itself is a capital of the communications industry, containing the headquarters of a TV network (NBC), several major publishing companies (Time-Warner, McGraw-Hill, Simon & Schuster), and the world's largest news-gathering organization, the Associated Press. Some of the complex's major sights include ☞ **Radio City Music Hall,** the ☞ **International Building,** the ☞ **Channel Gardens,** the ☞ **Lower Plaza,** and the ☞ **GE Building.** ☎ *212/632–3975 for Rockefeller Center information.*

★ 15 **St. Bartholomew's Church.** Like the Racquet & Tennis Club two blocks south, this handsome 1919 limestone-and-brick church vividly represents a generation of midtown Park Avenue buildings long since replaced by such modernist landmarks as the ☞ **Seagram** and the ☞ **Lever** buildings. The incongruous juxtaposition plays up the church's finest features—a McKim, Mead & White Romanesque portal from an earlier (1904) church and the intricately tiled Byzantine dome. St. Bart's sponsors music events throughout the year, including June and July's Festival of Sacred Music, which features full-length masses and other choral works; an annual Christmas concert; concerts by L'antic musica, an early music group; and an organ recital series, which showcases the church's 12,422-pipe organ, the largest in the city. ✉ *Park Ave. between 50th and 51st Sts.,* ☎ *212/378–0200; 212/378–0248 for music program information.* ⏲ *Daily 8–6.*

NEED A BREAK? **Café St. Bart's** (✉ Park Ave. and 50th St., ☎ 212/935–8434), a charming and tranquil spot for a relatively inexpensive meal or a glass of wine or beer, has an outdoor terrace open in summer (Monday nights in summer it doubles as a floor for tango dancing).

13 **Seagram Building.** Architect Ludwig Mies van der Rohe, a leading interpreter of the International Style, built this simple bronze-and-glass boxlike tower in 1958. The austere facade belies its wit: I-beams, used to hold buildings up, are here attached to the surface, representing the *idea* of support. The Seagram's ground-level plaza, an innovation at the time, has since become a common element in urban skyscraper design due partly to a 1961 New York City resolution encouraging such land use. It is a perfect place to contemplate the monumental brick-and-limestone neo-Renaissance Racquet & Tennis Club (1916) across the street, which exhibits a complementary restraint and classicism. Inside the Seagram Building is one of New York's most venerated restaurants, the **Four Seasons Grill and Pool Room** (☞ Chapter 6). ✉ *375 Park Ave., between 52nd and 53rd Sts.,* ☎ *212/572–7404.* 💵 *Free.* ⏲ *Tours Tues. at 3.*

11 **Sony Building.** Commissioned by AT&T, which has since decamped to New Jersey, the Sony Building was designed by architect Philip Johnson in 1984. Unlike the sterile ice-cube-tray buildings marching up 6th Avenue, Sony's rose-granite columns, its regilded statue of the winged *Golden Boy* in the lobby, and its giant-size Chippendale-style roof have made the skyscraper an instant landmark. The first floor, which is Sony Plaza, includes a public seating area, cafés, a newsstand, a music store, and the **Sony Wonder Technology Lab,** outfitted with interactive exhibits such as a recording studio, a video-game production studio, and a TV production studio. ✉ *550 Madison Ave., between 55th and 56th Sts.,* ☎ *212/833–8830 for Sony Wonder Technology Lab.* 💵 *Free.* ⏲ *Technology Lab: Tues.–Sat. 10–6, Sun. noon–6 (last entrance 5:30); Sony Plaza: daily 7 AM–11 PM.*

"21" Club. A trademark row of jockey statuettes parades along the wrought-iron balcony of this landmark restaurant, which has a burnished men's-club atmosphere, a great downstairs bar, and a power-broker clientele. In the movie *The Sweet Smell of Success,* Burt Lancaster as a powerful Broadway columnist held court at his regular table here, besieged by Tony Curtis as a pushy young publicist (☞ Chapter 6). ✉ *21 W. 52nd St.,* ☎ *212/582–7200.*

5TH AVENUE AND 57TH STREET

For better or for worse, there's an increasingly fine line between retail and entertainment along much of 5th Avenue upward from Rockefeller Center. This is still one of the world's great shopping districts, as evidenced by its many elegant shops as well as the international fashion firms that try to muscle in on this turf, and the rents are even higher along East 57th Street, where there's a parade of very exclusive boutiques and upscale art galleries. But in the past several years the area's character has begun to change as brand-name stores with novel decoration and entertainment schemes have moved in. Hype aside, these stores can be fun even if you don't want to buy anything, and the many shoppers they attract to the neighborhood are welcomed into the pricier stores, too, noticeably bringing down the snootiness level. This tour mentions all the obvious stores, both new and established, but for more information about these and others, *see* Chapter 10. Theme restaurants dominate 57th Street west of 5th Avenue (☞ Chapter 6).

Numbers in the text correspond to numbers in the margin and on the Midtown map.

A Good Walk

Start right across the street from Rockefeller Center's Channel Gardens (☞ Rockefeller Center and Midtown Skyscrapers, *above*), at the renowned **Saks Fifth Avenue** ⑯, the flagship of the national department store chain. Across 50th Street is the Gothic-style Roman Catholic **St. Patrick's Cathedral** ⑰. From outside, catch one of the city's most photographed views: the ornate white spires of St. Pat's against the black-glass curtain of Olympic Tower, a multiuse building of shops, offices, and luxury apartments.

Cartier displays its wares in a jewel-box turn-of-the-century mansion on the southeast corner of 52nd Street and 5th Avenue; similar houses used to line this street, and many of their residents were parishioners of **St. Thomas Church** ⑱, an Episcopal institution that has occupied the site at the northwest corner of 53rd Street and 5th Avenue since 1911. Continuing north, you'll see the imposing bulk of the **University Club** ⑲ at the northwest corner of 5th Avenue and 54th Street; this granite palace was built by New York's leading turn-of-the-century architects, McKim, Mead & White. It shares the block with the Peninsula, one of the city's fanciest hotels (☞ Chapter 7). Across the street is **Takashimaya New York** ⑳, a branch of a Japanese department store chain.

Fifth Avenue Presbyterian Church, a grand brownstone church (1875), sits on the northwest corner of 5th Avenue and 55th Street. On the same block is **Henri Bendel** ㉑, a bustling fashion store organized like a little tower of intimate boutiques. Next door is Harry Winston (⊠ 718 5th Ave.), with a spectacular selection of fine jewelry. Across the street, on the northeast corner of 5th Avenue and 55th Street, is the Disney Store (⊠ 711 5th Ave.), where you can buy everything Disney, from key chains and clothes to animation stills and even vacations. The Coca-Cola Store (⊠ 711 5th Ave.), next door, seems modest by comparison.

Trump Tower ㉒, on the east side of 5th Avenue between 56th and 57th streets, is an exclusive 68-story apartment and office building named for its developer, Donald Trump. Just north of it, the intersection of 5th Avenue and 57th Street is ground zero for high-class shopping. And what more fitting resident for this spot than **Tiffany & Co.** ㉓, the renowned jewelers. Around the corner on 57th Street, NikeTown (⊠ 6 E. 57th St.) is a shrine to sports; it even has TVs and scoreboards on the first floor, so you can check on how your team is doing. Neighboring Tourneau TimeMachine (⊠ 12 E. 57th St.) has three levels of timekeepers and the small Gallery of Time exhibit hall. It's next to 590 Madison Avenue, which to some is still the IBM Building (though the company sold it in 1996), a five-sided, 20-story sheath of dark gray-green granite and glass by Edward Larrabee Barnes. The public is still welcome inside, to view exhibits at **Newseum/NY** ㉔, a media-monitoring institution. In the building's atrium (⊠ Entrances on 57th St. and Madison Ave.), you can relax with a snack and enjoy the Alexander Calder sculptures.

Cross 57th Street and head back toward 5th Avenue on the north side of the street, with its stellar lineup of boutiques: the French shop Hermès (⊠ 11 E. 57th St.), the English shop Burberrys Ltd. (⊠ 9 E. 57th St.), the German Escada (⊠ 7 E. 57th St.), and the French classic Chanel (⊠ 5 E. 57th St.). Regular folk are less likely to feel outclassed at the watch store Swatch (⊠ 5 E. 57th), the Original Levi's Store (⊠ 3 E. 57th St.), and a Warner Brothers Studio Store (⊠ 1 E. 57th St.), an eight-story extravaganza filled with movie, television, and cartoon paraphernalia as well as interactive displays, movies, and even a café. From outside the Warner Brothers store, you can watch a larger-than-life Superman pushing up the elevator. Across 5th Avenue stands the elegant **Bergdorf Goodman** ㉕. The extravagant women's boutiques are on the west side of the avenue between 57th and 58th streets, the men's store on the east side at 58th Street. Van Cleef & Arpels jewelers is within Bergdorf's West 57th Street corner.

Cross 58th Street to **Grand Army Plaza** ㉖, the open space along 5th Avenue between 58th and 60th streets. Appropriately named **The Plaza** ㉗, the famous hotel at the western edge of this square is a National Historic Landmark, built in 1907. Across the street, on the southeast corner of 58th Street and 5th Avenue, is the legendary **F.A.O. Schwarz** ㉘ toy store, ensconced in the General Motors Building.

Now return to 57th Street and head west, where the glamour eases off a bit. The large red NO. 9 on the sidewalk, in front 9 West 57th Street, was designed by Ivan Chermayeff. You'll also pass the excellent Rizzoli Bookstore (⊠ 31 W. 57th St.), its interior as elegant as many of the art books it carries. From the corner of 57th Street and 5th Avenue you can see the sleek Harley-Davidson Cafe (⊠ 1370 6th Ave., at 56th St.) and the playfully menacing Jekyll and Hyde Club (⊠ 1409 6th Ave., at 57th St.).

Across 6th Avenue (remember, New Yorkers *don't* call it Avenue of the Americas, despite the street signs), you'll know you're in classical-music territory when you peer through the showroom windows at Steinway and Sons (⊠ 109 W. 57th St.). Many theme restaurants line the stretch between here and just beyond Carnegie Hall: Motown Cafe (⊠ 104 W. 57th St.), Planet Hollywood (⊠ 140 W. 57th St.), Brooklyn Diner (⊠ 212 W. 57th St.), and the Hard Rock Cafe (⊠ 221 W. 57th St.).

An old joke says it all: A tourist asks an old guy with a violin case, "How do you get to Carnegie Hall?" His reply: "Practice, practice, practice." Presiding over the southeast corner of 7th Avenue and 57th Street, **Carnegie Hall** ㉙ has been considered a premier international concert hall for decades. Devotees of classical music may want to head from here up to nearby Lincoln Center (☞ The Upper West Side, *below*).

A few blocks south and west is the old Ed Sullivan Theater (⊠ 1697 Broadway, between 53rd and 54th Sts.), home to the *David Letterman Show.* Many shopkeepers and restaurateurs on this block have become minor late-night celebrities as a result of the talk-show host's habit of wandering out onto the street to harass his neighbors. Standby tickets become available at the box office weekdays at noon.

TIMING

This walk isn't long and can be completed in about 1½ hours. Add at least an hour for basic browsing around stores and several more hours for serious shopping. Make sure the stores are open beforehand. If you want to eat at your favorite memorabilia-decked restaurant, plan on waiting up to an hour just for a table. Fifth Avenue is jam-packed with holiday shoppers from before Thanksgiving until New Year's.

Sights to See

㉕ **Bergdorf Goodman.** Good taste reigns supreme in this understated department store with dependable service—at a price. The seventh floor has room after exquisite room of wonderful linens, tabletop items, and gifts. ✉ *Main store: 754 5th Ave., between 57th and 58th Sts.; men's store: 745 5th Ave., at 58th St.,* ☎ *212/753–7300.*

★ 29 **Carnegie Hall.** Musical headliners have been playing Carnegie Hall since 1891, when its opening concert series included none other than Tchaikovsky conducting his own works. Designed by architect William Barnet Tuthill, who was also an amateur cellist, this renowned concert hall was paid for almost entirely by Andrew Carnegie. Outside it's a stout, square brown building with a few Moorish-style arches added, almost as an afterthought, to the facade. Inside, however, is a simply decorated 2,804-seat auditorium that is considered one of the finest in the world. The hall has attracted the world's finest orchestras and solo and group performers, from Arturo Toscanini and Leonard Bernstein (he made his triumphant debut in 1943 standing in for New York Philharmonic conductor Bruno Walter) to Duke Ellington, Ella Fitzgerald, Judy Garland, Frank Sinatra, Bob Dylan, the Beatles (playing one of their first U.S. concerts)—and thousands of others.

Carnegie Hall was extensively restored in the 1980s; a subsequent mid-1990s renovation removed concrete from beneath the stage's wooden floor (vastly improving the acoustics), increased the size of the lobby, and added the small **Rose Museum** (✉ 154 W. 57th St., ☎ 212/247–7800), which is free and open Thursday–Tuesday 11–4:30 and through intermission during concerts. It's just east of the main auditorium, displaying such mementos from the hall's illustrious history as a Benny Goodman clarinet and Arturo Toscanini's baton. Guided tours of Carnegie Hall are available (they last about one hour). A well-kept secret is that the hall is available for rent; call for details if you've always dreamed of singing from its stage. ✉ *W. 57th St. at 7th Ave.,* ☎ *212/247–7800.* *$6.* ⏲ *Tours Mon.– Tues. and Thurs.–Fri. at 11:30, 2, and 3 (performance schedule permitting).*

OFF THE BEATEN PATH

DAHESH MUSEUM – Fueled by funds and a collection of approximately 3,000 works from Lebanese Dr. Dahesh (1909–84), this small exhibition space is dedicated to the European academic tradition. Among the well-known painters represented in changing exhibitions here are Bonheur, Bouguereau, Gérôme, and Troyon—all painters who have since been upstaged by their contemporaries, the Impressionists, but who once claimed greater popularity. ✉ *601 5th Ave.,* ☎ *212/759–0606.* *Free.* ⏲ *Tues.–Sat. 11–6.*

★ 28 **F.A.O. Schwarz.** A fantastic mechanical clock stands right inside the front doors of this famous toy-o-rama, which offers a vast, wondrously fun selection. Browsing here brings out the child in everyone, as it did in the movie *Big,* when Tom Hanks and Robert Loggia got caught up in tap dancing on a giant keyboard ("Big" keyboards are still for sale). If the line to get in looks impossibly long, try walking around the block, past the fanciful window displays, to the Madison Avenue entrance, where the wait may be shorter (☞ Chapter 4 and 10). ✉ *767 5th Ave. at 58th St.,* ☎ *212/644–9400.*

26 **Grand Army Plaza.** Just before you get to Central Park, you'll reach this open space along 5th Avenue between 58th and 60th streets. The southernmost block features the **Pulitzer Fountain,** donated by publisher Joseph Pulitzer of Pulitzer Prize fame. Appropriately enough for this ritzy area, the fountain is crowned by a female figure representing Abundance. The block to the north holds Augustus Saint-Gaudens's gilded equestrian statue of Civil War general William Tecumseh Sherman; across the street is **Doris C. Freedman Plaza,** which features sculpture exhibits courtesy of the Public Art Fund, at the grand Schol-

ars' Gate entrance to Central Park (☞ Central Park, *below*). ☞ **The Plaza**, an internationally famous hotel, is at the western edge of the square. East of Grand Army Plaza, on 5th Avenue at 58th Street, stands the General Motors Building, a 50-story tower of white Georgian marble and glass. One section of the main floor is the flagship of the legendary ☞ **F.A.O. Schwarz** toy store.

21 **Henri Bendel.** Chic Henri Bendel sells whimsical, expensive clothing in a beautiful store. Inventive displays and sophisticated boutiques are hallmarks. The facade's René Lalique art-glass windows (1912) can be viewed at close range from balconies ringing the four-story atrium. The second-floor café is particularly charming. ✉ *712 5th Ave., between 55th and 56th Sts.,* ☎ *212/247–1100.*

24 **Newseum/NY.** A sister to the larger Newseum in Arlington, Virginia, the New York Newseum, operated by the Freedom Forum Foundation, offers changing exhibits as well as public roundtables and other programs related to journalism, free speech, and freedom of the press. Recent exhibits have included a selection of Harry Benson's photographs of First Families and Vietnam War photos taken by photographers who died there. ✉ *580 Madison Ave., between 56th and 57th Sts.,* ☎ *212/397–7596.* 🎟 *Free.* ⏲ *Mon.–Sat. 10–5:30.*

27 **The Plaza.** With Grand Army Plaza, 5th Avenue, *and* Central Park at its doorstep, this world-famous hotel claims one of Manhattan's prize real estate corners. A registered historical landmark built in 1907, the Plaza was designed by Henry Hardenbergh, who also built the Dakota apartment building (☞ The Upper West Side, *below*). Here he concocted a birthday-cake effect, with white-glazed brick busily decorated and topped with a copper-and-slate mansard roof. The hotel is home to Eloise, the fictional star of Kay Thompson's children's books, and has been featured in many movies, from Alfred Hitchcock's *North by Northwest* to *Arthur, Crocodile Dundee, Home Alone 2,* and, of course, *Plaza Suite*. Past real-life guests include the Duke and Duchess of Windsor and the Beatles. The Plaza's ballroom was the scene of Truman Capote's Black and White Ball of 1966, given in honor of *Washington Post* publisher Katharine Graham. Capote said that his guests had to be "either very rich, very talented, or very beautiful, and of course preferably all three." One attendee called it "the most exquisite of spectator sports," and the party has lived on in social annals as one of the great parties of the century. ✉ *5th Ave. at 59th St.,* ☎ *212/759–3000.*

★ 17 **St. Patrick's Cathedral.** The Gothic-style house of worship is the Roman Catholic cathedral of New York and one of New York's largest (seating approximately 2,400) and most striking churches. Dedicated to the patron saint of the Irish—then and now one of New York's principal ethnic groups—the white marble-and-stone structure was begun in 1859 by architect James Renwick and consecrated in 1879. Additions over the years include the archbishop's house and rectory, two 330-ft spires, and the intimate Lady Chapel. The original members of the congregation purposely chose the 5th Avenue location for their church, claiming a prestigious spot for themselves at least on Sunday—otherwise they would have been in the neighborhood largely as employees of the wealthy. Among the statues in the alcoves around the nave is a modern depiction of the first American-born saint, Mother Elizabeth Ann Seton. The steps outside are a convenient, scenic rendezvous spot. ✉ *5th Ave. at 50th St.,* ☎ *212/753–2261 rectory.* ⏲ *Daily 7 AM–8:45 PM.*

18 **St. Thomas Church.** This Episcopal institution with a striking French Gothic interior was consecrated on its present site in 1916. The impressive huge stone reredos behind the altar holds the statues of more

than 50 apostles, saints, martyrs, missionaries, and other church figures, all designed by Lee Lawrie. The church is also known for its men's and boys' choir; Christmas Eve services here have become a seasonal star. ✉ *5th Ave. at 53rd St.,* ☎ *212/757–7013.* ⏲ *Daily 7–6:30.*

16 **Saks Fifth Avenue.** On a breezy day the 14 American flags fluttering from the block-long facade of Saks' flagship store make for the happy-go-luckiest, most patriotic scene in town. The national department store chain's move here in 1926 solidified midtown 5th Avenue's new status as an upscale shopping mecca. At the time, this branch's name was meant to distinguish it from its earlier incarnation on Broadway. It remains a civilized favorite among New York shoppers. The eighth-floor Café SFA serves delicious snacks and lunches to go with the Rockefeller Center–5th Avenue view. Saks's annual Christmas window displays (on view from late November through the first week of the new year) are among New York's most festive. ✉ *611 5th Ave., between 49th and 50th Sts.,* ☎ *212/753–4000.*

20 **Takashimaya New York.** This elegant yet somewhat austere branch of Japan's largest department store chain features a garden atrium, a two-floor gallery, and a tearoom. It has four floors of men's and women's clothing, gifts, and accessories and also carries household items that combine Eastern and Western styles. ✉ *693 5th Ave., between 54th and 55th Sts.,* ☎ *212/350–0100.*

23 **Tiffany & Co.** One of the most famous jewelers in the world and the quintessential New York store, Tiffany's anchors the southeast corner of one of the city's great intersections. The Fort Knox–like Art Deco entrance and dramatic miniature window displays have been a fixture here since 1940, when the store moved from Herald Square, following five previous moves, each more uptown, since its inception in 1837 at 237 Broadway. The store's signature Tiffany blue (robin's-egg-color) bags are perennially in style and arouse great anticipation. The 1958 film, *Breakfast at Tiffany's,* based on Truman Capote's novella, opens with Audrey Hepburn dressed in a Givenchy evening gown and emerging from a yellow cab at dawn to stand here window-shopping with a coffee and Danish. ✉ *727 5th Ave., at 57th St.,* ☎ *212/755–8000.*

NEED A BREAK?

Mangia (✉ 50 W. 57th St., ☎ 212/582–5882), an Italian and American food shop, is a great place to stop for coffee and a snack, especially if good food is the only theme you want in a restaurant. Desserts are scrumptious, and the salad bar is exceptional. ⏲ *Closed Sun.*

22 **Trump Tower.** As he has done with other projects, developer Donald Trump named this exclusive 68-story apartment and office building after himself. The grand 5th Avenue entrance leads into a glitzy six-story shopping atrium paneled in pinkish-orange marble and trimmed with lustrous brass. A fountain cascades against one wall, drowning out the clamor of the city, while trees and ivy grow on the setbacks outside. ✉ *5th Ave. between 56th and 57th Sts.*

19 **University Club.** New York's leading turn-of-the-century architects, McKim, Mead & White, designed this 1899 granite palace for an exclusive midtown club for degree-holding men. Its popularity declined as individual universities built their own clubs and as clubs became less important features of the New York social scene, but the seven-story Renaissance Revival building (the facade looks as though it is three stories) is as grand as ever. The critic Paul Goldberger has called it Charles McKim's "best surviving work." The crests of various prestigious universities hang above its windows. ✉ *1 W. 54th St, at 5th Ave.*

42ND STREET

"Hear the beat of the dancing feet. It's the avenue I'm taking you to, 42nd Street!" exclaim the lyrics to an old Broadway song. It's been decades since 42nd Street inspired such eager anticipation, but the singing and dancing are on their way back to this once-lionized thoroughfare. Few streets in America claim as many landmarks as midtown Manhattan's central axis, from Times Square, Bryant Park, and the New York Public Library on its western half to Grand Central Terminal and the United Nations on its eastern flank. Yet as long ago as World War II, 42nd Street began to nosedive, as once-grand theaters around Times Square switched from showing burlesque and legitimate theater to second-run and pornographic movies. With that decline came pickpockets, prostitutes, and the destitute, and the area became synonymous with tawdry blight.

But all that began to change—slowly in the late '80s, and then more rapidly in the mid-'90s, as first Bryant Park and then the Deuce, as the block between 7th and 8th avenues has long been known (it refers to the 2 in the name), were nurtured back to life. 42nd Street is now poised to reclaim its fame as the metaphorical Broadway, and today each week brings new deals and new construction, theater reopenings, and new stores, hotels, and restaurants, many with entertainment themes, each visually louder than the last. In Times Square itself, the neon lights shine brighter than ever, as ads become as creative as technology allows. Some critics decry the Disney-fication of this part of town, but, really, what New York neighborhood is more appropriate for this over-the-top treatment?

Numbers in the text correspond to numbers in the margin and on the Midtown map.

A Good Walk

Begin at the corner of 42nd Street and 10th Avenue (or for the intrepid, at the *Intrepid* Sea-Air-Space Museum, four blocks north at the Hudson River). The block of 42nd Street stretching toward 9th Avenue is home to a string of thriving off-Broadway playhouses, called Theatre Row (☞ Chapter 5). Across 9th Avenue, at No. 330, stands the first McGraw-Hill Building, designed in 1931 by Raymond Hood, who later worked on Rockefeller Center (where there is a later McGraw-Hill building; ☞ Rockefeller Center and Midtown Skyscrapers, *above*). The lobby is an Art Deco wonder of opaque glass and stainless steel.

The monolithic Port Authority Bus Terminal, at the corner of 8th Avenue and 42nd Street, is itself much improved over the last few years (and slated to have a golf driving range appended to its roof), while the Deuce, the block just east of it, is in the throes of an astonishing, though still incomplete, transformation. Nine theaters once lined the street (some are actually on 41st and 43rd streets and present only slim entrances on 42nd Street), and for decades X-rated bookstores and peep shows were their only tenants. Some of those theaters have been immaculately restored or rehabilitated, their facades beaming with high-wattage signs, while others await their turn. The western half of the Deuce, nearest the Port Authority, is still largely under construction. Stretching across the northeast portion of the street, E Walk, a huge $300 million hotel, retail, and entertainment complex with 13 movie theaters, is scheduled for completion in 2001. Next door is the currently dark Times Square Theater (✉ 215 W. 42nd St.), where for two decades after its 1920 opening, top hits such as *Gentlemen Prefer Blondes, The Front Page,* and *Strike Up the Band* were staged; Noël

Coward's *Private Lives* opened here with Gertrude Lawrence, Laurence Olivier, and the author himself. Just east of Times Square are the new **Ford Center for the Performing Arts** ㉚ (which presents only a slim entrance on the Deuce—the main facade is on 43rd Street and well worth a detour) and the **New Victory Theater** ㉛, a reclaimed treasure that specializes in theatrical productions for children. On the Deuce's south side, what were once the Empire and Liberty theaters are in the process of being transformed into a movie house and a Madame Tussaud's exhibit, respectively. Farther east, across from the New Victory, is the **New Amsterdam Theater** ㉜, brought back to life by the Walt Disney Company.

Although it may not exactly be the Crossroads of the World, as it is often called, **Times Square** ㉝ is one of New York's principal energy centers, not least because of its dazzling billboards. Before continuing east on 42nd Street, head north through Times Square to **Duffy Square** ㉞, a triangle between 46th and 47th streets, the home of the TKTS discount ticket booth. On the east side of 7th Avenue, the **Times Square Visitors Center** is in the historic Embassy Theater and is an all-in-one resource for visitors. Return to 42nd Street, where Hotaling's News (☒ 142 W. 42nd St.) sells more than 220 daily newspapers (most issues only a day or two old) from throughout the world. At the intersection of 42nd Street and 6th Avenue, look north to see, on the side of a low 43rd Street building, the National Debt Clock, an electronic display established by the late real estate developer Seymour Durst to remind passersby of how much deeper in debt the United States gets every second. At 6th Avenue and 43rd Street you can visit a branch of the International Center of Photography (☞ Museum Mile, *below*), **ICP Midtown** ㉟.

A block north of that is a rather clubby section of 44th Street that you might want to peek into before returning to 42nd Street. First, you'll see the surprisingly unpretentious **Algonquin Hotel** ㊱, a celebrity haunt. Next door is the more humble (and cheaper) Iroquois Hotel (☒ 49 W. 44th St.), where struggling actor James Dean lived in the early 1950s. Across the street from them is the Royalton Hotel (☒ 44 W. 44th St.), a midtown hot spot chicly redone by French designer Philippe Starck (☞ Chapter 7). Its neighbor, at 42 West 44th Street, is the Association of the Bar of the City of New York, with an 1896 neoclassic facade resembling the courthouses where its members spend so much of their time. Back on the north side of the street, at 37 West 44th Street, is the New York Yacht Club (1900), the former longtime home of the America's Cup trophy. The swelling Beaux Arts window fronts look just like the sterns of ships, complete with stone-carved water splashing over the sill. Farther east is the redbrick Harvard Club (☒ 27 W. 44th St.); the newer Penn Club (☒ 30 W. 44th St.), with its elegant blue awning, is on the other side of the street. And, yes, something on this block is open to the public: the **General Society of Mechanics and Tradesmen Building** ㊲.

At the southwest corner of 5th Avenue and 44th Street, notice the 19-ft-tall 1907 sidewalk clock on a pedestal set in the 5th Avenue sidewalk, a relic of an era when only the wealthy could afford watches.

At 42nd Street at 6th Avenue, steps rise into the shrubbery and trees of the handsomely renovated **Bryant Park** ㊳, a perfect place to relax for a few minutes. The park has been adopted as the backyard of all midtown workers. It's directly behind the magnificent Beaux Arts central research building of the **New York Public Library Center for the Humanities** ㊴, and the library houses part of its collections under the green lawn.

Continue east on 42nd Street to **Grand Central Terminal** (40). This Manhattan landmark was saved from the wrecking ball in a precedent-setting case that established the legality of New York's landmark-preservation law. On the southwest corner of Park Avenue and 42nd Street, directly opposite Grand Central, the **Whitney Museum of American Art at Philip Morris** (41) occupies the ground floor of the Philip Morris Building. The museum abuts Pershing Square, the block of Park Avenue east of the viaduct. Attempts to make this area more pleasant have included turning it into a pedestrian zone during the day. The southeast corner of 42nd and Park is a major departure point for buses to the three New York area airports, and upstairs at 100 East 42nd Street is the Satellite Airlines Terminal, where most major U.S. airlines operate ticket counters. Next door is Green Point Savings Bank, in what's known as the Bowery Savings Bank building (built in 1923; ✉ 110 E. 42nd St.), whose massive arches and 70-ft-high marble columns give it a commanding presence; it more closely resembles a church than a bank. At the end of the block is the 1929 Chanin Building (✉ 122 E. 42nd St.), notable for the Art Deco patterns that adorn its facade. Across the street stands the Grand Hyatt (✉ Park Ave. at Grand Central Terminal), which was created by wrapping a black-glass sheath around the former Commodore Hotel.

Ask New Yorkers to name their favorite skyscraper, and most will choose the Art Deco **Chrysler Building** (42) at 42nd Street and Lexington Avenue. Although the Chrysler Corporation itself moved out long ago, this graceful shaft culminating in a stainless-steel spire still captivates the eye and the imagination. On the south side of 42nd Street and east one block, the **Daily News Building** (43), where the newspaper was produced until spring 1995, is another Art Deco tower with a lobby worth visiting. The **Ford Foundation Building** (44), on the next block, is more modern and encloses a 12-story, ⅓-acre greenhouse.

Climb the steps along 42nd Street between 1st and 2nd avenues to enter **Tudor City** (45), a self-contained complex of a dozen buildings featuring half-timbering and stained glass. From it you have a great view of the **United Nations headquarters** (46), which occupies a lushly landscaped 18-acre riverside tract just east of 1st Avenue between 42nd and 48th streets. To end this walk on a quiet note, walk up 1st Avenue and turn right on East 49th Street, where you will enter the rarefied world of **Beekman Place,** a lovely town house–lined oasis.

TIMING

This long walk covers vastly different types of sights, from frenzied Times Square to bucolic Bryant Park to majestic Grand Central Terminal to the inspiring United Nations. If you start at the *Intrepid,* you could easily eat up most of a day even before you reach 5th Avenue. If you can, time your sightseeing so you visit Times Square at night, perhaps for a meal or a show, to take in the neon spectacle.

Sights to See

36 **Algonquin Hotel.** Considering its history as a haunt of well-known writers and actors, this 1902 hotel is surprisingly unpretentious. Its most famous association is with what become known as the Algonquin Roundtable, a witty group of literary Manhattanites who gathered in its lobby and dining rooms in the 1920s—a clique that included short-story writer and critic Dorothy Parker, humorist Robert Benchley, playwright George S. Kaufman, journalist and critic Alexander Woollcott, and actress Tallulah Bankhead. One reason they met here was the hotel's proximity to the former offices of the *New Yorker* magazine at 28 West 44th Street (now at 20 West 43rd Street). Come here for tea in the lobby, a drink at the bar, or dinner and cabaret performances in

the intimate Oak Room. ✉ *59 W. 44th St., between 5th and 6th Aves.,* ☎ *212/840–6800.*

OFF THE BEATEN PATH

BEEKMAN PLACE – This secluded and exclusive two-block-long East Side enclave has an aura of unperturbably elegant calm. Residents of its refined town houses have included the Rockefellers, Alfred Lunt and Lynn Fontanne, Ethel Barrymore, Irving Berlin, and, of course, Auntie Mame, a character in the well-known Patrick Dennis play (and later movie) of the same name. Steps at 51st Street lead to an esplanade along the East River. ✉ *East of 1st Ave. between 49th and 51st Sts.*

★ 38 **Bryant Park.** Following a dramatic $9 million renovation in the early '90s, Bryant Park, midtown's only major green space, has become one of the best-loved and most beautiful small parks in the city. Named for the poet and editor William Cullen Bryant (1794–1878), the 7-acre park was originally known as Reservoir Square (the New York Public Library stands on the reservoir's former site). America's first World's Fair, the Crystal Palace Exhibition, was held here in 1853–54. Today century-old London plane trees and formal flower beds line the perimeter of its grassy central square, which is scattered with 2,000 green folding chairs. (The bucolic square doubles as a roof over subterranean book stacks of the ☞ **New York Public Library.**) In temperate months the park draws thousands of lunching office workers; in summer it hosts live jazz and comedy concerts and sponsors free outdoor film screenings on Monday at dusk (☞ Chapter 5). Each spring and autumn giant white tents spring up for the New York fashion shows. It is also home to the Bryant Park Grill (☞ Chapter 6) and the adjacent, open-air Bryant Park Café, which is open April 15–October 14. Kiosks at the west end of the park sell sandwiches and salads. ✉ *6th Ave. between W. 40th and W. 42nd Sts.,* ☎ *212/922–9393.* ⏲ *Nov.–Apr., daily 8–7; May and Aug., daily 7 AM–8 PM; June and July, daily 7 AM–9 PM; Sept.–Oct., daily 7–7.*

★ 42 **Chrysler Building.** An Art Deco masterpiece, built between 1928–30, the Chrysler Building is one of New York's most iconic, and beloved, skyscrapers. It is at its best at dusk, when the setting sun makes the stainless-steel spire glow, and at night, when its illuminated geometric design looks like the backdrop to an expensive Hollywood musical. The Chrysler Corporation moved out in the mid-1950s, but the building retains its name and many details from the company's cars—"gargoyles" shaped like car-hood ornaments sprout from the building's upper stories: wings from the 31st floor, eagle heads from the 61st. At 1,048 ft, the building only briefly held the world's-tallest title—for 40 days, when the Empire State Building (☞ Murray Hill to Union Square, *below*) unseated it. The Chrysler Building has no observation deck, but you can go into its elegant dark lobby, which is faced with African marble and covered with a ceiling mural that salutes transportation and human endeavor. ✉ *405 Lexington Ave., at 42nd St.*

43 **Daily News Building.** This Raymond Hood–designed Art Deco tower (1930) has brown-brick spandrels and windows that make it seem loftier than its 37 stories. The newspaper moved to the west side in 1995, but the famous illuminated globe, 12 ft in diameter, is still there. The floor is laid out as a gigantic compass, with bronze lines indicating air mileage from principal world cities to New York. ✉ *220 E. 42nd St.*

34 **Duffy Square.** This triangle at the north end of ☞ **Times Square** is named after World War I hero Father Francis P. Duffy (1871–1932), known as "the fighting chaplain," who later was pastor of Holy Cross Church on West 42nd Street. Besides the suitably military statue of Father Duffy,

there's also one of George M. Cohan (1878–1942), who wrote "Yankee Doodle Dandy." The square is the best place for a panoramic view of Times Square's riotous assemblage of signs. At the north end of the square, the **TKTS discount ticket booth** sells discounted tickets to Broadway and off-Broadway shows (☞ Chapter 5). ✉ *In traffic island between 46th and 47th Sts.*

30 **Ford Center for the Performing Arts.** A musical production of E. L. Doctorow's novel *Ragtime* inaugurated this spectacular $22.5 million theater in January 1998. On the site of two classic 42nd Street theaters, the Ford Center incorporates a landmark 43rd Street exterior wall from the Lyric (built in 1903) and architectural elements from the Apollo (1910), including its stage, proscenium, and dome (the rest of the theaters, which had fallen into disrepair, was demolished). A 1,119-seat orchestra, two 360-seat balconies, and a huge stage make it likely the Ford will be a leading venue for large-scale musical productions. Such a future is in keeping with the Lyric and Apollo's history: In the early part of this century, the top talents they attracted to their stages included the Marx Brothers, Fred Astaire, Ethel Merman, and W. C. Fields. ✉ *213–215 W. 42nd St., between 7th and 8th Aves.,* ☎ *212/307–4100 for tickets.*

44 **Ford Foundation Building.** Home to one of the largest philanthropic organizations in the world, the Ford Foundation Building, built by architects Kevin Roche, John Dinkeloo & Associates in 1967, is best known for its glass-walled, 130-ft-high atrium, which doubles as a ⅓-acre greenhouse. Its trees, terraced garden, and still-water pool make the atrium a respite from the crush around Grand Central Terminal. ✉ *320 E. 43rd St., with an entrance on 42nd St.* 🎫 *Free.* ⏲ *Weekdays 9–5.*

OFF THE BEATEN PATH

GARMENT DISTRICT – This district teems with warehouses, workshops, showrooms that manufacture and finish mostly women's and children's clothing, and countless fabric, button, and notions shops. On weekdays the streets are crowded with trucks, and the sidewalks swarm with daredevil deliverymen wheeling garment racks between factories and specialized subcontractors. ✉ *7th Ave. between 31st and 41st Sts., where it's also called Fashion Ave.*

37 **General Society of Mechanics and Tradesmen Building.** A turn-of-the-century prep-school building houses this still-active society, which sponsors a general-membership library. On display in the three-story hall are Colonial era steamer trunks, Civil War paraphernalia, and locks and keys as old as the United States. ✉ *20 W. 44th St.,* ☎ *212/840–1840.* 🎫 *Free.* ⏲ *Weekdays 10–4.*

★ 40 **Grand Central Terminal.** Grand Central is not only the world's largest transportation building (49 acres) and the nation's busiest (426,000 commuters and subway riders pass through it daily). It is also one of the world's greatest public spaces, "justly famous," as the critic Tony Hiss has said, "as a crossroads, a noble building, an essential part of midtown Manhattan, and an ingenious piece of engineering." A massive four-year, $300 million renovation, at press time scheduled for completion in November 1998, will restore the 1913 landmark to its original splendor—and then some. Dozens of restaurants and shops, many occupying spaces long closed to the public, will make Grand Central a major destination in its own right—similar to Union Station in Washington, D.C.

The south side of 42nd Street is the best vantage from which to admire the dramatic Beaux Arts facade, dominated by three 75-ft-high arched windows separated by pairs of fluted columns, a beautiful clock, and a crowning sculpture, *Transportation,* which depicts a soaring Mercury, flanked by Hercules and Minerva (the facade is particularly beautiful at night, when bathed in golden light). Doors on Vanderbilt Avenue and on 42nd Street lead to the cavernous **main concourse.** Larger than the nave of Paris's Cathedral of Notre Dame, this majestic space is 470 ft long, 160 ft wide, and 150 ft—roughly 15 stories—high. Corridors run through 60-ft-high arched windows. The celestial map on its ceiling gloriously displays the starlighted constellations of the zodiac (60 actually glow with fiber-optic lights). A new staircase, included in the original plans but never built, was grafted onto the concourse's east end. Restaurants on the balconies offer fine vantages from which to view this majestic space.

Underground, more than 60 ingeniously integrated railroad tracks lead trains upstate and to Connecticut via MetroNorth Commuter Rail. The renovated **dining concourse** has two dozen food vendors. In 1978 the U.S. Supreme Court upheld Grand Central's status as a landmark, affirming the city's tough landmark laws and preventing the station's owners from building an office tower on top of the terminal. The best time to visit is at rush hour, when the concourse crackles with the frenzy of scurrying commuters dashing every which way. (Remember the scene in the movie *The Fisher King,* when the crowd stopped running for trains, turned to each other, and waltzed instead?) ⊠ *Main entrance: E. 42nd St. at Park Ave.,* ☎ *212/935–3960.* 🎫 *Tour free (donations to the Municipal Art Society accepted).* ⊙ *Tours Wed. at 12:30 (meet in front of information booth inside terminal on main level).*

35 **ICP Midtown.** The midtown branch of the International Center of Photography presents several photography shows a year, including selections from its extensive permanent collection. ⊠ *1133 6th Ave., at 43rd St.,* ☎ *212/860–1777.* 🎫 *$4; Tues. 6–8 pay as you wish.* ⊙ *Tues. 11–8, Wed.–Sun. 11–6.*

***Intrepid* Sea-Air-Space Museum.** Formerly the U.S.S. *Intrepid,* this 900-ft aircraft carrier is serving out its retirement as the centerpiece of Manhattan's only floating museum. An A-12 Blackbird spy plane, lunar landing modules, helicopters, seaplanes, and other aircraft are on deck. Docked alongside, and also part of the museum, are the *Growler,* a strategic-missile submarine; the lightship *Nantucket;* and several other battle-scarred naval veterans. Kids will enjoy exploring the ships' skinny hallways and winding staircases, as well as manipulating countless knobs, buttons, and wheels. ⊠ *Hudson River, Pier 86 (12th Ave. and W. 46th St.),* ☎ *212/245–0072.* 🎫 *$10; free to U.S. military personnel.* ⊙ *May–Sept., weekdays 10–5, weekends 10–6; Oct.–Apr., Wed.–Sun 10–5.*

Japan Society Gallery. With newly renovated galleries, this wonderfully serene setting holds exhibitions from well-known Japanese and American museums, as well as private collections. Also offered are movies, lectures, classes, concerts, and dramatic performances. ⊠ *333 E. 47th St., between 1st and 2nd Aves.,* ☎ *212/832–1155.* 🎫 *$3 (suggested donation).* ⊙ *Tues.–Sun. 11–5.*

32 **New Amsterdam Theater.** The Deuce's most glorious theater, neglected for decades, triumphantly returned to life in 1997 following a breathtaking $35 million restoration. Built in 1903 by Herts & Tallant, the theater, dazzlingly decorated and boasting such innovative features as a cantilevered balcony, was the original home of the Ziegfeld Follies. Years of decay had left the theater structurally and aesthetically in near-total ruin. With the backing of its new tenant, the Walt Disney Company, which wanted a venue in which to stage its own musical

productions, the 1,814-seat Art Nouveau theater was painstakingly restored by Hardy, Holzman, Pfeiffer, the New York architectural firm that also rehabilitated the ☞ **New Victory Theater** and ☞ **Bryant Park.** Today the theater is "a magical place," the architecture critic Ada Louise Huxtable has said, "from the elaborate peacock proscenium arch to the nymphet heads illuminating columns with halos of incandescent lights." Outside, the 1940s-vintage Art Deco facade, installed when the theater became a movie house, was retained in the renovation. The stage version of *The Lion King,* which opened in 1997 to critical accolades and commercial success, is likely to run here for years to come. ✉ *214 W. 42nd St., between 7th and 8th Aves.* ☎ *212/282–2900*

★ ⓫ 31 **New Victory Theater.** Since its superb restoration in 1995, the New Victory can make three unique claims: It was the first 42nd Street theater to be renovated as part of the recent revitalization of Times Square, it is the oldest theater in New York still in operation, and it is the city's only theater devoted exclusively to productions for children. Oscar Hammerstein built the theater in 1900 (his more famous grandson, Oscar Hammerstein II, wrote the lyrics to such shows as *Oklahoma!* and *Carousel*). Acting legends Lionel Barrymore, Lillian Gish, Mary Pickford, and Tyrone Power strutted its stage, and in the 1930s it was Broadway's most famous burlesque house. Decades of neglect are now a fading memory, as yellow-and-purple signs beckon from its elegant Venetian facade, and a gracious double staircase rises to a second-floor entry. Inside, garland-strewn putti perch casually on the edge of the theater's dome, above gilded deep red walls—appropriate overseers to this theatrical treasure. ✉ *209 W. 42nd St., between 7th and 8th Aves.,* ☎ *212/239–6255 for tickets.*

★ 39 **New York Public Library (NYPL) Center for the Humanities.** This 1911 masterpiece of Beaux Arts design is one of the greatest research institutions in the world, with 6 million books, 12 million manuscripts, and 2.8 million pictures (materials do not circulate). Financed largely by a bequest from former New York governor Samuel J. Tilden, the NYPL's main 5th Avenue building, now a National Historic Landmark, combined the resources of two 19th-century libraries: the Lenox Library the Astor Library. The latter, founded by John Jacob Astor, was housed in a previous building downtown, which has since been turned into the Joseph Papp Public Theater (☞ East Village, *below*).

Although there is an entrance on 42nd Street, for a better experience walk around to 5th Avenue, where two marble lions—dubbed "Patience" and "Fortitude" by Mayor Fiorello La Guardia, who said he visited the facility to "read between the lions"—guard the flagstone plaza in front. Statues and inscriptions cover the white-marble neoclassic facade; in good weather the grand marble staircase, like the Metropolitan Museum of Art's 40 blocks uptown, are a perfect spot to people-watch.

Bronze front doors open into the magnificent marble **Astor Hall,** flanked by a sweeping double staircase. Free one-hour tours, each as individual as the library volunteer who leads it, leave from here Monday–Saturday at 11 and 2; sign up in advance at the information desk. If you are on your own, be sure to see the **DeWitt Wallace Periodicals Room** (to the left of the lobby, at the end of the hall), decorated with trompe l'oeil paintings by Richard Haas that commemorate New York's importance as a publishing center. Upstairs, the magisterial **Main Reading Room**—297 ft long (almost two full north–south city blocks), 78 ft wide, and just over 51 ft high—is one of the world's grandest library interiors; it is scheduled to reopen in February 1999 following a major renovation, with its original chandeliers, oak tables, and bronze reading lamps looking better than ever. Exhibitions are held regularly in the **Gottesman Exhibition Hall,** the **Edna B. Salomon Room,** the **Third Floor Galleries,** and the **Berg Exhibition Room** (exhibit information is available at 212/869–8089). Among the treasures you might see are Gilbert Stuart's portrait of George Washington, Charles Dickens's desk, and Charles Addams cartoons. ✉ *5th Ave. between 40th and 42nd Sts.,* ☎ *212/930–0800.* ⏲ *Mon. and Thurs.–Sat. 10–6, Tues.–Wed. 11–7:30 (exhibitions until 6).*

33 **Times Square.** Love it or hate it, you can't deny that Times Square is one of New York's white-hot energy centers. Hordes of people, mostly tourists, crowd it day and night to walk and gawk. Like many New York City "squares," it's actually two triangles formed by the angle of Broadway slashing across 7th Avenue between 47th and 42nd streets. Times Square (the name also applies to the general area, beyond the intersection of these streets) has been the city's main theater district since the turn of the century: From 44th to 51st streets, the cross streets west of Broadway are lined with some 30 major theaters; film houses joined the fray beginning in the 1920s.

Before the turn of the century, this was New York's horse-trading center, known as Long Acre Square. Substantial change came with the arrival of the subway, as well as the *New York Times,* then a less prestigious paper, which moved here in exchange for having its name grace the square. On December 31, 1904, the *Times* celebrated the opening of its new headquarters, at Times Tower (✉ W. 42nd St. between Broadway and 7th Ave.), with a fireworks show at midnight, thereby starting a New Year's Eve tradition. Now resheathed in Miami Beach marble and called **One Times Square Plaza,** the building's most famous feature is a rooftop pole, down which an illuminated 200-pound ball is lowered each December 31, to the wild enthusiasm of revelers below. (In the 1920s the *Times* moved to its present building, a green-copper-roofed neo-Gothic behemoth, at 229 West 43rd Street.)

Times Square is hardly more sedate on the other 364 nights of the year, mesmerizing visitors with its astonishingly high-wattage signage: five-story-high cups of coffee that actually steam, a 42-ft-tall bottle of Coca-Cola, huge billboards of underwear models, a mammoth, superfast digital display offering world news and stock quotes, and countless other technologically sophisticated signs beckoning for attention. Amazingly, the cleanup of Times Square is unlikely to turn out the lights, as current zoning *requires* buildings to sport ads, as they have for nearly a century. ☞ **Duffy Square** occupies the north end of Times Square and offers a fine vantage from which to take it all in. ✉ *42nd–47th Sts. at Broadway and 7th Ave.*

Times Square Visitors Center. When it opened in 1925, the Embassy Theater showed Metro-Goldwyn-Mayer films for upper-class patrons. In mid-1998 the landmark theater reopened for everyone, as a one-stop center for general Times Square information, sightseeing and full-price theater tickets, MetroCards, transit memorabilia, and much else. Free walking tours are given Friday at noon. Perhaps most important, its rest rooms are the only facilities in the vicinity open to the general public. ✉ *1560 7th Ave., between 46th and 47th Sts.* ⏲ *Daily 8–8.*

45 **Tudor City.** Built between 1925 and 1928 to attract middle-income residents, this private "city" centers around 12 buildings containing 3,000 apartments. On a bluff above 1st Avenue, Tudor City now affords great views of the United Nations and the East River, although two of the buildings originally had no east-side windows, so the tenants would not be forced to gaze at the slaughterhouses, breweries, and glue fac-

tories then along the river. The terrace at the end of 43rd Street overlooks the ☞ **United Nations headquarters** and stands at the head of **Sharansky Steps** (named for Natan—formerly Anatoly—Sharansky, the Soviet dissident). The steps run along **Isaiah Wall** (inscribed THEY SHALL BEAT THEIR SWORDS INTO PLOWSHARES); below are **Ralph J. Bunche Park** (named for the African-American former UN undersecretary) and **Raoul Wallenberg Walk** (named for the Swedish diplomat and World War II hero who saved many Hungarian Jews from the Nazis). ✉ *1st and 2nd Aves. from 40th to 43rd Sts.*

★ 46 **United Nations Headquarters.** Officially an "international zone" and not part of the United States, the U.N. Headquarters is a working symbol of global cooperation. The 18-acre riverside tract, now lushly landscaped, was bought and donated by oil magnate John D. Rockefeller Jr. in 1946. The headquarters were designed in 1947–53 by an international team of architects led by Wallace Harrison. The slim, 550-ft-tall green-glass Secretariat Building; the much smaller, domed General Assembly Building; and the Dag Hammarskjold Library (1963) form the complex, before which the flags of its member nations, from Afghanistan to Zimbabwe, fly in alphabetical order when the General Assembly is in session (mid-September to mid-December). Although the buildings may look a bit dated today, their windswept park and plaza remain visionary: There is a beautiful riverside promenade, a rose garden with 1,400 rosebushes, and sculptures donated by member nations.

An hour-long guided tour (given in 20 languages) is the main visitor attraction; it includes the General Assembly, the Security Council Chamber, the Trustee Council Chamber, and the Economic and Social Council Chamber, though some rooms may be closed on any given day. Displays on war, nuclear energy, and refugees also part of the tour; corridors overflow with imaginatively diverse artwork donated by member nations. Free tickets to assemblies are sometimes available on a first come, first served basis before sessions begin; pick them up in the General Assembly lobby. The Delegates Dining Room is open for lunch (jackets required for men; reservations required at least one day in advance). The public concourse, one level down from the visitor entrance, has a coffee shop, gift shops, bookstore, and a post office where you can mail letters with U.N. stamps. ✉ *Visitor entrance: 1st Ave. and 46th St.,* ☎ *212/963–7713.* 🎫 *Tour $7.50.* ⏲ *Tours Mar.–Dec., daily 9:15–4:45; Jan.–Feb., weekdays 9:15–4:45; 45-min tours in English leave General Assembly lobby every 30 mins. Children under 5 not permitted.*

41 **Whitney Museum of American Art at Philip Morris.** An enormous, 42-ft-high sculpture court with outstanding examples of 20th-century sculpture, many of which are simply too big for the Whitney's uptown base, is the centerpiece of the museum's midtown branch. Such Whitney icons as Claes Oldenberg and Alexander Calder have works here. In the adjacent gallery five shows annually cover all aspects of American art. An espresso bar and seating areas make it an agreeable place to rest. ✉ *120 Park Ave., at E. 42nd St.,* ☎ *212/878–2550.* 🎫 *Free.* ⏲ *Sculpture court: Mon.–Sat. 7:30 AM–9:30 PM, Sun. 11–7; gallery: Mon.–Wed. and Fri. 11–6, Thurs. 11–7:30.*

MURRAY HILL TO UNION SQUARE

As the city grew progressively north throughout the 19th century, one neighborhood after another had its fashionable heyday, only to fade from glory. But three neighborhoods, east of 5th Avenue roughly between 14th and 40th streets, have preserved much of their historic charm: Murray Hill's brownstone mansions and town houses; Madison Square's classic turn-of-the-century skyscrapers; and Gramercy Park's London-like leafy square. The Empire State Building is the only must-see along this route, but the walk as a whole is worth taking for the many moments en route when you may feel as if you've stepped back in time.

Numbers in the text correspond to numbers in the margin and on the Murray Hill to Union Square map.

A Good Walk

Begin on East 36th Street, between Madison and Park avenues, at the **Morgan Library** ①, where old-master drawings, medieval manuscripts, illuminated books, and original music scores are on opulent display. As you proceed south on Madison Avenue, at 35th Street you'll pass the **Church of the Incarnation** ②, a broodingly dark brownstone version of a Gothic chapel. Across the street and taking up the entire next block is the landmark **B. Altman Building** ③, home of the famous department store from 1906 to 1989 and now the site of the New York Public Library's most high-tech research center: the **Science, Industry, and Business Library.**

At 5th Avenue and 34th Street, you can't miss the **Empire State Building** ④, one of the world's best-loved skyscrapers. South of the Empire State, at 5th Avenue and 29th Street, is the **Marble Collegiate Church** ⑤. Cross the street and head east on 29th Street to the **Church of the Transfiguration** ⑥, better known as the Little Church Around the Corner. Continuing south along Madison Avenue, you'll come to the **New York Life Insurance Building** ⑦, which occupies the block between 26th and 27th streets on the east side of Madison, its distinctive gold top visible from afar. The limestone Beaux Arts courthouse, one block down at 25th Street, is the **Appellate Division, New York State Supreme Court** ⑧. The **Metropolitan Life Insurance Tower** ⑨, between 23rd and 24th streets, is another lovely, classically inspired insurance-company tower.

Across from these latter two sites, on the west side of Madison Avenue, is **Madison Square** ⑩, one of Manhattan's nicest green pockets. A walk through the square leads to one of New York's most photographed buildings—the Renaissance-style **Flatiron Building** ⑪, by architect Daniel Burnham. This distinguished building has lent its name to the now trendy Flatiron district, which lies to the south between 5th Avenue and Park Avenue South. The neighborhood's massive buildings, the last of the pre-skyscraper era and remnants of New York's Gilded Age, have had their ornate Romanesque facades gleamingly restored; hip boutiques and some of the city's best restaurants occupy their street levels, while advertising agencies, publishing houses, architects' offices, graphic design firms, residential lofts, and multimedia companies fill the upper stories.

Continue south on Broadway and turn east on 20th Street to the **Theodore Roosevelt Birthplace** ⑫, a reconstruction of the Victorian brownstone where Teddy lived until he was 15 years old. The prettiest part of this residential district, **Gramercy Park** ⑬, lies farther east, at the top of Irving Place between 20th and 21st streets. Alas, this picture-

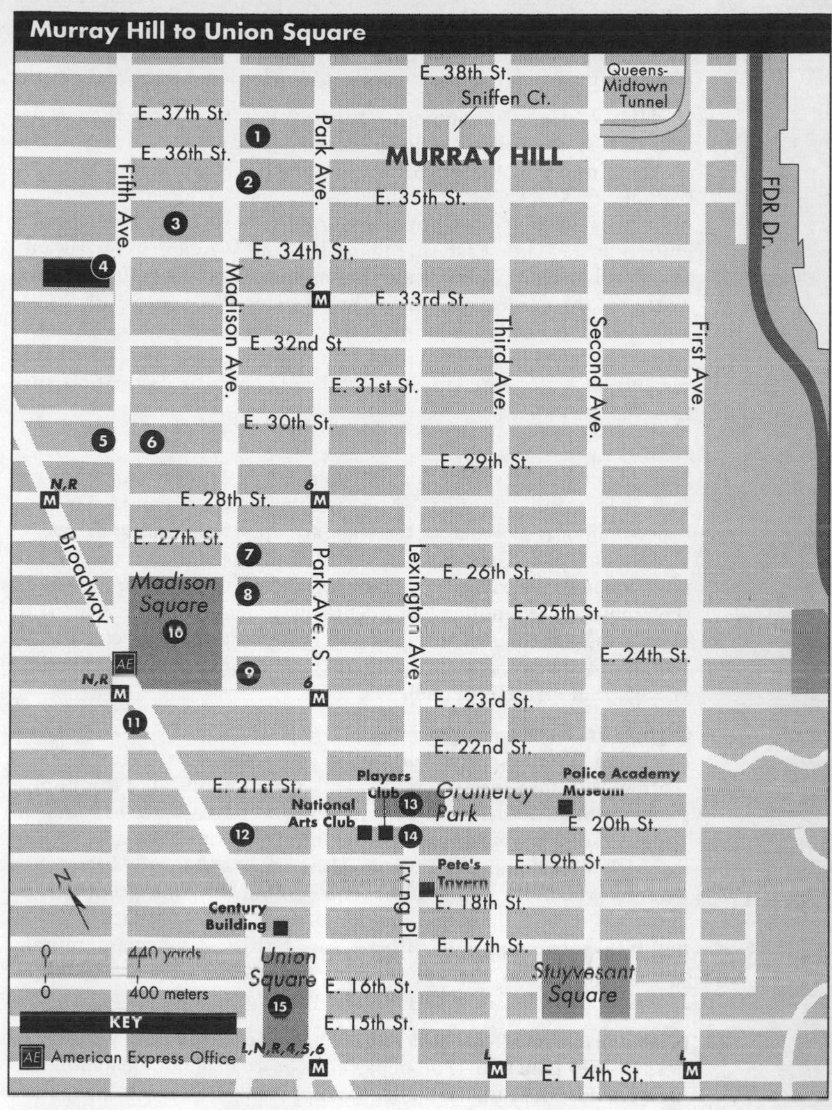

Appellate Division, New York State Supreme Court, **8**

B. Altman Building/ New York Public Library Science, Industry, and Business Library (SIBL), **3**

Church of the Incarnation, **2**

Church of the Transfiguration, **6**

Empire State Building, **4**

Flatiron Building, **11**

Gramercy Park, **13**

Irving Place, **14**

Madison Square, **10**

Marble Collegiate Church, **5**

Metropolitan Life Insurance Tower, **9**

Morgan Library, **1**

New York Life Insurance Building, **7**

Theodore Roosevelt Birthplace National Historic Site, **12**

Union Square, **15**

perfect park, with its flower beds, bird feeders, sundials, and cozy-looking benches, is accessible only to area residents who have keys. **Irving Place** ⑭, lined with charming brownstones, leads south from the park.

If you have made an appointment in advance, now is the time to detour east, to the **Police Academy Museum.** As an alternative, you can wander up to Lexington Avenue in the high 20s, a neighborhood affectionately known as Little India, which has a concentration of Indian restaurants, spice shops, imported-video stores, and clothing emporiums; Middle Eastern, Indonesian, and Vietnamese restaurants also dot the area, which has a strong multicultural flavor. If you make neither of these side trips, turn right off Irving Place onto 17th Street, which leads to **Union Square** ⑮. The square itself bustles with the Greenmarket, a farmers' market, four days a week, but fashionable restaurants, cafés, and stores make the area a great destination anytime.

TIMING

Half a day should suffice for this tour. Allow 1½ hours each for the Empire State Building and the Morgan Library. Keep in mind that some office buildings included in the walk are open only during the week. The Union Square Greenmarket, a must-visit, is open all day every Monday, Wednesday, Friday, and Saturday. Before traipsing to the top of the Empire State Building, consider the weather and how it is likely to affect visibility. Sunsets from the observation deck are spectacular, so you may want to end your day there (but be sure to factor in the time you'll spend waiting on line).

Sights to See

❽ **Appellate Division, New York State Supreme Court.** Figures representing "Wisdom" and "Justice" flank the main portal of this imposing Corinthian courthouse, built in 1900, on the east side of Madison Square. Great lawmakers of the past line the roof balustrade, including Moses, Justinian, Confucius, although a statue of Muhammad was removed in the 1950s at the request of local Islamic groups, as Islamic law forbids the representation of humans in sculpture or painting. Inside are exhibitions of New York historical ephemera, murals, and rooms with furniture by the Herter Brothers. ✉ *35 E. 25th St., at Madison Ave.,* ☎ *212/340–0400.* ⏲ *Weekdays 9–5.*

❸ **B. Altman Building/New York Public Library Science, Industry, and Business Library (SIBL).** In 1906 department-store magnate Benjamin Altman gambled that the fashionable shoppers who patronized his store at 6th Avenue and 18th Street would follow him uptown to large new quarters on 5th Avenue and 34th Street, then a strictly residential street. They indeed came, and other stores followed, but then moved uptown again, to the 50s, leaving this trailblazer behind. Green canopies reminiscent of old subway kiosks grace the building's elaborate entrances. In the wake of the B. Altman chain's 1989 bankruptcy, the landmark sat vacant for several years. In 1996 the New York Public Library transferred all scientific, technology, and business materials from its main 42nd Street building to a new state-of-the-art facility here, the **Science, Industry, and Business Library** (SIBL). In the entrance area, a wall of TVs tuned to business-news stations and an electronic ticker tape reporting the latest stock market prices set SIBL's high-tech tone, while electronic signs beam instructions to patrons. Hundreds of computers wired to the Internet and research databases are the library's hottest tickets. In the summer of 1999, the City University of New York Graduate School and University Center is slated to move into the building's 5th Avenue side. ✉ *188 Madison Ave., at 34th St.,* ☎ *212/592–7000.* ⏲ *Mon. and Fri.–Sat. 10–6, Tues.–Thurs. 11–7.*

❷ **Church of the Incarnation.** A broodingly dark brownstone version of a Gothic chapel on the outside, this 1864 Episcopal church boasts jewel-like stained glass inside that counteracts the building's dour effect. The north aisle's 23rd Psalm Window is by the Tiffany Glass works; the south aisle's two Angel windows, dedicated to infants, are by the 19th-century English writer-designer William Morris. ✉ *205 Madison Ave., at 35th St.*

❻ **Church of the Transfiguration.** Known as the Little Church Around the Corner, this Gothic Revival church complex (1849–1861) is set back in a shrub-filled New York version of an old English churchyard. It won its memorable appellation in 1870 when other area churches refused to bury actor George Holland, a colleague of well-known thespian Joseph Jefferson. Jefferson was directed to the "little church around the corner" to accomplish the burial, and the Episcopal institution has welcomed literary and theater types ever since. The south transept's stained-glass window, by John LaFarge, depicts 19th-century superstar actor Edwin Booth as Hamlet, his most famous role. ✉ *1 E. 29th St.,* ☎ *212/684–6770.* ⏲ *Sun. after 11 AM mass.*

★ ❹ **Empire State Building.** It may no longer be the world's tallest building (it currently ranks fifth), but it is certainly one of the world's best-loved skyscrapers, its pencil-slim silhouette a symbol for New York City. The Art Deco playground for King Kong opened in April 1931 after only about a year and a half of construction; the framework rose at a rate of 4½ stories per week, making the Empire State Building the fastest-rising major skyscraper ever built. Many floors were left completely unfinished, however, so tenants could have them custom-designed. The depression delayed this process, and critics deemed it the "Empty State Building." The crowning spire was originally designed as a mooring mast for dirigibles, but none ever docked here; in 1951 a TV transmittal tower was added to the top, raising the total height to 1,472 ft (its signals reach 8 million television sets in four states). Ever since the 1976 American bicentennial celebration, the top 30 stories have been spotlighted at night with seasonal colors. Today the holidays celebrated in lights include: Martin Luther King Jr. Day (red, black, and green); Valentine's Day (red and white); the Fourth of July (red, white, and blue); Columbus Day (red, white, and green); Hanukkah (blue and white); and Christmas (red and green). The building has appeared in more than 100 movies, among them 1933's unforgettable *King Kong* and 1957's *An Affair to Remember,* in which Cary Grant waited impatiently at the top for his rendezvous with Deborah Kerr, an event around which Nora Ephron built the entire screenplay of her 1993 hit, *Sleepless in Seattle.*

Today about 20,000 people work in the Empire State Building, and more than 3.8 million people visit its 86th- and 102nd-floor observation decks annually. Tickets are sold on the concourse level; on your way up admire the illuminated panels depicting the Seven Wonders of the World—with the Empire State brazenly appended as number eight—in the three-story-high marble lobby. If you choose one observatory, make it the 86th, which is open to the air; on clear days you can see up to 80 mi. The 102nd-floor spot is smaller, cramped, and glassed in. It's worth timing your visit for early or late in the day, when the sun is low on the horizon and the shadows are deep across the city. Morning is the least crowded time, while at night the views of the city's lights are dazzling. ✉ *350 5th Ave., at 34th St.,* ☎ *212/736–3100.* 🎫 *$6.* ⏲ *Daily 9:30 AM–midnight; last elevator up leaves at 11:30 PM.*

The Empire State Building's other major tourist attraction is the **New York Skyride.** A three-minute Comedy Central video presentation on the virtues of New York precedes a seven-minute motion-simulator ride above and around some of the city's top attractions, which are projected on a two-story-tall screen. The show, which leaves you feeling a little dizzy and disoriented, is not recommended for anyone who has trouble with motion sickness, and pregnant women are not admitted. ☎ *212/279–9777.* *$11.50; $14 for Skyride and Observatory.* *Daily 10–10.*

★ ⓫ **Flatiron Building.** When it opened in 1902, the Fuller Building, as it was originally known, was the tallest building in the world (a claim successively held by, among others, the Chrysler and Empire State buildings and the World Trade Center's twin towers). Architect Daniel Burnham made ingenious use of the triangular wedge of land and employed a revolutionary steel frame, which allowed for its unprecedented 20-story, 286-ft height. Covered with a limestone and terra-cotta skin in the Italian Renaissance style, the ship's-bow-like structure, appearing to sail intrepidly up the avenue, was the most popular subject of picture postcards at the turn of the century. Winds invariably swooped down at its 23rd Street tip, billowing up the skirts of women pedestrians on 23rd Street, and local traffic cops had to shoo away male gawkers—coining the phrase "23 skiddoo." It was immediately noticed that the building resembled the then-popular flatirons, and the popular nickname eventually became official. ✉ *175 5th Ave., bordered by 22nd and 23rd Sts., 5th Ave., and Broadway.*

NEED A BREAK? A good stop for coffee, hearty soups, salads, or sandwiches on thick, crusty bread is **La Boulangère** (✉ 49 E. 21st St., ☎ 212/475–8772), just 2½ blocks from the Flatiron Building. Madison or Union squares are both nearby take-out destinations.

⓭ **Gramercy Park.** New York's only surviving private square occupies what was originally swamp. In 1831 real estate developer Samuel B. Ruggles bought and drained the land and created a park, inspired by London's residential squares, for the exclusive use of those who would buy the surrounding lots. Sixty-six of the city's fashionable elite did just that, and no less than golden keys were provided for them to penetrate the park's 8-ft-high cast-iron fence. Although no longer golden, keys are still given only to residents. The parks' pristine lower beds, bird feeders, sundials, and benches may not be accessible, but its charms are apparent even to passersby.

Original 19th-century row houses in Greek Revival, Italianate, Gothic Revival, and Victorian Gothic styles still surround the south and west sides of the park. On the south side of the square stands a statue of actor Edwin Booth playing Hamlet; Booth lived at No. 16, which he remodeled in the early 1880s to serve as an actors' association, the **Players Club.** Stanford White, the architect for the renovation, was a member of the club, as were many other nonactors. Members over the years have included Mark Twain, Booth Tarkington, John and Lionel Barrymore, Irving Berlin, Winston Churchill, Sir Laurence Olivier, Frank Sinatra, Walter Cronkite, Jack Lemmon, and Richard Gere.

The **National Arts Club** (✉ 15 Gramercy Park S) was once the home of Samuel Tilden, a governor of New York and the 1876 Democratic presidential candidate (he won the popular vote but lost the election to Rutherford B. Hayes, whose one-vote plurality in the electoral college won him the presidency). Calvert Vaux, codesigner of Central Park, remodeled this building in 1884, conjoining two houses and creating a 40-room mansion. Among its Victorian Gothic decorations are medallions portraying Goethe, Dante, Milton, and Benjamin Franklin.

The club, founded in 1898 to bring together "art lovers and art workers," moved into the mansion in 1906. Early members included Woodrow Wilson and Theodore Roosevelt; Robert Redford and Martin Scorsese are more recent members. The Club now houses the Poetry Society of America, which sponsors poetry readings (☞ Chapter 5).

On the west end of the square, redbrick Greek Revival town houses with fanciful cast-iron verandas look like something out of New Orleans's French Quarter. Mayor James Harper (elected in 1888) lived at No. 4, behind the pair of street lanterns. Actor John Garfield died in 1952 while staying at No. 3.

At the northeast corner, the ornate white terra-cotta apartment building at **36 Gramercy Park East** (1910) is guarded by concrete knights in silver-paint armor. The turreted redbrick building at **34 Gramercy Park East** (1883) was one of the city's first cooperative apartment houses; its tenants have included actors James Cagney, John Carradine, and Margaret Hamilton, who played the Wicked Witch in *The Wizard of Oz*. The austere gray-brown Friends Meeting House at 28 Gramercy Park South (1859) became the **Brotherhood Synagogue** in 1974, and a narrow plaza just east of the synagogue contains a Holocaust memorial. No. **19 Gramercy Park South** (1845) was the home in the 1880s of society doyenne Mrs. Stuyvesant Fish, a fearless iconoclast who shocked Mrs. Astor and Mrs. Vanderbilt when she reduced the time of formal dinner parties from several hours to 50 minutes, thus ushering in the modern social era. ✉ *Lexington Ave. between 20th and 21st Sts.*

⓮ **Irving Place.** Like neighboring ☞ **Gramercy Park**, this short street is lined with charming row houses, many of which now house boutiques and restaurants. The street has a number of literary associations: It's claimed that O. Henry (pseudonym of William Sidney Porter) wrote "The Gift of the Magi" while sitting in the second booth to the right at **Pete's Tavern** (✉ 129 E. 18th St., at Irving Pl.), which also claims to be the oldest saloon in New York (1864); both assertions are disputed, but it's still a good spot for a drink in a Gaslight Era atmosphere. O. Henry lived at 55 **Irving Place** in a building long ago demolished.

The street takes its name from another famous New York chronicler, Washington Irving (1783–1859), who wrote *The Legend of Sleepy Hollow* more than a century before O. Henry was there. A plaque on the redbrick house at 17th Street and Irving Place erroneously identifies it as the home of Washington Irving; it was actually his nephew's house, but the famous writer did often visit (a sushi bar now occupies the ground floor). A huge bust of the writer is outside **Washington Irving High School** (✉ 40 Irving Pl.), alma mater of Claudette Colbert and Whoopi Goldberg.

❿ **Madison Square.** With a fine view of some of the city's oldest and most charming skyscrapers, this tree-filled 7-acre park mainly attracts dog owners and office workers, but it's a fine spot for people-watching or picnicking. Baseball was invented across the Hudson in Hoboken, New Jersey, but the city's first baseball games were played here circa 1845. On the north end an imposing 1881 statue by Augustus Saint-Gaudens memorializes Civil War naval hero Admiral Farragut. An 1876 statue of Secretary of State William Henry Seward (the Seward of the phrase "Seward's folly"—as Alaska was originally known) sits in the park's southwest corner, though it's rumored the sculptor placed a reproduction of the statesman's head on a likeness of Abraham Lincoln's body. ✉ *23rd to 26th Sts., between 5th and Madison Aves.*

5 **Marble Collegiate Church.** Built in 1854 for the Reformed Protestant Dutch Congregation first organized in 1628 by Peter Minuit, the canny Dutchman who bought Manhattan from the Native Americans for the equivalent of $24, this impressive Romanesque Revival church takes its name from the Tuckahoe marble that covers it. Dr. Norman Vincent Peale (*The Power of Positive Thinking*) was Marble Collegiate's pastor from 1932 to 1984. ✉ *1 W. 29th St., at 5th Ave., 212/686–2770.*

9 **Metropolitan Life Insurance Tower.** When it was added in 1909, the 700-ft tower, which re-creates the campanile of St. Mark's in Venice, made this building the world's tallest. Its clock's four dials are each three stories high, and their minute hands weigh half a ton each; it chimes on the quarter hour. A skywalk connects Met Life's North Building, between 24th and 25th streets. Its Art Deco loggias have attracted many film crews—the building has appeared in such films as *After Hours, Radio Days,* and *The Fisher King.* ✉ *1 Madison Ave., between 23rd and 24th Sts.*

★ 1 **Morgan Library.** One of New York's most patrician museums, the Morgan is a world-class treasury of medieval and Renaissance illuminated manuscripts, old-master drawings and prints, rare books, and autographed literary and musical manuscripts. Many of the crowning achievements produced on paper, from the Middle Ages to the 20th century, are here: letters penned by John Keats and Thomas Jefferson; a summary of the theory of relativity in Einstein's own elegant handwriting; three Gutenberg Bibles; drawings by Dürer, da Vinci, Rubens, Blake, and Rembrandt; the only known manuscript fragment of Milton's "Paradise Lost"; Thoreau's journals; and original manuscripts and letters by Charlotte Brontë, Jane Austen, Thomas Pynchon, and many others. Originally built for the collections of Wall Street baron J. Pierpont (J. P.) Morgan (1837–1913), the museum has at its core a Renaissance-style palazzo, completed in 1906 by McKim, Mead & White, which houses the opulent period rooms of Morgan's original library. The **East Room** (the main library) has dizzying tiers of handsomely bound rare books, letters, and illuminated manuscripts. The **West Room,** Morgan's personal study, contains a remarkable selection of mostly Italian Renaissance furniture, paintings, and other marvels within its red-damask-lined walls.

Changing exhibitions, drawn from the permanent collection, are often highly distinguished. In May–August 1999 the Library will mount its first full-scale loan exhibition of 20th-century works, which will include more than 120 drawings by Kandinsky, Matisse, Klee, Picasso, and de Kooning, among others, from many of New York's finest private collections. The library shop is within an 1852 Italianate brownstone, once the home of Morgan's son, J. P. "Jack" Morgan Jr., which is connected to the rest of the library by a graceful glass-roof garden court where lunch and afternoon tea are served. Outside, what was rumored to be architect Charles McKim's face is on the sphinx in the right-hand sculptured panel of the original library's facade, on 36th Street. ✉ *29 E. 36th St., at Madison Ave.,* ☎ *212/685–0008.* 🎫 *$7 (suggested donation).* ⏲ *Tues.–Thurs. 10:30–5, Fri. 10:30–8:00, Sat. 10:30–6, Sun. noon–6.*

7 **New York Life Insurance Building.** Cass Gilbert, better known for the Woolworth Building (☞ The Seaport and the Courts, *below*), capped this 1928 building with a gilded pyramid that is stunning when lighted at night. The soaring lobby's coffered ceilings and ornate bronze doors are equally sumptuous. P. T. Barnum's Hippodrome formerly occupied this site, and after that (1890–1925) Madison Square Garden, designed by architect and playboy Stanford White. White was shot in the

Garden's roof garden by Harry K. Thaw, a partner in White's firm and the jealous husband of actress Evelyn Nesbit, with whom White was purportedly having an affair—a lurid episode more or less accurately depicted in E. L. Doctorow's book *Ragtime*. ✉ *51 Madison Ave., between 26th and 27th Sts.*

Police Academy Museum. Law-enforcement memorabilia—uniforms, firearms, batons, badges, even counterfeit money dating to the time of the Dutch—fill the second floor of the city's police academy. ✉ *235 E. 20th St., between 2nd and 3rd Aves.,* ☎ *212/477–9753.* 💵 *Free.* ⏲ *Weekdays 9–3 by appointment only.*

OFF THE BEATEN PATH

SNIFFEN COURT – Just two blocks from the Morgan Library, the 10 Romanesque Revival former brick carriage houses that line this easily overlooked cul-de-sac are equal parts old London and New Orleans. Peer through the locked gate to admire the lovely buildings. ✉ *150–158 E. 36th St., between Lexington and 3rd Aves.*

12 **Theodore Roosevelt Birthplace National Historic Site.** Theodore Roosevelt, the 26th president and the only one from New York City, was born on this site in 1858. The original 1848 brownstone was demolished in 1916, but this Gothic Revival replica, built in 1923, is a near-perfect reconstruction of the house where Teddy lived until he was 15 years old. Now administered by the National Park Service, the house has a fascinating collection of Teddyana in five Victorian period rooms. Saturday-afternoon chamber music concerts are offered each fall, winter, and spring. ✉ *28 E. 20th St., between Broadway and Park Ave. S,* ☎ *212/260–1616.* 💵 *$2.* ⏲ *Wed.–Sun. 9–5; guided tours every hr until 4.*

15 **Union Square.** Its name, originally signifying the fact that two main roads crossed here, proved doubly apt in the late 19th and early 20th centuries, when the square became a rallying spot for labor protests and mass demonstrations; many unions, as well as fringe political parties, moved their headquarters nearby. A massive renewal program in the 1980s reclaimed the park from longtime neglect. A **statue of Gandhi,** stands in the northwest corner of the park. The restored 1932 **Pavilion** is now flanked by playgrounds and **Luna Park** (☎ 212/475–6299), an open-air café in operation from mid-May through October.

Union Square is at its best on Monday, Wednesday, Friday, and Saturday, when the largest of the city's two dozen **Greenmarkets** brings farmers and food purveyors from all over the Northeast to its western and northern edges. Crowds of nearby residents and office workers browse among the stands of fresh produce, flowers and plants, homemade bakery goods, cheeses, cider, New York State wines, and fish and meat.

Bustling restaurants and retail superstores like Bradlees and Toys "R" Us have moved into the area in recent years; some occupy the handsome, restored 19th-century commercial buildings that surround the park. Foremost among these is the redbrick and white-stone **Century Building** (built in 1881, ✉ 33 E. 17th St.), now a Barnes & Noble bookstore, which has preserved the building's original cast-iron columns and other architectural details. The building at 17th Street and Union Square East, now housing the New York Film Academy and the Union Square Theatre (☞ Chapter 5), was the final home of **Tammany Hall.** This organization, famous for its days as a fairly corrupt yet effective political machine, moved here just at the height of its power in 1929, but by 1943 it went bankrupt and had to sell the building. ✉ *14th to 17th Sts. between Broadway and Park Ave. S.*

MUSEUM MILE

Once known as Millionaires' Row, the stretch of 5th Avenue between 79th and 104th streets has been fittingly renamed Museum Mile, for it now contains New York's most distinguished cluster of cultural institutions. The connection is more than coincidental: Many museums are housed in what used to be the great mansions of merchant princes and wealthy industrialists. A large percentage of these buildings were constructed of limestone (it's cheaper than marble) and reflect the Beaux Arts style, which was very popular among the wealthy at the turn of the century.

Numbers in the text correspond to numbers in the margin and on the Museum Mile, Upper East Side map.

A Good Walk

This tour is a simple, straight walk up 5th Avenue, from 70th Street to 105th, and it covers nearly 2 mi. If you walk up the west side of the street (crossing over to visit museums, of course), you'll be under the canopy of Central Park and have a good view of the mansions and apartments across the street. If you're not sure whether you're interested in a particular museum, stop in its gift store; museum shops are usually good indicators of what's in the rest of the building. A brochure called "Museum Mile" is available at most institutions listed below; it provides brief descriptions of the various museums along the route as well as their opening hours.

Begin at 5th Avenue and 70th Street (technically not part of Museum Mile) with the **Frick Collection** ①, housed in an ornate, imposing Beaux Arts mansion built in 1914 for coke-and-steel baron Henry Clay Frick. It's several blocks north before you get to the next stop. On your way, be sure to admire the former mansions, some of them now converted into multiple-family dwellings, among them the Gothic Revival facade of the Ukrainian Institute of America, on the southeast corner of 5th Avenue at 79th Street. One block north is the **American Irish Historical Society** ②, another fine example of the French-influenced Beaux Arts style that was so popular at the turn of the century.

From here you can't miss the immense and impressive **Metropolitan Museum of Art** ③, one of the world's largest art museums, encroaching on Central Park's turf. The goings on around the steps that sweep you up into the museum merit at least casual observation—it's a favorite spot for performance artists, musicians, and souvenir sellers.

Across from the Met, between 82nd and 83rd streets, one Beaux Arts town house stands its ground amid newer apartment blocks. It now belongs to the Federal Republic of Germany, which has installed a branch of the **Goethe Institut** ④ here. At the corner of 85th Street is 1040 5th Avenue, the former home of Jacqueline Kennedy Onassis, from which she could view Central Park and the reservoir that now bears her name.

Frank Lloyd Wright's **Guggenheim Museum** ⑤ (opened in 1959) is the architect's only major New York building. A block north stands the **National Academy Museum** ⑥, an art museum and school (until recently known as the National Academy of Design) housed in a stately 19th-century mansion. At 91st Street you'll find the former residence of industrialist Andrew Carnegie, now a museum devoted to contemporary and historic design—the **Cooper-Hewitt National Design Museum** ⑦. Across 91st Street, the Convent of the Sacred Heart (⊠ 1 E.

Museum Mile
American Irish Historical Society (AIHS), **2**
Conservatory Garden, **12**
Cooper-Hewitt National Design Museum, **7**
El Museo del Barrio, **11**
Frick Collection, **1**
Goethe Institut, **4**
International Center of Photography (ICP), **9**
Jewish Museum, **8**
Metropolitan Museum of Art, **3**
Museum of the City of New York, **10**
National Academy Museum, **6**
Solomon R. Guggenheim Museum, **5**

The Upper East Side
Americas Society, **16**
Asia Society, **17**
Asphalt Green, **24**
Bloomingdale's, **13**
Carl Schurz Park, **22**
Carlyle Hotel, **20**
Gracie Mansion, **23**
Henderson Place Historic District, **21**
Polo/Ralph Lauren, **18**
Seventh Regiment Armory, **15**
Temple Emanu-El, **14**
Whitney Museum of American Art, **19**

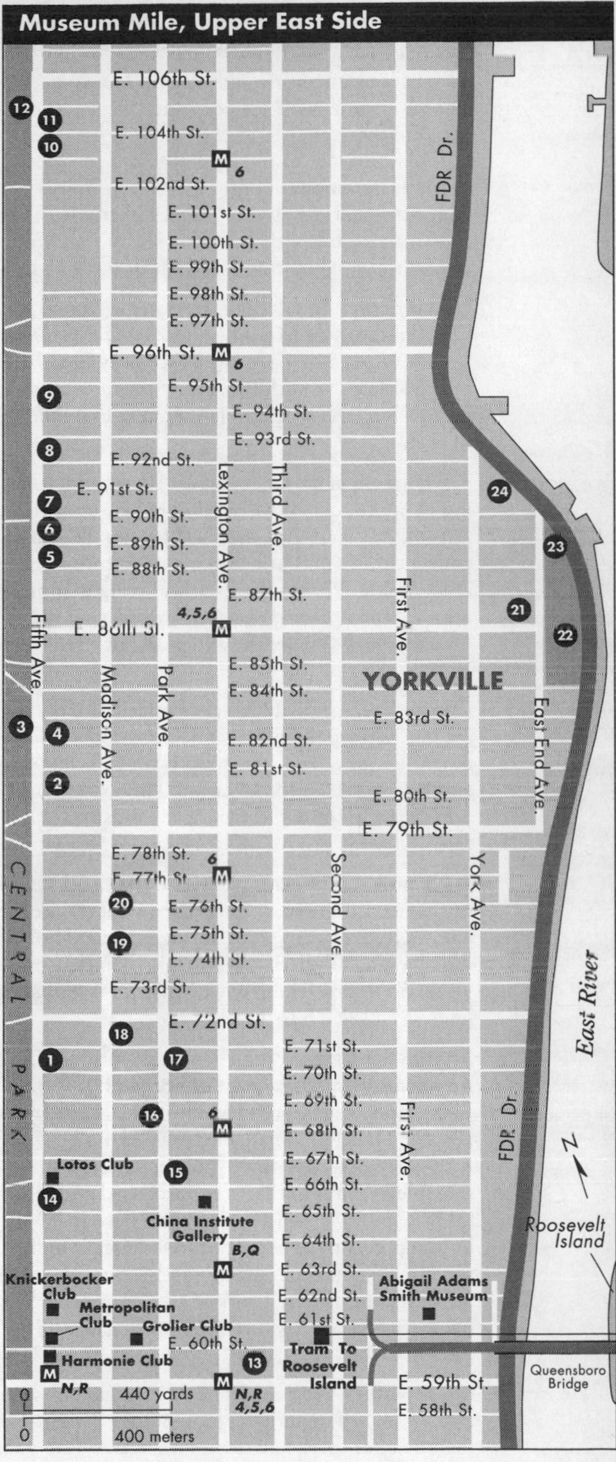

Museum Mile, Upper East Side

91st St.) is in a huge Italianate mansion originally built in 1918 for financier Otto Kahn, a noted patron of the arts.

As you continue north, the **Jewish Museum** ⑧, at 92nd Street, is next. The handsome, well-proportioned Georgian-style mansion on the corner of 5th Avenue and 94th Street was built in 1914 for Willard Straight, founder of the *New Republic* magazine. Today it is the home of the **International Center of Photography** ⑨. If you'd like some architectural variety as you proceed north on 5th Avenue, you may want to walk east on 97th Street to see the onion-dome towers of the St. Nicholas Russian Orthodox Cathedral (✉ 15 E. 97th St.), built in 1902.

Between 98th and 101st streets, 5th Avenue is dominated by the various buildings of Mount Sinai Medical Center, which was originally founded in 1852 by a group of wealthy Jewish citizens and moved here in 1904. The 1976 addition, the Annenberg Building, is a looming tower of Cor-Ten steel that has deliberately been allowed to develop a patina of rust.

The **Museum of the City of New York** ⑩, which has permanent and changing exhibits related to Big Apple history, is one of the homier museums on this tour. Another is **El Museo del Barrio** ⑪, founded in 1969, concentrating on Latin American culture in general, with a particular emphasis on Puerto Rican art. Having completed this long walk, you may want to reward yourself by crossing the street to Central Park's **Conservatory Garden** ⑫, a formal, enclosed tract in the rambling park.

TIMING

It would be impossible to do justice to all these collections in one outing; the Metropolitan Museum alone contains too much to see in a week, much less in a day. You may want to select one or two museums or exhibits in which to linger and simply walk past the others, appreciating their exteriors (this in itself constitutes a minicourse in architecture). Save the rest for another day—or for your next trip to New York.

Do be sure to pick the right day of the week for this tour: Most of these museums are closed at least one day of the week, usually Monday, but a few have free admission during extended hours on Tuesday or Thursday evening. Others have drinks, snacks, and/or music during late weekend hours. The Jewish Museum is closed Saturday; the Guggenheim is closed Thursday.

Sights to See

❷ **American Irish Historical Society (AIHS).** U.S. Steel president William Ellis Corey, who scandalized his social class by marrying musical comedy star Mabelle Gilman, once owned this heavily ornamented, mansard-roofed Beaux Arts town house; he died in 1934, and the building remained vacant until it was purchased and renovated by the AIHS (established 1897), who set up shop here in 1940. The society's library holdings chronicle people of Irish descent in the United States, and the society hosts talks approximately once a week in the summer; it also puts on exhibitions. Tours of the mansion are usually available on request. ✉ *991 5th Ave., at 80th St.,* ☎ *212/288–2263.* *Free.* ⏲ *Weekdays 10:30–5.*

★ ⓬ **Conservatory Garden.** Huge conservatories stood here between 1899 and 1934, when parks commissioner Robert Moses, citing their high maintenance costs, had them torn down. Today three gardens on 6 acres compose Central Park's most magnificent formal space (☞ Central Park, *below*). The garden's entrance leads through elaborate wrought-iron gates that once graced the midtown 5th Avenue mansion of Cornelius Vanderbilt II. The **Central Garden**, in the classic Italian style, has a deep green central lawn bordered by yew hedges and cool crab-apple allées. Across the lawn is the large Conservatory Fountain, beyond which a semicircular wisteria-draped pergola rises into the hillside. In the **North Garden,** in the French tradition, large numbers of like plants are marshaled into elaborate floral patterns. The three spirited girls dancing in the Untermeyer Fountain are at the heart of a huge circular bed where 20,000 tulips bloom in the spring and 5,000 chrysanthemums in the fall. The **South Garden,** restored in the early 1980s by celebrated garden designer Lynden B. Miller (who also redesigned Bryant Park and many other gardens), is a fine example of the contemporary American mixed border. ⊠ *Entrance at 105th St. and 5th Ave.,* ☎ *212/360–2766.* ⏲ *Daily 8–dusk, free tours on summer Sat. at 11.*

❼ **Cooper-Hewitt National Design Museum.** Andrew Carnegie sought comfort more than show when he built this 64-room house on what were the outskirts of town in 1901; he administered his extensive philanthropic projects from the first-floor study. (Note the low doorways—Carnegie was only 5 ft 2 inches tall.) The core of the museum's collection was begun in 1897 by the two Hewitt sisters, granddaughters of inventor and industrialist Peter Cooper; major holdings include drawings, prints, textiles, furniture, metalwork, ceramics, glass, woodwork, and wall coverings. The Smithsonian Institution took over the museum in 1967, and in 1976 the collection moved into the Carnegie mansion. The museum has been under renovation since 1995, forcing the closing of all or some exhibition galleries, but in June 1998 the project is expected to be complete; the museum's three buildings will be linked, a new Design Resource Center will open, and all galleries will reopen. The changing exhibitions, which focus on various aspects of contemporary or historical design, are invariably enlightening and often amusing. In summer some exhibits make use of the lovely courtyard. In winter 1999 the first-ever *Triennial* design exhibition debuts; it will showcase works in progress by American designers. ⊠ *2 E. 91st St.,* ☎ *212/849–8420.* 🎟 *$3; free Tues. 5–9.* ⏲ *Tues. 10–9, Wed.–Sat. 10–5, Sun. noon–5.*

⓫ **El Museo del Barrio.** *El barrio* is Spanish for "the neighborhood," and the museum is positioned on the edge of East Harlem, a largely Spanish-speaking, Puerto Rican neighborhood. It moved here in 1977, after eight years in various nearby locations. Though the museum focuses on Latin American and Latino culture and has objects from the Caribbean and Central and South America, its collection of Puerto Rican art is particularly strong. The 8,000-object permanent collection includes numerous pre-Columbian artifacts. ⊠ *1230 5th Ave., at 104th St.,* ☎ *212/831–7272.* 🎟 *$4 (suggested donation).* ⏲ *May–Sept., Wed. and Fri.–Sun. 11–5, Thurs. 11–8; Oct.–Apr., Wed.–Sun. 11–5.*

★ ❶ **Frick Collection.** Coke-and-steel baron Henry Clay Frick found a home for the superb art collection he was amassing far from the soot and smoke of Pittsburgh, where he'd made his fortune. The original mansion was designed by Thomas Hastings and built in 1913–14. Opened as a public museum in 1935 and expanded in 1977, it still resembles a gracious private home, albeit one with bona fide masterpieces in almost every room. The number of paintings traditionally found in art-history textbooks is astounding; you'll also see sculptures and decorative arts throughout the house. (Consider purchasing the Frick's *Guide to Works of Art on Exhibition* [$1], which provides brief but useful annotations about each piece of art.) Many treasures bear special mention. Édouard Manet's *The Bullfight* (1864) hangs in the Garden Court. Two of the Frick's three Vermeers—*Officer and Laughing Girl* (circa 1658) and *Girl Interrupted at Her Music* (1660–61)—hang by the front staircase. Fra Filippo Lippi's *The Annunciation* (circa 1440) hangs in the Octagon Room. Gainsborough and Reynolds portraits are in the dining room; canvases by Gainsborough, Constable, Turner, and Gilbert Stuart are in the library; and several Titians (including *Portrait of a Man in a Red Cap,* circa 1516), Holbeins, a Giovanni Bellini (*St. Francis in the Desert,* circa 1480), and an El Greco (*St. Jerome,* circa 1590–1600) are in the living room. Nearly 50 additional paintings, as well as much sculpture, decorative arts and furniture, are in the West and East galleries. Three Rembrandts, including *The Polish Rider* (circa 1655) and *Self-Portrait* (1658), as well as a third Vermeer, *Mistress and Maid* (circa 1667–68), hang in the former; paintings by Whistler, Goya, Van Dyck, Lorrain, David, and Corot in the latter. The tranquil indoor court with a fountain and glass ceiling is a lovely spot for a respite. ✉ *1 E. 70th St., at 5th Ave.,* ☎ *212/288–0700.* 🎟 *$5. Children under 10 not admitted.* ⏲ *Tues.–Sat. 10–6, Sun. 1–6.*

❹ **Goethe Institut.** This institute, which doubles as a German cultural center, offers art exhibitions as well as lectures, films, and workshops; its extensive library includes current issues of German newspapers and periodicals. ✉ *1014 5th Ave., at 82nd St.,* ☎ *212/439–8700.* 🎟 *Exhibitions free.* ⏲ *Tues. and Thurs. noon–7, Wed. and Sat. noon–5.*

❾ **International Center of Photography (ICP).** The city's leading photography-only venue, ICP is housed in a 1913 redbrick Georgian Revival mansion that once belonged to one of the founders of the *New Republic.* Founded in 1974 by photojournalist Cornell Capa (photographer Robert Capa's brother), ICP culls from its collection of 45,000 works for its changing exhibitions, both here and at its midtown branch (☞ 42nd Street, *above*). These often focus on the work of a single prominent photographer or one photographic genre (portraits, architecture, etc.). The bookstore carries an impressive array of photography-oriented books, prints, and postcards. ✉ *1130 5th Ave., at 94th St.,* ☎ *212/860–1777.* 🎟 *$4; Tues. 6–8 pay as you wish.* ⏲ *Tues. 11–8, Wed.–Sun. 11–6.*

❽ **Jewish Museum.** The permanent two-floor exhibition, which complements temporary shows, explores the development and meaning of Jewish identity and culture over the course of 4,000 years. The exhibition draws on the museum's enormous collection of artwork, ceremonial objects, and electronic media. An expansion completed in 1993 preserved the gray-stone Gothic-style 1908 mansion occupied by the museum since 1947 and enlarged the 1963 addition; a café and a larger shop were also added. At the same time, the mansion facade was extended, giving the museum the appearance of a late–French Gothic château. This museum sometimes has a line to get in that extends down the block, so try to arrive early in the day. In 1999 look for the exhibition on the beginning of modernism in Berlin. ✉ *1109 5th Ave., at 92nd St.,* ☎ *212/423–3230.* 🎟 *$7; Tues. free after 5.* ⏲ *Sun.–Mon. and Wed.–Thurs. 11–5:45, Tues. 11–8.*

★ ❸ **Metropolitan Museum of Art.** The largest art museum in the western hemisphere (it encompasses 2 million square ft), the Met is one of the city's supreme cultural institutions. Its permanent collection of nearly 3 million works of art from all over the world includes objects from the Paleolithic era to modern times—an assemblage whose quality and range make this one of the world's greatest museums.

Founded in 1870, the Met first opened its doors 10 years later, on March 30, 1880, but the original Victorian Gothic redbrick building by Calvert Vaux has since been encased in other architecture, which in turn has been encased in other architecture. The majestic 5th Avenue facade, designed by Richard Morris Hunt, was built in 1902 of gray Indiana limestone; later additions eventually surrounded the original building on the sides and back. (You can glimpse part of the museum's original redbrick facade in a room to the left of the top of the main staircase and on a side wall of the ground-floor European Sculpture Court.)

The 5th Avenue entrance leads into the **Great Hall,** a soaring neoclassic chamber that has been designated a landmark. Past the admission booths, a vast marble staircase leads up to the **European painting** galleries, whose 2,500 pre-19th-century works include Botticelli's *The Last Communion of St. Jerome,* Pieter Brueghel's *The Harvesters,* El Greco's *View of Toledo,* Johannes Vermeer's *Young Woman with a Water Jug,* Velázquez's *Juan de Pareja,* and Rembrandt's *Aristotle with a Bust of Homer.* The arcaded **European Sculpture Court** includes Auguste Rodin's massive bronze *The Burghers of Calais.*

The **American Wing,** in the northwest corner, is best approached from the first floor, where you enter through a refreshingly light and airy garden court graced with Tiffany stained-glass windows, cast-iron staircases by Louis Sullivan, and a marble Federal-style facade taken from the Wall Street branch of the United States Bank. Take the elevator to the third floor and begin working your way down through the rooms decorated in period furniture—everything from a Shaker retiring room to a Federal-era ballroom to the living room of a Frank Lloyd Wright house—and the excellent galleries of American painting.

In the realm of 20th-century art, the Met was a latecomer, allowing the Museum of Modern Art and the Whitney to build their collections with little competition until the Metropolitan's contemporary art department was finally established in 1967. The Met has made up for lost time, however, and in 1987 it opened the three-story **Lila Acheson Wallace Wing,** in the southwest corner. Pablo Picasso's portrait of Gertrude Stein (1906) is the centerpiece of this collection. The **Iris and B. Gerald Cantor Roof Garden,** above this wing and open during the summer, showcases a few contemporary sculptures each year and provides a unique view of Central Park.

There is much more to the Met than paintings, however. Visitors with a taste for classical art should go immediately to the left of the Great Hall on the first floor to see the **Greek and Roman galleries,** including dozens of significant statues and a large collection of rare Roman wall paintings excavated from the lava of Mt. Vesuvius. Directly above these galleries, on the second floor, you'll find room after room of Grecian urns and other classical vases. The Met's awesome **Egyptian collection,** spanning some 3,000 years, is on the first floor, directly to the right of the Great Hall. Its centerpiece is the **Temple of Dendur,** an entire Roman-period temple (circa 15 BC) donated by the Egyptian government in thanks for U.S. help in saving ancient monuments. Placed in a specially built gallery with views of Central Park, the temple faces east, as it did in its original location, and a pool of water has been installed at the same distance from it as the river Nile once stood. Another spot suitable for contemplation is directly above the Egyptian treasures, in the **Asian galleries:** The Astor Court Chinese garden reproduces a Ming dynasty (1368–1644) scholar's courtyard, complete with water splashing over artfully positioned rocks.

The **Armana Art Galleries** are near the Temple of Dendur, on the first floor past the staircase in the Great Hall. Armana was an Egyptian city founded during the reign of King Akhenaton on the east bank of the Nile, and the galleries contain works from 1353 BC to 1295 BC, including reliefs, sculptures, and paintings. There's also a fine arms-and-armor exhibit on the first floor (go through the medieval tapestries, just behind the main staircase, and turn right). The medieval collection here is lovely, but to see the real medieval treasures, don't miss a trip to the **Cloisters,** the Met's annex in Washington Heights (☞ Morningside Heights, *below*). Keep going straight from the medieval galleries until you enter the cool skylighted white space of the **Lehman Pavilion,** where the exquisite, mind-bogglingly large personal collection of the late donor, investment banker Robert Lehman, is displayed in rooms resembling those of his West 54th Street town house. The collection's strengths include old-master drawings; Renaissance paintings, including works by Rembrandt, El Greco, Goya, Petrus Christus, and Hans Memling; French 18th-century furniture; and 19th-century canvases by Ingres and Renoir. Even at peak periods, crowds tend to be sparse here (Lehman's insistence that his collection be exhibited in one place may be one of the reasons, for as great as the collections here are, it feels uncannily like an echo of the Met's main collections). The **Costume Institute,** one level below the main floor's Egyptian Art exhibit, has changing but always extremely well-done displays of clothing and fashion.

Although it exhibits roughly only a quarter of its vast holdings at any one time, the Met offers more than can reasonably be seen in one visit. The best advice for tackling the museum itself is to focus on two to four sections and know that somewhere, in some wing, there's an empty exhibit that just might be more rewarding than the one you can't see due to the crowds. Walking tours and lectures are free with your admission contribution. Tours covering various sections of the museum begin about every 15 minutes on weekdays, less frequently on weekends; they depart from the tour board in the Great Hall. Self-guided audio tours, which are recorded by Philippe de Montebello, the Met's longtime director, can be rented at a desk in the Great Hall and often at the entrance to major exhibitions. Lectures, often related to temporary exhibitions, are given frequently. ✉ *5th Ave. at 82nd St.,* ☎ *212/879–5500.* 🎫 *$8 (suggested donation).* ⏲ *Tues.–Thurs. and Sun. 9:30–5:15, Fri.–Sat. 9:30–8:45.*

NEED A BREAK?

The first American branch of the very popular Belgian café chain, **Le Pain Quotidien** (✉ 1131 Madison Ave., between 84th and 85th Sts., ☎ 212/327–4900) attracts Upper East Siders to its large, wide-plank pine communal table for croissants, tarts, brioche, and café au lait or simple meals of soup, open-face sandwiches, or salads. The quintessential Upper East Side café, **E.A.T.** (✉ 1064 Madison Ave., between 80th and 81st Sts., ☎ 212/772–0022) serves everything from carrot soup and tabbouleh salad to roast lamb sandwiches and fish pâté. Silver-painted columns and a black-and-white checkered floor enliven the light and airy room, which bustles with diners from 7 AM to 10 PM daily.

★ ⓾ **Museum of the City of New York.** One of the best ways to start any visit to this daunting metropolis is with a visit to this museum, set in a massive Colonial Georgian mansion built in 1930. From the Dutch settlers of Nieuw Amsterdam to the present day, with period rooms, dioramas, slide shows, films, prints, paintings, sculpture, and clever displays of memorabilia, the museum's got it all. An exhibit on the Port of New York illuminates the role of the harbor in New York's rise to greatness; the noteworthy Toy Gallery has several meticulously detailed dollhouses; maps, Broadway memorabilia, Currier & Ives lithographs, and furniture collections comprise other parts of the museum's vast exhibits. Weekend programs are oriented especially to children. Currently undergoing a $36 million renovation, the museum should be considerably brightened by the year 2000. ✉ *1220 5th Ave., at 103rd St.,* ☎ *212/534–1672.* 🎫 *$5 (suggested donation).* ⏲ *Wed.–Sat. 10–5, Sun. 1–5.*

6 **National Academy Museum.** The academy, which was founded in 1825, has always required each elected member to donate a representative work of art, which has resulted in a strong collection of 19th- and 20th-century American art. Members have included Mary Cassatt, Samuel F. B. Morse, Winslow Homer, John Singer Sargent, Frank Lloyd Wright, Jacob Lawrence, I. M. Pei, and Robert Rauschenberg. Changing shows of American art and architecture, some curated by member artists, are drawn from the permanent collection. The collection's home is a stately 19th-century mansion donated by members Archer Milton and Anna Hyatt Huntington in 1940. The Academy also schedules loan exhibits. ✉ *1083 5th Ave., at 89th St.,* ☎ *212/369–4880.* 🎫 *$5; free Fri. 5–8.* ⏲ *Wed.–Thurs. and weekends noon–5, Fri. noon–8.*

5 **Solomon R. Guggenheim Museum.** Frank Lloyd Wright's only major New York commission is one of the highlights of the modernist architectural tradition. Opened in 1959, shortly after Wright died, it is a controversial building—even many who love its six-story spiral will admit that it does not result in the best space in which to view art. Wright's attention to detail is everywhere evident—in the circular pattern of the sidewalk outside the museum, for example, the porthole-like windows on its south side, the smoothness of the hand-plastered concrete. Under a 92-ft-high glass dome, a ¼-mi-long ramp spirals down past changing exhibitions of modern art. The museum has especially strong holdings in Wassily Kandinsky, Paul Klee, and Pablo Picasso; the oldest pieces are by the French Impressionists. The Tower Galleries opened in 1992, creating additional gallery space to display the Panza di Buomo collection of minimalist art, among other works. The 10-story annex designed by Gwathmey, Siegel and Associates and based on Wright's original designs offers four spacious galleries that can accommodate the extraordinarily large art pieces that the Guggenheim owns but previously had no room to display. In 1992 the museum also received a gift from the Robert Mapplethorpe Foundation of more than 200 of the photographer's works, some of which are on view in the Guggenheim's SoHo branch (☞ SoHo and TriBeCa, *below*). If a visit here whets your appetite for Wright's work, be sure to visit the ☞ **Metropolitan Museum of Art**'s American Wing, which displays a complete living room from one of his finest houses. ✉ *1071 5th Ave., between 88th and 89th Sts.,* ☎ *212/423–3500.* 🎫 *$10, Fri. 6–8 pay as you wish; joint admission to both Guggenheim branches $15.* ⏲ *Sun.–Wed. 10–6, Fri.–Sat. 10–8.*

THE UPPER EAST SIDE

The words *Upper East Side* leave a bad taste in the mouths of many New Yorkers, connoting old money, conservative values, and general snobbery. For others, those same qualities make this neighborhood the epitome of the high-style, high-society way of life often associated with the Big Apple. Between 5th and Lexington avenues, up to about 96th Street or so, the trappings of wealth are everywhere apparent: well-kept buildings, children in private school uniforms, nannies wheeling grand baby carriages, dog walkers, limousines, doormen in braided livery. This is the territory where Sherman McCoy, protagonist of Tom Wolfe's *Bonfire of the Vanities,* lived in pride before his fall, and where the heroine of Woody Allen's movie *Alice* felt suffocated despite her money.

But like all other New York neighborhoods, this one is diverse, and plenty of local residents live modestly. The northeast section particularly, which is known as **Yorkville,** is more affordable and ethnic, a jumbled mix of high and low buildings, old and young people. Until the 1830s, when the New York & Harlem Railroad and a stagecoach line began racing through, this was a quiet, remote hamlet with a large German population. Over the years it has also welcomed waves of immigrants from Austria, Hungary, the Czech Republic, and Slovakia, and local shops and restaurants still bear reminders of this European heritage.

Numbers in the text correspond to numbers in the margin and on the Museum Mile, Upper East Side map.

A Good Walk

A fitting place to begin your exploration of the moneyed Upper East Side is that infamous shrine to conspicuous consumption, **Bloomingdale's** ⑬, at 59th Street between Lexington and 3rd avenues. Leaving Bloomingdale's, head west on 60th Street toward 5th Avenue. As you cross Park Avenue, look for a moment at the wide, neatly planted median strip. Railroad tracks once ran above ground here; they were not completely covered with a roadway until after World War I, and the grand, sweeping street that resulted became a distinguished residential address. Look south toward midtown, and you'll see the Met Life Building; squished up against it, the Helmsley Building looks small and frilly by comparison. Then turn to look uptown, and you'll see a thoroughfare lined with massive buildings that are more like mansions stacked atop one another than apartment complexes. Decorations such as colorful tulips in the spring and lighted pine trees in December in the "park" proclaimed by the street's name are paid for by residents.

On the northwest corner of 60th Street and Park Avenue is Christ Church United Methodist Church, built during the Depression but designed to look centuries old, with its random pattern of limestone blocks. Inside, the Byzantine-style sanctuary (open Sunday and holidays) glitters with golden handmade mosaics. Continue west on 60th Street to pass a grouping of clubs, membership-only societies that cater to the privileged. Most were formed in the 1800s, modeled after British gentlemen's clubs. Though the clubs remain exclusive, their admirable architecture is there for all to see. Ornate grillwork curls over the doorway of the scholarly **Grolier Club,** an exception in that it *is* open to the public. On the block right before the park is the **Harmonie Club,** and across the street is the even more lordly **Metropolitan Club.**

Take a right at 5th Avenue. At 61st Street you'll pass the Pierre, a hotel that opened in 1930 (☞ Chapter 7); notice its lovely mansard roof and tower. As you cross East 62nd Street, look at the elegant brick-and-limestone mansion (1915) at 2 East 62nd Street, the home of the **Knickerbocker Club,** another private social club.

Across the street is the Fifth Avenue Synagogue, a limestone temple built in 1959. Its pointed oval windows are filled with stained glass in striking abstract designs. You may want to detour down this elegant block of town houses; take special note of No. 11, which has elaborate Corinthian pilasters and an impressive wrought-iron entryway. Farther up 5th Avenue, at 65th Street, is another notable Jewish house of worship: **Temple Emanu-El** ⑭, one of the largest synagogues in the world. If you walk east from 5th Avenue on 65th Street, you'll reach the **China Institute Gallery,** which houses displays of Chinese art.

Turn right on 66th Street, past the site of the house (✉ 3 E. 66th St.) where Ulysses S. Grant spent his final years, before he moved permanently up to Grant's Tomb (☞ Morningside Heights, *below*). (If you are interested in presidential homes, you may want to detour over to 65th Street between Madison and Park avenues to 45–47 East 65th Street, a double town house built in 1908 for Sara Delano Roosevelt and her son, Franklin; FDR once lay recovering from polio at No. 47.) Next door, at 5 East 66th Street, is the **Lotos Club,** a private club whose members are devoted to arts and literature.

Continue east across Madison Avenue to Park Avenue. The large apartment building on the northeast corner of Madison Avenue and 66th Street was built from 1906 to 1908 with lovely Gothic-style detail. The red Victorian castle-fortress at 66th Street and Park Avenue is the **Seventh Regiment Armory** ⑮, now often used as an exhibition space.

Though houses have generally been replaced by apartment buildings along Park Avenue, a few surviving mansions give you an idea of how the neighborhood once looked. The grandly simple silvery-limestone palace on the southwest corner of 68th Street, built in 1919, now houses the prestigious Council on Foreign Relations (⊠ 58 E. 68th St.). The dark-redbrick town house on the northwest corner was built for Percy Pyne in 1909–11 by McKim, Mead & White and is now the **Americas Society** ⑯; its art gallery is open to the public. The three houses to the north—built during the following decade and designed by three different architects—carried on the Pyne mansion's Georgian design to create a unified block. Today these buildings hold the Spanish Institute (⊠ 684 Park Ave.), the Italian Cultural Institute (⊠ 686 Park Ave.), and the Italian Consulate (⊠ 690 Park Ave.). Two blocks north, on the east side of Park Avenue, is the **Asia Society** ⑰, a museum and educational center.

At this point shoppers may want to get down to business back on Madison Avenue. The catchphrase *Madison Avenue* no longer refers to the midtown advertising district (most major agencies have moved away from there anyway) but instead to uptown's fashion district, between 59th and 79th streets, an exclusive area of haute couture designer boutiques, patrician art galleries, and unique specialty stores. Many of these shops are small, intimate, expensive—and almost invariably closed on Sunday, but larger brand-name stores such as Calvin Klein (at 60th Street) and the Giorgio Armani Boutique (at 66th Street) have flocked to the prestigious neighborhood. Even if you're just window-shopping, it's fun to step inside the tony digs of **Polo/Ralph Lauren** ⑱, at 72nd Street, which hardly seems like a store at all. The **Whitney Museum of American Art** ⑲, a striking building whose base is smaller than its upper floors, looms on the right at 75th Street, its collection well worth seeing. At Madison Avenue and 76th Street is the **Carlyle Hotel** ⑳, one of the city's most elite and discreet properties.

The final leg of this tour is several blocks away. How you get through Yorkville is up to you, but we suggest walking four blocks east on 78th Street, then north on 2nd Avenue, and east again on 86th. The quiet blocks of 78th between Park and 2nd avenues are home to rows of well-maintained Italianate town houses from the late 1800s. Many shops and restaurants line 2nd Avenue, some reflecting the area's Eastern European heritage. At 81st Street, for example, is the Hungarian Meat Market (⊠ 1560 2nd Ave.), and at 86th Street, the German store Schaller & Weber (⊠ 1654 2nd Ave.), both recognizable by the array of sausages hanging in their windows. Secondhand stores sell all sorts of odds and ends discarded by the privileged (☞ Secondhand Shops *in* Chapter 10).

On 86th Street at East End Avenue, the **Henderson Place Historic District** ㉑ includes 24 small-scale town houses built in the 1880s in the Queen Anne style, which was developed in England by Richard Norman Shaw. As if these beautiful dwellings weren't enough, residents here are doubly blessed by the view of and easy access to **Carl Schurz Park** ㉒, across the street and overlooking the East River. **Gracie Mansion** ㉓, the mayor's house, sits at its north end. The park comes to a narrow stop at 90th Street, but the greenery continues at **Asphalt Green** ㉔, a concrete parabolic former asphalt plant that's now protected by landmark status and is part of a fitness center.

TIMING

This tour covers a lot of ground, but many sights require looking, not stopping. Allow about three leisurely hours for the walk. The art institutions—the Americas Society, Asia Society, and the Whitney Museum—may take more of your time if you like, so check their opening hours.

Sights to See

OFF THE BEATEN PATH

ABIGAIL ADAMS SMITH MUSEUM – Once the converted carriage house of the home of President John Adams's daughter Abigail and her husband, Colonel William Stephen Smith, this 18th-century treasure is now owned by the Colonial Dames of America and largely restored to its early 19th-century use as a day hotel. Nine rooms display furniture and articles of the Federal and Empire periods, and an adjoining garden is designed in 18th-century style. This stone house, complete with a lawn, is hidden among newer, taller structures a few blocks east of Bloomingdale's. ✉ *421 E. 61st St.,* ☎ *212/838–6878.* 🎫 $3. ⏲ *Sept.–May, Tues.–Sun. 11–4; June–July, Tues. 11–9, Wed.–Sun. 11–4.*

⓰ **Americas Society.** This McKim, Mead & White–designed town house was among the first on this stretch of Park Avenue (built 1909–11). It was commissioned by Percy Pyne, the grandson of noted financier Moses Taylor and a notable financier himself. From 1948 to 1963 the mansion was the Soviet Mission to the United Nations; when the Russians moved out, developers wanted to raze the town house, but in 1965 the Marquesa de Cuevas (a Rockefeller descendant) acquired the property and presented it to the Center for Inter-American Relations, now called the Americas Society, whose mission is to educate U.S. citizens about the rest of the western hemisphere. Its art gallery hosts changing exhibits. ✉ *680 Park Ave.,* ☎ *212/249–8950.* 🎫 *$3 (suggested gallery donation).* ⏲ *Tues.–Sun. noon–6.*

⓱ **Asia Society.** The eight-story red-granite building that houses this museum and educational center complements Park Avenue's older, more traditional architecture. This nonprofit educational society, founded in 1956 and headquartered here, offers a regular program of lectures, films, and performances, in addition to changing exhibitions. The permanent holdings comprise Mr. and Mrs. John D. Rockefeller III's collection of Asian art and are used along with pieces from other collections for exhibits that might feature South Asian stone and bronze sculptures; art from India, Nepal, Pakistan, and Afghanistan; bronze vessels, ceramics, sculpture, and paintings from China; Korean ceramics; and paintings, wooden sculptures, and ceramics from Japan. ✉ *725 Park Ave., at 70th St.,* ☎ *212/288–6400.* 🎫 *$4; free Thurs. 6–8.* ⏲ *Tues.–Wed. and Fri.–Sat. 11–6, Thurs. 11–8, Sun. noon–5.*

㉔ **Asphalt Green.** When this former asphalt plant was built by Kahn and Jacobs in 1941–44, it was the country's first reinforced concrete arch, and it will be here for the ages thanks to landmark status. The plant is now part of a fitness complex—there are often games on the bright green lawn out front, and the adjoining natatorium (AquaCenter) houses Manhattan's largest pool (☞ Chapter 9). ⊠ *90th St. between York Ave. and FDR Dr.*

13 **Bloomingdale's.** This noisy, trendy, and crowded block-long behemoth sells everything from designer clothes to high-tech teakettles in slick, sophisticated displays. Most selections are high quality, and sale prices on designer goods can be extremely satisfying. In addition to full his, hers, and home sections, Bloomingdale's has four restaurants, a chocolatier, and a coffee shop (☞ Chapter 10). ⊠ *59th St. between Lexington and 3rd Aves.,* ☎ *212/705–2000.*

22 **Carl Schurz Park.** During the American Revolution, a house on this promontory was used as a fortification by the Continental Army, then was taken over as a British outpost. In more peaceful times the land became known as East End Park. It was renamed in 1911 to honor Carl Schurz (1829–1906), a famous 19th-century German immigrant who eventually served the United States as a minister to Spain, a major general in the Union Army, and a senator from Missouri. During the Hayes administration, Schurz was secretary of the interior; he later moved back to Yorkville and worked as editor of the *New York Evening Post* and *Harper's Weekly.*

A curved stone staircase leads up to the wrought-iron railings at the edge of John Finley Walk, which overlooks the churning East River—actually just an estuary connecting the Long Island Sound with the harbor. You can see the Triborough, Hell's Gate, and Queensboro bridges, Wards, Randall's, and Roosevelt islands, and on the other side of the river, Astoria, Queens. The view is so tranquil you'd never guess you're directly above the FDR Drive. Behind you along the walk are raised flower beds planted with interesting blooms; there are also a few recreation areas and a playground in the park. Though it doesn't compare in size with the West Side's Riverside Park, this area is a treasure to Upper East Siders.

Stroll to the north end of Carl Schurz Park to reach ☞ **Gracie Mansion,** where the city's mayor resides. The park tapers to an end at 90th Street, where there is a dock from which ferry boats depart to lower Manhattan and up to Yankee Stadium (☞ Chapter 9). ⊠ *E. 84th to E. 90th St., between East End Ave. and East River.*

20 **Carlyle Hotel.** The mood here is English manor house. The hotel has the elegant Café Carlyle, where top performers such as Bobby Short, Barbara Cook, and Woody Allen (the latter on clarinet) appear regularly, and the more relaxed Bemelmans Bar, with murals by Ludwig Bemelmans, the famed illustrator of the Madeline children's books. Stargazers, take note: This hotel's roster of rich-and-famous guests has included Elizabeth Taylor, George C. Scott, Steve Martin, and Warren Beatty and Annette Bening. In the early 1960s President John F. Kennedy frequently stayed here; rumor has it he entertained Marilyn Monroe in his rooms (☞ Chapters 7 and 8). ⊠ *35 E. 76th St., at Madison Ave.,* ☎ *212/744–1600.*

China Institute Gallery. A pair of fierce, fat stone lions guards the doorway of this pleasant redbrick town house, where two museum-quality shows are mounted yearly, generally on Chinese history. ⊠ *125 E. 65th St.,* ☎ *212/744–8181.* 🎫 *$5 (suggested donation).* ⊙ *Mon. and Wed.–Sat. 10–5, Tues. 10–8, Sun. 1–5.*

23 **Gracie Mansion.** Surrounded by a small lawn and flower beds, this Federal-style yellow-frame residence, the official home of the mayor of New

York, still feels like a country manor house, which it was when built in 1779 by wealthy merchant Archibald Gracie. The Gracie family entertained many notable guests at the mansion, including Louis Philippe (later king of France), President John Quincy Adams, the Marquis de Lafayette, Alexander Hamilton, James Fenimore Cooper, Washington Irving, and John Jacob Astor. The city purchased Gracie Mansion in 1887, and after a period of use as the Museum of the City of New York, Mayor Fiorello H. La Guardia made it the official mayor's residence. Rudy Giuliani and his family are the current inhabitants. ✉ *Carl Schurz Park, East End Ave. opposite 88th St.,* ☎ *212/570–4751.* 🎫 *$4.* ⏲ *Guided tours late Mar.–mid-Nov., Wed.; all tours by advance reservation only.*

Grolier Club. Founded in 1884, this private club is named after the 16th-century French bibliophile Jean Grolier. Its members are devoted to the bookmaking crafts; one of them, Bertram G. Goodhue, designed this neatly proportioned Georgian-style redbrick building in 1917. The club presents public exhibitions on subjects related to books and has a specialized reference library of more than 100,000 volumes (open by appointment only). ✉ *47 E. 60th St., between Madison and Park Aves.,* ☎ *212/838–6690.* 🎫 *Free.* ⏲ *Gallery Mon.–Sat. 10–5.*

Harmonie Club. Originally a private club for German Jews, this was the city's first men's club to allow women at dinner. (Stephen Birmingham's *Our Crowd: The Great Jewish Families of New York* profiles the club's original generation.) The building is a pseudo-Renaissance palace built in 1906 by McKim, Mead & White. ✉ *4 E. 60th St.*

21 **Henderson Place Historic District.** Originally consisting of 32 small-scale town houses, Henderson Place still has 24 stone-and-brick buildings. They were built in the 1880s in the Queen Anne style, which was developed in England by Richard Norman Shaw. Designed to be comfortable yet romantic dwellings, they combine elements of the Elizabethan manor house with classic Flemish details. Note especially the lovely bay windows, the turrets marking the corner of each block, and the symmetrical roof gables, pediments, parapets, chimneys, and dormer windows. ✉ *East End Ave. between 86th and 87th Sts.*

NEED A BREAK? **Viand** (✉ 300 E. 86th St., at 2nd Ave., ☎ 212/879–9425), a diner with superlative service and an extensive menu, has just the drink, snack, or meal to tide you over on this long walk through the neighborhood.

Lotos Club. Founded in 1870, this private club has members devoted to the arts and literature. Its current home is a handsomely ornate French Renaissance mansion originally built in 1900 by Richard Howland Hunt for a member of the Vanderbilt family. ✉ *5 E. 66th St.*

Metropolitan Club. A lordly neoclassic edifice, this was built in 1894 by the grandest producers of such structures—McKim, Mead & White. Ironically, this exclusive club was established by J. P. Morgan when a friend of his was refused membership in the Union League Club; its members today include leaders of foreign countries and presidents of major corporations. ✉ *1 E. 60th St.*

18 **Polo/Ralph Lauren.** Ralph Lauren's flagship New York store, in the landmark, French Renaissance–style Rhinelander mansion, has preserved the grand house's walnut fittings, Oriental carpets, and family portraits as an aristocratic setting in which to display Lauren's to-the-manor-born clothing and home furnishings. (☞ Chapter 10). ✉ *867 Madison Ave., at 72nd St.,* ☎ *212/606–2100.*

OFF THE BEATEN PATH

ROOSEVELT ISLAND – This 2½-mi-long East River island was taken over by a residential complex in the 1970s, although only half the high-rise buildings originally planned have been built, and further funding is doubtful. Some fragments remain of the asylums, hospitals, and jails once clustered here, when it was known as Welfare Island and before that Blackwell's Island (Mae West and William "Boss" Tweed are among those who served time here). Walkways along the edge of the island provide fine river views, and it's surprisingly quiet, considering the city is so close. The real treat, however, is the 3½-minute ride over on an aerial tram; the entrance is at 2nd Avenue and 60th Street, a few blocks east of Bloomingdale's. The one-way fare is $1.50. ✉ *East River, from 48th to 85th St.*

15 **Seventh Regiment Armory.** The term *National Guard* derives from the Seventh Regiment, which has traditionally consisted of select New York men who volunteered for service. (The Seventh Regiment first used the term in 1824 to honor the Guarde National of Paris.) This huge structure, designed by Seventh Regiment veteran Charles W. Clinton in the late 1870s, is still used as an armory, though not exclusively—a homeless shelter, the Seventh Regiment Mess and Bar (☞ Chapter 6), and numerous exhibitions use its space. Two posh annual antiques shows take place in the expansive drill hall, for example. Both Louis Comfort Tiffany and Stanford White designed rooms in its surprisingly residential interior; go up the front stairs into the wood-paneled lobby and take a look around. Tours are available by appointment. ✉ *643 Park Ave.,* ☎ *212/744–2968 curator's office.*

14 **Temple Emanu-El.** The world's largest Reform Jewish synagogue seats 2,500 worshipers. Built in 1929 of limestone, it is covered with mosaics and designed in the Romanesque style, with Byzantine influences; the building features Moorish and Art Deco ornamentation. ✉ *1 E. 65th St., at 5th Ave.,* ☎ *212/744–1400.* ⏲ *Sabbath services Fri. 5, Sat. 10:30; weekday services Sun.–Thurs. 5:30; guided group tours of synagogue by appointment.*

19 **Whitney Museum of American Art.** This museum grew out of a gallery in the studio of the sculptor and collector Gertrude Vanderbilt Whitney, whose talent and taste were fortuitously accompanied by the wealth of two prominent families. In 1929 she offered her collection of 20th-century American art to the Met, but they turned it down, so she established an independent museum. The current building, opened in 1966, is a minimalist gray-granite vault separated from Madison Avenue by a dry moat; it was designed by Marcel Breuer, a member of the Bauhaus school (its manifesto called for architects and artists to work toward "the building of the future"). The monolithic exterior is much more forbidding than the interior, where changing exhibitions offer an intelligent survey of 20th-century American works. Following a recent renovation, the fifth floor now has eight galleries for permanent exhibitions from the museum's collection; the first, designed to resemble the museum's first building (on West 8th Street), includes Carl Waters's original entrance door panels from that location. The Stieglitz circle, urban artists, and abstract art and surrealism are focuses of other galleries. Three are devoted to specific artists: Edward Hopper, including *Early Sunday Morning* and *A Woman in the Sun*; Georgia O'Keeffe, with several of her famous flower paintings; and Alexander Calder, whose *Circus* sculpture has been moved here from the lobby. In spring of 1999, a massive exhibit will look back on the century's art. The Whitney also has a branch across from Grand Central Terminal (☞ 42nd Street, *above*). ✉ *945 Madison Ave., at 75th*

St., ☎ *212/570–3676.* 💵 *$8; free Thurs. 6–8.* ⏲ *Wed. and Fri.–Sun. 11–6, Thurs. 1–8.*

NEED A BREAK? The soft lighting, tasteful decor, and delicious, if somewhat pricey, pastries, chocolates, and drinks of **Payard Patisserie and Bistro** (✉ 1032 Lexington Ave., between 73rd and 74th Sts., ☎ 212/717–5252) are a perfect complement to a day on the chic Upper East Side. A full restaurant is in back, but you can nibble on sandwiches and desserts at the small café tables up front.

CENTRAL PARK

Many people consider Central Park the greatest—and most indispensable—part of New York City. Without the park's 843 acres of meandering paths, tranquil lakes, ponds, and open meadows, New Yorkers might be a lot less sane. Every day thousands of joggers, cyclists, inline skaters, and walkers make their daily jaunts around the park's loop, the reservoir, and various other parts of the park. Come summertime the park serves as Manhattan's Riviera, with sun worshipers crowding every available patch of grass. Throughout the year pleasure seekers of all ages come to enjoy horseback riding, softball, ice-skating or roller-skating, rock climbing, croquet, tennis, bird-watching, boating, chess, checkers, theater, concerts, skateboarding, folk dancing, and more—or simply to escape from the rumble of traffic, walk through the trees, and feel—at least for a moment—far from the urban frenzy.

Although it appears to be nothing more than a swath of rolling countryside exempted from urban development, Central Park was in fact the first artificially landscaped park in the United States. The design for the park was conceived in 1857 by park superintendent Frederick Law Olmsted and Calvert Vaux, one of the founders of the landscape architecture profession in the United States. Their design was one of 33 submitted in a contest arranged by the Central Park Commission—the first such contest in the country. The Greensward Plan, as it was called, combined pastoral, picturesque, and formal elements: Open rolling meadows complement fanciful landscapes and grand, formal walkways. The southern portion of the park features many formal elements, while the north end is deliberately more rustic. Four transverse roads—at 66th, 79th, 86th, and 96th streets—were designed to carry crosstown traffic beneath the park's hills and tunnels so that park goers would not be disturbed, and 40 bridges were conceived—each with its own unique design and name—to give strollers easy access to various areas.

The job of constructing the park was monumental. Hundreds of residents of shantytowns were displaced, swamps were drained, and great walls of Manhattan schist were blasted. Thousands of workers were employed to remove some 5 million cubic yards of soil and plant thousands of trees and shrubs in a project that lasted 16 years and cost $14 million. Today, thanks to the efforts of the Central Park Conservancy, a private, not-for-profit organization that took over the reconstruction and maintenance of the park in 1980, Olmsted and Vaux's green oasis looks better than at any time in its history.

In the years following the park's opening in 1857, more than half its visitors arrived by carriage. Today, with a little imagination, you can still experience the park as they did, by hiring a horse-drawn carriage at Grand Army Plaza or any other major intersection of Central Park South at 59th Street between 5th and 8th avenues. Rates, which are regulated, are $34 for the first half hour and $10 for every additional quarter hour.

Numbers in the text correspond to numbers in the margin and on the Central Park map.

A Good Walk

If you want to explore the park on foot, begin at the southeast corner, at Grand Army Plaza, at 59th Street. The first path off the main road (East Drive) leads to the **Pond** ①, where Gapstow Bridge provides a great vantage point for the oft-photographed midtown skyscrapers. Heading north on the road, you'll come to **Wollman Memorial Rink** ②, whose popularity is second only to that of the rink at Rockefeller Center. Turn your back to the rink, and you'll see the historic **Dairy** ③, which now serves as the park's visitor center. As you walk up the hill to the Dairy, you'll pass the Chess and Checkers House to your left, where gamesters gather on weekends (playing pieces are available at the Dairy on weekends, 11:30–3).

As you leave the Dairy, to your right (west) is the Playmates Arch—aptly named, since it leads to a large area of ball fields and playgrounds. Coming through the arch, you'll hear the jaunty music of the antique **Friedsam Memorial Carousel** ④, the second oldest on the East Coast.

Turning your back to the carousel, climb the slope to the left of the Playmates Arch and walk beside Center Drive, which veers to the right. Stop for a look at the **Sheep Meadow** ⑤, a 15-acre expanse that was used for grazing sheep until 1934, and the neighboring **Mineral Springs Pavilion** ⑥, one of the park's original refreshment stands. The grand, formal walkway east of the Sheep Meadow is the **Mall** ⑦, which is lined with statuary and magnificent American elms.

As you stroll up the Mall, note the contrast between the peaceful Sheep Meadow, to your left, and the buzzing path ahead, where joggers, rollerbladers, and cyclists speed by. This path is the 72nd Street transverse, the only crosstown street that connects with the East, Center, and West drives. The transverse cuts across the park at the north end of the Mall; you can either cross it or pass beneath it through a lovely tiled arcade—note the elaborately carved birds and fruit trees that adorn the upper parts of both staircases—to get to **Bethesda Fountain** ⑧, set on an elaborately patterned paved terrace on the edge of the lake.

If you're in the mood for recreation, take the path east from the terrace to **Loeb Boathouse** ⑨, where in season you can rent rowboats and bicycles. The path to the west of the terrace leads to **Bow Bridge** ⑩, a splendid cast-iron bridge arching over a neck of the lake. Across the bridge is the **Ramble** ⑪, a heavily wooded wild area laced with 37 acres of twisting, climbing paths. Then recross Bow Bridge and continue west along the lakeside path for a view of the lake from **Cherry Hill** ⑫.

Turn your back to the lake and follow the path back to the 72nd Street transverse; on the rocky outcrop across the road, you'll see a statue of a falconer gracefully lofting his bird. Turn to the right, and you'll see a more prosaic statue, the pompous bronze figure of Daniel Webster with his hand thrust into his coat. Cross Center Drive behind Webster, being careful to watch for traffic coming around the corner. You've now come to **Strawberry Fields** ⑬, a lush, 2½-acre landscape memorializing John Lennon.

At the top of Strawberry Fields' hill, turn right through a rustic wood arbor thickly hung with wisteria vines. From here follow the downhill path to Eaglevale Arch, the southern portal to **Naturalists' Walk** ⑭. After you've explored the varied landscapes of the walk, head back toward

The Arsenal, **23**
Belvedere Castle, **18**
Bethesda Fountain, **8**
Bow Bridge, **10**
Central Park Wildlife Center (Zoo), **24**
Cherry Hill, **12**
Cleopatra's Needle, **19**
Conservatory Water, **22**
The Dairy, **3**
Delacorte Theater, **16**
Friedsam Memorial Carousel, **4**
Great Lawn, **20**
Jacqueline Kennedy Onassis Reservoir, **21**
Loeb Boathouse, **9**
The Mall, **7**
Mineral Springs Pavilion, **6**
Naturalists' Walk, **14**
The Pond, **1**
The Ramble, **11**
Shakespeare Garden, **17**
Sheep Meadow, **5**
Strawberry Fields, **13**
Swedish Cottage, **15**
Wollman Memorial Rink, **2**

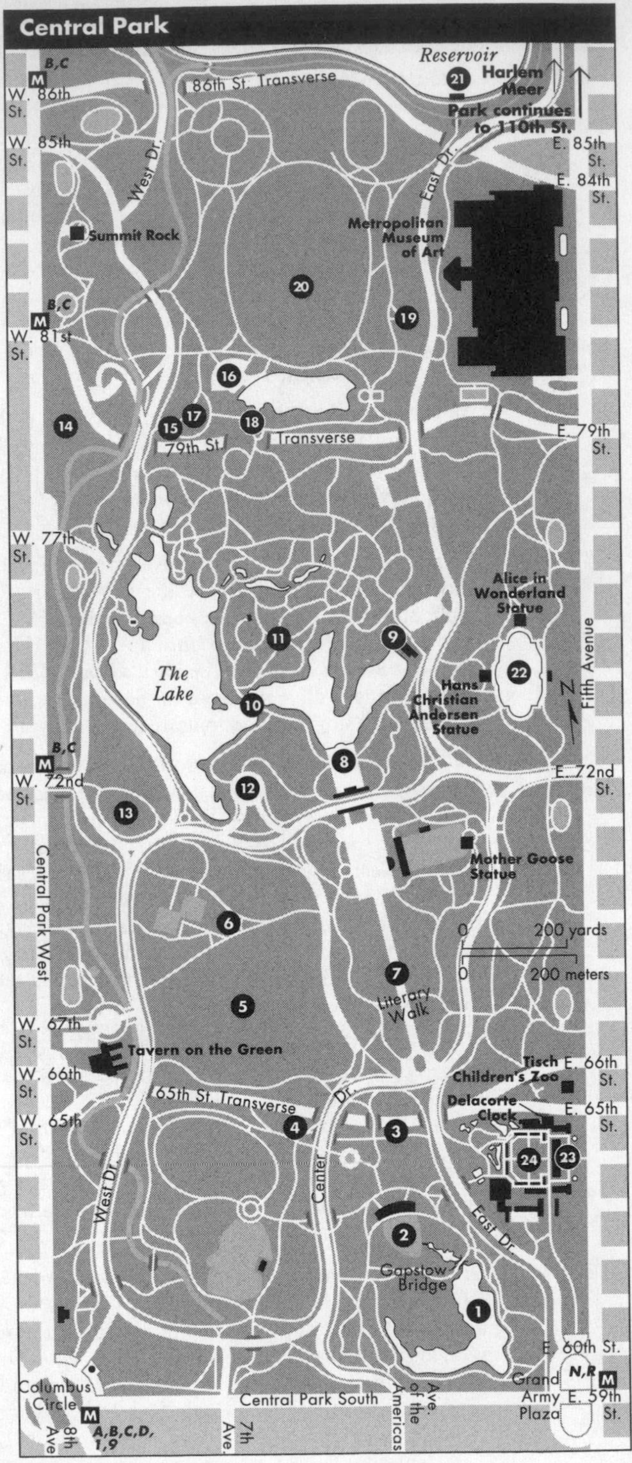

the Park Drive, where directly across the street you will see the quaint wooden **Swedish Cottage** ⑮, scene of marionette shows. Staying on the west side of the Drive, continue north along the path to Summit Rock, the highest natural point in the park. After you've enjoyed the view here, head down the other side of the promontory; a path will lead you back toward the Park Drive.

Cross the Park Drive, and you'll find yourself at the north end of the Great Lawn (☞ *below*), at the Arthur Ross Pinetum, a collection of pine trees and evergreens from around the world. Follow the path south along the Great Lawn to the open-air **Delacorte Theater** ⑯, where the Joseph Papp Public Theater performs each summer. Just south of the theater is **Shakespeare Garden** ⑰, a lush, landscaped hill covered with flowers and plants that have figured in the writings of the Bard. From the top of the hill you can follow a path to the aptly named Vista Rock, which is dominated by the circa-1872 **Belvedere Castle** ⑱. The castle is now used as a measurement station of the U.S. Weather Bureau; inside is a nature center.

From the castle's plaza, follow the downhill path east along the rehabilitated Turtle Pond, populated by fish, ducks, and dragonflies, in addition to turtles, of course. At the east end of the pond you'll pass a statue of King Jagiello of Poland; groups gather here for folk dancing on weekends. Follow the path north to **Cleopatra's Needle** ⑲, an Egyptian obelisk just east of the **Great Lawn** ⑳. Vigorous walkers may want to continue north to the **Jacqueline Kennedy Onassis Reservoir** ㉑ for a glimpse of one of the city's most popular and scenic jogging paths. Others can return south from Cleopatra's Needle, following the path to the left under Greywacke Arch, which leads around the back corner of the Metropolitan Museum.

Continuing south on the path that runs along the east side of the park, you'll come to one of the park's most formal areas: the symmetrical stone basin of the **Conservatory Water** ㉒, which is usually crowded with remote control model sailboats. Climb the hill at the far end of the water, cross the 72nd Street transverse, and follow the path south to the Tisch Children's Zoo; you'll pass under the Denesmouth Arch to the elaborately designed Delacorte Clock. A path to the left will take you around to the front entrance of the **Arsenal** ㉓, which houses various exhibits and some great WPA-era murals. Just past the clock is the **Central Park Wildlife Center** ㉔, formerly known as the zoo and home to polar bears, sea lions, monkeys, and more.

TIMING

Allow three to four hours for this route so that you can enjoy its pastoral pleasures in an appropriately leisurely mood. Bear in mind that the circular drive through the park is closed to auto traffic on weekdays 10–3 (except for the southeast portion of the road, up to 72nd Street) and 7–10, and on weekends and holidays. Nonautomotive traffic is often heavy and sometimes fast moving, so always be careful when you're crossing the road, and stay toward the inside when you're walking. Weekends are the liveliest time in the park—free entertainment is on tap, and the entire social microcosm is on parade. Weekend crowds make it safe to go into virtually any area of the park, although even on weekdays you should be safe anywhere along this tour. However, you're advised to take this walk during the day, since the park is fairly empty after dark. Despite its bad reputation, Central Park has the lowest crime rate of any precinct in the city—although the widely publicized and spectacularly ugly and frightening attacks on women in April 1989, September 1995, and June 1996 have reminded New Yorkers that the wisest course is to stay where the crowds are.

We've done our best to provide opening hours for the various park attractions, but schedules fluctuate according to the seasons, the weather, and special events schedules. If there's something you don't want to miss, call ahead to confirm the schedule before you set out for the park; you may also want to find out about scheduled events or ranger-led walks and talks. For park information and events, call 212/360–3444. For a recorded schedule of weekend walks and talks led by Urban Park Rangers, call 888/697–2757. Information booths are scattered about the park to help you find your way.

Food for thought: Although there are cafés connected with several attractions, as well as food stands near many entrances, most food choices are limited and predictable; a picnic lunch is usually a good idea. The Boathouse Cafe at the Loeb Boathouse (☞ *below*), however, is pleasant.

Sights to See

23 **The Arsenal.** Constructed between 1847 and the early 1850s, the Arsenal, built as a storage facility for munitions, predates the park and is the oldest extant structure within its grounds. Between 1869–77 it was the early home of the American Museum of Natural History (☞ The Upper West Side, *below*), and it now serves as headquarters of the Parks and Recreation Department. The downstairs lobby has some great WPA-era murals; an upstairs gallery features changing exhibitions relating to urban design and natural and organic themes; and a third-floor conference room houses the rendering of the Greensward Plan—the design that Olmsted and Vaux conceived for the park. ✉ *821 5th Ave.,* ☎ *212/360–8111.* ⏲ *Weekdays 9–4:30.*

18 **Belvedere Castle.** Standing regally atop Vista Rock, Belvedere Castle was built in 1872 of the same gray Manhattan schist that thrusts out of the soil in dramatic outcrops throughout the park (you can examine some of this schist, polished and striated by Ice Age glaciers, from the lip of the rock). From here you can also look down directly on the stage of the Delacorte and observe the picnickers and softball players on the Great Lawn. The castle itself, a typically 19th-century mishmash of styles—Gothic with Romanesque, Chinese, Moorish, and Egyptian motifs—was deliberately kept small so that when it was viewed from across the lake, the lake would seem bigger. (The Ramble's forest now obscures the lake's castle view.) Since 1919 it has been a U.S. Weather Bureau station; look for twirling meteorological instruments atop the tower. On the ground floor, the Henry Luce Nature Observatory has nature exhibits, children's workshops, and educational programs. ☎ *212/772–0210.* 🎟 *Free.* ⏲ *Mid-Apr.–mid-Oct., Tues.–Sun. 10–5; mid-Oct.–mid-Apr., Tues.–Sun. 10–4.*

★ 8 **Bethesda Fountain.** Few New York views are more romantic than the one from the top of the magnificent stone staircase that leads down to the ornate, three-tiered Bethesda Fountain. The fountain itself was dedicated in 1873 to commemorate the soldiers who died at sea during the Civil War, and it was named for the biblical pool in Jerusalem, which was supposedly given healing powers by an angel—hence the statue of an angel rising from the center. This statue, called *The Angel of the Waters,* figures prominently in Tony Kushner's epic drama *Angels in America,* which ends with a scene here. The four figures around the fountain's base symbolize Temperance, Purity, Health, and Peace. Beyond the terrace stretches the lake, filled with drifting swans and amateur rowboat captains.

10 **Bow Bridge.** This splendid cast-iron bridge arches over a neck of the lake to the ☞ **Ramble.** Stand here to take in the picture-postcard view

of the water reflecting a quintessentially New York image of vintage apartment buildings peeping above the treetops.

24 **Central Park Wildlife Center (Zoo).** Even a leisurely visit to this small but delightful menagerie, home to about a hundred species, will take only about an hour. The biggest specimens here are the polar bears—go to the Bronx Zoo (☞ Chapter 3) if you need tigers, giraffes, and elephants. Clustered around the central Sea Lion Pool are separate exhibits for each of the earth's major environments; the Polar Circle features a huge penguin tank and polar-bear floe; the open-air Temperate Territory is highlighted by a pit of chattering monkeys; and the Tropic Zone contains the flora and fauna of a miniature rain forest. The **Tisch Children's Zoo,** on the north side of the Denesmouth Arch, has interactive, hands-on exhibits where younglings and older wanna-be farmers can meet and touch such domestic animals as pigs, sheep, goats, and cows. Set above a redbrick arch near the Zoo is the **Delacorte Clock,** delightful glockenspiel that was dedicated to the city by philanthropist George T. Delacorte. Its fanciful bronze face is decorated with a menagerie of mechanical animals, including a dancing bear, a kangaroo, a penguin, and monkeys that rotate and hammer their bells when the clock chimes its tune every half hour. ✉ *Entrance at 5th Ave. and 64th St.,* ☎ *212/439–6500.* *$3.50. No children under 16 admitted without adult.* ⏲ *Apr.–Oct., weekdays 10–5, weekends 10:30–5:30; Nov.–Mar., daily 10–4:30.*

12 **Cherry Hill.** Originally a watering area for horses, this circular plaza with a small wrought-iron-and-gilt fountain is a great vantage point for the lake and the West Side skyline.

19 **Cleopatra's Needle.** This exotic, hieroglyphic-covered obelisk began life in Heliopolis, Egypt, around 1600 BC, was eventually carted off to Alexandria by the Romans in 12 BC, and landed here on February 22, 1881, when the khedive of Egypt made it a gift to the city. It stands, appropriately, near the glass-enclosed wing of the Metropolitan Museum (☞ Museum Mile, *above*), which houses the Egyptian Temple of Dendur. Ironically, a century in New York has done more to ravage the Needle than millennia of globe-trotting, and the hieroglyphics have sadly worn away to a *tabula rasa.* The copper crabs supporting the huge stone at each corner almost seem squashed by its weight.

22 **Conservatory Water.** Sophisticated model boats are raced each Saturday morning at 10 from spring through fall at this neo-Renaissance-style stone basin. At the north end is one of the park's most beloved statues, José de Creeft's 1960 bronze sculpture of **Alice in Wonderland,** sitting on a giant mushroom with the Mad Hatter, White Rabbit, and leering Cheshire Cat in attendance; kids are free to clamber all over it. On the west side of the pond, a bronze statue of **Hans Christian Andersen,** the Ugly Duckling at his feet, is the site of storytelling hours on summer weekends.

3 **The Dairy.** When it was built in the 19th century, the Dairy sat amid grazing cows and sold milk by the glass. Today the Dairy's painted, pointed eaves, steeple, and high-pitched slate roof harbor the **Central Park Visitor Center,** which has exhibits and interactive videos on the park's history, maps, and information about park events. ☎ *212/794–6564.* ⏲ *Apr.–Oct., Tues.–Sun. 10–5; Nov.–Mar., Tues.–Sun. 10–4.*

16 **Delacorte Theater.** Some of the best things in New York are, indeed, free, including summer performances by the Joseph Papp Shakespeare Theater Company (☞ Chapter 5) at this open-air theater. For free tickets (two per person), plan to arrive by mid-morning; the booth opens at 1 for that evening's performance. Same-day tickets are also given

away at the Joseph Papp Public Theater (✉ 425 Lafayette Ave.), also at 1. ☎ *212/539–8750 (seasonal).* ⏲ *Mid-June–Labor Day, Tues.–Sun. 8 PM.*

★ 4 **Friedsam Memorial Carousel.** Remarkable for the size of its hand-carved steeds—all 57 are three-quarters the size of real horses—this carousel was built in 1903 and moved here from Coney Island in 1951. Today it's considered one of the finest examples of turn-of-the-century folk art. The organ plays a variety of tunes, new and old. ☎ *212/879–0244.* *90¢.* ⏲ *Apr.–Oct., daily 10–6:30; Nov.–Mar., weekends 10–4:30, weather permitting.*

20 **Great Lawn.** After millions of footsteps, thousands of ball games, hundreds of downpours, dozens of concerts, and one papal mass, the Great Lawn had had it. In 1997 the Great Dust Bowl, as it had come to be known, underwent high-tech reconstructive surgery. The central 14-acre oval is now the stuff suburbanites dream—perfectly tended turf (a mix of rye and Kentucky bluegrass), state-of-the-art drainage systems, automatic sprinklers, and careful horticultural monitoring. The area hums with action on weekends and most summer evenings, when its softball fields and picnicking grounds provide a much-needed outlet for city dwellers of all ages.

OFF THE BEATEN PATH

HARLEM MEER – Those who never venture beyond 96th Street miss out on two of the park's most unusual attractions: the Conservatory Garden (☞ Museum Mile, *above*) and Harlem Meer, where as many as 100 people fish for stocked largemouth bass, catfish, golden shiners, and bluegills every day on a catch-and-release basis. At the north end of the meer is the Charles A. Dana Discovery Center, disguised as a petite Swiss chalet, where you can learn about geography, orienteering, ecology, and the history of the upper park. Within walking distance of the center are fortifications from the American Revolution and other historic sites, as well as woodlands, meadows, rocky bluffs, lakes, and streams. Fishing poles are available with identification from mid-April through October. ✉ *5th Ave. and 110th St.,* ☎ *212/860–1370.* ⏲ *Discovery Center: Apr.–Oct., Tues.–Sun. 10–5; Nov.–Mar., Tues.–Sun. 10–4.*

21 **Jacqueline Kennedy Onassis Reservoir.** This 106-acre reservoir (named for the former first lady after her death in 1994) takes up most of the center of the park, from 86th to 97th streets. The reservoir itself is more or less a holding tank; the city's main reservoirs are upstate. Around its perimeter is a 1.58-mi track popular with runners year-round (despite a badly needed renovation); if you come for a jog, observe local traffic rules and run counterclockwise. Even if you're not training for the New York Marathon, it's worth visiting for the stellar views of surrounding high-rises and the stirring sunsets; in fall and spring the hundreds of trees around it burst into color, and migrant waterfowl is plentiful.

9 **Loeb Boathouse.** At the brick neo-Victorian boathouse, on the east side of the park's 18-acre lake, you can rent a dinghy (or the one authentic Venetian gondola) or pedal off on a rented bicycle. ☎ *212/517–4723 boat rental; 212/861–4137 bicycle rental.* *Boat rental $10 per hr, $30 deposit; bicycle rental $8–$10 per hr, tandems $14 per hr, deposit required.* ⏲ *Mar.–Nov., weekdays 10–6, weekends 9–6, weather permitting.*

NEED A BREAK?

Characters in the movies *Three Men and a Little Lady, Postcards from the Edge,* and *The Manchurian Candidate* ate at the **Boathouse Cafe,** a waterside, open-air restaurant and bar. An adjacent cafeteria serves a good cheap breakfast, including freshly made scones, and lunch. Both are open from March through September. ✉ *East Park Dr. and E. 72nd St.,* ☎ *212/517–2233.*

❼ **The Mall.** A broad, formal walkway where fashionable ladies and men used to promenade around the turn of the century, the Mall looks as grand as ever. The south end of its main path, the **Literary Walk,** is covered by the grand canopy of the largest collection of American elms in North America and lined by statues of famous and not-so-famous men—not all of whom are literary. Included here are *The Indian Hunter,* sculpted in 1869 by John Quincy Adams Ward; this was the first piece of made-in-America sculpture to stand in the park. For statues of the other sex, look for **Alice in Wonderland** (☞ Conservatory Water, *above*) and **Mother Goose,** by East 72nd Street—but the female bronze stops there. East of the Mall, behind the Naumburg Bandshell, is the site of **SummerStage,** a free summertime concert series. ☎ *212/360–2777 for SummerStage information.*

❻ **Mineral Springs Pavilion.** The Moorish-style palace at the north end of the ☞ **Sheep Meadow** was designed by Calvert Vaux and J. Wrey Mould, who also designed Bethesda Terrace. Built as one of the park's four refreshment stands in the late 1860s, the pavilion still has a snack bar. Behind it are the **croquet grounds** and **lawn-bowling greens.** During the season (May–November) you can peer through gaps in the high hedges to watch the players, dressed in crisp white.

⓮ **Naturalists' Walk.** Starting at the West 79th Street entrance to the park across from the Museum of Natural History, this recently created nature walk is one of the best places to learn about local wildlife, bird life, flora, fauna, and geology. As you wind your way toward ☞ **Belvedere Castle,** you'll find the spectacular rock outcrops of Geology Walk, a stream that attracts countless species of birds, a woodland area with various native trees, stepping-stone trails that lead over rocky bluffs, and a sitting area.

❶ **The Pond.** Swans and ducks can sometimes be spotted on the calm waters of the Pond. For an unbeatable view of the city skyline, walk along the shore to **Gapstow Bridge.** From left to right, you'll see the peak-roofed brown Sherry-Netherland Hotel, the black-and-white General Motors Building, the rose-color Chippendale-style top of the Sony Building, the black-glass shaft of Trump Tower, and in front, the green gables of the Plaza hotel.

⓫ **The Ramble.** Across the ☞ **Bow Bridge** from the lake, the Ramble is a heavily wooded, wild 37-acre area laced with twisting, climbing paths, designed to resemble upstate New York's Adirondack Mountain region. This is prime bird-watching territory; a rest stop along a major migratory route, it shelters many of the more than 260 species of birds that have been sighted in the park. The Urban Park Rangers lead bird-watching tours here; call 212/988–4952 for details. Because the Ramble is so dense and isolated, however, it is not a good place to wander alone.

⓱ **Shakespeare Garden.** Inspired by the flora mentioned in the Bard's work, and nestled between Belvedere Castle and the Swedish Cottage, this somewhat hidden garden is a true find. Something is always in flower in the terraced hillside of lush, well-tended beds. Of particular note are the spring bulb display and June's peak bloom of antique roses.

❺ **Sheep Meadow.** A sheep grazing area until 1934, this grassy 15-acre meadow is now a favorite of picnickers and sunbathers. It's an officially designated quiet zone; the most vigorous sports allowed are kite flying and Frisbee tossing. Just west of the meadow, the famous **Tavern on the Green**, originally the sheepfold, was erected by Boss Tweed in 1870 and is now a Manhattan institution (☞ Chapter 6).

★ 13 **Strawberry Fields.** Called the "international garden of peace," this memorial to John Lennon, with its curving paths, shrubs, trees, and flower beds (donated from nearly every country of the world), creates a deliberately informal pastoral landscape, reminiscent of the English parks Lennon may have had in mind when he wrote the song "Strawberry Fields Forever" in 1967. Every year on December 8, Beatles fans gather around the star-shape, black-and-white tiled IMAGINE mosaic set into the sidewalk to mourn Lennon's 1980 murder, which took place across the street at the Dakota (☞ The Upper West Side, *below*), where he lived.

15 **Swedish Cottage.** Yet another newly renovated park feature, this traditional Swedish school house was imported in 1876 for the Philadelphia Exhibition and brought to Central Park soon thereafter. Marionette theater is performed regularly to the delight of young park visitors. ☎ *212/988–9093.* *$5.* *Shows Tues.–Fri. 10:30 and noon; Sat. 11, 1, and 3; call for reservations.*

2 **Wollman Memorial Rink.** Its music blaring out into the tranquility of the park can be a bit of a intrusion, but you can't deny that the lower park makes a great setting for a spin on the ice. Even if you don't want to join in, you can stand on the terrace here to watch ice-skaters throughout the winter and roller skaters and dancers in the summer (☞ Dance with Me! *in* Chapter 8). ☎ *212/396–1010.* *$7, skate rentals and lockers extra.* *Mid-Oct.–Mar., Mon. 10–4, Tues.–Thurs. 10–9:30, Fri. 10 AM–11 PM, Sat. 10 AM–11 PM; Sun. 10–9 for ice-skating; late Apr.–Sept., hrs are approximately the same for in-line skating. Call to confirm prices and hrs, as dates are subject to change due to weather.*

THE UPPER WEST SIDE

The Upper West Side—never as exclusive as the tony East Side—has always had an earthier appeal, even though it, too, has had many famous residents, past and present, along with a similar mix of real estate—large apartment buildings along Central Park West, West End Avenue, and Riverside Drive, and town houses on the shady, quiet cross streets—much of which is now protected by landmark status. The neighborhood's development largely followed the routes of mass transit, with an elevated train pioneering the way (1879) and subways coming around the turn of the century.

Once a haven for the Jewish intelligentsia and still a liberal stronghold, the West Side in the 1960s had become a rather grungy multiethnic community. In the 1970s actors, writers, and gays set in motion the area's gentrification, and today its restored brownstones and high-price co-op apartments are among the city's most coveted residences. The young professionals who gravitate to its small apartments graduate to its larger ones when they become young families. On weekends they cram the sidewalks as they push babies around in their imported strollers, but in the evenings the action moves inside, where singles from the city and suburbs mingle in bars and restaurants. Columbus Avenue is one such boutique-and-restaurant strip; Amsterdam Avenue is slowly following suit, its shop fronts a mix of bodegas, new restaurants, and boutiques. These lively avenues, the Upper West Side's many quiet tree- and brownstone-lined side streets, its two flanking parks—Central on its east flank, Riverside on its west, as well as such leading cultural attractions as the American Museum of Natural History and Lincoln Center, are all perennial attractions and make for a great variety of things to do in one relatively compact area.

Numbers in the text correspond to numbers in the margin and on the Upper West Side, Morningside Heights map.

A Good Walk

The West Side story begins at **Columbus Circle** ①, the bustling intersection of Broadway, 8th Avenue, Central Park West, and Central Park South. Cars enter this enormous circle from any one of seven directions (use caution and cross only at marked intersections). On the leafy southwest corner of Central Park, a line of horse-drawn carriages awaits fares. If you're in the mood for an ecclesiastical outing, stop in at the nearby **American Bible Society Gallery and Library,** home of the largest Bible collection in the United States.

With its parade of elegant, monumental apartment buildings on one side and Central Park on the other, Central Park West is one of the city's grandest avenues and the ideal place to begin a walk of the area. In the 1930s it was quite the rage to have your home address at the block-long Century (⊠ 25 Central Park W), which went up in 1931, taking with it one of the last large lots below 96th Street—only two buildings have gone up on this stretch since then. Continue past the solid brick-and-limestone New York Society for Ethical Culture buildings (⊠ 33 Central Park W), built 1903–1910, where lectures and concerts are held periodically, to 64th Street. The view up the avenue from here is particularly handsome. Turn west on 64th Street; on your left is the back of the West Side YMCA (⊠ 10 W. 64th St.), which has a neo-Moorish portal that sports tiny carved figures representing the worlds of sport (golfers, tennis players) *and* religion (St. George slaying the dragon). As you approach Broadway, **Lincoln Center** ②, New York's premier performing arts venue, widens into view. On summer nights the fountain in the central plaza with the Metropolitan Opera House behind is a lovely sight.

On the east side of Columbus Avenue just below 66th Street, stands the **Museum of American Folk Art** ③. Around the corner on 66th Street is the headquarters of the ABC television network; ABC owns several buildings along Columbus Avenue as well, including some studios where news shows and soap operas are filmed, so keep an eye out for your favorite daytime doctors, tycoons, and temptresses.

Turn right from Columbus Avenue onto **West 67th Street** and head toward Central Park along this handsome block of former artists' studios. Toward the end of the block on the left is the Elizabethan front of the Hotel des Artistes. At the end of the block, just inside Central Park, is Tavern on the Green (☞ Chapter 6).

Walk north on the east (park) side of Central Park West for the best view of the stately apartment buildings that line the avenue. Mixed among them is the **Spanish & Portuguese Synagogue, Shearith Israel** at 70th Street, thought to be the first synagogue built in the classical style of the Second Temple in Jerusalem. At 72nd Street cross back over Central Park West to get a close-up view of the **Dakota** ④, the apartment building–cum-château that presides over the block. Its neighbors to the north include several other famous apartment buildings and their famous residents: the Langham (⊠ 135 Central Park W), an Italian Renaissance–style high-rise designed by leading apartment architect Emery Roth in 1929–30; the twin-tower San Remo (⊠ 145–146 Central Park W), also designed by Roth in 1930 and over the years home to Rita Hayworth, Dustin Hoffman, Raquel Welch, Paul Simon, Barry Manilow, Tony Randall, and Diane Keaton; and the Kenilworth (built in 1908,

Upper West Side
American Museum of Natural History, **5**
Ansonia Hotel, **7**
Columbus Circle, **1**
The Dakota, **4**
Lincoln Center, **2**
Museum of American Folk Art, **3**
New-York Historical Society, **6**
Riverside Park, **9**
Subway kiosk, **8**

Morningside Heights
Barnard College, **12**
Cathedral of St. John the Divine, **10**
Columbia University, **11**
Grant's Tomb, **16**
Jewish Theological Seminary, **15**
Riverside Church, **17**
Teachers College, **13**
Union Theological Seminary, **14**

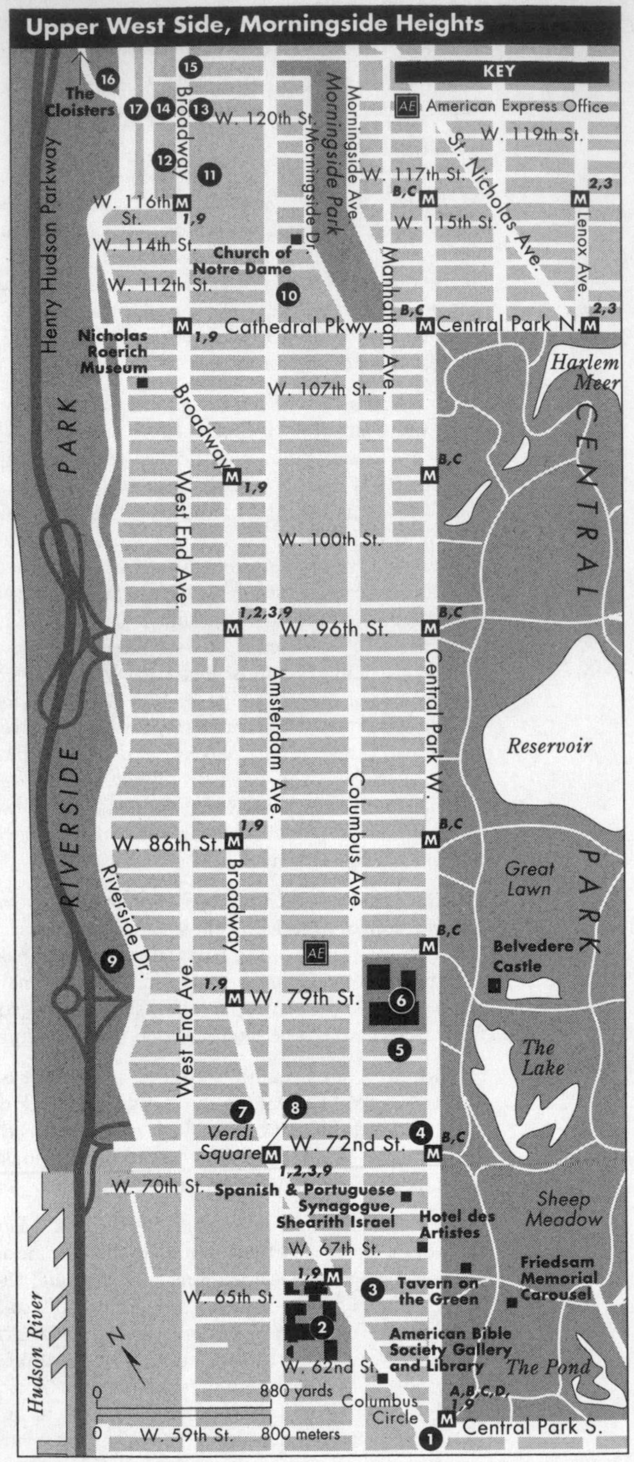

(✉ 151 Central Park W), with its immense pair of ornate front columns, once the address of Basil Rathbone (film's quintessential Sherlock Holmes) and Michael Douglas. The final beauty is the cubic Beresford (built in 1929, ✉ 211 Central Park W, at 81st St.), also by Emery Roth, whose lighted towers romantically haunt the night sky.

The buildings of Central Park West fold back at 77th and 81st streets to make room for the **American Museum of Natural History** ⑤, where past and present inhabitants of the entire world are on display. Before dashing off to fight the crowds there, however, consider a stop at the **New-York Historical Society** ⑥ for a quick history lesson on the city itself.

At this point you've covered the mandatory itinerary for the neighborhood. If you've had enough sightseeing, you could forsake the rest of this tour for shopping along Columbus Avenue (☞ Chapter 10), which is directly behind the museum. If you're here on a Sunday, check out the flea market at the southwest corner of 77th Street and Columbus Avenue. Food lovers should continue on to the four foodie shrines along the west side of Broadway: Zabar's (✉ 2245 Broadway, between 80th and 81st Sts.), where shoppers battle it out for exquisite delicatessen items, prepared foods, gourmet groceries, coffee, and cheeses as well as cookware, dishes, and small appliances; H & H Bagels (✉ 2239 Broadway, at 80th St.), which sells (and ships around the world) a dozen varieties of chewy bagels hot from the oven; Citarella (✉ 2135 Broadway, at 75th St.), with its intricate arrangements of seafood on shaved ice in the front window; and the bountiful but unpretentious Fairway Market (✉ 2127 Broadway, at 74th St.), where snack food, cheeses, and produce practically burst onto the street.

At 73rd Street and Broadway stands the white facade and fairy-castle turrets of the **Ansonia Hotel** ⑦, a turn-of-the-century luxury building. At 72nd Street, where Broadway cuts across Amsterdam Avenue, is triangular Verdi Square (named for Italian opera composer Giuseppe Verdi); here a marble statue of the composer is flanked by figures from Verdi's operas: *Aida, Otello,* and *Falstaff*. The triangle south of 72nd Street is Sherman Square (named for Union Civil War general William Tecumseh Sherman); the **subway kiosk** ⑧ here is an official city landmark.

Blocks like West 71st Street or West 74th Street between Broadway and Central Park West are perfect for casual strolling; Riverside Drive to 116th Street and Columbia University in Morningside Heights makes another fine walk. The latter leads past **Riverside Park** ⑨, which many neighborhood residents consider their private backyard. A long, slender green space along the Hudson River, Riverside, like Central Park, was landscaped by architects Frederick Law Olmsted and Calvert Vaux; its finest stretches are between 79th Street and Grant's Tomb (☞ Morningside Heights, *below*), at 122nd Street.

TIMING

Tree- and brownstone-lined park blocks are a main charm of this tour, which would easily take two or three hours at a relaxed clip. The exhibits at the Museum of American Folk Art and the New-York Historical Society shouldn't take more than an hour or so to view, but the mammoth and often crowded American Museum of Natural History can eat up most of a day. In bad weather you might want to limit your itinerary to what's covered between Lincoln Center and the Museum of Natural History.

Sights to See

American Bible Society Gallery and Library. With nearly 50,000 scriptural items in 2,000 languages, this is the largest Bible collection in the world outside the Vatican. The library, renovated in 1998, houses Helen Keller's massive 10-volume Braille Bible, leaves from a first edition Gutenberg Bible, and a Torah from China. ✉ *1865 Broadway, at 61st St.,* ☎ *212/408–1200.* ⏲ *Bookstore and gallery: Mon.–Wed. and Fri. 9–5, Thurs. 9–7, Sat. 10–2; library: Mon.–Sat. 9:30–4:30.*

★ 5 **American Museum of Natural History.** With more than 36 million artifacts and specimens, including its awe-inspiring collection of dinosaur skeletons, this wonderland is the world's largest and most important museum of natural history. Forty-two exhibition halls display something for everyone. Dinosaur-mania begins in the massive, barrel-vaulted **Theodore Roosevelt Rotunda,** where a 50-ft-tall skeleton of a barosaurus rears on its hind legs, protecting its fossilized baby from an enormous marauding allosaurus. Three spectacular $34 million dinosaur halls on the fourth floor—the **Hall of Saurischian Dinosaurs,** the **Hall of Ornithischian Dinosaurs,** and the **Hall of Vertebrate Origins**—use real fossils and interactive computer stations to present the most recent interpretations of how dinosaurs and pterodactyls might have behaved. The **Hall of Fossil Mammals** has interactive video monitors featuring museum curators explaining what caused the woolly mammoth to vanish from the earth and why mammals don't have to lay eggs to have babies. The **Hall of Human Biology and Evolution**'s wondrously detailed dioramas trace human origins back to Lucy and features a computerized archaeological dig and an electronic newspaper about human evolution. The **Hall of Meteorites** displays the 4-billion-year-old *Ahnighito,* the largest meteorite ever retrieved from the Earth's surface. The **Hall of Minerals and Gems** shows off the shimmering 563-carat Star of India sapphire. On Friday and Saturday evenings, when the museum stays open late, the **Hall of Ocean Life,** where a fiberglass replica of a 94-ft blue whale hangs from the ceiling, doubles as a cocktail lounge.

Films on the **IMAX Theater**'s 40-ft-high, 66-ft-wide screen are usually about nature (a jaunt through the Grand Canyon, a safari in the Serengeti, or a journey to the bottom of the sea to the wreck of the *Titanic*). The **Hayden Planetarium** is undergoing an extensive renovation and is slated to reopen in 2000 as the Center for Earth and Space. ✉ *Central Park W at W. 79th St.,* ☎ *212/769–5200 for museum tickets and programs, 212/769–5100 for museum general information, 212/769–5034 for IMAX Theater show times.* 🎫 *Museum $8 (suggested donation), IMAX Theater $15; combination tickets available.* ⏲ *Sun.–Thurs. 10–5:45; Fri.–Sat. 10–8:45.*

NEED A BREAK? For a diner-style cheeseburger or just a banana split, stop by **EJ's Luncheonette** (✉ 447 Amsterdam Ave., between 81st and 82nd Sts., ☎ 212/873–3444).

7 **Ansonia Hotel.** This 1904 Beaux Arts masterpiece, now a condominium apartment building, commands its corner of Broadway with as much architectural detail as good taste can stand. Inspiration for the Ansonia's turrets, mansard roof, and filigreed-iron balconies came from turn-of-the-century Paris. It was built as an apartment hotel, with suites without kitchens (and separate quarters for a staff that took care of the food). Designed to be fireproof, it has thick, soundproof walls that make it attractive to musicians; famous denizens of the past include Enrico Caruso, Igor Stravinsky, Arturo Toscanini, Florenz Ziegfeld,

Theodore Dreiser, and Babe Ruth. ✉ *2109 Broadway, between 73rd and 74th Sts.*

❶ **Columbus Circle.** This confusing intersection has never had the grandeur or the definition of Broadway's major intersections to the south, but it does have a 700-ton granite monument capped by a marble statue of Columbus himself in the middle of a traffic island. The monument had to be elaborately supported when the land underneath was torn up during the construction of the Columbus Circle subway station in the early 1900s. On the southwest quadrant of the circle is the **New York Coliseum,** a functional-looking white-brick building that served as the city's chief convention and trade-show venue before the Jacob Javits Center opened farther south on 11th Avenue. Redevelopment plans for the Circle have long been bitterly opposed by New Yorkers determined not to let the huge shadows of new skyscrapers be cast across Central Park. At press time the city is poised to choose from among six architects' designs for a new multiuse complex; once plans move forward, the Coliseum will be torn down.

On the northeast corner of the circle, standing guard over the entrance to Central Park, is the ***Maine Monument,***whose gleaming equestrian figures perch atop a formidable limestone pedestal. At the monument's foot, horse-drawn cabs await fares through Central Park, and a Victorian-style gazebo houses a 24-hour newsstand. The Trump International Hotel and Tower (☞ Chapter 7) fills the wedge of land between Central Park West and Broadway; Trump spent $250 million to gut the once marble-clad tower and rewrap it in a lamentable brown-glass curtain wall.

★ ❹ **The Dakota.** The most famous of all the apartment buildings lining Central Park West, the Dakota set a high standard for the many that followed it. Designed by Henry Hardenbergh, who also built the Plaza (☞ 5th Avenue and 57th Street, *above*), the Dakota was so far uptown when it was completed in 1884 that it was jokingly described as being "out in the Dakotas." Indeed, this buff-color château, with picturesque gables and copper turrets, housed some of the West Side's first residents. The Dakota is often depicted in scenes of old New York, and it was by looking out of a window here that Si Morley was able to travel back in time in Jack Finney's *Time and Again.* Its slightly spooky appearance was played up in the movie *Rosemary's Baby,* which was filmed here. The building's entrance is on 72nd Street; the spacious, lovely courtyard is visible beyond the guard's station. At the Dakota's gate, in December 1980, a deranged fan shot John Lennon as he came home from a recording session. Other celebrity tenants have included Boris Karloff, Rudolf Nureyev, José Ferrer and Rosemary Clooney, Lauren Bacall, Rex Reed, Leonard Bernstein, and Gilda Radner. ✉ *1 W. 72nd St., at Central Park W.*

★ ❷ **Lincoln Center.** A unified complex of pale travertine, Lincoln Center is the largest performing arts center in the world—so large it can seat nearly 18,000 spectators at one time in its various halls. The $165 million complex was built between 1962 and 1968. Local residents protested its construction in vain; a vast chunk of the area was razed to make way for it (*West Side Story* was filmed on the slum's gritty, deserted streets just before the demolition crews moved in), but that has long been forgotten by the artists who've since moved to the area, as well as their patrons. The complex's three principal venues are grouped around the central Fountain Plaza: To the left, as you face west, is Philip Johnson's **New York State Theater,** home to the New York City Ballet and the New York City Opera. To the center, Wallace Harrison's

Metropolitan Opera House, with its brilliantly colored Chagall murals visible through the arched lobby windows, is, of course, the Metropolitan Opera's stage, as well as that of the American Ballet Theatre. And to the north is Max Abramovitz's **Avery Fisher Hall,** host to the New York Philharmonic Orchestra. A great time to visit the complex is on summer evenings, when thousands of dancers trot and swing around the plaza during the Midsummer Night Swing. One-hour guided "Introduction to Lincoln Center" tours, given daily, cover the center's history and wealth of artwork and usually visit these three theaters, performance schedules permitting.

Lincoln Center encompasses much more than its three core theaters. Its major outdoor venue is **Damrosch Park,** on the south flank of the Met, where summer open-air festivals are often accompanied by free concerts at the **Guggenheim Bandshell.** Accessible via the walk between the Metropolitan and Avery Fisher is the North Plaza—the best of Lincoln Center's spaces—with a massive Henry Moore sculpture reclining in a reflecting pool. The long lines and glass wall of Eero Saarinen's **Vivian Beaumont Theater** stand behind the pool. It is officially considered a Broadway house, despite its distance from the theater district. Below it is the smaller **Mitzi E. Newhouse Theater,** where many award-winning plays originate. To the rear is the **New York Public Library for the Performing Arts,** a research and circulating library with an extensive collection of books, records, videos, and scores on music, theater, and dance; in mid-1998 the library is slated to close for a two-year renovation. An overpass leads from this plaza across 65th Street to the world-renowned **Juilliard School** (☎ 212/769–7406) for music and theater; actors Kevin Kline, Robin Williams, and Patti LuPone studied here. An elevator leads down to street level and **Alice Tully Hall,** home of the Chamber Music Society of Lincoln Center and the New York Film Festival. Or turn left from the overpass and follow the walkway west to Lincoln Center's **Walter Reade Theater,** one of the finest places in the city to watch films (☞ Chapter 5). ✉ *W. 62nd to 66th Sts. between Broadway and Amsterdam Ave.,* ☎ *212/546–2656 for general information, 212/875–5350 for tour schedule and reservations.* 🎫 *Tour $8.25.*

NEED A BREAK? Before or after a Lincoln Center performance, the pleasant **Cafe Mozart** (✉ 154 W. 70th St., ☎ 212/595–9797) is the closest place to stop for conversation with a friend. The operatic atmosphere and espresso at **Cafe La Fortuna** (✉ 69 W. 71st St., ☎ 212/724–5846) are just right.

❸ **Museum of American Folk Art.** The collection of this small museum includes arts and crafts from all over the Americas: native paintings, quilts, carvings, dolls, trade signs, painted-wood carousel horses, and a giant Indian-chief copper weather vane. Changing exhibits are often worth seeing. The gift shop has intriguing craft items, books, and great cards. ✉ *2 Lincoln Sq. (Columbus Ave. between 65th and 66th Sts.),* ☎ *212/595–9533.* 🎫 *$3 (suggested donation).* ⏲ *Tues.–Sun. 11:30–7:30.*

❻ **New-York Historical Society.** Founded in 1804, the New-York Historical Society is the city's oldest museum and one of its finest research libraries, with a collection of 6 million pieces of art, literature, and memorabilia. Exhibitions shed light on New York's—and America's—history, everyday life, art, and architecture. Highlights of the collection include George Washington's inaugural chair, 500,000 photographs from the 1850s to the present, original watercolors for John James Audubon's *Birds of America,* the architectural files of McKim, Mead & White, and the largest U.S. collection of Louis Comfort Tiffany's lamps (alas, until 2000 few are slated to be on display). From April to September

1999, the museum will mount *Dance in the City: 50 Years of the New York City Ballet*, to commemorate the founding of Lincoln Kirstein and George Balanchine's world-renowned company. ✉ *2 W. 77th St., at Central Park W,* ☎ *212/873–3400.* 💵 *Museum $5 (suggested donation).* ⏲ *Museum: Tues.–Sun. 11–5, library: Tues.–Sat. 11–5.*

9 **Riverside Park.** Long and narrow, tree-lined Riverside Park—laid out by Central Park's designers Olmsted and Vaux between 1873 and 1888—runs along the Hudson from 72nd Street to 159th Street. More manageable than Central Park—which can feel overwhelming to first-time visitors—Riverside Park is best visited on weekends, when Upper West Side residents and their children throng its walkways. A **statue of Eleanor Roosevelt** stands at the 72nd Street entrance. Locals gravitate to the **Promenade,** a broad formal walkway, extending from 80th Street to a few blocks north, with a stone parapet looking out over the river. The steps that descend here lead to an underpass beneath Riverside Drive and the **79th Street Boat Basin,** a rare spot in Manhattan where you can walk right along the river's edge, smell the salt air, and watch a flotilla of houseboats bobbing in the water. These boats must sail at least once a year to prove their seaworthiness. Behind the boat basin, the **Rotunda** occupies a wonderful circular space punctuated by a fountain.

At the end of the Promenade, a patch of its median strip explodes with flowers tended by nearby residents. To the right, cresting a hill along Riverside Drive at 89th Street, stands the Civil War **Soldiers' and Sailors' Monument,** an imposing 96-ft-high circle of white-marble columns. From its base is a refreshing view of Riverside Park, the Hudson River, and the New Jersey waterfront. *See also* Grant's Tomb *in* Morningside Heights, *below.* ✉ *72nd to 159th Sts. between Riverside Dr. and the Hudson River.*

Spanish & Portuguese Synagogue, Shearith Israel (Orthodox Jewish). Built in 1897, this is the fifth home of the oldest Jewish congregation in the United States, founded in 1654. The adjoining "Little Synagogue" is a replica of Shearith Israel's Georgian-style first synagogue. ✉ *8 W. 70th St., at Central Park W,* ☎ *212/873–0300.*

8 **Subway kiosk.** This brick and terra-cotta building with rounded neo-Dutch molding is one of two remaining control houses from the original subway line (the other is at Bowling Green in lower Manhattan [☞ Wall Street and the Battery, *below*]). Built in 1904–05, this was the first express station north of 42nd Street. ✉ *W. 72nd St. and Broadway.*

West 67th Street. On West 67th Street between Columbus Avenue and Central Park West, many of the apartment buildings were designed as "studio buildings," with high ceilings and immense windows that make them ideal for artists—these were the days when "studio apartment" allowed far more space than one room barely big enough for a futon. Gothic motifs, carved in white stone or wrought in iron, decorate several of these buildings at street level. Perhaps the finest apartment building on the block is the **Hotel des Artistes** (✉ 1 W. 67th St.), built in 1918 on the corner of Central Park West, with its elaborate mock-Elizabethan lobby. Its tenants have included Isadora Duncan, Rudolph Valentino, Norman Rockwell, Noël Coward, Fannie Hurst, and contemporary actors Joel Grey and Richard Thomas; another tenant, Howard Chandler Christy, designed the lush, soft-toned murals in the ground-floor restaurant, Café des Artistes, where Louis Malle's *My Dinner with André* was filmed (☞ Chapter 6).

MORNINGSIDE HEIGHTS

On the high ridge just north and west of Central Park, a cultural outpost grew up at the end of the 19th century, spearheaded by a triad of institutions: the relocated Columbia University, which developed the mind; St. Luke's Hospital, which cared for the body; and the Cathedral of St. John the Divine, which tended the soul. Idealistically conceived as an American Acropolis, the cluster of academic and religious institutions that developed here managed to keep these blocks stable during years when neighborhoods on all sides were collapsing. More recently, West Side gentrification has reclaimed the area to the south, while the areas north and east of here haven't changed as much. Yet within the gates of the Columbia or Barnard campuses or inside the hushed St. John the Divine or Riverside Church, the character of the city changes. This is an *uptown* student neighborhood—less hip than the Village, but friendly, fun, and intellectual.

Numbers in the text correspond to numbers in the margin and on the Upper West Side, Morningside Heights map.

A Good Walk

Broadway is the heartbeat of Morningside Heights, but many of the most remarkable sights will take you east and west of the main thoroughfare. Walk east from Broadway on grungy 112th Street and the massive **Cathedral of St. John the Divine** ⑩ will gradually loom up before you. You could easily spend an hour wandering through the church, gawking at its monumental architecture, inspecting its stained-glass windows, looking at its tapestries and art, and browsing in its gift store. Don't miss a stroll on the driveway just south of the nave. It doesn't look like much, but it leads back past a neoclassic building to the delightful Biblical Garden—an utter escape from the urban crush. Just south of the upper drive, the Peace Fountain sits in a circular plaza off Amsterdam Avenue at 111th Street.

From here swing east on 113th Street to secluded Morningside Drive. You'll pass the Beaux Arts–baroque 1896 core of St. Luke's Hospital, of which a jumble of newer buildings awkwardly grows. On Morningside Drive at 114th Street, the **Church of Notre Dame** nestles into its corner with as much personality but far less bulk than the other churches on this tour. At 116th Street, catercorner from Columbia's President's House, pause at the overlook on the right to gaze out at the skyline and down into Morningside Park, tumbling precipitously into a wooded gorge. Designed by Olmsted and Vaux of Central Park fame, the park has a lovely landscape, but since it is bordered by some rough blocks of Harlem, it would be safest not to get any closer.

Turn back toward Amsterdam Avenue on 116th Street, and walk past the Law School's streamlined Greene Hall to the eastern gates of **Columbia University** ⑪. Its quadrangle is hardly a respite from the urban activity around it, but it does have its share of collegiate grandeur. The university's renowned journalism school, founded by Joseph Pulitzer (the reason Columbia bestows Pulitzer Prizes each spring), holds classes in the building just south of the campus's west gates. The official college bookstore is at 115th Street and Broadway. Across Broadway from Columbia proper is its sister institution, **Barnard College** ⑫.

Institutes of higher learning abound as you follow Broadway on the east side of the street north to 120th Street—on the right is **Teachers College** ⑬, a part of Columbia, and on the left, on the west side of the street, is the interdenominational **Union Theological Seminary** ⑭. At the northeast corner of 122nd Street and Broadway, behind a large blank-walled redbrick tower that fronts the intersection at an angle, is the **Jewish Theological Seminary** ⑮. Walk west on 122nd Street; between Claremont Avenue and Broadway the prestigious Manhattan School of Music is on your right, with musical instruments carved into the stone beneath its upper-story windows. Between Claremont and Riverside Drive is Sakura Park, a quiet formal garden.

Cross Riverside Drive at West 122nd Street into Riverside Park (☞ The Upper West Side, *above*). The handsome white-marble **Grant's Tomb** ⑯ was one of the city's most popular sights around the last turn of the century. Finish the walk at **Riverside Church** ⑰, at Riverside Drive and 120th Street—any afternoon but Monday you can climb the tower for a view up the palisades across the Hudson River.

TIMING

Allow yourself about two hours to leisurely walk the tour. To get the true flavor of the neighborhood, which is often student dominated, come during the week, when classes are in session. You'll be able to visit campus buildings, sample café life, and because the major churches on the tour are active weeklong, you won't miss seeing them in action. If you visit on a Sunday, you could attend church services.

Sights to See

12 **Barnard College.** Established in 1889 and one of the former Seven Sisters of women's colleges, Barnard has steadfastly remained single-sex and independent from Columbia, although its students can take classes there (and vice versa). Note the bear (the college's mascot) on the shield above the main gates at 117th Street. Through the gates is **Barnard Hall**, which houses classrooms, offices, a pool, and dance studios. Its brick-and-limestone design echoes the design of Columbia University's buildings. To the right of Barnard Hall, a path leads through the narrow but neatly landscaped campus; to the left from the main gate is a quiet residential quadrangle. ☎ *212/854–2014.* ⏲ *Student tours Mon.–Sat. 10:30 and 2:30.*

★ 10 **Cathedral of St. John the Divine.** Everything about the Episcopal Cathedral of St. John the Divine is colossal, from its cavernous 601-ft-long nave, which can hold some 6,000 worshipers, to its 155-ft-tall domed crossing, which could comfortably contain the Statue of Liberty. When this Gothic behemoth is finished—the transepts and facade are the most noticeably uncompleted elements—it will be the largest cathedral in the world. To get the full effect of the building's mammoth size, approach it from Broadway on 112th Street. On the wide steps climbing to the Amsterdam Avenue entrance, five portals arch over the entrance doors. The central portal depicts St. John having his vision of the Lord. The bronze doors he presides over open only twice a year—on Easter and in October for the Feast of St. Francis, when animals as large as elephants and camels are brought in, along with cats and dogs, to be blessed. The doors have relief castings of scenes from the Old Testament on the left and the New Testament on the right. Statuary on the doorjambs, much of it still not finished, is currently the only part of the cathedral actually in progress—on weekdays from approximately April to October, you can watch masons carving.

The cathedral's first cornerstone was laid in 1892, and in 1911 a major change in architectural vision came at the hands of Ralph Adams Cram, a Gothic Revival purist who insisted on a French Gothic style for the edifice. The granite of the original Romanesque-Byzantine design is visible inside at the crossing, where it has yet to be finished with the Gothic limestone facing. Note that the finished arches are pointed—

Gothic—while the uncovered two are in the rounded Byzantine style. The one-two punch of the Great Depression and World War II brought construction to a halt.

Inside, along the cathedral's side aisles, some chapels display decorations with surprisingly contemporary outlooks: on sports, poetry, and AIDS, for example. The **Saint Saviour Chapel** contains a three-panel plaster altar with religious scenes by artist Keith Haring (this was his last work before he died of AIDS in 1990). The more conventional **baptistry,** to the left of the altar, is an exquisite octagonal chapel with a 15-ft-high marble font and a polychrome sculpted frieze commemorating New York's Dutch heritage. The altar area itself expresses the cathedral's interfaith tradition and international mission—with menorahs, Shinto vases, golden chests presented by the king of (then) Siam, and in the ring of chapels behind the altar, dedications to various ethnic groups.

A peaceful precinct of châteaulike Gothic-style buildings, known as the **Cathedral Close,** is behind the cathedral on the south side. In a corner by the Cathedral School is the delightful **Biblical Garden.** Perennials, roses, herbs, and an arbor are planted in and around the stone border of a Greek cross, bounded on the outside by the cathedral, a low stone wall, and a hedge. Around the bend from this garden, a small rose garden will thrill your nose with its spicy scents. Back at Amsterdam Avenue, the **Peace Fountain** depicts the struggle of good and evil. The forces of good, embodied in the figure of the archangel Michael, triumph by decapitating Satan, whose head hangs from one side. The fountain is encircled by small, whimsical animal figures cast in bronze from pieces sculpted by children.

Along with Sunday services (8, 9, 9:30, 11, and 1 and 7), the cathedral operates a score of community outreach programs, has changing museum and art gallery displays, supports artists-in-residence and an early music consortium, and presents a full calendar of nonreligious (classical, folk, solstice) concerts. Christmastime programs are especially worth looking into. ✉ *1047 Amsterdam Ave., at 112th St.,* ☎ *212/316–7540; 212/662–2133 box office; 212/932–7347 to arrange tours.* 🎫 *Tours $3 (suggested donation), vertical tours $10 (suggested donation).* ⏲ *Mon.–Sat. 7:15–6, Sun. 7 AM–8 PM; tours Tues.–Sat. at 11, Sun. at 1; vertical tours 1st and 3rd Sat. of month at noon and 2 (reservations required).*

NEED A BREAK? If St. John has filled your soul but your stomach is crying out for its share, head for the **Hungarian Pastry Shop** (✉ 1030 Amsterdam Ave., ☎ 212/866–4230) for tasty desserts and coffee.

Church of Notre Dame. A French neoclassic landmark building, this Roman Catholic church has a replica of the French grotto of Lourdes behind its altar. It once served a predominantly French community of immigrants, but like the neighborhood, today's congregation is more diverse ethnically, with Irish, German, Italian, African-American, Hispanic, and Filipino members. The building is open 30 minutes before masses, which are held weekdays at 8, 12:05, and 5:30; Saturdays at 5:30; and Sundays at 8:30, 10 (in Spanish), 11:30, and 5:30. ✉ *405 W. 114th St., at Morningside Dr.,* ☎ *212/866–1500.*

OFF THE BEATEN PATH **THE CLOISTERS** – Perched atop a wooded hill in Fort Tryon Park, near Manhattan's northernmost tip, the Cloisters houses the medieval collection of the Metropolitan Museum of Art in an appropriately medieval monastery-like setting. Colonnaded walks connect authentic French and

Spanish monastic cloisters, a French Romanesque chapel, a 12th-century chapter house, and a Romanesque apse. An entire room is devoted to the richly woven and extraordinarily detailed 15th- and 16th-century Unicorn Tapestries—a must-see. Three enchanting gardens shelter more than 250 species of plants similar to those grown during the Middle Ages, including herbs and medicinals; the Unicorn garden blooms with flowers and plants depicted in the tapestries. The Cloisters frequently hosts concerts of medieval music (☞ Music *in* Chapter 5). The Cloisters is easily accessible by public transportation: The M4 Cloisters–Fort Tryon Park bus provides a lengthy but scenic ride; catch it along Broadway, or take the A train to 190th Street. If you're traveling from below 110th Street, the M4 bus runs along Madison Avenue. ✉ *Fort Tryon Park,* ☎ *212/923–3700.* 🎟 *$8 (suggested donation).* ⏲ *Mar.–Oct., Tues.–Sun. 9:30–5:15; Nov.–Feb., 9:30–4:45.*

⓫ **Columbia University.** This wealthy, private, coed Ivy League school was New York's first college when it was founded in 1754. Back then, before American independence, it was called King's College—note the gilded crowns on the black wrought-iron gates at the Amsterdam Avenue entrance. The herringbone-pattern brick paths of College Walk lead into the refreshingly open main quadrangle, dominated by neoclassic **Butler Library** to the south and the rotunda-topped **Low Memorial Library** to the north. Butler, built in 1934, holds the bulk of the university's 5 million books. Low was built in 1895–97 by McKim, Mead & White, which laid out the general campus plan when the college moved here in 1897. Modeled on the Roman Pantheon, Low is now mostly offices, but on weekdays you can go inside to see its domed, templelike former Reading Room. Low Library also houses the visitor center, where you can pick up a campus guide or arrange a tour. The steps of Low Library, presided over by Daniel Chester French's statue *Alma Mater,* have been a focal point for campus life, not least during the student riots of 1968. The southwest corner of the quad is the site of a new **student center,** scheduled to open in September 1999. ✉ *Visitor Center, north of W. 116th St. between Amsterdam Ave. and Broadway,* ☎ *212/854–4900.* ⏲ *Weekdays 9–5. Tours begin 11 and 2 weekdays from Room 213, Low Library.*

Before Columbia moved here, this land was occupied by the Bloomingdale Insane Asylum; the sole survivor of those days is **Buell Hall,** the gabled orange-red brick house, east of Low Library. North of Buell Hall is the interdenominational **St. Paul's Chapel** (1907), an exquisite little Byzantine-style domed church laid out in the shape of a cross, with fine tiled vaulting inside. ☎ *212/854–3574.* ⏲ *Sept.–May, Sun.–Thurs. 10–10, Fri. 10 AM–1 AM, Sat. noon–1 AM; Sun. services 10:30–2:30 and 7–10. Greatly reduced hrs June–Aug. and during winter intercession, so call ahead for Sun. schedule. Free organ recitals selected Thurs. noon.*

NEED A BREAK? The exterior of **Tom's Restaurant** (✉ 2880 Broadway, at 112th St., ☎ 212/864–6137) made frequent appearances on the TV show *Seinfeld.* Whether or not you care about its fame, this diner is still a good place for a New York bite.

⓰ **Grant's Tomb.** This commanding position along the Hudson River, within Riverside Park, is Civil War general and two-term president Ulysses S. Grant and wife Julia Dent Grant's final resting place. Opened in 1897, almost 12 years after Grant's death, it was a more popular sight than the Statue of Liberty until the end of World War I. An architectural mishmash outside, the towering granite mausoleum is engraved with the words LET US HAVE PEACE, which recall Grant's speech to the Republican convention upon his presidential nomination. Under a small white dome, the Grants' twin black-marble sarcophagi are sunk into a deep circular chamber visible from above; minigalleries to the sides display photographs and Grant memorabilia. The surrounding plaza's benches, finished with 1960s-era mosaic designs by local schoolchildren, are a colorful counterpoint to the monument's Victorian bulk. ✉ *Riverside Dr. and 122nd St.,* ☎ *212/666–1640.* 🎫 *Free.* ⏲ *Daily 9–5, 20-min tours run on the hr.*

⓯ **Jewish Theological Seminary.** The seminary was founded in 1887 as a training ground for rabbis, cantors, and scholars of Conservative Judaism, but this complex wasn't built until 1930. The tower, gutted by fire in 1966 and only now undergoing restoration, formerly housed the seminary's excellent library, which holds frequent exhibits. ✉ *3080 Broadway, at 122nd St.,* ☎ *212/678–8000.* 🎫 *Free.* ⏲ *Library Sun.–Thurs. 9:30–5:30, Fri. 9:30–2.*

OFF THE BEATEN PATH

NICHOLAS ROERICH MUSEUM – An 1898 Upper West Side town house is the site of this small, eccentric museum dedicated to the work of Russian artist Nicholas Roerich, who emigrated to New York in the 1920s and quickly developed an ardent following. Some 200 of his paintings hang here—notably some vast canvases of the Himalayas. He also designed sets for Diaghilev ballets, such as *Rite of Spring,* photographs of which are also on view. ✉ *319 W. 107th St.,* ☎ *212/864–7752.* 🎫 *Free.* ⏲ *Tues.–Sun. 2–5.*

★ ⓱ **Riverside Church.** In this modern (1930) Gothic-style edifice, the smooth, pale limestone walls seem the antithesis of the rougher hulk of the Cathedral of St. John the Divine. Although most of the building is refined and restrained, the main entrance, on Riverside Drive, explodes with elaborate stone carvings (modeled on the French cathedral of Chartres, as are many other decorative details here). Inside, look at the handsomely ornamented main sanctuary, which seats only half as many people as St. John the Divine; if you're here on Sunday, take the elevator to the top of the 22-story, 356-ft **tower,** with its 74-bell carillon, the largest in the world. Although it is affiliated with the Baptist church and the United Church of Christ, Riverside is nondenominational, interracial, international, extremely political, and socially conscious. Its calendar includes political and community events, dance and theater programs, and concerts, along with regular Sunday services. ✉ *Riverside Dr. and 122nd St.,* ☎ *212/870–6700.* 🎫 *Church free, tower $1.* ⏲ *Mon.–Sat. 9–5, Sun. noon–4; service each Sun. 10:45; tower: Tues.–Sat. 11–4, Sun. noon–6;*

⓭ **Teachers College.** Redbrick Victorian buildings house Columbia University's Teachers College, founded in 1887 and still the world's largest graduate school in the field of education. Names of famous teachers throughout history line the frieze along the Broadway facade. ✉ *525 W. 120th St.*

⓮ **Union Theological Seminary.** Founded in 1836, the seminary moved here, to its rough, gray, collegiate Gothic quadrangle, in 1910; it has one of the world's finest theological libraries. Step inside the main entrance, on Broadway at 121st Street, and ask to look around the serene central quadrangle. ✉ *W. 120th to W. 122nd Sts., between Broadway and Claremont Ave.*

HARLEM

Harlem has been the mecca for African-American culture and life for nearly a century. Originally called Nieuw Haarlem and settled by Dutch farmers, Harlem was a well-to-do suburb in the 19th century; many Jews moved from the Lower East Side to Harlem in the late 1800s, and black New Yorkers began settling here in large numbers in about 1900, moving into a surplus of fine apartment buildings and town houses built by real estate developers for a middle-class white market that never materialized. By the 1920s Harlem (with one *a*) had become the most famous black community in the United States, perhaps in the world. In an astonishing confluence of talent known as the Harlem Renaissance, black novelists, playwrights, musicians, and artists, many of them seeking to escape discrimination and worse in other parts of the country, gathered here. Black performers starred in chic Harlem jazz clubs—which, ironically, only whites could attend. Throughout the Roaring '20s, while whites flocked here for the infamous parties and nightlife, blacks settled in for the opportunity this self-sustaining community represented. But the Depression hit Harlem hard. By the late 1930s it was no longer a popular social spot for downtown New Yorkers, and many African-American families began moving out to houses in the suburbs of Queens and New Jersey.

By the 1960s Harlem's population had dropped dramatically, and many of those who remained were disillusioned enough to join in civil rights riots. A vicious cycle of crowded housing, poverty, and crime turned the neighborhood into a simmering ghetto. Today, however, Harlem is restoring itself. Mixed in with some seedy remains of the past are old jewels such as the refurbished Apollo Theatre and such newer attractions as the Studio Museum. Black professionals and young families are restoring many of Harlem's classic brownstones and limestone buildings, bringing new life to the community.

Deserted buildings, burned out shop fronts, and yards of rubble still scar certain parts; although a few whites live here, some white visitors may feel conspicuous in what is still a largely black neighborhood. But Harlemites are accustomed to seeing tourists—white and otherwise—on their streets; only common traveler's caution is necessary during daytime excursions to any of the places highlighted. For nighttime outings it's smart to take a taxi, as in many other parts of the city. Bus tours may be a good way to see Harlem because they cover more areas than the central Harlem walk outlined below (☞ Sightseeing *in* the Gold Guide).

Note that the city's north–south avenues acquire different names up here, commemorating heroes of black history: 6th Avenue becomes Lenox Avenue or Malcolm X Boulevard, 7th Avenue is Adam Clayton Powell Jr. Boulevard, and 8th Avenue is Frederick Douglass Boulevard; 125th Street, the major east–west street, is also Martin Luther King Jr. Boulevard. Many people still use the streets' former names, but the street signs use the new ones.

Numbers in the text correspond to numbers in the margin and on the Harlem map.

A Good Walk

Beginning on West 115th Street and Adam Clayton Powell Jr. Boulevard, head west on the north side of the block to admire the facade of this branch of the **New York Public Library** ①. It's sufficiently interesting for you to make the trip even on Sunday, when the library is closed.

The next two stops, however, are most worthwhile on Sunday, because church is in session and gospel singers fill the sanctuaries with soulful, moving, often joyous gospel music. Memorial Baptist Church (☒ 141 W. 115th St., ☎ 212/663–8830) welcomes visitors at its two-hour service, which begins at 10:45. Gospel fans and visitors are also welcome at the 10:45 Sunday service at Canaan Baptist Church of Christ (☒ 132 W. 116th St., ☎ 212/866–0301), where Rev. Dr. Wyatt Tee Walker is senior minister.

On the southwest corner of 116th Street and Lenox Avenue, an aluminum onion dome tops the Malcolm Shabazz Mosque (☒ 102 W. 116th St.), a former casino that was converted in the mid-1960s to a black Muslim temple (Malcolm X once preached here). Several Muslim stores are nearby. Continuing north along Lenox Avenue and then east on 120th Street brings you to **Marcus Garvey Park** ②, which interrupts 5th Avenue between 120th and 124th streets. Stay outside the park, but be sure to notice its watchtower and the pretty row houses as you skirt its west side. At the north end of the park, walk east to 5th Avenue and then north one block to 125th Street.

Harlem's main thoroughfare is 125th Street (also known as Martin Luther King Jr. Boulevard), the chief artery of its cultural, retail, and economic life. Real estate values here have never come close to those downtown along 5th Avenue or even Broadway, and many commercial buildings rise only a few stories. But never fear—Harlem isn't missing out on the malling of America, as new businesses, many of them branches of national chains, have moved in of late, bringing new shop fronts along a retail row that used to see many FOR RENT signs. There's even a bona fide mall planned for the street—Harlem USA. Above the street-level stores is the home of the National Black Theatre (☒ 2033 5th Ave., between 125th and 126th Sts., ☎ 212/722–3800), which produces new works by contemporary African-American writers. A literary landmark, the **Langston Hughes House** is a quick detour away. Walking west along 125th Street you'll pass a number of African-themed stores. On Lenox Avenue between 126th and 127th streets is **Sylvia's Soul Food Restaurant,** owned by Sylvia Woods, New York's self-proclaimed "queen of soul food."

Continuing along 125th Street, you can't help but notice the modern, hulking State Office Building and, catercorner, the lovely **Theresa Towers** office building, formerly the Hotel Theresa, at the southwest corner of Adam Clayton Powell Jr. Boulevard. Both buildings tower over their neighbors. Another community showplace is also on the block between Lenox Avenue and Adam Clayton Powell Jr. Boulevard, the **Studio Museum in Harlem** ③, and on the next block across the street, the famous **Apollo Theatre** ④. One of Harlem's greatest landmarks, the Apollo was fantastically restored and brought back to life in the 1980s.

Return to Adam Clayton Powell Jr. Boulevard and continue north. Between 131st and 132nd streets you'll pass what is today the Williams Institutional (Christian Methodist Episcopal) Church. From 1912 to 1939 this was the Lafayette Theatre, which presented black revues in the 1920s and housed the WPA's Federal Negro Theater in the 1930s. A tree outside the theater was considered a lucky charm for black actors to touch, and it eventually became known as the Tree of Hope; though the original tree and then its live replacement were both cut down, it has been replaced by the colorful, abstract metal "tree" on the traffic island in the center of the street. A stump from the second tree is now a lucky charm for performers at the Apollo.

Abyssinian Baptist Church, **6**
Apollo Theater, **4**
Marcus Garvey Park, **2**
New York Public Library 115th Street Branch, **1**
Schomburg Center for Research in Black Culture, **5**
Strivers' Row, **7**
Studio Museum in Harlem, **3**

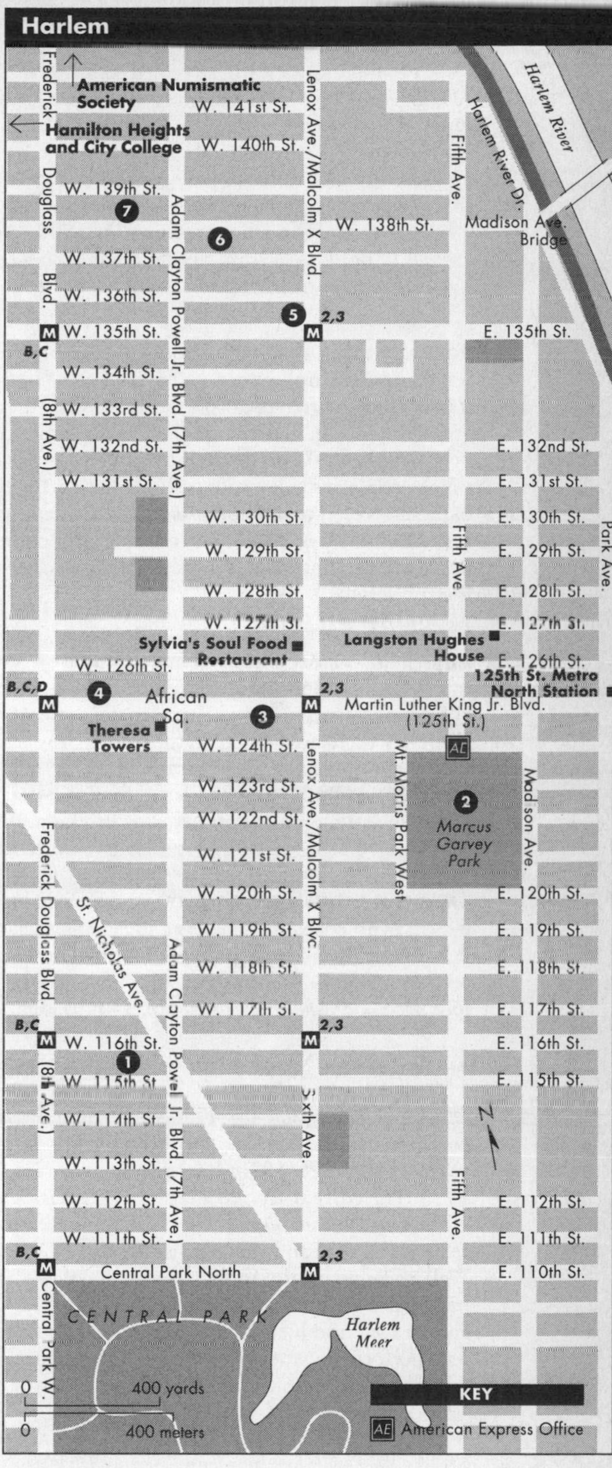

At 135th Street cross back east to Lenox Avenue. Notice the branch of the YMCA at 180 West 135th Street; writers Langston Hughes, Claude McKay, and Ralph Ellison all rented rooms here. At the corner of Lenox Avenue you'll find the **Schomburg Center for Research in Black Culture** ⑤, a research branch of the New York Public Library that also functions as a community center of sorts. Three blocks north is another neighborhood landmark, the **Abyssinian Baptist Church** ⑥, one of the first black institutions to settle in Harlem when it moved here in the 1920s; it was founded downtown in 1808. Across Adam Clayton Powell Jr. Boulevard from the church is St. Nicholas Historic District, a handsome set of town houses known as **Strivers' Row** ⑦.

TIMING

The walk takes about four hours, including stops at the Studio Museum and the Schomburg Center. Sunday is a good time to tour Harlem if you'd like to listen to gospel music at one of the area's many churches, and weekends in general are the liveliest time for walking around the neighborhood. If you do attend a church service, remember that most other people are there to worship and that they probably don't think of themselves or their church as tourist attractions. Be respectful of ushers, who may ask you to sit in a special section; don't take pictures; make a contribution when the collection comes around; and stay for the full service.

Sights to See

❻ **Abyssinian Baptist Church.** A famous family of ministers—Adam Clayton Powell Sr. and his son, Adam Clayton Powell Jr., the first black U.S. congressman—have presided over this Gothic-style bluestone church, which moved here in the 1920s. Stop in on Sunday to hear the gospel choir and the fiery sermon of its present activist minister, Reverend Calvin Butts. The baptismal font's Coptic Cross was a gift from Haile Selassie, then the emperor of Ethiopia. ✉ *132 Odell Clark Pl. W, at 138th St.,* ☎ *212/862–7474.* ⏲ *Sun. services 9 and 11.*

OFF THE BEATEN PATH

AMERICAN NUMISMATIC SOCIETY – The society, founded in 1858, displays its vast collection of coins and medals, including many that date from ancient civilizations, in one of several museums in the Audubon Terrace complex. ✉ *Broadway at 155th St.,* ☎ *212/234–3130.* 🎫 *Free (donations accepted).* ⏲ *Tues.–Sat. 9–4:30, Sun. 1–4.*

★ ❹ **Apollo Theatre.** When it opened in 1913, it was a burlesque hall for white audiences only, but after 1934 music greats such as Billie Holiday, Ella Fitzgerald, Duke Ellington, Count Basie, and Aretha Franklin performed at the Apollo. The theater fell on hard times and closed for a while in the early 1970s but has been renovated and in use again since 1983. The current Apollo's roster of stars isn't as consistent as it was in the past, but its regular Wednesday-night amateur performances at 7:30 are as wild and raucous as they were in the theater's heyday. The Wall of Fame, in the lobby, is a giant collage of Apollo entertainers. Included in an hour-long guided tour is a spirited, audience-participation-encouraged oral history of the theater, with many inside stories about past performers, as well as a chance to perform in a no-boos-allowed "Amateur Night" show. Tour goers also get to touch what's left of the Tree of Hope (☞ A Good Walk, *above*) as they walk across the stage. A gift shop sells Apollo clothing, gift items, jewelry, and recordings. ✉ *253 W. 125th St., between 7th and 8th Aves.,* ☎ *212/749–5838 for performance schedules; 212/222–0992 for tours.* 🎫 *Tours $8.*

NEED A BREAK? If you smell a sweet aroma, it's probably doughnuts frying at **Krispy Kreme** (✉ 280 W. 125th St., at Frederick Douglass Blvd., ☎ 212/531–0111), which has quickly become New York's favorite doughnut shop.

OFF THE BEATEN PATH **HAMILTON HEIGHTS AND CITY COLLEGE** – From Strivers' Row, you can see the beautiful neo-Gothic stone towers of City College along the ridge of Hamilton Heights (City College's center is 138th Street and Convent Avenue), and it's a short walk up the hill, on 141st Street past St. Nicholas Park, to this quiet neighborhood. City College's arched schist gates, green lawns, and white terra-cotta trim could easily be part of an Ivy League campus, but this has always been a public institution (tuition was free until the mid-1970s); the college moved to the George B. Post–designed campus from Lexington Avenue in 1907. Today, most classes are in the immense, institutional-like North Academic Building. The pretty row houses and churches that comprise Hamilton Heights were built around the turn of the century on land once owned by Alexander Hamilton. His Federal-style house, known as Hamilton Grange, is at 287 Convent Avenue (about 100 yards south of its original location). Wide sidewalks, quiet streets, green plantings, and well-maintained houses make this neighborhood a real charmer. ✉ *St. Nicholas Ave. to Hudson River, approx. 135th St. to 155th Sts.*

Langston Hughes House. From his top-floor apartment here, Harlem Renaissance master Langston Hughes (1902–1967) penned many of his Jesse B. Semple, or "Simple," columns about Harlem life, in addition to numerous plays, stories, and poems. Hughes lived in this Italianate brownstone from 1948 until his death in 1967. ✉ *20 E. 127th St., between 5th and Madison Aves.,* ☎ *212/534–5992.* ⏲ *By appointment only.*

2 **Marcus Garvey Park.** Originally Mount Morris Square, this rocky plot of land was renamed in 1973 after Marcus Garvey (1887–1940), who preached from nearby street corners and led the back-to-Africa movement. It's not known for being safe, so you should stay outside the park itself. From the street on its south side, however, you can see its three-tiered, cast-iron fire **watchtower** (Julius Kroel, 1856), the only remaining part of a now defunct citywide network useful in the days before the telephone. The handsome neoclassic row houses of the **Mount Morris Park Historic District** front the west side of the park and line side streets. ✉ *Interrupts 5th Ave. between 120th and 124th Sts., Madison Ave. to Mt. Morris Park W.*

1 **New York Public Library 115th Street Branch.** This bubbly Italian Renaissance–style row house was designed by McKim, Mead & White in 1908. The money for the construction of this and more than 60 other branch libraries was donated by Andrew Carnegie in 1901, and almost all of these were narrow, midblock structures—because Manhattan real estate was and still is so expensive. ✉ *203 W. 115th St., between 7th and 8th Aves.,* ☎ *212/666–9393.* ⏲ *Mon. and Wed. 10–6, Tues. noon–8, Thurs.–Fri. noon–6, Sat. 1–5.*

★ 5 **Schomburg Center for Research in Black Culture.** The New York Public Library's Division of Negro History bought the vast collection of Arturo Alfonso Schomburg, a scholar of black and Puerto Rican descent, in 1926. In 1940, after Schomburg died, this collection of more than 10,000 books, documents, paintings, and photographs recording black history was named after him. Later designated a research library, the ever-growing collection moved in 1980 into this modern redbrick building from the handsome Victorian one next door (designed by McKim, Mead & White and paid for by Andrew Carnegie), which is now an exhibit hall that's part of the Schomburg. Today more than 5 million items compose the collection. The expansion and renovation of the Schomburg building was completed in 1991 and includes the refurbished **American Negro Theatre** and increased gallery space. Just past the main entrance is an airy lobby, also the entrance to the **Langston Hughes Auditorium.** Inlaid in the floor is the artistic work *Rivers,* a memorial tribute to Hughes. The center's resources include rare manuscripts, art and artifacts, motion pictures, records, and videotapes. Regular exhibits in two halls, performing arts programs, and lectures continue to contribute to Harlem culture. ✉ *515 Lenox Ave., at 135th St.,* ☎ *212/491–2200.* 🎫 *Free.* ⏲ *Mon.–Wed. noon–8, Thurs.–Sat. 10–6; exhibits: Mon.–Wed. noon–6, Fri.–Sat. 10–6, Sun. 1–5.*

NEED A BREAK? A good place for coffee and maybe a bite to eat, whether it's grits, a delicious dessert, or fried chicken, is **Pan Pan Restaurant** (✉ 500 Lenox Ave., at 135th St., ☎ 212/926–4900), catercorner from the Schomburg Center.

★ 7 **Strivers' Row.** Since 1919 African-American doctors, lawyers, and other middle-class professionals have owned these elegant homes, designed nearly 30 years earlier by such notable architects as Stanford White (his neo-Renaissance contributions are on the north side of 139th Street). Behind each row are service alleys, a rare luxury in Manhattan. Musicians W. C. Handy ("The St. Louis Blues") and Eubie Blake ("I'm Just Wild About Harry") were among the residents here. The area, now officially known as the **St. Nicholas Historic District,** got its nickname because less affluent Harlemites felt that its residents were "striving" to become well-to-do. These quiet, tree-lined streets are a remarkable reminder of the Harlem that used to be. ✉ *W. 138th and W. 139th Sts. between 7th and 8th Aves.*

3 **Studio Museum in Harlem.** One of the community's showplaces, this small art museum houses a large collection of paintings, sculpture (there is a small, light-filled sculpture garden), and photographs (including historic photographs of Harlem by James Van Der Zee, popular in the 1930s, and works by Jacob Lawrence and Romare Bearden). The museum offers changing exhibitions, special lectures and programs, and its gift shop is full of black American and African-inspired books, posters, and jewelry. ✉ *144 W. 125th St., between 6th and 7th Aves.,* ☎ *212/864–4500.* 🎫 *$5, free 1st Sat. of month.* ⏲ *Wed.–Fri. 10–5, weekends 1–6.*

Sylvia's Soul Food Restaurant. Although there have been rumors about her retiring, personable Sylvia Woods still remains late most nights chatting with her customers. Southern specialties and cordiality are the rule here. Sylvia's own line of foods are now available at the restaurant and in neighborhood supermarkets. ✉ *328 Lenox Ave., between 126th and 127th Sts.,* ☎ *212/996–0660.*

Theresa Towers. Its former incarnation as Harlem's poshest place to stay, the Hotel Theresa, is still evident from the HT crests under some windows and a sign painted on its west side, which towers over the neighboring buildings. Fidel Castro left his midtown accommodations to stay here during his 1960 visit to the United Nations. Now an office building, Theresa Towers is home to several community organizations. ✉ *2090 Adam Clayton Powell Jr. Blvd., at 125th St.*

CHELSEA

Like the London district of the same name, New York's Chelsea has preserved its villagelike personality. Both have their quiet nooks where the 19th century seems to live on; both have been havens for artists, writers, and bohemians—New York's notables include Louise Bourgeois and Susan Sontag. Although London's Chelsea is a much more upscale chunk of real estate, New York's Chelsea is catching up, with town-house renovations reclaiming side-street blocks. Restored historic cast-iron buildings on 6th Avenue house superstore tenants that have revitalized the area. Seventh, 8th, and 9th avenues may never equal the shopping mecca of King's Road in London's Chelsea, but they have one-of-a-kind boutiques sprinkled among unassuming grocery stores and other remnants of the neighborhood's immigrant past.

Precisely speaking, the New York neighborhood was named not after Chelsea itself but after London's Chelsea Royal Hospital, an old soldiers' home. Running from 19th to 28th Street, from 8th Avenue west, it was one family's country estate until the 1830s, when Clement Clarke Moore saw the city moving north and decided to divide his land into lots. With an instinctive gift for urban planning, he dictated a pattern of development that ensured street after street of graceful row houses. A clergyman and classics professor, Moore is probably best known for his 1822 poem "A Visit from St. Nicholas"—"'Twas the night before Christmas. . . ." He composed it while bringing a sleigh full of Christmas treats from lower Manhattan to his Chelsea home.

Today's Chelsea extends west of 5th Avenue from 14th Street to 29th Street. Eighth Avenue now rivals Christopher Street in the West Village as a gay concourse: Shops, fitness clubs, and restaurants cater to a gay clientele on both sides of the street. Yet the thriving neighborhood also accommodates a multicultural population that has lived here for decades as well as a burgeoning art community west of 10th Avenue.

Numbers in the text correspond to numbers in the margin and on the Chelsea map.

A Good Walk

Begin on the corner of 6th Avenue and 18th Street. Sixth Avenue was once known as Ladies' Mile for its concentration of major department stores (also in the late 19th century, elevated tracks cast their shadow along this street). After the stores moved uptown in the early 1900s, the neighborhood declined, and the grand old store buildings stood empty and dilapidated. The 1990s, however, brought a renaissance to the Flatiron district to the east (☞ Murray Hill to Union Square, *above*), and 6th Avenue's grandest buildings once again purvey wares of all kinds. On the east side of the avenue, between 18th and 19th streets, stands the former **Siegel-Cooper Dry Goods Store** ①.

Between 18th and 19th streets on the west side of the avenue is the 1877 cast-iron **B. Altman Dry Goods Store** ②, now occupied by Today's Man. Continue walking north to 20th Street. The Gothic-style Church of the Holy Communion, an Episcopal house of worship dating from 1846, is on the northeast corner of the avenue. To the horror of some preservationists, it was converted several years ago into the Limelight, a notorious nightclub that is now closed (though, at press time, slated to reopen). On the west side of the avenue between 20th and 21st streets stands another former cast-iron retail palace, the **Hugh O'Neill Dry Goods Store** ③.

B. Altman Dry Goods Store, **2**
Chelsea Hotel, **12**
Chelsea Piers Sports and Entertainment Complex, **11**
Cushman Row, **8**
Dia Center for the Arts, **9**
404 West 20th Street, **7**
General Theological Seminary, **6**
Hugh O'Neill Dry Goods Store, **3**
Joyce Theater, **4**
London Terrace Apartments, **10**
St. Peter's Episcopal Church, **5**
Siegel-Cooper Dry Goods Store, **1**

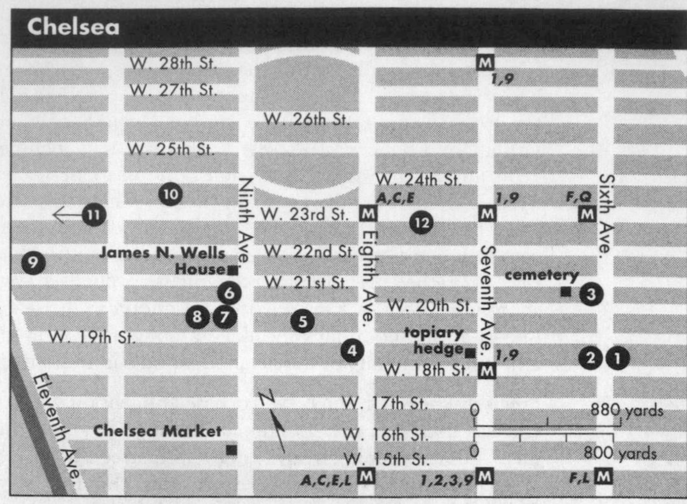

On weekends, 6th Avenue between 24th and 27th streets is the site of the city's longest-running outdoor flea market (☞ Chapter 10). Next, turn left from 6th Avenue onto 21st Street (on the south side of the street) for a look at the Third Cemetery of the Spanish & Portuguese Synagogue, Shearith Israel, these days a neglected spot with upset marble gravestones adjacent to a parking lot. In use from 1829 to 1851, it is one of three graveyards created in Manhattan by this congregation (☞ Greenwich Village *and* Little Italy and Chinatown, *below*).

At 7th Avenue cross the street and detour down to Chadwin House, No. 140, between 18th and 19th streets. In front of a very ordinary Chelsea building, stands a fabulous, Edward Scissorhands–like display of fanciful topiary.

Back up on 21st Street, continue west to 8th Avenue, where the Chelsea Historic District officially begins. Between 19th and 23rd streets, from 8th to 10th avenues, are examples of all of Chelsea's architectural periods: Greek and Gothic Revival, Italianate, and 1890s apartment buildings. To get a quick feel for 8th Avenue, head down to 19th Street to the Art Deco **Joyce Theater** ④, primarily a dance venue. Its presence, along with the burgeoning lesbian and gay community here, helped attract many good moderately priced restaurants to 8th Avenue.

On 20th Street between 8th and 9th avenues, you'll find the brick parish house, fieldstone church, and rectory of 19th-century **St. Peter's Episcopal Church** ⑤, which houses the well-known Atlantic Theater Company (☞ Chapter 5). Next, head west on 20th Street to 9th Avenue; on the west side of the avenue between 20th and 21st streets is the **General Theological Seminary** ⑥, the oldest Episcopal seminary in the United States. A block north at 21st street on the northwest corner is the **James N. Wells House,** once the home of the man who planned Chelsea. The café on its first floor is great for a neighborhood break.

Across the street from the seminary, **404 West 20th Street** ⑦ is the oldest house in the historic district. The residences next door, from 406 to 418 West 20th Street, are called **Cushman Row** ⑧ and are excellent examples of Greek Revival town houses. Farther down West 20th Street, stop to look at the fine Italianate houses from Nos. 446 to 450. The arched windows and doorways are hallmarks of this style, which prized circular forms—not least because the expense required to build them showed off the owner's wealth.

West 22nd Street has a string of handsome old row houses just east of 10th Avenue. No. 435 was the longtime residence of actors Geraldine Page and Rip Torn; they nicknamed it the Torn Page. In 1987, a year after winning an Oscar for *The Trip to Bountiful,* Page suffered a fatal heart attack here.

Between 10th and 11th avenues stretching from 20th to 29th Street, you can explore the **Chelsea galleries.** A good place to begin is 22nd Street, home to **Dia Center for the Arts** ⑨, the anchor of Chelsea's renaissance as an art community. Besides 22nd Street, 21st and 24th streets also have an ever-growing contingent of galleries large and small, including several relocated from SoHo. From the gallery zone return to 10th Avenue and walk to 23rd Street. Occupying the entire block between 10th and 9th avenues and 23rd and 24th streets, the **London Terrace Apartments** ⑩ is a vast 1930 complex containing 1,670 apartments. As you walk along 23rd Street, notice the lions on the arched entrances; from the side they look as if they're snarling, but from the front they have wide grins.

If you walk west on 23rd Street as far as you can go, you'll come to the mammoth new **Chelsea Piers Sports and Entertainment Complex** ⑪, where you can take a breath of sea air and look at Chelsea's slice of the Hudson River waterfront. The entrance is at 23rd Street. If you don't head to the river, continue east on 23rd Street. During the 1880s and Gay '90s, the street was the heart of the entertainment district, lined with theaters, music halls, and beer gardens. Today it is an undistinguished commercial thoroughfare. Among the relics of its proud past is the **Chelsea Hotel** ⑫.

TIMING

Allow yourself at least three to four hours to explore Chelsea. If your schedule permits, plan to spend the day so you have ample time to browse the stores and galleries and have a leisurely lunch.

Sights to See

❷ **B. Altman Dry Goods Store.** Built in 1877 with additions in 1887 and 1910, this ornate cast-iron giant originally housed B. Altman Dry Goods until the business moved in 1906 to its imposing quarters at 5th Avenue and 34th Street (☞ Murray Hill to Union Square, *above*). ✉ *621 6th Ave., between 18th and 19th Sts.*

Chelsea galleries. Extending from 20th to 29th Street between 10th and 11th avenues, the Chelsea art scene has expanded dramatically in the past couple of years. Several of the most recent additions are large, upscale places. Because each gallery keeps its own hours, it's best to call ahead about openings and closings. Begin exploring on 22nd Street, which has the ☞ **Dia Center for the Arts** and seven other galleries. You'll probably want to stop at the **Matthew Marks Gallery** (✉ 522 W. 22nd St., ☎ 212/243–0200) and three spaces at 530 West 22nd Street: **Morris-Healy** (☎ 212/243–3753), the **Pat Hearn Gallery** (☎ 212/727–7366), and **Annina Nosei** (☎ 212/741–8695). At 504 West 22nd Street you'll find the **Jessica Fredericks Gallery** (☎ 212/633–6555), **Xavier La Boulbenne** (☎ 212/462–4111), and **Linda Kirkland Gallery** (☎ 212/627–3930), all featuring younger artists; the same building also houses **Art Resources Transfer** (☎ 212/691–5956), which publishes books based on conversations with artists and sponsors art-related video screenings and readings. There are also an exhibition space and a bookstore.

Contemporary art mavens will also want to visit SoHo transplant the **Paula Cooper Gallery** (⊠ 534 W. 21st St., ☎ 212/255–1105), and on 24th Street also between 10th and 11th avenues, **Barbara Gladstone** (⊠ 515 W. 24th St. ☎ 212/206–9300), **Metro Pictures** (⊠ 519 W. 24th St., ☎ 212/206–7100), and **Matthew Marks**'s second Chelsea gallery space (⊠ 523 W. 24th St., ☎ 212/243–0200); the latter three major players, known collectively as M. G. M., all represent high-profile creators. Among the smaller, no-frills operations in the area are **Clementine Gallery** (⊠ 526 W. 26th St., 2nd floor, between 10th and 11th Aves., ☎ 212/243–5937) in a building overflowing with artists' and photographers' studios and **Viewing Room Exhibitions** (⊠ 515 W. 29th St., 3rd floor, between 10th and 11th Aves., ☎ 212/290–8117), run by two painters.

12 **Chelsea Hotel.** Constructed of red brick with lacy wrought-iron balconies and a mansard roof, this 11-story neighborhood landmark opened in 1884 as a cooperative apartment house. It became a hotel in 1905, although it has always catered to long-term tenants, with a tradition of broad-mindedness that has attracted many creative types. Its literary roll call of former live-ins includes Mark Twain, Eugene O'Neill, O. Henry, Thomas Wolfe, Tennessee Williams, Vladimir Nabokov, Mary McCarthy, Brendan Behan, Arthur Miller, Dylan Thomas, William S. Burroughs, and Arthur C. Clarke (who wrote the script for *2001: A Space Odyssey* while living here). In 1966 Andy Warhol filmed artist Brigid Polk in her Chelsea Hotel room, which eventually became *The Chelsea Girls*. More recently, the hotel was seen on screen in *I Shot Andy Warhol* (1996) and *Sid and Nancy* (1986), a dramatization of the true-life Chelsea Hotel murder of Nancy Spungen, who was stabbed to death here, allegedly by her boyfriend, drugged punk rocker Sid Vicious. The shabby aura of the Chelsea Hotel is part of its allure. Read the commemorative plaques outside and then step into the lobby to see the 10-floor-high, skylighted open stairwell and the unusual artwork, some of it donated in lieu of rent by residents down on their luck. ⊠ *222 W. 23rd St., between 7th and 8th Aves.,* ☎ *212/243–3700.*

11 **Chelsea Piers Sports and Entertainment Complex.** Beginning in 1910, the Chelsea Piers were the launching point for a new generation of big ocean liners; they were also the destination of the *Titanic,* which never arrived, and the departure point for the last sailing of the *Lusitania,* the British liner sunk by a German submarine in 1915. Decades-long neglect ended with the transformation of the four piers' old buildings along the Hudson River into a 1.7-million-square-ft state-of-the-art facility, providing a huge variety of activities (☞ Chapter 9 for details). The complex has a wall of historical photographs, sporting goods shops, and several restaurants with river views, including the Crab House (☞ Chapter 6) and the Chelsea Brewing Company. ⊠ *Piers 59–62 on the Hudson River from 17th to 23rd Sts.; entrance at 23rd St.,* ☎ *212/336–6666.*

8 **Cushman Row.** Built by dry-goods merchant Don Alonzo Cushman, a friend of Clement Clarke Moore, who made a fortune developing Chelsea, this string of homes between 9th and 10th avenues represents some of the country's most perfect examples of Greek Revival town houses. The residences retain such original details as small wreath-encircled attic windows, deeply recessed doorways with brownstone frames, and striking iron balustrades and fences. Pineapples, a traditional symbol of welcome, perch atop the newels in front of Nos. 416 and 418. ⊠ *406–418 W. 20th St., between 9th and 10th Aves.*

★ **9** **Dia Center for the Arts.** This facility provides contemporary artists with the chance to develop new work or to mount an organized exhibit on a full floor for extended time periods, usually an entire year. Besides installations by diverse artists, you might find an exhibit from Dia's permanent collection, which includes creations by Joseph Beuys, Walter De Maria, Dan Flavin, Blinky Palermo, Cy Twombly, Richard Serra, and Andy Warhol. Installed outside on the roof is a fascinating exhibition designed by Dan Graham, which consists of a two-way mirror glass cylinder inside a cube. ✉ *548 W. 22nd St., between 10th and 11th Aves.,* ☎ *212/989–5912.* 💵 *$4 (suggested donation).* ⏲ *Thurs.–Sun. noon–6.*

NEED A BREAK? The shiny **Empire Diner** (✉ 210 10th Ave., ☎ 212/243–2736) gleefully lights up the corner of 22nd Street and 10th Avenue. Though the food is somewhat overpriced, the authentic diner atmosphere here is cheerful and friendly, and it's open 24 hours.

7 **404 West 20th Street.** At 10th Avenue is the oldest house in the historic district, which was built between 1829 and 1830 in the Federal style. It still has one clapboard side wall; over the years it acquired a Greek Revival doorway and Italianate windows on the parlor floor, and the roof was raised one story.

6 **General Theological Seminary.** When Chelsea developer Clement Clarke Moore divided his estate, he deeded a large section to this Episcopal seminary, where he had taught Hebrew and Greek; the religious oasis still occupies a block-long stretch. The stoutly fenced campus is accessible through the modern building on 9th Avenue; during off-hours you can view the grounds from West 20th Street. The 1836 **West Building** is a fine early example of Gothic Revival architecture. Most of the rest of the complex was completed in 1883–1902, when the school hired architect Charles Coolidge Haight to design, in the style known as English Collegiate Gothic, which Haight had pioneered, a campus that would rival those of most other American colleges of the day. Today the quiet interior gardens are a welcome green spot in park-poor Chelsea. A 1960s era building facing 9th Avenue houses administrative offices, a bookstore, and the 210,000-volume **St. Mark's Library,** generally considered the nation's greatest ecclesiastical library; it has the world's largest collection of Latin Bibles. ✉ *175 9th Ave., at W. 20th St.,* ☎ *212/243–5150.* ⏲ *Grounds weekdays noon–3; call for information on using the library.*

3 **Hugh O'Neill Dry Goods Store.** Constructed in 1875, this cast-iron building, originally an emporium, features Corinthian columns and pilasters; its corner towers were once topped with huge bulbous domes. The name of the original tenant is proudly displayed on the pediment. ✉ *655–671 6th Ave., between 20th and 21st Sts.*

James N. Wells House. This 1833 2½-story brick house was the home of Clement Clarke Moore's property manager, the man who planned Chelsea. Wells was responsible for the strict housing codes that created the elegant residential neighborhood by prohibiting stables and manure piles and requiring tree planting. ✉ *401 W. 21st St.*

NEED A BREAK? At **Le Gamin** (✉ 183 9th Ave., at 21st St., ☎ 212/243–8864), a rustic French café where soup-bowl size café au lait, crepes, and salads are de rigueur, you can sit for hours without being disturbed.

4 **Joyce Theater.** The former Elgin movie house, built in 1942, was gutted and in 1982 transformed into this sleek modern theater that pays tribute to its Art Deco origins. It is one of the city's leading modern-dance venues (☞ Chapter 5). ✉ *175 8th Ave., at W. 19th St.,* ☎ *212/242–0800.*

10 **London Terrace Apartments.** When this vast block-long brick complex first opened in 1930, the doormen dressed as London bobbies. London Terrace is actually made up of two rows of 14 interconnected 16-story buildings, which enclose a private garden. ✉ *W. 23rd to W. 24th Sts. between 9th and 10th Aves.*

5 **St. Peter's Episcopal Church.** St. Peter's Greek Revival–style **rectory** (1832), to the right of the main church, originally served as the sanctuary. Four years after it was built, the congregation had already laid foundations for a bigger church when, it is said, a vestryman returned from England bursting with excitement over the Gothic Revival that had just taken hold there. The fieldstone **church** that resulted is one of New York's earliest examples of Gothic Revival architecture. The church "welcomes all faiths and uncertain faiths." To the left of the church, the brick **parish hall** is an example of the so-called Victorian Gothic style; its churchlike front was added in 1871. It's now the home of the Atlantic Theater Company, founded by playwright David Mamet (☞ Chapter 5). The wrought-iron fence framing the three buildings once enclosed St. Paul's Chapel downtown (☞ The Seaport and the Courts, *below*). ✉ *344 W. 20th St., between 8th and 9th Aves.,* ☎ *212/929–2390.*

1 **Siegel-Cooper Dry Goods Store.** Built in 1896, much later than its neighbors, this impressive building adorned with glazed terra-cotta encompasses 15½ acres of space, yet it was built in only five months. In its retail heyday, the store's main floor featured an immense fountain—a circular marble terrace with an enormous white-marble-and-brass replica of *The Republic,* the statue Daniel Chester French displayed at the 1883 Chicago World's Fair—which became a favorite rendezvous point for New Yorkers. During World War I the building was a military hospital. The recent renovation brought back attention to its splendid ornamentation: round wreathed windows, Corinthian and Doric pilasters, Romanesque rounded arches, lion heads, and more. Today its principal tenants are Bed, Bath & Beyond, Filene's Basement, and T. J. Maxx. ✉ *620 6th Ave., between 18th and 19th Sts.*

NEED A BREAK? **La Petite Abeille** (✉ 107 W. 18th St., ☎ 212/604–9350), just west of 6th Avenue, serves tasty café standards in addition to traditional Belgian waffles, chocolates, and cookies.

GREENWICH VILLAGE

Greenwich Village, which New Yorkers almost invariably speak of simply as "the Village," enjoyed a raffish reputation for years. Originally a rural outpost of the city—a haven for New Yorkers during early 19th-century smallpox and yellow fever epidemics—many of its blocks still look somewhat pastoral, with brick town houses and low rises, tiny green parks and hidden courtyards, and a crazy-quilt pattern of narrow, tree-lined streets (some of which follow long-ago cow paths). In the mid-19th century, however, as the city spread north of 14th Street, the Village became the province of immigrants, bohemians, and students (New York University [NYU], today the nation's largest private university, was planted next to Washington Square in 1831). Its politics were radical and its attitudes tolerant, which is one reason it remains a home to such a large lesbian and gay community.

Several generations of writers and artists have lived and worked here: in the 19th century, Henry James, Edgar Allan Poe, Mark Twain, Walt Whitman, and Stephen Crane; at the turn of the century, O. Henry, Edith Wharton, Theodore Dreiser, and Hart Crane; and during the 1920s and '30s, John Dos Passos, Norman Rockwell, Sinclair Lewis, John Reed, Eugene O'Neill, Edward Hopper, and Edna St. Vincent Millay. In the late 1940s and early 1950s, the Abstract Expressionist painters Franz Kline, Jackson Pollock, Mark Rothko, and Willem de Kooning congregated here, as did the Beat writers Jack Kerouac, Allen Ginsberg, and Lawrence Ferlinghetti. The 1960s brought folk musicians and poets, notably Bob Dylan and Peter, Paul, and Mary.

Today, block for block, the Village is still one of the most vibrant parts of the city. Well-heeled professionals occupy high-rent apartments and town houses side by side with bohemian, longtime residents, who pay cheap rents thanks to rent-control laws, as well as NYU students. Locals and tourists rub elbows at dozens of small restaurants, cafés spill out onto sidewalks, and an endless variety of small shops please everyone. Except for the area immediately around the west end of Christopher Street, where young outer-borough gays congregate and a few adult-entertainment shops remain, the Village is as scrubbed as posher neighborhoods.

Numbers in the text correspond to numbers in the margin and on the Greenwich Village and the East Village map.

A Good Walk

Begin your tour of Greenwich Village at the foot of 5th Avenue at Washington Arch in **Washington Square** ①, a hugely popular 9½-acre park that provides a neighborhood oasis for locals and tourists alike. Most buildings bordering Washington Square belong to NYU. On Washington Square North, between University Place and MacDougal Street, stretches the **Row** ②, composed of two blocks of lovingly preserved Greek Revival and Federal-style town houses.

On the east side of the square, you can take in a contemporary art exhibit at **Grey Art Gallery** ③, housed in NYU's main building. If you walk to the south side of the square, a trio of red sandstone hulks represents an abortive 1960s attempt to create a unified campus look for NYU, as envisioned by architects Philip Johnson and Richard Foster. At one time plans called for all the Washington Square buildings to be refaced in this red stone; fortunately, the cost proved prohibitive. At La Guardia Place and Washington Square South, the undistinguished modern Loeb Student Center stands on the site of a famous boardinghouse that had been nicknamed the House of Genius for the talented writers who lived there over the years: Theodore Dreiser, John Dos Passos, and Eugene O'Neill, among others. A block west of the student center, at the corner of Washington Square South and Thompson Street, is the square-towered **Judson Memorial Church** ④.

From Washington Square Arch and the park, cross Washington Square North to the east side of 5th Avenue. On your right, at the northeast corner of Washington Square North and 5th Avenue, is the portico entrance to 7–13 Washington Square North. Beyond the white columns of this entrance is the small, attractive Willy's Garden. A statue of Miguel de Cervantes, the author of *Don Quixote,* stands at the far end. The likeness, cast in 1724, was a gift from the mayor of Madrid.

Another half a block north, on the east side of 5th Avenue, is **Washington Mews,** a cobblestone private street. A similar Village mews, MacDougal Alley, can be found between 8th Street and the square just off MacDougal Street, one block west. Continue up the west side of 5th

Greenwich Village and the East Village

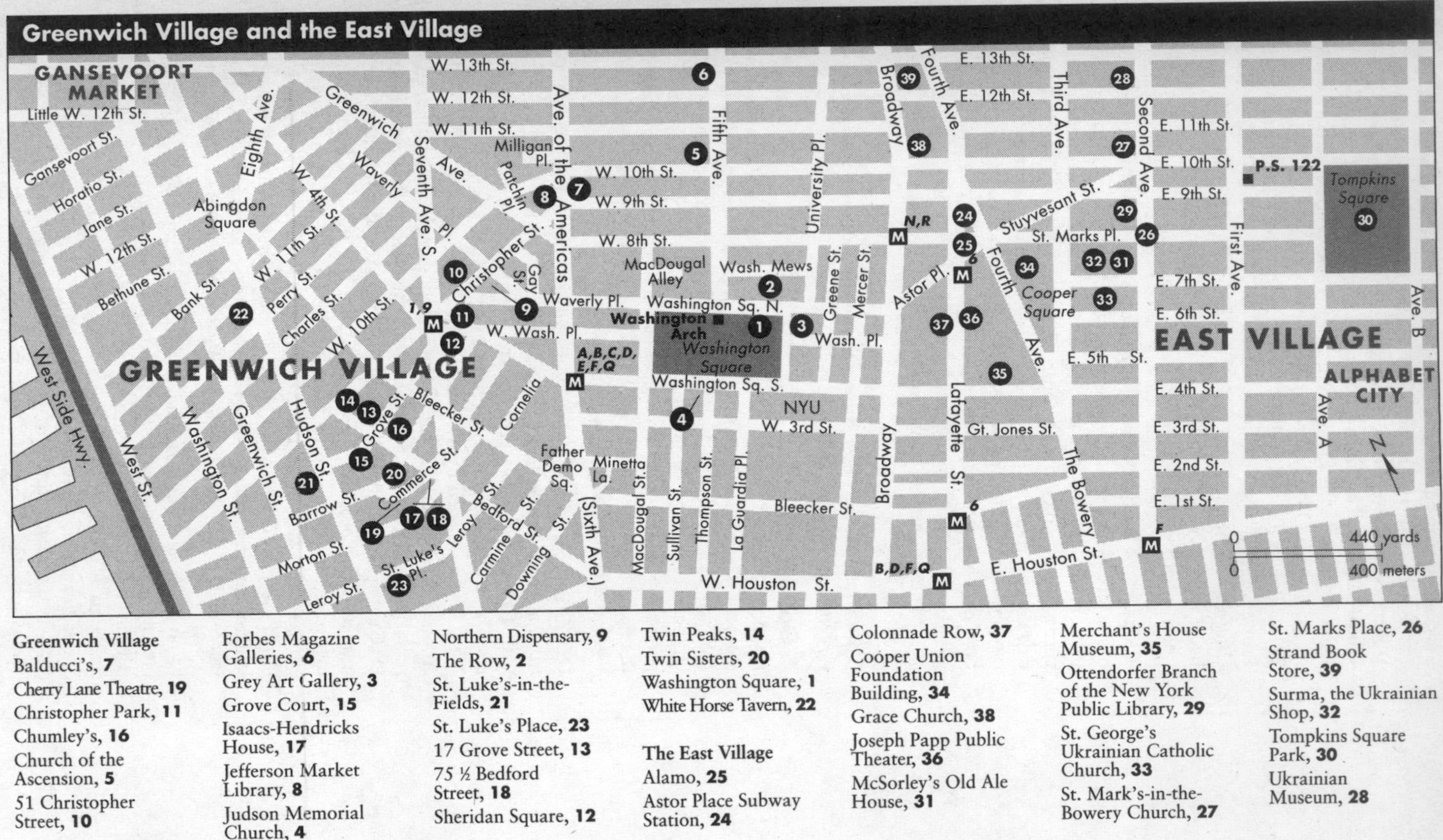

Greenwich Village
Balducci's, **7**
Cherry Lane Theatre, **19**
Christopher Park, **11**
Chumley's, **16**
Church of the Ascension, **5**
51 Christopher Street, **10**
Forbes Magazine Galleries, **6**
Grey Art Gallery, **3**
Grove Court, **15**
Isaacs-Hendricks House, **17**
Jefferson Market Library, **8**
Judson Memorial Church, **4**
Northern Dispensary, **9**
The Row, **2**
St. Luke's-in-the-Fields, **21**
St. Luke's Place, **23**
17 Grove Street, **13**
75 ½ Bedford Street, **18**
Sheridan Square, **12**
Twin Peaks, **14**
Twin Sisters, **20**
Washington Square, **1**
White Horse Tavern, **22**

The East Village
Alamo, **25**
Astor Place Subway Station, **24**
Colonnade Row, **37**
Cooper Union Foundation Building, **34**
Grace Church, **38**
Joseph Papp Public Theater, **36**
McSorley's Old Ale House, **31**
Merchant's House Museum, **35**
Ottendorfer Branch of the New York Public Library, **29**
St. George's Ukrainian Catholic Church, **33**
St. Mark's-in-the-Bowery Church, **27**
St. Marks Place, **26**
Strand Book Store, **39**
Surma, the Ukrainian Shop, **32**
Tompkins Square Park, **30**
Ukrainian Museum, **28**

Avenue; you'll pass the **Church of the Ascension** ⑤, a Gothic Revival brownstone building. At 5th Avenue and 12th Street you can stop in the **Forbes Magazine Galleries** ⑥, which house the late publisher Malcolm Forbes's unusual personal collection.

Backtrack on 5th Avenue to West 11th Street and turn right to see one of the best examples of a Village town-house block. One exception to the general 19th-century redbrick look is the modern, angled front window of 18 West 11th Street, usually occupied by a stuffed bear whose outfit changes from day to day. This house was built after the original was destroyed in a 1970 explosion of a basement bomb factory, which had been started by members of the radical Weather Underground faction. At the end of the block, behind a low gray-stone wall on the south side of the street, is the Second Shearith Israel graveyard, used by the country's oldest Jewish congregation after the original cemetery in Chinatown (☞ Little Italy and Chinatown, *below*) and before the one in Chelsea (☞ Chelsea, *above*).

On Avenue of the Americas (6th Avenue), turn left to sample the wares at **Balducci's** ⑦, a high-end gourmet food store. Directly opposite, the triangle formed by West 10th Street, 6th Avenue, and Greenwich Avenue originally held a market, a jail, and the magnificent towered courthouse that is now the **Jefferson Market Library** ⑧. Just west of 6th Avenue on 10th Street is the wrought-iron gateway to a tiny courtyard called **Patchin Place**; around the corner, on 6th Avenue just north of 10th Street, is a similar cul-de-sac, Milligan Place.

Next, proceed to Christopher Street, which veers off from the south end of the library triangle. Christopher Street has long been the symbolic heart of New York's gay and lesbian community. Before you proceed just a few steps, you'll see **Gay Street** on your left. This quiet curved thoroughfare of early 19th-century row houses was immortalized in Ruth McKinney's book *My Sister Eileen.* Continuing west on Christopher Street, cross Waverly Place, where on your left you'll pass the 1831 brick **Northern Dispensary** ⑨ building, which at one time provided health care to poor neighborhood residents. Across the street is **51 Christopher Street** ⑩, where the historic Stonewall riots marked the beginning of the gay rights movement. Across the street is a green triangle named **Christopher Park** ⑪, not to be confused with **Sheridan Square** ⑫, another landscaped triangle to the south.

Across the busy intersection of 7th Avenue South, Christopher Street has many bars and stores; several cater to a gay clientele, but the street is by no means off-limits to other people. Two shops worth a visit are McNulty's Tea and Coffee Co. (✉ 109 Christopher St.), with a large variety of tea and coffee blends, and Li-Lac Chocolate Shop (✉ 120 Christopher St.), a longtime favorite in the area for its homemade chocolate and butter crunch. West of 7th Avenue South, the Village turns into a picture-book town of twisting tree-lined streets, quaint houses, and tiny restaurants. Follow Grove Street from Sheridan Square west past the house where Thomas Paine died (✉ 59 Grove St.)—now the site of Marie's Crisis Cafe—and the boyhood home of poet Hart Crane (✉ 45 Grove St.). At this point you'll be close to the intersection of Grove and Bleecker streets. You may now choose to take a leisurely stroll along the portion of Bleecker Street that extends west of 7th Avenue South from Grove to Bank Street, heading northwest toward Abingdon Square. This section of Bleecker Street is full of crafts and antiques shops, coffeehouses, and small restaurants.

If you choose to forego Bleecker Street, continue your walk west on Grove Street. The secluded intersection of Grove and Bedford streets seems to have fallen through a time warp into the 19th century. On the northeast corner stands **17 Grove Street** ⑬, one of the few remaining clapboard structures in Manhattan. Behind it, at 102 Bedford Street, is **Twin Peaks** ⑭, an early 19th-century house that resembles a Swiss chalet. Heading west, Grove Street curves in front of the iron gate of **Grove Court** ⑮, a group of mid-19th-century brick-front residences.

At Bedford Street, turn left and walk down until you get to No. 86. Behind the unmarked door is **Chumley's** ⑯, a former speakeasy. Walk a couple of blocks farther down to the **Isaacs-Hendricks House** ⑰, the oldest house in the Village. The place next door, **75½ Bedford Street** ⑱, at 9½ ft wide, is New York's narrowest house. Bedford Street intersects Commerce Street, one of the Village's most romantic untrod lanes, and home to the historic **Cherry Lane Theater** ⑲. Across the street stand two nearly identical brick houses separated by a garden and popularly known as the **Twin Sisters** ⑳. Across the street, Grange Hall (⊠ 50 Commerce St.) serves comfort food in a restored speakeasy (☞ Chapter 6).

Turn left from Commerce Street onto Barrow Street, which next intersects with Hudson Street, so named because this was originally the bank of the Hudson River. The block to the northwest is owned by **St. Luke's-in-the-Fields** ㉑, built in 1822 as a country chapel for downtown's Trinity Church. Writer Bret Harte once lived at 487 Hudson Street, at the end of the row. If your feet are getting tired, you can head north on Hudson Street for four blocks and take a rest at the legendary **White Horse Tavern** ㉒, at 11th Street.

If you choose to continue, head south on Hudson Street for two blocks until you reach Leroy Street. East of Hudson Street, for the length of a block, Leroy Street becomes **St. Luke's Place** ㉓, a row of classic 1860s town houses shaded by graceful gingko trees. Across 7th Avenue South, St. Luke's Place becomes Leroy Street again, which terminates in an old Italian neighborhood at Bleecker Street. Amazingly unchanged amid all the Village gentrification, Bleecker Street between 6th and 7th avenues seems more vital these days than Little Italy does. For authentic Italian ambience, stop into one of the fragrant Italian bakeries, such as A. Zito & Sons (⊠ 259 Bleecker St.) and Rocco's (⊠ 243 Bleecker St.), or look inside the old-style butcher shops, such as Ottomanelli & Sons (⊠ 285 Bleecker St.) and Faicco's (⊠ 260 Bleecker St.). New Yorkers swear by John's Pizzeria (⊠ 278 Bleecker St.), the original of what are now four branches citywide. Be forewarned, however: no slices; whole pies only.

Head east on Bleecker, and you'll come to Father Demo Square (at Bleecker Street and 6th Avenue). Across Bleecker Street you'll see the Church of Our Lady of Pompeii, where Mother Cabrini, a naturalized Italian immigrant who became the first American saint, often prayed. Head up 6th Avenue to 3rd Street and check out the playground caged there within a chain-link fence. NBA stars of tomorrow learn their moves on this patch of asphalt, where city-style basketball is played all afternoon and evening in all but the very coldest weather. Return along Washington Square South to MacDougal Street and turn right. The Provincetown Playhouse (⊠ 133 MacDougal St.) premiered many of Eugene O'Neill's plays. Louisa May Alcott wrote *Little Women* while living at 130–132 MacDougal Street. The two houses at 127 and 129 MacDougal Street were built for Aaron Burr in 1829; notice the pineapple newel posts, a symbol of hospitality.

At Minetta Tavern (⊠ 113 MacDougal St.), a venerable Village watering hole, turn right onto Minetta Lane, which leads to narrow Minetta Street, another former speakeasy alley. Both streets follow the course of Minetta Brook, which once flowed through this neighborhood and still bubbles deep beneath the pavement. The foot of Minetta Street returns you to the corner of 6th Avenue and Bleecker Street, where you will have reached the stomping grounds of 1960s-era folksingers (many performed at the now-defunct Folk City, one block north on West 3rd Street). This area still attracts a young crowd—partly because of the proximity of NYU—to its cafés, bars, jazz clubs, coffeehouses, theaters, and cabarets, not to mention its long row of unpretentious ethnic restaurants.

TIMING

Greenwich Village moves at a slower pace than the rest of the city, so allow yourself most of a day to explore its backstreets and stop at shops and cafés.

Sights to See

7 **Balducci's.** From the vegetable stand of the late Louis Balducci Sr. sprouted this full-service gourmet food store. Along with more than 80 Italian cheeses and 50 kinds of bread, the family-owned enterprise features imported Italian specialties and first-rate take-out foods. ⊠ *121 6th Ave., at 9th St.,* ☎ *212/673–2600.*

19 **Cherry Lane Theatre.** One of the original off-Broadway houses, this 1817 building was converted into a theater in 1923, thanks to Edna St. Vincent Millay and a group of theater artists. Over the years it hosted American premieres of works by O'Neill, Beckett, Ionesco, Albee, Pinter, and Mamet. The playhouse was modernized in 1996, but it still contains the original audience seats. At nearby 48 Commerce Street stands a handsome, renovated Greek Revival building originally constructed in 1844 for merchant prince Alexander T. Stewart. ⊠ *38 Commerce St.,* ☎ *212/989–2020.*

11 **Christopher Park.** Sometimes mistaken for ☞ **Sheridan Square,** this pleasant triangular oasis contains a bronze statue of Civil War general Philip Sheridan and striking sculptures designed by George Segal of a lesbian couple sitting on a bench and gay male partners standing near them; both couples appear to be having a conversation. ⊠ *Bordered by Washington Pl. and Grove and Christopher Sts.*

16 **Chumley's.** A speakeasy during the Prohibition era, this still-secret tavern behind an unmarked door on Bedford Street retains its original ambience with oak booths, a fireplace once used by a blacksmith, and subdued lighting. For years Chumley's attracted a literary clientele (John Steinbeck, Ernest Hemingway, Edna Ferber, Simone de Beauvoir, and Jack Kerouac), and the book covers of their publications were proudly displayed (and still appear) on the walls. There's another "secret" entrance in Pamela Court, accessed at 58 Barrow Street around the corner. ⊠ *86 Bedford St., near Barrow St.,* ☎ *212/675–4449.*

5 **Church of the Ascension.** A mural depicting the Ascension of Jesus and stained-glass windows by John LaFarge, as well as a marble altar sculpture by Louis Saint-Gaudens, are the highlights of this 1841 Gothic Revival–style brownstone church designed by Richard Upjohn. In 1844 President John Tyler married Julia Gardiner here. ⊠ *36–38 5th Ave., at W. 10th St.,* ☎ *212/254–8620.*

10 **51 Christopher Street.** On June 27, 1969, a gay bar at this address named the Stonewall Inn was the site of a clash between gay men (some in drag) and the New York City police. As the bar's patrons were being

forced into police wagons, sympathetic gay onlookers protested and started fighting back, throwing beer bottles and garbage cans. Every June the Stonewall Riots are commemorated around the world with parades and celebrations that honor the gay rights movement. A clothing store now occupies the site of the bar; a more recent bar named Stonewall is next door at No. 53.

★ 6 **Forbes Magazine Galleries.** The late publisher Malcolm Forbes's idiosyncratic personal collection fills the ground floor of the limestone Forbes Magazine Building, once the home of Macmillan Publishing. Exhibits change in the large painting gallery and one of two autograph galleries, while permanent highlights include U.S. presidential papers, more than 500 intricate model boats, 12,000 toy soldiers, and some of the oldest Monopoly game sets ever made. Perhaps the most memorable permanent display contains exquisite items created by the House of Fabergé, including 12 jeweled eggs designed for the last of the Russian czars. ✉ *62 5th Ave., at 12th St.,* ☎ *212/206–5548.* *Free.* *Tues.–Wed. and Fri.–Sat. 10–4.*

NEED A BREAK? If you're yearning for a *pain au chocolat* or a madeleine, stop by **Marquet Patisserie** (✉ 15 E. 12th St., ☎ 212/229–9313), a sleek, friendly café that serves irresistible French pastries, great coffee, and satisfying sandwiches, salads, and quiches.

OFF THE BEATEN PATH **GANSEVOORT MARKET** – Each morning otherwise undistinguished warehouse buildings become the meat market for the city's retailers and restaurants. Racks of carcasses make a fascinating, if not very pretty, sight. Action peaks on weekdays between 5 AM and 9 AM. ✉ *Between 9th Ave. and the Hudson River, from Gansevoort St. north to 14th St.*

Gay Street. A curved lane lined with small row houses circa 1810, one-block-long Gay Street was originally a black neighborhood and later a strip of speakeasies. In the 1930s the short thoroughfare and nearby Christopher Street became famous nationwide when Ruth McKinney published her somewhat zany autobiographical stories in the *New Yorker,* based on what happened when she and her sister moved to Greenwich Village from Ohio (they appeared in book form as *My Sister Eileen* in 1938). McKinney wrote in the basement of No. 14. Also on Gay Street, Howdy Doody was designed in the basement of No. 12. ✉ *Between Christopher St. and Waverly Pl.*

3 **Grey Art Gallery.** On the east side of Washington Square, New York University's main building contains a welcoming street-level space with changing exhibitions usually devoted to contemporary art. ✉ *100 Washington Sq. E,* ☎ *212/998–6780.* *$2.50 (suggested donation).* *Tues. and Thurs.–Fri. 11–6, Wed. 11–8, Sat. 11–5.*

15 **Grove Court.** Built between 1853 and 1854, this enclave of brick-front town houses was intended originally as apartments for employees at neighborhood hotels. Grove Court used to be called Mixed Ale Alley because of the residents' propensity to pool beverages brought from work. It now houses a more affluent crowd. ✉ *10–12 Grove St.*

17 **Isaacs-Hendricks House.** Originally built as a Federal-style wood-frame residence in 1799, this immaculate structure is the oldest remaining house in Greenwich Village. Its first owner, Joshua Issacs, a wholesale merchant, lost the farmhouse to creditors; the building then belonged to copper supplier Harmon Hendricks. The village landmark was remodeled twice; it received its brick face in 1836, and the third floor was added in 1928. ✉ *77 Bedford St., at Commerce St.*

8 **Jefferson Market Library.** Critics variously termed this magnificent towered courthouse's hodgepodge of styles Venetian, Victorian, or Italian; Villagers, noting the alternating wide bands of red brick and narrow strips of granite, dubbed it the "lean bacon style." Over the years the structure has housed a number of government agencies (public works, civil defense, census bureau, police academy); it was on the verge of demolition when local activists saved it and turned it into a public library in 1967. Note the fountain at the corner of West 10th Street and 6th Avenue, and the seal of the City of New York on the east front; inside are handsome interior doorways and a graceful circular stairway. If the gate is open, visit the flower garden behind the library, a project run by local green thumbs. ✉ *425 6th Ave., at 10th St.,* ☎ *212/243–4334.*

4 **Judson Memorial Church.** Designed by celebrated architect Stanford White, this Italian Roman-Renaissance church has long attracted a congregation interested in the arts and community activism. Funded by the Astor family and John D. Rockefeller and constructed in 1892, the yellow-brick and limestone building was the brainchild of Edward Judson, who hoped to reach out to the poor immigrants in adjacent Little Italy. The church has stained-glass windows designed by John LaFarge and a 10-story campanile. ✉ *51–54 Washington Sq. S, at Thompson St.,* ☎ *212/477–0351.* ⏲ *To gain access to sanctuary weekdays 10–6, inquire at parish office, 241 Thompson St.; also open for Sun. service at 11.*

9 **Northern Dispensary.** Constructed for $4,700 in 1831, this triangular Georgian brick building originally served as a health-care clinic for indigent Villagers. Edgar Allan Poe was a frequent patient. In more recent times the structure has housed a dental clinic and a nursing home for AIDS patients. Note that the Dispensary has *one* side on *two* streets (Grove and Christopher streets where they meet) and *two* sides facing *one* street—Waverly Place, which splits in two directions. ✉ *165 Waverly Pl.*

Patchin Place. This charming cul-de-sac off 10th Street between Greenwich and 6th avenues has 10 miniature row houses dating from 1848. Around the corner on 6th Avenue is a similar dead-end street, **Milligan Place,** consisting of four small homes completed in 1852. The houses in both quiet enclaves were originally built for the waiters (mostly Basques) who worked at 5th Avenue's high-society Brevoort Hotel, long demolished. Patchin Place later attracted numerous writers, including Theodore Dreiser, e.e. cummings, Jane Bowles, and Djuna Barnes. John Reed and Louise Bryant also lived there. Milligan Place eventually became the address for several playwrights, including Eugene O'Neill.

★ 2 **The Row.** Built from 1829 through 1839, this series of beautifully preserved Greek Revival town houses along Washington Square North, on the two blocks between University Place and MacDougal Street, once belonged to merchants and bankers; now the buildings serve as NYU offices and faculty housing. Developers were not so tactful when they demolished 18 Washington Square North, once the home of Henry James's grandmother, which he later used as the setting for his novel *Washington Square* (Henry himself was born just off the square, in a long-gone house on Washington Place). The oldest building on the block, 20 Washington Square North, was constructed in 1829 in the Federal style, and with Flemish bond brickwork—alternate bricks inserted with the smaller surface (headers) facing out—which before 1830 was considered the best way to build stable walls. ✉ *1–13 Washington Sq.*

N, between University Pl. and 5th Ave.; 19–26 Washington Sq. N, between 5th Ave. and MacDougal St.

★ 21 **St. Luke's-in-the-Fields.** The first warden of St. Luke's, which was constructed in 1822 as a country chapel for downtown's Trinity Church, was Clement (" 'Twas the Night Before Christmas") Clarke Moore, who figured so largely in Chelsea's history (☞ Chelsea, *above*). An unadorned structure of soft-colored brick, the chapel was nearly destroyed by fire in 1981, but a flood of donations, many quite small, from residents of the West Village financed restoration of the square central tower. Bret Harte once lived at 487 Hudson Street (today the St. Luke's parish house), at the end of the row. The Barrow Street Garden on the chapel grounds is worth visiting. ⊠ *485 Hudson St., between Barrow and Christopher Sts.,* ☎ *212/924–0562.* ⏲ *Grounds open daily 9–dusk.*

★ 23 **St. Luke's Place.** This often peaceful street has 15 classic Italianate brownstone and brick town houses (1852–53), shaded by graceful gingko trees. Novelist Theodore Dreiser wrote *An American Tragedy* at No. 16, and poet Marianne Moore resided at No. 14. Mayor Jimmy Walker (first elected in 1926) lived at No. 6; the lampposts in front are "mayor's lamps," which were sometimes placed in front of the residences of New York mayors. This block is often used as a film location, too: No. 12 was shown as the Huxtables' home on *The Cosby Show* (although the family lived in Brooklyn), and No. 4 was the setting of the Audrey Hepburn movie *Wait Until Dark.* Before 1890 the playground on the south side of the street was a graveyard where, according to legend, the dauphin of France—the lost son of Louis XVI and Marie Antoinette—is buried. ⊠ *Between Hudson St. and 7th Ave. S.*

NEED A BREAK?

The **Anglers and Writers Café** (⊠ 420 Hudson St., at St. Luke's Pl., ☎ 212/675–0810) lives up to its name with bookshelves, fishing tackle, and pictures of Door County, Wisconsin, hung on the walls. It's an ideal spot to linger over a pot of tea and a slice of cake.

13 **17 Grove Street.** William Hyde, a prosperous window-sash maker, built this clapboard residence in 1822; a third floor was added in 1870. Hyde added a workshop behind the house in 1833. The building has since served many functions; it housed a brothel during the Civil War. The structure is the Village's largest remaining wood-frame house. ⊠ *17 Grove St., at Bedford St.*

18 **75½ Bedford Street.** Rising real estate rates inspired the construction of New York City's narrowest house—just 9½ ft wide—in 1873. Built on a lot that was originally a carriage entrance of the ☞ **Isaacs-Hendricks House** next door, this sliver of a building has been home to actor John Barrymore and poet Edna St. Vincent Millay, who wrote the Pulitzer Prize–winning *Ballad of the Harp-Weaver* during her tenure here from 1923 to 1924. ⊠ *75½ Bedford St., between Commerce and Morton Sts.*

12 **Sheridan Square.** At one time an unused asphalt space, this lovely green triangle was recently landscaped following an extensive dig by urban archaeologists, who unearthed artifacts dating to the Dutch and Native American eras. ⊠ *Bordered by Washington Pl. and W. 4th, Barrow, and Grove Sts.*

14 **Twin Peaks.** In 1925 financier Otto Kahn gave money to a Village eccentric named Clifford Daily to remodel an 1835 house for artists' use. The building was whimsically altered with stucco, half-timbers, and the addition of a pair of steep roof peaks. The result was something

that might be described as an ersatz Swiss chalet. ✉ *102 Bedford St., between Grove and Christopher Sts.*

20 **Twin Sisters.** These attractive Federal-style brick homes connected by a walled garden were said to have been erected by a sea captain for two daughters who loathed each other. Historical record insists that they were built in 1831 and 1832 by a milkman who needed the two houses and an open courtyard for his work. The striking mansard roofs were added in 1873. ✉ *39 and 41 Commerce St.*

Washington Mews. This cobblestone private street is lined on one side with the former stables of the houses on the Row on Washington Square North. Writer Walter Lippmann and artist-patron Gertrude Vanderbilt Whitney (founder of the Whitney Museum) once had homes in the mews; today it's mostly owned by NYU. ✉ *Between 5th Ave. and University Pl.*

★ 1 **Washington Square.** The physical and spiritual heart of the Village, 9½-acre Washington Square started out as a cemetery, principally for yellow fever victims—an estimated 10,000–22,000 bodies lie below. In the early 1800s it was a parade ground and the site of public executions; bodies dangled from a conspicuous Hanging Elm that still stands at the northwest corner of the square. Made a public park in 1827, the square became the focus of a fashionable residential neighborhood and a center of outdoor activity. Today it's a maelstrom of playful activity, shared by earnest-looking NYU students, Frisbee players, street musicians, skateboarders, jugglers, stand-up comics, joggers, chess players, and bench warmers, watching the grand opera of it all. A huge outdoor art fair is held here each spring and fall.

Dominating the square's north end is the triumphal **Washington Arch,** beyond which lies the start of glorious 5th Avenue. Designed by Stanford White, a wooden version of Washington Arch was built in 1889 to commemorate the 100th anniversary of George Washington's presidential inauguration and was originally placed about half a block north of its present location. The arch was reproduced in Tuckahoe marble in 1892, and the statues—*Washington at War* on the left, *Washington at Peace* on the right—were added in 1916 and 1918, respectively. The civilian version of Washington was the work of Alexander Stirling Calder, father of the renowned artist Alexander Calder. Bodybuilder Charles Atlas modeled for *Peace.* ✉ *5th Ave. between Waverly Pl. and W. 4th St.*

22 **White Horse Tavern.** Built in 1880, this amiable bar with a black-painted front occupies one of the city's few remaining wood-frame structures. Formerly a speakeasy and a seamen's tavern, the White Horse has been popular with artists and writers for decades; its best-known customer was Welsh poet Dylan Thomas who had a room named after him here after his death in 1953. ✉ *567 Hudson St., at 11th St.,* ☎ *212/243–9260.*

THE EAST VILLAGE

The gritty tenements of the East Village—an area bounded by 14th Street on the north, 4th Avenue or the Bowery on the west, Houston Street on the south, and the East River—provided inexpensive living places for artists, writers, and actors after real estate prices in SoHo zoomed sky-high in the 1980s. New residents brought in their wake new restaurants, shops, and somewhat cleaner streets, while the old East Villagers maintained the trappings of the counterculture. Longtime bastions of the arts, such as the theaters Classic Stage Company and La MaMa, and St. Mark's-in-the-Bowery Church were joined by newer institutions such as P.S. 122, and several "hot" art galleries opened in narrow East Village storefronts. But the East Village scene lasted only a couple of years—just long enough to drive up rents substantially on some blocks but not long enough to drive out all the neighborhood's original residents. Today an interesting mix has survived: artistic types in black leather and longtime members of various immigrant enclaves, principally Polish, Ukrainian, Slovene, Puerto Rican, and other Latino groups. More recent arrivals come from the Dominican Republic, Japan, and the Philippines. The neighborhood has also long had its share of homeless people and addicts (more so as you head deeper east into the run-down buildings along Avenues B, C, and D, but the arrival of Kmart (☒ 770 Broadway) in 1997 is a clear indication of the gentrification sweeping through the neighborhood.

Numbers in the text correspond to numbers in the margin and on the Greenwich Village and the East Village map.

A Good Walk

Begin at the intersection of East 8th Street, 4th Avenue, and Astor Place, where you'll see two traffic islands. One of these contains an ornate cast-iron kiosk, a replica of a Beaux Arts subway entrance, which provides access to the **Astor Place Subway Station** ㉔. Go down into the station to see the authentically reproduced wall tiles with a beaver motif. On the other traffic island stands the **Alamo** ㉕, a huge black cube sculpted by Bernard Rosenthal.

Go straight east from the Alamo to **St. Marks Place** ㉖, the name given to 8th Street in the East Village. This often crowded thoroughfare has long attracted assorted fringe elements—punks, hyperkinetic club crawlers, and washed-out counterculture types.

Second Avenue, which St. Marks crosses after one block, was called the Yiddish Rialto in the early part of this century. At this time eight theaters between Houston and 14th streets presented Yiddish-language productions of musicals, revues, and heart-wrenching melodramas. Two survivors from that period are the Orpheum (☒ 126 2nd Ave., at 8th St.) and the neo-Moorish Yiddish Arts Theatre, now the multiscreen Village East Cinemas (☒ 189 2nd Ave., at 12th St.), which has preserved the original ornate ceiling. In front of the Second Avenue Deli (☒ 2nd Ave. and 10th St.), Hollywood-style squares have been embedded in the sidewalk to commemorate Yiddish stage luminaries.

Second Avenue is also home to a neighborhood landmark, **St. Mark's-in-the-Bowery Church** ㉗, a stately Episcopal church on the corner of 10th Street that serves as a community cultural center and public meeting hall. From in front of the church, you can take a quiet detour to investigate the facades of handsome redbrick row houses on **Stuyvesant Street,** which stretches southwest to 9th Street. If you continue north up 2nd Avenue from St. Mark's-in-the-Bowery Church, you'll reach the **Ukrainian Museum** ㉘, a modest upstairs gallery celebrating the cultural heritage of Ukraine.

Next, walk south on 2nd Avenue to 9th Street. At 135 2nd Avenue, between 9th Street and St. Marks Place, is the **Ottendorfer Branch of the New York Public Library** ㉙. A leisurely stroll east on 9th Street from 2nd Avenue to Avenue A will take you past a number of cafés and small, friendly shops selling designer and vintage clothing, housewares, toys, herbs, leather goods, recordings, and much more.

At the northeast corner of 1st Avenue and 9th Street stands P.S. 122 (✉ 150 1st Ave.), a former public school building transformed into a complex of spaces for avant-garde entertainment (☞ Chapter 5). If you continue east on 9th Street or St. Marks Place, you're heading toward **Alphabet City,** the area's nickname; here the avenues are named A, B, C, and D. St. Marks Place between 1st Avenue and Avenue A is lined with inexpensive cafés catering to a late-night younger crowd. Across from St. Marks Place on Avenue A is **Tompkins Square Park** ㉚, a fairly peaceful haven.

Next, head back west and follow 7th Street away from the southwest corner of Tompkins Square Park, surveying the mix of small stores and restaurants to get a reading on the neighborhood's culture-in-flux. At 1st Avenue swing down to 6th Street, where the whole south side of the block belongs to dozens of Indian restaurants serving inexpensive subcontinental fare (New Yorkers joke that they all share a single kitchen). On the other side of 2nd Avenue is the future home of the Ukrainian Museum. Turning right on Taras Shevchenko Place (named for the Ukrainain Shakespeare) takes you to **McSorley's Old Ale House** ㉛, one of New York's oldest bars. Just past McSorley's is **Surma, the Ukrainian Shop** ㉜, selling all sorts of Ukrainian-made goods. Across the street is the copper- domed **St. George's Ukrainian Catholic Church** ㉝.

Across 3rd Avenue, the massive brownstone **Cooper Union Foundation Building** ㉞, a tuition-free school for artists, architects, and engineers, overlooks Cooper Square, a large open space. Across the street from the west side of the Cooper Union Building is the enormous Carl Fischer Music Store (✉ 62 Cooper Sq.), where musicians select from an infinitude of sheet music and confer with the knowledgeable staff. Just south of this music store are the offices of the liberal downtown *Village Voice* newspaper (✉ 36 Cooper Sq.). If you're here from Sunday through Thursday, walk south on Cooper Square and turn right on 4th Street to visit the **Merchant's House Museum** ㉟, where 19th-century family life can be viewed thanks to the preservation of the original furnishings and architecture.

One block west of Cooper Square is Lafayette Street. The long block between East 4th Street and Astor Place contains on its east side a grand Italian Renaissance–style structure housing the New York Shakespeare Festival's **Joseph Papp Public Theater** ㊱ in the 19th century the city's first free library opened here. Across the street note the imposing marble Corinthian columns fronting **Colonnade Row** ㊲, a stretch of four crumbling 19th-century Greek Revival houses. Walking north on Lafayette Street brings you back to Astor Place; heading west brings you to Broadway. To the left (south) is a busy downtown shopping strip, with several clothing shops; chain stores such as Star Magic and the Body Shop; and Tower Records. Above street level the old warehouses here have mostly been converted into residential lofts. North on Broadway from Astor Place lies **Grace Church** ㊳, on the corner of Broadway and 10th Street, which has a striking marble spire. If you continue north on the same side of the street as the church, you'll pass a few of the many antiques stores in the area. You can end your walk at the popular **Strand Book Store** ㊴, the largest secondhand bookstore in the city and an absolutely necessary stop for anyone who loves to read.

TIMING

Allow about three hours for the walk. If you plan to stop at museums, add one hour, and at least another hour to browse in shops along the way. If you end your walk at the Strand Book Store, you may want to stop somewhere for coffee before perusing the bookshelves, which can easily eat up another hour or more of your time.

Sights to See

25 **Alamo.** Created by Bernard Rosenthal in 1967, this massive black cube made of steel was originally part of a temporary citywide exhibit, but it became a permanent installation thanks to a private donor. Balanced on a post, the "Cube," as it is locally known, was one of the first abstract sculptures in New York City to be placed in a public space. ✉ *On traffic island at Astor Pl. and Lafayette St.*

Alphabet City. Beyond 1st Avenue, the north–south avenues all labeled with letters, not numbers, give this area its commonly used nickname. Until fairly recently, Alphabet City was a burned-out territory of slums and drug haunts, but some blocks and buildings were gentrified during the height of the East Village art scene in the mid-'80s. The reasonably priced restaurants with their bohemian atmosphere on St. Marks Place and Avenue A attract a mix of locals, visitors "slumming it" from other parts of the city, and tourists. A close-knit Puerto Rican community lies east of Avenue A, lending a Latin flavor to many of the local dining spots and businesses. You'll find a number of grungy bars, such as Lakeside Lounge (✉ 162–4 Ave. B, between 10th and 11th Sts.), and trendy, cheap cafés, such as Cafe Rainbow (✉ 190 Ave. B, near 12th St.) and Kate's Joint (✉ 58 Ave. B, between 4th and 5th Sts.). ✉ *Alphabet City extends approximately from Ave. A to the East River, between 14th and Houston Sts.*

NEED A BREAK? **Old Devil Moon** (✉ 511 E. 12th St., between Aves. C and D, ☎ 212/475–4357) is a delightfully snug, dimly lighted hangout with whimsical decor where you can stop for a drink, snack, or something more substantial.

24 **Astor Place Subway Station.** At the beginning of this century, almost every Independent Rapid Transit (IRT) subway entrance resembled the ornate cast-iron replica of a Beaux Arts kiosk that covers the stairway leading to the uptown No. 6 train. In the station itself, authentically reproduced ceramic tiles of beavers, a reference to the fur trade that contributed to John Jacob Astor's fortune, line the walls. Milton Glaser, a Cooper Union graduate, designed the station's attractive abstract murals. ✉ *On traffic island at 8th St. and 4th Ave.*

37 **Colonnade Row.** Marble Corinthian columns front this grand sweep of four Greek Revival mansions (originally nine) constructed in 1833, with stonework accomplished by Sing Sing penitentiary prisoners. In their time these once-elegant homes served as residences to millionaires John Jacob Astor and Cornelius Vanderbilt until they moved uptown. Writers Washington Irving, William Makepeace Thackeray, and Charles Dickens all stayed here at one time or another; more recently, writer Edmund White lived here. Today three houses are occupied on street level by restaurants, while the northernmost building houses the Astor Place Theatre. ✉ *428–434 Lafayette St., between Astor Pl. and E. 4th St.*

34 **Cooper Union Foundation Building.** This impressive eight-story brownstone dominates Cooper Square, a large open space situated where 3rd and 4th avenues merge into the Bowery. A statue of industrialist Peter Cooper, by Augustus Saint-Gaudens, presides over the square. Cooper founded this college in 1859 to provide a forum for public opinion and free technical education for the working class; it still offers tuition-free education in architecture, art, and engineering. Cooper Union was the first structure to be supported by steel railroad rails—rolled in Cooper's

own plant. Two galleries in the building are open to the public, presenting changing exhibitions during the academic year. ✉ *E. 7th St. to Astor Pl., 4th Ave. to the Bowery at Cooper Sq.,* ☎ *212/353–4200.* 🎫 *Free.* ⏲ *Weekdays noon–7, Sat. noon–5.*

★ 38 **Grace Church.** Topped by a finely ornamented octagonal marble spire, this Episcopal church, designed by James Renwick Jr. has excellent Pre-Raphaelite stained-glass windows. The building—a fine mid-19th-century example of an English Gothic Revival church—fronts a small green yard facing Broadway. The church has been the site of many society weddings (including that of P. T. Barnum show member Tom Thumb). ✉ *802 Broadway, at E. 10th St.,* ☎ *212/254–2000.* ⏲ *Weekdays 10–6, Sat. noon–4, Sun. 8:30–1.*

36 **Joseph Papp Public Theater.** In 1854 John Jacob Astor opened the city's first free library in this expansive redbrick and brownstone Italian Renaissance–style building, which was renovated in 1967 as the Public Theater to serve as the permanent home of the New York Shakespeare Festival. The theater opened its doors with the popular rock musical *Hair.* Under the leadership of the late Joseph Papp, the Public's five playhouses built a fine reputation for bold and innovative performances; the long-running hit *A Chorus Line* had its first performances here, as have many less commercial plays. Today director and producer George C. Wolfe heads the Public, which continues to present controversial modern works and imaginative Shakespeare productions. The Public produces the three annual summer productions in Central Park's Delacorte Theater (☞ Central Park, *above,* and Chapter 5). ✉ *425 Lafayette St., between E. 4th St. and Astor Pl.,* ☎ *212/260–2400.*

31 **McSorley's Old Ale House.** One of several claimants to the distinction of being New York's oldest bar, this often-crowded saloon attracts many collegiate types enticed by McSorley's own brands of ale. The mahogany bar, gas lamps, and potbelly stove all hark back to decades past. McSorley's opened in 1854 but didn't admit women until 1970. Joseph Mitchell immortalized the spot in short stories he wrote for the *New Yorker.* ✉ *15 E. 7th St., between 2nd and 3rd Aves.,* ☎ *212/473–9148.*

35 **Merchant's House Museum.** Built in 1831–32, this redbrick house, combining Federal and Greek Revival styles, offers a rare glimpse of family life in the mid-19th century. Retired merchant Seabury Tredwell and his descendants lived here from 1835 right up until it became a museum in 1933. The original furnishings and architectural features remain intact; family memorabilia are also on display. The Greek Revival–style parlors have 13-ft ceilings with intricate plasterwork, freestanding Ionic columns, a mahogany pocket-door screen, and black-marble fireplaces. Self-guided tour brochures are always available, and guided tours are given on Sunday. ✉ *29 E. 4th St., between Bowery and 2nd Ave.,* ☎ *212/777–1089.* 🎫 *$3.* ⏲ *Sun.–Thurs. 1–4.*

29 **Ottendorfer Branch of the New York Public Library.** The first Manhattan building to be constructed as a free public library, this 1884 structure designed by William Schickel incorporates elements from several late Victorian styles; the early use of molded terra-cotta interior remains untouched. The rust-color building dates from a time when the East Village was heavily populated by German immigrants and was a gift from Oswald Ottendorfer, a rich German philanthropist and newspaper editor. It began as the German-language branch of the Free Circulating Library (hence the words FREIE BIBLIOTHEK UND LESEHALLE on its facade) and eventually became part of the city's public library system. ✉ *135 2nd Ave., near St. Marks Pl.,* ☎ *212/674–0947.*

33 **St. George's Ukrainian Catholic Church.** Notable for its copper dome and the three brightly colored religious murals on its facade, this ostentatious modern church serves as a central meeting place for the old local Ukrainian population. Built in 1977, it took the place of the more modest Greek Revival–style St. George's Ruthenian Church. An annual Ukrainian folk festival occurs here in the spring. ✉ *30 E. 7th St., between 2nd and 3rd Aves.,* ☎ *212/674–1615.*

27 **St. Mark's-in-the-Bowery Church.** A Greek Revival steeple and a cast-iron front porch were added to this 1799 fieldstone country church, which occupies the former site of the family chapel of the old Dutch governor Peter Stuyvesant. St. Mark's is the city's oldest continually used Christian church building (Stuyvesant and Commodore Perry are buried here). Its interior had to be completely restored after a disastrous fire in 1978, and stained-glass windows were added to the balcony in 1982. Over the years St. Mark's has hosted much countercultural activity. In the 1920s a forward-thinking pastor injected the Episcopal ritual with Native American chants, Greek folk dancing, and Eastern mantras. William Carlos Williams, Amy Lowell, and Carl Sandburg once read here, and Isadora Duncan, Harry Houdini, and Merce Cunningham also performed here. During the hippie era St. Mark's welcomed avant-garde poets and playwrights, including Sam Shepard. Today dancers, poets, and performance artists cavort in the main sanctuary, where pews have been removed to accommodate them. ✉ *131 E. 10th St., at 2nd Ave.,* ☎ *212/674–6377.*

NEED A BREAK? Bright and bustling **Veselka** (✉ 144 2nd Ave., at 9th St., ☎ 212/228–9682), a longtime East Village favorite, serves bagels, muffins, Italian coffee, egg creams, and Ben & Jerry's ice cream alongside good, traditional Ukrainian fare such as borscht, kielbasa, and veal goulash.

26 **St. Marks Place.** St. Marks Place, as 8th Street is called between 3rd Avenue and Avenue A, is the longtime hub of the hip East Village. During the 1950s beatniks such as Allen Ginsberg and Jack Kerouac lived and wrote in the area; the 1960s brought Bill Graham's Fillmore East concerts, the Electric Circus, and hallucinogenic drugs. The black-clad, pink-haired, or shaved-head punks followed, and some remain today. St. Marks Place between 2nd and 3rd avenues is lined with ethnic restaurants, jewelry stalls, leather shops, and stores selling books, posters, and eccentric clothing. The street vendors who line the sidewalk daily add to the bazaarlike atmosphere, although the presence of a Gap store helps to take some of the edge off.

At 80 St. Marks Place, near 1st Avenue, is the Pearl Theatre Company, which performs classic plays from around the world. The handprints, footprints, and autographs of such past screen luminaries as Joan Crawford, Ruby Keeler, Joan Blondell, and Myrna Loy are embedded in the sidewalk. At 96–98 St. Marks Place (between 1st Avenue and Avenue A), stands the building that was photographed for the cover of Led Zeppelin's *Physical Graffiti* album. The cafés between 1st Avenue and Avenue A attract customers late into the night.

★ 39 **Strand Book Store.** Serious book lovers from around the world make pilgrimages to this secondhand book emporium with a stock of some 2 million volumes, including thousands of collector's items. (The slogan "Eight Miles of Books" calls out from the store's sign.) Opened in 1929 by Ben Bass, the Strand was originally on 4th Avenue's Book Row until it moved to its present location on Broadway in 1956. Review copies of new books sell for 50% off, and used books are often priced at much less. A separate rare-book room is on the third floor at 826 Broadway, to the immediate north of the main store. ✉ *828 Broadway, at 12th St.,* ☎ *212/473–1452.* ⏲ *Main store: Mon.–Sat. 9:30–9:30, Sun. 11–9:30; rare books: Mon.–Sat 9:30–6, Sun. 11–6:30.*

★ **Stuyvesant Street.** This block-long thoroughfare, the hypotenuse of two triangles bounded by 2nd and 3rd avenues and East 9th and 10th streets, has a unique claim in Manhattan: It is the oldest street laid out precisely along an east–west axis. (This grid never caught on, and instead a street grid following the island's geographic orientation was adopted.) The area was once Governor Peter Stuyvesant's *bouwerie,* or farm; among the handsome redbrick row houses are the Federal-style **Stuyvesant-Fish House** (✉ 21 Stuyvesant St.), which was built in 1804 as a wedding gift for a great-great-granddaughter of the governor, and **Renwick Triangle,** an attractive group of carefully restored one- and two-story brick and brownstone residences originally constructed in 1861. At press time the George Hecht Viewing Gardens were being constructed at 3rd Avenue and 9th Street, with one side of the gardens bordering Stuyvesant Street.

32 **Surma, the Ukrainian Shop.** The exotic stock at this charming little store includes Ukrainian books, magazines, cassettes, and greeting cards, as well as musical instruments, painted eggs, and an exhaustive collection of peasant blouses. ✉ *11 E. 7th St., between 2nd and 3rd Aves.,* ☎ *212/477–0729.*

30 **Tompkins Square Park.** This leafy oasis amid the East Village's crowded tenements is the physical, spiritual, and political heart of the radical East Village. The square takes its name from four-time governor Daniel Tompkins, an avid abolitionist and vice president under James Monroe, who once owned this land from 2nd Avenue to the East River. Its history is long and violent: The 1874 Tompkins Square Riot involved some 7,000 unhappy laborers and 1,600 police. In 1988 riots again broke out, as police followed then-mayor David Dinkins's orders to clear the park of the many homeless who had set up makeshift homes here, and homeless rights and antigentrification activists armed with sticks and bottles fought back. After a yearlong renovation, the park reopened in 1992 with a midnight curfew, still in effect today. The park fills up with locals on clement days year-round, partaking in minipicnics, drum circles, rollerblade basketball, and, for dog owners, a large dog run. East of the park at 151 Avenue B, near 9th Street, stands an 1849 four-story white-painted brownstone, where renowned jazz musician Charlie Parker lived from 1950 to 1954. ✉ *Bordered by Aves. A and B and 7th and 10th Sts.*

NEED A BREAK? At the northwest corner of the park is **Life Cafe** (✉ 343 E. 10th St., at Ave. B, 212/477–8791), a frequently busy local hangout that is featured in the hit Broadway musical *Rent.* Two of the city's best Italian pastry shops are nearby. **De Robertis Pasticceria** (✉ 176 1st Ave., between 10th and 11th Sts., ☎ 212/674–7137) offers exceptional cheesecake and cappuccinos in its original 1904 setting, complete with glistening mosaic tiles. Opened in 1894, the popular **Veniero Pasticceria** (✉ 342 E. 11th St., ☎ 212/674–7264) has rows and rows of fresh cannoli, fruit tarts, cheesecakes, cookies, and other elaborate desserts on display in glass cases; there's a separate café section.

28 **Ukrainian Museum.** Ceramics, jewelry, hundreds of brilliantly colored Easter eggs, and an extensive collection of Ukrainian costumes and textiles are the highlights of this small collection, nurtured by Ukrainian Americans in exile throughout the years of Soviet domination. The museum is scheduled to move to a new quarters, at 222 East 6th Street,

in late 1999. ✉ *203 2nd Ave., between 12th and 13th Sts.,* ☎ *212/228-0110.* 🎫 *$1.* ⏲ *Wed.–Sun. 1–5.*

SOHO AND TRIBECA

Today the names of these two downtown neighborhoods are virtually synonymous with a certain eclectic elegance—an amalgam of black-clad artists, young Wall Streeters, expansive loft apartments, hip art galleries, and packed-to-the-gills restaurants. It's all very urban, very cool, very now. Twenty-five years ago, though, these two areas were virtual wastelands. SoHo (so named because it is the district *So*uth of *Ho*uston Street, bounded by Broadway, Canal Street, and 6th Avenue) was regularly referred to as "Hell's Hundred Acres" because of the many fires that raged through the untended warehouses crowding the area. It was saved by two factors: first, preservationists here discovered the world's greatest concentration of cast-iron architecture and fought to prevent demolition; and second, artists discovered the large, cheap, well-lighted spaces that cast-iron buildings provide.

All the rage between 1860 and 1890, cast-iron buildings were popular because they did not require massive walls to bear the weight of the upper stories. Since there was no need for load-bearing walls, these buildings had more interior space and larger windows. They were also versatile, with various architectural elements produced from standardized molds to mimic any style—Italianate, Victorian Gothic, neo-Grecian, to name but a few visible in SoHo. At first it was technically illegal for artists to live in their loft studios, but so many did that eventually the zoning laws were changed to permit residence.

By 1980 SoHo's galleries, trendy shops, and cafés, together with its marvelous cast-iron buildings and vintage Belgian-block pavements (the 19th-century successor to traditional cobblestones), had made SoHo such a desirable residential area that only the most successful artists could afford it. Seeking similar space, artists moved downtown to another half-abandoned industrial district, for which a new, SoHo-like name was invented: TriBeCa (the *Tri*angle *Be*low *Ca*nal Street, although in effect it goes no farther south than Murray Street and no farther east than West Broadway). The same scenario played itself out again, and TriBeCa's rising rents are already beyond the means of most artists, who have moved instead to west Chelsea, Long Island City, areas of Brooklyn, or New Jersey. But despite their gentrification, SoHo and TriBeCa retain some of their gritty bohemianism—one local store terms it "shabby chic"—that has come to dominate the downtown scene. In the case of SoHo, however, the arrival of large chain stores such as Pottery Barn and J. Crew has given some blocks the feeling of an outdoor suburban shopping mall.

Numbers in the text correspond to numbers in the margin and on the SoHo, TriBeCa, Little Italy, Chinatown map.

A Good Walk

Starting at Houston (pronounced *how*-ston) Street, walk south down Broadway, stopping at the many museums that crowd both sides of the street between Houston and Prince streets. The most noteworthy of these is the **Guggenheim Museum SoHo** ①, which opened in 1992—but also worthwhile are the **Alternative Museum** ②, whose political and sociopolitical themes make for lively discussion; the **Museum for African Art** ③, whose handsome two-story building complements its high-quality exhibits; and the **New Museum of Contemporary Art** ④, which is devoted exclusively to living artists. Several art galleries share these blocks as well, most notably at 568 Broadway, which has 13 galleries and the trendy Armani Exchange store on the ground level.

Just south of Prince Street, 560 Broadway on the east side of the block is another popular exhibit space, home to some 20 galleries. Across the street, Ernest Flagg's 1904 Little Singer Building (⊠ 561 Broadway) shows the final flower of the cast-iron style, with wrought-iron balconies, terra-cotta panels, and broad expanses of windows. On the ground floor of this building is Kate's Paperie, where handmade paper is elevated to a high art form. One block south of the Little Singer Building, between Spring and Broome streets, a cluster of lofts that were originally part of the 1897 New Era Building (⊠ 495 Broadway) boast an Art Nouveau copper mansard; La Boulangère bakery now resides on the street level. At the northeast corner of Broadway and Broome Street is the **Haughwout Building** ⑤, a restored classic of the cast-iron genre. At the southeast corner of Broadway and Broome Street, the former Mechanics and Traders Bank (⊠ 486 Broadway) is a Romanesque and Moorish Revival building with half-round brick arches. At the northwest corner of Broadway and Grand Street, the popular SoHo Antiques Fair draws about 100 dealers selling everything from used bicycles to vintage posters and prints on weekends from 9 to 5.

For a taste of pre-gentrified SoHo, detour west from Broadway to Mercer Street or east to Crosby Street, where Belgian paving stones, multiple loading docks, and a patchwork of fire escapes recall the days when these streets were used as service thoroughfares. If you head east and you have youngsters in tow, continue one more block east to the **Children's Museum of the Arts** ⑥, where the interactive exhibits should provide a welcome respite from SoHo's mostly grown-up pursuits.

As an alternative, you can head west from Broadway on Grand Street, which leads to **Greene Street,** where cast-iron buildings abound, such as the **Queen of Greene Street** ⑦ and the **King of Greene Street** ⑧. Several of SoHo's better exhibition spaces run by younger and more innovative dealers and artists are clustered on the south end of Greene and Wooster streets near Grand Street.

Greene Street between Prince and Spring streets is notable for the SoHo Building (⊠ 104–110 Greene St.); towering 13 stories, it was the neighborhood's tallest building until the SoHo Grand Hotel went up in 1996. On this block you'll also find Anna Sui (⊠ 113 Greene St.), a boutique whose pricey avant-garde fashions are among New York's most cutting-edge. At Prince Street, walk one block west to Wooster Street, which, like a few other SoHo streets, still has its original Belgian paving stones. Going south on Wooster, shoppers will find a retail paradise in the blocks between Prince and Spring streets (☞ Chapter 10). Also in this vicinity is one of Manhattan's finest photography galleries, Howard Greenberg (⊠ 120 Wooster St.). Proceeding even farther south on Wooster, between Broome and Grand streets and Grand and Canal streets, you'll find more art worth checking out at the Drawing Center (⊠ 35 Wooster St.), Spencer Brownstone (⊠ 39 Wooster St.), and Basilico Fine Arts and Friedrich Petzel (⊠ 26 Wooster St.). Right nearby, between Wooster and Greene streets, also stop at Deitch Projects (⊠ 76 Grand St.).

Now head back north on Wooster Street to the blocks between West Houston and Prince streets. Here you may investigate the **New York Earth Room** ⑨ and the Gagosian Gallery (⊠ 136 Wooster St.), operated by prominent uptown dealer Larry Gagosian.

From Wooster Street walk one block west on Prince Street to SoHo's main drag, West Broadway, with galleries and stores galore. In the block

SoHo and TriBeCa
Alternative Museum, **2**
Children's Museum of the Arts, **6**
Duane Park, **11**
Guggenheim Museum SoHo, **1**
Haughwout Building, **5**
Hudson River Park, **15**
Independence Plaza, **13**
King of Greene Street, **8**
Museum for African Art, **3**
New Museum of Contemporary Art, **4**
New York Earth Room, **9**
Queen of Greene Street, **7**
SoHo Grand Hotel, **10**
TriBeCa Film Center, **12**
Washington Market Park, **14**

Little Italy and Chinatown
Asian American Arts Centre, **26**
Chatham Square, **23**
Church of the Transfiguration, **21**
Columbus Park, **22**
Confucius Plaza, **25**
First Shearith Israel graveyard, **24**
Mott Street, **20**
Mulberry Street, **16**
Museum of Chinese in the Americas (MCA), **19**
New York City Police Headquarters, **17**
San Gennaro Church, **18**

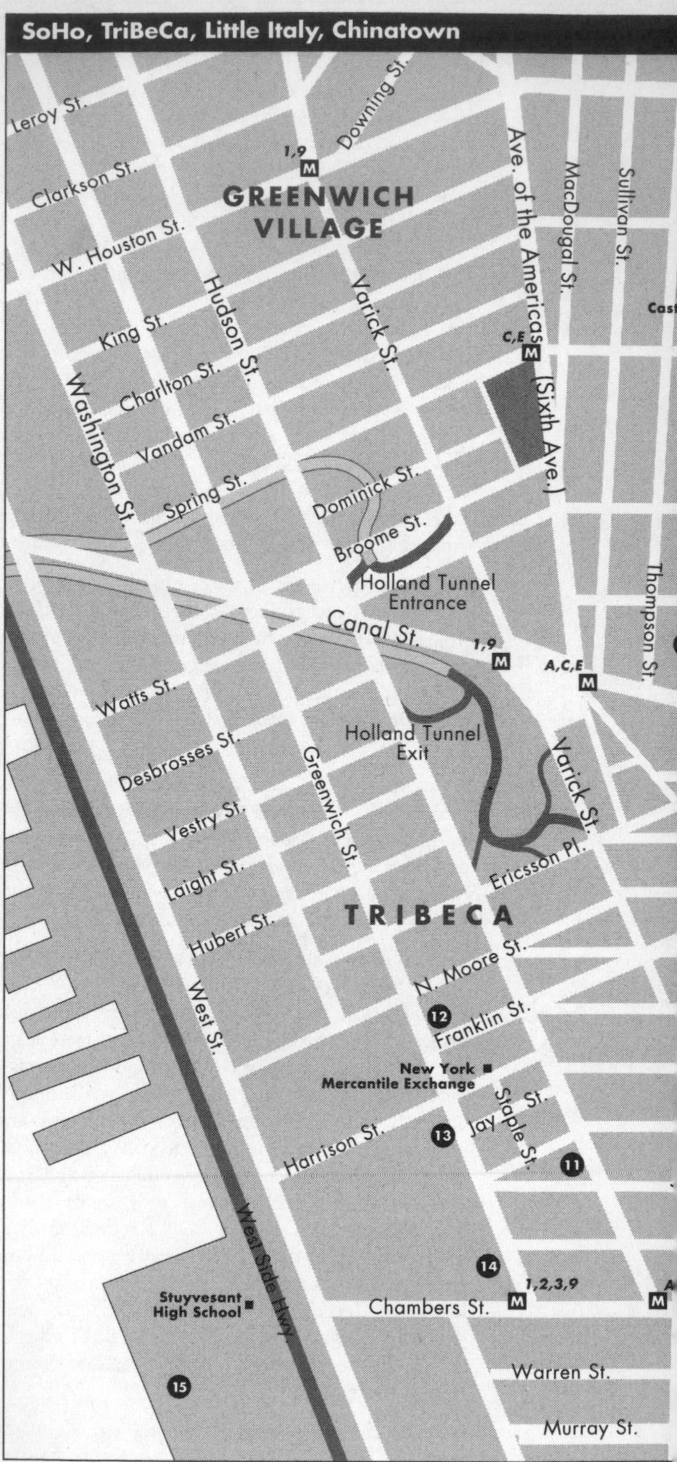

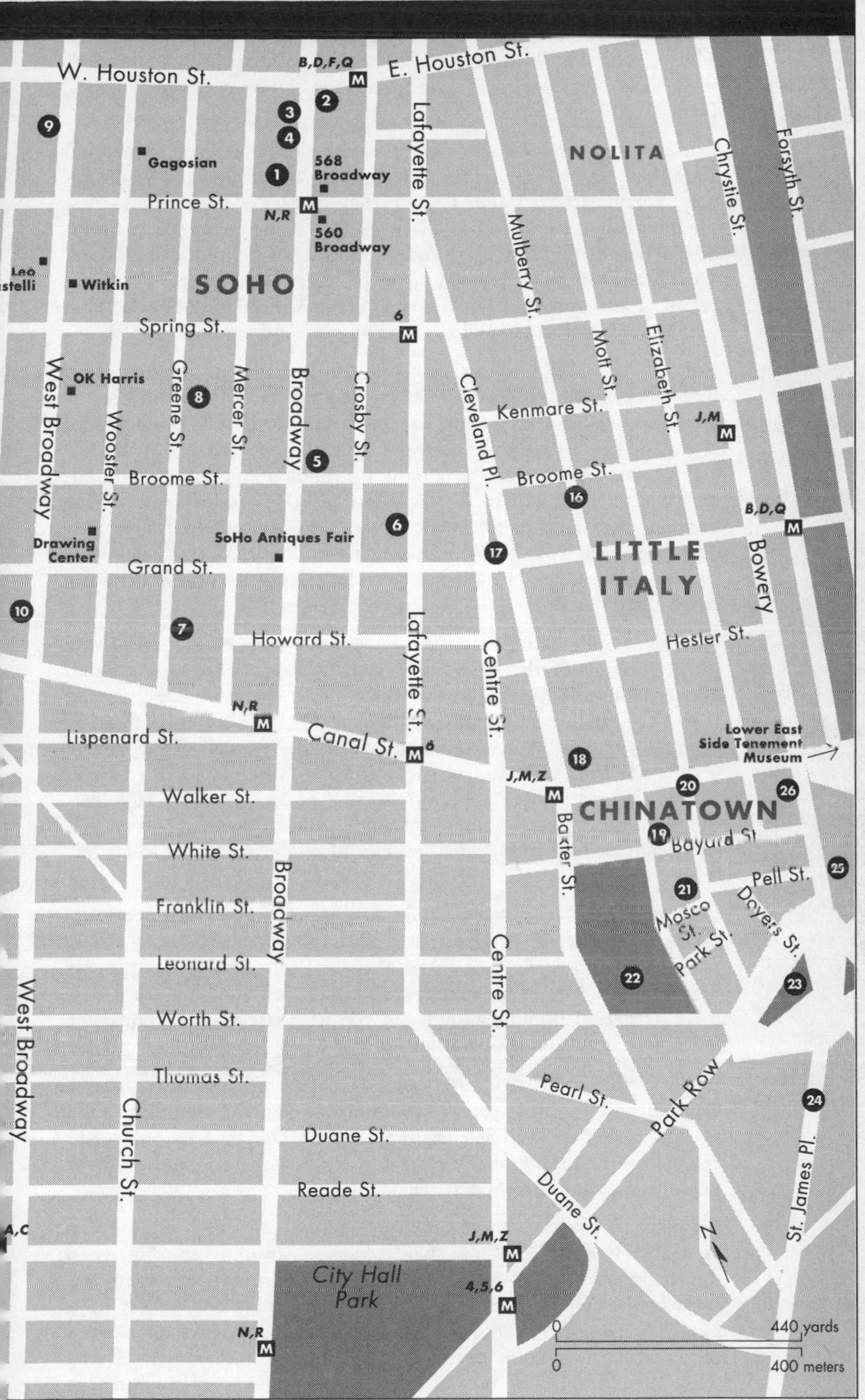
W. Houston St.
E. Houston St.
B,D,F,Q
NOLITA
Gagosian
568 Broadway
560 Broadway
Prince St.
N,R
Leo
astelli
Witkin
SOHO
Spring St.
6
Lafayette St.
Mulberry St.
Chrystie St.
Forsyth St.
Mott St.
Elizabeth St.
OK Harris
West Broadway
Wooster St.
Greene St.
Mercer St.
Broadway
Crosby St.
Cleveland Pl.
Kenmare St.
J,M
Broome St.
B,D,Q
Drawing Center
SoHo Antiques Fair
Grand St.
LITTLE ITALY
Bowery
Howard St.
Centre St.
Hester St.
Canal St.
Lispenard St.
Lower East Side Tenement Museum
J,M,Z
Walker St.
CHINATOWN
Baxter St.
Bayard St.
White St.
Pell St.
Franklin St.
Mosco St.
Doyers St.
Park St.
Leonard St.
Worth St.
Thomas St.
Pearl St.
Park Row
Church St.
Duane St.
Reade St.
St. James Pl.
A,C
City Hall Park
4,5,6
N
0
440 yards
400 meters

between Prince and Spring streets alone, you'll find Nancy Hoffman (✉ 429 W. Broadway); the gallery complex at 415 West Broadway, which includes the Witkin Gallery for photography; and 420 West Broadway, with six separate galleries, including two of the biggest SoHo names, Leo Castelli and the Sonnabend Gallery.

Continue south on West Broadway to the blocks between Spring and Broome streets, where you'll find Robert Lee Morris (✉ 400 W. Broadway), carrying the designer's jewelry, handbags, and home accessories; the immense OK Harris art gallery (✉ 383 W. Broadway); and Smith & Hawken (✉ 392 W. Broadway), a gardener's emporium. Stay on West Broadway on the west side of the street and proceed south; between Grand and Canal streets stands the **SoHo Grand Hotel** ⑩, the first major hotel to be built in the neighborhood since the 1880s.

From here TriBeCa is less than one block away; just follow West Broadway south to Canal Street, the neighborhood's official boundary. Stop to marvel at the life-size iron Statue of Liberty crown rising above the kitschy white-tile entrance to El Teddy's (✉ 219 W. Broadway), a gourmet Mexican restaurant. Continuing south on West Broadway to Duane Street, you'll pass Worth Street, once the center of the garment trade and the 19th-century equivalent of today's 7th Avenue. The area to the west, near the Hudson River docks, was once the heart of the wholesale food business; a few wholesalers such as Bazzini's (☞ *below*) still remain.

On Duane Street you'll find the calm, shady **Duane Park** ⑪. Walk one block north on Hudson Street. On your right you'll see the Art Deco Western Union Building (✉ 60 Hudson St.), where 19 subtly shaded colors of brick are laid in undulating patterns. Turn left from Hudson Street onto quiet Jay Street and pause at narrow Staple Street, whose green pedestrian walkway overhead links two warehouses. If you continue west on Jay Street, you'll pass the loading docks of a 100-year-old food wholesaler, Bazzini's Nuts and Confections, where an upscale retail shop peddles nuts, coffee beans, and candies; there are also a few tables where you can enjoy a light snack.

On Greenwich Street at Franklin Street is the **Tribeca Film Center** ⑫, owned by Robert De Niro. As you walk south down Greenwich Street, on your right is a surprising row of early 19th-century town houses nestled in the side of **Independence Plaza** ⑬, a huge high-rise apartment complex. Continuing south on Greenwich Street, you'll soon come to the 2½-acre **Washington Market Park** ⑭, a pleasant, landscaped oasis.

At the corner of the park, turn west on Chambers Street, heading west toward the Hudson River. A five-minute walk will bring you to the overpass across the West Side Highway. Here, behind the huge Stuyvesant High School building, you'll reach the north end of the **Hudson River Park** ⑮, a great place for a stroll.

TIMING

To see SoHo and TriBeCa at their liveliest, visit on a Saturday, when the fashionable art crowd is joined by smartly dressed uptowners and suburbanites who come down for a little shopping and gallery hopping. If you want to avoid crowds, take this walk during the week. Keep in mind that most galleries are closed on Sunday and Monday. If you allow time for leisurely browsing in several galleries and museums, as well as a stop for lunch, this tour can easily take up to an entire day.

Sights to See

❷ **Alternative Museum.** As the sign outside says, this two-room gallery SEEKS TO EXHIBIT THE WORK OF THOSE ARTISTS WHO HAVE BEEN DISEN-

FRANCHISED BECAUSE OF IDEOLOGY, RACE, GENDER, OR ECONOMIC INEQUALITY. It presents some of the most interesting and engaging (and occasionally offensive or confrontational) art in SoHo. ✉ *594 Broadway, near E. Houston St.,* ☎ *212/966–4444.* *$3 (suggested donation).* ⏲ *Wed.–Sat. 11–6.*

OFF THE BEATEN PATH

CHARLTON STREET – The city's longest stretch of redbrick town houses preserved from the 1820s and 1830s runs along the north side of this street, which is west of 6th Avenue and south of West Houston Street and has high stoops, paneled front doors, lead-glass windows, and narrow dormer windows all intact. While you're here, stroll along the parallel King and Vandam streets for more fine Federal houses. This quiet enclave was once an estate called Richmond Hill, whose various residents included George Washington, John and Abigail Adams, and Aaron Burr.

6 **Children's Museum of the Arts.** In a bi-level space in SoHo, children 1–10 have the chance to become actively involved in visual and performing arts (☞ Chapter 4). ✉ *182 Lafayette St., between Grand and Broome Sts.,* ☎ *212/274–0986.* *$4 weekdays, $5 weekends.* ⏲ *Tues.–Fri. noon–6, weekends 11–5.*

11 **Duane Park.** The city bought this calm, shady triangle from then-owner Trinity Church (☞ Wall Street and the Battery, *below*) in 1797 for $5. Cheese, butter, and egg warehouses have surrounded this oasis for more than 100 years. ✉ *Bordered by Hudson, Duane, and Staple Sts.*

NEED A BREAK?

For a real New York story, duck into the **Odeon** (✉ 145 W. Broadway, ☎ 212/233–0507), an Art Deco restaurant-bar. With black-and-red banquettes, chrome mirrors, neon-lighted clocks, and ceiling fans, this place has a distinctively slick atmosphere. Come for a drink at the bar or a snack anytime from noon to 2 AM.

Greene Street. Cast-iron architecture is at its finest here; the block between Canal and Grand streets (✉ 8–34 Greene St.) represents the longest row of cast-iron buildings anywhere. Handsome as they are, these buildings were always commercial, containing stores and light manufacturing, principally textiles. Along this street notice the iron loading docks and the sidewalk vault covers that lead into basement storage areas. Two standout buildings on Greene Street are the so-called ☞ **Queen of Green Street** and the ☞ **King of Greene Street.** Even the lampposts on Greene Street are architectural gems: Note their turn-of-the-century bishop's-crook style, adorned with various cast-iron curlicues from their bases to their curved tops.

NEED A BREAK?

Space Untitled Espresso Bar (✉ 133 Greene St., near W. Houston St., ☎ 212/260–8962) serves coffee, tea, sweets, and lunch sandwiches, as well as wine and beer, in a minimalist gallery setting.

1 **Guggenheim Museum SoHo.** Since it opened in 1992, this downtown branch of the uptown museum has displayed a revolving series of exhibitions, both contemporary work and pieces from the Guggenheim's permanent collection. The museum occupies space in a landmark 19th-century redbrick structure with its original cast-iron storefronts and detailed cornice. Arata Isozaki designed the two floors of stark, loftlike galleries as well as the museum store facing Broadway. ✉ *575 Broadway, at Prince St.,* ☎ *212/423–3500.* *$8.* ⏲ *Wed.–Fri. and Sun. 11–6, Sat. 11–8.*

NEED A BREAK? Diagonally across from the Guggenheim Museum SoHo, **Dean & DeLuca** (✉ 560 Broadway, at Prince St., ☎ 212/431–1691), the gourmet emporium, brews superb coffee and tea, but it gets crowded fast.

5 **Haughwout Building.** Nicknamed the Parthenon of Cast Iron, this Venetian palazzo–style structure was built in 1857 to house Eder Haughwout's china and glassware business. Inside, the building once contained the world's first commercial passenger elevator, a steam-powered device invented by Elisha Graves Otis. ✉ *488 Broadway, at Broome St.*

★ 15 **Hudson River Park.** A landscaped oasis with playgrounds, promenades and walkways, handball and basketball courts, and grassy areas, this park on the river at the corner of Chambers and West streets and north of the World Financial Center fills with downtown residents soaking up rays on sunny days. **The Real World** sculpture garden at its north end, by Tom Otterness, playfully pokes fun at the area's capitalist ethos. The Stuyvesant High School building (1992) is also at this end of the park; on its north side begins the paved river esplanade that extends to Gansevoort Street in the West Village. The **esplanade** is full of skaters, joggers, and strollers at all hours, and the benches along the path are terrific spots from which to watch the sunset over New Jersey. The park is part of plans for an even larger park to extend north to midtown, managed by the Hudson River Park Conservancy (☞ A New Breeze Is Blowing, Down by the Riverside, *below*).

13 **Independence Plaza.** These high-rise towers at the intersection of Greenwich and Harrison streets are the fruit of a pleasant, if somewhat utilitarian, project of the mid-1970s that was supposed to be part of a wave of demolition and construction—until the preservationists stepped in. For several years Independence Plaza remained a middle-class island stranded downtown, far from stores, schools, and neighbors. With TriBeCa's increasingly chic reputation, however, plus the development of Battery Park City to the south, it has become a much more desirable address. The three-story redbrick houses that share Harrison Street with Independence Plaza were moved here from various sites in the neighborhood when, in the early 1970s, the food wholesalers' central market nearby was razed and moved to the Bronx. ✉ *Greenwich St. between Duane and N. Moore Sts.*

8 **King of Greene Street.** This five-story Renaissance-style 1873 building has a magnificent projecting porch of Corinthian columns and pilasters. Today the King (now painted ivory) houses the M-13 art gallery, Alice's Antiques, and Bennison Fabrics. ✉ 72–76 *Greene St., between Spring and Broome Sts.*

3 **Museum for African Art.** Dedicated to contemporary and traditional African art, this small but expertly conceived museum is housed in a handsome two-story space designed by Maya Lin, who also designed Washington, D.C.'s Vietnam Veterans Memorial. Exhibits may include contemporary sculpture, ceremonial masks, architectural details, costumes, and textiles. The entertaining museum store features African crafts, clothing, and jewelry. ✉ *593 Broadway, near Houston St.,* ☎ *212/966–1313.* *$5.* ⏲ *Tues.–Fri. 10:30–5:30, weekends noon–6.*

4 **New Museum of Contemporary Art.** The avant-garde exhibitions here, all by living artists (many from outside the United States), are often radically innovative and socially conscious. A 1997 renovation added a second-floor gallery, a bookstore, and no-admission-charge exhibition space in the basement devoted to participatory art (all of which

can be touched). ✉ *583 Broadway, between Houston and Prince Sts.,* ☎ *212/219–1222.* 💵 *$5; free Thurs. 6 PM–8 PM.* 🕐 *Wed., Fri., and Sun. noon–6., Thurs. and Sat noon–8.*

9 **New York Earth Room.** Walter de Maria's 1977 avant-garde work consists of 140 tons of gently sculpted soil (22 inches deep) filling 3,600 square ft of space of a second-floor gallery. ✉ *141 Wooster St., between Houston and Prince Sts.,* ☎ *212/473–8072.* 💵 *Free.* 🕐 *Jan.–mid-June and mid-Sept.–Dec., Wed.–Sat. noon–6.*

7 **Queen of Greene Street.** The regal grace of this 1873 cast-iron beauty is exemplified by its dormers, columns, window arches, projecting central bays, and Second Empire–style roof. ✉ *28–30 Greene St., between Grand and Canal Sts.*

10 **SoHo Grand Hotel.** The first major hotel to appear in the area since the 1800s, the 15-story SoHo Grand, which opened in 1996, was designed to pay tribute to the neighborhood's architectural history, particularly the cast-iron historic district. Manhattan's only "dog bar," a 17-century French stone basin, stands at the hotel's entrance to signal that pets are welcome. A staircase—made of translucent bottle glass and iron and suspended from the ceiling by two cables—links the entryway with the second-floor 7,000-square-ft lobby, which has 16-ft-high windows and massive stone columns supporting the paneled mercury mirror ceiling (☞ Chapter 7). ✉ *310 W. Broadway, at Grand St.,* ☎ *212/965–3000.*

NEED A BREAK? For a taste of SoHo shabby chic, head for **Scharmann's** (✉ 386 W. Broadway, between Spring and Broome Sts., ☎ 212/219–2561), where the hip drink tea from gleaming brass pots on oversize couches, mismatched chairs, and a bean bag or two.

Staple Street. Little more than an alley, Staple Street was named for the eggs, butter, cheese, and other staple products unloaded here by ships in transit that didn't want to pay duty on any extra cargo. Framed at the end of the alley is the redbrick **New York Mercantile Exchange** (✉ 6 Harrison St.), its square corner tower topped by a bulbous roof. On the ground floor is the acclaimed French restaurant Chanterelle (☞ Chapter 6).

12 **TriBeCa Film Center.** Robert De Niro created this complex of editing, screening, and production rooms, where Miramax Films, Stephen Spielberg, Quincy Jones, and De Niro keep offices. Like many of the other chic buildings in this area, it's inside a former factory, the old Coffee Building. On the ground floor is the Tribeca Grill restaurant (☞ Chapter 6), also owned by Robert De Niro. ✉ *375 Greenwich St., between Franklin and N. Moore Sts.*

14 **Washington Market Park.** This much-needed recreation space for TriBeCa was named after the great food market that once sprawled over the area. It is now a green, landscaped oasis with a playground and a gazebo. Just across Chambers Street from the park, **P.S. 234,** a public elementary school, has opened to serve TriBeCa's younger generation. At the corner, a stout little red tower resembles a lighthouse, and iron ship figures are worked into the playground fence—reminders of the neighborhood's long-gone dockside past. ✉ *Greenwich St. between Chambers and Duane Sts.*

LITTLE ITALY AND CHINATOWN

Mulberry Street is the heart of Little Italy; in fact, at this point it's virtually the entire body. In 1932 an estimated 98% of the inhabitants of this area were of Italian birth or heritage, but since then the growth and expansion of neighboring Chinatown have encroached on the Italian neighborhood to such an extent that merchants and community leaders of the Little Italy Restoration Association (LIRA) negotiated a truce in which the Chinese agreed to let at least Mulberry remain an all-Italian street.

In the second half of the 19th century, when Italian immigration peaked, the neighborhood stretched from Houston Street to Canal Street and the Bowery to Broadway. During this time Italians founded at least three Italian parishes, including the Church of the Transfiguration (now almost wholly Chinese); they also operated an Italian-language newspaper, *Il Progresso.*

In 1926 immigrants from southern Italy celebrated the first Feast of San Gennaro along Mulberry Street—a 10-day street fair that still takes place every September. Dedicated to the patron saint of Naples, the festival transforms Mulberry Street into a virtual alfresco restaurant, as wall-to-wall vendors sell traditional fried sausages and pastries. Today the festival is one of the few reminders of Little Italy's vibrant history as the neighborhood continues to change. (If you want the flavor of a completely Italian neighborhood, you'd do better to visit Carroll Gardens in Brooklyn or Arthur Avenue in the Bronx [☞ Chapter 3]—or rent a video of the Martin Scorsese movie *Mean Streets,* which was filmed in Little Italy in the early 1970s.)

In the meantime, quiet but dramatic change has set in hereabouts in the last year. Mulberry, Mott and Elizabeth streets between Houston and Spring streets are the core of Nolita, an up-and-coming, newly christened neighborhood whose name comes from "*No*rth of *Li*ttle *It*aly." Trendy clothing, design, and secondhand boutiques as well as restaurants and cafés have opened up and down these few blocks, and many new ventures continue to debut, making this area a sort of undiscovered SoHo. Though the neighborhood lacks big-draw exploring sights, its cutting-edge stores are worth exploring (☞ Chapter 10).

Throughout Little Italy and Nolita, note the many tenement buildings with fire escapes projecting over the sidewalks. Most are of the late-19th-century New York style known as railroad flats: six-story buildings on 25- by 90-ft lots, with all the rooms in each apartment placed in a straight line like railroad cars. This style was common in the densely populated immigrant neighborhoods of lower Manhattan until 1901, when the city passed an ordinance requiring air shafts in the interior of buildings.

Visibly exotic, Chinatown is a popular tourist attraction, but it is also a real, vital community where about half the city's population of 300,000 Chinese still live. Its main businesses are restaurants and garment factories; some 55% of its residents speak little or no English. Theoretically, Chinatown is divided from Little Italy by Canal Street, the bustling artery that links the Holland Tunnel (to New Jersey) and the Manhattan Bridge (to Brooklyn). However, in recent years an influx of immigrants from the People's Republic of China, Taiwan, and especially Hong Kong has swelled Manhattan's Chinese population, and Hong Kong residents have poured capital into Chinatown real estate. Consequently, Chinatown now spills over its traditional borders into Little Italy to the north and the formerly Jewish Lower East Side to the east.

The first Chinese immigrants were primarily railroad workers who came from the West in the 1870s to settle in a limited section of the Lower East Side. For nearly a century anti-immigration laws prohibited most men from having their wives and families join them; the neighborhood became known as a "bachelor society," and for years its population remained static. It was not until the end of World War II, when Chinese immigration quotas were increased, that the neighborhood began the outward expansion that is still taking place today.

Chinatown is now livelier than ever—a virtual marketplace crammed with souvenir shops and restaurants in funky pagoda-style buildings and crowded with pedestrians day and night. From fast-food noodles or dumplings to sumptuous Hunan, Szechuan, Cantonese, Mandarin, and Shanghai feasts, every imaginable type of Chinese cuisine is served here. Sidewalk markets burst with stacks of fresh seafood and strange-shaped vegetables in extraterrestrial shades of green. Food shops proudly display their wares: If America's motto is "A chicken in every pot," then Chinatown's must be "A roast duck in every window."

Numbers in the text correspond to numbers in the margin and on the SoHo, TriBeCa, Little Italy, Chinatown map.

A Good Walk

Start your tour at the intersection of Spring and Mulberry streets, which still has a residential feel. Take a moment to poke your nose into the DiPalma Bread Outlet (✉ 45 Spring St.), one of the last coal-oven bakeries in the United States. Walk down **Mulberry Street** ⑯ to Broome Street, a gastronomic thoroughfare. East of Mulberry Street, the building at 375 Broome Street is known for its sheet-metal cornice that bears the face of a distinguished, albeit anonymous, bearded man.

To see the ornate Renaissance Revival former **New York City Police Headquarters** ⑰, walk west on Broome Street to Centre Street, between Broome and Grand streets. Then work your way back to the corner of Grand and Mulberry streets and stop to get the lay of the land. Facing north (uptown), on your right you'll see a series of multistory houses from the early 19th century, built long before the great flood of immigration hit this neighborhood between 1890 and 1924. Turn and look south along the east side of Mulberry Street to see Little Italy's trademark railroad-flat-style tenement buildings.

On the southeast corner of Grand Street, E. Rossi & Co. (✉ 191 Grand St.), established in 1902, is an antiquated little shop that sells housewares, espresso makers, embroidered religious postcards, and jocular Italian T-shirts. Two doors east on Grand Street is Ferrara's (✉ 195 Grand St.), a pastry shop opened in 1892 that ships its creations—cannoli, peasant pie, Italian rum cake—all over the world. Another survivor of the pre-tenement era is the two-story, dormered brick Van Rensselaer House, now Paolucci's Restaurant (✉ 149 Mulberry St.); built in 1816, it is a prime example of the Italian Federal style.

One block south of Grand Street, on the corner of Hester and Mulberry streets, you'll reach the site of what was once Umberto's Clam House (✉ 129 Mulberry St.), best known as the place where mobster Joey Gallo was munching scungilli in 1973 when he was fatally surprised by a task force of mob hit men. Turn left onto Hester Street to visit yet another Little Italy institution, Puglia (✉ 189 Hester St.), a restaurant where guests sit at long communal tables, sing along with house entertainers, and enjoy southern Italian specialties with quantities of homemade wine. (For other Little Italy restaurants, *see* Chapter 6.) One street west, on Baxter Street about three-quarters of a block toward Canal Street, stands the **San Gennaro Church** ⑱, which each autumn sponsors Little Italy's keynote event, the annual Feast of San Gennaro.

To reach Chinatown from Little Italy, cross Canal Street at Mulberry Street. A good place to get oriented is the **Museum of Chinese in the Americas** ⑲, in a century-old schoolhouse at the corner of Bayard and Mulberry streets. For a taste of Chinatown-style commercialism, walk one block north to Canal Street, where restaurants and markets abound. If Chinese food products intrigue you, stop to browse in **Kam Man** (⊠ 200 Canal St.) and then head east to **Mott Street** ⑳, the principal business street of the neighborhood.

Turn right from Canal Street onto Mott Street and walk three blocks. On the corner of Mott and Mosco streets, you'll find the **Church of the Transfiguration** ㉑, where the faithful have worshiped since 1801. From here turn right from Mott Street onto Mosco Street, proceeding downhill to Mulberry Street, where you'll see **Columbus Park** ㉒. This peaceful spot occupies the area once known as the Five Points, a tough 19th-century slum ruled by Irish gangs.

Across Mott Street from the church is a sign for Pell Street, a narrow lane of wall-to-wall restaurants whose neon signs stretch halfway across the thoroughfare. Halfway up Pell is **Doyers Street,** the site of turn-of-the-century gang wars. At the end of Doyers you'll find the **Bowery.** Cross the street to **Chatham Square** ㉓, where the Kimlau Arch honors Chinese casualties in American wars, and a statue pays homage to Lin Zexu, a 19th-century Chinese official who banned opium from the mainland. From Chatham Square cross over the east side, past Park Row. Take a sharp right turn onto St. James Place to find two remnants of this neighborhood's pre-Chinatown past. On St. James Place is the **First Shearith Israel graveyard** ㉔, the first Jewish cemetery in the United States. Walk a half block farther, turn left on James Street, and you'll see St. James Church (⊠ 32 James St.), a stately 1837 Greek Revival edifice where Al Smith, who rose from this poor Irish neighborhood to become New York's governor and a 1928 Democratic presidential candidate, once served as altar boy.

Return to Chatham Square once again and walk north up the Bowery to **Confucius Plaza** ㉕, where a statue of the Chinese sage stands guard. Then cross the Bowery back to the west side of the street; at the corner of Pell Street stands 18 Bowery, which is one of Manhattan's oldest homes—a Federal and Georgian structure built in 1785 by meat wholesaler Edward Mooney. Farther north up the Bowery, a younger side of Chinatown is shown at the **Asian American Arts Centre** ㉖, which displays current work by Asian-American artists.

Continue north. At the intersection of the Bowery and Canal Street, a grand arch and colonnade mark the entrance to the Manhattan Bridge, which leads to Brooklyn. This corner was once the center of New York's diamond district. Today most jewelry dealers have moved uptown, but you can still find some pretty good deals at jewelers on the Bowery and the north side of Canal Street.

TIMING

Since Little Italy consists of little more than one street, a tour of the area shouldn't take more than one hour. Most attractions are food-related, so plan on visiting around lunchtime. Another fun time to visit is during the San Gennaro Festival, around mid-September. Come on a weekend to see Chinatown at its liveliest; locals crowd the streets from dawn until dusk, along with a slew of tourists. For a more relaxed experience, opt for a weekday instead. Allowing for stops at the two local museums and a lunch break, a Chinatown tour will take about three additional hours.

Sights to See

26 **Asian American Arts Centre.** This space offers impressive contemporary works by Asian-American artists, annual Chinese folk-art exhibitions during the Chinese New Year, Asian-American dance performances, and videotapes of Asian American art and events. The center also sells unique art objects from Asia. There's no sign out front, and the door reads KTV-CITY; ring buzzer No. 1. ✉ *26 Bowery, between Bayard and Canal Sts.,* ☎ *212/233–2154.* 🎫 *Free.* ⏲ *Tues.–Fri. 1–6, Sat. 4–6.*

The Bowery. Now a commercial thoroughfare lined with stores selling light fixtures and secondhand restaurant equipment, in the 17th century this broad boulevard was a farming area north of the city; its name derives from *bowerij,* the Dutch word for farm. As the city's growing population moved northward, the Bowery became a broad, elegant avenue lined with taverns and theaters. In the late 1800s the placement of an elevated subway line over the Bowery and the proliferation of saloons and brothels led to its demise as an elegant commercial thoroughfare; by the early 20th century it had become infamous as a skid row full of indigents and crime. After 1970 efforts at gentrification had some effect, and the neighborhood's indigent population dispersed. Today the Bowery is a major, if forgotten, artery through lower Manhattan.

23 **Chatham Square.** Ten streets converge at this labyrinthine intersection, creating pandemonium for cars and a nightmare for pedestrians. A memorial, the **Kimlau Arch,** honoring Chinese casualties in American wars, stands on an island in the eye of the storm. A new statue on the square's eastern edge pays tribute to a Quin Dynasty official named Lin Zexu. Erected in late 1997, the 18-ft, 5-inch tall granite statue reflects Chinatown's growing population of mainland immigrants and their particular national pride: The Fujianese minister is noted for his role in sparking the Opium War by banning the drug. The base of his statue reads, SAY NO TO DRUGS. On the far end of the square, at the corner of Catherine Street and East Broadway, there's a **Republic National Bank**—originally a branch of the Manhattan Savings Bank. It was built to resemble a pagoda.

21 **Church of the Transfiguration.** Built in 1801 as the Zion Episcopal Church, this is an imposing Georgian structure with Gothic windows. It is now a Chinese Catholic church distinguished by its trilingualism: Here Mass is said in Cantonese, Mandarin, and English. ✉ *29 Mott St.,* ☎ *212/962–5157.*

NEED A BREAK?

Right across from the Church of the Transfiguration, at the corner of Mott and Mosco Streets, you'll see a red shack, **Cecilia Tam's Hong Kong Egg Cake Company,** where Ms. Tam makes mouthwatering small, round egg cakes for $1 a portion, between Tuesday and Sunday from early morning until 5. At 35 Pell Street, off Mott Street, is **May May Chinese Gourmet Bakery** (☎ 212/267–0733), a local favorite, with Chinese pastries, rice dumplings wrapped in banana leaves, yam cakes, and other sweet treats. A colorful flag hangs outside the entrance of the **Chinatown Ice Cream Factory** (✉ 65 Bayard St., between Mott and Elizabeth Sts., ☎ 212/608–4170), where the flavors range from red bean to litchi to green tea. Prepare to eat your scoop on the run, since there's no seating.

22 **Columbus Park.** Mornings bring groups of elderly Chinese practicing the graceful movements of tai chi to this shady, paved space; during afternoons the park's tables fill for heated games of mah-jongg. One hundred years ago the then-swampy area was known as the Five Points—after the intersection of Mulberry Street, Anthony (now Worth) Street, Cross (now Park) Street, Orange (now Baxter) Street, and Little Water Street (no longer in existence)—and was notoriously ruled by dangerous Irish gangs. In the 1880s a neighborhood-improvement campaign brought about the park's creation.

25 **Confucius Plaza.** At this open area just north of ☞ **Chatham Square,** a bronze statue of Confucius presides before the redbrick high-rise apartment complex named for him. The statue was originally opposed by leftist Chinese immigrants, who considered the sage a reactionary symbol of old China. ✉ *Intersection of Bowery and Division St.*

Doyers Street. The "bloody angle"—an unexpected sharp turn halfway down this little alleyway—was the site of turn-of-the-century battles between Chinatown's Hip Sing and On Leon tongs, gangs who fought for control over the local gambling and opium trades. Today the street is among Chinatown's most colorful, lined with tea parlors and barbershops.

24 **First Shearith Israel graveyard.** Consecrated in 1656 by the country's oldest Jewish congregation, this small burial ground bears the remains of Sephardic Jews (of Spanish-Portuguese extraction) who emigrated from Brazil in the mid-17th century. The second and third Shearith Israel graveyards are in Greenwich Village and Chelsea, respectively. ✉ *55 St. James Pl.*

OFF THE BEATEN PATH

LOWER EAST SIDE TENEMENT MUSEUM – America's first urban living-history museum preserves and interprets the life of immigrants and migrants in New York's Lower East Side. A guided tour (reservations suggested) takes you to a partially restored 1863 tenement building at 97 Orchard Street, where you can view the apartments of Natalie Gumpertz, a German-Jewish dressmaker (dating from 1878); Adolph and Rosaria Baldizzi, Catholic immigrants from Sicily (1935); the Rogarshevsky family from Eastern Europe (1918); and the Confino family, Sephardic Jews from Kastoria, Turkey, which is now part of Greece (1916). The Confino family apartment has been reconstructed from a child's point of view, and children and adults can actually touch items in the exhibit. The museum also leads historic walking tours around Orchard Street. If you wish to forego the tours, you can watch a free slide show tracing the history of the tenement building and the neighborhood as well as a video with interviews of Lower East Side residents past and present. The gallery (free) has changing exhibits relating to Lower East Side history, in addition to a list of the former residents. (The museum may be reached by subway by taking the F train to Delancey Street, the B, D, or Q to Grand Street, or the J, M, or Z to Essex Street; or take the M15 bus to Allen and Delancey streets.) ✉ *90 Orchard St.,* ☎ *212/431–0233.* 🎟 *Tenement tour $8, tenement and Orchard St. walking tours $12.* ⏲ *Museum: Tues.–Fri. noon–5, weekends 11–5; tenement tours: Tues.–Fri. 1, 2, and 3, weekends every 45 mins 11–4:15; walking tours: weekends 1:30 and 2:30. Tour are limited to 15 people.*

20 **Mott Street.** The main commercial artery of Chinatown, Mott Street has appeared in innumerable movies and television as the street that exemplifies the neighborhood. It's also so well known to New Yorkers that it's been immortalized in the lyrics of "Manhattan," a song by Rodgers and Hart. Chinatown began in the late 1880s when Chi-

nese immigrants (mostly men) settled in tenements in a small area that included the lower portion of Mott Street as well as nearby Pell and Doyer streets. Today the street is often crowded during the day and especially on weekends; it overflows with fish and vegetable markets, restaurants, bakeries, and souvenir shops.

Opened in 1891, **Quong Yuen Shing & Co.** (✉ 32 Mott St.), also known as the Mott Street General Store, is one of Chinatown's oldest curio shops, with porcelain bowls, teapots, and cups for sale. Next door is one of Chinatown's best and oldest bakeries, **Fung Wong** (✉ 30 Mott St.), where you can stock up on almond cookies, sticky rice cakes, sweet egg tarts, roast pork buns, and other goodies. If you've never tried dim sum (Chinese dumplings and other small dishes), now's your chance; **20 Mott Street** and **Mandarin Court** (✉ 61 Mott St.) are good bets.

16 **Mulberry Street.** Crowded with restaurants, cafés, bakeries, imported-food shops, and souvenir stores, Mulberry Street is where Little Italy lives and breathes. The blocks between Houston and Spring streets fall within the newly named neighborhood of Nolita, and are home to an increasing number of up-to-the-moment stores and restaurants, which are side by side with others that seem dedicated to staying exactly as their old customers remember them.

NEED A BREAK? You can savor cannoli and other sweet treats at **Caffè Roma** (✉ 385 Broome St., ☎ 212/226–8413), a traditional neighborhood favorite with wrought-iron chairs and a pounded-tin ceiling.

19 **Museum of Chinese in the Americas (MCA).** In a century-old schoolhouse that once served Italian-American and Chinese-American children, MCA is the only U.S. museum devoted to preserving the history of the Chinese people throughout the western hemisphere. The permanent exhibit—*Where's Home? Chinese in the Americas*— explores the Chinese-American experience by weaving together displays of artists' creations and personal and domestic artifacts with historical documentation. Slippers for binding feet, Chinese musical instruments, a reversible silk gown (circa 1900) worn at a Cantonese opera performance, items from a Chinese laundry, and antique business signs are some of the unique objects on display; changing exhibits fill a second room. MCA sponsors workshops, walking tours, lectures, and family events. Its archives (open by appointment only) dedicated to Chinese-American history and culture include 2,000 volumes. ✉ *70 Mulberry St., 2nd floor,* ☎ *212/619–4785.* *$3.* *Tues.–Sat. noon–5.*

17 **New York City Police Headquarters.** This magnificent Renaissance Revival structure with baroque embellishments and a striking dome served as the New York City police headquarters from its construction in 1909 until 1973; in 1988 it was converted into a high-priced condominium complex. Known to New Yorkers today as "240 Centre Street," its big-name residents have included Cindy Crawford, Winona Ryder, and Steffi Graf, among others. ✉ *240 Centre St., between Broome and Grand Sts.*

18 **San Gennaro Church.** Every autumn San Gennaro Church—officially called the Most Precious Blood Church, National Shrine of San Gennaro—sponsors the Feast of San Gennaro, the biggest event in Little Italy (☞ Festivals and Seasonal Events *in* Chapter 1). (The community's other big festival celebrates St. Anthony of Padua in June; the church connected to the festival is at Houston and Sullivan streets, in what is now SoHo.) ✉ *113 Baxter St., near Canal St.*

WALL STREET AND THE BATTERY

Island city that it is, much of Manhattan strangely turns its back on the rushing waters that surround it—not so the Battery. From waterside walks in Battery Park, you can look out on the confluence of the Hudson and East River estuaries where bustling seaborne commerce once glutted the harbor that built the "good city of old Manhatto," Herman Melville's moniker from the second chapter of *Moby-Dick*. It was here that the Dutch established the colony of Nieuw Amsterdam in 1625; in 1789 the first capital building of the United States found itself here. The city did not really expand beyond these precincts until the middle of the 19th century. Today this historic heart of New York continues to be dominated by Wall Street, which is both an actual street and a shorthand name for the vast, powerful financial community that clusters around the New York and American stock exchanges. A different but equally awe-inspiring type of sight can be found at the tip of the island as you gaze across the great silvery harbor to the enduring symbols of America: the Statue of Liberty and Ellis Island, port of entry for countless immigrants to a new land.

Numbers in the text correspond to numbers in the margin and on the Lower Manhattan map.

A Good Walk

The immediate vicinity of the Staten Island Ferry Terminal (just outside the South Ferry subway station on the 1 and 9 lines) is a little unsightly, but that doesn't detract from the pleasure of a ride on the **Staten Island Ferry** ①. The 20- to 30-minute ride across New York Harbor provides great views of the Manhattan skyline, Ellis Island, the Statue of Liberty, the Verrazano-Narrows Bridge, and the New Jersey coast—and the blue-and-orange boats are a delight (plus, rides are free).

Just north of the Staten Island Ferry Terminal, the tall white columns and curved brick front of the 1793 **Shrine of St. Elizabeth Ann Seton at Our Lady of the Rosary** are a dignified sight. The house used to be one of many mansions lining State Street. To the left of the shrine, the verdant **Battery Park** ②, Manhattan's green toe, curves up the west side of the island. It is filled with sculpture and monuments, one of which is the circular **Castle Clinton** ③. The venerable fort is where you buy tickets for the ferries to the **Statue of Liberty** ④ and **Ellis Island** ⑤. From Castle Clinton follow the rose-color walk toward **Bowling Green,** an oval greensward at the foot of Broadway that became New York's first public park in 1733. Across State Street, facing the south flank of Bowling Green, is the Beaux Arts Alexander Hamilton U.S. Custom House, home of the **National Museum of the American Indian** ⑥.

Next follow Whitehall Street down the east side of the American Indian museum. A left turn onto Bridge Street will bring into focus a block of early New York buildings. As you approach Broad Street, the two-tone Georgian **Fraunces Tavern** ⑦ will appear. The complex of five largely 19th-century buildings houses a museum, restaurant, and bar. Across Pearl Street, 85 Broad Street pays homage to urban archaeology with a transparent panel in the sidewalk showing the excavated foundations of the 17th-century Stadt Huys, the Old Dutch City Hall. The course of old Dutch Stone Street is marked in the lobby with a line of brown paving stones.

Head north on Pearl Street to **Hanover Square,** a quiet tree-lined plaza, then head inland on William Street to the triangular convergence of South William and Beaver streets. On the right, 20 Exchange Place towers and adds street-level interest with weighty Art Deco doorways depicting the engines of commerce. Two blocks farther north, William Street crosses **Wall Street,** a jaw-dropping display of the money that built Manhattan—the massive arcade of 55 Wall Street alone speaks volumes. Developers' greed backfired here—they built on every inch of land only to have property values decrease once people realized how stultifying the results were.

One block west on Wall Street, where Broad Street becomes Nassau Street, a regal statue of George Washington stands on the steps of the **Federal Hall National Memorial** ⑧. Across the street is an investment bank built by J. P. Morgan in 1913. By building only four stories, Morgan was in effect declaring himself above the pressures of Wall Street real estate values. Now **Morgan Guaranty Trust,** the building bears pockmarks near the fourth window on the Wall Street side; these were created when a bomb that had been placed in a pushcart exploded in 1920. The temple-fronted **New York Stock Exchange** ⑨ is the central shrine of Wall Street (even though its address is officially on Broad Street). From its visitor center you can watch stressed-out traders gesture wildly in the name of making deals.

The focal point at the west end of Wall Street is the brownstone **Trinity Church** ⑩. Just north of the church is tiny Thames Street, where a pair of skyscrapers playfully called the Thames Twins—the Trinity and U.S. Realty buildings—display early 20th-century attempts to apply Gothic decoration to skyscrapers. Across the street at 120 Broadway, the 1915 Equitable Building rises 30 stories straight from its base with no setback; its overpowering shadow on the street helped persuade the city government to pass the nation's first zoning law. Large public plazas around the bases of skyscrapers have helped to alleviate this problem, at the same time creating space for public sculpture.

Four sculpture installations make for an interesting side tour. The first is on Broadway between Cedar and Liberty streets, where the black-glass Marine Midland Bank (1971) heightens the drama of the red-and-silver Isamu Noguchi sculpture *Cube* in its plaza. Two blocks east, near the William Street edge of the plaza surrounding the 65-story Chase Manhattan Bank Building (1960), stands Jean Dubuffet's striking black-and-white *Group of Four Trees.* Inset in the plaza is another Noguchi installation, a circular sculpture garden with his signature carved stones, located slightly south of the Dubuffet. Just north of the Chase plaza, where Liberty Street converges with William Street and Maiden Lane under the Federal Reserve Bank, the triangular Louise Nevelson Plaza contains four pieces of her black-welded-steel abstract sculpture: three of moderate size and one 70-footer.

The massive, rusticated **Federal Reserve Bank of New York** ⑪, directly across the street, recalls Florence's Palazzo Strozzi and looks the way a bank ought to: solid, imposing, and absolutely impregnable. Walk west back toward Broadway on Maiden Lane, which will turn into Cortland Street. The contrast between the Federal Reserve's 1924 vision of architectural power and that of the 1,350-ft-tall towers of the **World Trade Center** ⑫ couldn't be more striking. The 16-acre, 12-million-square-ft complex contains New York's tallest buildings. During the towers' construction more than a million cubic yards of rock and soil were excavated—then moved across West Street to help beget **Battery Park City.** The pedestrian overpass north of 1 World Trade Center leads to Battery Park City's centerpiece, the **World Financial Center** ⑬, a four-tower complex designed by Cesar Pelli. Just north of the basin is the terminal for ferry service to Hoboken, New Jersey. Beyond the ferry terminal is the south end of the Hudson River Park (☞ SoHo and

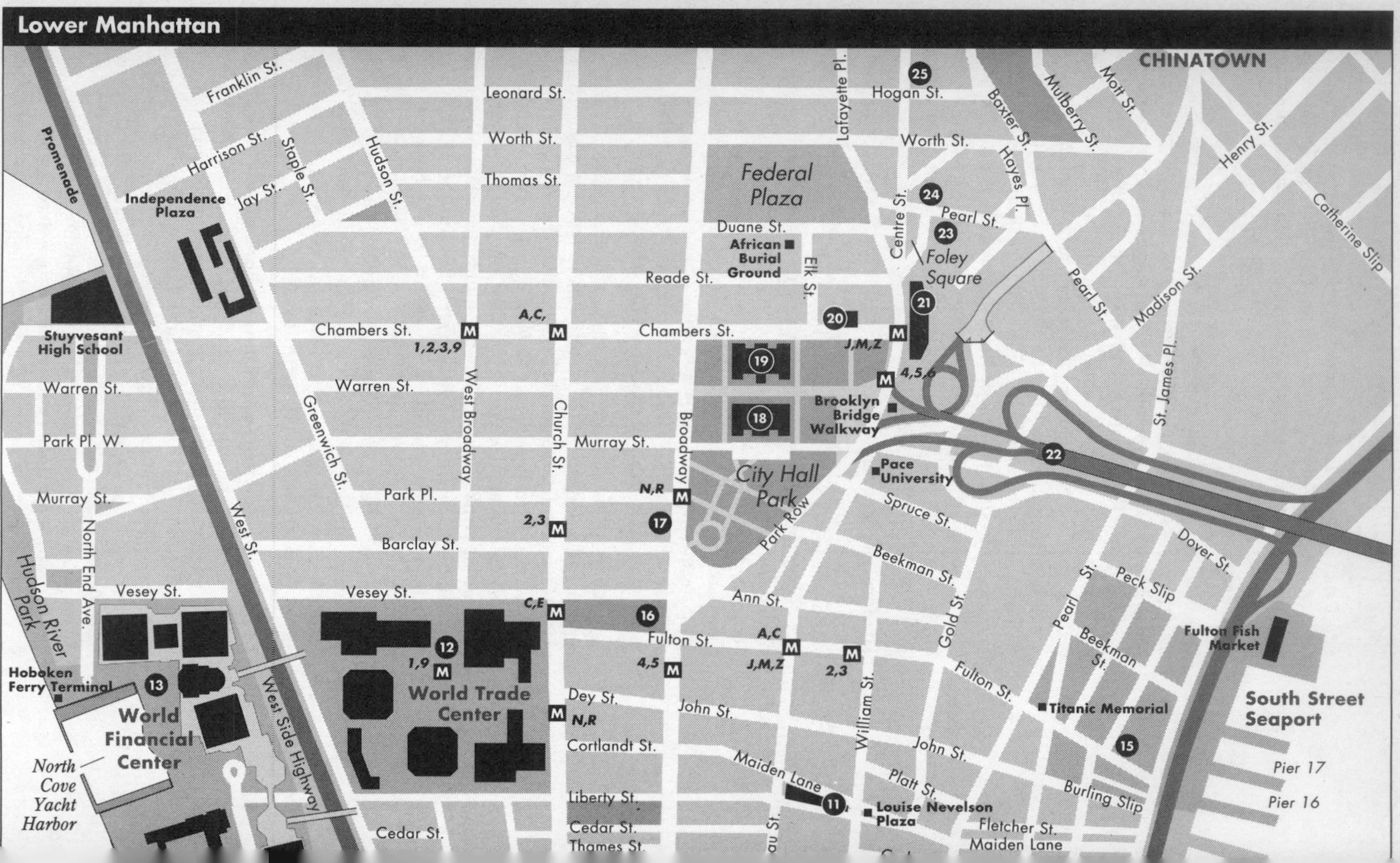

Lower Manhattan
CHINATOWN
Franklin St.
Leonard St.
Worth St.
Thomas St.
Harrison St.
Staple St.
Hudson St.
Jay St.
Independence Plaza
Promenade
Stuyvesant High School
Warren St.
Park Pl. W.
Murray St.
North End Ave.
Hudson River Park
Vesey St.
Hoboken Ferry Terminal
World Financial Center
North Cove Yacht Harbor
West St.
West Side Highway
Greenwich St.
Chambers St.
1,2,3,9
Warren St.
West Broadway
A,C,
Church St.
Park Pl.
2,3
Barclay St.
Vesey St.
C,E
1,9
World Trade Center
Cedar St.
Dey St.
N,R
Cortlandt St.
Liberty St.
Cedar St.
Thames St.
Federal Plaza
Duane St.
African Burial Ground
Reade St.
Elk St.
Chambers St.
Murray St.
Broadway
N,R
City Hall Park
Park Row
Fulton St.
4,5
John St.
A,C
J,M,Z
2,3
William St.
Maiden Lane
Louise Nevelson Plaza
Lafayette Pl.
Hogan St.
Worth St.
Centre St.
Pearl St.
Foley Square
J,M,Z
4,5,6
Brooklyn Bridge Walkway
Pace University
Spruce St.
Beekman St.
Ann St.
Gold St.
Fulton St.
John St.
Platt St.
Fletcher St.
Maiden Lane
Baxter St.
Hayes Pl.
Mulberry St.
Mott St.
Henry St.
Catherine Slip
Pearl St.
Madison St.
St. James Pl.
Dover St.
Peck Slip
Pearl St.
Beekman St.
Titanic Memorial
Burling Slip
Fulton Fish Market
South Street Seaport
Pier 17
Pier 16

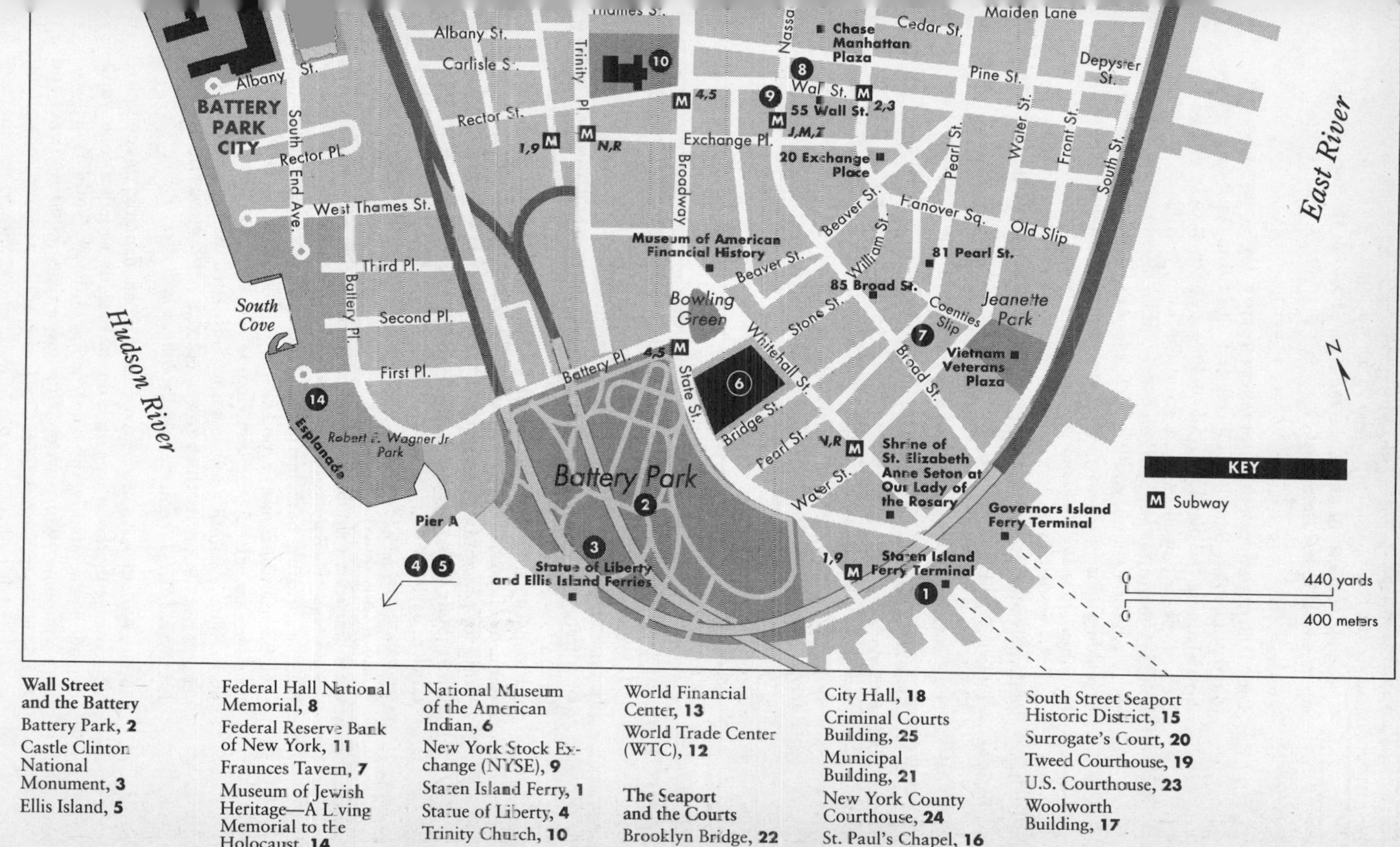

Wall Street and the Battery
Battery Park, **2**
Castle Clinton National Monument, **3**
Ellis Island, **5**
Federal Hall National Memorial, **8**
Federal Reserve Bank of New York, **11**
Fraunces Tavern, **7**
Museum of Jewish Heritage—A Living Memorial to the Holocaust, **14**
National Museum of the American Indian, **6**
New York Stock Exchange (NYSE), **9**
Staten Island Ferry, **1**
Statue of Liberty, **4**
Trinity Church, **10**
World Financial Center, **13**
World Trade Center (WTC), **12**

The Seaport and the Courts
Brooklyn Bridge, **22**
City Hall, **18**
Criminal Courts Building, **25**
Municipal Building, **21**
New York County Courthouse, **24**
St. Paul's Chapel, **16**
South Street Seaport Historic District, **15**
Surrogate's Court, **20**
Tweed Courthouse, **19**
U.S. Courthouse, **23**
Woolworth Building, **17**

TriBeCa, *above*). To the south, a longer riverside esplanade accompanies the residential part of Battery Park City and connects with **Robert F. Wagner Jr. Park,** home to the **Museum of Jewish Heritage—A Living Memorial to the Holocaust** ⑭.

TIMING
The Manhattan side of this tour takes most of a day—allow more time to ferry out to the Statue of Liberty and Ellis Island. Visit on a weekday to capture the district's true vitality—but expect to be jostled on the crowded sidewalks if you stand too long, peering at the great buildings that surge skyward on every corner. If you visit on a weekend, on the other hand, you'll feel like a lone explorer among a canyon of buildings. Either way, winds from the harbor whipping around the buildings can make this area feel markedly colder than other parts of the city—a great thing in summer—so dress accordingly. Start early, preferably making the first ferry, to try to beat the crowds to Liberty and Ellis islands. Get tickets by lunchtime if you plan to visit the Stock Exchange, which is open only on weekdays until 4. The best place to end the day is looking west over the Hudson for the sunset.

Sights to See

❷ **Battery Park.** Jutting out as if it were Manhattan's green toe, Battery Park (so named because a battery of 28 cannons was placed along its shore in Colonial days to fend off the British) is built on landfill and has gradually grown over the centuries. The park's main structure is ☞ **Castle Clinton National Monument,** the takeoff point for ferries to the ☞ **Statue of Liberty** and ☞ **Ellis Island.** The park is loaded with various other monuments and statues, some impressive, some downright obscure. Starting near the Staten Island Ferry Terminal, head north along the water's edge to the **East Coast Memorial,** a statue of a fierce eagle that presides over eight granite slabs inscribed with the names of U.S. servicemen who died in the western Atlantic during World War II. Climb the steps of the East Coast Memorial for a fine view of the main features of **New York Harbor**; from left to right: **Governors Island,** a former Coast Guard installation whose future, as of press time, was undecided; hilly **Staten Island** (☞ Chapter 3) in the distance; the **Statue of Liberty,** on Liberty Island; **Ellis Island,** gateway to the New World for generations of immigrants; and the old railway terminal in **Liberty State Park,** on the mainland in Jersey City, New Jersey. On crystal-clear days you can see all the way to Port Elizabeth's cranes, which seem to mimic Lady Liberty's stance. Continue north past a romantic **statue of Giovanni da Verrazano,** the Florentine merchant who piloted the ship that first sighted New York and its harbor in 1524. The **Verrazano-Narrows Bridge,** between Brooklyn and Staten Island—so long that the curvature of the earth had to be figured into its dimensions—is visible from here, just beyond Governors Island. At the park's northernmost edge, Pier A, the last Victorian fireboat pier in the city, was undergoing restoration at press time; it is slated to offer a visitor center and restaurant. Its clock tower, erected in 1919, was the nation's first World War I memorial. ⊠ *Broadway at Battery Pl.*

Battery Park City. An impressive feat of urban planning, this complete 92-acre neighborhood was built on the roughly 1 million cubic yards of landfill generated by the construction of the ☞ **World Trade Center**'s whopping twin towers. With more than 5,000 residents and 20,000 workers, Battery Park City is almost like a separate city within the city, with high-rises, town houses, shops, and green squares—though it's not a very exciting place to visit. Its commercial centerpiece is the ☞ **World Financial Center.**

Bowling Green. This oval greensward at the foot of Broadway became New York's first public park in 1733. On July 9, 1776, a few hours after citizens learned about the signing of the Declaration of Independence, rioters toppled a statue of British king George III that had occupied the spot for 11 years; much of the statue's lead was melted down into bullets. In 1783, when the occupying British forces fled the city, they defiantly hoisted a Union Jack on a greased, uncleated flagpole so it couldn't be lowered; patriot John Van Arsdale drove his own cleats into the pole to replace the flag with the Stars and Stripes. The entrance to the subway station here is the original one, built in 1904–05.

❸ **Castle Clinton National Monument.** This circular red-stone fortress first stood on an island 200 ft from shore as a defense for New York Harbor. In 1824 it became Castle Garden, an entertainment and concert facility that reached its zenith in 1850 when more than 6,000 people (the capacity of Radio City Music Hall) attended the U.S. debut of the Swedish Nightingale, Jenny Lind. After landfill connected it to the city, Castle Clinton became, in succession, an immigrant processing center, an aquarium, and now a restored fort, museum, and ticket office for ferries to the ☞ **Statue of Liberty** and ☞ **Ellis Island.** (The ferry ride is one loop; you can get off at Liberty Island, visit the statue, then reboard any ferry and continue on to Ellis Island, boarding another boat once you have finished exploring the historic immigration facility there.) Inside the old fort are dioramas of lower Manhattan in 1812, 1886, and 1941. Outside the landward entrance is a statue titled *The Immigrants,*at the beginning of a broad mall that leads back across the park to the **Netherlands Memorial Flagpole,** which depicts the bead exchange that bought from the Native Americans the land to establish Fort Amsterdam in 1626. Inscriptions describe the event in English and Dutch. ☎ *212/344–7220 Castle Clinton; 212/269–5755 ferry information.* 🎫 *Castle Clinton: free; ferry: $7 round-trip.* ⏲ *Daily 8:30–5; ferry departures daily every 30 mins 9:30–3:30 (more departures and extended hrs in summer).*

★ ❺ **Ellis Island.** Approximately 16 million men, women, and children first set foot on U.S. soil at this 27½-acre island's federal immigration facility between 1892 and 1924. In all, by the time Ellis Island closed for good in 1954, it had processed the ancestors of more than 40% of Americans living today. The island's main building, now a national monument, reopened in 1990 as the **Ellis Island Immigration Museum.** At its heart is the **Registry Room,** where inspectors once attempted to screen out "undesirables"—polygamists, criminals, the utterly destitute, and people suffering from contagious diseases. The cavernous **Great Hall,** where immigrants were registered, has gorgeous tiled arches by Rafael Guastavino; white-tile dormitory rooms overlook this grand space. The **Railroad Ticket Office** at the back of the main building houses exhibits on the *Peopling of America,* recounting 400 years of immigration history, and *Forced Migration,* focusing on the slave trade. The old kitchen and laundry building has been stabilized rather than restored so you can see what the island's buildings looked like prior to the restoration. Perhaps the most moving exhibit is the **American Immigrant Wall of Honor,** where the names of 420,000 immigrant Americans are inscribed along an outdoor promenade overlooking the Statue of Liberty and the Manhattan skyline. The names include Miles Standish, Priscilla Alden, George Washington's grandfather, Irving Berlin—and possibly an ancestor of yours. In 1998 the Supreme Court ruled that about 90% of Ellis Island is in New Jersey. For ferry information *see* Castle Clinton National Monument, *above.* ☎ *212/363–3200 for Ellis Island or 212/883–1986 for Wall of Honor information.* 🎫 *Free.*

8 **Federal Hall National Memorial.** On the steps of this Greek Revival building stands a regal statue, created in 1883, of George Washington, who on that site—then also Federal Hall—was sworn in as the nation's first president in 1789. The likeness was made by noted sculptor and relative of the president, John Quincy Adams Ward. After the capital moved to Philadelphia in 1790, the original Federal Hall became New York's City Hall, then was demolished in 1812 when the present City Hall (☞ The Seaport and the Courts, *below*) was completed. The current structure, built as a U.S. Customs House in 1842, were modeled on the Parthenon, a potent symbol for a young nation striving to emulate classic Greek democracy. It's now a museum featuring exhibits on New York and Wall Street. Guided site tours are sometimes available on request, and you can also pick up brochures that lead you on differently themed self-guided walking tours of downtown. ⊠ *26 Wall St.,* ☎ *212/825–6888.* 🎫 *Free.* ⏲ *Weekdays 9–5.*

11 **Federal Reserve Bank of New York.** Built in 1924, and enlarged in 1935, this neo-Renaissance structure made of sandstone, limestone, and ironwork goes five levels underground. The gold ingots in the vaults here are worth roughly $140 billion—reputedly a third of the world's gold reserves. The bank was the setting for a robbery scene in the 1995 movie *Die Harder with a Vengeance.* Tours of the bank end at the $750,000 visitor center, which opened in 1997. Its dozen or so interactive computer terminals and displays provide almost as much information as an Economics 101 course—explaining such points as what the Federal Reserve Bank does (besides store gold), what the money supply is, and what causes inflation. ⊠ *33 Liberty St.,* ☎ *212/720–6130.* 🎫 *Free.* ⏲ *1-hr tour by advance (at least 5 days) reservation, weekdays at 10:30, 11:30, 1:30, and 2:30.*

7 **Fraunces Tavern.** Redbrick along one side, cream-color brick along the other, the main corner building is a stately Colonial house with a white-marble portico and coffered frieze, built in 1719 and converted to a tavern in 1762. It was the meeting place for the Sons of Liberty until the Revolutionary War. This was also the site where in 1783 George Washington delivered a farewell address to his officers celebrating the British evacuation of New York. Later the building housed some offices of the fledgling U.S. government. Today a museum, restaurant, and bar compose this historic five-building complex. Fraunces Tavern contains two fully furnished period rooms and other displays of 18th- and 19th-century American history. The museum also offers family programs (such as crafts workshops and a scavenger hunt), lectures, workshops, and concerts. ⊠ *54 Pearl St., at Broad St.,* ☎ *212/425–1778.* 🎫 *Museum $2.50.* ⏲ *Museum weekdays 10–4:45, weekends noon–4.*

NEED A BREAK? The **brick plaza behind 85 Broad Street** is flanked by a variety of small restaurants. Order a take-out meal or snack and eat it out here on the benches, where you can watch busy office workers milling past and enjoy not being one of them.

Hanover Square. When the East River ran past present-day Pearl Street, this quiet tree-lined plaza stood on the waterfront and was the city's original printing-house square—on the site of 81 Pearl Street, William Bradford established the first printing press in the colonies. The pirate Captain Kidd lived in the neighborhood, and the graceful brownstone **India House** (1851–54), a private club at No. 1, used to house the New York Cotton Exchange.

OFF THE BEATEN PATH **MUSEUM OF AMERICAN FINANCIAL HISTORY** – On the site of Alexander Hamilton's law office (today the Standard Oil Building), this four-room museum displays artifacts of the financial market's history, including vintage ticker-tape machines and ticker tape from "Black Tuesday," October 29, 1929—the worst crash in the stock market's history. ✉ *28 Broadway, just north of Bowling Green,* ☎ *212/908–4519.* 🎫 *Free.* ⏲ *Weekdays 11:30–3:30, or by appointment.*

★ 14 **Museum of Jewish Heritage–A Living Memorial to the Holocaust.** Housed in a granite hexagon rising 85 ft above ☞ **Robert F. Wagner Jr. Park,** just below ☞ **Battery Park City,** downtown's newest museum, opened in late 1997 after more than 15 years of planning, pays tribute to the 6 million Jews who perished in the Holocaust. Architect Kevin Roche's Star of David–shape building has three floors of exhibits demonstrating the dynamism of 20th-century Jewish culture. Artifacts of early 20th-century Jewish life are on the first floor: elaborate screens painted by a Budapest butcher for the fall harvest festival of Sukkoth, wedding invitations, and tools used by Jewish tradesmen. *The War Against the Jews,* on the second floor, details the rise of Nazism, the period's anti-Semitism, and the ravages of the Holocaust. A gallery covers the doomed voyage of the *St. Louis,* a ship of German Jewish refugees that crossed the Atlantic twice in 1939 in search of a safe haven. Signs of hope are on display, as well, including a trumpet that Louse Bannet (the "Dutch Louis Armstrong") played for three years in the Auschwitz-Birkenau inmate orchestra, and a pretty blue-and-white checked dress sewn in 1945 by Fania Bratt at the newly liberated Dachau concentration camp. The third floor covers postwar Jewish life and is devoted to the theme of Jewish renewal. The exhibition space's final gallery leads to a usually light-filled room lined with southwest-facing windows with a view of the harbor and the Statue of Liberty. ✉ *18 1st Pl., Battery Park City,* ☎ *212/968–1800.* 🎫 *$7.* ⏲ *Sun.–Wed. 9–5., Thurs. 9–8., Fri. and eve of Jewish holidays 9–2.*

★ 6 **National Museum of the American Indian.** This museum, a branch of the Washington, D.C.–based Smithsonian Institution, is the first of its kind to be dedicated to Native American culture. Well-mounted exhibits examine the history and the current cultures of native peoples from all over the Americas through literature, dance, lectures, readings, film, and crafts. Contemporary Native Americans participate in visiting programs and work at all levels of the staff. George Gustav Heye, a wealthy New Yorker, amassed most of the museum's collection—more than a million artifacts including pottery, weaving, and basketry from the southwestern United States, painted hides from the Plains Indians of North America, carved jade from the Mexican Olmec and Maya cultures, and contemporary Native American paintings. The museum is in one of lower Manhattan's finest buildings: the ornate Beaux Arts **Alexander Hamilton U.S. Custom House** (1907). Above its base, massive granite columns rise to a pediment topped by a double row of statuary. Daniel Chester French, better known for the sculpture of Lincoln in the Lincoln Memorial in Washington, D.C., carved the lower statues, which symbolize various continents (left to right: Asia, the Americas, Europe, Africa). The upper row represents the major trading cities of the world. Inside, the display of white and colored marble couldn't be more remarkable. The semicircular side staircases are equally breathtaking. ✉ *1 Bowling Green,* ☎ *212/668–6624.* 🎫 *Free.* ⏲ *Mon.–Wed. and Fri.–Sun. 10–5, Thurs. 10–8.*

9 **New York Stock Exchange (NYSE).** The largest securities exchange in the world, the NYSE nearly bursts from this relatively diminutive neo-

classic 1903 building with an august Corinthian entrance—a fitting temple to the almighty dollar. Today's "Big Board" can handle a trillion shares of stock per day; in today's market-obsessed media, how those stocks do each day is news broadcast around the world. The third-floor interactive education center, which was completely renovated in 1997, has a self-guided tour, touch-screen computer terminals, video displays, a 15-minute-long film detailing the history of the exchange, and live guides to help you interpret the seeming chaos you'll see from the visitors' gallery overlooking the immense (50-ft-high) trading floor. ✉ *Tickets available at 20 Broad St.,* ☎ *212/656–5165.* 🎫 *Free tickets distributed beginning at 8:45; come before 1 PM to assure entrance.* ⏲ *Weekdays 9–4.*

★ **Robert F. Wagner Jr. Park.** The link in the chain of parks that stretch from ☞ **Battery Park** to above the ☞ **World Financial Center,** this newest addition to the downtown waterfront may be the best of the bunch. Lawns, walks, gardens, and benches spill right down to the river. Behind these, a brown-brick structure rises two stories to provide river and harbor panoramas. A stream of runners and bladers flows by, making it a toss-up which is better: the people-watching or the views of the Statue of Liberty and Ellis Island. ✉ *Between Battery Pl. and the Hudson River.*

Shrine of St. Elizabeth Ann Seton at Our Lady of the Rosary. The rectory of the shrine is a redbrick Federal-style town house, an example of the mansions that used to line the street, with a distinctive portico shaped to fit the curving street. This house was built in 1793 as the home of the wealthy Watson family; Mother Seton and her family lived here from 1801 to 1803. She joined the Catholic Church in 1805, after the death of her husband, and went on to found the Sisters of Charity, the first American order of nuns. In 1975 she became the first American-born saint. Masses are held here daily. ✉ *7–8 State St.,* ☎ *212/269–6865.* ⏲ *Weekdays 6:30–5, weekends by appointment.*

★ ❶ **Staten Island Ferry.** The best transit deal in town is the Staten Island Ferry, a free 20- to 30-minute ride across New York Harbor, which provides great views of the Manhattan skyline, the Statue of Liberty, the Verrazano-Narrows Bridge, and the New Jersey coast. The classic blue-and-orange ferries embark on various schedules: every 15 minutes during rush hours, every 20–30 minutes most other times, and every hour after 11 PM and on weekend mornings. A word of advice, however: The ferry service runs swift, new low-slung craft that ride low in the water and have no outside deck space, so wait for one of the higher, more open old-timers. ☎ *718/390–5253.*

★ ❹ **Statue of Liberty.** Millions of immigrants to America first glimpsed their new land when they laid eyes on the Statue of Liberty, a monument that still ennobles all those who encounter it. *Liberty Enlightening the World,* as the statue is officially named, was sculpted by Frederic-Auguste Bartholdi and presented to the United States as a gift from France in 1886. Since then she has become a near-universal symbol of freedom and democracy, standing a proud 152 ft high on top of an 89-ft pedestal (executed by Richard Morris Hunt), on Liberty Island in New York Harbor. Emma Lazarus's sonnet *The New Colossus* ("Give me your tired, your poor, your huddled masses . . .") is inscribed on a bronze plaque attached to the statue's base. Gustav Eiffel designed the statue's iron skeleton. In anticipation of her centennial, Liberty underwent a long-overdue restoration in the mid-'80s and emerged with great fanfare on July 4, 1986.

The top of the statue is accessible in two ways: An elevator ascends 10 stories to the top of the pedestal, or if you're in good shape, you can climb 354 steps (the equivalent of a 22-story building) to the crown. (Visitors cannot go up into the torch.) Be forewarned that in summer, two- to four-hour waits to walk up to the crown have become commonplace; come prepared to contend with the heat, both outside waiting in line (where there is no overhead protection) and in the statue. Because the park service occasionally closes off the line to the crown as early as 2, it is vital to catch an early ferry out of ☞ **Castle Clinton National Monument**; the earliest leaves at 9:30 (9:15 in summer). Exhibits inside illustrate the statue's history, including videos of the view from the crown for those who don't make the climb. There are also life-size models of the Liberty's face and foot for the blind to feel and a pleasant outdoor café. ✉ *Liberty Island,* ☎ *212/363–3200; 212/269–5755 for ferry information.* 💵 *Free; ferry: $7 round-trip.*

10 **Trinity Church.** The present Trinity Church, the third on this site since an Anglican parish was established here in 1697, was designed in 1846 by Richard Upjohn. It ranked as the city's tallest building for most of the second half of the 19th century. The three huge bronze doors were designed by Richard Morris Hunt to recall Lorenzo Ghiberti's doors for the Baptistery in Florence, Italy. The church's Gothic Revival interior is surprisingly light and elegant. On the church's north side is a 2½-acre graveyard: Alexander Hamilton is buried beneath a white-stone pyramid, and a monument commemorates Robert Fulton, the inventor of the steamboat (he's actually buried in the Livingstone family vault, with his wife). ✉ *74 Trinity Pl. (Broadway at the head of Wall St.),* ☎ *212/602–0872.* ⏲ *Weekdays 7–6, Sat. 8–4, Sun. 7–4.*

OFF THE BEATEN PATH

VIETNAM VETERANS MEMORIAL – At this 14-ft-high, 70-ft-long rectangular memorial (1985), moving passages from news dispatches and the letters of servicemen and servicewomen have been etched into a wall of greenish glass. The brick plaza around it is often desolate on weekends. ✉ *At end of Coenties Slip, between Water and South Sts.*

Wall Street. Named after a wooden wall built across the island in 1653 to defend the Dutch colony against the native Indians, ⅓-mi-long Wall Street is arguably the most famous thoroughfare in the world—shorthand for the vast, powerful financial community that clusters around the New York and American stock exchanges. "The Street," as it's also widely known, began its financial career with stock traders conducting business along the sidewalks or at tables beneath a sheltering buttonwood tree. Today it's a dizzyingly narrow canyon—look to the east, and you'll glimpse a sliver of East River waterfront; look to the west, and you'll see the spire of Trinity Church, tightly framed by skyscrapers, at the head of the street. For a startlingly clear lesson in the difference between Ionic and Corinthian columns, look at **55 Wall Street**, the former Citibank building (at press time, slated to become a luxury hotel). The lower stories were part of an earlier U.S. Customs House, built in 1836–42; it was literally a bullish day on Wall Street when oxen hauled its 16 granite Ionic columns up to the site. When the National City Bank took over the building in 1899, it hired architects McKim, Mead & White to redesign the building and in 1909 added the second tier of columns but made them Corinthian.

13 **World Financial Center.** The four towers of this complex, each between 34 and 51 stories high and topped with a different geometric shape, were designed by Cesar Pelli and serve as headquarters for companies including Merrill Lynch, American Express, and Dow Jones. The highlight for visitors is the soaring **Winter Garden** atrium, where

pink-marble steps cascade down into a vaulted plaza with 16 giant palm trees. A vast arched window overlooking the Hudson fills the Winter Garden's west facade, and 45 shops and restaurants surround the atrium, which is a great place to beat the summer heat. The center hosts traveling exhibits and performances (they often tie in with the exhibits), which take place within the atrium and in a nearby gallery. The outdoor plaza right behind the Winter Garden curls around a tidy little yacht basin; take in the view of the Statue of Liberty and read the stirring quotations worked into the iron railings.

At the northwest corner of the World Financial Center, the **New York Mercantile Exchange**, opened in 1997, houses the world's largest energy and precious metals market. A ground-floor museum details the history of the exchange; a second-floor gallery with a 150-ft-long window overlooks the trading floors. ✉ *1 North End Ave.,* ☏ *212/299–2000.* *Free.* *Weekdays 9–5.*

At the end of North End Avenue, on the water's edge, is the terminal for **ferry service** to Hoboken, New Jersey (☏ 212/564–8846), across the Hudson River. It's a $2, eight-minute ride to Frank Sinatra's hometown, with a spectacular view of lower Manhattan.

To the south, a longer riverside **Esplanade** begins at the residential part of Battery Park City and connects with ☞ **Robert F. Wagner Jr. Park** and ☞ **Battery Park.** Especially noteworthy among the artwork populating the Esplanade are Ned Smyth's columned plaza with chessboards and the South Cove (a collaborative effort), a romantic curved stage set of wooden piers and a steel-frame lookout. ✉ *World Financial Center: West St. between Vesey and Liberty Sts.,* ☏ *212/945–0505.*

NEED A BREAK? Although the World Financial Center courtyard also offers several full-service restaurants, for a quick bite head for **Minters** (☏ 212/945–4455)—and be sure to leave room for great ice cream cones.

★ 12 **World Trade Center (WTC).** The mammoth WTC boasts New York's two tallest buildings, the third tallest in the world. Unlike some of the city's most beloved skyscrapers—the Empire State, the Chrysler, or the Flatiron buildings—the WTC's two 1,350-ft towers, designed by Minoru Yamasaki and built in 1972–73, are more engineering marvel than architectural masterpiece. To some they are an unmitigated disaster—"totalitarian-modernist monstrosity," complains the *Wall Street Journal*'s Raymond Sokolov; to others their brutalist design and sheer magnitude give them the beauty of modern sculpture, and at night when they're lighted from within, they particularly dominate the Manhattan skyline. The worldwide notoriety of these two buildings reached an all-time high on February 26, 1993, when a Ryder van loaded with explosives detonated in one of the underground parking garages, killing six and injuring more than 1,100 people. Today, with the WTC reconstruction completed, the only reminders of the explosion (the first major foreign terrorist attack on American soil) are the metal detectors that all employees and visitors must now pass and a small granite **memorial** embedded in the sidewalk of the outdoor plaza.

The WTC, though, is much more than its most famous twins: It's a 16-acre, 12-million-square-ft complex resembling a miniature city, with a daytime population of 140,000 (including 40,000 employees and 100,000 business and leisure visitors). The WTC has seven buildings in all, arranged around a plaza modeled after, and larger than, Venice's Piazza San Marco; summer concerts are held on the plaza. Underground is a giant mall with 70 stores and restaurants and a network of subway and other train stations. A TKTS booth sells discount tickets to Broadway and off-Broadway shows (☞ Chapter 5) in the mezzanine of 2 WTC, open weekdays 11–5:30, Saturday 11–3:30.

The WTC's biggest draw is **Top of the World,** the newly renovated 107th-floor observation deck at 2 World Trade Center, from which the view potentially extends 55 mi (signs at the ticket window disclose how far you can see that day and whether the outdoor deck is open). The elevator ride alone is worth the price of admission, as you hurl a quarter of a mile into the sky in only 58 seconds. Recent additions to the deck include three helicopter simulation theaters with moving seats and a nightly laser light show. On nice days you can ride up another few floors to the Rooftop Observatory, the world's highest outdoor observation platform. It's offset 25 ft from the edge of the building and surrounded with a barbed-wire electric fence. Notice that planes and helicopters are flying *below* you. *Ticket booth: 2 World Trade Center, mezzanine level,* ☎ *212/323–2340.* 🎫 *$12.* ⏲ *June–Aug., daily 9:30 AM–11:30 PM; Sept.–May, daily 9:30–9:30.*

THE SEAPORT AND THE COURTS

New York's role as a great seaport is easiest to understand downtown, with both the Hudson River and East River waterfronts within walking distance. Although the deeper Hudson River came into its own in the steamship era, the more sheltered waters of the East River saw most of the action in the 19th century, during the age of clipper ships. This era is preserved in the South Street Seaport restoration, centered on Fulton Street between Water Street and the East River. Only a few blocks away you can visit another seat of New York history: the City Hall neighborhood, which includes Manhattan's magisterial court and government buildings.

Numbers in the text correspond to numbers in the margin and on the Lower Manhattan map.

A Good Walk

Begin at the intersection of Water and Fulton streets. Water Street was once the shoreline; the latter thoroughfare was named after the ferry to Brooklyn, which once docked at its foot (the ferry itself was named after its inventor, Robert Fulton [1765–1815]). On the 19th-century landfill across the street is the 11-block **South Street Seaport Historic District** ⑮, created in 1967 to preserve the area's heritage as a port and to prevent it from being completely overtaken by skyscrapers.

Return to Fulton Street and walk away from the river to Broadway, to **St. Paul's Chapel** ⑯, the oldest (1766) surviving church in Manhattan. Forking off to the right is **Park Row,** which was known as Newspaper Row from the mid-19th to early 20th centuries, when most of the city's 20 or so daily newspapers had offices there. In tribute to that past, a statue of Benjamin Franklin (who was, after all, a printer) stands in front of Pace University, farther up on Park Row. Two blocks north on Broadway is one of the finest skyscrapers in the city, the Gothic **Woolworth Building** ⑰, for which Frank Woolworth paid $13 million—in cash.

Between Broadway and Park Row is triangular **City Hall Park,** originally the town common, which gives way to a slew of government offices. **City Hall** ⑱, built between 1803 and 1812, is unexpectedly modest. Lurking directly behind it is the **Tweed Courthouse** ⑲, named for the notorious politician William Marcy "Boss" Tweed. The small plaza east of Tweed Courthouse is used as a farmers' market on Tuesday and Friday, and it contains a Big Apple novelty that just might be

Close-up

A NEW BREEZE IS BLOWING, DOWN BY THE RIVERSIDE

NEW YORK IS A CITY OF islands, surrounded by ocean, bay, river, and sound. Its waterfront measures 578 mi around the perimeter of the five boroughs, making it the longest and most diverse of any municipality in the country. Down by the water, the air is salty and fresh, the views exhilarating, the mood peaceful and quiet. Yet New Yorkers have ventured to the city's edges only in the last decades, coinciding with the decline of the maritime industry and a new appreciation of its perspectives and open spaces. Today the waterfront's history is being rediscovered and its leisure opportunities invented anew.

New York grew up on the water, a shipping and shipbuilding town. After the opening of the Erie Canal in 1825, which connected it to the Great Lakes and the West for trade, the city became the preeminent port in the country, the gateway to the continent for exports and imports, the "golden door" for immigrants. At the turn of the last century, New York Harbor, crisscrossed with ferries, barges, tugs, canal boats, freighters and passenger liners, was the busiest in the world.

The waterfront still resonates with the illustrious past. At the southern tip of Manhattan, near ☞ **Battery Park,** the street names suggest the contours of the island before settlers began to fill in the wetlands: Pearl Street, where mother-of-pearl shells were collected; Water Street, Front Street. The port was first centered near the ☞ **South Street Seaport** on the East River, where the 18th-century streetscape and historic sailing vessels recall the clipper ship era. It then moved to the wider, less turbulent Hudson, named in 1609 by the explorer Henry Hudson; it was here where Robert Fulton launched the first steamboat, where the ironclad Civil War ship *Monitor* was built, where generations of Americans boarded ever grander transatlantic ocean liners from vast imperial piers.

NEW YORK'S RIVERS STILL churn with cruise ships, freighters, barges, and tugs, but plans are underway to create a new "greenbelt" around the edges where industry once ruled, with long promenades for cyclists, rollerbladers and joggers, marinas for boating, and an expanded 500-acre ☞ **Hudson River Park.** Today, moving north from ☞ **Battery Park City,** you can stroll along an interim greenway the length of the proposed park (imagining the tow pounds and parking lots as leafy spaces with playgrounds and beaches). At Christopher Street, walk out on ☞ **Greenwich Village**'s sunbathing pier for the view back toward a Victorian-era panorama of warehouses, factories, and sailors' hotels—the last semblance of a 19th-century waterfront in Manhattan. At 14th Street, remember Herman Melville, who worked as a customs inspector nearby. Just south of the ☞ **Chelsea Piers,** note the remains of the pier house where the *Titanic* was scheduled to conclude its maiden voyage. In summer, like a forecast of the future, other old piers spring to life with public events—movies, dances, food festivals. (Call the **Hudson River Park Conservancy** [212/353–0366] for information.) For kayaking, boating, and parasailing on the Hudson, *see* Chapter 9.

–Elizabeth Hawes

worth the 25¢ it costs to get in—a public-toilet kiosk, like those found in Paris.

Directly opposite the Tweed Courthouse on the north side of Chambers Street incongruously sits an eight-story Beaux Arts château, the 1911 **Surrogate's Court** ⑳, also called the Hall of Records (✉ 31 Chambers St.). Across Centre Street from the château is the city government's first skyscraper, the imposing **Municipal Building** ㉑, built in 1914 by McKim, Mead & White. Just steps south of the Municipal Building, a ramp curves up into the pedestrian walkway over the **Brooklyn Bridge** ㉒. How romantic it would be to look out from the bridge on the docks of the "mast-hemmed Manhattan" of Walt Whitman's "Crossing Brooklyn Ferry." By the time the bridge was built, the Fulton Ferry was making more than 1,000 crossings per day. The East River is far quieter now, but the river-and-four-borough views from the bridge are no less wondrous.

Foley Square, a name that has become synonymous with the New York court system, opens out north of the Municipal Building. On the right, the orderly progression of the Corinthian colonnades of the **U.S. Courthouse** ㉓ and the **New York County Courthouse** ㉔ is a fitting reflection of the epigraph carved in the latter's frieze: THE TRUE ADMINISTRATION OF JUSTICE IS THE FIRMEST PILLAR OF GOOD GOVERNMENT. Turn to look across Foley Square at Federal Plaza, which sprawls in front of the gridlike skyscraper of the Javits Federal Building. The black-glass box to the left houses the U.S. Court of International Trade. Just south of it, at the corner of Duane and Elk streets, is the site of the **African Burial Ground,** where thousands of African-Americans from the Colonial period were laid to rest.

Continue north up Centre Street past neoclassic civic office buildings to 100 Centre Street, the **Criminal Courts Building** ㉕, a rather foreboding construction with Art Moderne details. In contrast, the Civil and Municipal Courthouse (1960), across the way at 111 Centre Street, is an uninspired modern cube, although it, too, has held sensational trials. On the west side of this small square is the slick black-granite Family Court, built in 1975 (✉ 60 Lafayette St.), with its intriguing angular facade.

Turn left onto Leonard Street, which runs just south of the Family Court, and take a look at the ornate Victorian building that runs the length of the block on your left. This is the old New York Life Insurance Company headquarters (✉ 346 Broadway), an 1870 building that was remodeled and enlarged in 1896 by McKim, Mead & White. The ornate clock tower facing Broadway is now occupied by the avant-garde Clocktower Gallery, which is currently used as rehearsal space by various artists and is therefore not open to the public. The stretch of Broadway south of here is the subject of what is believed to be the oldest photograph of New York. The picture focuses on a paving project—to eliminate the morass of muddy streets—that took place in 1850.

From here a tasty day's-end meal in Chinatown (☞ Little Italy and Chinatown, *above*) is only a few blocks north and east. Or continue on Leonard Street to reach TriBeCa.

TIMING

You can easily spend a half day at the Seaport, or longer if you browse in shops. The rest of the tour is just walking and takes about 1½ hours. The real Seaport opens well before the sun rises and clears out not much after, when fishmongers leave to make way for the tourists. Unless you're really interested in wholesale fish, however, you're best off visiting the Seaport when its other attractions are open. Try to do this during the week, so that the government offices will be open, too. Also, consider walking across the Brooklyn Bridge in the late afternoon for dramatic contrasts of light.

Sights to See

African Burial Ground. This grassy corner is part of the original area used to inter the city's earliest African-Americans—an estimated 20,000 were buried here until the cemetery was closed in 1794. The site was discovered during a 1991 construction project, and by an act of Congress it was made into a National Historical Landmark, dedicated to the people who were enslaved in the city between 1626 and Emancipation Day in New York, July 4, 1827. ✉ *Duane and Elk Sts.*

★ 22 **Brooklyn Bridge.** "A drive-through cathedral" is how the critic James Wolcott describes this engineering marvel, one of New York's noblest landmarks. Spanning the East River, the Brooklyn Bridge connected Manhattan island to the then-independent city of Brooklyn; before its opening, Brooklynites had only the Fulton Street Ferry to shuttle them across the river. John Augustus Roebling—a visionary architect, legendary engineer, metaphysical philosopher, and fervid abolitionist—is said to have first conceived of the bridge on an icy winter's day in 1852, when the frozen river prevented him from getting to Brooklyn, although, to be sure, he was by no means the first person so inconvenienced. Roebling spent the next 30 years designing, raising money for, and building the bridge. Alas, its construction was fraught with peril. Work began in 1867; two years later Roebling died of gangrene, after a wayward ferry boat rammed his foot, while he was at work on a pier. His son, Washington, took over the project and was himself permanently crippled—like many others who worked on the bridge, he suffered from the bends. With the help of his wife, Emily, Washington nonetheless saw the bridge's construction through to completion. The long struggle to build the span so captured the imagination of the city that when it opened in 1883, it was promptly crowned the "Eighth Wonder of the World." Its twin Gothic-arched towers, with a span of 1,595½ ft, rise 272 ft from the river below; the bridge's overall length of 6,016 ft made it four times longer than the longest suspension bridge of its day. From roadway to water is about 133 ft, high enough to allow the tallest ships to pass. The roadway is supported by a web of steel cables, hung from the towers and attached to block-long anchorages on either shore.

A walk across the bridge's promenade—a boardwalk elevated above the roadway and shared by pedestrians, in-line skaters, and bicyclists—takes about 40 minutes, from Manhattan's civic center to the heart of Brooklyn Heights (☞ Chapter 3); it is well worth traversing for the astounding views. Midtown's jumble of spires loom to the north, to the left of the Manhattan Bridge, and are especially scenic at night, when bright, variously hued lights show off the buildings to great effect. Mostly newer skyscrapers crowd lower Manhattan, while the tall ships docked at their feet, at South Street Seaport, appear to have sailed in straight from the 19th century. Governors Island sits forlornly in the middle of the harbor, which sweeps open dramatically toward Lady Liberty and off in the distance, the Verrazano-Narrows Bridge (its towers are more than twice as tall as those of the Brooklyn Bridge). A word of caution to pedestrians: Do obey the lane markings on the promenade—pedestrians on the north side, bicyclists on the south—as the latter often pedal furiously.

18 **City Hall.** Reflecting not big-city brawn but the classical refinement and civility of Enlightenment Europe, New York's surprisingly decorous City Hall is a diminutive palace with a facade punctuated by arches

and columns and a cupola crowned by a statue of Lady Justice. Built between 1803 and 1812, it was originally clad in white marble only on its front and sides, while the back was faced in more modest brownstone because city fathers assumed the city would never grow farther north than this. Limestone now covers all four sides. A sweeping marble double staircase leads from the domed rotunda to the second-floor public rooms. The small, clubby Victorian-style **City Council Chamber** in the east wing, has mahogany detailing and ornate gilding; the **Board of Estimate chamber,** to the west, has Colonial paintings and church-pew-style seating; and the **Governor's Room** at the head of the stairs, used for ceremonial events, is filled with historic portraits and furniture, including a writing table that George Washington used in 1789 when New York was the U.S. capital. The **blue room,** which was traditionally the mayor's office, is on the ground floor; it is now used for mayoral press conferences (an exact replica can be seen on the Michael J. Fox sitcom, *Spin City,* about a fictional New York City mayor and his deputy). On either side of the building are free interactive video machines that dispense information on area attractions, civic procedures, City Hall history, mass transit, and other topics. ✉ *City Hall Park,* ☎ *212/788–6865 for tour information.* 🎫 *Free.* ⏲ *Weekdays 9–5; reservations required for tours, given at 10, 11, and 2.*

City Hall Park. Known in Colonial times as the Fields or the Common, this green spot has hosted hangings, riots, and demonstrations; it is also the finish line for ticker-tape parades up lower Broadway (though nowadays ticker tape is replaced with shredded computer paper). A bronze statue of patriot Nathan Hale, who was hanged in 1776 as a spy by the British troops occupying New York City, stands on the Broadway side of the park. ✉ *Between Broadway, Park Row, and Chambers St.*

25 **Criminal Courts Building.** Fans of the TV show *NYPD Blue* may recognize this rather grim Art Deco tower, which is connected by a skywalk (New York's Bridge of Sighs) to the detention center known as the Tombs. In *The Bonfire of the Vanities,* Tom Wolfe wrote a chilling description of this court's menacing atmosphere. ✉ *100 Centre St.*

21 **Municipal Building.** Who else but the venerable architecture firm McKim, Mead & White would the city government trust to build its first skyscraper in 1914? The roof section alone is 10 stories high, bristling with towers and peaks and topped by a 25-ft-high gilt statue of Civic Fame. New Yorkers come here to pay parking fines and get marriage licenses (and to get married, in a civil chapel on the second floor). An immense arch straddles Chambers Street (traffic used to flow through here). ✉ *1 Centre St., at Chambers St.*

24 **New York County Courthouse.** With its stately columns, pediments, and 100-ft-wide flight of steps, this 1912 classical temple front is yet another spin-off on Rome's Pantheon. It deviates from its classical parent in its hexagonal rotunda, shaped to fit an irregular plot of land. The courtroom drama *Twelve Angry Men* was filmed here, as was the film *Legal Eagles.* The courthouse also hosts thousands of marriages a year. ✉ *60 Centre St., Foley Sq.*

16 **St. Paul's Chapel.** The oldest (1766) extant church in Manhattan, this Episcopal house of worship, built of rough Manhattan brownstone, was modeled on London's St. Martin-in-the-Fields (a columned clock tower and steeple were added in 1794). A prayer service here followed George Washington's inauguration as president; Washington's pew is in the north aisle. The gilded crown adorned with plumes above the pulpit is thought to be the only vestige in the city of British rule. In the

adjoining cemetery, 18th-century headstones crumble in the shadows of glittering skyscrapers. ✉ *Broadway and Fulton St.,* ☎ *212/602–0874.* ⏲ *Weekdays 9–3, Sun. 8–3.*

★ 15 **South Street Seaport Historic District.** Had it not been declared a historic district in 1967, this charming, cobblestone corner of the city would likely have been gobbled up by skyscrapers. The Rouse Corporation, which had already created Boston's Quincy Market and Baltimore's Harborplace, was hired to restore and adapt the existing historic buildings, preserving the commercial feel of centuries past. The result is a hybrid: part historic museum and part shopping mall. Many of its streets' 18th-, 19th-, and early 20th-century architectural details re-create the city's historic seafaring era.

At the intersection of Fulton and Water streets, the gateway to the Seaport, stands the ***Titanic*** Memorial, a small white lighthouse that commemorates the sinking of the RMS *Titanic* in 1912. Beyond it, Fulton Street, cobbled in blocks of Belgian granite, turns into a busy pedestrian mall. Just to the left of Fulton, at 211 Water Street, is **Bowne & Co.,** a reconstructed working 19th-century print shop. Continue down Fulton around to Front Street, which has wonderfully preserved old brick buildings—some dating from the 1700s. Directly across Front Street is the **Fulton Market Building,** a modern building full of shops and restaurants that updates the bustling atmosphere of the old victual markets, which occupied this site from 1822 on. On the south side of Fulton Street is the seaport's architectural centerpiece, **Schermerhorn Row,** a redbrick terrace of Georgian- and Federal-style warehouses and countinghouses built in 1811–12. Today the ground floors are occupied by upscale shops, bars, and restaurants, and the **South Street Seaport Museum,** which hosts walking tours and fantastic programs for kids (☞ Chapter 4). ✉ *12 Fulton St.,* ☎ *212/748–8600 for museum; 212/732–7678 for events and shopping information.* 🎟 *$6 (to ships, galleries, walking tours, Maritime Crafts Center, films, and other seaport events).* ⏲ *Museum Apr.–Sept., daily 10–6, Thurs. 10–8; Oct.–Mar., Wed.–Mon. 10–5.*

Cross South Street under an elevated stretch of the FDR Drive to **Pier 16,** where the historic ships are docked, including the *Pioneer,* a 102-ft schooner built in 1885; the *Peking,* the second-largest sailing ship in existence; the full-rigged *Wavertree*; and the lightship *Ambrose.* The Pier 16 ticket booth provides information and sells tickets to the museum, the ships, tours, and exhibits. Pier 16 also hosts frequent concerts and performances, has an ice rink in winter, and is the departure point for the one-hour Seaport Liberty Cruise (☎ 212/630–8888), which runs from late March through mid-December. The fare is $12; combination fare for cruise and other attractions is $15.

To the north is **Pier 17,** a multilevel dockside shopping mall featuring standard-issue national chain retailers like the Gap, Banana Republic, and Nine West, among many others. Its weathered-wood rear decks make a splendid spot from which to sit and contemplate the river.

As your nose will surmise, the blocks along South Street north of the museum complex still house a working fish market, which has been in operation since the 1770s. More than 200 species of fish—from swordfish to sea urchin roe—are sold by the hundreds of fishmongers of the **Fulton Fish Market.** Get up early (or stay up late) if you want to see it: The action begins around 3 AM and ends by 8 AM. ☎ *212/748–8590.* 🎟 *$10.* ⏲ *1st and 3rd Thurs. every month May–Sept. at 6 AM; tours by reservation only.*

NEED A BREAK? The cuisine at the fast-food stalls on Pier 17's third-floor **Promenade Food Court** is nonchain eclectic: Pizza on the Pier, Wok & Roll, Simply Seafood, and Salad Mania. What's really spectacular is the view from the tables in a glass-walled atrium.

20 **Surrogate's Court.** Also called the **Hall of Records,** this 1911 building is the most ornate of the City Hall court trio. In true Beaux Arts fashion, sculpture and ornament seem to have been added wherever possible to the basic neoclassic structure, yet the overall effect is graceful rather than cluttered. Filmmakers sometimes use its ornate lobby in opera scenes. A courtroom here was the venue for *Johnson* v. *Johnson,* where the heirs to the Johnson & Johnson fortune waged their bitter battle. ✉ *31 Chambers St., at Centre St.*

19 **Tweed Courthouse.** Under the corrupt management of notorious politician William Marcy "Boss" Tweed (1823–78), this Anglo-Italianate gem, one of the finest designs in the City Hall area, took some $12 million and nine years to build (it was finally finished in 1872, but the ensuing public outrage drove Tweed from office). Although it is imposing, with its columned classical pediment outside and seven-story rotunda inside, almost none of the boatloads of marble that Tweed had shipped from Europe made their way into this building. Today it houses municipal offices; it has also served as a location for several films, most notably *The Verdict.* ✉ *52 Chambers St.*

23 **U.S. Courthouse.** Cass Gilbert built this in 1936, convinced that it complemented the much finer nearby Woolworth Building, which he had designed earlier. Granite steps climb to a massive columned portico; above this rises a 32-story tower topped by a gilded pyramid, not unlike that with which Gilbert crowned the New York Life building uptown (☞ Murray Hill to Union Square, *above*). This courthouse has been the site of such famous cases as the tax-evasion trial of hotel queen Leona Helmsley. ✉ *40 Centre St., Foley Sq.*

★ 17 **Woolworth Building.** Called the Cathedral of Commerce, this ornate white terra-cotta edifice was, at 792 ft, the world's tallest building when it opened in 1913; it still houses the Woolworth (now Venator Group) corporate offices, even though its eponymous stores closed in 1997. The spectacular **lobby**'s extravagant Gothic-style details include sculptures set into arches in the ceiling; one of them represents an elderly F. W. Woolworth pinching his pennies, while another depicts the architect, Cass Gilbert, cradling in his arms a model of his creation. ✉ *233 Broadway, at Park Pl.*

3 Exploring the Other Boroughs

Trips to the city's four other boroughs offer quintessential experiences: a free ride on the Staten Island Ferry, a bracing walk across the noble Brooklyn Bridge, a subway ride along elevated tracks to Queens. Once you arrive, the pleasures are many: the Bronx's Wave Hill and world-renowned zoo; Brooklyn's world-class botanical garden and historic brownstone neighborhoods; Queens' s lively Greek neighborhood and museum of film; and Staten Island's far-from-the-madding-crowd Richmondtown and its Tibetan Museum.

By Amy McConnell and Matthew Lore

Updated by Margaret Mittelbach and Matthew Lore

MANY VISITORS TO MANHATTAN notice the four outer boroughs—Brooklyn, Queens, the Bronx, and Staten Island—only from an airplane window or the deck of a Circle Line cruise, leaving those areas to remain ciphers. "Don't fall asleep on the subway," the unschooled tourist tells himself, "or you may end up in the Bronx!"

Manhattanites themselves, many driven over the river by astronomical rents, discovered the outer boroughs in the late 1970s and 1980s. They found sky, trees, and living space among the 19th-century brownstones, converted industrial lofts, Art Deco apartment palaces, and tidy bungalows. They also found fascinating ethnic enclaves and a host of museums and parks.

The reality is that Manhattan is only a small part of New York City. Its population of about 1.48 million is smaller than that of either Brooklyn (2 million) or Queens (1.95 million) and only slightly larger than that of the Bronx (1.2 million). Staten Island may be less populous (391,000), but it's 2½ times the size of Manhattan.

There are things to see and do in the outer boroughs that you simply won't find in Manhattan, and most are just a subway ride from midtown. Manhattanites may try to put you off such a journey, but don't be daunted. After a couple of beers, those same people may rave about their favorite place for cheesecake (Junior's on Flatbush Avenue in Brooklyn) or a great outdoor barbecue they had at their sister-in-law's mock-Tudor brick house (in Forest Hills, Queens); you may even have to listen to a story about their life's peak experience—found in the bleachers of Yankee Stadium in . . . the Bronx.

THE BRONX

The only of New York's boroughs attached to the North American mainland, the Bronx has been an emblem of urban decay for the past 30 years, but it is actually as diverse and rich in personality as the rest of the city. The borough is home to the city's most famous botanical garden and its oldest and largest zoo. In addition, there's the friendly Italian neighborhood of Belmont, and wealthy Riverdale, with its riverside estates; and of course, Yankee Stadium, the home of the New York Yankees.

The New York Botanical Garden, the Bronx Zoo, and Belmont

Within the 5-mi vicinity covered in this tour, you can stroll among gardens of roses (250 kinds), peonies (58 varieties), and medicinal herbs; watch red pandas swing from tree to tree; and sample biscotti at a third-generation bakery where patrons greet customers by name.

Numbers in the text correspond to numbers in the margin and on the New York Botanical Garden and Bronx Zoo map.

A Good Walk

The most direct route to the **New York Botanical Garden** ① is via Metro North to the Botanical Garden stop, which is right across from the garden's pedestrian entrance (cross Kazimiroff Boulevard to the garden's Mosholu Gate). As an alternative, take the D train or the No. 4 to Bedford Park Boulevard. From the subway station continue east on Bedford Park Boulevard (a 10-minute walk) to the Kazimiroff Boulevard entrance of the garden, where you may be tempted to spend the

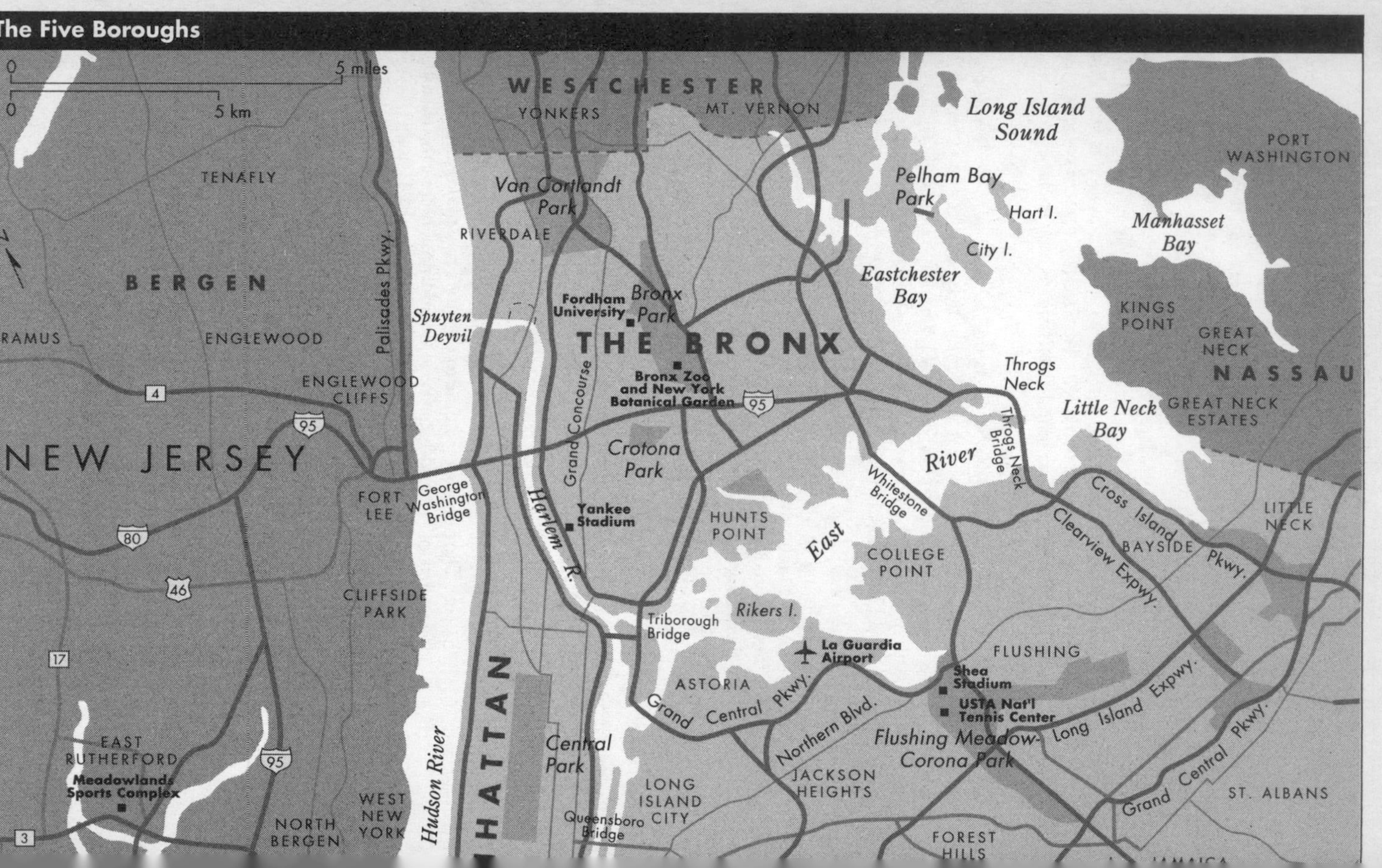
The Five Boroughs
0 5 miles
0 5 km
WESTCHESTER
YONKERS
MT. VERNON
Long Island Sound
PORT WASHINGTON
Pelham Bay Park
Hart I.
City I.
Manhasset Bay
Van Cortlandt Park
RIVERDALE
TENAFLY
BERGEN
Eastchester Bay
KINGS POINT
GREAT NECK
NASSAU
Palisades Pkwy.
Spuyten Deyvil
Fordham University
Bronx Park
THE BRONX
PARAMUS
ENGLEWOOD
ENGLEWOOD CLIFFS
Bronx Zoo and New York Botanical Garden
Grand Concourse
Throgs Neck
Little Neck Bay
GREAT NECK ESTATES
4
95
NEW JERSEY
Crotona Park
River
Throgs Neck Bridge
FORT LEE
George Washington Bridge
Harlem R.
Yankee Stadium
HUNTS POINT
East
Whitestone Bridge
COLLEGE POINT
Cross Island Pkwy.
BAYSIDE
LITTLE NECK
Clearview Expwy.
80
46
CLIFFSIDE PARK
Rikers I.
Triborough Bridge
La Guardia Airport
FLUSHING
17
ASTORIA
Shea Stadium
USTA Nat'l Tennis Center
Grand Central Pkwy.
Northern Blvd.
Long Island Expwy.
HATTAN
EAST RUTHERFORD
Meadowlands Sports Complex
Hudson River
Central Park
Flushing Meadow-Corona Park
JACKSON HEIGHTS
LONG ISLAND CITY
Queensboro Bridge
ST. ALBANS
WEST NEW YORK
NORTH BERGEN
3
FOREST HILLS

BERGEN
FOREST HILLS
JAMAICA
SPRINGFIELD GARDENS
SECAUCUS
WEEHAWKEN
Queens-Midtown Tunnel
495
LYNDHURST
Lincoln Tunnel
GREENPOINT
QUEENS
Van Wyck Expwy.
Woodhaven Blvd.
Southern Pkwy.
17
UNION CITY
East River
MASPETH
Inter Boro Pkwy.
WILLIAMSBURG
OZONE PARK
SOUTH OZONE PARK
J.F.K. International Airport
HUDSON
HOBOKEN
Williamsburg Bridge
Holland Tunnel
Manhattan Bridge
BEDFORD-STUYVESANT
KEARNY
9
1
Brooklyn Bridge
BROOKLYN HEIGHTS
Atlantic Ave.
EAST NEW YORK
Cross Bay Blvd.
280
Pulaski Skyway
COBBLE HILL
Eastern Pkwy.
JERSEY CITY
Liberty State Park
Ellis I.
Brooklyn-Battery Tunnel
CARROLL GARDENS
Brooklyn Museum and Brooklyn Botanic Garden
Linden Blvd.
Jamaica Bay Wildlife Refuge
Statue of Liberty
PARK SLOPE
Governors I.
Prospect Park
Liberty I.
Brooklyn
CANARSIE
NEWARK
MID-WOOD
ESSEX
Flatbush Ave.
78
Upper Bay
Queens Expwy
BROOKLYN
Floyd Bennett Field
95
Newark Bay
Ocean Pkwy
Marine Park
Newark International Airport
BAYONNE
BAY RIDGE
The Narrows
Kill Van Kull
Ferry Terminal
Snug Harbor Cultural Center
BENSONHURST
Rockaway Inlet
Jacob Riis Park
ELIZABETH
Belt Pkwy.
Bayonne Bridge
UNION
CONEY ISLAND
Verrazano-Narrows Bridge
STATEN ISLAND
ATLANTIC OCEAN
Goethals Bridge
Lower Bay

Belmont, **3**
Bronx Zoo (International Wildlife Conservation Center), **2**
Dominick's, **5**
Fordham University, **6**
New York Botanical Garden, **1**
Our Lady of Mt. Carmel Roman Catholic Church, **4**

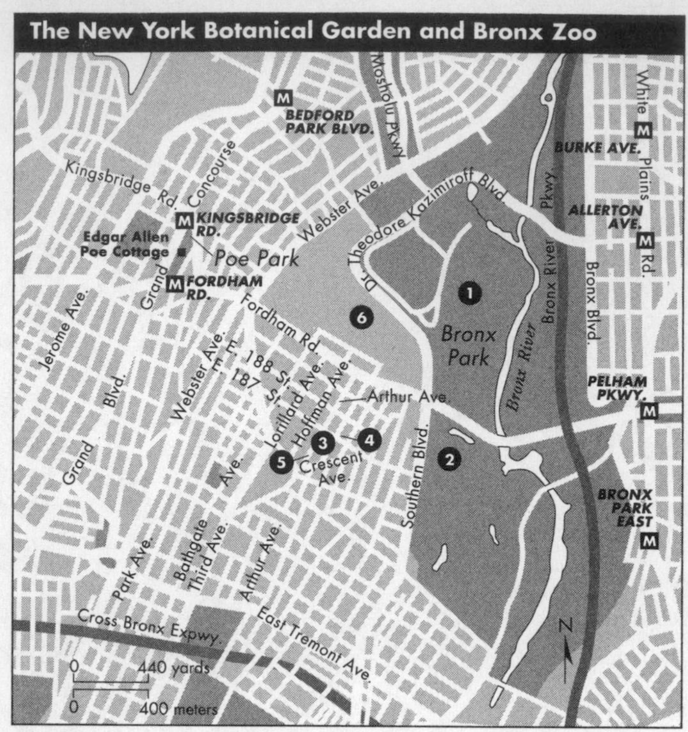

whole day. When you're ready to leave the garden grounds, exit via the main gate. Turn left and walk along Southern Boulevard (10 minutes); turn left onto Fordham Road and continue (5 minutes) to the Rainey Gate entrance of the **Bronx Zoo** ②—another must-see sight that could easily hold you for most of the day.

Exit the zoo via Southern Boulevard, turn right, and walk two blocks to East 187th Street; this will lead you straight into the heart of **Belmont** ③, an Italian neighborhood. You'll know you're in the right place when you see the imposing brick structure of **Our Lady of Mt. Carmel Roman Catholic Church** ④ (at Belmont Avenue and East 187th Street), the spiritual heart of the neighborhood—but for the true Belmont experience, a walk through the **Arthur Avenue Retail Market** and a dish of pasta at **Dominick's** ⑤ are essential.

Fordham University ⑥ occupies a large plot of land north of Belmont. Backtrack on Arthur Avenue to East Fordham Road (head toward the tall Gothic tower in the distance) and turn left. For a peek at the handsome inner campus, turn right on Bathgate Avenue; this will lead you to the college gate, which is manned by a security guard. Otherwise, continue on East Fordham Road three blocks to chaotic Fordham Plaza, nicknamed the Times Square of the Bronx. To return to Manhattan take the Metro North at East Fordham Road and Webster Avenue, or continue on East Fordham Road about four blocks up to the Fordham Road subway station (at the Grand Concourse) for the D train.

TIMING

The Bronx Zoo and the New York Botanical Garden are each vast and interesting enough to merit half a day or more. If you plan to visit both, start early and plan on a late lunch or early dinner in Belmont. Saturday is the best day to see the Italian neighborhood at its liveliest; on Sunday most stores are closed. The zoo and the botanical garden are less crowded on weekdays—except Wednesday, when admission to both is free.

Sights to See

3 **Belmont.** Often called the Little Italy of the Bronx, Belmont is where some 14,500 families socialize, shop, work, and eat, eat, eat. On Saturday afternoons, as residents rush around buying freshly baked bread and homemade salami, you may as well be in a small market town in Italy. Don't be surprised to hear people speaking Italian in the neighborhood's tidy streets. ✉ *Bordered by E. Fordham Rd., Southern Blvd., Crescent and 3rd Aves.*

Across from ☞ **Our Lady of Mt. Carmel Roman Catholic Church,** the **Catholic Goods Center** (✉ 630 E. 187th St.) sells multilingual Bibles and greeting cards as well as religious art. Next to the Catholic Goods Center, **Borgatti's Ravioli & Egg Noodles** (✉ 632 E. 187th St.) is known for its homemade pastas. **Danny's Pork Store** (✉ 626 E. 187th St.) has homemade sausages. One block down, **Mount Carmel Wines & Spirits** ✉ (612 E. 187th St.) has a tremendous selection of Italian wines and grappas in beautiful bottles. On Arthur Avenue, the gastronomic temptations continue: The brick ovens at **Madonia Bros. Bakery** (✉ 2348 Arthur Ave.) have been turning out golden-brown loaves since 1918; they'll fill cannoli fresh on request.

An indoor shed sheltering more than a dozen stalls, the **Arthur Avenue Retail Market** (✉ 2344 Arthur Ave.) is one of the last bastions of old-time New York. Here, amid piles of fresh produce, market vendors still sell fresh beef hearts and occasionally burst into song. There's also fresh rabbit and tripe, 15 kind of olives, gnocchi *freschi, bufula* mozzarella, and low-price ceramic pasta ware imported from Italy. Stop for a quick lunch—or at least a pizza square with toppings fresh from the market—at the Cafe al Mercato.

★ 2 **Bronx Zoo.** Opened in 1899 (and now officially called the International Wildlife Conservation Center), this 265-acre spread is the world's largest urban zoo. The zoo's 4,000 animals, representing roughly 600 species, mostly live in naturalistic, parklike settings, often separated from you by no more than a moat. Among the best exhibits are "Jungle World," an indoor tropical rain forest complete with five waterfalls, millipedes, flowering orchids, and pythons; "Wild Asia," where tigers and elephants roam free on nearly 40 acres of open meadows and dark forests; and "the World of Darkness," a windowless building that offers a rare glimpse into the "nightlives" of such nocturnal creatures as fruit-eating bats and naked mole rats. Three different rides, including a shuttle bus, a monorail, and an aerial tram, offer various perspectives of the grounds during summer. The **Children's Zoo** has many hands-on learning activities, as well as a large petting zoo. Youngsters are encouraged to mingle with prairie dogs in kid-size tunnels and try on a turtle's shell for size. To get to the zoo, take the No. 2 subway to Pelham Parkway and walk three blocks west to the zoo's Bronxdale entrance. You can also take the Metro North train (☎ 212/532–4900) from Grand Central Terminal (☞ 42nd Street *in* Chapter 2) or catch the Liberty Line Bronx M11 express bus (☎ 718/652–8400) from mid-Manhattan. ✉ *Bronx River Pkwy. and Fordham Rd.,* ☎ *718/367–1010.* 🎫 *Apr.–Oct., Thurs.–Tues. $6.75; Nov.–Mar., Thurs.–Tues. $3; free Wed.; Children's Zoo $2.* ⏲ *Apr.–Oct., weekdays 10–5, weekends 10–5:30; Nov.–Mar., daily 10–4:30; Children's Zoo Apr.–Oct. (same hrs as main zoo); last ticket sold 1 hr before closing.*

5 **Dominick's.** There are no menus and no wine lists at this neighborhood favorite, where the question "What do you have?" is most often an-

swered with "What do you want?" What you'll want is a heaping dish of traditional spaghetti with meatballs—some of the best you'll find in New York City—along with crusty bread and wine poured from a jug. The same family has been cooking at Dominick's since the 1940s, serving loyal fans at congested communal tables with red-and-white checked cloths. Expect to pay about $50 for two people. ✉ *2335 Arthur Ave., at 187th St.,* ☎ *718/733–2807. Closed Tues.*

OFF THE BEATEN PATH

EDGAR ALLAN POE COTTAGE – If you finish your tour while it's still light out, venture up Fordham Road to East Kingsbridge Road, turn right, and walk the short block to Poe Park, where the Bronx County Historical Society maintains the Edgar Allan Poe Cottage, open weekends only. It was here that Poe and his sickly wife, Virginia, sought refuge from Manhattan and from the vicissitudes of the writerly life between 1846 and 1849. He wandered the countryside on foot and listened to the sound of the church bells at nearby St. John's College Church (now Fordham University); word has it that these bells inspired one of his most famous poems, "The Bells." At night the park attracts loiterers; visit only by day. ✉ *E. Kingsbridge Rd. and Grand Concourse,* ☎ *718/881–8900.* *$2.* ⏲ *Mid-Jan.–mid-Dec., Sat. 10–4, Sun. 1–5.*

❻ **Fordham University.** A small enclave of distinguished Collegiate Gothic architecture in the midst of urban sprawl, this university opened in 1841 as a Jesuit college and was, for a time, one of the country's preeminent schools. Fordham now has an undergraduate enrollment of nearly 6,000 and a second campus near Lincoln Center. Enter the grounds via Bathgate Avenue, a few blocks west of Arthur Avenue (the security guard may require you to show ID), to see **Old Rose Hill Manor Dig**; the **University Church,** whose stained glass was donated by King Louis Philippe of France (1773–1850); the pleasant **Edward's Parade** quadrangle in the center of campus; and **Keating Hall,** sitting like a Gothic fortress in the center of things. Maps are posted around the campus and are available in the security office on your left inside the gate.

★ ❶ **New York Botanical Garden.** Considered one of the leading botany centers of the world, this 250-acre garden built around the dramatic gorge of the Bronx River is one of the best reasons to make a trip to the Bronx. The garden was founded by Dr. Nathaniel Lord Britton and his wife, Elizabeth. After visiting England's Kew Gardens in 1889, they returned full of fervor to create a similar haven in New York. The grounds encompass the historic **Lorillard Snuff Mill,** built by two French Huguenot manufacturers in 1840 to power the grinding of tobacco for snuff. Nearby, the Lorillards grew roses to supply fragrance for their blend. A path along the Bronx River from the mill leads to the garden's 40-acre **Forest,** the only surviving remnant of the forest that once covered New York City. Outdoor plant collections include the **Peggy Rockefeller Rose Garden,** with 2,700 bushes of 230 varieties; the spectacular rock garden, which displays alpine flowers; and the **Everett Children's Adventure Garden,** 8 acres of plant and science exhibits for children, including a boulder maze, giant animal topiaries, a wild wetland trail, and a plant discovery center.

In 1997 the historic **Enid A. Haupt Conservatory**—a Victorian-era glass house with 17,000 individual panes—reopened following a four-year, $24 million renovation. Inside are year-round re-creations of misty tropical rain forests, arid deserts, and the Australian outback. Other indoor attractions can be found at the **Museum Building,** which houses a gardening shop, a library, and a world-renowned herbarium holding 6 million dried plant specimens.

To get to the Botanical Garden, take the Metro North train (☎ 212/532–4900) to the garden from Grand Central Terminal (☞ 42nd Street *in* Chapter 2); or take the D train or the No. 4 to the Bedford Park Boulevard stop and walk eight blocks east to the entrance on Kazimiroff Boulevard. ✉ *200th St. and Kazimiroff Blvd.,* ☎ *718/817–8700.* *Nov.–Mar. $1.50, Apr.–Oct. $3; free Sat. 10–noon and Wed.; Enid A. Haupt Conservatory $3.50; parking $4.* ⏲ *Nov.–Mar., Tues.–Sun. 10–4; Apr.–Oct., Tues.–Sun. 10–6.*

4 **Our Lady of Mt. Carmel Roman Catholic Church.** Rising like a beacon of faith above the neighboring food stores and restaurants, this is the spiritual center of Belmont. In 1907, when an Irish priest who spoke Italian successfully petitioned the archdiocese for an Italian church to serve the new immigrant community, many Italian residents of the neighborhood volunteered to help build the church in order to keep the costs down. ✉ *627 E. 187th St., between Hughes and Belmont Aves.,* ☎ *718/295–3770.* ⏲ *Weekdays 7:30–1 and 4–8:30, Sat. 7:30 AM–8:30 PM, Sun. 7:30–2 and 6–8:30.*

NEED A BREAK?

At **Egidio's Pastry Shop** (✉ 622 E. 187th St., ☎ 718/295–6077), a neighborhood favorite, you can sample handmade Italian pastries, washed down with a strong shot of espresso. The homemade gelatos next door are top-notch.

OFF THE BEATEN PATH

CITY ISLAND – At the extreme east end of the Bronx is a bona fide island measuring 230 acres wide. (To reach City Island, take the No. 6 subway to Pelham Bay Parkway and then catch the No. 29 bus.) Back in 1761, a group of the area's residents planned a port to rival New York's, but when that scheme hit the shoals, they returned to the perennial maritime pursuits such as fishing and boatbuilding. City Island–produced yachts have included a number of America's Cup contenders. Connected to Pelham Bay Park by bridge, City Island has a maritime atmosphere, fishing boat rentals, and good seafood restaurants. Worth visiting is the **North Wind Undersea Museum,** with its displays devoted to marine mammal rescue and deep-sea diving. ✉ *610 City Island Ave.,* ☎ *718/885–0701.* *$3.* ⏲ *Mar. 15–Nov. 15, Mon.–Sat. 10–5; Nov. 16–Mar 14., Thurs.–Sun. 10–4.*

WAVE HILL – In the mid- to late-19th century, Manhattan millionaires built summer homes in the Bronx suburb of Riverdale, which, perched on a ridge above the Hudson River, offered stirring views of the New Jersey Palisades. Wave Hill, a 28-acre estate built in 1843, then lavishly expanded by J. P. Morgan's conservation-minded partner George Perkins, is the only one of these old estates open to the public. At various times Theodore Roosevelt, Mark Twain, and Arturo Toscanini all rented the property, which was donated to the city in 1960. Today 18 acres of exquisite herb, wildflower, and aquatic gardens, which change from year to year, attract green thumbs from all over the world. Grand beech and oak trees adorn wide lawns, and the rugged Palisades looms across the Hudson, by turns framed by elegant pergolas and hidden along curving pathways. Additional draws are a greenhouse and conservatory, gardening and crafts workshops, a summertime dance series, and changing art exhibits. A car is the best way to get here: From Manhattan take the Henry Hudson Parkway to Exit 21 and follow the signs to Wave Hill. Or you can take the Metro North Harlem line train to the Riverdale stop and walk up West 254th Street to Sycamore Avenue, turn right, and continue to Independence Avenue. ✉ *W. 249th St. and Independence Ave.,* ☎ *718/549–2055.* *Mid-Mar.–mid-Nov. $4; Sat. AM and Tues. free; mid-Nov.–mid-Mar. free.* ⏲ *Mid-May–mid-Oct., Tues.–*

Thurs. and weekends 9–5:30, Fri. 9–dusk; mid-Oct.–mid-May, Tues.–Sun. 9–4:30; free garden tours Sun. 2:15.

BROOKLYN

New York City's most populous borough is also its most popular—aside from Manhattan, that is. More people visit Brooklyn than any of the other outer boroughs. Several Brooklyn neighborhoods, particularly Brooklyn Heights, Park Slope, Cobble Hill, and Carroll Gardens, are more popular than ever with young families, lawyers, publishing and media people, and other professionals, who are drawn by the dignified brownstone- and tree-lined streets, water views, handsome parks, friendly neighborhood businesses, and less frenetic pace of life.

Brooklyn Heights, Cobble Hill, and Carroll Gardens

"All the advantages of the country, with most of the conveniences of the city." So ran the ads for a real-estate development that sprang up in the 1820s just across the East River from downtown Manhattan. Brooklyn Heights—named for its enviable hilltop position—was New York's first suburb, linked to the city originally by ferry and later by the Brooklyn Bridge. Feverish construction led by wealthy industrialists and shipping magnates quickly transformed the airy heights into a fashionable upper-middle-class community.

The Heights deteriorated in the 1930s. In the 1940s and 1950s, the area became an alternative to the bohemian haven of Greenwich Village—home to writers including Carson McCullers, W. H. Auden, Arthur Miller, Truman Capote, Richard Wright, Alfred Kazin, Norman Mailer, and Hart Crane. Given the neighborhood's European feel and convenient setting, it's not hard to imagine why they came.

Thanks to the vigorous efforts of preservationists in the 1960s, much of the Heights was designated as New York's first historic district. Some 600 buildings more than 100 years old, representing a wide range of American building styles, are in excellent condition today.

Cranberry and Pineapple are just two of the unusual street names in the Heights. Word has it that these names were created by a certain Sarah Middagh, who despised the practice of naming streets for the town fathers and instead named them after various fruits.

A short hop across Atlantic Avenue from Brooklyn Heights, Cobble Hill is another quiet residential area of leafy streets lined with notable town houses built, like those in the Heights, by 19th-century New York's upper middle class. The neighborhood is rapidly becoming one of Brooklyn's most sought-after; on weekends the sidewalks are busy with residents pushing strollers, walking dogs, or chatting with their neighbors. A bit farther south, around President Street, Cobble Hill turns into the historically Italian, working-class section of Carroll Gardens, a neighborhood distinguished by deep blocks that allow for front yards that are unusually large, at least by New York standards. On nice days, residents can be found tending their front-yard gardens or sitting on their stoops as they watch life go by.

Numbers in the text correspond to numbers in the margin and on the Brooklyn Heights, Cobble Hill, and Carroll Gardens map.

A Good Walk

Take the No. 2 or 3 subway from Manhattan to Clark Street, or the No. 6 to Borough Hall and walk up Court Street to Clark Street. From Clark turn left on Henry Street toward Pineapple Street. From here you'll be able to see the blue towers of the Manhattan Bridge, linking Brooklyn to Manhattan, and a view of the Brooklyn Bridge will soon come into view. (As an alternative, walk across the Brooklyn Bridge (☞ The Seaport and the Courts *in* Chapter 2). At the bridge's terminus at Tillary Street, turn right, walk two blocks to Cadmon Plaza West, jog right to Clark Street, where you'll see the No. 2 or 3 subway entrance.)

Turn left onto Orange Street. On the north side of the block (the right-hand side of the street) between Henry and Hicks streets is a formidable institution, the **Plymouth Church of the Pilgrims** ①, the vortex of abolitionist sentiment in the years before the Civil War. Turn right on Hicks Street and follow it to Middagh Street (pronounced *mid*-awe). At its intersection with Willow Street is **24 Middagh Street** ②, the oldest home in the neighborhood. Venture a few steps west on Middagh to watch neighborhood children and their parents playing at the pleasant Harry Chapin Playground, named after the late singer-songwriter.

Backtrack on **Willow Street** and observe the outstanding architecture between Clark and Pierrepont streets (Nos. 149, 155, 157, and 159 are especially notable). As you turn right on Pierrepont Street heading toward the river, glance down Columbia Heights to your right, where the brownstones are particularly elegant.

Pierrepont Street ends at the **Brooklyn Heights Promenade** ③, one of the most famous vista points in all of New York City. This is a great place for a picnic, with take-out food from one of the many Montague Street restaurants or provisions from the exotic food stores on nearby Atlantic Avenue; try Sahadi Importing (☞ Need a Break?, *below*) in particular. As you leave the Promenade (via Montague Street), look left to see Nos. 2 and 3 Pierrepont Place, two brick-and-brownstone palaces built in the 1850s by a China trader and philanthropist and used as a location for John Huston's film *Prizzi's Honor.* On your right lies Montague Terrace, where Thomas Wolfe lived when he was finishing *You Can't Go Home Again.* Auden lived a few doors away.

After you've soaked in the views from the Promenade, leave it via Montague Street, the commercial spine of the Heights, heading east past restaurants representing a multitude of ethnic cuisines. At the northeast corner of Montague and Clinton streets is **St. Ann's and the Holy Trinity Church** ④, known for its historic stained-glass windows and performing-arts center.

Beyond Clinton on the north side of Montague Street, note an interesting row of banks: Chase (✉ 177 Montague St.), a copy of the Palazzo della Gran Guardia in Verona, Italy; a Citibank (✉ 181 Montague St.) that looks like a latter-day Roman temple; and the Art Deco Municipal Credit Union (✉ 185 Montague St.). Continue east on Montague Street if you wish to visit the historic **Brooklyn Borough Hall** ⑤ or detour a block north up Clinton Street to the elegant redbrick **Brooklyn Historical Society** ⑥, slated to be closed for renovation throughout 1999.

Return south along Clinton Street, and then turn right onto Remsen Street. At the corner of Remsen and Henry streets, stop to take in the Romanesque Revival **Our Lady of Lebanon Maronite Church** ⑦. Continue west on Remsen Street and then turn left onto Hicks Street to visit the 1847 Gothic Revival Grace Church at No. 254. Across Hicks Street is Grace Court Alley, a traditional mews with a score of beautifully restored redbrick carriage houses, which were once stables for the mansions on Remsen and Joralemon streets.

Brooklyn Borough Hall, **5**
Brooklyn Heights Promenade, **3**
Brooklyn Historical Society, **6**
Christ Church, **10**
Cobble Hill Park, **9**
F. G. Guido Funeral Home, **11**
New York City Transit Museum, **8**
Our Lady of Lebanon Maronite Church, **7**
Plymouth Church of the Pilgrims, **1**
St. Ann's and the Holy Trinity Church, **4**
24 Middagh Street, **2**

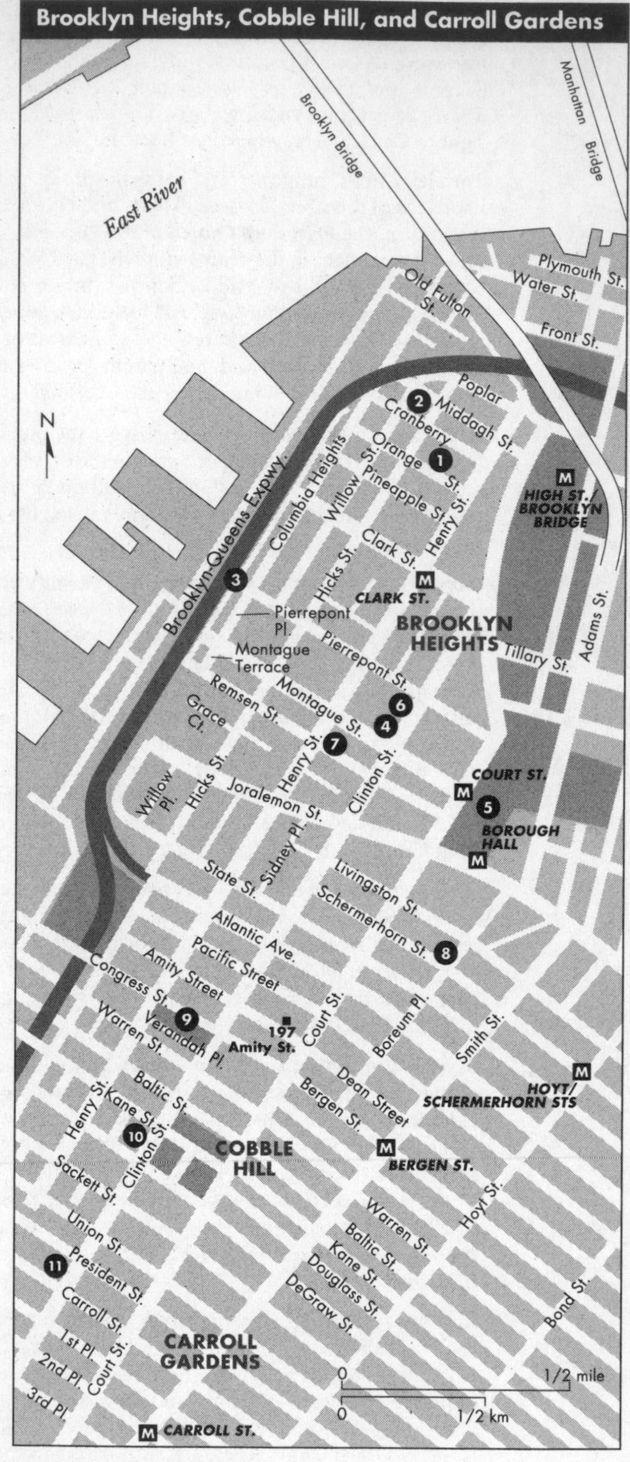

Just a few more steps down Hicks Street, turn right and stroll down cobblestoned Joralemon Street, noting Nos. 29–75, a row of modest brick row houses that delicately sidestep their way down the hill toward the river and the piers beyond the expressway. Follow Willow Place south along the peaceful block between Joralemon and State streets. Watch for the quietly elegant former Willow Place Chapel, built in 1876, and Nos. 43–49, four redbrick houses linked by a majestic two-story colonnade that looks transplanted from an antebellum southern mansion.

At the end of Willow Place, turn left on State Street and follow it past Hicks and Henry streets back to Clinton Street. If you're so inclined, make a left on Clinton and then the next right on Schermerhorn Street to visit the **New York City Transit Museum** ⑧. Otherwise turn right down Clinton to Atlantic Avenue, a busy thoroughfare crowded with Middle Eastern restaurants and, a few blocks farther east between Hoyt and Bond streets, 18 antique furniture stores.

Atlantic Avenue is the official dividing line between the neighborhoods of Brooklyn Heights and Cobble Hill. For a taste of the latter, go two blocks south down Clinton Street to Amity Street. You may want to turn left to **197 Amity Street,** where Jennie Jerome, the mother of Winston Churchill, was born in 1854.

Return to Clinton and go one more block south, where on the west side of the street is **Cobble Hill Park** ⑨, bordered by Verandah Place, a charming row of converted stable buildings where Thomas Wolfe once lived. Proceed south down Clinton Street to observe block after block of distinguished row houses, ranging from Romanesque Revival to neoclassic to Italianate brownstone. Three blocks south of the park, at 320 Clinton Street, is the Episcopal **Christ Church** ⑩, designed by Richard Upjohn.

About four blocks farther down Clinton Street, toward President Street, Cobble Hill gives way to the largely Italian Carroll Gardens. Wander down President, Carroll, and 1st and 2nd places to see the lovingly tended gardens where the abundance of religious statuary attests to the largely Catholic makeup of the neighborhood.

Before leaving Clinton Street, stop for a look at the **F. G. Guido Funeral Home** ⑪ (on the northwest corner of Carroll and Clinton streets), one of the city's finest examples of a Greek Revival town house. Turn left (east) on Carroll Street to Court Street, the main commercial thoroughfare of the neighborhood. Carroll Gardens peters out about five blocks south (to the right); from here it's about 10 blocks back to Atlantic Avenue, to the north.

If you have the stamina to continue on to the Park Slope tour, take the F train from the Carroll Street subway station (at the intersection of Carroll and Smith streets) three more stops, in the direction of Coney Island, to the 7th Avenue stop.

TIMING

Allow three to four hours for a leisurely tour of these three neighborhoods, more if you plan on stopping for a picnic along the Promenade or a meal along Montague Street. Try to come on a clear, sunny day, when the view from the Promenade is most spectacular.

Sights to See

★ ❺ **Brooklyn Borough Hall.** Built in 1848 and thoroughly restored in the late 1980s, this Greek Revival landmark is arguably Brooklyn's handsomest building. The hammered-brass top of the cast-iron cupola (a successor to the original wooden one, which burned in 1895) was restored by the same French craftsmen who restored the Statue of Liberty. The stately building boasts Tuckahoe marble both inside and out; other highlights are the square rotunda and the two-story Beaux Art courtroom with plaster columns painted to look like wood. Today the hall serves as the office of Brooklyn's borough president. On Tuesday and Saturday a city Greenmarket sets up on the flagstone plaza in front, where bundles of fresh flowers and produce tempt local office workers and shoppers from the Heights. ✉ *209 Joralemon St.,* ☎ *718/875–4047.* *Free.* ⏲ *Tours Tues. 1–2:30; groups should telephone ahead.*

★ ❸ **Brooklyn Heights Promenade.** East–west streets—from Orange Street, on the north, to Remsen Street, on the south—end at this ⅓-mi-long sliver of park, which hangs over Brooklyn's industrial waterfront like one of Babylon's fabled gardens. Cantilevered over two lanes of the Brooklyn–Queens Expressway and a service road, the esplanade offers enthralling views of the Manhattan skyline. Circling gulls squawk, tugboats honk, and the city seems like a magical place. This is a terrific vantage point from which to admire the Brooklyn Bridge, the historic steel suspension bridge designed by John Augustus Roebling and completed in 1883 (☞ The Seaport and the Courts *in* Chapter 2). The small island to your left is Governors Island, a former military installation, the future of which is now being hotly debated.

❻ **Brooklyn Historical Society.** Erected in 1878–80, this elegant redbrick museum and library was the first major structure in New York to feature terra-cotta ornamentation, which includes lifelike busts, capitals, and friezes. The building is undergoing a major renovation and is slated to be closed through 1999. Neither its exhibits on Brooklyn history nor its impressive library will be accessible during the renovation, but other programs, Saturday neighborhood walking tours, and off-site exhibitions are planned; call for details. ✉ *128 Pierrepont St.,* ☎ *718/624–0890.*

❿ **Christ Church.** This sandstone Episcopal church, with its lean tower-dominated facade, was designed by the prolific architect Richard Upjohn, who lived nearby at 296 Clinton Street. (He also designed Grace Church, at 254 Hicks Street, and ☞ **Our Lady of Lebanon Maronite Church.**) The pulpit, lectern, and altar are the work of Louis Comfort Tiffany. The setting, on a tree-embowered patch of green enclosed by a wrought-iron fence, has the tranquil air of an English churchyard. ✉ *320 Clinton St., at Kane St.,* ☎ *718/624–0083.* ⏲ *Wed. 6:30 PM, Sun. 11 AM.*

❾ **Cobble Hill Park.** This lovely green oasis, one of the first vest-pocket parks in the city, has marble columns at its entrances, antique benches and tables, and a playground at one end. Bordering the park's south side is **Verandah Place,** a charming row of converted stable buildings; Thomas Wolfe once resided in the basement of No. 40 (one of his many residences in the borough). ✉ *Congress St. between Clinton and Henry Sts.*

NEED A BREAK?

Between Court and Clinton streets on Atlantic Avenue are a half dozen Middle Eastern gourmet markets and eateries. The best of these is 45-year-old **Sahadi Importing** (✉ 187–189 Atlantic Ave., ☎ 718/624–4550), where serious cooks stock up on cheap and delicious dried fruits, nuts, oils, olives, and spices, among other things. **Damascus Bread & Pastry** (✉ 195 Atlantic Ave., ☎ 718/625–7070) purveys stellar baklava and spinach pie.

Columbia Heights. Among the majestic residences on this street, **Nos. 210–220** compose a brownstone grouping often cited as the most graceful in New York. Norman Mailer lives on this street, and from a rear window in **No. 111,** John Roebling's son Washington, who in 1869 succeeded his father as chief engineer for the Brooklyn Bridge, directed the building of the bridge from his sickbed.

Court Street. The main commercial thoroughfare of Cobble Hill and Carroll Gardens, Court Street overflows with activity, with its cafés, restaurants, bookstores, old-fashioned bakeries, and a multiplex movie theater. In Cobble Hill, the **Attic** (✉ 220 Court St., ☎ 718/643–9535) is a small antiques store particularly worth seeking out. In Carroll Gardens, fresh pasta, mozzarella, sausages, olives, and prepared dishes are available at a number of shops, including **Pastosa Ravioli** (✉ 347 Court St., ☎ 718/625–9482), where the gnocchi is particularly good, and **Caputo's Dairy** (✉ 460 Court St., ☎ 718/855–8852), with a wide selection of homemade pastas and sauces. Italian sausages, *soppressata* (pork sausage), and homemade mozzarella can be had at **G. Esposito's & Sons** (✉ 357 Court St., ☎ 718/875–6863), the neighborhood's best meat store.

NEED A BREAK?

With its whirring ceiling fans, painted tin ceiling, and old wooden tables, the **Roberto Cappuccino Caffè and Tea Room** (✉ 221 Court St., at Wycoff St., ☎ 718/858–7693) is a charming spot for soup, sandwiches, coffee, and tea. At **Shakespeare's Sister** (✉ 270 Court St., at Kane St., ☎ 718/694–0084), a gift shop-cum-café chock-full of scented candles and handmade cards, you can soothe yourself with any one of a great variety of teas and light snacks while viewing art exhibits—usually featuring work by women.

11 **F. G. Guido Funeral Home.** Once the John Rankin residence, this freestanding three-story redbrick building, built in 1840, is considered one of the city's finest examples of a Greek Revival town house. Its recessed portal, bordered by limestone and topped with a fanlight, is particularly distinguished. ✉ *440 Clinton St.*

8 **New York City Transit Museum.** Inside a converted 1930s subway station, the Transit Museum displays 18 restored classic subway cars and has an operating signal tower. Its gift shop is a mother lode of subway-inspired memorabilia. ✉ *Boerum Pl. at Schermerhorn St.,* ☎ *718/243–3060.* 🎫 *$3.* ⏲ *Tues.–Fri. 10–4, weekends noon–5.*

197 Amity St. Jennie Jerome, the mother of Winston Churchill, was born in this modest house in 1854. (A plaque at 426 Henry Street, southwest of here, incorrectly identifies *that* building as the famous woman's birthplace. The Henry Street address is actually where Jennie's parents lived before she was born.)

7 **Our Lady of Lebanon Maronite Church.** One of the oldest Romanesque Revival buildings in the country, this Congregational church was designed by Richard Upjohn in 1844. Its doors, which depict Norman churches, were salvaged from the 1943 wreck of the ocean liner *Normandie.* ✉ *113 Remsen St., at Henry St.,* ☎ *718/624–7228.* ⏲ *Sun. 8:30–noon or by appointment.*

1 **Plymouth Church of the Pilgrims.** Thanks to the stirring oratory of Brooklyn's most eminent theologian, Henry Ward Beecher (brother of Harriet Beecher Stowe, author of *Uncle Tom's Cabin*), this house of worship was the vortex of abolitionist sentiment in the years before the Civil War. Because it provided refuge to American slaves, the church, which was built in 1850, is known as the Grand Central Terminal of the Underground Railroad. Its windows, like those of many other neighborhood churches, were designed by Louis Comfort Tiffany. Beside the church is a courtyard (locked, alas) with a statue of Beecher, which you can see through the gate. Nearby, at **22 Willow Street,**

Beecher's house still stands—a prim Greek Revival brownstone. ✉ *Orange St. between Henry and Hicks Sts.,* ☎ *718/624–4743.* ⏲ *Tours Sun. 12:15 or by appointment.*

4 **St. Ann's and the Holy Trinity Church.** The church, a National Historic Landmark, claims 60 of the first stained-glass windows made in the United States. More than two-thirds have been restored to date; through the **St. Ann's Center for Restoration and the Arts,** visitors can see the restoration process up close. In 1980 the church created its own performing arts center, Arts at St. Ann's, referred to in *Rolling Stone* as "New York's hippest hall." A wide variety of nonclassic music—jazz, blues, world and new music, musical theater, and experimental opera—is performed March–May and October–December. The church is open only for performances and Sunday at 11 AM for Episcopal worship services. ✉ *157 Montague St., at Clinton St.,* ☎ *718/834–8794 for tours; 718/858–2424 for box office.* ⏲ *Box office Tues.–Sat. noon–6.*

2 **24 Middagh Street.** This 1824 Federal-style clapboard residence with a mansard roof is the oldest home in the neighborhood. Peer through a door in the wall on the Willow Street side for a glimpse of the cottage garden and carriage house in the rear.

Willow Street. One of the prettiest and most architecturally varied blocks in Brooklyn Heights is Willow Street between Clark and Pierrepont streets. **Nos. 155–159** are three distinguished brick Federal row houses that were allegedly stops on the Underground Railroad.

Coney Island

Named Konijn Eiland (Rabbit Island) by the Dutch for its wild rabbit population, Coney Island has a boardwalk, a 2½-mi-long beach, a huge amusement park, the city's only aquarium, and easy proximity to Brighton Beach, a Russian enclave drenched in old-world atmosphere. Although Coney Island may have declined from its glory days early in this century—when visitors lunched at an ocean-side hotel built in the shape of an elephant, glided across the nation's biggest dance floor at Dreamland, or toured a replica of old Baghdad called Luna Park—it's still a great place to experience the sounds, smells, and sights of summer: hot dogs, suntan lotion, crowds, fried clams, girls and boys necking under the boardwalk, and old men staring vacantly out to sea, not to mention the heart-stopping roll of the king of roller coasters, the Cyclone, and the Wonder Wheel.

A Good Walk

Coney Island is the last stop on the B and F trains heading toward Brooklyn. The Coney Island boardwalk still remains the hub of the action; amble along it to take in the local color. For a taste of times gone by, stop at the **Sideshows by the Seashore and the Coney Island Museum,** where fire-eaters and sword swallowers carry on the traditions of what was once billed as the "World's Largest Playground." Entertainment of a more natural sort can be had at the **Aquarium for Wildlife Conservation,** where five beluga whales and some 10,000 other creatures of the sea make their home. From here, so-called Little Odessa is just a short walk away. To get there, take Surf Avenue to Brighton Beach Avenue, where a community of some 90,000 Russian, Ukrainian, and Georgian emigrés operate countless inexpensive restaurants. This is the place to find borscht and blinis, not to mention caviar, at prices that put Petrossian to shame.

TIMING

Coney Island is at its liveliest on weekends, when crowds come out to play, and in summer. Brighton Beach is a vibrant neighborhood year-round. Allow most of a day for this trip, since the subway ride from Manhattan (one-way) takes at least an hour.

Sights to See

★ **Aquarium for Wildlife Conservation.** Moved to Coney Island in 1955 from its former digs at Battery Park, New York City's only aquarium is worth a trip in itself. Here otters, walruses, penguins, and seals lounge on a replicated Pacific coast; a 180,000-gallon seawater complex hosts beluga whales; and dolphins and sea lions perform in the Aquatheater. ✉ *W. 8th St. and Surf Ave.,* ☎ *718/265–3474.* *$7.75.* *Daily 10–4:45.*

Sideshows by the Seashore and the Coney Island Museum. A lively traditional circus sideshow, complete with a fire-eater, sword swallower, snake charmer, and contortionist, can be seen here. On the first Saturday after summer solstice, the cast of the sideshow and an amazing array of local legends take part in the Mermaid Parade, in which 50 antique cars, six marching bands, and artistic floats with a mermaid theme throng the Boardwalk and Surf Avenue. Upstairs from Sideshows, the Coney Island Museum has historic Coney Island memorabilia and a wealth of tourist information. ✉ *Sideshows: W. 12th St. and Surf Ave.; museum: 1208 Surf Ave.;* ☎ *718/372–5159 for both.* *Sideshows $3, museum 99¢.* *Memorial Day–Labor Day, Wed.–Sun. noon–midnight; Labor Day–Memorial Day, weekends noon–5.*

Park Slope and Prospect Park

Park Slope grew up in the late 1800s and is today one of Brooklyn's most sought-after places to live. The largely residential neighborhood has row after row of dazzlingly well-maintained brownstones dating from its turn-of-the-century heyday, when Park Slope had the nation's highest per-capita income. The "Park" in Park Slope refers to Prospect Park, one of New York's most revered green spaces, encompassing 526 acres of meadow, woodland, and water; miles of drives and paths; and home to a zoo, skating rink, concert band shell, and much more. Just beyond the park's borders are the outsized Grand Army Plaza, with its Arc de Triomphe–style Soldiers' and Sailors' Memorial Arch; the stately Brooklyn Museum and Brooklyn Library; and the scenic Brooklyn Botanic Garden, a worthwhile destination virtually any time of year.

Numbers in the text correspond to numbers in the margin and on the Park Slope and Prospect Park map.

A Good Walk

Start your tour at **7th Avenue,** the neighborhood's commercial center, accessible by the D or F train (7th Ave. stops) and by the Nos. 2 and 3 (Grand Army Plaza stop). The beginning of this walk is closer to the D, 2, or 3 train. Turn east from 7th Avenue onto Lincoln Place to find the **Montauk Club** ①, whose sumptuous Venetian-palace style belies its standing as one of Brooklyn's most prestigious men's clubs. Make your way south along 8th Avenue, sampling the brownstones on various streets along the way (President and Carroll streets are especially handsome), until you reach **Montgomery Place** ②, with its remarkable row of Romanesque Revival brownstones.

From Montgomery Place, walk one block east along Prospect Park West to **Grand Army Plaza** ③, whose center is dominated by the Soldiers' and Sailors' Memorial Arch, patterned on the Arc de Triomphe in Paris. Southeast of the plaza is the main entrance to the 526-acre **Prospect Park,** designed by Frederick Law Olmsted and Calvert Vaux, who also created Manhattan's Central Park. The best way to experience the park is to walk the entirety of its 3.3-mi circular drive and make detours

Boathouse, **7**
Brooklyn Botanic Garden, **11**
Brooklyn Museum of Art (BMA), **12**
Brooklyn Public Library, **10**
Grand Army Plaza, **3**
Lefferts Homestead Children's Museum, **8**
Litchfield Villa, **4**
Montauk Club, **1**
Montgomery Place, **2**
Prospect Park Wildlife Center, **9**
Tennis House, **5**
Wollman Memorial Rink, **6**

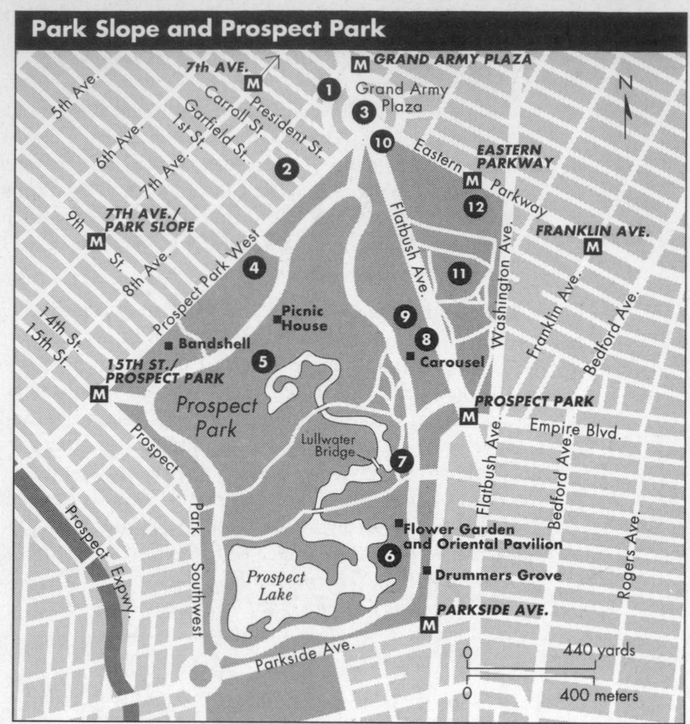

off it as you wish. On summer evenings and weekends year-round, when the drive is closed to vehicular traffic, joggers, skaters, and bicyclists have it to themselves and make a high-energy parade. Immediately upon entering the park, veer right on the circular drive. Take a moment to admire the 75-acre Long Meadow, one of New York's greatest open spaces and a haven for picnickers, kite fliers, and dog lovers on nice weekends. Remarkably, more than 130 years after the park's construction, the view down the Long Meadow from here still takes in no buildings—only grass, trees, and sky. A short distance down the drive, just beyond a circular playground on your right, a small access road leads you around to the **Litchfield Villa** ④, an elaborate Italianate mansion and home of the park's administrative offices.

Continuing on the circular drive from the villa, you'll next come to two popular park structures on your left—the Picnic House, frequently rented for weddings, and, a moment later, the **Tennis House** ⑤, home to the Brooklyn Center for Urban Education. Off to the right, just a few steps farther, is the band shell, site of the park's enormously popular free summer performing-arts series. Continue around the circular drive, which curves to the left around the park's half dozen baseball diamonds, in continuous use by local leagues between Memorial Day and Labor Day; the diamonds mark the far southern end of the Long Meadow. Down the hill on your left is the glorious 60-acre Prospect Lake, a refuge for waterfowl, including a few resident swans. Beyond the Ocean Parkway/Coney Island Avenue park entrance, as you reach the lake's outer reaches, in swift succession you'll come upon the **Drummers Grove** on the right, and, on the left, the **Wollman Memorial Rink** ⑥, Flower Garden, Oriental Pavilion, and **Boathouse** ⑦.

Not far beyond the Boathouse, off on the eastern edge of the park (to your right) is the carousel, and beyond that the **Lefferts Homestead Chil-**

In case you want to see the world.
At American Express, we're here to make your journey a smooth one. So we have over 1,700 travel service locations in over 120 countries ready to help. What else would you expect from the world's largest travel agency?
do more
AMERICAN EXPRESS
Travel
http://www.americanexpress.com/travel

dren's Museum ⑧ and the **Prospect Park Wildlife Center** ⑨, a small zoo. From here, you're just a short walk up the last of the circular drive back to Grand Army Plaza, at which point you've come full circle around the park. To the east of the park's main entrance, you will find the main branch of the **Brooklyn Public Library** ⑩. A couple hundred yards east on the grand **Eastern Parkway** lie the entrances to two of Brooklyn's most important cultural offerings: the beautifully tended **Brooklyn Botanic Garden** ⑪, which occupies 52 acres across Flatbush Avenue from Prospect Park, and the world-class **Brooklyn Museum of Art** ⑫. To return to Manhattan, you can take the No. 2 or 3 subway from the station right in front of the museum.

TIMING

You could spend a whole day at the Brooklyn Museum alone—and another day exploring Prospect Park and the Brooklyn Botanic Garden. If you do choose to fit everything into one trip, break up your wanderings with a visit to 7th Avenue, where restaurants and cafés abound. Weekends are the best time to observe local life along 7th Avenue and to enjoy the park, when it's closed to vehicles. The Botanic Garden reaches its prime during spring, when the cherry blossoms bloom like pink snow, although its gardens and greenhouses have been designed to offer year-round pleasures.

Sights to See

❼ **Boathouse.** Styled after Sansovino's 16th-century Library at St. Mark's in Venice, this 1905 lakefront structure in Prospect Park, built about 40 years after the park was first created, sits opposite the **Lullwater Bridge,** which affords a lovely view of it, particularly on evenings when the light is just right and the lake reflects an exact image of the building. Unfortunately, its white-glazed terra-cotta facade has been heavily water-damaged, and the building has been unattractively fenced off and will be closed at least through 1999. Just steps from the Boathouse (on the left as you face the Cleft Ridge Span) and unaffected by its closure is the lovely **Camperdown Elm,** immortalized by the poet Marianne Moore, who in the 1960s was an early park preservationist.

★ ⓫ **Brooklyn Botanic Garden.** A major attraction at this 52-acre botanic garden, one of the finest in the country, is the beguiling **Japanese Garden**—complete with a blazing red *torii* gate and a pond laid out in the shape of the Chinese character for "heart." The Japanese cherry arbor in the Japanese Garden turns into a heart-stopping cloud of pink every spring. You can also wander through the **Cranford Rose Garden** (5,000 bushes, 1,200 varieties); the **Fragrance Garden,** designed especially for the blind; the **Shakespeare Garden,** featuring more than 80 plants immortalized by the Bard (including many kinds of roses); and **Celebrity Path,** Brooklyn's answer to Hollywood's Walk of Fame, with the names of homegrown stars—including Mel Brooks, Woody Allen, Mary Tyler Moore, Barbra Streisand, Mae West, and Maurice Sendak—inscribed on stepping-stones. The **Steinhardt Conservatory,** a complex of handsome greenhouses, holds thriving desert, tropical, temperate, and aquatic vegetation, as well as a display charting the evolution of plants over the past 140 million years. The extraordinary **C. V. Starr Bonsai Museum** in the Conservatory exhibits about 80 miniature Japanese specimens. Free tours are given weekends at 1 PM, except for holiday weekends. ✉ *1000 Washington Ave., between Empire Blvd. and south side of Brooklyn Museum,* ☎ *718/622–4433.* *$3; free Tues.* ⏲ *Garden Apr.–Sept., Tues.–Fri. 8–6, weekends 10–6; Oct.–Mar., Tues.–Fri. 8–4:30, weekends 10–4:30. Steinhardt Conservatory Apr.–Sept., Tues.–Sun. 10–5:30; Oct.–Mar., Tues.–Sun. 10–4.*

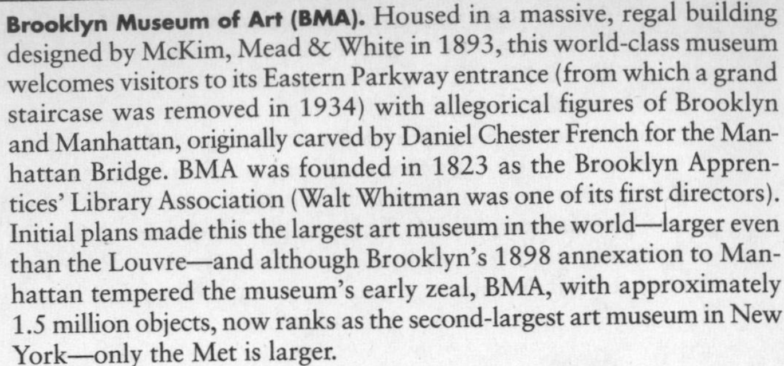
★ 12 **Brooklyn Museum of Art (BMA).** Housed in a massive, regal building designed by McKim, Mead & White in 1893, this world-class museum welcomes visitors to its Eastern Parkway entrance (from which a grand staircase was removed in 1934) with allegorical figures of Brooklyn and Manhattan, originally carved by Daniel Chester French for the Manhattan Bridge. BMA was founded in 1823 as the Brooklyn Apprentices' Library Association (Walt Whitman was one of its first directors). Initial plans made this the largest art museum in the world—larger even than the Louvre—and although Brooklyn's 1898 annexation to Manhattan tempered the museum's early zeal, BMA, with approximately 1.5 million objects, now ranks as the second-largest art museum in New York—only the Met is larger.

Collection highlights include **Egyptian Art** (third floor), considered one of the best of its kind and slated to be reinstalled by late 1999; and **African and Pre-Columbian Art** (first floor), another one recognized worldwide. In the gallery of **American painting and sculpture** (fifth floor), *Brooklyn Bridge* by Georgia O'Keeffe hangs alongside nearly 200 first-rate works by Winslow Homer, John Singer Sargent, Thomas Eakins, George Bellows, and Milton Avery. The **Period Rooms** (fourth floor) include the complete interior of the Jan Martense Schenck House, built in the Brooklyn Flatlands section in 1675, as well as a Moorish-style room from the 54th Street mansion of John D. Rockefeller (the MoMA sculpture garden now occupies the mansion's former site). **Asian Art** (second floor) includes galleries devoted to Chinese, Korean, Indian, and Islamic works. Outdoors, the **Frieda Schiff Warburg Memorial Sculpture Garden** showcases architectural fragments from demolished New York buildings, including Penn Station. BMA is working hard to significantly boost attendance, with more blockbuster shows, extended Saturday hours, film screenings, readings, and musical performances, all intended to put it at the top of New York's hyper-competitive museum heap. ✉ *200 Eastern Pkwy.,* ☎ *718/638–5000.* 💵 *$4 (suggested donation).* ⏲ *Wed.–Fri. 10–5, Sat. 11–9, Sun. 11–6.*

10 **Brooklyn Public Library.** Built in 1941, this grand neoclassic edifice was designed to resemble an open book, with a gilt-inscribed spine on Grand Army Plaza that opens out to Eastern Parkway and Flatbush Avenue. Bright limestone walls, perfect proportions, and ornate decorative details make this a unique 20th-century New York building. The 15 bronze figures over the entrance, representing favorite characters in American literature, were sculpted by Thomas Hudson Jones, who also designed the Tomb of the Unknown Soldier in Arlington National Cemetery. ✉ *Grand Army Plaza at intersection of Flatbush Ave. and Eastern Pkwy.,* ☎ *718/780–7700.* ⏲ *Tues.–Thurs. 9–8; Mon., Fri., and Sat. 10–6; Sun. 1–5.*

Drummers Grove. Designated as an official ☞ **Prospect Park** site in 1996, this area has long been a popular informal weekend gathering spot for Caribbean and African-American musicians, many of whom live in the neighborhood bordering the park's eastern flank. Sunday afternoons from mid-March through mid-September, dozens of drummers, chanters, dancers, and other revelers get down, joined by an audience of stalled bicyclists, joggers, and skaters lulled by the mesmerizing beat, beat, beat of the tom-tom.

Eastern Parkway. The first six-lane parkway in the world, which originates at Grand Army Plaza, this major boulevard mimics the grand sweep of the boulevards of Paris and Vienna; Frederick Law Olmsted and Calvert Vaux conceived the design in 1866, in tandem with their plans for the park; at that time the parkway ended at Ralph Avenue, then the border of Brooklyn. Today Eastern Parkway continues to play an important role in Brooklyn culture: Every Labor Day weekend it hosts the West Indian American Day Parade (☞ Festivals and Seasonal Events *in* Chapter 1), the biggest and liveliest carnival outside the Caribbean.

❸ **Grand Army Plaza.** Prospect Park West, Eastern Parkway, and Flatbush and Vanderbilt avenues radiate outward from this geographic star. At the center stands the **Soldiers' and Sailors' Memorial Arch,** honoring Civil War veterans and patterned on the Arc de Triomphe in Paris. Three heroic sculptural groupings adorn the arch: atop, a four-horsed chariot by Frederick MacMonnies, so dynamic that it seems on the verge of catapulting off the arch; to the sides, the victorious Union Army and Navy of the Civil War. Inside are bas-reliefs of presidents Abraham Lincoln and Ulysses S. Grant, sculpted by Thomas Eakins and William O'Donovan, respectively. Crossing the broad streets around here can be hazardous; beware. On some spring and fall weekends the top of the arch is accessible; call 718/965–8999 for information.

To the northwest of the arch, Neptune and a passel of debauched Tritons leer over the edges of the **Bailey Fountain,** where tulle-drenched brides and grooms in Technicolor tuxes pose after exchanging vows. On Saturday year-round, the second-largest of the city's Greenmarkets (after Union Square's in downtown Manhattan) sets up in the plaza; heaps of locally grown produce, flowers and plants, baked goods, and other foodstuffs attract throngs of neighborhood residents.

❽ **Lefferts Homestead Children's Museum.** Built in 1783 and moved to ☞ **Prospect Park** in 1918, this gambrel-roof Dutch colonial farmhouse contains a historic house museum for children. Adults will enjoy the two period rooms furnished with antiques, while children love playing in the four rooms with period reproduction furniture. Nearby is a restored 1912 **carousel.** ☎ *718/965–6505 museum.* *Free.* *Mid-Apr.–mid-Dec., Thurs. and weekends 1–5, Fri. 1–4; mid-Dec.–Mar. by appointment. Hrs vary, so call ahead.* *Carousel 50¢ per ride on weekends; closed mid-Oct.–early Apr.*

❹ **Litchfield Villa.** The most important sight on the western border of ☞ **Prospect Park,** this Italianate mansion built in 1857 was designed by Alexander Jackson Davis, considered the foremost architect of his day, for a prominent railroad magnate. It has housed the park's headquarters since 1883, but visitors are welcome to step inside and view the domed octagonal rotunda. Not far from the Litchfield Villa on the park's circular drive is the **Picnic House,** one of the park's less architecturally distinguished buildings, used mostly for private functions. ✉ *Prospect Park W and 3rd St.,* ☎ *718/965–8999 for park hot line.*

❶ **Montauk Club.** The home of a venerable men's club (and newly developed condominium apartments on its upper floors), this 1891 mansion designed by Francis H. Kimball is modeled on Venice's Ca' d'Oro and other Gothic Venetian palaces. It is Park Slope's most impressive building and easily rivals the showcase mansions with more prestigious addresses on Manhattan's Upper East Side. Notice the friezes of Montauk Indians and the 19th-century private side entrance for members' wives. ✉ *25 8th Ave.*

❷ **Montgomery Place.** This block-long street between 8th Avenue and Prospect Park West is considered to be one of Park Slope's finest thoroughfares; it's lined with picturesque town houses designed by the Romanesque Revival genius C. P. H. Gilbert.

Prospect Park. When they initiated construction of this 526-acre park in 1866, Frederick Law Olmsted and Calvert Vaux considered their plan superior to that of Central Park (☞ Chapter 2)—which was being completed as they started work here—because no streets divided it and no bordering skyscrapers infringed on its borders. It is regarded by Olmsted aficionados as among his very best creations, and although its fortunes have risen and fallen over the last 130 years, a large number of restoration projects now planned or in progress are helping to revitalize the park. The largest of these involves the **Ravine,** the wooded core of the park. Though just steps from the Long Meadow (the main path from the park's 9th Street entrance leads right down to it), it vividly conveys a sense of wilderness and demonstrates Olmsted's genius at juxtaposing vastly different landscapes. Currently undergoing a monumental multiphase restoration, the Ravine is scheduled to be closed at least through 2000, although one path is open through the area, and seasonal guided tours are given (call the park hot line for details).

A rewarding visit to the park need not involve any specific destination, as the park's winding paths and drives, undulating hills, unexpected vistas, and open spaces serve up unanticipated pleasures at every turn. But visitors desiring specific destinations won't be disappointed; key attractions include the ☞ **Tennis House,** the ☞ **Wollman Memorial Skating Rink,** the ☞ **Prospect Park Wildlife Center,** and the **band shell.** At the Park's 9th Street entrance (at Prospect Park West), the band shell is the home of the annual Celebrate Brooklyn Festival, which from mid-June through Labor Day sponsors free performances—with an emphasis on music—to please every taste, from African-Caribbean jazz to Kurt Weill, from the Brooklyn Philharmonic playing Duke Ellington to bluegrass and zydeco groups. A performance here on a glorious summer evening is *the* best way to enjoy the park and the Slope at their finest. ✉ *Band shell, Prospect Park W and 9th St.,* ☎ *718/965–8999 for park hot line; 718/855–7882, ext. 52 for Celebrate Brooklyn Festival .* 🎟 *Free.* ⏲ *Concerts late June–Labor Day, Fri.–Sat. 7 PM, some Sun. 2 PM, plus additional times. Call for details.*

NEED A BREAK? In the historic Pavilion Theater (once a single-screen grandam and now a five-plex cinema), the **Living Room Café** (✉ 188 Prospect Park W, at 14th St., ☎ 718/369–0824) is just a short walk from the band shell. You can gaze out the oversize windows overlooking the park as you nibble on crepes, sandwiches, a sundae, or an egg cream from the Ben & Jerry's Ice Cream Parlor.

9 **Prospect Park Wildlife Center.** Small, friendly, and educational, this children's zoo off the main road of ☞ **Prospect Park** has just the right combination of indoor and outdoor exhibits along with a number of unusual and endangered species among its 390 inhabitants. The central sea-lion pool is a hit with youngsters, as are the indoor exhibits—"Animal Lifestyles," which explains habitats and adaptations, and "Animals in Our Lives," showcasing animals that make good pets and animals used on the farm. There's also an outdoor discovery trail with a simulated prairie-dog burrow and a naturalistic pond. The zoo is run by the Wildlife Conservation Society, which also oversees the Bronx Zoo (☞ The Bronx, *above*). ☎ *718/399–7339.* 🎟 *$2.50.* ⏲ *Nov.–Mar., daily 10–4:30; Apr.–Oct., weekdays 10–5, weekends 10–5:30.*

Seventh Avenue. Restaurants, groceries, bookstores, cafés, bakeries, churches, and many other neighborhood businesses stretch continuously down Park Slope's commercial spine from Flatbush Avenue roughly to 14th Street, where things peter out. A leisurely stroll will yield finds for browsers and buyers of all interests, but a few choice spots—beginning at the north (Flatbush) end and moving south—include the **New Prospect** (✉ 52 7th Ave.), the best place to pick up some ready-made food; **Prints Charming** (✉ 54 7th Ave.), offering a good selection of both framed and unframed prints; **Cousin John's Bakery** (✉ 70 7th Ave.), one of the neighborhood's best; **Leaf & Bean** (✉ 83 7th Ave.), a charming tea and coffee shop with lots of hard-to-find paraphernalia; **Leon Paley Ltd. Wines & Spirits** (✉ 88 7th Ave.), a fine wine store; the **Clay Pot** (✉ 162 7th Ave.), which sells a distinctive array of handmade American crafts and jewelry; and **Connecticut Muffin** (✉ 171 7th Ave.), a popular people-watching spot.

A bit farther down, closer to 9th Street (where the F train stops), be sure not to miss another branch of **Cousin John's Bakery** (✉ 343 7th Ave.); and the funkiest store in the Slope, **Scouting Party** (✉ 349 7th Ave., at 10th St.), a riotous mix of toys and doodads that will appeal to kids and adults alike, plus a small but well-chosen selection of jewelry, crafts, cards, and used books.

NEED A BREAK? **Second Street Café** (✉ 189 7th Ave., at 2nd St., ☎ 718/369–6928) is a homey restaurant and coffee bar with lunch on weekdays, brunch on weekends, and counter-service coffee-bar fare in late afternoons and evenings. Try the raisin-studded bread pudding or heartwarming soups such as curry pumpkin. The coffee house of choice around here is **Ozzie's Coffee & Tea** (✉ 57 7th Ave., at Lincoln Pl., ☎ 718/398–6695), a converted drugstore with its apothecary cases still intact.

5 **Tennis House.** The most prominent of several neoclassic structures in the park, this 1910 limestone and yellow brick building postdates by 40 years the more rustic structures favored by Olmsted and Vaux, few of which survive. The Tennis House's most elegant features are the triple-bay Palladian arches on both its north and south facade, and its airy terra-cotta barrel-vaulted arcade on the south side. The building's large tiled central court has amazing acoustics—shout "hello" and listen to your voice bounce back at you. The house sits atop a modest knoll overlooking the south end of the Long Meadow, where from spring through fall you can almost always catch a baseball or softball game at one of the nearby diamonds. In the basement is the **Brooklyn Center for the Urban Environment,** which houses rotating exhibits about urban issues. ☎ *718/788–8500.* *Free.* *Weekdays 8:30–5 (Tennis House only) and weekends noon–4 (Tennis House and BCUE gallery, when an exhibit is up).*

6 **Wollman Memorial Rink.** A cousin to Wollman Rink in Central Park (☞ Chapter 2), this is one of ☞ **Prospect Park**'s most popular destinations. Besides skating in the winter, pedal boat rentals are available here weekends and holidays from April through the middle of October (☎ 718/282–7789); the cost is $10 per hour. The rink is directly across the circular drive from the ☞ **Drummers Grove** and adjacent to the **Flower Garden,** the most formally laid-out area of the park. Unfortunately, the construction of the Wollman Rink destroyed this area's original close connection with the lake. In the early days an orchestra would play on an island just off the shore while spectators strolled along the terraces and radial pathways among busts of composers including Mozart and Beethoven or sat beneath the beautiful **Oriental Pavilion,** an open shelter supported by eight hand-painted wrought-iron columns and illuminated within by a central stained-glass skylight. Today this area is usually unwelcomingly deserted, and during the winter music blares from the rink. ☎ *718/287–5538.* *$4; $3.50 skate rental.* *Mid-Nov.–early Mar., Mon.–Thurs. 8:30–2, Fri. 8:30–8:30, Sat. 10–1, 2–6 and 7–10, Sun. 10–1 and 2–6.*

QUEENS

Home of the La Guardia and John F. Kennedy International airports and many of Manhattan's bedroom communities, Queens is perhaps New York City's most underappreciated borough. It's certainly the most diverse, for the borough's countless ethnic neighborhoods continue to attract immigrants from all over the world—its inhabitants represent 117 different nationalities and speak scores of languages, ranging from Hindi to Hebrew. Queens communities, such as Astoria (Greek and Italian), Jackson Heights (Colombian and Indian), Sunnyside (Turkish), and Flushing (Korean), are fascinating to explore, particularly if you're interested in experiencing some of the city's tastiest—and least expensive—cuisine. In addition, these areas often feature little-known historic sites, many of them just 10 minutes by subway from Grand Central Terminal.

Astoria

Home to a vital community of some 35,000 Greeks, Astoria is a place where people socialize on their front lawns at dusk and where mom-and-pop businesses thrive. Here you can buy Cypriot cured olives and feta cheese from store owners who will tell you where to go for the best spinach pie; or you can sit outside at one of the many *xaxaroplasteion* (pastry shops), eating baklava and watching the subway's elevated trains speed by.

Originally German, then Italian, Astoria earned the nickname Little Athens in the late 1960s; by the early 1990s Greeks accounted for nearly half the population. Today there are also substantial numbers of Asians, Eastern Europeans, Irish, and Hispanic immigrants in Astoria, not to mention an ever-growing contingent of former Manhattan residents in search of cheaper rents and a safer, friendlier atmosphere. It may seem ironic that such a melting pot made history as the center of America's flashiest industry—namely, show business. Before Hollywood, in the 1920s, such stars as Gloria Swanson, Rudolph Valentino, and the Marx Brothers came to this neighborhood to work at "the Big House," Paramount's moviemaking center in the east. At that time the Kaufman-Astoria Studios were the largest and most important filmmaking studios in the country; today they remain the largest in the East, and they're still used for major films and television shows.

Numbers in the text correspond to numbers in the margin and on the Astoria map.

A Good Tour

By subway, take the N train from Manhattan to the Broadway stop. Walk five blocks along Broadway to 36th Street; turn right and walk two blocks to 35th Avenue (bear with the confusion of intersecting streets, drives, and avenues). Here you'll find the **American Museum of the Moving Image** ①, where you can spend hours studying its exhibits on film production and catching bits of the regularly scheduled film series and directors' talks. Next door, the imposing 13-acre Kaufman-Astoria Studios (☒ 34–12 36th St.), a former powerhouse in the American movie industry, has been used for the filming of *The Cotton Club* and *Sabrina* and television series such as *Cosby* and *Sesame Street*.

Head back to the heart of the Greek community by wandering along Broadway between 31st and 36th streets. Here Greek pastry shops and coffeehouses abound, and the elevated subway brings a constant stream of activity. Farther up, 30th Avenue has every kind of food store imaginable; between 35th and 36th streets alone you'll find a *salumeria,* a

American Museum of the Moving Image, **1**
Isamu Noguchi Sculpture Museum, **3**
Socrates Sculpture Park, **2**

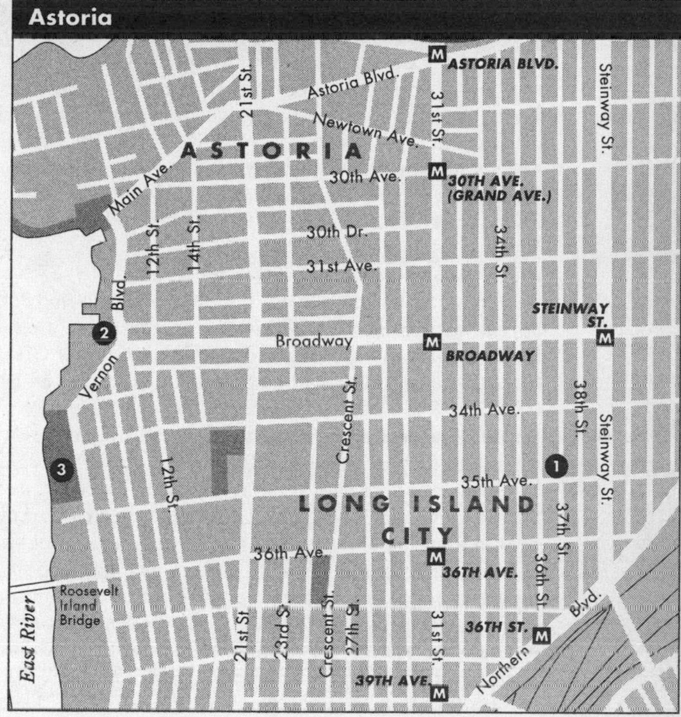

meat market, a bakery, a wholesale international food store, and more. The largest Orthodox community outside Greece worships at St. Demetrios Cathedral (✉ 30-11 30th Dr.), just off 30th Avenue.

Anyone interested in sculpture won't want to miss the funky **Socrates Sculpture Park** ② and the more refined **Isamu Noguchi Sculpture Museum** ③. From the Broadway subway station, walk eight blocks (about 15 minutes) toward the river. At Vernon and Broadway the Socrates Sculpture Park at first almost appears to be an urban hallucination, with its large, abstract artwork framed by the Manhattan skyline. Three blocks to the left on Vernon Boulevard, with its entrance on 33rd Road, the Isamu Noguchi Sculpture Museum has hundreds of Noguchi's works displayed in an indoor-outdoor setting that evokes the tranquillity of a Zen garden.

TIMING

To see Greek Astoria at its finest, visit on a Saturday, when sidewalk culture comes to life. Weekdays are also pleasant, as the neighborhood's quiet pace offers a welcome alternative to frenetic Manhattan. Allow at least three hours for a leisurely visit to the American Museum of the Moving Image and a tour of Greek Astoria; add another hour or two if you plan to visit the more distant Socrates Sculpture Park and Isamu Noguchi Sculpture Museum (the latter is closed in winter).

Sights to See

★ ❶ **American Museum of the Moving Image.** The nation's only museum devoted to the art, technology, and history of film, TV, and digital media is alone worth a visit to Astoria. Its core exhibition, "Behind the Screen," takes you step by step through the process of producing, marketing, and exhibiting moving images through a combination of artifacts, texts, live demonstrations, and video screenings. You can make your own video flip book, edit sound effects, dub dialogue, and create animation through 13 computer-based interactive experiences. The museum's collection of movie memorabilia includes 70,000 items; in the costume display are outfits worn by Marlene Dietrich, Marilyn Monroe, and Robin Williams. The museum also presents changing exhibits, lectures, and provocative film programs, including major artist-oriented retrospectives, Hollywood classics, experimental videos, and TV documentaries (☞ Film and Video *in* Chapter 5). ✉ *35th Ave. between 36th and 37th Sts.*, ☎ *718/784–0077.* *$8.* ⏲ *Tues.–Fri. noon–5, weekends 11–6.*

NEED A BREAK? At the **Omonia Café** (✉ 32–20 Broadway, ☎ 718/274–6650) you can watch the constant activity on Broadway while nursing coffee and honey-sweet pastries. At Broadway and 34th Street, **Uncle George's** (✉ 33–19 Broadway, ☎ 718/626–0593) is a 24-hour Greek diner where rotisserie-roasted lamb and other Greek classics can be had for a song.

★ ❸ **Isamu Noguchi Sculpture Museum.** In 1961 Japanese-American sculptor Isamu Noguchi (1904–88) rented a studio across the street from this space, a former photo engraver's factory he subsequently purchased, and which, in 1985, became a museum devoted to his sculpture. A large, open-air garden and two floors of gallery space hold more than 250 of Noguchi's pieces in stone, bronze, wood, clay, and steel. Videos document his long career; there are also models, drawings, and even stage sets for dances by Martha Graham. Weekend bus service ($5) to the museum leaves every hour on the half hour, 11:30–3:30, from the Asia Society (☞ The Upper East Side *in* Chapter 2). ✉ *32–61 Vernon Blvd., at 33rd Rd., Long Island City,* ☎ *718/204–7088.* *$4 (suggested donation).* ⏲ *Apr.–Nov., Wed.–Fri. 10–5, weekends 11–6.*

OFF THE BEATEN PATH **Queens Museum of Art** – It's worth trekking to Flushing Meadows–Corona Park to see the knock-your-socks-off New York City panorama, a 9,335-square-ft model of the five boroughs, made for the 1964–65 World's Fair, which faithfully replicates all five boroughs of the city, building by building, on a scale of 1 inch per 100 ft. The model's tiny brownstones and skyscrapers are updated periodically to look exactly like the real things. The museum's other exhibits examine the history of the World's Fair, and its frequent art exhibitions often reflect the cultural diversity of Queens. The park's New York City Building, which houses the museum, was also the site of several United Nations meetings between 1939 and 1964. The 140-ft-high **Unisphere**, a 380-ton stainless-steel sculpture of the Earth also made for the World's Fair, is here, gracing the back entrance to the new U.S. Tennis Center, home of the U.S. Open. The New York Hall of Science (☞ Chapter 4) is nearby. To get here, take the No. 7 subway from Times Square or Grand Central Station to the 111th Street Station. ✉ *Flushing Meadows–Corona Park,* ☎ *718/592–9700.* *$3.* ⏲ *Wed.–Fri. 10–5, weekends noon–5.*

❷ **Socrates Sculpture Park.** The ancient Greeks excelled in the art of sculpture, which was often displayed in outdoor temples. It is appropriate, then, that Astoria should have an outdoor sculpture park. In 1985 local residents rallied to transform what had been an illegal dump site into this 4.2-acre park, devoted to the display of public art. Today a superb view of the river and the Manhattan skyline beyond frames huge works of art made of scrap metal, old tires, and other recycled products. ✉ *Vernon Blvd. at Broadway,* ☎ *718/956–1819.* ⏲ *Daily 10 AM–sunset.*

STATEN ISLAND

Even though Staten Island is officially a borough of New York City, it is, to many New Yorkers, the forgotten borough. Its claims to fame are as the city's official garbage dump, and as the borough that is perpetually agitating to secede from New York City. Permanently settled in 1661 as a farming community by the Dutch, Staten Island today still feels provincial and even old-fashioned compared with the rest of the city; indeed, time stands still in the two re-created villages of Richmondtown and Snug Harbor. Although it's less convenient to get here than the other boroughs, the 20-minute ferry ride across New York Harbor affords phenomenal views of lower Manhattan and the Statue of Liberty—and it's free. On weekend mornings (until 11:30 AM), ferries leave the southern tip of Manhattan every hour on the half hour; on weekdays and weekend afternoons you can catch one at least every half hour. Call 718/815–2628 for schedules and directions.

Snug Harbor and Beyond

Just 2 mi from the ferry terminal, the restored sailor's community of Snug Harbor is by far the most popular of Staten Island's attractions. For a highly enjoyable daytime outing, take the scenic ferry ride from Manhattan and visit Snug Harbor and two small but engaging nearby museums; then stop perhaps for a meal at Adobe Blues.

Numbers in the text correspond to numbers in the margin and on the Staten Island map.

A Good Tour

From the Staten Island Ferry terminal, a seven-minute (2-mi) ride on the S40 bus will take you to the **Snug Harbor Cultural Center** ①, an 83-acre complex with an art gallery, a botanical garden, a children's museum, and a colorful history. Signal the driver as soon as you glimpse the black iron fence along the edge of the property.

If the day is still young after you've toured Snug Harbor, return to the ferry terminal and catch the S51–Bay Street bus for the 15-minute ride to Hylan Boulevard to see the turn-of-the-century photographs displayed in the picturesque **Alice Austen House Museum** ②. Italian history buffs should head to the **Garibaldi-Meucci Museum** ③, where war general Giuseppe Garibaldi lived in exile with his friend Antonio Meucci—the true inventor of the telephone.

TIMING

The Snug Harbor Cultural Center alone will take at least half a day, including the ferry commute; add to that the Alice Austen House and the Garibaldi-Meucci Museum, and you're in for a whole-day adventure. If you're interested in visiting all three attractions, plan your visit toward the end of the week, when both the museums are open. The Garibaldi-Meucci Museum is closed in winter.

Sights to See

❷ **Alice Austen House Museum.** Photographer Alice Austen (1866–1952) defied tradition when, as a girl of 10, she received her first camera as a gift from an uncle and promptly began taking pictures of everything around her. Austen went on to make photography her lifetime avocation, recording on film a vivid social history of Staten Island in the early part of the century; one of the local ferries is actually named for her. The cozy, ivy-covered Dutch-style cottage known as Clear Comfort, where she lived almost all her life, has been restored, and many of her photographs are on display. ✉ *2 Hylan Blvd.,* ☎ *718/816–4506.* 💳 *$3 (suggested donation).* ⏲ *Mar.–Dec., Thurs.–Sun. noon–5.*

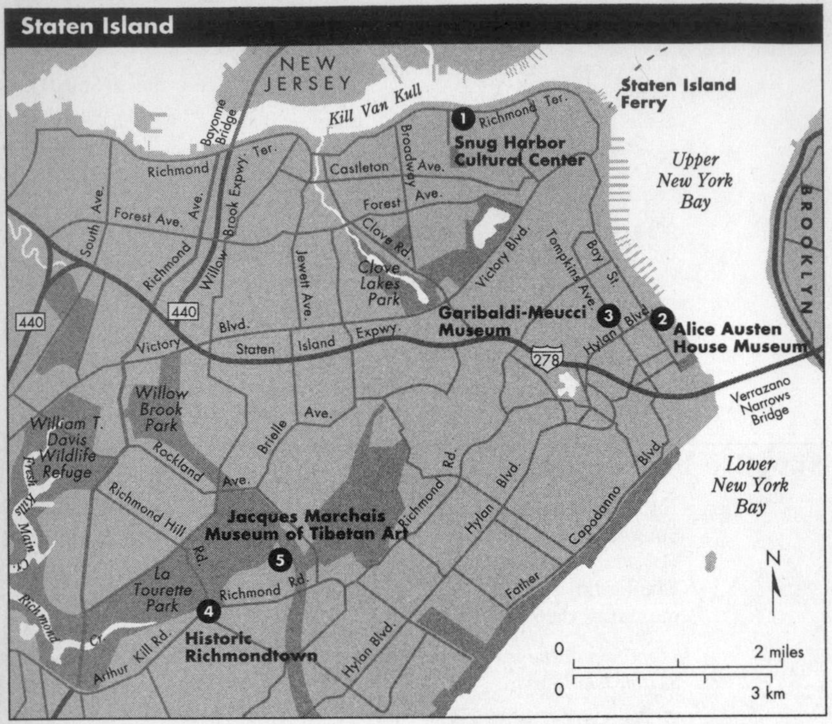

❸ **Garibaldi-Meucci Museum.** Housed in an altered Federal farmhouse, this small museum is full of letters and photographs from the life of fiery Italian patriot Giuseppe Garibaldi; it also documents Antonio Meucci's claim that he invented the telephone before Alexander Graham Bell did. Appropriately, the museum is in the heart of the Italian neighborhood of Rosebank; the colorful, if kitschy, **Our Lady of Mount Saint Carmel Society Shrine** is just around the corner, at 36 Amity Street. Ask the curator for directions. ✉ *420 Tompkins Ave.,* ☎ *718/442–1608.* 🎫 *Free; donations accepted.* ⏲ *Apr.–Nov., Tues.–Fri. 1–5; other times by appointment.*

★ ❶ **Snug Harbor Cultural Center.** Once part of a sprawling farm, then a home for "aged, decrepit, and worn-out sailors," this 83-acre property is based around a row of five columned Greek Revival temples, built between 1831 and 1880, and consists of 28 historic buildings, most of which have been restored. Its newly renovated **Music Hall,** the second-oldest hall in the city (after Carnegie, built in 1892), offers frequent performances; and the former chapel houses the 210-seat **Veterans Memorial Hall,** site of many indoor concerts and gatherings, including an annual music festival.

Snug Harbor's Main Hall—the oldest building on the property, dating from 1833—holds the **Newhouse Center for Contemporary Art,** which features changing exhibitions. Next door is the **John A. Noble Collection** of maritime art, with paintings, lithographs, photographs, and drawings. The complex has a gift shop and a cafeteria. The ☞ **Staten Island Botanical Gardens** and the ☞ **Staten Island Children's Museum** are also on the grounds. ✉ *1000 Richmond Terr.,* ☎ *718/448–2500; 718/447–6490 for John A. Noble Collection.* 🎫 *Cultural Center grounds free, Newhouse Center $2 (suggested donation), John A. Noble Collection $2 (various charges for special events), free guided tours weekends 2 PM.* ⏲ *Grounds 8 AM–dusk, Newhouse Center Wed.–*

Sun. 12–5, John A. Noble Collection weekdays 9–2 and by appointment.

Staten Island Botanical Gardens. On the grounds of the ☞ Snug Harbor Cultural Center, this 83-acre haven includes a perennial garden, a greenhouse, a vineyard, 10 acres of natural marsh habitat, a fragrance garden for the physically challenged, and a rose garden. An authentic Chinese Scholars' Garden, with a meditation area and a water garden, is in progress. ✉ *Snug Harbor Cultural Center, 1000 Richmond Terr.,* ☎ *718/273–8200.* *Free.* ⏲ *Dawn–dusk.*

Staten Island Children's Museum. Five galleries at this popular museum are devoted to hands-on exhibitions that introduce children to such diverse topics as news and media, storytelling, and insects. Portia's Playhouse, an interactive children's theater, invites tykes to step up to the stage and even try on costumes. ✉ *Snug Harbor Cultural Center, 1000 Richmond Terr.,* ☎ *718/273–2060.* *$4.* ⏲ *Tues.–Sun. noon–5.*

NEED A BREAK? Those with a powerful thirst should head straight to **Adobe Blues** (✉ 63 Lafayette St., just off Richmond Terr., ☎ 718/720–2583), a southwestern-style saloon and restaurant with more than 200 beers and a killer chili con carne.

Historic Richmondtown

Hilly and full of green space, the scenic southern part of the island is far from the ferry terminal but worth the trip. Sprawling Historic Richmondtown takes you on a vivid journey into Staten Island's past, and the hilltop Jacques Marchais Museum of Tibetan Art transports you to the hilltop mountains of Central Asia.

A Good Tour

Take the S74–Richmond Road bus from the ferry terminal to **Historic Richmondtown** ④ (about 25 minutes), whose 27 historic buildings date from the 17th, 18th, and 19th centuries. Afterward, grab lunch at the Parsonage restaurant, or walk about a half mile east on Richmond Road and up steep Lighthouse Avenue to the **Jacques Marchais Museum of Tibetan Art** ⑤, which has the largest collection of such art outside Tibet.

TIMING

Set aside the better part of a day for a trip to Historic Richmondtown, which is on the opposite end of the island from the ferry terminal; add on a couple of hours for the Tibetan Museum. The latter is closed Monday and Tuesday; in winter its hours are subject to change, so call ahead. Historic Richmondtown hosts a variety of seasonal celebrations, including an autumn crafts fair and a Christmas celebration; in summer some of the staff dresses in old-fashioned costumes.

Sights to See

★ ❹ **Historic Richmondtown.** These 27 buildings constructed as early as 1685 are situated in a 100-acre complex that was the site of Staten Island's original county seat. The buildings have been restored inside and out; some were here originally, while others were relocated from other spots on the island. Many buildings, such as the Greek Revival courthouse, which serves as the **visitor center,** date from the 19th century; other architectural styles on site range from Dutch colonial to Victorian Gothic Revival. During the warmer months costumed staff members demonstrate Early American crafts and trades such as printing, tinsmithing, and baking.

The Voorlezer's House, built in 1695, is the oldest elementary schoolhouse still standing in the United States; it looks like the mold from which all little red schoolhouses were cast.

The **Staten Island Historical Society Museum,** built in 1848 as the second county clerk's and surrogate's office, now has in its archives American china, furniture, toys, and tools, plus a collection of Staten Island photographs.

During a summer visit you might want to make reservations for the 19th-century dinner, cooked outdoors and served with utensils of the period. The Autumn Celebration shows off craftspeople demonstrating their skills; the annual Encampment in July is a reenactment of a Civil War battle; and December brings a monthlong Christmas celebration. Richmondtown regularly hosts other fairs, flea markets, and tours of the historic buildings. A tavern on the grounds of the historic village hosts a Saturday-night concert series showcasing ethnic and folk music; call the visitor center for details. ✉ *441 Clarke Ave.,* ☎ *718/351–1611.* 🎫 *$4.* ⏲ *Sept.–June, Wed.–Sun. 1–5; July–Aug., Wed.–Fri. 10–5, weekends 1–5.*

NEED A BREAK? For a taste of Richmondtown cuisine, head to the **Parsonage** (✉ 74 Arthur Kill Rd., ☎ 718/351–7879), which serves escargot du jour, chilled spicy shrimp, and walnut-crusted pork chops in a fully restored 19th-century parish house.

5 **Jacques Marchais Museum of Tibetan Art.** One of the largest private, nonprofit collections of Tibetan sculpture, scrolls, and paintings outside of Tibet is displayed in a museum resembling a Tibetan temple. Try to visit on a day when the monks bless the temple—and you. ✉ *338 Lighthouse Ave.,* ☎ *718/987–3500.* 🎫 *$3; occasionally an additional $3 charge for special Sun. programs.* ⏲ *Apr.–Nov., Wed.–Sun. 1–5; Dec.–Mar., Wed.–Fri. 1–5 (but call first, because winter hrs are sometimes restricted).*

4 Exploring New York City with Children

Including Children's Shopping

New York is as magical a place for children as it is for adults. Although hotels and restaurants tend to be geared firmly to the grown-ups, when provision has been made for children, it is usually accomplished in a grand way. The world's best and largest toy store, the biggest dinosaur skeletons, the biggest and best park, the nicest city seaport, the best burgers, and, of course, some of the world's tallest buildings are here.

By Kate Sekules

Updated by Rebecca Knapp Adams, Amy McConnell, Jennifer Paull, Tom Steele, and J. Walman

BESIDES NEW YORK'S CHILD-PLEASING SIGHTS, there are rare ambient treats to stumble upon—from brightly colored pictograms in Chinatown to the spectacular four-story-high neon signs in Times Square, from Central Park squirrels to Greenwich Village street musicians good enough to appear on television (and sometimes they do).

To get children psyched for a New York trip, give them *Eloise,* by Kay Thompson; *A Cricket in Times Square,* by George Selden; *From the Mixed-up Files of Mrs. Basil E. Frankweiler,* by E. L. Konigsburg; *My New York,* by Kathy Jakobsen; or *Stuart Little,* by E. B. White.

SIGHTSEEING

In no other city are you more likely to entertain offspring simply by wandering: Surprising pockets of street sculpture, graffiti art, quirky or distinguished building facades, and appealing shop windows may be found on almost every block. The sheer size of the buildings is astonishing to children not raised here or in other large cities. Getting around in quintessential New York ways—riding cabs, or even buses and subways (especially in the first or last car, with a view of the track and tunnels)—can also be thrilling. To get a feeling for turn-of-the-century New York, ride in a **horse-drawn carriage** around Central Park. Carriages line up on Grand Army Plaza (at the corner of 5th Avenue and 59th Street) and along 59th Street between 5th and 7th avenues. The cost is city-regulated at $34 for the first half hour, $10 for each quarter hour after that; the fare is calculated by time, not per passenger.

Ferry rides are great fun. For a close-up view of the boats, islands, and other sights of New York Harbor, try the free ride on the **Staten Island Ferry** (⊠ Terminal in Battery Park). Or for $2 ($1 for kids 6–11) take the scenic **Port Imperial Ferry** (⊠ Terminal at World Financial Center, ☎ 212/564–8846) across the Hudson River to Hoboken and catch a free shuttle bus to the Liberty Science Center (☞ Museums, *below*). For a special water-bound excursion, the restored 19th-century schooner the ***Pioneer***(⊠ South Street Seaport, ☎ 212/748–8786) sails from May 4 through September 27; cost for two hours is $20 for adults, $12 for children under 12; reservations are required.

The **Roosevelt Island Aerial Tramway** (⊠ 2nd Ave. at 60th St., ☎ 212/832–4543) across the East River costs the same as a subway ride. Trams run every 15 minutes during regular hours and every 7½ minutes during rush hours.

Kids also enjoy New York's opportunities for vertical travel. Take the elevator to the 107th floor of the **World Trade Center** (⊠ 1 World Trade Center, ☎ 212/323–2340) for a panoramic view 1,350 ft above the city (☞ Wall Street and the Battery *in* Chapter 2). The favorite midtown high-level view is from the 86th floor of the **Empire State Building** (⊠ 350 5th Ave., at 34th St., ☎ 212/736–3100) (☞ Murray Hill to Union Square *in* Chapter 2).

Museums

Although almost every major museum in New York City has something to interest children, and many offer special programs, certain ones hold special appeal. At the top of the list is the **American Museum of**

Natural History (✉ Central Park W at W. 79th St., ☎ 212/769–5100), with its lifelike dioramas and collection of giant dinosaurs, including a huge Tyrannosaurus rex (☞ The Upper West Side *in* Chapter 2).

The **Children's Museum of Manhattan** is a creative learning center (a kind of indoor playground), where kids 1–10 can climb, crawl, paint, make collages, try on costumes, and even film their own newscasts. The admission price includes daily workshops. ✉ *212 W. 83rd St., between Amsterdam Ave. and Broadway,* ☎ *212/721–1234.* 🎫 *$5.* ⏲ *Wed.–Sun. 10–5.*

The **Children's Museum of the Arts,** in a loftlike space in SoHo, allows kids 1–10 to become actively involved in visual and performing arts. Highlights include the Monet Ball Pond, where kids can play with brightly colored balls near a water-lily mural; the Music Garden and Wonder Theater, where performances are held; a reading nook with cushions and futons; and daily art activities. ✉ *118 Mercer St.,* ☎ *212/274–0986.* 🎫 *$4 weekdays and $5 weekends for adults under 65 and children over 18 months.* ⏲ *Tues.–Fri. noon–6, weekends 11–5.*

At the *Intrepid* **Sea-Air-Space Museum** (☞ 42nd Street *in* Chapter 2), kids can inspect the vintage and modern aircraft parked wing to wing on the flight deck, try the navy flight simulator, and fly their own F-18 mission. Admission also includes access to the submarine *Growler* and the destroyer *Edson.* ✉ *Pier 86, at 12th Ave. and W. 46th St.,* ☎ *212/245–0072.* 🎫 *$10 adults, $5 children 6–11, $1 children 2–5, free, children under 2 and active military personnel.* ⏲ *May–Sept., Mon.–Sat. 10–5, Sun. 10–6; Oct.–Apr., Wed.–Sun. 10–5 (last admission 1 hr before closing).*

In the nautical vein, the **South Street Seaport Museum** is an 11-square-block "museum without walls" with a fleet of historic sailing ships, cobblestone streets, 19th-century architecture, an old print shop, a maritime crafts center, and a children's center with hands-on exhibits about the history of ships and the sea. ✉ *Museum Visitors' Center, 12 Fulton St.,* ☎ *212/748–8600.* 🎫 *$6 adults, $3 children under 12.* ⏲ *Apr.–Sept., daily 10–6; Oct.–Mar., Wed.–Mon. 10–5.*

Aspiring heroes appreciate the **New York City Fire Museum,** with its comprehensive collection of authentic firefighting tools from the 18th, 19th, and 20th centuries. Hand-pulled and horse-drawn apparatus, engines, sliding poles, uniforms, and fireboat equipment are all display; real firefighters give the tours. ✉ *278 Spring St., near Varick St.,* ☎ *212/691–1303.* 🎫 *$4 (suggested donation).* ⏲ *Tues.–Sun. 10–4.*

Kids like the **Forbes Magazine Galleries** for the collections of Monopoly games, toy soldiers, model boats, and the rooms with the bejeweled Fabergé eggs (☞ Greenwich Village *in* Chapter 2). ✉ *62 5th Ave., at 12th St.,* ☎ *212/206–5548.*

For children eight and older, the **Sony Wonder Technology Lab** is an interactive science and communications technology exhibit that allows kids to log on to computers, play sound engineer, and be on TV. ✉ *550 Madison Ave., at 56th St.,* ☎ *212/833–8100.* 🎫 *Free.* ⏲ *Tues.–Sat. 10–6, Sun. noon–6 (last entrance 30 mins before closing).*

Meanwhile, don't ignore the city's outer boroughs and environs, which can be easily reached by mass transit. The **Brooklyn Children's Museum** is a fully interactive museum with tunnels to crawl through and animals to pet. ✉ *145 Brooklyn Ave.,* ☎ *718/735–4432.* 🎫 *$3 (suggested donation).* ⏲ *June–Aug., Mon. and Wed.–Sun. noon–5; Sept.–May, Wed.–Fri. 2–5, weekends noon–5.*

Underground in an old subway station in downtown Brooklyn, the **New York City Transit Museum** houses full-size, turn-of-the-century and modern subway cars and working miniature subway trains. ✉ *Boerum Pl. at Schermerhorn St.,* ☎ *718/243–3060.* *$3 adults, $1.50 children.* ⏲ *Tues.–Fri. 10–4, weekends noon–5.*

The **New York Hall of Science,** in Flushing Meadows–Corona Park, Queens (☞ Chapter 3), is one of the nation's top 10 science museums. Budding scientists can examine more than 160 hands-on experiments on subjects ranging from lasers to microbes. Outside, the Science Playground features more than 20 outdoor experiments to coax kids into learning about science while they're horsing around. (In the old days, seesaws were for playing; now they're lessons in balance and leverage.) ✉ *111th St. at 46th Ave.,* ☎ *718/699–0005.* *$6 adults, $4 children and seniors; free Thurs. and Fri. 2–5.* ⏲ *Mon.–Wed. 9:30–2, Thurs.–Fri. 9:30–5, weekends 11–5.*

The hands-on exhibits of the **Staten Island Children's Museum** (✉ 1000 Richmond Terr., ☎ 718/273–2060), on everything from the five senses to high technology, will particularly enthrall younger kids (☞ Staten Island *in* Chapter 3). Children with a strong sense of the past may enjoy **Historic Richmondtown** (✉ 441 Clarke Ave., ☎ 718/351–1611), which has a Museum of Childhood with displays of antique dolls, toys, and children's furniture (☞ Staten Island *in* Chapter 3).

Just across the Hudson River in Liberty State Park, New Jersey, the **Liberty Science Center** is the largest science museum in the New York metropolitan area. Highlights include an insect zoo, a 100-ft touch tunnel, an amazing 700-pound geodesic globe, the Kodak OMNI Theater for viewing IMAX movies on a gigantic screen, and "Web of Life," a 3-D laser show. ✉ *Liberty State Park, 251 Philip St., Jersey City, NJ,* ☎ *201/200–1000.* *$9.50 adults, $6.50 children 2–12; OMNI Theater: $7 adults, $5 children under 12; Williams Theater: $2; combined admission to exhibits and theaters $15 adults, $11 children 2–12; pay what you wish 1st Wed. of month 1 PM–closing.* ⏲ *Apr.–Labor Day., daily 9:30–5:30; Labor Day–Mar., Tues.–Sun. 9:30–5:30. Call center for directions by car, PATH train, or ferry.*

Parks and Playgrounds

New York's great outdoors sounds like a contradiction in terms, especially when you add children to the equation. But in **Central Park,** children can ride bicycles, row boats, go horseback riding, ice-skate, rollerblade, skateboard, fly kites, throw Frisbees, and much more (☞ Central Park *in* Chapter 2 and 9). Favorite destinations include the **Conservatory Water,** which attracts owners of large, remote-controlled model boats; it is near the statues of Alice in Wonderland and Hans Christian Andersen. Younger children enjoy the hands-on activities at the park's fairy-tale-like **Belvedere Castle** (☎ 212/772–0210). The antique **Carousel** (✉ Central Park at 65th St., ☎ 212/879–0244), complete with painted steeds that prance to jaunty organ music, costs only 90¢ a ride. The pretty **Wollman Memorial Rink** (☎ 212/396–1010) has outdoor rollerblading classes and sessions—ice-skating in winter (☞ Chapter 9). At the beautifully restored **Harlem Meer** (☎ 212/860–1370), kids of all ages are encouraged to fish along the shore for bass and sunfish, which must be thrown back. Free fishing poles and bait are given out at the Charles A. Dana Discovery Center; valid identification is needed to borrow poles.

At Brooklyn's 526-acre **Prospect Park,** kids enjoy kite flying and picnicking on the 90-acre Long Meadow (☞ Brooklyn *in* Chapter 3). The cherry trees, giant glass greenhouses, and spicy herbs at the **Brooklyn Botanic Garden** (✉ 1000 Washington Ave., ☎ 718/622–4433) will please both kids and parents (☞ Brooklyn *in* Chapter 3).

In the Bronx, adjacent to the Bronx Zoo, the **New York Botanical Garden** (✉ 200th St. and Southern Blvd., ☎ 718/817–8700) is one of the world's largest botanical gardens, with a large conservatory, 12 outdoor gardens, walking trails, and 40 acres of forest, as well as the Everett Children's Adventure Garden, an 8-acre botanical science garden for children. (☞ The Bronx *in* Chapter 3).

Manhattan has wonderful state-of-the-art playgrounds. **Central Park**'s 21 playgrounds are full of slides, bridges, bars, swings, towers, and tunnels; they're carpeted with sand or soft rubber matting and often cooled in summer by sprinklers, fountains, or running water. Good ones can be found along 5th Avenue at 67th Street near the zoo, at 71st and 77th streets, at 85th Street near the Metropolitan Museum, and at 96th Street. Along Central Park West, the best ones are at 68th, 82nd, 85th, 93rd (with a Wild West theme), and 96th streets. The **Heckshер Playground,** in Central Park at 62nd Street, is the park's largest.

Top-rated by Manhattan kids is the playground at **Hudson River Park** (✉ West St. south of Vesey St.), which has kid-size bronze sculptures of people and animals integrated into the parkscape. Not far from the financial district, **Washington Market Park** (✉ Greenwich St. between Chambers and Duane Sts.) features a pretty tree-filled layout and great play equipment. **Washington Square Park** (✉ South end of 5th Ave. between Waverly Pl. and W. 4th St.) has a popular and shady playground, as well as live jugglers and magicians in summertime. In **Riverside Park,** west of Riverside Drive, the best playgrounds are at 77th and 91st streets; the one at 77th Street has a circle of spouting elephant fountains. The **Asser Levy Playground** (✉ 23rd St., 1 block from East River) is the first in Manhattan to cater fully to children with disabilities, with giant, multicolor mazelike structures; helter-skelter slides with wheelchair stations; and textured pavement for children who are blind.

Coney Island in Brooklyn boasts great outdoor playgrounds: **Astroland** (✉ 1000 Surf Ave., ☎ 718/372–0275) and **Deno's Wonderwheel Park** (✉ 3059 W. 12th St.,, ☎ 718/449–8836) are two of Coney Island's finest old amusement parks, with a distinctly Brooklyn feel. Both are free; fares are $1–$4 per ride at Astroland and $1.75 per ride or 10 rides for $15 at Deno's.

At indoor playgrounds, kids can burn up energy no matter what the weather. **Playspace** (✉ 2473 Broadway, at 92nd St., ☎ 212/769–2300) provides sandboxes, toys, games, and room to run for youngsters six months–six years; the cost is $5.50 per person (including parents, second adult free). **Kidmazeum** (✉ 80 East End Ave., at 83rd St., ☎ 212/327–4800) offers a sprawling maze, children's village, and Lego room for children eight and under; entry costs $8 per child and is free for adults.

Zoos

The **Central Park Zoo** (✉ Off 5th Ave. at 64th St., ☎ 212/861–6030), officially called the Central Park Wildlife Center and now including the Tisch Children's Zoo, is of a very manageable size, even for toddlers. The children's zoo has interactive exhibits and domestic animals to pet and feed (☞ Central Park *in* Chapter 2). The antics of the Japanese snow monkeys—which live here on their own island—are endlessly fascinating, but the diving and swimming polar bears steal the show.

The **Bronx Zoo** is the largest zoo in the United States. Most of the animals here live in replicas of their natural habitats (☞ The Bronx *in* Chapter 3). ✉ *2300 Southern Blvd.,* ☎ *718/367–1010.*

Brooklyn's **Prospect Park Wildlife Center** focuses on small animals, such as prairie dogs and red pandas (☞ Brooklyn *in* Chapter 3). ✉ *Flatbush Ave. at Empire Blvd.,* ☎ *718/399–7339.*

The **Queens Wildlife Center** shows American animals in approximations of their natural habitats. The inhabitants include spectacled bears, mountain lions, sea lions, bobcats, coyotes, bison, and elk. ✉ *53–51 111th St., Flushing Meadows Park,* ☎ *718/271–7761.* 🎫 *$2.50 adults, 50¢ children 3–12.* ⏲ *Weekdays 10–5, weekends 10–5:30.*

The small but high-quality **Staten Island Zoo** features one of the world's finest collections of venomous snakes and the African Savannah Tropical Forest Exhibit and Aquarium, as well as a separate Children's Zoo. ✉ *Barrett Park, 614 Broadway, Staten Island,* ☎ *718/442–3100.* 🎫 *$3 adults, $2 children 3–11; pay as you wish Wed. 2–4:45.* ⏲ *Daily 10–4:45.*

In Brooklyn, the **Aquarium for Wildlife Conservation** has nearly 300 different marine creatures, including dolphins, sharks, walruses, and whales (☞ Brooklyn *in* Chapter 3). ✉ *Surf Ave. at W. 8th St., Coney Island,* ☎ *718/265–3474.*

THE ARTS AND ENTERTAINMENT

In New York theater groups exist just for children, art museums organize special programs, and kids can choose among art classes, summer courses, the circus, music concerts, storytelling, parades, and puppet shows.

Circuses

Ringling Bros. and Barnum & Bailey Circus (check local newspapers for dates, times, and ticket information) pitches its tents each spring at Madison Square Garden (✉ 7th Ave. between 31st and 33rd Sts., ☎ 212/465–6000). The **Big Apple Circus** (✉ 35 W. 35th St., 10001, ☎ 212/268–2500) charms the toughest New Yorkers in locations all over the city during spring and summer and is in residence at Lincoln Center from October through January. Each summer **Circus Amok** (☎ 718/486–7432), a socially progressive troupe that uses dance, puppetry, and music, presents an hour-long, topically themed series of skits and antics in parks around the city.

Film

Several museums sponsor special film programs aimed at families and children, including the Museum of Modern Art, the Museum of Television and Radio (☞ Rockefeller Center *in* Chapter 2), and the American Museum of the Moving Image (☞ Queens *in* Chapter 3). At the **Sony IMAX Theater** (✉ 1998 Broadway, at 68th St., ☎ 212/336–5000) audience members strap on high-tech headgear that makes nature and specially created feature films appear in 3-D. To experience the **Cinema Ride** (✉ 1481 Broadway, at 42nd St., ☎ 212/391–6550), in Times Square, moviegoers slip on 3-D glasses and enter a "motion simulation" capsule that rocks and rolls with such films as the *Atlantis Submarine Race* and *Galactic Flight*. Kids thrill at the amazing nature films shown on the huge screen in the **IMAX Theater** (✉ Central Park W and 79th St., ☎ 212/769–5034) at the American Museum of Natural History (☞ Upper West Side *in* Chapter 2). The **Walter Reade The-**

ater (✉ 165 W. 65th St., at Broadway, ☎ 212/875–5600) shows feature films for children on weekends and sponsors children's film festivals.

Libraries and Storytelling

The **Donnell Library Center of the New York Public Library** (✉ 20 W. 53rd St., ☎ 212/621–0618) is home of the original Winnie-the-Pooh bear, as well as companions Kanga, Eeyore, Tigger, and Piglet; the display case is in the Central Children's Room. Inquire about storytelling dates and times. **Books of Wonder** (✉ 16 W. 18th St., ☎ 212/989–3270) has storytelling on Sunday at 11:45. **Barnes & Noble** (☞ Readings and Lectures *in* Chapter 5) hosts frequent readings for kids.

Music

The **Little Orchestra Society** (✉ 220 W. 42nd St., ☎ 212/704–2100) organizes concert series that introduce classical music to children ages 3–5 at Florence Gould Hall (✉ 55 E. 59th St.) and ages 5–12 at Lincoln Center. The Metropolitan Opera offers its **Growing Up with Opera** program (☎ 212/769–7008) and also sponsors an out-of-doors summer arts program, with plenty in it for children. To introduce parents and their kids to jazz music, Jazz at Lincoln Center (✉ 140 W. 65th St., ☎ 212/875–5299) hosts an annual **Jazz for Young People** concert series hosted by Wynton Marsalis.

Puppet Shows

Marionette Theater (✉ Swedish Cottage, Central Park at W. 81st St., ☎ 212/988–9093) features programs Tuesday–Saturday. **Puppet Playhouse** (✉ Asphalt Green, 555 E. 90th St., ☎ 212/369–8890) offers weekend shows with puppets and marionettes. **Puppetworks** (✉ 338 6th Ave., Park Slope, Brooklyn, ☎ 718/965–3391) presents marionettes performing classic children's stories.

Theater

Miss Majesty's Lollipop Playhouse (✉ Grove Street Playhouse, 39 Grove St., between W. 4th St. and 7th Ave., ☎ 212/741–6436) brings fairy tales and nursery rhymes to life on weekend afternoons. **New York Children's Theater** (✉ Lincoln Square Theater, 250 W. 65th St., ☎ 212/496–8009) is determinedly realistic in style and explores topics such as literacy and aging. **New Victory Theater** (✉ 209 W. 42nd St., ☎ 212/239–6255) presents plays and performances oriented specifically to children. The **Paper Bag Players** (✉ Sylvia and Danny Kaye Playhouse, Hunter College, 68th St. between Park and Lexington Aves., ☎ 212/772–4448) is the longest-running children's theater group in the nation. **Tada!** (✉ 120 W. 28th St., ☎ 212/627–1732) is a popular children's group with a multiethnic perspective. **Theaterworks/USA** (✉ Promenade Theater, Broadway at 76th St., ☎ 212/647–1100) mounts classic stories and original musicals based on well-known children's books. The **13th Street Theater** (✉ 50 W. 13th St., ☎ 212/675–6677) presents its children's offerings on weekends. **West End Kids Productions** (✉ West End Gate Children's Theater, 2911 Broadway, ☎ 212/877–6115; ✉ Caroline's, 1626 Broadway, ☎ 212/757–4100) stages whimsical weekend performances for young audiences. West End Kids also presents Kids 'n Comedy, programs in which 8- to 15-year-olds do stand-up comedy. Newcomers are welcome.

DINING

By J. Walman

If you're looking for a low-key place to park the kids for a quick bite, the city's coffee shops (which is the local term for a diner) are probably your best bets. Usually featuring comfy booths and lunch counters with stools that swivel, coffee shops don't offer gourmet food, but with their ready supply of hamburgers and pancakes served 24 hours a day, they may end up being your kids' favorite culinary moments. For more exotic fare try the following eateries that appeal to young appetites.

Lower Manhattan and Chinatown

The younger ones should enjoy **Minter's Fun Food and Drink** (✉ 250 Vesey St., at 4 World Financial Center, ☎ 212/945–4455) for chocolate beverages. The surprising charms of the only **McDonald's** branch with doorman and pianist (✉ 160 Broadway, between Maiden La. and Liberty St., ☎ 212/385–2063) are obvious. In Chinatown don't miss the green-tea or red-bean ice cream at the **Chinatown Ice Cream Factory** (✉ 65 Bayard St., between Mott and Elizabeth Sts., ☎ 212/608–4170). Chinatown is also a good place to take the whole family for lunch or dinner at reasonable prices. **Mandarin Court** (✉ 61 Mott St., ☎ 212/608–3838) serves dim sum every day until 3.

SoHo and TriBeCa

In SoHo the airy decor at **Jerry's** (✉ 101 Prince St., ☎ 212/966–9464) is popular with local artists and their young protégés. The **Cupping Room Café** (✉ 359 W. Broadway, near Broome St., ☎ 212/925–2898) provides waffles throughout the day. In TriBeCa **Bubby's** (✉ 120 Hudson St., at N. Moore, ☎ 212/219–0666) has casual dining and great baked goods.

Greenwich Village and the East Village

In the West Village **Arturo's** (✉ 106 W. Houston St., at Thompson St., ☎ 212/677–3820) serves coal-fired pizza with child-friendly aplomb. **Aggie's** (✉ 146 W. Houston St., at MacDougal St., ☎ 212/673–8994) is a funky coffee shop with sprightly soups and sandwiches. **Elephant and Castle** (✉ 68 Greenwich Ave., near W. 11th St., ☎ 212/243–1400) has burgers and great french fries. For huge Cal-Tex servings at low prices, try **Benny's Burritos** (✉ 113 Greenwich Ave., at Jane St., ☎ 212/727–0584). The **Cowgirl Hall of Fame** (✉ 519 Hudson St., at W. 10th St., ☎ 212/633–1133) dishes up both Cajun cooking and cowgirl memorabilia.

In the East Village the **Time Cafe** (✉ 380 Lafayette St., at Great Jones St., ☎ 212/533–7000) is sunny, relaxed, and fantastic for brunch, when it serves heavenly southern-style biscuits. Kids will love **Stingy Lulus** (✉ 129 St. Mark's Pl., between 1st Ave. and Ave. A, ☎ 212/674–3545), a raucous diner that raided the middle America truck stops for its blue-plate-special decor. **Two Boots** (✉ 37 Ave. A, between 2nd and 3rd Sts., ☎ 212/505–2276), which refers to the geographical "boots" of Italy and Louisiana, serves both pizza and jambalaya.

Gramercy Park and Chelsea

Just off Union Square is **America** (✉ 9 E. 18th St., ☎ 212/505–2110), where everything is huge—menu, portions, spaces—except your check. The **Royal Canadian Pancake House** (✉ 180 3rd Ave., between 16th and 17th Sts., ☎ 212/777–9288) has more than 50 flavors, including peanut-butter pancakes with real maple syrup. On Chelsea's bustling 6th Avenue, the 1940s-style **Hot Tomato** (✉ 676 6th Ave., at 21st St., ☎ 212/691–3535) serves up tomato soup, meat loaf, and mashed potatoes. For kids who are 10-going-on-30, **Campagna** (✉ 24 E. 21st St., ☎ 212/460–0900) serves large portions of home-style Italian food in a grown-up atmosphere. (A low-price children's menu, with half portions, is served Sunday.)

Midtown

The **American Festival Café** (✉ Rockefeller Center, 20 W. 50th St., ☎ 212/332–7620) is the essential New York City family dining experience. With its displays of designer gowns, the **Fashion Cafe** (✉ 51st St. between 5th and 6th Aves., in Rockefeller Plaza, ☎ 212/765–3131) will enthrall would-be supermodels. In the theater district the **Stage Delicatessen** (✉ 834 7th Ave., at 54th St., ☎ 212/245–7850) will wow kids with its enormous piles of corned beef.

"Theme-park" restaurants dominate on 57th Street east of Carnegie Hall. Young music fans will be impressed by the **Hard Rock Cafe** (✉ 221 W. 57th St., ☎ 212/459–9320), **Planet Hollywood** (✉ 140 W. 57th St., ☎ 212/333–7827), and **Motown Cafe** (✉ 104 W. 57th St., ☎ 212/581–8030). The motorcycle-oriented **Harley-Davidson Cafe** (✉ 1370 6th Ave., at 56th St., ☎ 212/245–6000) bills itself as the "newest American legend." Kids can star in their own TV show and take the tape home (for a price) at **Television City** (✉ 70 W. 50th St., ☎ 212/333–3388). **Mickey Mantle's** (✉ 42 Central Park S, near 6th Ave., ☎ 212/688–7777) excites ball-crazy kids. If Groucho Marx stops you and inquires, "How'd ya like the show?" you must be in front of **Comedy Nation** (✉ 1626 Broadway, between 49th and 50th Sts., ☎ 212/757–4100), part of the Caroline's Comedy Club complex.

Lincoln Center and the Upper West Side

Fiorello's Roman Café (✉ 1900 Broadway, near 63rd St., ☎ 212/595–5330) has individual pizzas and outside seating. A good bet near Lincoln Center is the **Saloon** (✉ 1920 Broadway, at 64th St., ☎ 212/874–1500), with a long menu and the occasional skating waiter. The extensive menu at **China Fun** (✉ 246 Columbus Ave., between 71st and 72nd Sts., ☎ 212/580–1516) should satisfy the most finicky young eaters. Fun, messy ribs and chicken entice youngsters at **Dallas BBQ** (✉ 27 W. 72nd St., ☎ 212/873–2004). **Big Nick's** pizza joint (✉ 2175 Broadway, at 77th St., ☎ 212/724–2010) gives out balloons that say "Big Nick Loves Me." **Mad Fish** (✉ 2182 Broadway, at 77th St., ☎ 212/787–0202) serves up high-quality seafood as well as fish-and-chips. Family-style meat loaf (served whole) plus kid-size portions are the hallmarks of **Main Street** (✉ 446 Columbus Ave., between 81st and 82nd Sts., ☎ 212/873–5025). **Firehouse** (✉ 522 Columbus Ave., between 85th and 86th Sts., ☎ 212/595–3139) has good Buffalo wings, chili, and burgers, plus gooey desserts. Very child-friendly, the **Popover Cafe** (✉ 551 Amsterdam Ave., at 87th St., ☎ 212/595–8555) has comfortable booths, hearty food, and teddy bears lurking in odd corners. At the brasserie-style **Boulevard** (✉ 2398 Broadway, at 88th St., ☎ 212/874–7400), kids can eat spaghetti and draw on the tablecloths.

Upper East Side

Serendipity 3 (✉ 225 E. 60th St., ☎ 212/838–3531), "the ice cream parlor to the stars," is perfect for a light meal or dessert. **Jackson Hole** (✉ 232 E. 64th St., ☎ 212/371–7187) is a reliable, pleasant burger joint with other branches around town. **China Fun** (✉ 1239 2nd Ave., at 65th St., ☎ 212/752–0810), like its Upper West Side counterpart, has an extensive Chinese menu. Central Park's **Boathouse Café** (✉ East Park Dr. and E. 72nd St., ☎ 212/517–3623) can be somewhat pricey, but it's wonderfully soothing. **EJ's Luncheonette** (✉ 1271 3rd Ave., at 73rd St., ☎ 212/472–0600) serves good meat loaf and other blue-plate specials. The **Barking Dog Luncheonette** (✉ 1678 3rd Ave., at 94th St., ☎ 212/831–1800) has a festive menu of sandwiches, burgers, salads, and shakes as well as a special drinking fountain for dogs.

LODGING

Since the vast majority of hotels are in midtown Manhattan, your choice of which neighborhood to pick for a family stay is limited. Hotels near Central Park offer easy access to the carousel, the zoo, the boat pond, and several playgrounds. Consider booking a room or suite with a kitchenette so you can prepare snacks or formula in the comfort of your own room. As in any other big city, most Manhattan hotels will provide an extra bed, baby-sitting, and stroller rental—all the common requirements of families traveling with young children—but call ahead.

A very limited number of hotels have facilities especially for kids. (*See* Chapter 7 for details about the following hotels.) **The Paramount** has a small playroom with children's videos and furniture made of Tweety Bird and Pink Panther stuffed animals. Kids might also enjoy the **Hotel Wales,** with its whimsical Pied Piper parlor. Other good choices, thanks to their rooftop swimming pools, are **The Peninsula, Le Parker Meridien, the Regal U.N. Plaza,** and the **Millenium Hilton.** Any of the **Manhattan East Suite Hotels** (☎ 212/465–3690) properties would make good choices, since they resemble tiny apartments.

SHOPPING

Adults and children alike find shopping nirvana in New York. Highlighted here are children's clothing stores, as well as unique kid-friendly specialty shops. For additional stores featuring toys, games, magic, and general gizmos, *see* Fun and Games *and* Toys *in* Chapter 10. It's also worth visiting the toy and clothing sections of some department stores. **Macy's** carries a huge spread of everything from sleepwear to poufy dresses. **Bloomingdale's** doesn't skimp on quantity either; preteens can tear through the trends, from little flips of rayon to CK and Guess? denim. **Barneys New York** has a small children's area with an appropriately label-conscious selection: teeny Polo pants, cashmere sweaters appliquéd with race cars, even diminutive Dries van Noten dresses. The trick is steering kids around all the breakable housewares on the same floor. **Saks Fifth Avenue** is a great source for girls' dress-up clothes, but there is no preteen boys' section. (☞ Department Stores *in* Chapter 10). Refer to the maps in Chapter 10 for the locations of the stores listed below.

Lower Manhattan and SoHo

Lilliput. You'll find Curious George T-shirts and toys, as well as "vintage" (to kids) clothes like Dick Tracy raincoats. ✉ *265 Lafayette St., between Prince and Spring Sts.,* ☎ *212/965–9567.*

Quest Toys. The wooden toys and trains here will intrigue both kids and adults. ✉ *225 Liberty St., at 2 World Financial Center,* ☎ *212/945–9330.*

The Stork Club. While the name spins off from one of Old New York's most famous watering holes, this little store is geared for comfort, not sophistication. Chenille sweaters, painters' pants, and overalls share space with nostalgic-inducing toys. ✉ *142 Sullivan St.,* ☎ *212/505–1927.*

Greenwich Village, the East Village, Gramercy Park, and Chelsea

Books of Wonder. A friendly staff can help select gifts for all reading levels from the extensive stock here; Oziana is a specialty (☞ Libraries and Storytelling *in* the Arts and Entertainment, *above*). ✉ *16 W. 18th St.,* ☎ *212/989–3270.*

Dinosaur Hill. You'll find unusual handmade clothes for newborns to eight-year-olds, as well as discovery toys. ✉ *306 E. 9th St., between 1st and 2nd Aves.,* ☎ *212/473–5850.*

Ibiza Kidz. This section of the Ibiza women's clothing shop is filled with comfortable, not too dressy kids' clothes, like flowered Kenzo dresses and French-made striped T-shirts and overalls. ✉ *46 University Pl., between 9th and 10th Sts.,* ☎ *212/533–4614.*

Space Kiddets. The funky (Elvis-print rompers) mixes with the tried-and-true (fringed cowboy/cowgirl outfits) at this casual, trendsetting store. ✉ *46 E. 21st St., between Broadway and Park Ave.,* ☎ *212/420–9878.*

Tootsie's Children's Bookstore. Classics like Babar are sold alongside nature books and discovery games at this store with an appealing combo of books, videos, and toys. ✉ *554 Hudson St., between Perry and 11th Sts.,* ☎ *212/242–0182.*

Midtown

F.A.O. Schwarz. One of the world's best and best-loved toy stores is probably destination number one for young consumers. With two seemingly endless floors of toys, your kids may be hypnotized into inaction for a minute or two. Once recovered, they can storm the huge selections of stuffed animals, action figures, games, and Barbies, and if they aren't already hyper enough, steer them to the F.A.O. Schweetz area by the Madison Avenue entrance; the candy here encompasses old-faithfuls (jawbreakers) and the latest sweets (aqua and silver M&Ms). And yes, you can still find the *Big* floor keyboards. (☞ Toys *in* Chapter 10). ✉ *767 5th Ave.,* ☎ *212/644–9400.*

Wynken, Blynken & Nod's. The clothes here, which are especially kid friendly, include "My Little Friend" sweaters, which have a secret pocket with a small doll inside. ✉ *306 E. 55th St., between 1st and 2nd Aves.,* ☎ *212/308–9299.*

Upper West Side

CLOTHING

CO2. Hipster preteens wiggle into Go Girl, Greed Girl, and Dollhouse outfits at this girls-clothes-only store. ✉ *284 Columbus Ave., between 73rd and 74th Sts.,* ☎ *212/721–4966.*

Greenstones et Cie. Catering to junior yuppies, these stores offer some handsome clothes, particularly sweaters. ✉ *442 Columbus Ave., between 81st and 82nd Sts.,* ☎ *212/580–4322;* **Greenstones Too!** ✉ *1184 Madison Ave., between 86th and 87th Sts.,* ☎ *212/427–1665.*

Morris Bros. This gold mine of boys' and girls' active wear has Bear down jackets, mesh shorts, Quiksilver swim trunks, and stacks of Levi's. They can supply name tapes for camp-bound kids. ✉ *2322 Broadway, at 84th St.,* ☎ *212/724–9000.*

Shoofly. Children's shoes and accessories range from Mary Janes, moc crocs, and wing tips to hats, socks, tights, and jewelry. ✉ *465 Amsterdam Ave., between 82nd and 83rd Sts.,* ☎ *212/580–4390;* ✉ *42 Hudson St., between Thomas and Duane Sts.,* ☎ *212/406–3270.*

Z'Baby Company. Fun clothes like Suss Design chenille sweaters are a specialty here. ✉ *100 W. 72nd St., at Columbus Ave.,* ☎ *212/579–2229.*

OTHER

Bellini. One of the world's few children's stores to share the name of a cocktail, Bellini specializes in layettes, furniture, and bedding. ✉ *110 W. 86th St., between Columbus and Amsterdam Aves.,* ☎ *212/580–3801;* ✉ *1305 2nd Ave., between 68 and 69th Sts.,* ☎ *212/517–9233.*

Cozy's Cuts for Kids. This is an inspired combination of toy store and children's hair salon, where kids can perch in a model Jeep instead of a barber's chair. Many of the toys make great party favors. ✉ *448 Amsterdam Ave. at 81st St.,* ☎ *212/579–2600;* ✉ *1125 Madison Ave., at 84th St.,* ☎ *212/744–1716.*

West Side Kids. Classics (Legos, arts-and-crafts sets, rubber animal figures) share shelf space with up-to-date, multicultural family hand puppets. ✉ *498 Amsterdam Ave., at 84th St.,* ☎ *212/496–7282.*

Upper East Side

CLOTHING

Au Chat Botté. Besides the little-princess party dresses, this store has delicate, snowy layettes. ✉ *1192 Madison Ave., at 87th St.,* ☎ *212/722–6474.*

Bambini. Mostly European imports, the clothes here are sophisticated in the traditional way for children, with beautiful fabrics and cuts. ✉ *1367 3rd Ave., at 78th St.,* ☎ *212/717–6742.*

Bébé Thompson. This store is apparently for mamas who want their babies to grow up to be Euro—there are Cacharel dresses, Kenzo jeans, Sonia Rykiel backpacks, even TSE cashmere cardigans. ✉ *1216 Lexington Ave., at 82nd St.,* ☎ *212/249–4740.*

Bonpoint. The sophistication here lies in the beautiful designs and impeccable workmanship—full-skirted dresses with puffed sleeves, linen shifts threaded with velvet ribbon, appliquéd sweaters, and pristine layettes. ✉ *1269 Madison Ave., at 91st.,* ☎ *212/722–7720;* ✉ *811 Madison Ave., at 68th St.,* ☎ *212/879–0900.*

The Chocolate Soup. This crammed, casual store has party dresses, rain boots, and play clothes, plus some tried-and-true toys like kazoos and washcloth puppets. ✉ *946 Madison Ave., between 74th and 75th Sts.,* ☎ *212/861–2210.*

Exclusive Oilily Store. Brightly colored play and school clothes designed in Holland supposedly make children unwilling to wear anything else (so the ad copy proclaims). ✉ *870 Madison Ave., between 70th and 71st Sts.,* ☎ *212/628–0100.*

Infinity. Infinity carries slinky Les Tout Petits dresses, Baby-G watches, and Paris Blues jeans. A bulletin board covered with magazine pictures of preteen heartthrobs hovers near the register; purchases are stashed in replicas of Chinese food cartons. ✉ *1116 Madison Ave., at 83rd St.,* ☎ *212/517–4232.*

Jacadi. Jacadi stocks adorable toddler-size clothes from Paris, as well as fashions for older children, and stuffed animals. ✉ *787 Madison Ave., at 67th St.,* ☎ *212/535–3200;* ✉ *1281 Madison Ave., at 91st St.,* ☎ *212/369–1616.*

La Petite Etoile. These *petit* French imports might cost as much as dinner at one of the neighboring French bistros, but they are unique and very well made. ✉ *746 Madison Ave.,* ☎ *212/744–0975.*

Little Eric. Hip adult styles—loafers with silver bits, velvet slippers, and brogues—inspire the kids' shoes here. Prices can approach grown-up levels, too. ✉ *1331 3rd Ave., at 76th St.,* ☎ *212/288–8987;* ✉ *1118 Madison Ave.,* ☎ *212/717–1513.*

OTHER

Big City Kite Co. Sport kites, twisters, and technique books are the specialty here. The salespeople can talk winglets and wind windows or suggest a kite that can withstand crashing. ✉ *1210 Lexington Ave., at 82nd St.,* ☎ *212/472–2623.*

Dollhouse Antics. Besides the rows of miniature furnishings, there are build-your-own dollhouse kits, ready-made houses, and model homes for inspiration. ✉ *1343 Madison Ave., at 94th St.,* ☎ *212/876–2288.*

Store of Knowledge. This public-television-affiliated store caters to the curious, with 3-D puzzles, crafts sets, and science kits. Favorite PBS characters Wallace and Gromit, Mr. Bean, and Barney are here in droves; grown-ups can riffle through PBS videos, including the *Prime Suspect* series. ✉ *1091 3rd Ave., at 64th St.,* ☎ *212/223–0018.*

5 The Arts

For lovers of the performing arts, New York is a kind of paradise. Theater fans can choose among Broadway productions, revivals of classics, and works by emerging playwrights off-Broadway. Music devotees have the chance to see the world's top performers appearing in incomparable showcases such as Carnegie Hall and the Metropolitan Opera House. For dance aficionados, there are two first-rate ballet troupes and a fine array of modern-dance venues. Film fanatics can indulge in a full line of Hollywood releases, classics, foreign movies, and independent works.

By David Low

Updated by Tom Steele

IN A CITY AS LARGE AS NEW YORK, urban hassles sometimes appear insurmountable. When it's pouring rain, every cab seems engaged or off-duty. Waiting at the post office, supermarket, and even the cash machine almost always takes longer than you expected. Even buying a pair of socks can become a chore when a store is busy, which is usually the case. But in the end, New Yorkers put up with all the stress for at least one obvious reason: the city's unrivaled artistic life. Despite the immense competition and the threat of cuts in city aid to the arts, great artists from all disciplines continue to come to the city in droves to find their peers and to produce and perform their work. Audiences benefit greatly.

New York has somewhere between 200 and 250 legitimate theaters, and many more ad hoc venues—parks, churches, universities, museums, lofts, galleries, streets, and rooftops—where performances ranging from Shakespeare to sword dancing take place. The city is, as well, a revolving door of festivals and special events: summer jazz, one-act-play marathons, international film series, and musical celebrations from the classical to the avant-garde, to name just a few.

Arts Centers

New York's most renowned centers for the arts are tourist attractions in themselves.

Brooklyn Academy of Music (BAM; ⊠ 30 Lafayette Ave., Brooklyn, ☎ 718/636–4100), America's oldest performing arts center, began in 1859, but its reputation today is far from stodgy, thanks to its daring and innovative dance, music, opera, and theater productions. The main performance spaces are the 2,000-seat Opera House, a white-brick Renaissance Revival palace built in 1908, and the 900-seat Majestic Theatre, a restored vaudeville house around the corner. The BAM Café, which opened in the Opera House in 1997, is a convenient spot to grab a bite; it is part of a $20 million renovation slated to be completed by the end of 1998 that will also add a multiplex movie theater and a bookstore.

Carnegie Hall (⊠ 881 7th Ave., at 57th St., ☎ 212/247–7800) is world famous as a premier hall for concerts. Performances are held in both its 2,804-seat main auditorium and in the far more intimate Weill Recital Hall, where young talents often make their New York debuts. Although the emphasis is on classical music, Carnegie Hall also hosts jazz, cabaret, and folk music series (☞ 5th Avenue and 57th Street *in* Chapter 2).

City Center (⊠ 131 W. 55th St.; mailing address for ticket orders: CityTix, 130 W. 56th St., 4th floor, 10019, ☎ 212/581–1212), under its eccentric, tiled Spanish dome (built in 1923 by the Ancient and Accepted Order of the Mystic Shrine and saved from demolition in 1943 by Mayor Fiorello La Guardia), presents dance troupes such as Alvin Ailey and Paul Taylor, as well as concert versions of American musicals (the current Broadway hit revival of *Chicago* originated here). The Manhattan Theatre Club (☞ Theater, *below*) also resides here, with its highly regarded and popular program of innovative contemporary drama.

Lincoln Center (⊠ W. 62nd to 66th Sts., Broadway to Amsterdam Aves., ☎ 212/875–5000) is a 14-acre complex that houses the Metropolitan Opera, the New York Philharmonic, the Juilliard School, the New York City Ballet, the American Ballet Theatre, the New York City Opera, the Film Society of Lincoln Center, the Chamber Music Society of Lincoln Center, the Lincoln Center Theater, the School of American Ballet, and the New York Public Library's Library and Museum of the Performing Arts. Tours of Lincoln Center are available (☎ 212/875–5350; ☞ The Upper West Side *in* Chapter 2).

In 1996 the complex inaugurated the **Lincoln Center Festival** (☎ 212/875–5928) an international summer performance event (held mostly in July) under the direction of arts critic and writer John Rockwell. The program includes classical music concerts, contemporary music and dance presentations, stage works, and non-Western arts performances.

Madison Square Garden (✉ W. 31st to W. 33rd Sts. on 7th Ave., ☎ 212/465–6741), atop Penn Station, includes a renovated 20,000-seat arena and the sleek 5,600-seat Paramount Theater. The complex welcomes Ringling Bros. and Barnum & Bailey Circus each spring, hosts sports events such as basketball, ice hockey, tennis, and boxing, and draws crowds to pop/rock music concerts by stars as diverse as Barbra Streisand, Paul Simon, the Rolling Stones, and Elton John. Some rock bands that bypass Madison Square Garden appear at its suburban sister halls, **Nassau Veterans Memorial Coliseum** (✉ Uniondale, Long Island, ☎ 516/794–9300) and the Meadowlands's **Continental Airlines Sports Arena** (✉ East Rutherford, NJ, ☎ 201/935–3900).

Radio City Music Hall (✉ 1260 6th Ave., at 50th St., ☎ 212/247–4777), an Art Deco gem, opened in 1932; it has 6,000 seats, a 60-ft-high foyer, 2-ton chandeliers, and a powerful Wurlitzer organ. On this vast stage you'll find everything from rock and pop concerts to Christmas extravaganzas (featuring the celebrated Rockettes kick line), and star-studded TV specials and awards ceremonies. Tours (☎ 212/632–4041) are conducted daily (☞ Rockefeller Center and Midtown Skyscrapers *in* Chapter 2).

Manhattan has several small-scale yet important arts centers:

The Kitchen (✉ 512 W. 19th St., between 10th and 11th Aves., ☎ 212/255–5793) showcases avant-garde videos, music, performance art, and dance in its 170-seat space.

Merkin Concert Hall (✉ 129 W. 67th St., between Columbus Ave. and Broadway, ☎ 212/501–3330) mainly features chamber music concerts.

92nd Street Y (✉ 1395 Lexington Ave., at 92nd St., ☎ 212/996–1100), known for its classical-music concerts, also sponsors readings by famous writers, and the Lyrics and Lyricists series.

Sylvia and Danny Kaye Playhouse (✉ Hunter College, 68th St. between Park and Lexington Aves., ☎ 212/772–4448), a lovely concert hall, has a varied calendar of music, dance, opera, and theater events.

Symphony Space (✉ 2537 Broadway, at 95th St., ☎ 212/864–5400), a cavernous converted movie theater, schedules an eclectic offering that ranges from folk music to short stories read by celebrities.

Town Hall (✉ 123 W. 43rd St., between 6th Ave. and Broadway, ☎ 212/840–2824) hosts a diverse program of chamber, choral, popular, and world music; an annual cabaret festival; and literary events.

Tribeca Performing Arts Center (✉ 199 Chambers St., ☎ 212/346–8510) presents a lively and distinctive program of theater, dance, and music events.

Getting Tickets

Prices for tickets in New York, especially for Broadway shows, never seem to stop rising. Major concerts and recitals, however, can be equally expensive. The top Broadway ticket prices for musicals are $80; the best seats for nonmusicals can cost as much as $65.

On the positive side, tickets for New York City's arts events usually aren't too hard to come by—unless, of course, you're dead set on seeing the season's hottest shows, which are often sold out. Generally, a theater or concert hall's box office is the best place to buy tickets, since in-house ticket sellers make it their business to know about their theaters and shows and can point out (on a chart) where you'll be seated. It's always a good idea to purchase tickets in advance to avoid disappointment, especially if you're traveling a long distance. For advance purchase, send the theater or hall a certified check or money order, several alternate dates, and a self-addressed, stamped envelope.

You can also pull out a credit card and call **Tele-charge** (☏ 212/239–6200) or **Ticketmaster** (☏ 212/307–4100) to reserve tickets for Broadway and off-Broadway shows—newspaper ads generally will specify which you should use for any given event. Both services will give you seat locations over the phone upon request. A surcharge ($2–$6.75 per ticket) will be added to the total in addition to a handling fee from Ticketmaster (up to $3). You can arrange to have your tickets mailed to you or have them waiting for you at the theater.

For those willing to pay top dollar to see that show or concert everyone's talking about but no one can get tickets for, try a ticket broker. Recently, some brokers charged $100–$150 per ticket for *Rent* and *The Lion King*; had the same seats been available at the box office, they would have sold for $80 each. Among the brokers to try are **Continental/Golden and Leblangs Theatre Tickets** (☏ 212/944–8910 or 800/299–8587) and **West Side Ticket Agency** (☏ 212/719–2566). Also, check the lobbies of major hotels for ticket-broker outlets.

You may be tempted to buy from ticket scalpers. But beware: They have reportedly sold tickets to the big hits for as much as $200 when seats were still available at the box office for much less. Bear in mind that ticket scalping is against the law in New York. Also, these scalpers may even sell you phony tickets.

Off- and off-off-Broadway theaters have their own joint box office called **Ticket Central** (✉ 416 W. 42nd St., between 9th and 10th Aves., ☏ 212/279–4200). It's open daily between 1 and 8. Although there are no discounts here, tickets to performances in these theaters are usually less expensive than Broadway tickets, and they cover an array of events, including legitimate theater, performance art, and dance.

Discount Tickets

The **TKTS booth** in Duffy Square (✉ Traffic island at 47th St. and Broadway, ☏ 212/768–1818) is New York's best-known discount source. TKTS sells day-of-performance tickets for Broadway and off-Broadway plays at discounts that, depending on a show's popularity, are usually 25% off and often 50% off the usual price, plus a $2.50 surcharge per ticket. The names of shows available on that day are posted on electronic boards in front of the booth. For evening performances Monday–Saturday, the booth is open 3–8; for Wednesday and Saturday matinee performances, 10–2; for Sunday matinee and evening performances, 11–closing. *Note: TKTS accepts only cash or traveler's checks—no credit cards.*

The wait is generally pleasant (weather permitting), as the bright lights and babble of the reborn Times Square surround you. (Lines, however, can be long, especially on weekends.) You're likely to meet friendly theater lovers in line eager to share opinions about shows they've recently seen; often you'll even meet struggling actors who can give you the inside scoop. By the time you get to the booth, you may be willing to take a gamble on a show you would otherwise never have picked, and it just might be more memorable than one of the long-running hits.

An **auxiliary TKTS booth** operates in the World Trade Center (✉ 2 World Trade Center mezzanine). The branch is open weekdays 11–5:30, Saturday 11–3:30. For matinees and Sunday, you have to purchase tickets between 11 and closing the day before the performance. The lines at the downtown TKTS booth are usually shorter than those at Duffy Square, though the uptown booth usually has a larger selection of plays.

Discounts on well-known long-running shows (such as *Miss Saigon* and *Les Misérables*) are often available if you can lay your hands on a couple of **"twofers"**—discount ticket coupons found on various cash registers around town, near the lines at TKTS, at the Times Square Visitors Center (✉ 1560 7th Ave., between 46th and 47th Sts.), at the New York Visitors and Convention Bureau (✉ At 2 Columbus Circle), and at the **Hit Show Club** (✉ 630 9th Ave., 8th floor, ☎ 212/581–4211), which is open weekdays 9–4.

Some theaters, such as **Classic Stage Company** (✉ 136 E. 13th St., ☎ 212/677–4210) and the **Joseph Papp Public Theater** (✉ 425 Lafayette St., ☎ 212/260–2400), offer reduced rates on unsold tickets the day of the performance, usually a half hour before curtain time. Other shows have front-row orchestra seats available at a reduced price (about $20) the day of the performance. These special discounts are sometimes noted in the newspaper theater listings or ads. Occasionally, box offices offer same-day standing-room tickets ($10–$20) for sold-out shows; check with the particular theater for more information.

Some Broadway and off-Broadway shows sell reduced-priced tickets for performances scheduled before opening night. Look at newspaper ads for discounted previews or consult the box office. Tickets may cost less at matinees, particularly on Wednesday.

Finding Out What's On

To find out who or what's playing where, your first stop should be the newsstand. The *New York Times* isn't a prerequisite for finding out what's going on around town, but it comes in pretty handy, especially on Friday, with its two "Weekend" sections (Fine Arts and Leisure, and Movies and Performing Arts). The Sunday "Arts and Leisure" section features longer articles on everything from opera to sitcoms—and a lot more theater ads, plus a full, detailed survey of cultural events for the upcoming week.

The *New Yorker* magazine has long been known for its discerning and often witty listings called "Goings On About Town"—a section at the front of the magazine that contains ruthlessly succinct reviews of theater, dance, art, music, film, and nightlife. *New York* magazine's "Cue" listings are extremely helpful, covering everything from art to the written word.

For adventurous, more unconventional tastes, consult ***Time Out New York,*** a comprehensive guide to all kinds of entertainment happenings around town, with particularly good coverage of the downtown scene. The free weekly newspaper the ***Village Voice*** is a lively information source; its club listings and "Choices" section are both reliable. ***The New York Blade, LGNY, Time Out New York, Paper,*** and the ***Village Voice*** illuminate the gay and lesbian scene.

The League of New York Theatres and Producers and ***Playbill*** magazine publish a twice-monthly ***Broadway Theatre Guide,*** available in hotels and theaters around town. For information on the lower Manhattan cultural scene, write for a ***Downtown Arts Activities Calendar*** (⊠ Lower Manhattan Cultural Council, 15 World Trade Center, Suite 9325, 10048, ☎ 212/432–0900).

The **Broadway Line** (☎ 212/302–4111 in the tri-state area; 888/411-2929 elsewhere), a new comprehensive Broadway information service, provides show times, plot summaries, theater addresses, ticket prices, and special offers; it can also connect you directly with Tele-Charge and Ticketmaster (☞ Getting Tickets, *above*). **NYC/ON STAGE** (☎ 212/768–1818) is the Theatre Development Fund's 24-hour information service.

THEATER

The theater—not the Statue of Liberty or the Empire State Building—is the city's number one tourist attraction, and uptown or downtown you can spot theater folk pursuing their work with passion and panache. It should come as no surprise that the renovation of some of the city's oldest and grandest theaters on 42nd Street has catapulted the long-awaited revitalization of Times Square and environs into the national—and global—consciousness, and that here in the heart of the theater world, as in decades long past, is where everyone wants to be.

Broadway Theater District

To most people, New York theater means Broadway, that region bounded by 42nd and 53rd streets, between 7th and 9th avenues, where bright lights shine on newly restored theaters, gleaming entertainment complexes, theme stores, and restaurants, and a few remaining porn theaters.

Some old playhouses are as interesting for their history as for their current offerings. The **St. James** (⊠ 246 W. 44th St.), for instance, is where Lauren Bacall was an usherette in the '40s and where a sleeper of a musical called *Oklahoma!* woke up as a hit. At the **Shubert Theatre** (⊠ 225 W. 44th St.), Barbra Streisand made her 1962 Broadway debut in *I Can Get It for You Wholesale,* and the long-run record breaker, *A Chorus Line,* played for 15 years. The **Martin Beck Theatre** (⊠ 302 W. 45th St.), built in 1924 in Byzantine style, is the stage that served up premieres of Eugene O'Neill's *The Iceman Cometh,* Arthur Miller's *The Crucible,* and Tennessee Williams's *Sweet Bird of Youth*. Theater names read like a roll call of American theater history: Edwin Booth, the Barrymores (Ethel, John, and Lionel), Eugene O'Neill, George Gershwin, Alfred Lunt and Lynn Fontanne, Richard Rodgers, and Neil Simon, among others.

As you stroll around the theater district, you may also see **Shubert Alley,** a shortcut between 44th and 45th streets where theater moguls used to park their limousines, today the site of a jam-packed Great White Way memorabilia store called One Shubert Alley (☎ 212/944–4133). Farther west is **Restaurant Row** (⊠ 46th St. between 8th and 9th Aves.), which offers plenty of choices (☞ Chapter 6).

The resuscitation of the 42nd Street houses between Broadway and 8th Avenue continues to make headlines. The **New Victory** (⊠ 209 W. 42nd St.), previously known both as the Theater Republic and the Belasco Theater, is the oldest surviving playhouse in New York, with a lovely Venetian facade; reopened in 1995 and now completely modernized, it stages exciting productions for kids. The **Ford Center for the Performing Arts** (⊠ 213–215 W. 42nd St.), a lavish 1,839-seat theater constructed on the site of two classic houses, the Lyric and the Apollo, incorporates original architectural elements from both theaters, along with state-

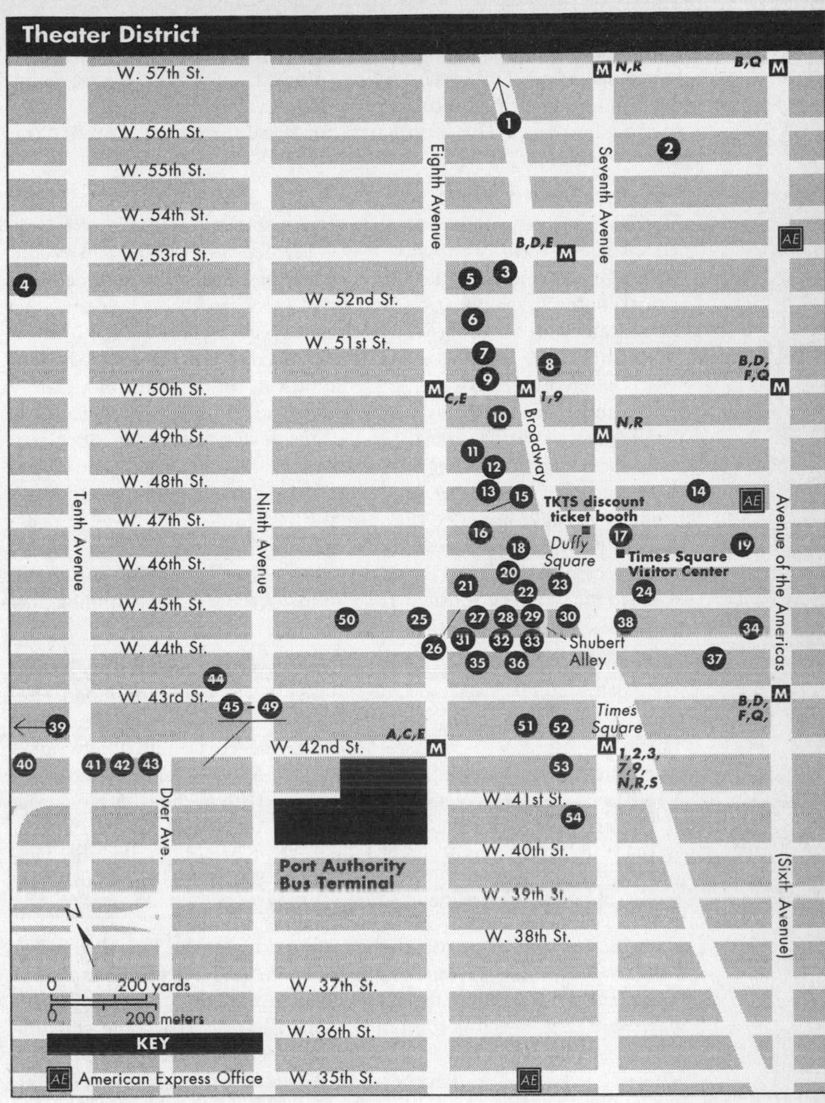

Ambassador, **10**
American Place, **19**
Belasco, **34**
Booth, **29**
Broadhurst, **32**
Broadway, **3**
Brooks Atkinson, **16**
Circle in the Square, **9**
Cort, **14**
Douglas Fairbanks, **43**
Ensemble Studio, **4**
Ethel Barrymore, **15**
Eugene O'Neill, **11**
Ford Center for the Performing Arts, **51**
Gershwin, **7**
Harold Clurman, **48**
Helen Hayes, **36**
INTAR, **46**
Imperial, **21**
John Golden, **26**
John Houseman, **41**
Judith Anderson, **45**
Kaufman, **40**
Lamb's, **37**
Lincoln Center Theater: Vivian Beaumont, Mitzi E. Newhouse, **1**
Longacre, **13**
Lunt-Fontanne, **18**
Lyceum, **24**
Majestic, **31**
Manhattan Theatre Club (City Center), **2**
Marquis, **23**
Martin Beck, **25**
Minskoff, **30**
Music Box, **22**
Nat Horne, **42**
Nederlander, **54**
Neil Simon, **6**
New Amsterdam, **53**
New Victory, **52**
Palace, **17**
Playwrights Horizons, **47**
Plymouth, **28**
Primary Stages, **50**
Richard Rodgers, **20**
Roundabout Theatre Company (Criterion Center), **38**
Royale, **27**
Samuel Beckett, **49**
St. James, **35**
Shubert, **33**
Signature Theatre Company, **39**
Virginia, **5**
Walter Kerr, **12**
Westside, **44**
Winter Garden, **8**

of-the-art facilities to accommodate grand-scale musical shows. Across the street, the Walt Disney Company has refurbished the Art Nouveau **New Amsterdam** (✉ 214 W. 42nd St.). Eddie Cantor, Will Rogers, Fanny Brice, and the Ziegfeld Follies once drew crowds here; today it is the spectacular den of *The Lion King* (For these three theaters, *see* 42nd Street *in* Chapter 2).

Beyond Broadway

Not all that long ago it was relatively simple to categorize the New York stage beyond Broadway. It was divided into off-Broadway and off-off-Broadway, depending on a variety of factors that included theatrical contract type, location, and ticket price. Today such distinctions seem strained, as off-Broadway prices have risen and the quality of some off-off-Broadway productions has improved. Off- and off-off-Broadway is where Eric Bogosian, Ann Magnuson, John Leguizamo, Danny Hoch, and Laurie Anderson often make their home and where *Rent, Driving Miss Daisy, Steel Magnolias,* and *Jeffrey* were first conceived. Attendance and ticket sales remain relatively healthy, proving how vital this segment of the theater world is to New York culture. Recent long-running hits have included the surreal *Blue Man Group; Stomp,* a percussion performance piece; and *Forbidden Broadway Strikes Back!,* an evening of parodies of Broadway shows. Off-Broadway is also still home to the romantic musical *The Fantasticks,* the longest-running play in U.S. theater history.

One of the major off-Broadway enclaves is Theatre Row, a collection of small houses (100 seats or fewer)—such as the **John Houseman Theatre** (✉ 450 W. 42nd St., ☎ 212/967–9077), the **Douglas Fairbanks Theatre** (✉ 432 W. 42nd St., ☎ 212/239–4321), and **Playwrights Horizons** (✉ 416 W. 42nd St., ☎ 212/279–4200)—on the downtown (south) side of 42nd Street between 9th and 10th avenues. A block east of Theatre Row is the **Westside Theatre** (✉ 407 W. 43rd St., ☎ 212/307–4100). Other small playhouses west of Broadway include **Theatre Four** (✉ 424 W. 55th St., ☎ 212/757–3900) and the **47th Street Theatre** (✉ 304 W. 47th St., ☎ 212/239–6200).

Name actors appear in top-flight productions at the two theaters at Lincoln Center: the **Vivian Beaumont** (considered a Broadway playhouse) and the more intimate **Mitzi E. Newhouse** (✉ 65th St. and Broadway, ☎ 212/239–6200 for both), which has scored some startling successes, including John Guare's *Six Degrees of Separation,* Tom Stoppard's *Arcadia,* and acclaimed revivals of *Carousel, The Heiress,* and *Ivanov.*

Downtown in the East Village, at the **Joseph Papp Public Theater** (✉ 425 Lafayette St., ☎ 212/260–2400), renamed in 1992 to honor its late founder and longtime guiding genius, producer George C. Wolfe continues the tradition of innovative theater, mounting new and classic plays. In the summertime the Public raises its sets in Central Park's open-air **Delacorte Theater** (☎ 212/539–8750 [seasonal]) for productions of plays and musicals (a decade-long cycle of Shakespeare's plays ended in 1997, so more varied fare is planned). Free tickets for evening performances are handed out to those who have waited in line beforehand at around 1 PM on the day of performance downtown at the Public and uptown at the Delacorte. If you want to see a popular show, get in line well before 1.

Greenwich Village, around Sheridan Square, is another off-Broadway neighborhood. Its theaters include the **Actors Playhouse** (✉ 100 7th Ave. S, ☎ 212/239–6200), the **Cherry Lane Theatre** (✉ 38 Commerce St., ☎ 212/989–2020), the **Lucille Lortel Theatre** (✉ 121 Christopher

St., ☎ 212/239–6200), the **Minetta Lane Theatre** (✉ 18 Minetta La., ☎ 212/420–8000), the **Players Theater** (✉ 115 MacDougal St., ☎ 212/254–5076), and the **Sullivan Street Playhouse** (✉ 181 Sullivan St., ☎ 212/674–3838).

Many estimable **off-Broadway theaters** are flung across the Manhattan map: the **Astor Place Theatre** (✉ 434 Lafayette St., ☎ 212/254–4370); the **Orpheum Theatre** (✉ 126 2nd Ave., at 8th St., ☎ 212/477–2477); the **Variety Arts Theatre** (✉ 110 3rd Ave., at 14th St., ☎ 212/239–6200); the **Union Square Theatre** (✉ 100 E. 17th St., ☎ 212/505–0700); the **American Place Theatre** (✉ 111 W. 46th St., ☎ 239–6200); the **Lamb's Theatre** (✉ 130 W. 44th St., ☎ 212/997–1780); the **Triad Theatre** (✉ 158 W. 72nd St., between Columbus and Amsterdam Aves., ☎ 212/799–4599); and the **Promenade Theatre** (✉ Broadway at 76th St., ☎ 212/580–1313).

THEATER COMPANIES

Several off- and off-off-Broadway theater groups are worth keeping your eye on:

American Jewish Theatre (✉ 307 W. 26th St., off 8th Ave., ☎ 212/633–9797) stages contemporary plays and revivals of musicals, more often than not with a Jewish theme.

Atlantic Theater Company (✉ 33 W. 20th St., at 5th Ave., ☎ 212/645–1242), founded by playwright David Mamet and actor William H. Macy, is dedicated to producing controversial new plays.

Classic Stage Company (CSC; ✉ 136 E. 13th St., between 3rd and 4th Aves., ☎ 212/677–4210) provides a showcase for the classics—some arcane, others European—in new translations and adaptations.

Drama Dept. (✉ Administrative office: 450 W. 42nd St., ☎ 212/629–3014) doesn't have a permanent home, but the energetic company of young actors, playwrights, and other theater artists has won high acclaim for its lively, imaginative revivals of overlooked plays.

Ensemble Studio Theatre (✉ 549 W. 52nd St., between 10th and 11th Aves., ☎ 212/247–3405), with its tried-and-true roster of players, stresses new dramatic works. It also presents an annual marathon of one-act plays.

Irish Repertory Theatre (✉ 132 W. 22nd St., between 6th and 7th Aves., ☎ 212/727–2737) stages classic and contemporary Irish plays.

Jean Cocteau Repertory (✉ Bouwerie Lane Theatre, 330 Bowery, at Bond St., ☎ 212/677–0060), founded in 1971, reinvents international classics, intelligently performed by its resident acting troupe.

Jewish Repertory Theatre (✉ Playhouse 91, 316 E. 91st St., between 1st and 2nd Aves., ☎ 212/831–2000), begun in 1972, produces plays and musicals about Jewish life such as *Crossing Delancey,* the basis for the hit film.

Manhattan Theatre Club (✉ At City Center, 131 W. 55th St., ☎ 212/581–1212) stages some of the most talked-about new plays and musicals in town; Terrence McNally, Athol Fugard, and Stephen Sondheim have all had their work produced here.

New York Theater Workshop (✉ 79 E. 4th St., between 2nd and 3rd Aves., ☎ 212/460–5475) produces challenging new theater by American and international playwrights like Jonathan Larson, Tony Kushner, and Caryl Churchill.

Pan Asian Repertory Theatre (✉ Playhouse 46 in St. Clement's Church, 423 W. 46th St., between 9th and 10th Aves., ☎ 212/245–2660), a center for Asian and Asian-American artists, focuses on new works or adapted Western plays.

Pearl Theatre Company (✉ 80 St. Marks Pl., between 2nd and 3rd Aves., ☎ 212/598–9802) is the intimate home of a troupe of resident players who concentrate on classics from around the globe; the works of such masters as Molière, Ibsen, Shakespeare, and Sophocles have found a new life here.

Primary Stages (✉ 354 W. 45th St., ☎ 212/333–4052) puts the spotlight on new work by American playwrights, such as David Ives and Donald Margulies.

Repertorio Español (✉ Gramercy Arts Theatre, 138 E. 27th St., between 3rd and Lexington Aves., ☎ 212/889–2850) is an Obie award–winning Spanish-arts repertory theater; performances are in Spanish.

Roundabout Theater Company (☎ 212/869–8400) produces classic plays and musicals at various theaters; in late 1999 it will take occupancy of the renovated Selwyn Theater, on 42nd Street.

Second Stage (✉ McGinn/Cazale Theatre, 2162 Broadway, at W. 76th St., ☎ 212/873–6103) is committed to new works and recent plays that may not have been given a fair chance their first time around.

Signature Theatre Company (✉ 555 W. 42nd St., between 10th and 11th Aves., ☎ 212/244–7529) devotes each season to the sensitive productions of the works of one American playwright; past seasons have recognized the plays of Edward Albee, Horton Foote, Adrienne Kennedy, and Sam Shepard.

Vineyard Theater (✉ 108 E. 15th St., between Park Ave. S and Irving Pl., ☎ 212/353–3366) features innovative new plays and musicals by established and emerging artists.

WPA Theatre (✉ 519 W. 23rd St., between 10th and 11th Aves., ☎ 212/206–0523) showcases new works by American playwrights, such as Paul Rudnick and Charles Busch.

York Theatre Company (✉ Theatre at St. Peter's Church, 54th St. at Lexington Ave., ☎ 212/935–5820) presents acclaimed revivals of plays and musicals in addition to new theater works.

Avant-Garde

Last, but not at all least, is New York's fabled theatrical avant-garde. The experimental theater movement's founders may no longer be the long-haired hippies they were when they first started doing mixed-media productions and promoting off-center playwrights (such as Sam Shepard and John Guare) in the '60s, but they continue at the forefront.

Ellen Stewart, also known—simply and elegantly—as La Mama, started the theater complex **La MaMa E.T.C.** (✉ 74A E. 4th St., off 2nd Ave., ☎ 212/475–7710) in 1961. Over the past three-plus decades, her East Village organization has branched out to import European innovators and has grown physically as well. It now encompasses the First Floor Theater, the Annex Theater, and a club. Productions include everything from African fables to new-wave opera to reinterpretations of the Greek classics; past triumphs have included the original productions of *Godspell* and *Torch Song Trilogy.*

A four-theater cultural complex is home to the experimentalist **Theater for the New City** (✉ 155 1st Ave., between 9th and 10th Sts., ☎ 212/254–1109), which devotes its productions to new playwrights. The complex also sponsors a free street-theater program, arts festivals, and Christmas and Halloween spectacles.

Hailed by the *New York Times* as "a first-class magician of the avant-garde," Richard Foreman oversees the **Ontological-Hysteric Theater** (✉ St. Mark's-in-the-Bowery Church, 131 E. 10th St., at 2nd Ave., ☎ 212/533–4650), whose unconventional productions illuminate the human condition, often exploring the realm of dreams and nightmares. During the summer the theater sponsors the Blueprint Series, which allows novice directors to test their skills in front of an audience.

Performance Art

Intentionally difficult to categorize, performance art is a curious mélange of artistic disciplines blending music and sound, dance, video and lights, words, and whatever else comes to the performance artist's mind to produce events of erratic success—sometimes fascinating, sometimes deadening. Performance art is almost exclusively a downtown endeavor, though it is also showcased in the outer boroughs, especially Brooklyn, where the **Brooklyn Academy of Music** (✉ 30 Lafayette Ave., Brooklyn, ☎ 718/636–4100) has built its considerable reputation on its annual **Next Wave Festival,** which features performance works.

Manhattan has a few notable performance art showcases:

Dixon Place (✉ 258 Bowery, between Houston and Prince Sts., ☎ 212/219–3088) presents an eccentric, eclectic schedule, including comedy acts, musicians, and readings.

The Kitchen (✉ 512 W. 19th St., between 10th and 11th Aves., ☎ 212/255–5793) is perhaps *the* Manhattan center for performance art, although video, dance, and music have their moments here, too.

P.S. 122 (✉ 150 1st Ave., at 9th St., ☎ 212/477–5288) occupies a former public school that was comedian George Burns's alma mater. This vibrant East Village venue presents exhibitions and productions that come and go quickly, and they're never boring. Look especially for its annual marathon in February, in which scores of dazzling downtowners take part.

DANCE

Ballet

Visiting balletomanes live out their dreams in New York, where two powerhouse companies—the New York City Ballet and the American Ballet Theatre—continue to please and astonish.

The New York City Ballet (NYCB), founded by Lincoln Kirstein and George Balanchine in 1948, celebrates its 50th anniversary in 1998–99, which it plans to mark with a full calendar of special events and programs (details not yet available at press time). NYCB's winter season runs from mid-November through February—with its beloved annual production of George Balanchine's *The Nutcracker* ushering in the December holiday season—while its spring season lasts from late April through June. The company continues to stress dance as a whole above individual ballet stars, though that hasn't stopped a number of principal dancers (such as Kyra Nichols, Darci Kistler, Damian Woetzel, and Jock Soto) from standing out. The company has more than 90 dancers and performs and maintains an active repertoire of 20th-century works unmatched in the world, including works by Balanchine, Jerome Robbins, Ballet Master-in-Chief Peter Martins, and others. NYCB performs in Lincoln Center's **New York State Theater** (☎ 212/870–5570).

Across the plaza at Lincoln Center, the **Metropolitan Opera House** (☎ 212/362–6000) is home to the **American Ballet Theatre (ABT),** renowned for its brilliant renditions of the great 19th-century classics (*Swan Lake, Giselle, The Sleeping Beauty,* and *La Bayardère*) as well as for the unique scope of its eclectic contemporary repertoire (including works by all the 20th-century masters—Balanchine, Tudor, Robbins, and de Mille, among others). Since its inception in 1940, the company has included some of the greatest dancers of the century, such as Mikhail Baryshnikov, Natalia Makarova, Rudolf Nureyev, Gelsey Kirkland, and Cynthia Gregory. Since 1992 the ABT has been directed by Kevin McKenzie, one of the company's leading male dancers in the 1980s. It has two New York seasons—eight weeks beginning in early May and two weeks beginning in late October; the fall performances are at **City Center** (✉ 131 W. 55th St., ☎ 212/581–1212).

The varied bill at **City Center** (✉ 131 W. 55th St., ☎ 212/581–1212) often includes touring ballet companies.

Modern Dance

At **City Center** (✉ 131 W. 55th St., ☎ 212/581–1212), the moderns hold sway. In seasons past the **Alvin Ailey Dance Company, Twyla Tharp and Dancers,** the **Martha Graham Dance Company,** the **Paul Taylor Dance Company,** the **Dance Theater of Harlem,** and the **Merce Cunningham Dance Company** have performed here. The **Brooklyn Academy of Music** (BAM; ✉ 30 Lafayette Ave., Brooklyn, ☎ 718/636–4100) features both American and foreign contemporary dance troupes as part of its **Next Wave Festival** every fall; virtually every New York performance of the **Mark Morris Dance Group** has been at BAM.

The **Joyce Theater** (✉ 175 8th Ave., at 19th St., ☎ 212/242–0800), housed in a former Art Deco movie theater in Chelsea, has emerged as a major international modern-dance center. The Joyce is the permanent home of **Ballet Tech,** founded as Feld Ballet/NY in 1974 by Eliot Feld, an upstart ABT dancer who went on to become a principal fixture on the dance scene. Recent featured companies have included the startling **Parsons Dance Company,** the lyrical **Lar Lubovitch Dance Company,** the passionate **Ballet Hispánico,** and the fantastical **Momix** troupe. The Joyce has an eclectic program, including tap, jazz, ballroom, and ethnic dance, and it often showcases emerging choreographers. It has another space downtown, the **Joyce SoHo** (✉ 155 Mercer St., between Houston and Prince Sts., ☎ 212/431–9233), which hosts a number of performances by highly talented local dancers.

Manhattan has several other small-scale, mostly experimental and avant-garde dance forums:

Dance Theater Workshop (✉ 219 W. 19th St., between 7th and 8th Aves., ☎ 212/924–0077) serves as one of New York's most successful laboratories for new dance.

Danspace Project (✉ St. Mark's-in-the-Bowery Church, 131 E. 10th St., at 2nd Ave., ☎ 212/674–8194) sponsors a series of avant-garde choreography that runs from September through June.

Merce Cunningham Studio (✉ 55 Bethune St., ☎ 212/691–9751) showcases performances by cutting-edge modern dance companies.

92nd St. Y Harkness Dance Project (✉ 1395 Lexington Ave., at 92nd St., ☎ 212/996–1100) presents emerging dance troupes with discussion following performances.

P.S. 122 (✉ 150 1st Ave., at 9th St., ☎ 212/477–5288) programs dance events that often border on performance art.

Repertorio Español (✉ Gramercy Arts Theatre, 138 E. 27th St., between 3rd and Lexington Aves., ☎ 212/889–2850) is often visited by the famed Spanish stylist Pilar Rioja.

Sylvia and Danny Kaye Playhouse (✉ Hunter College, 68th St. between Park and Lexington Aves., ☎ 212/772–4448) hosts up-and-coming dance companies.

Symphony Space (✉ 2537 Broadway, at 95th St., ☎ 212/864–5400) often focuses on ethnic dance.

Tribeca Performing Arts Center (✉ 199 Chambers St., ☎ 212/346–8510) presents dance troupes from around the world.

MUSIC

"Gentlemen," conductor Serge Koussevitzky once told the assembled Boston Symphony Orchestra, "maybe it's good enough for Cleveland or Cincinnati, but it's not good enough for New York." In a nutshell that summarizes New York's place in the musical world.

New York possesses not only the country's oldest symphony, the New York Philharmonic, but also three renowned conservatories—the Juilliard School, the Manhattan School of Music, and Mannes College of Music—plus myriad other musical performance groups. Since the turn of the century, the world's great orchestras and soloists have made Manhattan a principal stopping point.

If you're visiting the city for its music, New York has an overwhelming number of happenings to keep you busy. In an average week, between 50 and 150 events—everything from zydeco to Debussy, from Cole Porter and Kurt Weill to reggae—appear in newspaper and magazine listings, and weekly concert calendars are published in all the major newspapers. Record and music shops serve as music information centers. These shops include the cavernous **Tower Records** (✉ 692 Broadway, at 4th St., ☎ 212/505–1500; ✉ Trump Tower, 725 5th Ave., at 57th St., ☎ 212/838–8110; ✉ 1961 Broadway, at 66th St., ☎ 212/799–2500); **HMV** (✉ 2081 Broadway, at 72nd St., ☎ 212/721–5900; ✉ 1280 Lexington Ave., at 86th St., ☎ 212/348–0800; ✉ 565 5th Ave., at 46th St., ☎ 212/681–6700; ✉ 59 W. 34th St., off 5th Ave., ☎ 212/629–0900); the burgeoning **J & R Music World** (✉ 15–33 Park Row, across from City Hall, ☎ 212/238–9000); the reliable **Bleecker Bob's Golden Oldies** (✉ 118 W. 3rd St., at MacDougal St., ☎ 212/475–9677), and the classy **Joseph Patelson Music House** (✉ 160 W. 56th St., between 6th and 7th Aves., ☎ 212/582–5840).

Classical Music

Lincoln Center (✉ W. 62nd St. to 66th Sts., Broadway to Amsterdam Ave.) remains the city's musical nerve center, especially when it comes to the classics.

Avery Fisher Hall (☎ 212/875–5030), designed by Max Abramovitz, opened at Lincoln Center in 1961 as Philharmonic Hall but underwent drastic renovation in 1976 to improve the acoustics (at a price tag of $5 million). The result is an auditorium that follows the classic European rectangular pattern. To its stage come the world's great musicians; to its boxes, the black tie and diamond tiara set.

The **New York Philharmonic** (☎ 212/875–5656), led by music director Kurt Masur, performs at Avery Fisher Hall from late September to early June. In addition to its magical concerts showcasing exceptional guest artists and the works of specific composers, the Philharmonic also schedules weeknight Rush Hour Concerts at 6:45 and Casual Saturdays Concerts at 2; these special events, offered throughout the season, last one hour and are priced lower than the regular subscription concerts. Rush Hour Concerts are followed by receptions with the conductor on the Grand Promenade, and Casual Saturdays Concerts feature discussions after the performances. A note for New York Philharmonic devotees: In season and when conductors and soloists are amenable, weekday orchestra rehearsals at 9:45 AM are open to the public for $10.

During the summer at Avery Fisher Hall, the popular **Mostly Mozart** (☎ 212/875–5135) festival presents an impressive roster of classical performers.

Near Avery Fisher is **Alice Tully Hall** (✉ Broadway at 65th St., ☎ 212/875–5050), an intimate "little white box," considered as acoustically perfect as a concert hall can get. Here you can hear to the **Chamber Music Society of Lincoln Center**, promising Juilliard students, chamber music ensembles, music on period instruments, choral music, famous soloists, and concert groups.

Lincoln Center's outdoor **Damrosch Park** and nearby **Bruno Walter Auditorium** (in the Library of the Performing Arts, ☎ 212/870–1630) often offer free concerts.

Although Lincoln Center is only some 30 years old, another famous classical music palace—**Carnegie Hall** (✉ W. 57th St. at 7th Ave., ☎ 212/247–7800)—recently celebrated its 100th birthday (☞ 5th Avenue and 57th Street *in* Chapter 2).

In addition to Lincoln Center and Carnegie Hall, the city has many other prime classical music locales around the city:

Aaron Davis Hall at City College (✉ W. 133rd St. at Convent Ave., ☎ 212/650–6900) is an uptown venue for world music events and a variety of classical concerts and dance programs.

Bargemusic at the Fulton Ferry Landing in Brooklyn (☎ 718/624–4061) keeps chamber music groups busy year-round on an old barge with a fabulous skyline view.

Brooklyn Academy of Music (✉ 30 Lafayette Ave., Brooklyn, ☎ 718/636–4100) is the home of the Brooklyn Philharmonic, which under music director Robert Spano has the city's most adventurous symphonic programming.

Church of St. Ignatius Loyola (✉ 980 Park Ave., at 84th St., ☎ 212/288–2520) hosts choral and organ concerts about twice a month from September to April.

Merkin Concert Hall at the Abraham Goodman House (✉ 129 W. 67th St., between Columbus Ave. and Broadway, ☎ 212/550–3330) is almost as prestigious for performers as the concert halls at Lincoln Center.

The **Metropolitan Museum of Art** (✉ 5th Ave. at 82nd St., ☎ 212/570–3949) holds concerts in three venues—the Temple of Dendur, the Grace Rainey Rogers Auditorium, and, at Christmas, the Medieval Sculpture Hall—with leading vocal, chamber, and jazz musicians. Recent performers have included Chanticleer, Dawn Upshaw, and Billy Taylor. Access to concerts on evenings other than Friday or Saturday (when the museum is open until 8:45) is through the street-level entrance at 83rd Street and 5th Avenue.

Miller Theatre (✉ Columbia University, Broadway at 116th St., ☎ 212/854–7799) features a varied program of classical performers, such as the New York Virtuosi Chamber Symphony.

92nd St. Y (✉ 1395 Lexington Ave., at 92nd St., ☎ 212/996–1100) showcases star recitalists and chamber music groups.

Sylvia and Danny Kaye Playhouse (✉ Hunter College, 68th St. between Park and Lexington Aves., ☎ 212/772–4448) presents a varied program of events, including distinguished soloists and chamber music groups, in a small state-of-the-art concert hall.

Early Music

New York's early music scene has increased dramatically over the last few years. A half dozen performing groups and presenting organizations offer concerts throughout the year in many venues, including various churches.

BachWorks (☎ 212/259–9496) performs works by Johann Sebastian Bach and other 18th-century baroque composers at the German Evangelical-Lutheran Church of St. Paul (✉ 315 W. 22nd St., between 8th and 9th Aves.)

Concerts at the Cloisters (☎ 212/650–2290) presents sacred and secular music from the middle ages in the Cloisters' 12th-century chapel.

Gotham Early Music (☎ 212/595–4036; 800/627–0655 for tickets) presents top international early music groups; the season runs from October through April at venues from Alice Tully Hall to neighborhood churches.

Lionheart (☎ 718/638–0041), a New York–based male a cappella sextet, performs medieval, Renaissance, and contemporary music at various venues, including the Church of the Heavenly Rest (✉ 2 E. 90th St., at 5th Ave.).

Music Before 1800 (☎ 212/666–9266) performs seven concerts a year; all are Sunday at 4 at Corpus Christi Church (✉ 529 W. 121 St.).

New York's Ensemble for Early Music (☎ 212/749–6600), celebrating its 25th anniversary in 1998–99, performs about 20 medieval and Renaissance music concerts in the Cathedral of St. John the Divine, where they are in residence, and in the Cloisters (☞ Morningside Heights *in* Chapter 2 for both).

Voices of Ascension (☎ 212/254–8553), well known through its recordings, performs choral concerts of all periods, mostly at the Church of the Ascension (✉ 5th Ave. at 10th St.).

Outdoor Concerts

Weather permitting, the city presents myriad musical events in the great outdoors. Each August the plaza around Lincoln Center explodes with the **Lincoln Center Out-of-Doors** (☎ 212/875–5108) series. In the summertime both the Metropolitan Opera and the New York Philharmonic appear in municipal parks to play free concerts, filling verdant spaces with the haunting strains of *La Bohème* or the thunder of the *1812 Overture* (for information call Lincoln Center, ☎ 212/875–5400, or the City Parks Special Events Hotline, ☎ 212/360–3456).

Central Park SummerStage (✉ Rumsey Playfield, Central Park at 72nd St., ☎ 212/360–2777 or 800/201–7275) presents free music programs, ranging from world music to alternative rock, generally on Saturday and Sunday afternoons from June through August. The **Museum of Modern Art** hosts free Friday- and Saturday-evening concerts of 20th-century music in its sculpture garden as part of the **Summergarden** series (☎ 212/708–9480), held from mid-June through August. A **Jazzmobile** (☎ 212/866–4900) transports jazz and Latin music to parks throughout the five boroughs in July and August; Wednesday-evening concerts are held at **Grant's Tomb** (✉ Riverside Dr. and 122nd St.). Prospect Park comes alive with the sounds of its annual **Celebrate Brooklyn Concert Series** (✉ 9th Street band shell, 9th St. and Prospect Park W, Park Slope, Brooklyn, ☎ 718/855–7882, ext. 52). **Pier 16 at South Street Seaport** (☎ 212/732–7678) becomes the setting for a cornucopia of musical entertainment from Thursday through Saturday evenings from Memorial Day to Labor Day; it also sponsors holiday music concerts from late November through January 1 on weekday evenings and weekend afternoons.

Lunchtime Concerts

During the workweek lunchtime concerts provide musical midday breaks at public atriums all over the city. Events are generally free, and bag-lunching is encouraged. Check out the **World Financial Center's Winter Garden Atrium** (across the West Side Highway from the World Trade Center). Of course, everywhere—in parks, on street corners, and on subway platforms—aspiring musicians of all kinds hold forth, their instrument cases thrown open for contributions. True, some are hacks, but others are bona fide professionals: moonlighting violinists, Broadway chorus members indulging their love of the barbershop quartet, or horn players prowling around after leaving their clubs.

You can take a midtown music break at **St. Peter's Lutheran Church** (✉ 619 Lexington Ave., at the Citicorp Center, ☎ 212/935–2200), with its Wednesday series of lunchtime jazz at 12:30 and organ concerts on Friday at 12:45.

Downtown, venerable **St. Paul's Chapel** (✉ Fulton St. and Broadway, ☎ 212/602–0874) presents lunchtime concerts on Monday at noon. **Trinity Church** (✉ 74 Trinity Pl., ☎ 212/602–0873) also has concerts every Thursday at 1. Programs at both churches may include classical or contemporary music. A $2 contribution is suggested.

OPERA

These are good times for opera lovers in New York, as the city's two major companies, the Metropolitan Opera and New York City Opera, are in splendid form. The titan of U.S. opera companies, **Metropolitan Opera** (the Met; ☎ 212/362–6000) brings the world's leading singers to its massive stage for productions by the world's greatest directors, stage designers, costume designers, and lighting directors. Under the direction of James Levine, the Met's principal conductor and artistic director, and new principal guest conductor Valery Gergiev, the opera orchestra performs with an intensity and quality that rival the world's finest symphonic orchestras. All performances, including operas sung in English, are unobtrusively subtitled on small screens on the back of each seat (and which can be turned off).

The Met performs its vaunted repertoire from October to mid-April, and though tickets can cost more than $100, many less expensive seats and standing room are available. The top-price tickets are the center box seats, which are few in number and rarely available without a subscription. The Met has several different price levels, with some 600 seats sold at $24; weekday prices are slightly lower than weekend prices. Standing-room tickets for the week's performances go on sale on Saturday. Saturday-matinee performances from early December through the end of the season are simulcast around the world over the Texaco radio network; it can be thrilling to be in the audience for a performance you know is being broadcast.

Although it is not as widely known to non-natives as the Met, the **New York City Opera** is as vital to the city's operagoers as its more famous next-door neighbor. Under the leadership of its new artistic director, Paul Kellogg, City Opera had a glorious 1997–98 season, and bets are on that the company will continue to blossom. At the least, City Opera continues its tradition of offering a diverse repertoire, including rarely seen baroque operas, adventurous new works such as *The Voyage of Marco Polo* and *The Times of Harvey Milk,* and the beloved classic operas—*La Bohème, Carmen,* and the like. The company has consistently nurtured the talent of young American stars-to-be. A surprising number of the world's finest singers, such as Placido Domingo, Frederica von Stade, and Beverly Sills, began their careers at City Opera—and if recent performances are any indication, the next generation of great voices is on its way to joining these elevated ranks. City Opera performs from September through November and in March and April at Lincoln Center's **New York State Theater** (☎ 212/870–5570). All performances of foreign-language operas have supertitles—line-by-line English translations electronically displayed above the stage.

Opera aficionados should also keep track of the **Carnegie Hall** (☎ 212/247–7800) schedule for debuting singers and performances by the **Opera Orchestra of New York** (☎ 212/799–1982), which specializes in presenting rarely performed operas in concert form, often with star soloists. A libretto of the opera performed is provided, and lights are kept up enough for reading.

The **Brooklyn Academy of Music** (✉ 30 Lafayette Ave., Brooklyn, ☎ 718/636–4100) has emerged as an outstanding venue for opera, particularly less famous baroque masterpieces by such composers as Rameau, Gluck, and Handel. Productions here are typically staged by such leading European and American artists as William Christie, Christopher Hogwood, and Mark Morris.

The city has a few lesser-known opera groups:

Amato Opera Theatre (✉ 319 Bowery, ☎ 212/228–8200) is an intimate 50-year-old showcase for rising singers. The theater seats only 107, and the performances of Verdi, Mozart, and other composers of the standard opera repertory are often sold out.

New York Gilbert and Sullivan Players (✉ 302 W. 91st St., ☎ 212/769–1000 or 212/864–5400 for box office) presents lively productions of G&S classics, usually at **Symphony Space** (✉ 95th and Broadway).

New York Grand Opera (✉ 154 W. 57th St., Suite 125, ☎ 212/245–8837) mounts free summer performances of Verdi operas—with a full orchestra and professional singers—at Central Park SummerStage at Rumsey Playfield (✉ Central Park at E. 72nd St.).

Opera at the Algonquin (✉ 59 W. 44th St., ☎ 212/840–6800), a new Sunday series in the fabled Algonquin hotel's venerable Oak Room, hosts prominent singers who perform following dinner.

FILM AND VIDEO

On any given week New York City might be described as a kind of film archive featuring all the major new releases, classics renowned and obscure, unusual foreign offerings, small independent flicks, and cutting-edge experimental works. Alas, the city may be the global capital of cineastes, and so sold-out shows have become common. If you do get tickets, you may have to stand awhile in a line that winds around the block, but even that can be entertaining—conversations overheard in such queues are often more entertaining than the previews of coming attractions. Note, however, that these lines are generally for people who have already bought their tickets; if you see a line as you approach the theater, be sure to ask if it's for ticket holders or tickets buyers.

For information on first-run movie schedules and show times at the theater nearest you, call the **MovieFone** (☎ 212/777–3456). You can also call this number to order tickets in advance with a credit card; not all movie theaters participate, however, and the surcharge is $1.50 per ticket. At press time (spring 1998), three New York cinemas have instituted reserved seating for all shows: **United Artists 64th and 2nd** (✉ 1210 2nd Ave.), **Cineplex Odeon Chelsea West Cinemas** (✉ 333 W. 23rd St., between 8th and 9th Aves.), and **Cineplex Odeon Ziegfield Theatre** (✉ 141 W. 54th St., at 6th Ave.). Reservations are available at the box offices or through MovieFone.

Festivals and Seasonal Screenings

New York's leading annual film event is the **New York Film Festival,** conducted by the Film Society of Lincoln Center every September and October at Alice Tully and Avery Fisher halls (☎ 212/875–5600). Its program includes exceptional movies, most never before seen in the

United States; the festival's hits usually make their way into local movie houses over the ensuing couple of months. This festival has presented the U.S. premieres of such memorable movies as Martin Scorsese's *Mean Streets,* François Truffaut's *Day for Night,* Quentin Tarantino's *Pulp Fiction,* and Mike Leigh's *Secrets and Lies.* Each March the Film Society joins forces with the Museum of Modern Art (MoMA) to produce a **New Directors/New Films** series, where the best works by up-and-coming directors get their moment to flicker. Several movies included in this festival have gone on to become box-office successes. The series is held at MoMA's Roy and Niuta Titus theaters (✉ 11 W. 53rd St., between 5th and 6th Aves., ☎ 212/708–9480).

During the summer you can bring a picnic and blankets to **Bryant Park** (✉ 6th Ave. between W. 40th and 42nd Sts., ☎ 212/512–5700) on Monday just after sunset, when classics like *On the Waterfront, Singing in the Rain,* and *King Kong* are shown for free. There's always a crowd, so arrive early.

Museums

The **American Museum of the Moving Image** (✉ 35th Ave. at 36th St., Astoria, Queens, ☎ 718/784–0077) presents changing exhibits, lectures, and provocative film programs, including major artist-oriented retrospectives, Hollywood classics, experimental videos, and TV documentaries (☞ Queens *in* Chapter 3). More than 300 screenings per year are held in the intimate 195-seat Riklis Theater—among them tributes to Hollywood directors, cinematographers, writers, and stars. Shorts or vintage film serials are shown every hour in Tut's Fever Movie Palace, a garish re-creation of an Egyptian-style picture palace of the 1930s, designed by Red Grooms and Lysiane Luong.

In midtown Manhattan, the **Museum of Television & Radio** (✉ 25 W. 52nd St., ☎ 212/621–6800) houses a gigantic collection of 75,000 radio and TV shows, from the golden past to the present. The museum's library provides 96 consoles where you can watch or listen to whatever you wish for up to two hours at a time. The museum presents scheduled theater screenings, gallery exhibits, and series for children.

First-Run Houses

Suburban-style **multiscreen complexes** are all over town, even in such hip urban neighborhoods as SoHo (Houston and Mercer Sts.), the East Village (2nd Ave. at 12th St. and 3rd Ave. at 11th St.), the Flatiron District (890 Broadway, at 19th St.), and Hell's Kitchen (Worldwide Plaza, 320 W. 50th St.). Manhattan's most impressive multiplex movie house, **Sony Theatres Lincoln Square** (✉ Broadway and 68th St., ☎ 212/336–5000), has 12 state-of-the-art theaters designed to recall grand old movie palaces and an eight-story, 600-seat IMAX Theatre that is equipped not only for large-scale formatted films but also for 3-D imagery. *Across the Sea of Time,* an exciting journey into New York's past, is one of several short films on view at the IMAX Theatre.

The Lincoln Square theater has the illusion of the size and allure of movie houses of the past, but two New York theaters, both recently renovated, actual preserve this heritage. **The Ziegfeld** (✉ 141 W. 54th St., west of 6th Ave., ☎ 212/765–7600) has a huge screen, brilliant red decor, and an awesome sound system. **Radio City Music Hall** (✉ 1260 6th Ave., at 50th St., ☎ 212/247–4777) with its Art Deco setting, 34-ft-high screen, and 4,500-watt projector, is occasionally used for movie screenings (watch for an August film series).

Revival Houses

One of the best places to see old films in Manhattan is the **Walter Reade Theater** at Lincoln Center (✉ 70 Lincoln Center Plaza, Broadway at

65th St., ☎ 212/875–5600), operated by the Film Society of Lincoln Center. This comfortable movie house presents concurrent series devoted to the films of single nations, themes, or directors; movies for kids are featured on Saturday morning. Current mainstream movies are open-captioned for the deaf and shown once a month. The auditorium has excellent sight lines, and tickets can be purchased at the box office weeks in advance.

Revivals can also be found at:

American Museum of the Moving Image (✉ 35th Ave. at 36th St., Astoria, Queens, ☎ 718/784–0077) offers American film series, often in historical contexts. Programs also honor overlooked artists, such as cinematographers and screenwriters.

Anthology Film Archives (✉ 32 2nd Ave., at 2nd St., ☎ 212/505–5181) shows movies that have made a significant contribution to film history.

Film Forum (✉ 209 W. Houston St., ☎ 212/727–8110) has three screens showing often quirky films organized in series based on movie genres or directors and other film artists.

The Museum of Modern Art (✉ 11 W. 53rd St., ☎ 212/708–9480) includes rare classic films in its many excellent revival series. Tickets, free with the price of admission, are distributed at the main information desk in the lobby on the day of the performance (tickets for evening screenings are available beginning at 1; they often go fast).

Foreign and Independent Films

Between the interest generated by the New York Film Festival, the city's population of foreign executives and diplomats, a resident corps of independent filmmakers, and a large contingent of cosmopolitan cinemaniacs, there's always an audience here for foreign films and for innovative new American films and videos that buck the Hollywood currents. New York has several cinemas that more or less specialize in such films.

Angelika Film Center (✉ W. Houston and Mercer Sts., ☎ 212/995–2000) offers several screens devoted to offbeat independent and foreign films, as well as a lively café catering to a youthful crowd.

Anthology Film Archives (✉ 32 2nd Ave., at 2nd St., ☎ 212/505–5181) presents esoteric independent and foreign fare seldom shown elsewhere.

Cinema Village (✉ 12th St. between 5th Ave. and University Pl., ☎ 212/924–3363) schedules innovative independent features and occasional animation festivals. Programs concentrating on movies produced in Hong Kong are particularly popular.

Eastside Playhouse (✉ 919 3rd Ave., between 55th and 56th Sts., ☎ 212/755–3020) usually shows first-run art films.

Film Forum (✉ 209 W. Houston St., ☎ 212/727–8110) presents some of the best new independent films and hard-to-see foreign movies.

Lincoln Plaza (✉ Broadway between 62nd and 63rd Sts., ☎ 212/757–2280) has six cinemas playing long-run foreign and independent hits.

Millennium (✉ 66 E. 4th St., ☎ 212/673–0090) focuses on the avant-garde.

Quad Cinema (✉ 13th St. between 5th and 6th Aves., ☎ 212/255–8800) plays first-run art and foreign films on very small screens.

Screening Room (✉ 54 Varick St., at Canal St., ☎ 212/334–2100) screens provocative independent movies in a theater that adjoins a restaurant.

68th Street Playhouse (✉ 3rd Ave. at 68th St., ☎ 212/734–0302) has exclusive extended runs of critically acclaimed films.

Sony Paris (✉ 58th St. between 5th and 6th Aves., ☎ 212/980–5656) is an exquisite showcase for much-talked-about new American and foreign entries.

Village East Cinemas (✉ 2nd Ave. at 12th St., ☎ 212/529–6799) presents cutting-edge independent features alongside mainstream Hollywood productions.

Foreign and independent films and videos frequently run at cultural societies and museums around town, including the following:

Asia Society (✉ 725 Park Ave., at 70th St., ☎ 212/288–6400) shows excellent films from countries all over Asia.

The Brooklyn Museum of Art (✉ 200 Eastern Pkwy., Brooklyn, ☎ 718/638–5000) screens foreign films on Saturday afternoon.

French Institute (✉ Florence Gould Hall, 55 E. 59th St., ☎ 212/355–6160) presents retrospectives of French movies, often devoted to a particular theme or director.

Goethe House (✉ 1014 5th Ave., between 82nd and 83rd Sts., ☎ 212/439–8700) screens movies by leading German filmmakers.

Japan Society (✉ 333 47th St., between 8th and 9th Aves., ☎ 212/752–3015) focuses on Japanese films rarely available in other parts of the city.

The Museum of Modern Art (✉ 11 W. 53rd St., ☎ 212/708–9480) frequently shows foreign classics and hard-to-see independent films.

Whitney Museum of American Art (✉ Madison Ave. at 75th St., ☎ 212/570–3676) is a forum for experimental and independent films.

READINGS AND LECTURES

New York is the center of American publishing, and as a result many international writers—however reclusive—eventually find reason to come here, either to visit or to live. If you're interested in seeing the written word and catching a glimpse of the people who create books, a New York prose or poetry reading can be fun and is often inspirational. Readings unfold all over the city—in bookstores, libraries, museums, bars, and legitimate theaters—attracting debuting talents and some of the top names in contemporary literature, including such writers as John Updike, Don DeLillo, Toni Morrison, Frank McCourt, Philip Roth, Kazuo Ishiguro, and many others.

Poetry Calendar(✉ 611 Broadway, Suite 905, 10012, ☎ 212/260–7097), published monthly from September through June, provides extensive listings of prose and poetry readings around the city. The calendar is available by subscription or for free at several Manhattan bookstores. You can also check the listings of readings in *New York* magazine, the *New Yorker, Time Out New York,* and the *Village Voice.*

Authors, poets, lyricists, and playwrights take the stage at the **92nd St. Y** (✉ 1395 Lexington Ave., at 92nd St., ☎ 212/996–1100). **Symphony Space** (✉ Broadway at 95th St., ☎ 212/864–5400) holds a number of readings, including the Selected Shorts series of stories read by prominent actors. Manhattan Theatre Club sponsors **Writers in Performance** (✉ 131 W. 55th St., ☎ 212/399–3000), a provocative program of dramatic readings and roundtable discussions that showcase novelists, poets, and playwrights from the United States and abroad.

Downtown, rising young scribes appear at **Limbo** (✉ 47 Ave. A, between 3rd and 4th Sts., ☎ 212/477–5271), a coffee bar. **Dixon Place** (✉ 258 Bowery, between Houston and Prince Sts., ☎ 212/219–3088) and the **Kitchen** (✉ 512 W. 19th St., between 10th and 11th Aves., ☎ 212/255–5793) both sponsor readings regularly, some of which border on performance art.

Distinguished series of poetry readings are sponsored by several organizations in Manhattan, including the **Academy of American Poets** (✉ 580 Broadway, ☎ 212/274–0343), **Dia Center for the Arts** (✉ 548 W. 22nd St., ☎ 212/989–5566), the **Poetry Project** (✉ St. Mark's-in-the-Bowery Church, 131 E. 10th St., at 2nd Ave., ☎ 212/674–0910), **Poetry Society of America** (✉ 15 Gramercy Park S, ☎ 212/254–9628), and **Poets House** (✉ 72 Spring St., ☎ 212/431–7920).

Informal poetry readings, sometimes with an "open-mike" policy that allows audience members to read their own work, continue to crop up with frequency in New York City clubs and bars. These events are fairly popular, particularly with a younger crowd. There may be a low cover charge ($2–$5), and food and drink are usually available. Some reliable spots include **Biblio's** (✉ 317 Church St., ☎ 212/334–6990); **Ear Inn** (✉ 326 Spring St., ☎ 212/226–9060), on Saturday afternoon; **Cornelia Street Café** (✉ 29 Cornelia St., ☎ 212/989–9319); the **Knitting Factory** (✉ 74 Leonard St., ☎ 212/219–3055); and **Nuyorican Poets Café** (✉ 236 E. 3rd St., ☎ 212/505–8183), with a variety of multicultural poets scheduled weekly and their Poetry Slam competition each Friday (you may also find Latin jazz, comedy, and play readings here).

Many Manhattan bookstores organize evening readings by authors of recently published books. Best bets are **Barnes & Noble** (✉ 1280 Lexington Ave., at 86th St., ☎ 212/423–9900; ✉ Citicorp Bldg., 54th St. at 3rd Ave., ☎ 212/750–8033; ✉ 2289 Broadway, at 82nd St., ☎ 212/362–8835; ✉ 1960 Broadway, at 66th St., ☎ 212/595–6859; ✉ 605 5th Ave., at 48th St., ☎ 212/765–0590; ✉ 675 6th Ave., at 22nd St., ☎ 212/727–1227; ✉ 33 E. 17th St., at Union Sq., ☎ 212/253–0810; ✉ 4 Astor Pl., ☎ 212/420–1322); **Borders** (✉ 5 World Trade Center, ☎ 212/839–8049); **Posman Books** (✉ 1 University Pl., between Waverly Pl. and 8th St., ☎ 212/533–2665); **Rizzoli** (✉ 454 W. Broadway, between Prince and Houston Sts., ☎ 212/674–1616); **Shakespeare and Co.** (✉ 739 Lexington Ave., between 68th and 69th Sts., ☎ 212/570–0201), **Three Lives and Co.** (✉ 154 W. 10th St., at Waverly Pl., ☎ 212/741–2069); and **Tower Books** (✉ 383 Lafayette St., at 4th St., ☎ 212/228–5100). For readings by gay and lesbian authors, try **A Different Light** (✉ 151 W. 19th St., between 6th and 7th Aves., ☎ 212/989–4850).

A major reading and talk series is held at the **Lincoln Center Library for the Performing Arts** (☎ 212/870–1630), specializing in presentations by musicians, directors, singers, and actors. Several branches of the **New York Public Library** (NYPL) present lectures and reading events. A monthly calendar of free library readings is available at each branch.

At the **Metropolitan Museum of Art** (✉ 5th Ave. at 82nd St., ☎ 212/570–3949), seasonal lectures regularly draw sellout crowds. Artists and world-eminent art historians speak here.

6 Dining

With Coffee Bars and Cafés

Dining out is one of New York's greatest pleasures. Because of the city's prominence as an international financial and cultural center, you can easily sample a multitude of foreign cuisines in the span of a week as well as regional dishes from around the United States. Manhattan has a restaurant to suit any taste or pocketbook—from extravagant caviar and sushi bars to trendsetting TriBeCa haunts to affordable bistros, trattorias, coffee shops, and delis. If you're looking for innovative cuisine, you'll discover it prepared by some of the best chefs anywhere, yet you can find places that serve traditional meals as well.

By J. Walman

THESE ARE HEADY DAYS for New York diners. Food is one of the city's joys, and it may be that more restaurants are spreading more joy to more people than at any earlier time in its history. What's happened to make this a golden age for Big Apple gourmands? A constellation of reasons: A sustained boom on Wall Street continues to gild the pockets of many New Yorkers. Superstar chefs by the dozen, having turned their kitchens into shrines to invention, devise cutting-edge cuisine that everyone wants to be the first to taste—and they're garnering accolades and loyal followings in the process. Architects and designers are doing their part, creating environments of unprecedented bravura—a breathtakingly sumptuous dining room here, a dazzlingly abuzz communal dining table there—and generating for these spectacular settings as many oohs and ahs as the food they're meant to showcase. And out-of-towners by the millions are flooding into the city, in their largest numbers in decades, doing as the natives do—looking for the hottest seat at the hottest spot in town.

Of course, there'd be no restaurants if there weren't individuals willing to sacrifice great chunks of their lives to them—and today legions of creative entrepreneurs deserve attention. At the top of the heap, New York's most celebrated chefs now garner almost as much ink as Hollywood celebrities: Jean-Georges Vongerichten, Nobu Matsuhisa, Daniel Boulud, François Payard, Alfred Portale, Diane Forley, Matthew Kenney, Larry Forgione, Anne Rosenzweig, Gray Kunz—the list grows longer seemingly by the hour. Hundreds of sous chefs and apprentices who have cooked beside these and other masters have left their nests. Everyone has benefited from their journeys, as virtually every Manhattan neighborhood and many in Brooklyn and Queens now have at least one eatery where adventuresome and sometimes absolutely top-flight fare can be had, often in casual surroundings.

It's also worth remembering that thousands of the city's anonymous cooks, whose names never appear in the *Times,* are, like their more celebrated counterparts, immigrants, and they, too, contribute mightily to the life of the city's restaurants. The mix of small ethnic eating spots continues to change constantly, following shifting immigration patterns. Besides its hundreds of French, Italian, and Chinese eateries, New York today also offers hundreds, if not thousands of restaurants serving the foods of Afghanistan, Korea, Malaysia, Senegal, Spain, Thailand, Turkey, and Vietnam. Caribbean, Middle Eastern, and African cuisines are also well represented. Watch for more African-American restaurants opening in neighborhoods well beyond Harlem, as well as more restaurants devoted to a single region—the cuisines of Italy, France, and other European nations especially lend themselves to this specialization.

At the traditional end of the spectrum, hotel dining rooms are roaring back, and many high-profile restaurants are setting up within hotels—Le Cirque 2000 in the New York Palace is the most visible example. There's no end in sight to the bistro and trattoria craze—but no one's complaining, as many are as excellent as they are inexpensive and abundant. New York restaurateurs have gone clone-crazy: spinning off eat-alikes (Coco Pazzo, Coco Opera, and Coco Pazzo Teatro, for instance) faster than Starbucks can draw a *macchiato.* Wall Streeters and other highfliers are storming the city's outstanding dozen-plus steak houses. Kosher is easier to find than ever, with the appellation now preceding such diverse cuisines as Japanese, Persian, and Indian. Brazilian cuisine is playing a very fast game of catch-up—marvelous all-you-can eat barbecues called *churrascarias* are cropping up in Manhattan and

Queens. Microbreweries, wine/champagne/cigar bars, and club lounges are all now an integral part of the landscape, dissolving the distinction between restaurant and nightclub. Sports bars, theme restaurants, and other restaurants where the food is not the main attraction continue to proliferate, especially in and around a rejuvenated Times Square.

When it comes to breakfast, New York's best choices are not limited to so-called tablecloth restaurants. Dozens of Greek-owned coffee shops pride themselves on perfectly scrambled eggs, savory hash browns, and that New York institution, the toasted bagel. Chinatown's teahouses go nonstop from 8 AM till 5 PM, and Little Korea, a string of amazingly inexpensive possibilities centered on West 32nd Street between 5th and 7th avenues, is open around the clock. The coffeehouse explosion offers a civilized respite from Manhattan frenzy (☞ Coffee Bars and Cafés, *below*) day and night.

With the menus of many restaurants changing often (sometimes daily), the signature dish is becoming a thing of the past. It's the kitchen's style that counts, so if a dish described here sounds appealing but is no longer served, look for similar preparations or ingredients. Bottom line? Take a chance. Not every venture will be a success, but the whole experience will be rewarding. That's a promise.

Wine

New York won't disappoint on this score. Generally, the most expensive wines have the smallest markup, the mid-price spectrum offers the best values, and the least-expensive offerings are poor values. Half bottles are hard to find. Wine by the glass is ubiquitous—younger restaurants as well as old-timers offer serious vintages at sensible prices this way. If the wine list is large, have an aperitif and take your time in ordering. Remember: You're the buyer. Many restaurants allow you to bring your own bottle; virtually all charge a corkage fee from $5 to $25, but some are experimenting with discontinuing this surcharge.

Prices

The world of $15 appetizers, $35 entrées, and $10 desserts has arrived. Granted, only the very top tier of New York's restaurants can command such stratospheric prices, but the numbers that can continue to rise. Expect prices roughly half of these at hot spots serving all kinds of cuisines all over town. Ethnic eateries still generally offer the greatest opportunity to eat well for less than your monthly mortgage payment.

CATEGORY	COST*
$$$$	over $60
$$$	$40–$59
$$	$20–$39
$	under $20

**per person for a three-course meal, excluding drinks, service, and 8¼% sales tax*

Restaurants marked with a price range ($–$$, for example) include both modest restaurants where choosing the most expensive dishes can push your check into the next category and pricier restaurants where you can lower your tab by going for lunch or brunch rather than dinner, opting for the less expensive fare, or choosing a prix-fixe meal (although most prix-fixe menus don't include coffee or drinks).

One dining bargain has become a virtual New York institution. In 1991 gourmet restaurants came up with the idea of charging $19.91 for a prix-fixe lunch for one week in June. It was a huge success, and eight years later you can find $19.99 lunches (and some dinners) at restaurants throughout the city not only in June but year-round. One warning: Some restaurants making this special offer are greedy (and unfriendly), although others make it an outstanding value.

Rather than being sensibly attached to the menu, European-style, specials are often recited by the waiter with no mention of cost. So if you're watching your budget, always ask the price of specials and avoid an unexpectedly costly check.

Finally, always review your bill. Mistakes do occur (and not always in the restaurant's favor).

Tipping

Rules are simple. Never tip the maître d' unless you're out to impress your companion. In most restaurants, tip the waiter at least 15% to 20%. (To figure the amount quickly, just double the tax noted on the check—it's 8¼% of your bill—and round slightly up or down.) Tip at least $1 per coat checked.

Dress

Use common sense. Dress up for grand restaurants and wear neat but casual clothes for casual spots. Midtown is more conservative than residential neighborhoods, SoHo and TriBeCa trendier than the Upper East and Upper West sides. Shorts are appropriate only in summer and in the most casual spots. When in doubt, call ahead.

Reservations

Make a reservation. If you change your mind, cancel—it's only courteous. Tables can be hard to come by between 7 and 9, but if you eat early or late, you may be able to take advantage of a prix-fixe not offered at peak hours. Many restaurants will ask you to call the day before your scheduled meal to reconfirm: Remember to do so. If your original time isn't ideal, ask when you confirm if a better one has become available. Eating after a play or concert is quite common in New York, and there's no shortage of options. And don't be afraid to speak up if you prefer to sit in a certain area or if you want a special table. When you call, double-check that the service information listed below hasn't changed. Credit cards, hours of operation, chefs, and prices can be ephemeral.

Smoking

New York has one of the country's strictest smoking laws: Smoking is not allowed in most restaurants, though you may be able to smoke at the bar or at a table outdoors, if such seating is available; call ahead for details. Many restaurants have added areas for smoking cigars, and some establishments are devoted solely to this pastime. Cigar bars, a recent phenomenon, often stock a superb selection of single-malt Scotches, cognacs, wines, and champagnes along with elegant sandwiches, salads, tapas, caviar, or other snacks. Restaurant owners or patrons who break the smoking law are subject to a fine. Call 212/442–9666 for information or with complaints.

MANHATTAN RESTAURANTS

Lower Manhattan

New York grew from its base and went north, so it should be no surprise that history—coupled with finance, lower Manhattan's all-powerful engine—rather than gastronomy, is the order of the day here. Still, you can eat well by being selective.

American

$$ ✕ **Fraunces Tavern.** Opened as a tavern in 1762 by Samuel Fraunces, George Washington's steward, this Georgian brick landmark dates from 1719; George Washington delivered his farewell address to his officers here when the British evacuated New York (☞ Chapter 2). Today the place has a clubby bar and faithful Colonial decor; it's a nice spot for cocktails (they're rather good) and for basic eggs-bacon-and-oatmeal breakfasts. Any other time, stick to steaks or, on Wednesday, pot roast. ✉ *54 Pearl St., at Broad St.,* ☎ *212/269–0144. Reservations essential. AE, DC, MC, V. Closed weekends.*

Chinese

$$–$$$ ✕ **Au Mandarin.** One of the best bets in Manhattan for haute Chinese, this World Financial Center restaurant has a courtyard-like setting, an exotic fish tank, and classy furnishings. The dining experience combines a polished atmosphere with careful service. You might start with vegetarian dumplings or Shanghai buns, then move on to Shanghai prawns, followed by Peking duck, tangerine beef, or delicate rice noodles with julienne vegetables. ✉ *200–250 Vesey St. (World Financial Center),* ☎ *212/385–0313. AE, DC, MC, V.*

Contemporary

$$$–$$$$ ✕ **Hudson River Club.** Spacious wood-paneled rooms with paisley-print banquettes, spectacular views of the Hudson River and the Statue of Liberty, and a spirited bar with piano music distinguish this consistently top-flight World Financial Center restaurant. The kitchen celebrates Hudson River valley produce in such dishes as mint-cured apple-smoked salmon Napoleon and veal shank with horseradish mashed potatoes. Desserts—like the signature tower of chocolate (combining brownie, mousse, and meringue)—are edible sculptures, while the New York State cheese plate with walnut bread and nut muffins is a perfect foil to the magnificent wines from the regional American wine list. ✉ *4 World Financial Center, 250 Vesey St.,* ☎ *212/786–1500. Reservations essential. AE, DC, MC, V. No lunch Sat.*

$$$–$$$$ ★ ✕ **Windows on the World.** Pages dressed in rainbow colors and an impressive 38-ft-wide bead curtain await on the 107th floor of One World Trade Center—a fitting introduction to this monumental restaurant complex, with several entertaining options (☞ Chapter 8). In the intimate Cellar in the Sky, a prix-fixe dinner is served, accompanied by an optional selection of good wines. The 240-seat main dining room has artwork by Milton Glaser, banquettes upholstered in apricot, ceilings wrapped with origami fabric, and panoramic windows with stunning Manhattan views. Executive chef Michael Lomonaco turns out updated American fare: roasted vegetable salad ring with spiced walnuts and Winesap apples encrusted with white cheddar cheese, North Carolina roasted quail with black-truffle risotto and mushroom stew, and the decadent chocolate dome with brandied cherries. ✉ *1 World Trade Center, 107th floor,* ☎ *212/524–7011; 212/938–0030 for Cellar in the Sky. Reservations essential. Jacket required. AE, DC, MC, V.*

Seafood

$$ ✕ **Gianni's.** South Street Seaport is not noted for gastronomic excellence; this is its most earnest restaurant. Pastas, salads, out-of-the-ordinary sandwiches, and seafood work best. There's an outdoor café in summer. ✉ *15 Fulton St.,* ☎ *212/608–7300. AE, DC, MC, V.*

SoHo and TriBeCa

With the wonderful loft spaces available in SoHo and TriBeCa, restaurants here tend to be large and dramatic. It's arguably Manhattan's best dining district.

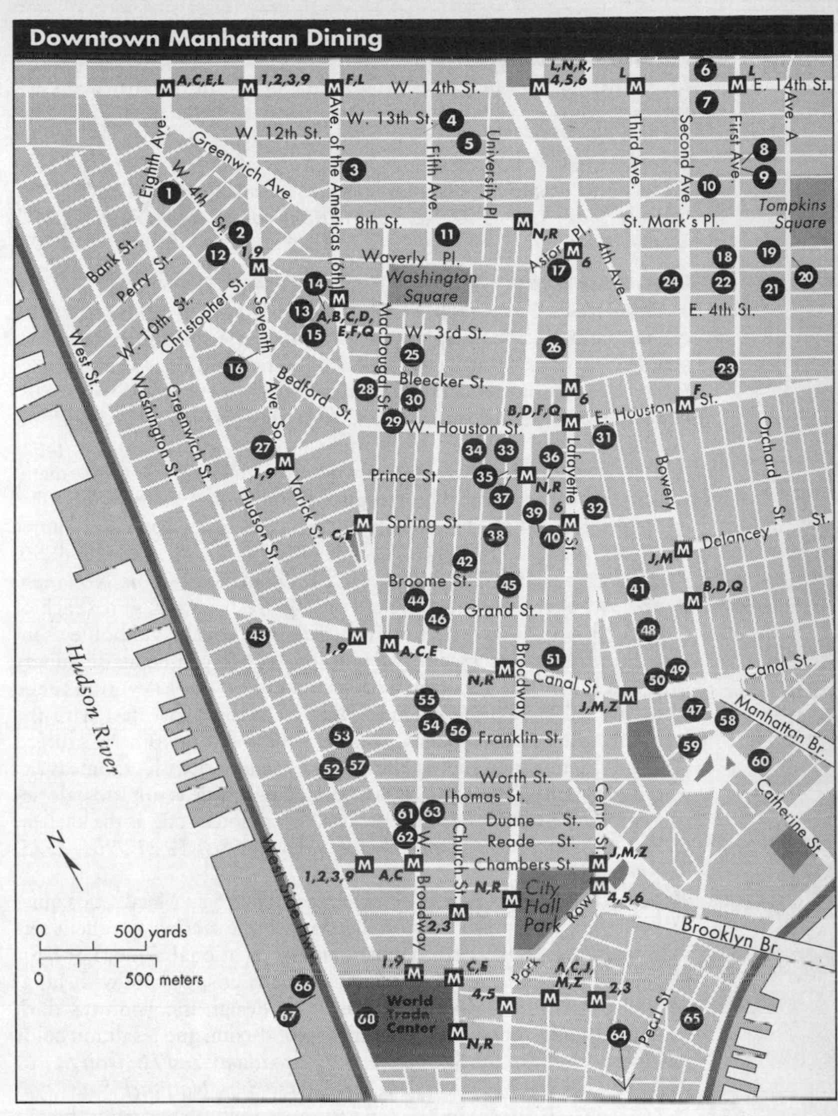

Acme Bar and Grill, **26**
Agrotikon, **7**
Arturo's, **29**
Au Mandarin, **67**
Ballato's, **31**
Balthazar, **39**
Boca Chica, **23**
Bouley Bakery, **62**
Brothers Bar-B-Q, **27**
Café Fès, **12**
Caffè Lure, **30**
Capsouto Frères, **43**
Casa La Femme, **34**
Cendrillon Asian Grill and Mamba Bar, **45**
Chanterelle, **57**
Chez Jacqueline, **28**
Clementine, **11**
Cornelia Street Café, **14**
Corsica, **1**
Da Nico, **41**
Drovers Tap Room, **13**
Duane Park Café, **61**
El Pollo, **42**
El Teddy's, **54**
Félix, **44**
First, **22**
Fraunces Tavern, **64**
French Roast, **3**
Gianni's, **65**
Global 33, **24**
Golden Unicorn, **60**
Gotham Bar & Grill, **5**
Grand Ticino, **25**
The Grange Hall, **16**
Home, **15**
Hudson River Club, **66**
Il Cortile, **50**
Indochine, **17**
Joe's Shanghai, **47**
Lanza Restaurant, **9**
Layla, **56**
Le Jardin Bistro, **32**
Lucky Strike, **46**
Manila Garden, **6**
Match, **33**
Mirezi, **4**
Montrachet, **55**
Monzù, **35**
Moomba, **2**
New York Noodletown, **58**
Nobu, **53**
Odeon, **63**
Pacifica, **51**
Penang SoHo, **38**
Pisces, **20**
Roettelle A. G., **19**
Sal Anthony's S.P.Q.R., **48**
Savoy, **36**
Second Avenue Deli, **10**
Spring Street Natural Restaurant & Bar, **40**
Sweet 'n' Tart Cafe, **49**
Takahachi, **21**
Teresa's, **18**
Tribeca Grill, **52**
20 Mott Street, **59**
Windows On The World, **68**
Xunta,**8**
Zoë, **37**

American/Casual

$–$$ ✕ **Lucky Strike.** One of Manhattan's funkiest small restaurants, this unadorned SoHo boîte doesn't look like much. In the crowded back room, specials and available wines are written on wall mirrors. Homemade bread (and great bread pudding) excels, as does steak and *pommes frîtes* (french fries). A young, hip crowd mobs the bar (☞ Chapter 8). ✉ *59 Grand St., between Wooster St. and W. Broadway,* ☎ *212/941–0479 or 212/941–0772. Reservations not accepted. AE, DC, MC, V.*

Contemporary

$$$$ ★ ✕ **Chanterelle.** Soft peach walls, luxuriously spaced tables, towering ceilings, and glorious displays of flowers set the stage for what is arguably New York's finest new American restaurant. Unassuming, flawless service complements chef David Waltuck's meticulously prepared, beautifully presented inventions. Although the signature seafood sausage, charred on the outside and succulent within, and the Japanese-style raw seafood are both always available, the rest of the menu is dictated by the season. The exceptional sommelier can help find value in the discriminating, beautifully chosen wine list. Lunch and dinner are prix fixe. ✉ *2 Harrison St., near Hudson St.,* ☎ *212/966–6960. Reservations essential. AE, DC, MC, V. Closed Sun.–Mon. No lunch.*

$$$–$$$$ ✕ **Bouley Bakery.** Under a vaulted ceiling, fresh flowers grace each of the 12 enormously coveted tables at celebrated chef David Bouley's informally elegant bakery-cum-restaurant. Service can be maddeningly slow, but the results are often worth the wait. Bouley's devotion to the freshest local (and often organic) produce is most manifest with the sparkling clams and oysters. Unlikely combinations like a sautéed skate with fennel and figs or thin rings of calamari with crabmeat exemplify his innovative style. A hot chocolate soufflé is not too calorie-packed to end a meal. The wine list, alas, isn't as interesting as the kitchen. ✉ *120 W. Broadway, between Duane and Reade Sts.,* ☎ *212/964–2525. AE, DC, MC, V.*

$$$ ✕ **Duane Park Café.** Owned by its Japanese chef, Seiji Maeda, this quiet TriBeCa find can spoil you with its comfortable seating, excellent service, serious but fairly priced wines, and international menu. Look for marinated duck and arugula salad as well as crispy skate with Japanese-inspired *ponzu* sauce. The pleasing design incorporates dark columns, maple-veneered walls, cherrywood-trim, and a salmon color scheme. ✉ *157 Duane St., between W. Broadway and Hudson St.,* ☎ *212/732–5555. AE, D, DC, MC, V. Closed Sun. No lunch Sat.*

$$$ ✕ **Tribeca Grill.** Subtly lighted and anchored by the bar from the old Maxwell's Plum, this cavernous brick-walled restaurant displays art by the late Robert De Niro Sr. who opened it with various celebrity partners and now owns it with Montrachet's Drew Nieporent. The best dishes are the simplest ones—crisp fried oysters with anchovy aioli and herb-crusted rack of lamb with oven-roasted vegetables; desserts are amicable (try banana tart with milk-chocolate ice cream), as is the staff. ✉ *375 Greenwich St., near Franklin St.,* ☎ *212/941–3900. Reservations essential. AE, DC, MC, V. No lunch Sat.*

$$$ ✕ **Zoë.** Thalia and Stephen Loffredo's colorful, high-ceiling SoHo eatery with cast-iron columns and terra-cotta floor has an open kitchen that produces impressive food, such as grilled yellowfin tuna on wok-charred vegetables. Zoë also has an exceptionally well-organized wine list and a fine group of carefully tended wines by the glass. This is one of Manhattan's better places for weekend brunch. ✉ *90 Prince St., between Broadway and Mercer St.,* ☎ *212/966–6722. Reservations essential. AE, DC, MC, V.*

$\$\$–\$\$\$$ ★ ✕ **Savoy.** Chef-owner Peter Hoffman serves an eclectic mix of dishes inspired by the Mediterranean regions and Latin America in this cozy houselike restaurant on a quiet cobblestone corner. A bronze wire-mesh ceiling, and arched wood lend the downstairs space an arts-and-crafts feel, the perfect setting for such down-to-earth dishes as baby chicken with Moroccan sausage or penne with rabbit. Upstairs, the original tin ceiling, artwork, and open hearth are the backdrop to a nightly prix fixe menu, which includes a special grilled dish (meat, fish, or poultry), gussied up with attractive vegetable garnishes and contemporary sauces (butter and cream free). The wine list emphasizes small producers from Italy, France, California, and South America. ✉ *70 Prince St., at Crosby St.,* ☎ *212/219–8570. Reservations essential. AE.*

$\$\$$ ✕ **Match.** This bi-level restaurant-lounge is hot enough to scorch the heels of a fire walker. Open beams and machine fixtures, blond-wood paneling, and snug booths hugging the wall preserve the memory of the building's industrial past (Match is housed in the former home of New York's oldest electrical company). The dim sum platter excels, while the raw bar teems with fabulous presentations of fresh shellfish, sushi, sashimi, and caviar. There's also a **Match Uptown** (✉ 33 E. 60th St., between Park and Madison Aves., ☎ 212/906–9173). ✉ *160 Mercer St., between Houston and Prince Sts.,* ☎ *212/343–0020. AE, MC, V.*

$\$\$$ ✕ **Odeon.** Established in 1980, this was downtown's first destination restaurant, and it's still one of the neighborhood's best. Neon, vinyl banquettes, and Formica tables make for a striking art deco setting, and the pleasant service, relatively low prices, and well-chosen wine list are all pluses. Tantalizing options include crab-and-potato fritters with soy-daikon sauce, and grilled lamb and leek sandwich on country bread. ✉ *145 W. Broadway, at Thomas St.,* ☎ *212/233–0507. AE, DC, MC, V.*

French

$\$\$\$–\$\$\$\$$ ★ ✕ **Montrachet.** Enterprising restaurateur Drew Nieporent's trendsetting first restaurant (☞ Tribeca Grill, *above, and* Layla *and* Nobu, *below*), still one of New York's finest, keeps the food at center stage. Pastel walls, plush mauve banquettes, and engaging works of art set an unpretentious tone. Two three-course menus as well as a five-course tasting affair are offered. For a satisfying dinner, start with rabbit salad with roasted peppers, then try the signature truffle-crusted salmon in red-wine fumé, and finish off with the puddinglike banana-chocolate gratin, quickly finished under the grill. The distinguished wine list emphasizes diminutive regional vineyards. Bargain hunters take note: A $19.99 lunch is offered on Friday year-round. ✉ *239 W. Broadway, between Walker and White Sts.,* ☎ *212/219–2777. Reservations essential. AE. Closed Sun. No lunch Mon.–Thurs. or Sat.*

$\$\$\$$ ★ ✕ **Balthazar.** This SoHo brasserie is currently one of the most difficult reservations to score in town. Restaurant impresario Keith McNally (of Pravda and the Odeon) has gone to extraordinary lengths to create a direct-from-Paris appearance whose authenticity will stop you dead in your tracks: red canvas awnings, gold-and-black decal writing on the windows, wall-filling framed mirrors, marble-top tables. Despite the need to placate a steady stream of celebrities, average diners are treated quite well. Nightly specials are based on classic French dishes; Tuesday it's *choucroute garni* (veal and garlic sausages, smoked meats, sauerkraut, and spices, among other ingredients, all simmered in white Alsatian wine). The chicken sauté with spaetzle and vegetables is flavorful and generous. Wonderful bread is baked in the restaurant's own bakery; you can ask to take home what's left in your bread basket or buy some at the tiny bakery next door. Prices are not exorbitant by today's standards, and the wine list is fair. ✉ *80 Spring St., between Broadway and Crosby St.,* ☎ *212/965–1414. Reservations essential. AE, DC, MC, V. No lunch Mon.*

$$–$$$ ★ ✕ **Capsouto Frères.** You'd never guess this romantic spot with exposed brick walls, tall columns, and wooden floors was once a warehouse. With its top-notch service, classical music, and interesting wine specials, this 1891 TriBeCa landmark is also a winner. Chef Charles Tutino prepares classics with a solid, contemporary touch—for instance, terrine Provençale and Peking duck in cassis-ginger sauce. Dessert soufflés around town pale against the light, delicious versions here. ✉ *451 Washington St., near Watts St.,* ☎ *212/966–4900. Reservations essential. AE, DC, MC, V. No lunch Mon.*

$$ ★ ✕ **Caffé Lure.** The small, rough, and raffish room has a tin ceiling, tables topped with brown paper and flacons of water, and walls festooned with vintage advertising signs and the fishing lures that give this spot its name. Seafood gets top billing—try baby lobster with spinach and port sauce or roast monkfish with black-olive pureed potatoes and mushrooms. You can also enjoy outstanding brick-oven pizza. Owner Jean Claude Iacovelli earned his stripes at Bouley. ✉ *169 Sullivan St., between Houston and Bleecker Sts.,* ☎ *212/473–2642. No credit cards.*

$–$$ ✕ **Félix.** No, you haven't traveled 3,000 mi to Paris's Left Bank; this charming bistro is in SoHo, a taxi ride from midtown. Whether you dine inside or alfresco, the service is friendly and the contemporary bistro fare is attractively presented. Try the steak with thin, crunchy french fries. ✉ *340 W. Broadway, at Grand St.,* ☎ *212/431–0021. AE. No lunch Mon.*

$–$$ ✕ **Le Jardin Bistro.** Gerard and Pamela Maurice's welcoming house with a lovely garden and grape arbor belongs in a small French village. There's no pretension—just hearty portions of French food. A tin ceiling, ceiling fans, an antique mirror, and lace café curtains grace the small, charming interior. Light and grease-free pommes frîtes accompany the fine steak tartare. You can't go wrong with any of the pleasant house wines or homemade desserts. ✉ *25 Cleveland Pl., near Spring St.,* ☎ *212/343–9599. Reservations essential. AE, DC, MC, V.*

Health

$–$$ ✕ **Spring Street Natural Restaurant and Bar.** Ceiling fans, overhead globe lights, wooden floors, and a long bar gussy up the big, open room of this comfortable restaurant, which you needn't be a health nut to appreciate. Two vegetarian dishes are standouts: corn-fried organic *seitan* (also known as *wheat meat*), in two dipping sauces, and a crispy tempeh. The desserts are heavenly yet healthy. ✉ *62 Spring St., at Lafayette St.,* ☎ *212/966–0290. AE, DC, MC, V.*

Italian

$$$ ✕ **Monzù.** Under the Guggenheim Museum SoHo, Monzù (the name refers to what chefs were once called on traditional Sicilian estates) is an airy, spacious, casually elegant restaurant. Each of the various dining areas, including a wine-cellarlike alcove, has an intimate feel. Executive chef Matthew Kenney re-interprets Sicilian cooking with panache. Homemade flat bread, sea urchin on *bruschetta,* and linguine with cauliflower, currants, pine nuts, and first-press olive oil give some idea of the expansiveness of the menu. For dessert go for the homemade cookies, risotto gelato, or *sorbetto.* ✉ *142 Mercer St., at Prince St.,* ☎ *212/343–0333. Reservations essential. AE, MC, V.*

Japanese

$$$$ ★ ✕ **Nobu.** A curved wall of river-worn black pebbles, bare wood tables, birch trees, and a hand-painted beech floor set an appropriately dramatic stage at this scorchingly hot spot, the brightest star in Drew Nieporent's constellation. Nobu Matsuhisa is the enormously celebrated chef (he also presides over restaurants in Los Angeles and London). It's difficult to decide in which direction to go on his menu: rock-shrimp tempura, black cod with miso, new-style sashimi—all are tours de force. The tiny onyx-face sushi bar is perfect for solo diners. Sake is the drink of choice. The only drawback: It's extremely difficult to get a reservation. ✉ *105 Hudson St., off Franklin St.,* ☎ *212/219–0500 or 212/219–8095 for same-day reservations. Reservations essential. AE, DC, MC, V. Closed Sun. No lunch.*

Latin

$ ✕ **El Pollo.** The ceiling soars above mission-style tables and chairs and walls decorated with Peruvian carvings and oil paintings in this SoHo trilevel eatery. The menu, a good introduction to Peruvian cuisine, includes such specialties as whole chicken, marinated in garlic, wine, pepper, lemon, oregano, vinegar, and spices, and then rotisserie-roasted. For an appetizer, try the traditional cold potatoes, prepared in a zesty cheese sauce. El Pollo has an unassuming **uptown counterpart** (✉ 1746 1st Ave., between 90th and 91st Sts., ☎ 212/996–7810). ✉ *482 Broome St., at Wooster St.,* ☎ *212/431–5666. AE, DC, MC, V.*

Malaysian

$$ ✕ **Penang SoHo.** With a dramatic waterfall, palm trees and tropical flowers, bar seat backs made of hoe handles, and individual huts that accommodate small groups, Penang is a Technicolor fantasy. The menu includes such relatively authentic culinary masterpieces as *sarang burung* (fried taro filled with scallops, squid, shrimp, and vegetables). For dessert try the pancake filled with ground peanuts and sweet corn. *See also* Penang Columbus on the Upper West Side, *below.* ✉ *109 Spring St., between Greene and Mercer Sts.,* ☎ *212/274–8883. AE, MC, V.*

Mexican

$$ ✕ **El Teddy's.** With its mirrors, tiles, glitter, and grotesque use of colors, this is a Mexican restaurant like no other. The margaritas get high marks, and the food is mostly wonderful, revealing both authentic Mexican subtleties and contemporary creativity, from the smoked chicken and goat-cheese quesadilla to the grilled rare yellowfin tuna. Almond flan and flourless chocolate cake top the roster of inventive desserts. ✉ *219 W. Broadway, between Franklin and White Sts.,* ☎ *212/941–7070. Reservations essential. AE, MC, V. No lunch weekends.*

Middle Eastern

$$$ ✕ **Layla.** Mosaics made of pottery shards form exotic collages within this leviathan space, a campy takeoff on the Middle East. Owned by Drew Nieporent (☞ Tribeca Grill, Nobu, *and* Montrachet, *above*) and actor Robert De Niro, it's complete with live belly dancers and lifelike mannequins of hookah smokers. Try the chef's feast, consisting of various hot and cold Middle Eastern appetizers such as stuffed baby calamari and sardines wrapped in phyllo to dip in black-olive oil. ✉ *211 W. Broadway, at Franklin St.,* ☎ *212/431–0700. Reservations essential. AE, DC, MC, V. No lunch weekends.*

$$–$$$ ✕ **Casa La Femme.** Currently the theme is Egyptian in this enterprising restaurant, with burgundy banquettes and tables under flowing white tents. But every six months the theme changes, and so does the decor and the menu, so you never know what you'll find. In season there's a sidewalk café. Recent standout dishes include meze, the Middle Eastern equivalent of mixed hors d'oeuvres, and the vegetarian version of

the spicy Moroccan stew known as *tagine.* ✉ *150 Wooster St., between Houston and Prince Sts.,* ☎ *212/505–0005. AE, DC, MC, V.*

Philippine

$$ ★ ✕ **Cendrillon Asian Grill and Marimba Bar.** Cendrillon means Cinderella in French, so the slipper-shape bar is apropos, as is the delicacy of the inlay designs in the beautiful wood tables that punctuate the dining room, which is full of exposed red brick. Don't miss the spring rolls, Asian barbecues (duck, spareribs, chicken), black rice salad, and adobo—the national dish of the Philippines, prepared here with quail and rabbit in the traditional vinegar and garlic sauce. ✉ *45 Mercer St., between Broome and Grand Sts.,* ☎ *212/343–9012. AE, DC, MC, V. Closed Sun.*

Chinatown, Little Italy, Lower East Side, and Nolita

Chinatown has all but overtaken Little Italy on its southern flank, while in the last year or so the newly christened Nolita has begun to bleed into the neighborhood from Houston Street, at its northern border. Chinatown has treasures galore; Little Italy, mostly old-fashioned bulwarks of *cucina tradizionale;* Nolita, an eclectic, quickly developing mix of mostly tiny places; the Lower East Side, slightly cheaper options.

Chinese

$$ ✕ **Golden Unicorn.** If you're dining en masse and can pay three days in advance, consider this Hong Kong–style restaurant for its outstanding 12-course banquet—a real bargain if shared by 10. Served in a small private room, it may include such dishes as roast suckling pig, scallops and seafood in a noodle nest, whole steamed fish, fried rice with raisins, lobster with ginger, and unusual desserts based on warm or chilled fruit or rice soups. For something less elaborate, sit in the regular dining room and order à la carte. ✉ *18 E. Broadway, at Catherine St.,* ☎ *212/941–0911. AE, MC, V.*

$$ ✕ **Pacifica.** Knowledgeable people crowd this elegant sleeper, one of Chinatown's best-kept secrets, on the second floor of the Holiday Inn Downtown (☞ Greenwich Village, SoHo, Chinatown, *in* Chapter 7). Ignore the pastas and choose from the selection of simple classics, including fresh fish from the tank (prepared in a variety of styles) and heady dessert soups. The dim sum is some of Manhattan's finest. ✉ *138 Lafayette St., between Canal and Howard Sts.,* ☎ *212/941–4168. AE, DC, MC, V.*

$$ ★ ✕ **20 Mott Street.** An excellent choice for dim sum, this neat if nondescript three-story restaurant has above-average service (though it helps to have someone who speaks Chinese in your party). To get food that's authentic, you must insist on it (look around and point); when you do, you may be served fabulous steamed dumplings or deep-fried eel with orange peel and spicy XO sauce (a Hong Kong specialty that's rare here)—or different but equally novel dishes. ✉ *20 Mott St., between Bowery and Pell St.,* ☎ *212/964–0380. AE, MC, V.*

$–$$ ✕ **New York Noodletown.** With its window full of hanging cooked ducks, this unassuming spot remains one of Chinatown's best small restaurants. Its soup and noodles are unbeatable—try the delicious shrimp, Chinese greens, and soft egg noodles served in a seafood broth. Watch what you order—if you're not careful, you can spend more than the no-nonsense coffee-shop decor suggests. Solo diners may end up at a communal table. ✉ *28½ Bowery, at Bayard St.,* ☎ *212/349–0923. Reservations not accepted. No credit cards.*

$ ★ ✕ **Joe's Shanghai.** Joe's Shanghai started in Queens, but buoyed by the accolades accorded its dumplings, which contain not only ground pork or crab but also piping-hot broth—it's now in Manhattan, too.

Also recommended are Shanghai fried flat noodles—long, winding doughy miracles served in an intense brown sauce—and stewed pork balls, big puffy blobs of meats embellished with steamed baby Chinese cabbage. The unadorned room is clean and modern. ✉ *9 Pell St., between Bowery and Mott St.,* ☎ *212/233–8888. No credit cards.*

$ ✕ **Sweet 'n' Tart Cafe.** Furnished with Formica tables and a counter resembling the inside of a pink seashell, this rathskeller snack shop serves some 20 curative soups: little white bowls composed of such exotica as quail eggs, almonds and Asian pears, snow fungi, and spooky-sounding herbs that actually taste quite wonderful. *Congee,* the porridgelike concoction eaten for breakfast in Hong Kong, is another must-try—especially if accompanied by a terrific sugarless cruller. Dim sum and fresh-fruit shakes are also available. ✉ *76 Mott St., at Canal St.,* ☎ *212/334–8088. No credit cards.*

Italian

$$–$$$ ✕ **Il Cortile.** With its statues, brick wall, sprays of fresh flowers, and skylit courtyard, the setting resembles an Italian palazzo. Rack of veal de Georgio, made with sausage, herbs, and prosciutto sauce, is the house specialty. ✉ *125 Mulberry St., between Canal and Hester Sts.,* ☎ *212/226–6060. Reservations essential. AE, DC, MC, V.*

$$ ✕ **Ballato's.** A Mark Kostabi painting, red-oak floors, and an enclosed garden create an atmospheric setting for the well-prepared food at this old-timer. The menu's earthy pastas and daily specials give good value; Ballato's tripe, prepared in a superb marinara sauce, is particularly worth trying. ✉ *55 E. Houston St., between Mott and Mulberry Sts.,* ☎ *212/274–8881. AE, DC, MC, V. No lunch Sun.*

$$ ✕ **Da Nico.** Outstanding rotisserie grills and charred thin-crust coal-oven pizza distinguish this Little Italy restaurant. Delicious roast chicken and any of the delectable pizzas can be savored up front by the marble bar or in the comfortable back room, which has a skylight. ✉ *164 Mulberry St., between Grand and Broome Sts.,* ☎ *212/343–1212. AE, DC, MC, V.*

$$ ✕ **Sal Anthony's S.P.Q.R.** This inviting spot with spacious tables and lots of brick and fresh flowers is one of the few restaurants with good food in Little Italy, an area noted more for fun than food. In addition to the good pasta, there's a terrific veal chop and a phenomenal cheesecake. ✉ *133 Mulberry St., between Hester and Grand Sts.,* ☎ *212/925–3120. AE, DC, MC, V.*

East Village and NoHo

The East Village, no longer the province of New York University students, artists, and immigrants, is an increasingly upscale downtown neighborhood with nightspots and restaurants that attract patrons from all over the city. NoHo (*No*rth of *Ho*uston Street), a transitional area between the East and West villages, has benefited from the rise in retail activity along Broadway between 14th and Houston streets.

American

$$ ✕ **First.** The only surprising thing about this quintessentially elegant New York milieu—hammered-metal tables juxtaposed against horseshoe-shape silk banquettes, with photographs shot by locals hanging at the bar—is that it's in the heart of the still-funky East Village. The open kitchen turns out intriguing American fare, with amusing presentations like tiny 'tinis (baby martinis) and s'mores served with a miniature hibachi, interspersed with great crab cakes and one of the best pork chops in town. Several fine vintages from the carefully chosen wine list are available by the glass. Late hours prevail, and on Sunday there's a fun brunch and a one-of-a-kind roast suckling pig dinner. ✉ *87 1st*

Ave., between 5th and 6th Sts., ☎ 212/674–3823. Reservations essential. AE, MC, V. No lunch.

$ ✕ **Acme Bar and Grill.** Chicago blues and jazz blast from the sound system, and bottles of hot sauce line the shelves at this boisterous NoHo eatery. The appropriately Cajun-influenced menu embraces chicken, ribs, crab cakes, catfish, and shrimp—either steamed in Old Bay spice, barbecued, or blackened. The coleslaw, a mix of different colored cabbages and onions all coarsely cut and blended with mayo, is worth a detour. ✉ *9 Great Jones St., between Broadway and Lafayette St., ☎ 212/420–1934. DC, MC, V.*

Contemporary

$$ ✕ **Global 33.** With vinyl, pewter, Lucite, and cast-concrete decor, this ultrahip restaurant looks like an airport lounge furnished by Bloomingdale's. Would-be jet-setters can enjoy generous retro cocktails and tapas-size goodies. Even the blasting music becomes tolerable when you try the luscious herbed rack of lamb with mashed potatoes, followed by chocolate espresso torte. ✉ *93 2nd Ave., between 5th and 6th Sts., ☎ 212/477–8427. AE. No lunch.*

Delicatessens

$–$$ ✕ **Second Avenue Deli.** Hollywood-style squares embedded in the sidewalk outside and memorabilia inside commemorate the stage luminaries who performed at the Yiddish-language theaters that once reigned along this stretch of 2nd Avenue. The deli's bevy of Central and Eastern European classics includes chicken in the pot, matzo ball soup, chopped liver, Romanian tenderloin, and *cholent* (a dish of meat, beans, and grain). ✉ *156 2nd Ave., at 10th St., ☎ 212/677–0606. AE.*

Eastern European

$ ✕ **Teresa's.** Homesick Poles mix with cost-conscious students at this Polish luncheonette. Comfort your tummy with *bigos,* the Polish national stew—sauerkraut layered with fresh and smoked meats and sausage—and the hearty, stick-to-the-ribs dumplings known as pierogi, filled with meat, fish, cheese, or mushrooms, boiled or fried and served with sour cream. ✉ *103 1st Ave., between 6th and 7th Sts., ☎ 212/228–0604. No credit cards.*

Greek

$–$$ ★ ✕ **Agrotikon.** Designed by artist Anna Lascari, this immaculate white, blue, and green dining room with two fireplaces has been whimsically decorated with decals of fruit and tiny blue fish. Owner and executive chef Kostis Tsingas oversees the most inventive Greek restaurant in Manhattan. Baby calamari meatballs and whole red snapper served with dandelion greens are standouts. ✉ *322 E. 14th St., ☎ 212/473–2602. AE, DC, MC, V. Closed Mon.*

Italian

$ ✕ **Lanza Restaurant.** From it decor—large wall paintings, ceiling fans, and an inviting garden—to its menu—traditional antipasti, pastas, and desserts, Lanza's evokes an Italian trattoria more faithfully than anywhere else in the East Village. The three-course fixed-price ($12) menu, offered nightly after 9, makes this one of Manhattan's greatest restaurant bargains and a spot worth seeking out. ✉ *168 1st Ave., between 10th and 11th Sts., ☎ 212/674–7014. AE, DC, MC, V.*

Japanese

$ ★ ✕ **Takahachi.** One of Manhattan's least expensive but best small Japanese restaurants, Takahachi serves terrific fresh sushi plus such distinctive dishes as seared tuna with black pepper and mustard sauce; bravura daily specials are not to be missed. The early bird special, served until 7, is a bargain, but they take no reservations. ✉ *85 Ave. A, between 5th and 6th Sts.,* ☎ *212/505–6524. AE, MC, V. No lunch.*

Latin

$ ★ ✕ **Boca Chica.** Assertively seasoned food from several Latin American nations at giveaway prices is the forte of this raffish East Villager. Start with a potent *caipirinha* (Brazilian rum, lime juice, and sugar). Check out the plantains, served as croquettes or filled with spicy meat; the soupy Puerto Rican chicken-rice stew; or the Cuban sandwiches, which blend roast pork, ham, and pickles. Lively music and dancing have their way on weekends, and watch your step—there's often an equally lively boa constrictor by the bar. ✉ *13 1st Ave., at 1st St.,* ☎ *212/473–0108. AE, DC, MC, V. No lunch Mon.–Sat.*

Philippine

$ ✕ **Manila Garden.** A grand piano, a seasonal garden, and fresh orchids on every table complement the authentic Philippine cuisine, which combines Asian and Spanish flavors. On Tuesday, you can take advantage of the bargain buffet at lunch and dinner. Other times, enjoy wonderful *lechon* (roasted pig), *lumpia* Shanghai (pork egg roll), and chicken adobo. For dessert order the flan, which is richer than its Spanish counterpart, or *halo halo* (ice cream topped with fruit). ✉ *325 E. 14th St., between 1st and 2nd Aves.,* ☎ *212/777–6314. AE, DC, MC, V.*

Seafood

$$ ✕ **Pisces.** Pisces's arrival on Avenue A in 1993 heralded the arrival of the eastward-moving gentrifying forces into Alphabet City. Its sophisticated menu, reasonable prices, and, weather permitting, outdoor café seating and floor-to-ceiling windows that turn the entire restaurant into an alfresco setting all make this a worthwhile destination. Brunch is served on weekends; a two-course early bird prix-fixe at dinner (until 7 weeknights, 6:30 weekends) is worth seeking out. ✉ *95 Ave. A, at 6th St.,* ☎ *212/260–6660. AE, DC, MC, V. No lunch weekdays.*

Spanish

$ ✕ **Xunta.** Fishnets cover the ceiling of this dining room where dried peppers fringe the brick bar and seating is on high stools at tables made of wine barrels. Of the 32 tapas, don't miss the superb tortilla *española con cebolla* (classic potato omelet with onions). Other good bets: grilled shrimp, tuna or codfish empanadas, and sautéed *cigalas* (a shellfish in white wine and tomato sauce). ✉ *174 1st Ave., between 10th and 11th Sts.,* ☎ *212/614–0620. AE, DC, MC, V.*

Swiss

$ ★ ✕ **Roettelle A. G.** This charming East Village town house's dining rooms, with hidden nooks, cozy bar, and garden arbor, are all ideal places to savor hearty Swiss fare and wine. House specialties include *viande de Grisons* (Swiss dried beef), raclette (mild melted cheese served with boiled potatoes and tiny pickles), and delicious sauerbraten with spaetzle and red cabbage. Apple strudel and Linzer torte are exceptionally good desserts. The two-course fixed-price dinner is a bargain. ✉ *126 E. 7th St., between 1st Ave. and Ave. A,* ☎ *212/674–4140. Reservations essential. AE, D, DC, MC, V. Closed Sun.*

Vietnamese

$$ ★ ✕ **Indochine.** Palm leafs painted on cream-color walls, black-and-white tile floors, mirrors, leather banquettes, and live palm trees team up with some of the most fascinating food this side of Saigon. Select from among such savory soups as *pho* (sliced fillet of beef, rice noodles, bean sprouts) and *noum protchok namya* (fish, scallops, shrimp, coconut milk, and rice vermicelli). The *banh cuon* (steamed Viet-

namese ravioli filled with chicken, shiitake, and bean sprouts) is celestial. ✉ *430 Lafayette St., between 4th St. and Astor Pl.,* ☎ *212/505–5111. Reservations essential. AE, DC, MC, V. No lunch.*

Greenwich Village

Restaurants in the Village have long been more noted for their atmosphere than for their cuisine. But culinary interest is blooming in areas such as Cornelia Street, full of quaint bistros, oyster bars, North African dives and just about everything in between. Stroll around the neighborhood and take potluck—you can't go too far wrong.

American

$$ ✕ **Cornelia Street Café.** For a real Left Bank atmosphere, you can't beat this intimate artist-owned restaurant with a working fireplace and exposed brick walls hung with antique farm implements. Start with a light-as-a-feather quiche, studded with roasted fennel and ham and enriched with cheddar cheese, accompanied by an excellent mesclùn salad—a meal in itself. The garlic and rosemary roasted chicken is delivered crisp with terrific mashed potatoes and broccoli, and the cornmeal-coated fried catfish comes in a roasted tomato and caper sauce, with lovely grilled green and yellow squash and fluffy brown rice. There's a jazz club downstairs. ✉ *29 Cornelia St., between Bleecker and W. 4th Sts.,* ☎ *212/989–9319. AE, DC, MC, V.*

$$ ✕ **Drovers Tap Room.** A red tin ceiling and walls hung with chef-owner David Page's family snapshots set the stage for his honest, Midwestern-style food. The bar pours generous and inventive house cocktails; the affordable, wine list includes interesting offerings from New York State. Notable entrées include country-style pork ribs with smoked onion, bourbon barbecue sauce, baked beans and coleslaw, and daily specials such as the roasted Long Island duckling with slow-cooked cabbage. Don't leave without sampling the homemade desserts, especially the drop-dead butterscotch pudding. ✉ *9 Jones St., between Bleecker and W. 4th Sts.,* ☎ *212/627–1233. AE, MC, V.*

$$ ✕ **Home.** In this sliver of a storefront restaurant, David Page (☞ Drovers Tap Room, *above*) cooks with rare authority and honesty, utilizing recipes from his Midwestern background. Check out the superb blue cheese fondue with caramelized shallots and rosemary toast and the moist roast chicken and spiced onion rings. The creamy chocolate pudding and homemade cookies won't disappoint. Home also offers an interesting wine list and brunch on weekends. ✉ *20 Cornelia St., between Bleecker and W. 4th Sts.,* ☎ *212/243–9579. AE. Closed Mon.*

$–$$ ★ ✕ **Grange Hall.** Updated all-American cuisine, affordable prices, and a buzzing, booth-lined Frank Lloyd Wright–esque room draw New York–size crowds nightly to this former speakeasy on one of Greenwich Village's most charming, tucked-away streets. You can order one of the small plates for starters, like potato pancakes with chive-spiked sour cream, or combine several to form a satisfying meal. Entrées—including the delicious, center-cut cranberry-glazed pork chops and grilled salmon—may be ordered by themselves or with a choice of soup or a field-greens salad for a couple of dollars more; classic American side dishes such as creamed spinach are the perfect complement. Excellent iced devil's food cake is a dessert staple. ✉ *50 Commerce St., at Barrow St.,* ☎ *212/924–5246. Reservations essential. AE.*

Barbecue

$ ✕ **Brothers Bar-B-Q.** This huge bi-level barnlike space has a lounge decorated in the style of the American South circa 1949, with hair dryers, tacky period plastic furniture, signs from Texaco, Esso, and Shell, even a garage door. On Monday night, it's all-you-can-eat; sample puffy hush puppies with hot sauce, smoked sausage over black-eyed peas, fried wings and smoked rib tips in bourbon sauce, shrimp po'boy sandwiches, and terrific chicken and ribs. There's enough of a selection of tequila shots to satisfy Pancho Villa, plus 11 bottled beers and seven on tap. ✉ *225 Varick St., at Clarkston St.,* ☎ *212/727–2775. AE.*

Contemporary

$$$$ ★ ✕ **Gotham Bar & Grill.** Every plate that comes out of celebrated chef Alfred Portale's kitchen is an artfully presented edible tower—he originated the now much-copied vertical style of food presentation. One-of-a-kind dishes and fresh takes on classics share space on the eclectic new American menu. Rack of lamb is always dependable, and the Gotham chocolate cake, served with toasted almond ice cream, should not be overlooked. Gotham's loftlike, multilevel space was *the* prototype for New York restaurants in the go-go 1980s, and although its warm salmon-and-green color scheme, diffused lighting, and large window overlooking a courtyard are still attractive, it lacks the refined elegance and sumptuousness of newer hot spots. ✉ *12 E. 12th St., between 5th Ave. and University Pl.,* ☎ *212/620–4020. Reservations essential. AE, DC, MC, V. No lunch weekends.*

$$–$$$ ★ ✕ **Clementine.** This innovative new American eatery offers pleasant service, affordable prices, and magnificent food, without a cliché in sight. The mobbed bar serves generous, beautifully executed drinks. Co-owner and executive chef John Schenk, formerly of the Monkey Bar (☞ Midtown, *below*), serves up melt-in-your-mouth entrées like braised lamb shank with tasty cauliflower gratin and expertly grilled lamb chops with terrific mustard scalloped potatoes, plus one unbeatable appetizer: fried green tomatoes with spareribs salad. Pastry chef Heather Ho's lemon caramel icebox cake puts Clementine's squarely on the New York dessert lovers' map. The well-chosen wine list has many selections under $25, and the main dining room, with its honey gold walls and bubbling rock garden and pool, is most agreeable. ✉ *1 5th Ave., at 8th St.,* ☎ *212/539–0877. Reservations essential. AE.*

French

$$ ✕ **Chez Jacqueline.** With its specials written on the blackboard outside and cast of regulars at the bar, this charming bistro could be in a faraway French village. Owner Jacqueline Zini greets you like an old friend, and you'll want to become part of her family after sampling the delectable Provençale dishes, such as *soupe de poisson,* a creamy puree of seafood and vegetables; *jarret de veau,* or veal shank braised with tomatoes, potatoes, zucchini, garlic, endive, and olives in marrow sauce; veal kidneys; and the celebrated upside-down apple tart. The prix-fixe dinner is a good buy. ✉ *72 MacDougal St., between W. Houston and Bleecker Sts.,* ☎ *212/505–0727. Reservations essential. AE, MC, V. No lunch weekends.*

$$ ✕ **Corsica.** If you want the perfect Greenwich Village restaurant, look no further than this French country bistro, with its exposed brick, copper pots, and stone floors. Try the Corsican country dishes including *torta,* a tart of Swiss chard and onions; the rabbit braised in white wine with onions, capers, olives, and parsley; and the cheesecake, made with the Corsican cheese *bruceio*. There's also a charming sidewalk café, weather permitting. ✉ *310 W. 4th St., between W. 12th and Bank Sts.,* ☎ *212/242–4705. AE, MC, V. Closed Mon. Nov.–Mar. No lunch.*

$$ ✕ **Moomba.** The improbable name of this up-to-the-minute hot spot refers to the aboriginal phrase that translates into English as "Let's get together and have fun." You enter through a greenhouse patio, followed by a raw bar, and a choice of ground floor or mezzanine dining rooms. (There's also a lounge upstairs for cigars and spirits.) Executive chef

Frank Falcinelli's sophisticated fare includes a salad of crisp sweetbreads, Maytag blue cheese, *frisée,* and preserved shallot-hazelnut vinaigrette and a foie gras preparation of the day. Seafood aficionados should try the tuna glazed with molasses and raw sugar in a puddle of roasted jalapeño salsa. Desserts, by Wendy Israel, are devastating: the Moomba bar, a mélange of dark chocolate torte, cocoa pudding, and toasted almond caramel mousse is a whimsical riff on a frozen Milky Way. ✉ *133 7th Ave. S, at 10th St.,* ☎ *212/989–1414. Reservations essential. AE, DC, MC, V. No lunch.*

$ ✕ **French Roast.** This casual, around-the-clock spot with a Left Bank ambience charges bargain prices for some very good bistro dishes rarely encountered elsewhere, such as poached beef marrow finished with bread crumbs and served in broth. The *croque monsieur* (a melted cheese sandwich, done in the style of French toast) is first rate. Near several Village movie houses, it's a convenient place to rendezvous for brunch, coffee, or dessert, but service can be sluggish. A sister spot is on the Upper West Side (✉ 2340 Broadway, at 85th St., ☎ 212/799–1533). ✉ *458 6th Ave., at 11th St.,* ☎ *212/533–2233. AE, MC, V.*

Italian

$$ ✕ **Grand Ticino.** Remember the quaint little Italian restaurant in the movie *Moonstruck?* Here it is, complete with the hunter green walls and romantic lighting. Named after the Swiss Canton of Ticino, it served its first meal in 1919 and has been a home-away-from-home to many artists and writers (Eugene O'Neill and Edna St. Vincent Millay were regulars). The menu includes excellent pasta, a wonderfully simple broiled chicken, and very good calves' liver. ✉ *228 Thompson St., between W. 3rd and Bleecker Sts.,* ☎ *212/777–5922. Reservations essential. AE, DC, MC, V. Closed Sun.*

Moroccan

$$ ✕ **Café Fès.** Named after co-owner and chef Drissa Rafael's hometown, this amiable Moroccan restaurant is on one of Greenwich Village's most charming streets. She and husband Jean Roger have created a perfect setting for this sensuous cuisine, with peach walls, Moroccan lanterns, a tin ceiling, and a small fountain. The cold mixed salad, made with pureed eggplant and spinach, is a delectable beginning. Classic couscous is served in three variations; *tajine,* is a delectable stew made of lamb with prunes or artichokes and fava beans. ✉ *246 W. 4th St., at Charles St.,* ☎ *212/924–7653. AE, DC, MC, V. No lunch.*

Pan-Asian

$$ ✕ **Mirezi.** The name of this cutting-edge pan-Asian bistro and grill is Korean for "future land," and the bi-level setting delivers on the promise of the name. It's stark and simple throughout; the walls in the striking, dimly lighted main dining room are punctuated with miniature TV screens. You can sit there or downstairs at the sake/Asian tapas bar. Try *bibimbap,* a Korean dish served in a clay pot brimming with rice, beef, and Asian vegetables. ✉ *59 5th Ave., between 12th and 13th Sts.,* ☎ *212/242–9710. AE, DC, MC, V. No lunch Mon.–Sat.*

Pizza

$ ✕ **Arturo's.** Few guidebooks list this brick-wall Village landmark, but the body-to-body crowds teetering on the wobbly wooden chairs suggest good things. The pizza is terrific, cooked in a coal-fired oven. Basic pastas as well as seafood, veal, and chicken concoctions with mozzarella and lots of tomato sauce come at giveaway prices. ✉ *106 W. Houston St., off Thompson St.,* ☎ *212/677–3820. AE, MC, V.*

Gramercy Park, Murray Hill, Chelsea, and the Flatiron District

The newly gentrified Flatiron District is the hub of a slew of super-trendy restaurants where the dress code is black, metropolitans are the libation, and cigars are the smoke of choice. Chelsea has surpassed Greenwich Village as the city's most fashionable lesbian and gay quarter; gay-friendly restaurants line 8th Avenue from 17th to 23rd streets; prices tend to be lower here than downtown. With its signature private park, Gramercy Park exudes a lovely old New York ambience; its southern spine, Irving Place, is lined with historic houses and is one of Manhattan's most charming destinations. Murray Hill's undeniable old-world charm includes its proximity to some lovely small hotels and to midtown, but sans the crowds.

American

$$$–$$$$ ★ ✕ **Gramercy Tavern.** Although Gramercy's look—wooden beams, white walls, and country artifacts—recalls an English tavern, the food is decidedly new American, and the service is smooth. The main dining room is a hard-to-get reservation, thanks in large measure to executive-chef Tom Colicchio's innovative fare. The $58 three-course dinner menu is supplemented seasonally by special four- to nine-course tasting menus. The tavern area, dominated by a splendid 91-ft-long mural of fruits and vegetables, does not take reservations and offers some terrific (and less expensive) dishes from the wood-burning grill—a hanger steak sandwich, for one. A fine cheese board and libations from a stellar wine list are served throughout. Gramercy is co-owned by Danny Meyer (of Union Square Cafe [☞ *below*] fame). ✉ *42 E. 20th St., between Broadway and Park Ave. S,* ☎ *212/477–0777. Reservations essential. AE, DC, MC, V.*

$$$–$$$$ ★ ✕ **Union Square Cafe.** New Yorkers consistently rate Union Square as one of their favorite restaurants—thanks in large measure to executive-chef Michael Romano's inventive creations and to its consistently unpretentious disposition and friendly service. Mahogany moldings outline white walls hung with bright modern paintings; in addition to the three main dining areas, there's a long bar—perfect for solo diners. Breads are delicious, and appetizers sparkle, particularly the iced oysters on the half shell with shallot vinaigrette. Although dinner entrées are conscientious—roasted leg of lamb with artichokes, for one, the sandwiches served at lunch—for example, fresh tuna club on Tom Cat white bread with slab bacon, arugula, and herb-potato chips—approach the divine. ✉ *21 E. 16th St., between 5th Ave. and Union Sq. W,* ☎ *212/243–4020. Reservations essential. AE, DC, MC, V. No lunch Sun.*

$$$ ★ ✕ **An American Place.** Executive chef Larry Forgione, one of the original and most influential practitioners of new American cooking, keeps An American Place in the top class of New York's —and the country's— restaurants by preparing classic dishes to perfection day after day. The menu ranges from fresh Maine deviled crab spring roll to cedar-planked salmon with seasonal vegetables. A high-ceiling room, Art Deco brasserie-style light fixtures, colorful Mikasa china, generously spaced tables, and Frank Stella paintings impart a sense of luxury at its most effortless. Kindly service puts a finishing sheen that makes this all add up to a stellar experience. ✉ *2 Park Ave., at 32nd St.,* ☎ *212/684–2122. Reservations essential. AE, DC, MC, V. No lunch weekends.*

$$$ ★ ✕ **Verbena.** Two small rooms with fireplaces, an olive, beige, and mustard color scheme, windows dotted with small pots of herbs, and a quiet garden are among the pleasures of this small, romantic restaurant in the historic Inn at Irving Place (☞ Chelsea and Gramercy Park, *in* Chapter 7). Executive chef Diane Forley's inventive yet severely simple style shines in such dishes as foie gras with salsify, prunes, and pearl

onions; chopped endive salad with melted Taleggio cheese tart; and beer-braised ribs of beef with horseradish dumplings. Crème brûlée scented with verbena is a perfect finish to a meal here. ✉ *54 Irving Pl., at 17th St.,* ☎ *212/260–5454. Reservations essential. AE, DC, MC, V. No lunch Mon.–Sat.*

$$–$$$ ✕ **Granville.** The decor—wrought-iron chandeliers, Asian carpets, and mahogany and leather furniture—brings to mind an English men's club. Nonsmokers are obliged to dine downstairs. Upstairs are individual humidor lockers, a large bar with a different DJ every night, a superlative cigar lounge with overstuffed chairs and couches, and a dining room with a red-and-green tin ceiling. The savory entrées include cured sea bass on a sheet of nori, with ponzu sauce, and roasted monkfish in green curry. ✉ *40 E. 20th St., between Broadway and Park Ave.,* ☎ *212/253–9088. AE, DC, MC, V. No lunch weekends.*

$$ ★ ✕ **Blue Water Grill.** A copper-and-tile raw bar anchors one end of this sweeping room (formerly the central hall of a bank), with its warm hues of indigo blue, sienna, and yellow and original 1904 molded ceiling and marble. The menu is strong on seafood, served neat (chilled whole lobster; shrimp in the rough), in various international styles (Moroccan-spiced red snapper, Maryland crab cakes, warm shrimp cocktail in bamboo steamers with Japanese and Shanghai sauces), or in simple preparations from a wood-burning oven. For dessert go for the brownie ice cream sundae. ✉ *31 Union Sq. W, at 16th St.,* ☎ *212/675–9500. Reservations essential. AE, DC, MC, V.*

American/Casual

$$ ✕ **Park Avalon.** The flagship restaurant of Steven Hanson (owner of Isabella's [☞ Upper West Side, *below*] and Blue Water Grill [☞ *above*]) has two dining levels, huge alabaster-shaded light fixtures, massive mirrors, and a bar area with floor-to-ceiling wine cases and a dramatic display of lighted candles. The menu includes such au courant pasta creations as homemade cracked black-pepper fettuccine with grilled Portobello mushrooms, spinach, and cheese; grilled free-range chicken with roasted garlic crust, sautéed broccoli rabe, and rosemary mashed potatoes is another highlight. There are several low-fat desserts as well as marvelously intense sorbets. ✉ *225 Park Ave. S, between 18th and 19th Sts.,* ☎ *212/533–2500. AE, DC, MC, V.*

Contemporary

$$$ ★ ✕ **Water Club.** This glass-enclosed barge in the East River is decidedly dramatic, with its long wood-paneled bar, blazing fireplace, appetizing shellfish display, and panoramic water views. Food is ingeniously presented: Tuna tartare with marinated shiitake mushrooms, wasabi, spicy ocean salad, and flying-fish roe arrives on a porthole with a tiny anchor supporting a jar of caviar. Or order the exemplary sautéed red snapper fillet with lobster dumpling fennel and saffron bouillon. Sample any dessert your conscience desires: Chocolate flourless cake with peppermint-stick ice cream will sweeten even the sourest disposition. Sunday brunch is winsome. ✉ *500 E. 30th St.,* ☎ *212/683–3333. Reservations essential. Jacket required. AE, DC, MC, V.*

$$–$$$ ✕ **Flowers.** The intimate Tuscan-style dining room resembles a country-barn interior. Baskets of dried flowers adorn the walls, and copper light fixtures exude a comforting glow that dims as the evening progresses. The menu is a synthesis of three cuisines: Asian (crispy shrimp roll with soy-ginger vinaigrette and spaghetti vegetables), Caribbean (roasted baby lamb chops with Jamaican spices), and Italian (risotto of seasonal wild mushrooms, asparagus, rosemary, and white-truffle oil). Desserts are lovely—especially the baked Alaska. ✉ *21 W. 17th St., between 5th and 6th Aves.,* ☎ *212/691–8888. AE, DC, MC, V. Closed Sun. No lunch Sat.*

$$–$$$ ✕ **Lola.** Here, beautiful people dance to loud music when they're not sipping wine at the bar or languishing romantically on the main dining room's striped banquettes, which have bouquets of fresh flowers. Perhaps you could start with a stack of ribbon onion rings, and then follow with the signature Lola fried chicken and Cuban-style black beans. ✉ *30 W. 22nd St., between 5th and 6th Aves.,* ☎ *212/675–6700. AE, DC, MC, V. No lunch Sat.*

$$ ✕ **147.** If you managed to score a reservation at Balthazar, it may be because the trendsetters have moved on to this jazz-club/restaurant/cigar lounge in a former firehouse in Chelsea. Caviar is the supreme devil-may-care starter, but the freshly steamed crab cake or the light, chilled vegetable rolls are fine substitutes. Filet mignon in a deep red-wine sauce and roast chicken with mashed potatoes are both hearty entrées. Desserts such as the remarkable mango cheesecake are a highlight. The wine list is well chosen and affordable. Cliff Williams, the charming maître d' hôtel (Nell's and Bowery Bar) will probably greet you; if you're allergic to noise, ask him to seat you away from the earsplitting front room. ✉ *147 W. 15th St., between 6th and 7th Aves.,* ☎ *212/929–5000. Reservations essential. AE, DC, MC, V. No lunch weekends.*

French

$$–$$$ ★ ✕ **Les Halles.** Strikingly unpretentious, this French-American steak house is one of the best bistros in town. Its homey interior has posters plastered on antique walls, a tin ceiling, and a windowed kitchen. A good bet is the extraordinary *côte de boeuf,* with béarnaise sauce, a massive rib steak for two served from a wooden board. Other top choices include crispy duck-leg confit and *frisée* salad, warm sausages with lentils, and heaping plates of garlicky cold cuts. ✉ *411 Park Ave. S, between 28th and 29th Sts.,* ☎ *212/679–4111. AE, DC, MC, V.*

Indian

$–$$ ✕ **Mavalli Palace.** Arguably the best small southern Indian (it's also vegetarian) restaurant in New York, Mavalli is a pretty place with exposed brick walls, blond wood, and fresh flowers on each table. Singular appetizers include *iddly,* steamed lentil and rice cake served with *sambar* (lentils and vegetables), chutney, and spicy fried cashew nuts. The standout entrée is *dosai,* a colossal crepe made with lentils and rice flour, wrapped around potatoes and a fiery chutney. Desserts, especially *kulfi* (homemade ice cream) and *kheer,* a luscious rice pudding, are admirable. Service may be a bit slow, but the gentle prices and short but affordable wine list more than compensate. ✉ *46 E. 29th St., between Madison and Park Ave. S,* ☎ *212/679–5535. AE, DC, MC, V. Closed Mon.*

Italian

$$$ ★ ✕ **Follonico.** You'll like the vintage wainscoting, muted Tuscan colors, open kitchen, and wood-burning oven—but most of all, you'll like the food, chef-owner Alan Tardi's personal interpretation of Tuscan cuisine. The deep-fried oysters crowned with horseradish cream and osetra caviar are so good you'll want to overindulge, but save room for one of the unusual pastas, such as *fazzoletto,* a handkerchief pasta imprinted with fresh herbs. For a third course try the whole red snapper baked in a rock-salt crust. Fresh fruit granita is refreshing, but it would be a shame to leave without dunking a *biscotti* into a compatible dessert wine and drinking some bracing espresso. ✉ *6 W. 24th St., between 5th and 6th Aves.,* ☎ *212/691–6359. Reservations essential. AE, DC, MC, V. Closed Sun. No lunch Sat.*

$$$ ✕ **I Trulli.** Rough-hewn gold walls, a fireplace, a garden for summer dining, and a whitewashed open grill with the traditional beehive shape of early Pugliese houses distinguish this Italian winner from its competitors. An out-of-the-ordinary glass of wine from a little-known producer and one of the enticing appetizers—baked oysters with pancetta, Tallegio cheese, and bread crumbs—are a great way to start. Specialties use game, meat, and fish cooked in the wood-fired oven. ✉ *122 E. 27th St., between Lexington and Park Ave. S,* ☎ *212/481–7372. Reservations essential. AE, DC, MC, V. Closed Sun. No lunch Sat.*

$$$ ✕ **Le Madri.** The Tuscan-style space with a vaulted ceiling and wood-burning pizza oven is the creation of Pino Luongo (of Coco Pazzo [☞ Upper East Side, *below*]). Fried calamari and zucchini with spicy roast-pepper tomato sauce might be a prelude to braised veal shank with Portobello mushrooms and saffron risotto. Impeccable desserts, such as *tortino* (a warm chocolate-hazelnut cake), and top-flight service add up to a lovely experience. ✉ *168 W. 18th St., at 7th Ave.,* ☎ *212/727–8022. Reservations essential. AE, DC, MC, V.*

$$ ★ ✕ **Caffé Bondí Ristorante.** This small, one-of-a-kind restaurant with a garden boasts something special—a menu, written with the assistance of a food historian, that re-creates the cooking of southern Italy in the 18th and 19th centuries. Standouts are artichokes braised in almond sauce, pumpkin and ricotta ravioli, oven-roasted boar chops, quail stuffed with grapes, and a memorable chocolate almond torte. The wine list is short, excellent, and fairly priced. ✉ *7 W. 20th St., between 5th and 6th Aves.,* ☎ *212/691–8136. AE, MC, V.*

Latin

$$$ ✕ **Asia de Cuba.** This remarkable space, designed by Philippe Starck, in the eclectic Morgans Hotel (☞ Murray Hill, *in* Chapter 7), is the definitive lounge-cum-restaurant. Up front is a striking bar area with slipcovered chairs. A marble communal "share-table" is the central feature of the main dining room, which also has a huge color blowup of a Chinese waterfall and bare marble tables. There are potent exotic drinks and a short, well-designed wine list. Wonder of wonders, the food is very good: A knockout foie gras with yucca-bread French toast, cashews, and tropical salsa or a glorious whole fish, cooked-to-a-turn and stuffed with crab *escabèche* (pickled). Desserts have playful names like "Latin Lover" (a chocolate-espresso mousse with espresso-Anglaise). Two appetizers, one entrée, and a side are more than enough food for two. ✉ *237 Madison Ave., between 37th and 38th Sts.,* ☎ *212/726–7755. Reservations essential. AE, MC, V.*

$$$ ★ ✕ **Patria.** Executive chef Doug Rodriquez performs culinary magic in this rousing trilevel Caribbean café, painted in striking earth tones, with handsome mosaics and an open grill. The fluctuating menu offers variations of several ethnic entrées, such as meat, vegetable, or seafood empanadas, as well as soups and seafood (look for the crispy red snapper with coconut-conch rice). Even nonsmokers may be tempted by the signature dessert, a chocolate cigar with edible matches. The wine list focuses on Spain, Argentina, and California. ✉ *250 Park Ave. S, at 20th St.,* ☎ *212/777–6211. Reservations essential. AE, MC, V.*

Pan-Asian

$ ✕ **Republic.** Downtown epicureans on the run flock to this innovative Asian noodle emporium. At one of the two long bluestone bars, you can simultaneously dine and enjoy the spectacle of chefs scurrying amid clouds of steam in the open kitchen. The menu contains chiefly rice dishes or noodles, stir-fried with hints of ginger, peanuts, and coriander or served in savory broths made with coconut milk, lemongrass, Asian basil, and lime leaf. There's also an **uptown branch** (✉ 2290 Broadway, between 82nd and 83rd Sts., ☎ 212/579–5959). ✉ *37A Union Sq. W, between 16th and 17th Sts.,* ☎ *212/627–7172. AE, DC, MC, V.*

Pizza

$–$$ ✕ **La Pizza Fresca.** With its wood-burning brick oven, brick walls, and red-clay floor tiles, this Flatiron District gem offers some of Manhattan's most authentic pizza. The 12-inch *Napoletana* pizza, with fresh tomato sauce, mozzarella, and a traditional thin crust, is a crispy standard. Salads are fresh and inviting; the tiramisu is perfect. The staff, though somewhat unfocused, is friendly, and there is an adequate selection of reasonably priced Italian wines. ✉ *31 E. 20th St., between Broadway and Park Ave. S,* ☎ *212/598–0141. AE, MC, V.*

Seafood

$–$$ ✕ **Crab House.** Part of a national chain, this large restaurant with 650 seats at Chelsea Piers has knotty-pine walls, waterfront dining, and spectacular views of the Statue of Liberty and the Verrazano-Narrows Bridge. You can't go wrong with the all-you-can-eat salad bar or the tender cod, fried in a crispy beer batter and served with fries. The Crab House has a sports bar called Madison Square Garden, where you can sample fine locally brewed beers. ✉ *Chelsea Pier 61, 23rd St. near the Hudson River,* ☎ *212/366–4111. AE, DC, MC, V. No lunch Jan.–May.*

Senegalese

$ ✕ **Ngone.** At this pleasant dining spot, colorful African-patterned cloths cover the tables, and the walls display tapestries and painted scenes of the countryside filled with elephants and wild game. Among the appealingly hot dishes are traditional *boulettes* (appetizers of boneless fish, seasoned with parsley and spices), chicken *yassa* (cooked with lemon, ginger, carrots, and potatoes), and lamb in a creamy peanut sauce. The Senegalese version of French toast makes a comforting conclusion to your meal. Although the Muslim staff abstains from liquor, you may bring your own wine or beer. ✉ *823 6th Ave., between 28th and 29th Sts.,* ☎ *212/967–7899. No credit cards. Closed Sun. BYOB.*

Southwestern

$$$ ✕ **Mesa Grill.** Chef Bobby Flay and owner Jerome Kretchmer have Manhattan foodies in the palms of their hands in this former bank, now done up with vinyl banquettes, green-and-yellow walls, and industrial fans. You can't go wrong with the small menu. Try the shrimp with a roasted garlic and corn tamale, or the chili-crusted rabbit with sweet-potato polenta and caramelized mango sauce. Chocolate–peanut butter ice cream cake with roasted marshmallows is just one of the unbeatable desserts. ✉ *102 5th Ave., between 15th and 16th Sts.,* ☎ *212/807–7400. Reservations essential. AE, MC, V.*

Spanish

$$$ ✕ **Bolo.** With its tile-edged brick oven, vivid gold, red, and cobalt color scheme, open kitchen, and polished wood bar, Bolo's design fuses Manhattan and Madrid. Bobby Flay's Spanish-inspired food aims at New York palates: Oven-roasted baby shrimp with toasted garlic is garnished with fragrant sprigs of thyme, and curried shellfish paella unites bivalves with sausage, chicken, and rice. If you're not in the mood for the perfect house sangria, select from the well-priced wine list. ✉ *23 E. 22nd St., between Broadway and Park Ave. S,* ☎ *212/228–2200. Reservations essential. AE, MC, V. No lunch weekends.*

Turkish

$–$$ ★ ✕ **Turkish Kitchen.** Manhattan's best Turkish restaurant is housed in a striking multilevel room with lipstick-red walls, chairs with skirted slipcovers, framed prints, and kilims covering the walls and floor. The young staff dressed in long white chefs' aprons serves delicate and authentic food. For appetizers choose from such delectable offerings as velvety char-grilled eggplant salad, panfried calves' liver, and fried calamari. The stuffed cabbage and bulgur-wheat patties, filled with ground lamb, pine nuts, and currants, are both highly recommended. The newer, smaller **Turkish Grill** (✉ 193 Bleecker St., at MacDougal St., ☎ 212/674–8833) is less expensive but has only a few tables. ✉ *386 3rd Ave., between 27th and 28th Sts., ☎ 212/679–1810. AE, DC, MC, V. No lunch weekends.*

Vegetarian

$–$$ ★ ✕ **Zen Palate.** Walls made from squares of fragile rice paper, wooden beams, and bamboo chairs set an appropriately minimalist tone at these vegetarian, Pan-Asian café-restaurants (the cafés are less expensive and serve takeout). Taro spring rolls, Vietnamese-style autumn rolls, and marinated seaweed are among the resplendent appetizers. Entrées have poetic names like "Festival on a Roll" (seasoned spinach in soybean crepes with a spicy sauce) and "Dreamland" (layers of spinach linguine, bean sprouts, and shredded black mushrooms). ✉ *34 Union Sq. E, at 16th St., ☎ 212/614–9291;* ✉ *663 9th Ave., at 46th St., ☎ 212/582–1669;* ✉ *2170 Broadway, between 76th and 77th Sts., ☎ 212/501–7768. AE, MC, V.*

Midtown

The locale of most big New York sights and therefore a big draw for tourists, this area offers perhaps the widest choice of restaurants in all price ranges, styles, and dress codes.

Afghan

$–$$ ★ ✕ **Pamir.** Gold-leaf chandeliers, hanging brass pots, Asian rugs, and brass sconces are the backdrop for New York's best Afghan cuisine (roughly, a combination of Italian, Chinese, and Middle Eastern cooking). The most memorable dishes include delicate deep-fried turnovers with stuffing of pumpkin or carrot; scallion-filled dumplings topped with yogurt and meat sauce; and a mélange of seasoned lamb garnished with pistachio nuts, almonds, orange strips, cardamom, and rose water. ✉ *1065 1st Ave., at 58th St., ☎ 212/644–9258;* ✉ *1437 2nd Ave., between 74th and 75th Sts., ☎ 212/734–3791. AE, DC, MC, V. No lunch Sat.–Mon.*

American

$$$$ ✕ **Rainbow Room.** This $25 million dinner-and-dancing room on the 65th floor remains a monument to glamour and fantasy—one of New York's quintessential spaces. Beneath the domed ceiling from which hangs an immense crystal chandelier, waiters in tuxedos weave through silver-lamé-clad tables that rise in tiers around a revolving dance floor; aubergine walls frame panoramic 50-mi views through floor-to-ceiling windows. At press time, plans for 1999 called for the restaurant to be open to the public only on a limited basis, although a bar will serve food. The Rainbow & Stars cabaret will become a restaurant. ✉ *30 Rockefeller Plaza, between 49th and 50th Sts., ☎ 212/632–5000 or 212/632–5100. Reservations essential. Jacket and tie. AE, DC, MC, V. Closed Mon. (Sun.–Mon. in summer).*

$$$$ ★ ✕ **"21" Club.** It's exciting to hobnob with celebrities and tycoons at this four-story brownstone landmark, a former speakeasy, which first opened on December 31, 1929. Executive chef Erik Blauberg turns out some of New York's most inventive new American and Asian-fusion food. With its banquettes, red-checked tablecloths, and a ceiling hung with toys, the Grill Room is *the* place to be; it serves such standbys as the signature "21" burger (also available in a clever miniature rendition), Asian-style seared tuna, and seasonal game preparations. Sauces

are based on fresh vegetable-juice reductions rather than butter and cream, dramatic desserts and specialty coffee flambés bring flair to meal's end, and service is seamless. For a once-in-a-lifetime splurge, the entire wine cellar—it's one of the world's greats, with some 50,000 bottles—can be reserved for a chef's tasting dinner (seating is up to 20), which includes appropriate wines. ✉ *21 W. 52nd St., between 5th and 6th Aves.,* ☎ *212/582–7200. Reservations essential. Jacket and tie. AE, DC, MC, V. Closed Sun. No lunch Sat.*

$$$–$$$$ ✕ **Fifty Seven Fifty Seven.** Designed by I. M. Pei, the Four Seasons Hotel (☞ Chapter 7), which houses this room, is strikingly sleek, and its 22-ft coffered ceilings, inlaid maple floors, and onyx-studded bronze chandeliers set the tone for superbly served urbane food. Imaginative appetizers like lobster Caesar salad are exceptional, and it's hard to choose between the perfectly timed herb-roasted rack of lamb and the moist rack of veal with its crispy onion garnish. ✉ *57 E. 57th St., between Madison and Park Aves.,* ☎ *212/758–5757. AE, DC, MC, V.*

$$–$$$ ★ ✕ **JUdson Grill.** Another venture of Jerome Kretchmer (of Gotham Bar and Grill fame), the airy space with a bar and balcony has red velour banquettes, mirrored walls, lofty ceilings, engaging John Parks murals, and immense gold vases. The open kitchen produces sumptuous dishes like seared New York State foie gras and inventive fish entrées, yet the more down-to-earth preparations—salads, sandwiches, and steaks—are equally well executed. The wine list is beautifully organized and eminently agreeable. ✉ *152 W. 52nd St., between 6th and 7th Aves.,* ☎ *212/582–5252. AE, DC, MC, V. Closed Sun. No lunch Sat.*

$$–$$$ ✕ **Maloney & Porcelli.** Pictures of eagles and a large fish suspended from the ceiling brighten up this lively two-level space, decorated in a green-and-beige color scheme with wood accents. A large, square bar marks the center of the room. The definitive dish is a huge, juicy crackling pork shank, served on a bed of poppy-seed sauerkraut, with a mason jar of tangy, homemade "Firecracker" jalapeño-spiced apple sauce. Drunken doughnuts, served with three small pots of liqueur-flavored jam, are one of the fun desserts. The inventive wine list includes 40 wines priced under $40. ✉ *37 E. 50th St., between Madison and Park Aves.,* ☎ *212/750–2233. AE, DC, MC, V.*

$$ ★ ✕ **Ambassador Grill.** If it's Sunday, head for the Regal U.N. Plaza (☞ Chapter 7) for one of the city's finest brunch buffets. Black-and-white tile floors, pink tablecloths, abundant plants, and an open kitchen make an elegant, modern statement within the greenhouse-inspired space. The char over wilted Atlantic greens is a fine choice for your main dish if you indulge in the appetizer buffet. Try the fruit tart of the day for dessert. An early bird two-course prix-fixe dinner gives excellent value. ✉ *1 United Nations Plaza, at 44th St.,* ☎ *212/702–5014. Reservations essential. AE, DC, MC, V.*

$$ ✕ **Billy's.** In this quintessential New York neighborhood restaurant, established in 1870, straightforward burgers, steaks, fish, and pasta dishes take second place to such down-home specials as chicken potpie, turkey with real mashed potatoes, and corned beef and cabbage. Billy's moneyed neighborhood means the people-watching is often as satisfying as the comfort food and vintage setting. ✉ *948 1st Ave., between 52nd and 53rd Sts.,* ☎ *212/753–1870. AE, DC, MC, V.*

American/Casual

$–$$ ✕ **Commonwealth Brewing Company.** Blond-wood floors, huge beer vats behind a glass wall, maroon padded booths, and black wood tables—it's the basic brew-pub look, but Commonwealth does it better than average. Its European-style ales and lagers include Rockefeller Red, Gotham City Gold, Lady Liberty Lager, and a wheat brew, enhanced by a twist of lemon. Hearty appetites will be readily satisfied by the

Alamo, **79**
Amarone, **55**
Ambassador Grill, **80**
An American Place, **99**
Anche Vivolo, **6**
Aquavit, **41**
Asia de Cuba, **97**
Barbetta, **59**
Bar Nine, **29**
Ben Benson's, **30**
Billy's, **50**
Blue Water Grill, **117**
Bolo, **108**
Bouterin, **1**
Bryant Park Grill and Bryant Park Café, **96**
Café Botanica, **18**
Cafe Centro, **93**
Caffé Bondí Ristorante, **107**
Carnegie Deli, **24**
Chiam, **85**
Churrascaria Plataforma, **65**
Cité, **70**
Commonwealth Brewing Company, **90**
Crab House, **123**
Dawat, **7**
Diwan Grill, **78**
Docks Oyster Bar, **81**
Felidia, **5**
Fifty Seven Fifty Seven, **12**
Film Center Cafe, **62**
Firebird, **60**
Flowers, **120**
Follonico, **105**
Four Seasons Grill and Pool Room, **52**
Frico Bar, **64**
Gallagher's Steak House, **31**
Girafe, **8**
Gramercy Tavern, **111**
Granville, **109**
Haikara Grill, **49**
Halcyon, **25**
Hard Rock Cafe, **22**
Il Nido, **48**
Inagiku, **76**
Ipanema, **88**
Island Spice, **63**
I Trulli, **101**
Jean Lafitte, **14**
Jewel of India, **91**
Jimmy Sung's, **82**
Joe Allen, **61**
JUdson Grill, **35**
La Caravelle, **39**
La Côte Basque, **40**
La Pizza Fresca, **110**
Lattanzi Ristorante, **58**
Le Bernardin, **33**
Le Cirque 2000, **71**
Le Colonial, **9**
Le Madri, **122**

Le Marais, **67**
Le Perigord, **51**
Les Célébrités, **17**
Les Halles, **104**
Lespinasse, **44**
Lola, **106**
Maloney & Porcelli, **74**
Mangia e Bevi, **28**
Manhattan Ocean Club, **13**
March, **2**
Marichu, **83**
Mavalli Palace, **103**
Mesa Grill, **119**
Meskerem, **56**
Monkey Bar, **73**
Morton's, **92**
Motown Cafe, **15**
Naples 45, **94**
New York Kom Tang Soot Bul House, **98**
Ngone, **102**
Oceana, **46**
Official All Star Cafe, **66**
147, **121**
Osteria al Doge, **69**
Osteria del Circo, **37**
Otabe, **11**
Palio, **34**
Pamir, **4**
The Park, **10**
Park Avalon, **113**
Patria, **112**
Patroon, **84**
Peacock Alley, **75**
Petrossian, **19**
Planet Hollywood, **16**
Pomaire, **57**
Rainbow Room, **86**
Remi, **26**
Republic, **114**
Rosa Mexicano, **3**
Ruth's Chris Steak House, **32**
San Domenico, **21**
San Pietro, **42**
SeaGrill, **87**
Seryna, **43**
Shaan, **89**
Smith & Wollensky, **77**
Stage Deli, **27**
Tang Pavillion, **38**
Tapika, **23**
"21" Club, **53**
Trattoria Dell'Arte, **20**
Tse Yang, **72**
Turkish Kitchen, **100**
Typhoon Brewery, **45**
Uncle Nick's, **54**
Union Square Cafe, **118**
Verbena, **115**
Victor's Cafe 52, **36**
Virgil's Real BBQ, **68**
Vong, **47**
Water Club, **95**
Zen Palate, **116**

ambitious menu. The contents of the sampler, served on a multitiered rack, change daily, but it may include German beer and cheese dip, tuna tartare, Asian chicken sticks, or crab cakes. ✉ *10 Rockefeller Plaza, at 48th St.,* ☎ *212/977–2269. AE, DC, MC, V. No lunch weekends.*

Brazilian

$$ ✕ **Churrascaria Plataforma.** This sprawling, boisterous shrine to meat, best experienced with a group, is a popular Brazilian spot. Order a full pitcher of *caipirinhas,* the Brazilian national cocktail, and head for the center of the room, where a vast salad bar beckons with greens and vegetables plus hot tureens of paella and octopus and daily specials. But exercise restraint—the real show begins with the barrage of lamb, beef, chicken, ham, sausage, and innards; only a paddle, marked green on one side (MORE!), red on the other (STOP!) can bring relief. Side dishes include plantains, french fries, rice, yucca flour, and a tangy vinegar sauce. The heavy, gooey desserts are a little too much, but the strong Brazilian coffee is perfect. ✉ *316 W. 49th St., between 8th and 9th Aves.,* ☎ *212/245–0505. AE, DC, MC, V.*

$–$$ ✕ **Ipanema.** Vivid oil paintings of Rio and Bahia decorate the white and peach-hued walls of this snug, modern restaurant, a comfortable place to sample Brazil's exotic cuisine. Feijoada, the national meal—black beans with smoked meats, collard greens, oranges, chili peppers, and a comforting grain called *farofa*—is good here. And don't miss the great drinks made with *cachaça* (Brazilian rum)—caipirinhas and *batidas* (with coconut milk). ✉ *13 W. 46th St., between 5th and 6th Aves.,* ☎ *212/730–5848. AE, DC, MC, V.*

Chinese

$$$–$$$$ ✕ **Tse Yang.** There are Tse Yangs in Paris, Geneva, and Beverly Hills, but this one is perhaps the most dramatic, with its dark wood, dim lighting, elegant tableware, and exotic fish tank. One of the joys of dining here is experimenting with wine and food combinations. Try the crisp whole sea bass with an equally crisp sauvignon blanc or the Peking duck, served traditionally with *doilies* (thin pancakes) and skin, with a spicy gewürztraminer. ✉ *34 E. 51st St., between Madison and Park Aves.,* ☎ *212/688–5447. Reservations essential. AE, DC, MC, V.*

$$–$$$ ✕ **Chiam.** Although purists argue that the only worthy Chinese eateries are in Chinatown, such venues as this, with its polished service, make a persuasive case for the more Westernized uptown experience. The stylish setting includes natural wood, an understated white-and-black motif, and a courtyard view. The wine list is extraordinary for a Chinese restaurant (inquire about special wine-tasting dinners). Enlist the services of the congenial captain, who will select from such diverse menu options as squab *soon* (minced pigeon in lettuce leaves) and steamed lotus-wrapped chicken. ✉ *160 E. 48th St., between Lexington and 3rd Aves.,* ☎ *212/371–2323. AE, DC, MC, V.*

$$–$$$ ✕ **Jimmy Sung's.** Four dramatic peacock-fountain chandeliers cast off restrained lighting at this elegant Chinese restaurant with rich carpeting, patterned wallpaper, and gleaming cherrywood paneling. The menu concentrates on Manchurian, Shanghai, and Mandarin cuisine, all discreetly served on lovely china. Begin your dinner with vegetarian pie with house pancake—crisp sheets of bean curd are stuffed in a puffy pancake, accompanied by plum sauce and scallions. Next, choose among such entrées as salt-baked fresh cuttlefish, shrimp or scallops with chili pepper, or sliced prawn served with an egg-white sauce. ✉ *219 E. 44th St., between 2nd and 3rd Aves.,* ☎ *212/682–5678. AE, DC, MC, V.*

$$–$$$ ★ ✕ **Tang Pavilion.** Outside of Chinatown, this is the most authentic Chinese restaurant in Manhattan, featuring the cuisine of Shanghai and Soo Chow. Request the Shanghai menu, which is presented in English as well as Chinese. Go with a group on your first visit so you may share the crisp baby eel, drunken chicken, Tung-Po pork stuffed in incredibly light, doughy buns; jumbo shrimp with walnuts in a slightly sweet, slightly spicy sauce; and green beans and tofu sheets (reminiscent of pasta). ✉ *65 W. 55th St., between 5th and 6th Aves.,* ☎ *212/956–6888. Reservations essential. AE, DC, MC, V.*

Contemporary

$$$$ ★ ✕ **Four Seasons Grill and Pool Room.** Mies van der Rohe's landmark-designated modernist Seagram Building houses one of New York's most famous restaurants, designed by architect Philip Johnson in a timeless contemporary style. The starkly masculine Grill Room, a longtime bastion of the power lunch, has inviting leather banquettes, rosewood walls, a renowned floating sculpture, and one of the best bars in New York. Illuminated trees, a Carrera marble gurgling pool, and undulating chain curtains distinguish the more romantic Pool Room. As the name implies, the eclectic international menu changes seasonally; the pre-theater prix-fixe dinner ($43.50) is a relatively inexpensive way to experience it. Superb service and an aristocratic wine list keep this at the top of its class. ✉ *99 E. 52nd St., between Park and Lexington Aves.,* ☎ *212/754–9494. Reservations essential. Jacket required. AE, DC, MC, V. Closed Sun. No lunch Sat.*

$$$$ ✕ **Lespinasse.** The opulent (some call it stuffy) Louis XV decor of the dining room at the opulent St. Regis (☞ Midtown East, *in* Chapter 7), with its oil paintings and commodious seating in satin chairs, is an ideal setting for the refined cuisine of Gray Kunz, who honed his craft under Switzerland's celebrated Frédy Girardet. Kunz's Singapore past as chef of Hong Kong's Regent Hotel dining room is evident in some of the entrées with Asian accents. A less adventurous repast might begin with herbed risotto and mushroom fricassee, move on to rack of lamb on curried eggplant tart, and conclude with a warm chocolate tartlet with orange-grapefruit coulis. ✉ *2 E. 55th St., between 5th and Madison Aves.,* ☎ *212/339–6719. Jacket required. AE, DC, MC, V. Closed Sun.*

$$$$ ★ ✕ **March.** With its travertine floor, working fireplace, and burled teak and elm wainscoting, this singular restaurant is elegantly understated. Co-owner Joseph Salice supervises the polished service, and the cuisine of chef Wayne Nish is at once restrained and inspired, demonstrating a mastery of classical technique coupled with artful contemporary presentations. Nish's innovative menu entirely replaces entrées with tasting portions. Dishes include a Japanese-influenced sashimi of Japanese yellowfin tuna with olive oil and soy sauce and such luxury offerings as the whimsical "Beggar's Purses," filled with lobster and truffles. ✉ *405 E. 58th St., between 1st Ave. and Sutton Pl.,* ☎ *212/754–6272. Reservations essential. AE, DC, MC, V. No lunch.*

$$$$ ✕ **Patroon.** Multiple lounges, a New York menu, and a retro-luxe look and feel distinguish this bastion of high-flying capitalists (*patroon* is Dutch for "landowner"). The formal dining room has private dining nooks, Spanish-cedar humidors (they rent to cigar aficionados for $1,500 a year), taupe velvet banquettes, and damask curtains and wall coverings. The big wine list is awkward to negotiate at the smallish tables, but you can't fault the contemporary European-inspired dishes, such as a light and elegant lobster and cod cake with braised parsnips and a spit-fired roasted chicken with truffled mashed potatoes. There's also the obligatory wood-grilled rib of beef for two. From the dessert menu, try the roasted pear bread pudding with mascarpone and port

wine sauce. ✉ *160 E. 46th St., between Lexington and 3rd Aves.,* ☎ *212/883–7373. Reservations essential. Jackets required. AE, DC, MC, V. No lunch weekends.*

$$$–$$$$ ★ ✕ **Le Cirque 2000.** Impresario Sirio Maccioni, whose Le Cirque was an '80s New York highflier, presides over this spectacular new restaurant, one of the most talked-about of the decade. Set in the landmark Villard Houses, it features Adam Tihany's sumptuous, futuristic decor, which contrasts with the original gilded, coffered ceilings. If you haven't secured a reservation, at least drop by the bar for a drink and something from the bar menu—earthy tripe or bargain-priced fresh Beluga caviar. Two elaborately paneled dining rooms—the plush and elegantly sedate Gold Room, with modern velvet banquettes, and the sprightlier Red Room and Grill, with a view of the open kitchen and wall-to-wall celebrities—set a dramatic stage for executive chef Sootha Khunn's classic French-Italian cuisine with contemporary overtones. Each weeknight brings its own specials; Thursday brings the classic Italian *bollito misto,* an aromatic mix of meats, sausage, brains, root vegetables, contrasting condiments, and coarse salt. Celebrated pastry chef Jacques Torres's over-the-top creations—try the drum roll, an apricot and strawberry parfait—keep the fireworks going to meal's end. Wine director Ralph Hersom has assembled an affordable list that spans the spectrum of the world's varietals. ✉ *455 Madison Ave., between 50th and 51st Sts., in the New York Palace Hotel,* ☎ *212/303–7788. Reservations essential. Jacket and tie. AE, DC, MC, V. No lunch Sun.*

$$$ ★ ✕ **Monkey Bar.** Cobalt blue bread plates and glasses, etched-glass panels of the Manhattan skyline, velvet banquettes with a colorful palm-tree design, and cute little monkeys hanging from the lighting fixtures all contribute to the lively atmosphere of this buzzing midtowner in the subdued Hotel Elysée (enter through the hotel to bypass the mobbed bar). There's no monkey business going on with Austrian-born executive chef Kurt Gutenbrunner's innovative combinations of ingredients, which result in such dishes as Kutnatnoto oysters with yellowfin tuna and osetra caviar, and Maine lobster, root vegetables, chanterelle and hedgehop mushrooms in a bouillabaisse sauce. The signature dessert is baked Alaska with chocolate cake and caramel ice cream; the wine list offers a broad international selection and the knowledgeable wine waiter can help you select wisely. ✉ *60 E. 54th St., between Madison and Park Aves.,* ☎ *212/838–2600. Reservations essential. Jacket required. AE, DC, MC, V. No lunch weekends.*

$$–$$$ ✕ **Bryant Park Grill and Bryant Park Café.** Stone fountains, Parisian chairs, and a 200-seat outdoor garden precede the more formal grill area, graced with rare lacquered woods, slate floors, and velvet leaf-patterned banquettes. The food is reasonably good, considering the volume demand on the kitchen. A typical dinner: calamari salad, Joe's special (scrambled eggs, sautéed spinach, ground sirloin, and mushrooms), and chocolate soufflé. The outdoor Bryant Park Café (open April 15–October 14) has a menu of light fare; after 5 its bar overflows with raucous revelers, so if you visit in the early evening, ask for a table at the 42nd Street end. ✉ *25 W. 40th St., between 5th and 6th Aves.,* ☎ *212/840–6500. AE, DC, MC, V.*

$$–$$$ ★ ✕ **The Park.** Next to the Lombardy Hotel (once owned by William Randolph Hearst), this restaurant has a spectacular setting: Baccarat chandeliers and cool blue and golden-beet walls, accented with pale salmon touches and plush green-velvet banquettes. Rudy Vallee once performed in what is now the bar area, which now features cool jazz. Tamboril, an elegant cigar lounge, is also under the roof. The cuisine, under the direction of executive chef Fabrizzio Salerni (formerly of Lespinasse), rivals the best in Manhattan. Begin with a crabmeat salad with bourbon-tomato dressing on a bed of avocado relish and continue

with ravioli filled with Portobello mushrooms in a light sauce of parsley juice and tomato glaze. Desserts, by Patience Dadz Kamen, are no less dazzling, especially the hazelnut bomb with milk chocolate sauce, praline parfait, and accents of chocolate on a nutty hazelnut cookie. ✉ *109 E. 56th St., between Park and Lexington Aves.,* ☎ *212/750–5656. AE, DC, MC, V.*

French

$$$$ ★ ✕ **La Côte Basque.** When this landmark in French dining moved to new quarters in 1995, many elements of the original restaurant came too, including the dark wooden cross beams, murals by Bernard Lamotte, faux windows, and even the revolving door. Executive chef–owner Jean-Jacques Rachou has lightened the cuisine but retained the generous portions. Begin with the trio of pâtés or one of the gossamer soufflés. The signature roast duckling with honey, Grand Marnier, and black-cherry sauce is prepared for two, and carved table-side. A reasonable (for such quality) fixed-price, three-course dinner is a great value. ✉ *60 W. 55th St., between 5th and 6th Aves.,* ☎ *212/688–6525. Reservations essential. Jacket and tie. AE, DC, MC, V. No lunch Sun.*

$$$–$$$$ ★ ✕ **La Caravelle.** Rita and André Jammet's celebration of the good life is New York's most Parisian restaurant. The appealing main dining room comes alive with Jean Pagés murals, their colors spilling over to the pink-peach banquettes. Mirrors, flowers, and the Caravelle coat of arms add to the scene, as does the most professional service staff in town. Enjoy truffled pike dumplings in lobster sauce, the perfectly roasted chicken in a delicate bath of champagne and cream, and one of the irresistible cloudlike soufflés (which must be requested at the beginning of the meal). ✉ *33 W. 55th St., between 5th and 6th Aves.,* ☎ *212/586–4252. Reservations essential. Jacket and tie. AE, DC, MC, V. Closed Sun. No lunch Sat.*

$$$–$$$$ ✕ **Le Perigord.** When you enter this luxurious restaurant, you're greeted with dusty rose walls, well-spaced tables, and an inviting display of hors d'oeuvres and desserts. The international clientele demands first-class food at a fair price, and that's what owner–maitre d'hôtel Georges Briguet provides. Fresh foie gras is worth the modest surcharge on the prix-fixe dinner, and there's a juicy sautéed beef fillet in red wine and bone-marrow sauce. Homemade tarts and cakes tempt from the Lyonnaise dessert cart. ✉ *405 E. 52nd St., between 1st Ave. and FDR Dr.,* ☎ *212/755–6244. Reservations essential. Jacket and tie. AE, DC, MC, V. No lunch weekends.*

$$$–$$$$ ★ ✕ **Peacock Alley.** Outside France it's nearly impossible to find such distinguished entrées as a boned rack of lamb, baked in clay, with Swiss chard and apricots, yet at the Waldorf-Astoria's flagship restaurant, it's standard fare. Under chef de cuisine Laurent Gras (formerly of Monaco's celebrated Louis XV), this luxurious room, embellished with delicate murals of peacocks, now offers one of New York's top hotel-dining experiences. Gras performs miracles with every course: A savory soup—pumpkin consommé with sweet and sour chicken wings, cockscombs, and San Danielle ham—is a triumph, as is a dessert soup, garnished with passion-fruit sorbet and tropical fruits. Tranquil lighting, banquette seating, roomy tables, fine china, professional service, and a comprehensive wine cellar add up to a bravura performance. ✉ *301 Park Ave., between 49th and 50th Sts.,* ☎ *212/872–4895. Reservations essential. AE, DC, MC, V. Closed Sun. No lunch Sat.*

$$$ ★ ✕ **Bouterin.** Baskets of apples and copper pans adorn the walls, adding a warm touch to chef-owner Antoine Bouterin's (formerly of Le Perigord [☞ *above*]) Provençal restaurant, just south of the Queensboro Bridge. Unpretentious dishes dominate on the short menu—an old-fashioned lamb stew, cooked for seven hours and best eaten with a spoon,

is a highlight. ✉ *420 E. 59th St., off 1st Ave.,* ☎ *212/758–0323. Reservations essential. Jacket required. AE, DC, MC, V. No lunch.*

$$–$$$ ✕ **Cité.** Alan Stillman (of Smith & Wollensky, Manhattan Ocean Club, Post House, and Park Avenue Café fame) offers an incredible deal. His Art Deco Parisian-style brasserie with crystal chandeliers and imported grillwork (not to be confused with the more casual adjoining bistro) pours four wines with dinner free of charge. The wines change, but they're always top drawer. An excellent three-course dinner is served 8–midnight. The food ranges from American steak house to Mediterranean, and since there's a real chef in the kitchen, you needn't stick to the excellent roast beef and sparkling shrimp or lobster cocktail. ✉ *120 W. 51st St., between 6th and 7th Aves.,* ☎ *212/956–7100. AE, DC, MC, V.*

$$ ✕ **Cafe Centro.** The terrazzo floors, gold-leaf columns, and a glass-enclosed kitchen of this pleasant café evoke a French brasserie. The eclectic menu includes a good three-pound T-bone steak, Moroccan-inspired *tajines* (stews), a wood-grilled dish of the day, and an array of desserts, including some of the most toothsome cookies around. A separate beer bar offers more than 30 selections and has its own attractively priced menu with fun snacks. ✉ *200 Park Ave., between 45th St. and Vanderbilt Ave., in the Met Life Bldg.,* ☎ *212/818–1222. AE, DC, MC, V. Closed Sun. No lunch Sat.*

Indian

$$–$$$ ★ ✕ **Dawat.** One of the city's finest Indian restaurants, this classy, understated spot with roomy tables really stands out for consultant Madhur Jaffrey's creative cuisine. Provocative choices include shrimp in mustard seeds with curry leaves; parsi-style salmon, steamed in a banana leaf with coriander chutney. The *kulcha,* an onion-stuffed bread flavored with fresh coriander, is particularly good. Dawat demonstrates the charms of Indian sweets; try the puddinglike carrot halvah, the pistachio-studded rice pudding known as *kheer,* and *kulfi,* a delicate frozen dessert. ✉ *210 E. 58th St., between 2nd and 3rd Aves.,* ☎ *212/355–7555. Reservations essential. AE, DC, MC, V. No lunch Sun.*

$$–$$$ ★ ✕ **Diwan Grill.** Low-key lighting, comfortable oversize booths, and esoteric wall hangings add mystery to the main dining room of this Manhattan offspring of the Jackson Diner in Queens, one of New York's best small Indian restaurants. The food—whether the remarkable tandoori breads, grilled chicken, lamb sausage, tandoori vegetables or the beautifully spiced curries—is always superb, as is the nurturing service. Bring your vegetarian friends for the traditional *thali,* a complete dinner of small vegetable curries, condiments, breads, and desserts, served on a round tray. ✉ *148 E. 48th St., between Lexington and 3rd Aves.,* ☎ *212/593–5425. AE, MC, V.*

$$–$$$ ✕ **Shaan.** Shaan means "pride" in Hindi, and owners Victor Khubani and Bhushan Arora have good reason to feel that sentiment about their elegant Rockefeller Center palace, furnished with hand-carved doors, tapestries, and roomy banquettes. The spicing ranges from subtle to fiery, and the northern cuisine, prepared by a Bengali-born chef, includes splendid tandoori lobster, rack of lamb, or quail, which are marinated in yogurt and spices and cooked in a clay oven. ✉ *57 W. 48th St., between 5th and 6th Aves.,* ☎ *212/977–8400. AE, DC, MC, V.*

$$ ✕ **Jewel of India.** Jewel of India specializes in the fare of northern India, which trades in the south's vegetarian dishes for such subtle meat preparations as lamb cooked with yogurt, nuts, and a touch of fresh tomato sauce. The marvelous herb-scented breads and knockout tandoori show off the kitchen's prowess. The main dining room overflows with wall hangings, exotic sculptures, and carved rosewood screens. An attractive lounge and bar area and popular luncheon buffet ensure

a loyal following. ✉ *15 W. 44th St., between 5th and 6th Aves.,* ☎ *212/869–5544. Reservations essential. AE, DC, MC, V.*

Italian

$$$$ ★ ✕ **Felidia.** Manhattanites frequent this celebrated *ristorante* as much for the winning enthusiasm of Lidia Bastianich, who owns it with her husband, Felix, as for the food, which emphasizes the authentic regional cuisine of Italy, with a bow to dishes from Ms. Bastianich's homeland, Istria, on the Adriatic. There are three dining options: an attractive front room with a wooden bar, a rustic room beyond, and a skylighted balcony. Regional and seasonal masterpieces include dishes featuring white truffles and exceptional game preparations (in fall). Fresh homemade pasta, roasted whole fish, and an elite wine list representing Italy's finest vineyards can always be counted on. ✉ *243 E. 58th St., between 2nd and 3rd Aves.,* ☎ *212/758–1479. Reservations essential. Jacket and tie. AE, DC, MC, V. Closed Sun. No lunch Sat.*

$$$–$$$$ ✕ **Il Nido.** This fashionable restaurant, with wood beams set in rough plaster walls, strives to create the interior of a Tuscan farmhouse. Hands-on restaurateur Adi Giovanetti finishes pastas, whisks zabaglione, and prepares the masterful blend of Gorgonzola and cognac to spread on toast. His preparations will please traditionalists: salmon carpaccio, *malfatti* (a ravioli-like pasta), and baked red snapper. Be prepared to wait for your table. ✉ *251 E. 53rd St., between 2nd and 3rd Aves.,* ☎ *212/753–8450. Reservations essential. AE, DC, MC, V. Closed Sun. No lunch Sat.*

$$$–$$$$ ✕ **San Pietro.** Specialties of the Amalfi Coast and southern Italy are the highlight at this stylish midtowner. Look for unusual pastas with surprising ingredients: Homemade strips of buckwheat pasta with fontina and savoy cabbage and chickpea-flour noodles with pesto. Similarly masterful are the grilled whole snapper and roast suckling pig rolled around fresh minced herbs in white wine sauce. There are good wines by the glass and wonderful homemade tarts and cheesecake. ✉ *18 E. 54th St., between 5th and Madison Aves.,* ☎ *212/753–9015. Reservations essential. Jacket. AE, DC, MC, V. Closed Sun.*

$$$ ✕ **Girafe.** A 20-ft-high metal statue of the namesake of this restaurant stands outside this otherwise traditional northern Italian restaurant. A standout dish is hay and straw (green and white vermicelli) in a bath of cream, prosciutto, and peas, served with a thick, juicy veal chop. The house tiramisu qualifies as one of Manhattan's best. ✉ *208 E. 58th St., between 2nd and 3rd Aves.,* ☎ *212/752–3054. Reservations essential. Jacket required. AE, DC, MC, V. Closed Sun. No lunch Sat.*

$$ ✕ **Anche Vivolo.** Austrian shades and big clay pots of fresh flowers help create the feel of an enclosed garden in this restaurant, one of the best deals in an expensive part of town. Huge portions of such well-prepared dishes as linguine *Francesco* (with garlic, anchovies, basil, tomatoes, and oregano) would cost at least 50% more at most other restaurants on this Italianate block. The best entrée is often a special. ✉ *222 E. 58th St., between 2nd and 3rd Aves.,* ☎ *212/308–0112. AE, DC, MC, V. Closed Sun. No lunch Sat.*

$–$$ ✕ **Naples 45.** The main dining room with three pizza ovens named after volcanoes is brightened by shelves of appetizing take-out items and gleaming white tiles softened by bands of terra-cotta. Equally tempting are the risotto cake, stuffed with meat ragout and boiled egg, and pizza, which is served by the half "metre" or as a whole pie for four or more. The long bar serves terrific wines by the glass and an interesting selection of antipasti and other appetizers. There's also a colorful outdoor patio. ✉ *200 Park Ave., at E. 45th St., in the Met Life Bldg.,* ☎ *212/972–7001. AE, DC, MC, V. Closed weekends.*

Japanese

$$$$ ✕ **Inagiku.** The casually elegant interiors of this venerable Japanese restaurant in the Waldorf-Astoria combine artistic restraint with creativity: A massive red-grain chandelier hangs over the bar, yin and yang symbols appear on fabric, glass, and stone, and inventive sconces and sculptures dot the traditional tatami rooms. Tuna served three ways—tartar, seared over daikon, or minced—is a fine introduction to the playful food. Dramatically presented sashimi mimics everything from the World Trade Center to the East River. You can spend a small fortune to sample the butter-tender *wagu* beef, but steak *Ishiyaki* (grilled table-side on a stone) is an affordable substitute. There are some interesting sakes, especially a rare brown one; otherwise beer or champagne work best. Service is sweet if at times distracted; desserts, alas, are an afterthought. ✉ *111 E. 49th St., between Lexington and Park Aves.,* ☎ *212/355–0440. AE, DC, MC, V. No lunch weekends.*

$$$$ ✕ **Otabe.** In this sleek dining room with spacious seating, you can order traditional Kyoto cuisine (a tasting menu of several small dishes) or in a room in back, experience superbly rendered authentic *teppan* (barbecue-style grill) cooking. Grilled eel on a bed of cucumber with a bouquet of fresh ginger or deep-fried tofu and eggplant are two appealing appetizers. Slices of raw tuna sashimi brushed with garlic-flavored soy sauce sparkle, while Kobe beef is so tender knives are unnecessary. ✉ *68 E. 56th St., between Madison and Park Aves.,* ☎ *212/223–7575. AE, DC, MC, V. No lunch weekends.*

$$$$ ★ ✕ **Seryna.** Although the sushi is superbly fresh at this superexpensive spot, the specialty is steak *ishiyaki,* cooked table-side on a smoldering rock. In the six-course *wagyu* dinner, you can choose between it and *shabu shabu,* another mealtime dish-cum-event: You begin with a broth, to which you add meat (which you then eat), then vegetables, then noodles, and conclude by sipping the bracing soup. Cocktails are served in small carafes that come buried in crushed ice. Service is superb. Earth tones and comfortable seating at big wooden tables cast a serene glow over the proceedings. ✉ *11 E. 53rd St., between 5th and Madison Aves.,* ☎ *212/980–9393. Reservations essential. AE, DC, MC, V. Closed Sun. No lunch Sat.*

Korean

$$–$$$ ✕ **Haikara Grill.** Haikara means "high-class" in Japanese, and Manhattan's first kosher sushi bar is certainly opulent, starting in the main dining room with its wall of mirrors, Japanese prints, and striking framed kimono. The traditional *bento,* a partitioned Japanese dinner box, contains a bowl of soup, raw fish rolls, steak, blanched vegetables, and sesame noodles. ✉ *1016 2nd Ave., between 53rd and 54th Sts.,* ☎ *212/355–7000. AE, DC, MC, V. Closed Fri. No dinner, no lunch Sat.*

$ ★ ✕ **New York Kom Tang Soot Bul House.** Specializing in barbecue, this is one of the best Korean restaurants on a street jammed with them, and dinner is a show. So come ready for charades (little English is spoken); wear clothes you don't mind getting smoky (from the hibachis in the center of the communal tables); and insist on the more attractive second floor. Dinner starts with 10 delicious side dishes, including kimchi (peppery Korean pickle). Afterward there's soup, then the main event: You cook thin slices of beef or chicken over red-hot coals, top them with hot chilies and raw garlic, and wrap them all up with lettuce. ✉ *32 W. 32nd St., between 5th and 6th Aves.,* ☎ *212/947–8482. AE, MC, V.*

Mexican

$$–$$$ ✕ **Rosa Mexicano.** Owner Josefina Howard is serious about her profession, and her authentic restaurant, with its carefully executed food, is a charmer. Duck enchiladas and chicken steamed in beer stand out among the interesting regional dishes; guacamole prepared table-side and a cold seafood platter are stellar standbys. The chocolate-chili mousse cake has real kick. ✉ *1063 1st Ave., at 58th St.,* ☎ *212/753–7407. Reservations essential. AE, DC, MC, V. No lunch.*

$ ✕ **Alamo.** The Alamo's creative riffs on Mexican and Texas-style cooking are served in the unpretentious main dining room, bright with piñatas and Mexican posters, and the even more comfortable second level, with big comfy booths. Chunky guacamole is made to order table-side. *Chili relleno* (green chili pepper stuffed with cheese and batter fried) is a vegetarian standout. ✉ *304 E. 48th St., between 1st and 2nd Aves.,* ☎ *212/759–0590. AE, DC, MC, V. Closed Sun. No lunch Sat.*

Pan-Asian

$$$ ✕ **Vong.** Jean-Georges Vongerichten's (☞ Jean Georges *and* Jo Jo, both *below*) stint at Bangkok's Oriental Hotel inspired this radiant restaurant with its potted palms and gold-leaf ceiling. Presentation is vital: The food is showcased on dazzling dishes of varying size, color, and shape. Although the menu changes often, reliable standbys include the lobster and daikon roll with rosemary-ginger dip, lobster in Thai spices, and the distinctive rabbit curry braised with carrots and cumin seed. The tab can be kept down by ordering a second appetizer in lieu of an entrée. ✉ *200 E. 54th St.,* ☎ *212/486–9592. Reservations essential. AE, DC, MC, V. No lunch weekends.*

Scandinavian

$$$–$$$$ ✕ **Aquavit.** Although prices in the upstairs café are only half as much, the striking downstairs room in the late Nelson Rockefeller's town house—with its atrium, Roger Smith kites, and waterfall—*is* Aquavit. The Swedish fare has been stripped of its homeyness and decked out in contemporary garb, with impressive results. Roasted-lobster salad and the more traditional herring plate are terrific appetizers, cherry-crusted rack of lamb and uncommon tea-smoked duck breast worthwhile follow-ups. New York's largest selection of aquavits keeps company with the well-chosen wine list. ✉ *13 W. 54th St., between 5th and 6th Aves.,* ☎ *212/307–7311. Reservations essential downstairs. AE, DC, MC, V.*

Seafood

$$$–$$$$ ✕ **Manhattan Ocean Club.** Picasso ceramics from owner Alan Stillman's collection embellish this sophisticated bi-level eatery. Impeccably fresh shellfish by the piece is a perfect starter. Tuna arrives seared and rare inside, with lattice potatoes and a green salsa. Other admirable entrées may include roasted blackfish with shiitake mushrooms, shallots, and penne pasta, or perfectly grilled swordfish. Comfortable seating may entice you to linger over a luscious warm chocolate tart. ✉ *57 W. 58th St., between 5th and 6th Aves.,* ☎ *212/371–7777. Reservations essential. AE, DC, MC, V. No lunch weekends.*

$$$–$$$$ ★ ✕ **Oceana.** Warm wood decor, contemporary lighting, bright murals, and posters of luxury ocean liners make a pretty, perfect setting for one of Manhattan's best fish restaurants. Crab cakes, lobster ravioli, bouillabaisse, and salmon tartare wrapped in smoked salmon all score high marks. The three-course prix-fixe lunch and dinner menus offer good value, as does the six-course tasting menu (dinner only). More than 100 whites are offered on the first-rate wine list; white Bordeaux are especially choice. ✉ *55 E. 54th St., between Madison and Park Aves.,* ☎ *212/759–5941. Reservations essential. Jacket required. AE, DC, MC, V. Closed Sun. No lunch Sat.*

$$$–$$$$ ★ ✕ **SeaGrill.** Famous restaurants with extraordinary views are often suspect when it comes to the food. But *this* famous restaurant, with a spectacular view of the Rockefeller Center ice rink in winter and captivating patio dining in summer, can stand tall. Master chef Ed Brown (of JUd-

son Grill [☞ Midtown, *above*]) turns out some of Manhattan's best seafood dishes, including charred, moist sugarcane shrimp on skewers with buttery rice. The key lime pie is the best this side of the Keys. ✉ *19 W. 49th St., between 5th and 6th Aves.,* ☎ *212/332–7610. Reservations essential. AE, DC, MC, V. Closed Sun. No lunch Sat.*

$$ ✕ **Docks Oyster Bar.** The large brass-trimmed bar of this terraced, high-ceiling, Art Deco brasserie displays scrupulously fresh shellfish presented on tiered platters. Cooked preparations run the gamut from traditional American to inventive-eclectic. Steamers in beer broth and Maryland crab cakes are generally available as appetizers. For the main course, go for what's fresh that day. Lobster is as good as it gets in Manhattan. ✉ *633 3rd Ave., at 40th St.,* ☎ *212/986–8080;* ✉ *2427 Broadway, at 89th St.,* ☎ *212/724–5588. Reservations essential. AE, DC, MC, V. No lunch Sat.*

Spanish

$$$ ✕ **Marichu.** Natural brick, old beams from Connecticut, and a lovely garden grace New York's only Basque restaurant, an overlooked find steps from the U.N. A fascinating list of Spanish wine nicely complements the refined and elegant Basque cuisine, which is particularly strong on seafood. There's no better way to start than with Rioja peppers stuffed with a puree of cod. Such changing house specials as mixed seafood in a green herb sauce provide a welcome relief from the ever-present grilled tuna. ✉ *342 E. 46th St., between 1st and 2nd Aves.,* ☎ *212/370–1866. AE, DC, MC, V. No lunch weekends.*

Steak

$$$–$$$$ ✕ **Morton's.** Although famous for its steaks, New York has never seen any place like this branch of Chicago's famous steak house. The masculine, softly lighted room has comfortable booths. Steaks, chops, chicken, seafood, and even the vegetables are presented to diners for inspection, before being prepared. Service is enthusiastic, and the bar knows how to make a drink, but the big draws are the steaks, chops, double-cut prime rib, and the 4½-pound lobsters. Hash browns and fresh asparagus are also terrific; for dessert go straight to the cheesecake or the rich chocolate-velvet cake. The wine list offers hundreds of extraordinary reds, and there is an excellent single-malt Scotch list. ✉ *551 5th Ave., at 45th St.,* ☎ *212/972–3315;* ✉ *90 West St., between Albany and Cedar Sts.,* ☎ *212/732–5665. Reservations essential. AE, DC, MC, V. No lunch weekends.*

$$$–$$$$ ✕ **Smith & Wollensky.** This archetypal New York–style steak house, with its bold and unabashedly masculine setting, gargantuan portions, and lofty list of wines (strong in red Bordeaux and California cabernets), is one of the best. Meat is dry-aged in-house, and sirloin, porterhouse, and double sirloin steaks arrive cooked to a turn. Order a side of hash browns or cottage fries and creamed or sautéed spinach, but skip the perfunctory appetizers and desserts. There is a generous selection of single-malt Scotch. The bustling, less pricey Wollensky's Grill next door has pleasant sidewalk seating in summer. ✉ *201 E. 49th St., at 3rd Ave.,* ☎ *212/753–1530; 212/753–0444 for Grill. Reservations essential. AE, DC, MC, V. No lunch weekends at restaurant.*

Thai

$$ ✕ **Typhoon Brewery.** Typhoon lays claim to being New York's only Thai restaurant–brew pub. Downstairs a satay bar serves raw and cooked appetizers, and a long brew bar offers six beers (including India pale ale, nut brown ale, and American amber) and 30 wines, all by the glass. Upstairs in a brick-walled area with exposed pipes, you dine at galvanized-steel tabletops in wonderful circular booths surrounded by industrial metal cages. The excellent Thai dishes include shell-on shrimp with garlic and pepper and seasonal Thai vegetables in green curry. For dessert don't miss the banana fritters with banana ice cream. ✉ *22 E. 54th St., between 5th and Madison Aves.,* ☎ *212/754–9006. AE, DC, MC, V. No lunch weekends.*

Vietnamese

$$–$$$ ✕ **Le Colonial.** With its rattan chairs, potted palms, ceiling fans, shutters, and period photographs, the dining room is straight out of a book by Somerset Maugham. The food, although Westernized, is usually well prepared: A superb starter is *bahn cuon*—steamed Vietnamese ravioli with chicken, shrimp, and mushrooms; crisp-seared whole snapper with spicy and sour sauce excels among the entrées. The sorbets, ice creams, and fruit-based puddings are right on, and the Vietnamese coffee—strong black brew over a layer of condensed milk is nirvana in a cup. ✉ *149 E. 57th St., between Lexington and 3rd Aves.,* ☎ *212/752–0808. Reservations essential. AE, DC, MC, V.*

Times Square, Clinton, Hell's Kitchen, and Carnegie Hall

The neighborhoods that make up and surround the theater district offer more pre- and post-theater choices than ever before. Times Square's revival has spawned a new generation of huge, noisy theme restaurants. "Restaurant Row," a seamless strip of restaurants on 46th Street between 8th and 9th avenues offers dozens of choices, including new upscale contenders plus several cabaret venues. Hell's Kitchen and Clinton, two overlapping neighborhoods that share 9th Avenue as their spine, both burst with eateries. Low-cost Italian, Latin, and other ethnic spots dominate, but new spots open (and sometimes close) virtually every week—for an eating adventure on one of New York's least gentrified frontiers, this is the place to come.

American/Casual

$–$$ ✕ **Hard Rock Cafe.** The signature marquee of vintage Cadillac fins, rock-star memorabilia, loud rock music, oversize burgers, and teenyboppers: Hard Rock virtually invented the theme-restaurant genre (and created a worldwide T-shirt franchise to boot). Truth be told, the food is quite tasty. The pork barbecue, listed as pig sandwich, is as good as you often find in North Carolina. Like everything else on the menu, the club sandwich—crispy bacon, roast chicken, lettuce, tomato, and mayo between huge slabs of icebox bread—is huge and can be split. To avoid waits, go at opening hours and avoid school holidays. ✉ *221 W. 57th St., between Broadway and 7th Ave.,* ☎ *212/489–6565. AE, MC, V.*

$–$$ ✕ **Joe Allen.** With its brick walls, dark wood bar, and showbiz posters, it looks like a pub, but the food warrants the smart white tablecloths. The menu has several satisfying offerings: a marvelous meat-loaf sandwich and an exceptional grilled calves' liver, thinly cut and served with creamy mashed potatoes. You might even glimpse a celebrity or two. ✉ *326 W. 46th St., between 8th and 9th Aves.,* ☎ *212/581–6464. Reservations essential. MC, V.*

$–$$ ✕ **Official All Star Cafe.** Andre Agassi's ponytail is among the sports memorabilia displayed in this theme restaurant; an entire room is devoted to actor Charlie Sheen's baseball collection (which includes Babe Ruth's 1927 World Series ring). The stadium-like dining room has a 60-ft ceiling, circled by a miniature blimp on a track, and around its perimeter are some 30 giant video screens playing memorable moments in sports. The huge circular booths may make you feel as if you're sitting inside oversize catchers' mitts. The menu is strictly American: T-bone steak, homemade corned-beef hash, and burgers (beef, turkey, or vegetable) with a choice of 17 toppings. ✉ *1540 Broadway, at 45th St.,* ☎ *212/840–8326. AE, MC, V.*

$–$$ ✕ **Planet Hollywood.** Bruce Willis, Demi Moore, Sylvester Stallone, Keith Barish, and Arnold Schwarzenegger are stakes in this café. The walls are full of celebrity handprints outside and movie memorabilia inside. Who cares that the place rates a 10 on the decibel scale? The food is adequate; you'll be happiest if you stick with the southwestern-style nachos, the fajitas, and the playful pizzas. ✉ *140 W. 57th St., between 6th and 7th Aves.,* ☎ *212/333–7827. AE, DC, MC, V.*

$ ✕ **Film Center Cafe.** Seating here is at vintage Formica tables and in cozy booths, surrounded by authentic Art Deco decor, pink neon lights, old radios, film reels, and wall murals of 20th Century Fox, Paramount, and MGM logos. The good diner food includes chili and meat loaf, both served with soothing mashed potatoes. From 11 to 4 on Sunday, a limited retro-priced menu offers unlimited cocktails, home-style brunch, and a hot cup of java. ✉ *635 9th Ave., between 44th and 45th Sts.,* ☎ *212/262–2525. AE, DC, MC, V. No lunch Sat.*

$ ✕ **Motown Cafe.** This three-level restaurant is home to the biggest record in the world: a classic 45 that's 27 ft in diameter and revolves on the ceiling. The stairway to the mezzanine is actually a ladder of gold records honoring Motown singers. Although the food isn't Grammy material, desserts really rock and roll—the homemade ice cream sandwich plays lead, while fabulous peach cobbler and sweet potato–pecan pie do great backup. ✉ *104 W. 57th St., between 6th and 7th Aves.,* ☎ *212/581–8030. AE, DC, MC, V.*

Barbecue

$ ✕ **Virgil's Real BBQ.** Clever neon and lots of Formica set the scene at this massive roadhouse in the theater district. Start with stuffed jalapeños or buttermilk onion rings with blue-cheese dip. Then go for the "pig out"—a rack of pork ribs, Texas hot links, pulled pork, rack of lamb, chicken, and more. There's a good list of top beers from around the world. ✉ *152 W. 44th St., between 6th Ave. and Broadway,* ☎ *212/921–9494. Reservations essential. AE, MC, V.*

Caribbean

$ ★ ✕ **Island Spice.** This altogether delightful spot, with green walls and plastic tablecloths, serves some of New York's best Caribbean fare. The kitchen's gastronomic reggae shows up in dishes like the zesty jerk pork and chicken curry; whole red snapper, panfried and then steamed with peppers, onions, and tomatoes; and the tender curried goat, eaten stuffed into Indian flat bread. Brunch is served on Sunday. ✉ *402 W. 44th St.,* ☎ *212/765–1737. Reservations essential. AE, DC, MC, V.*

Contemporary

$$$ ★ ✕ **Halcyon.** Peacock-green banquettes line the perimeter of the room, dominated by a domed ceiling painted to resemble the sky; looking up, you'll see gold star bursts and an antique brass chandelier. Despite the elaborate setting, the food is refreshingly simple, starting with such standards as hearts of romaine Caesar salad and roasted rack of lamb. Sunday brunch in the Marketplace in the Sky, on the 53rd floor, offers one of the best views (and buffets) in town. ✉ *151 W. 54th St., between 6th and 7th Aves., in the Rihga Royal Hotel,* ☎ *212/468–8888. AE, DC, MC, V.*

$$–$$$ ✕ **Café Botanica.** This glorious café, airy as a country garden with its high ceilings, wicker chairs, soft green tablecloths, and ravishing Central Park views, serves inventive and elegant food. The pretheater dinner is an exceptional value, and the wine list is priced fairly. The fixed-price lunch and Sunday brunch are as splendid as dinner. ✉ *160 Central Park S, between 6th and 7th Aves., in the Essex House Hotel,* ☎ *212/484–5120. Reservations essential. AE, DC, MC, V.*

Delicatessens

$ ✕ **Carnegie Deli.** Although not what it once was, this no-nonsense spot is still one of midtown's two best delis, a species distinguished by crowds, noise, impatient service, and jumbo sandwiches. Ask the counterman to hand-slice your corned beef or pastrami; the extra juiciness and superior texture warrant the extra charge. To drink? Try cream soda or celery tonic. ⊠ *854 7th Ave., between 54th and 55th Sts.,* ☎ *212/757–2245. No credit cards.*

$ ✕ **Stage Deli.** One taste of its chopped liver and pickles, and you'll know why this monument to corned beef and pastrami, founded in 1936 by Russian immigrant Max Asnas, transcends the tourist-trap syndrome. It personifies the New York theater culture. Bossy waiters and regular guests like Milton Berle and Eddie Cantor were once legion. Today the waitstaff seems almost genteel, but the sandwiches are more gargantuan than ever. ⊠ *834 7th Ave., between 53rd and 54th Sts.,* ☎ *212/245–7850. AE, DC, MC, V. No lunch Sat.*

Ethiopian

$ ✕ **Meskerem.** Ethiopian art adorns the yellow walls in this no-nonsense Hell's Kitchen storefront. The tasty Ethiopian delicacies include *kitfo,* similar to steak tartare, which can be ordered raw, rare, or well done, and *yebeg alecha,* tender pieces of lamb, marinated in Ethiopian butter (flavored with curry, rosemary, and a special herb called *kosart*) and then sautéed with fresh ginger and a bit more curry. The vegetarian combination, an array of five vegetable and grain preparations served on *injera* (a yeasty flat bread) is a terrific deal. ⊠ *468 W. 47th St., at 10th Ave.,* ☎ *212/664–0520. AE, DC, MC, V.*

French

$$$$ ★ ✕ **Le Bernardin.** Since 1986 this French seafood restaurant has been a trendsetter with inventive, meticulously prepared fish creations. The plush, expansive, and softly lighted teak-paneled room—with its well-spaced tables, huge bouquets of flowers, late-19th-century French oil paintings, and low noise level—is as popular as ever. Service is impeccable, and the food dazzles: Spanish mackerel tartare with osetra caviar, red snapper in sherry vinaigrette, and some of the finest desserts in town. The wine list is strong on white burgundies. ⊠ *155 W. 51st St., between 6th and 7th Aves.,* ☎ *212/489–1515. Reservations essential. Jacket required. AE, DC, MC, V. Closed Sun. No lunch Sat.*

$$$$ ✕ **Les Célébrités.** From the moon-shape banquettes and the plush red carpets to the careful lighting and paintings by celebrity artists, this intimate restaurant in the Essex House hotel (☞ Central Park South/59thStreet, *in* Chapter 7) is among the city's most lavish. The glassed-in kitchen, discretely hidden by a painting (of the fabled French ocean liner the *Normandy*), opens occasionally to reveal executive chef Christian Delouvrier busily preparing such specialties as a playful foie-gras burger, in which Granny Smith apple slices replace bread and elegant goose liver subs for beef. The six-item tasting dinner showcases his strengths. The wine list is extensive (and expensive), but there is also a good selection by the glass. ⊠ *160 Central Park S, between 6th and 7th Aves.,* ☎ *212/484–5113. Reservations essential. Jacket and tie. AE, DC, MC, V. Closed Sun.–Mon. No lunch.*

$$$–$$$$ ★ ✕ **Petrossian.** This Art Deco caviar bar and restaurant is like no other New York dining spot, with its fur-trimmed banquettes, granite bar, profusion of marble, and contributions of Erté and Lalique. Start with gobs of fresh caviar: beluga (the largest egg and most popular with Americans), Sevruga (smaller and a favorite of the British), or osetra (yellowish and highly prized by Russians on buttered toast or *blini,* a puffy pancake), with no competing garnishes. Petrossian offers an outstanding prix-fixe dinner (one of the world's great bargains in luxury dining) all evening; the supplement for 30 grams of Sevruga is relatively small. You may drink vodka with the caviar or champagne throughout. ✉ *182 W. 58th St., at 7th Ave.,* ☎ *212/245–2214. Reservations essential. AE, DC, MC, V.*

$$ ✕ **Jean Lafitte.** Owned by Eric Demarchelier and his brother, Patrick, the esteemed photographer, this popular spot has an attractively priced prix-fixe menu. The setting, with its abundance of wood, mirrors, and brass railings, and its Art Nouveau tulip-shape lighting fixtures, is straight out of Paris. You'll also welcome the sprightly bar scene. ✉ *68 W. 58th St., at 6th Ave.,* ☎ *212/751–2323. Reservations essential. AE, DC, MC, V. No lunch weekends.*

Greek

$–$$ ★ ✕ **Uncle Nick's.** This inexpensive taverna's long room has a navy blue pipe-lined tin ceiling, an exposed kitchen, and a wood floor, plus appetizing displays of whole red snapper, porgy, and striped bass. Uncle Nick's owners, Tony and Mike Vanatakis, prepare each fish selection with simplicity and care. A few excellent appetizers—crispy fried smelts, tender grilled baby octopus, marvelous sweetbreads, and giant lima beans with tomatoes and herbs—make a satisfying meal. In temperate weather there's outdoor dining in a quiet rear garden. ✉ *747 9th Ave., between 50th and 51st Sts.,* ☎ *212/245–7992. MC, V.*

Italian

$$$$ ★ ✕ **Palio.** Named after the 800-year-old Italian horse race that celebrates the Assumption of the Virgin, this is an exceptional restaurant, starting with the striking 13-ft Sandro Chia mural in the busy bar area downstairs. An elevator leads to the hushed second-floor dining room, a luxurious salon paneled in light oak, with generously spaced tables set with Frette linen and Riedel crystal. The cuisine excels, from a regional six-course menu from Siena to one based on aged balsamic vinegar. The wine selection and service match the posh setting. ✉ *151 W. 51st St., between 6th and 7th Aves.,* ☎ *212/245–4850. Reservations essential. Jacket and tie. AE, DC, MC, V. Closed Sun. No lunch Sat.*

$$$–$$$$ ★ ✕ **Barbetta.** New York's oldest restaurant still operated by its founding family (it opened in 1906) was one of the first to produce northern Italian food in America, and it remains faithful to tradition. The *carne cruda* (hand-chopped raw veal with lemon juice and olive oil) and handmade *agnolotti* (pasta stuffed with meat or vegetables and folded in half like turnovers) are superb. Besides the well-priced, carefully selected short wine list, there is a long version with many bottles dating from 1880. Housed in two antiques-furnished town houses on Restaurant Row, the restaurant has an enchanting garden; it's an island of civility in the neighborhood. ✉ *321 W. 46th St., between 8th and 9th Aves.,* ☎ *212/246–9171. Reservations essential. AE, DC, MC, V. Closed Sun. No lunch Mon.*

$$$–$$$$ ★ ✕ **San Domenico.** Owner Tony May presides over one of New York's most distinguished Italian restaurants. Terra-cotta floors, leather chairs, and lots of earthy hues set an understated, elegant tone in the villalike setting. Soft egg ravioli with truffle butter (the signature pasta) and loin of veal in smoked-bacon cream sauce exemplify the rich fare. Polenta *nera,* a chocolate hazelnut dessert soufflé, splendidly concludes a meal. The huge wine list showcases Italy's great vintages. Dining here can be a *very* expensive experience; prix-fixe dinners, especially on Sunday, help contain costs. ✉ *240 Central Park S, between Broadway and 7th Ave.,* ☎ *212/265–5959. Reservations essential. Jacket and tie required except on Sun. AE, MC, DC, V. No lunch weekends.*

$$$ ✕ **Osteria del Circo.** A festive atmosphere prevails in this restaurant run by the Maccioni family (owners of Le Cirque 2000 [☞ Midtown, *above*]). On the center pillar, architect Adam Tihany has arrayed a batch

of large monkeys that do tricks, and from the ceiling orange and red flags are suspended alongside a ropelike ladder; large metallic statues float over the open kitchen. The signature pizza pazza Circo (crazy pizza) has a delicate layer of mascarpone cheese and tomato, topped with thin prosciutto di Parma. Mama Egi's ravioli is filled with herbed spinach in delicate sage sauce. Don't miss the Circo cappuccino cup, espresso mousse in a coffee cup. ✉ *120 W. 55th St., between 6th and 7th Aves.,* ☎ *212/265–3636. Reservations essential. AE, DC, MC, V. No lunch Sun.*

$$$ ★ ✕ **Remi.** This stylish Italian restaurant—designed by architect Adam Tihany, who co-owns it with chef Francesco Antonucci—is striking with its nautical decor, skylighted open atrium-garden, blue-and-white-striped banquettes, Venetian-glass chandeliers, and soaring room-length mural of Venice by Paulin Paris. The accompanying contemporary Venetian cuisine is beautifully presented. Fresh sardines make a lovely beginning, with their contrasting sweet-and-sour onion garnish, and you can't go wrong with the expertly prepared rack of lamb or any of the wonderful desserts. ✉ *145 W. 53rd St., between 6th and 7th Aves.,* ☎ *212/581–4242. Reservations essential. AE, DC, MC, V. No lunch weekends.*

$$$ ✕ **Trattoria Dell'Arte.** This popular trattoria near Carnegie Hall still displays the oversize renderings of body parts, alongside portraits of Italian artists, in its three dining rooms. No matter the competition from the decor, the food commands attention, from the mouthwatering antipasti on the bar to the tasty pasta, pizza, hot focaccia sandwiches, and grilled double veal chop served with shoestring potatoes. Check out the wonderful cannoli, great wine list, and flavored grappas. ✉ *900 7th Ave., between 56th and 57th Sts.,* ☎ *212/245–9800. Reservations essential. AE, DC, MC, V.*

$$–$$$ ✕ **Lattanzi Ristorante.** An elegant Restaurant Row town house with several exposed-brick rooms, candles, flowers, and one of Manhattan's most romantic gardens is the setting for unusual Italian-Jewish cuisine. Notable dishes include the baby artichokes, flattened like a pancake and parchment-fried, so that even the leaves are edible. Homemade noodles with artichoke sauce and pecorino cheese is a pasta standout. Breads are remarkable, especially the huge, flat unleavened sheet of homemade matzo and the garlicky bread sticks. The napoleon is a glorious way to finish a meal. ✉ *361 W. 46th St., between 8th and 9th Aves.,* ☎ *212/315–0980. Reservations essential. AE. Closed Sun. No lunch Sat.*

$–$$ ★ ✕ **Amarone.** Named after the lush Italian red wine, this unpretentious trattoria is arguably the best Italian eatery on the Hell's Kitchen strip. The antipasti doesn't just look pretty, as in so many storefront pasta parlors—it's tasty, too. Inquire about such delectable specials as the chef's grandmother's country-style *cavatelli* (pasta shells) with sausage, carrots, and potatoes, or the excellent rabbit cacciatore. The wine list is also noteworthy, emphasizing numerous bottles of the namesake wine from top producers in fine vintages. ✉ *686 9th Ave., between 47th and 48th Sts.,* ☎ *212/245–6060. AE, MC, V.*

$–$$ ✕ **Frico Bar.** Owned by Lidia Bastianich of Felidia (☞ Midtown, *above*) and son Joseph, this casual place serves an array of tempting snacks ranging from thin-crust pizza to the house specialty, *frico,* a crustless pizza of griddle-crisped cheese stuffed with potatoes and vegetables. As in the Friulian countryside, wine comes on tap, along with 10 excellent beers. The restaurant has an engaging decor: tile floors and a moon-and-star logo that adorns the attractive wooden tables. ✉ *402 W. 43rd St., off 9th Ave.,* ☎ *212/564–7272. AE, DC, MC, V.*

$–$$ ✕ **Mangia e Bevi.** In this down-to-earth slice of Naples, murals of Italy, ceiling fans, checkered tablecloths, an open kitchen, and a wood-burning oven set the scene. Pizza aficionados will be happy (try the white four-cheese pizza), and there's also good bread to smear with virgin olive oil and focaccia with herb-marinated Mediterranean olives. Among the bargain-priced pastas, try rigatoni *Amatriciana*—brimming with homemade tomato sauce, Italian bacon, and spices. Waiters in T-shirts are helpful, as the music blares and customers slap tambourines and join in the fun. ✉ *800 9th Ave., at 53rd St.,* ☎ *212/956–3976. AE, DC, MC, V.*

$–$$ ✕ **Osteria al Doge.** Warm yellow walls and a two-tiered room with a charming balcony, long mahogany bar, colorful framed posters, and bare oak family tables conjure Tuscany in Times Square, as do the marvelous risottos and the thin-crust pizza with mozzarella, fresh tomatoes, arugula, and prosciutto. Leave room for warm pecan tart and cinnamon ice cream. ✉ *142 W. 44th St., between Broadway and 6th Ave.,* ☎ *212/944–3643. Reservations essential. AE, DC, MC, V.*

$ ✕ **Bar Nine.** Period antiques and sofas, wonderful mix-and-match chandeliers, and photos of saluting World War I servicemen create an offbeat setting for constrastingly simple yet contrasting food—it's basically American with European overtones. Warm bread arrives with olive oil, salt, red and black pepper, and a sprig of fresh rosemary that's meant to be used as a brush. Caesar salad and sautéed skate are perfectly done. In the evening a deejay spins contemporary music till the wee hours, and on weekends it's a great place for an inexpensive brunch. ✉ *809 9th Ave., at 54th St.,* ☎ *212/399–9336. AE, MC, V.*

Kosher

$$$ ★ ✕ **Le Marais.** The appetizing display of raw meats and terrines at the entrance and the bare wood floors may remind you of a Parisian bistro. Tables covered with butcher paper, French wall posters, and maroon banquettes reinforce that image. Yet the clientele (mostly male) is strictly kosher. A cold *terrine de boeuf en gelée façon pot au feu* (marinated short ribs) starts the meal on the right note, and rib steak for two is cooked to a turn, tender and juicy. The accompanying fries are perfect. ✉ *150 W. 46th St., between 6th and 7th Aves.,* ☎ *212/869–0900. AE, MC, V. No dinner Fri., no lunch Sat.*

Latin

$$–$$$ ✕ **Victor's Café 52.** This Technicolor Cuban restaurant has big high-back booths, a tile floor, and a raised back room with skylight. The blasting Latin American music and an atmosphere harking back to movie musicals set in old Havana seem not to bode well for serious dining. But the food is often fine, a contemporary transcription of Cuban, Puerto Rican, and Latino signature dishes: hearty paella, black bean soup, and fried bananas. ✉ *236 W. 52nd St., between Broadway and 8th Ave.,* ☎ *212/586–7714. AE, DC, MC, V.*

$ ✕ **Pomaire.** Named after a small village in Chile renowned for its pottery (in which many of the dishes are served), Manhattan's only Chilean restaurant has exposed brick, handmade rugs, a faux skylight, and attractive paintings; live music is occasionally offered. The intriguing dinner options include *pastel de choclo,* a casserole of beef, olives, chicken, onions, and egg that is covered with a corn puree, dusted with sugar, and baked in a clay pot. Leave room for *torta de mil hojas*—leaves of pastry layered with caramel. ✉ *371 W. 46th St., between 8th and 9th Aves.,* ☎ *212/956–3056. AE, DC, MC, V. No lunch.*

Russian

$$–$$$$ ★ ✕ **Firebird.** Housed in two brownstones renovated to emulate a St. Petersburg mansion, with eight dining rooms full of objets d'art and period antiques, Firebird has captured the Russian Tearoom celebrity crowd. Staples of the Russian regional cuisine range from caviar and *zakuska* (assorted Russian hors d'oeuvres) to tea with cherry pre-

serves, and signature desserts (an assortment of terrific Russian cookies steal the show). Don't fail to sample the extraordinary vodka selection, and inquire about the attractively priced pretheater selection of zakuska. Firebird Cafe, next door, has become a fashionable cabaret nightspot and serves desserts as well as vodkas. ✉ *365 W. 46th St., between 8th and 9th Aves.,* ☎ *212/586–0244. AE, DC, MC, V.*

Southwestern

$$–$$$ ✕ **Tapika.** Tapika's adobe-brown walls, faux pony-skin bar stools, branded wood, and steel light fixtures with Native American cutout designs pay fanciful tribute to the American West. To suit the setting, chef David Walzog expertly reinvents southwestern cuisine with such dishes as barbecued short ribs (falling off the bone), wild mushroom tamale, and incendiary ground-vegetable chili rellenos, served with smoked tomato salsa and crumpled cheese. The margaritas are terrific. ✉ *950 8th Ave., at 56th St.,* ☎ *212/397–3737. DC, MC, V.*

Steak

$$$–$$$$ ★ ✕ **Ben Benson's.** Not only are steaks, chops, and accompaniments first-rate here, there is also a real chef in the kitchen. Witness such contemporary steak-house fare as cold lobster cocktail and Maryland crab cakes, steaks, chops, and the fabulous prime rib, as well as such excellent daily specials as Friday's crusted fish hash. Don't miss the horseradish mashed potatoes or the home fries. The wine list improves with each visit. This convivial spot has a masculine interior—brass plaques inscribed with names of celebrities, framed pictures of animals. ✉ *123 W. 52nd St., between 6th and 7th Aves.,* ☎ *212/581–8888. Reservations essential. AE, DC, MC, V. No lunch weekends.*

$$$–$$$$ ✕ **Gallagher's Steak House.** The most casual of New York steak houses, with checkered tablecloths and photos of sports greats on the walls, Gallagher's has almost no pretensions and nothing to hide—even the meat-aging room is visible through the window. You won't be disappointed with the famous aged sirloin steaks, oversize lobsters, or any of the fabulous potato dishes (try the potatoes O'Brien with sweet pepper and onion). Don't miss the creamy rice pudding. ✉ *228 W. 52nd St., between Broadway and 8th Ave.,* ☎ *212/245–5336. Reservations essential. AE, DC, MC, V.*

$$$–$$$$ ✕ **Ruth's Chris Steak House.** Manhattan's genteel addition to this group of more than 40 so-named restaurants around the world is giving other steak houses around town a run for their money. With its Impressionist-style oil paintings, dark red walls, and crisp white napkins and tablecloths on well spaced tables, it's much more inviting than its location at the base of a nondescript office tower might suggest. Moreover, the steaks and chops, served sizzling in butter unless you specify otherwise, are tops. The menu defines degrees of doneness according to temperature and color, and the kitchen serves just what you request. ✉ *148 W. 51st St., between 6th and 7th Aves.,* ☎ *212/245–9600. Reservations essential. AE, DC, MC, V. No lunch weekends.*

Upper East Side

Beware the silk-stocking district, where overpriced, stuffy rooms have tables too close together and food just not up to standard. But if you look hard, you can find some really wonderful restaurants; the area is peppered with small storefront cafés and trattorias with passable pastas at surprisingly low prices.

Afghan

$ ✕ **Afghan Kebab House #2.** At this cavelike Afghan restaurant, scenic posters, copper platters, and Afghan rugs cover the walls. Newcomers to this cuisine should enjoy the *aushak,* or boiled dumplings, filled with scallions, herbs, and spices and topped with yogurt; the spiced half-chicken, marinated in fresh grated spices and hot peppers; and the vegetable combination plate. Menus are similar at two other locations, in Clinton (✉ 764 9th Ave., between 51st and 52nd Sts., ☎ 212/307–1612; no credit cards) and midtown (✉ 155 W. 46th St., ☎ 212/768–3875), but the decor at these is less dramatic. ✉ *1345 2nd Ave., between 70th and 71st Sts.,* ☎ *212/517–2776. AE, DC, MC, V. BYOB.*

American/Casual

$$$ ✕ **Lobster Club.** This two-story town-house restaurant resembles a New England inn with its bleached-wood beamed ceilings and inlaid mosaic floors, and, in the more formal second floor, the fireplace and vaulted ceiling. Chef Anne Rosenzweig (☞ Arcadia *in* French, *below*) has created an appealing menu of updated comfort food. The signature dish is the lobster club sandwich, a luxurious play on a classic, accompanied by plantain chips. ✉ *24 E. 80th St., between 5th and Madison Aves.,* ☎ *212/249–6500. Reservations essential. AE, MC, V. No lunch Sun.*

$–$$ ★ ✕ **Hi-Life Restaurant and Lounge.** Young East Siders wait in line to sit down at one of the spacious half-moon-shape booths at this bi-level Art Deco café. The draw? Soothing prices, huge portions, and some of the best martinis in town. Join the crowd and polish off sushi or something from the raw bar before you proceed to the filet mignon, sliced and served with potato salad or heaping bowls of *pad thai* (fried noodles with chicken or shrimp). Hi-Life's West Side location serves similar fare (✉ 477 Amsterdam Ave., at 83rd St., ☎ 212/787–7199). ✉ *1340 1st Ave., at 72nd St.,* ☎ *212/249–3600. AE, DC, MC, V.*

$–$$ ✕ **Serendipity 3.** This whimsical store-cum-café has been producing excellent burgers, foot-long hot dogs (with or without chili), French toast, omelets, salads, and other interesting if overly complicated plates since 1954. But most people come for the fantasy sundaes—huge, naughty, and decadent—and Serendipity's signature dessert, frozen hot chocolate. ✉ *225 E. 60th St., between 2nd and 3rd Aves.,* ☎ *212/838–3531. AE, DC, MC, V. BYOB.*

$–$$ ✕ **Seventh Regiment Mess and Bar.** The fourth floor of the historic Seventh Regiment Armory (☞ Chapter 2) is home to this restaurant with high ceilings and appropriately militaristic motifs. The homey food—-chicken à la king, pork chops, roast beef, and mustardy deviled beef bones—is served at rock-bottom prices. ✉ *643 Park Ave., at 66th St.,* ☎ *212/744–4107. AE, MC, V. Closed Sun.–Mon. No lunch.*

Chinese

$–$$ ✕ **Evergreen Cafe.** Come here for the Chinatown-style dumplings (try asparagus or seafood fillings) and the full range of noodle and rice dishes, such as Singapore-style curry-flavor noodles or diced chicken in salted fish-flavor fried rice. This attractive restaurant has blond-wood tables, ceiling fans, and an illuminated emerald sculpture; the back dining room tends to be quieter. ✉ *1288 1st Ave., at 69th St.,* ☎ *212/744–3266. AE, DC, MC, V.*

Contemporary

$$$$ ✕ **Aureole.** Charles Palmer's fashionable restaurant, with its alluring bas-reliefs, striking floral displays, and swank town-house location, is one of the town's toughest reservations. Appetizers are fetching: the signature sea scallop sandwich (between shredded potatoes and then deep fried) is always available and a fricassee of lobster with Provençale artichokes or pepper-seared tuna on green onion risotto will most certainly please. Desserts are visual masterpieces—bittersweet chocolate and praline "opera" with caramelized hazelnut nougats is a high-rise wonder that requires some dexterity to dissect

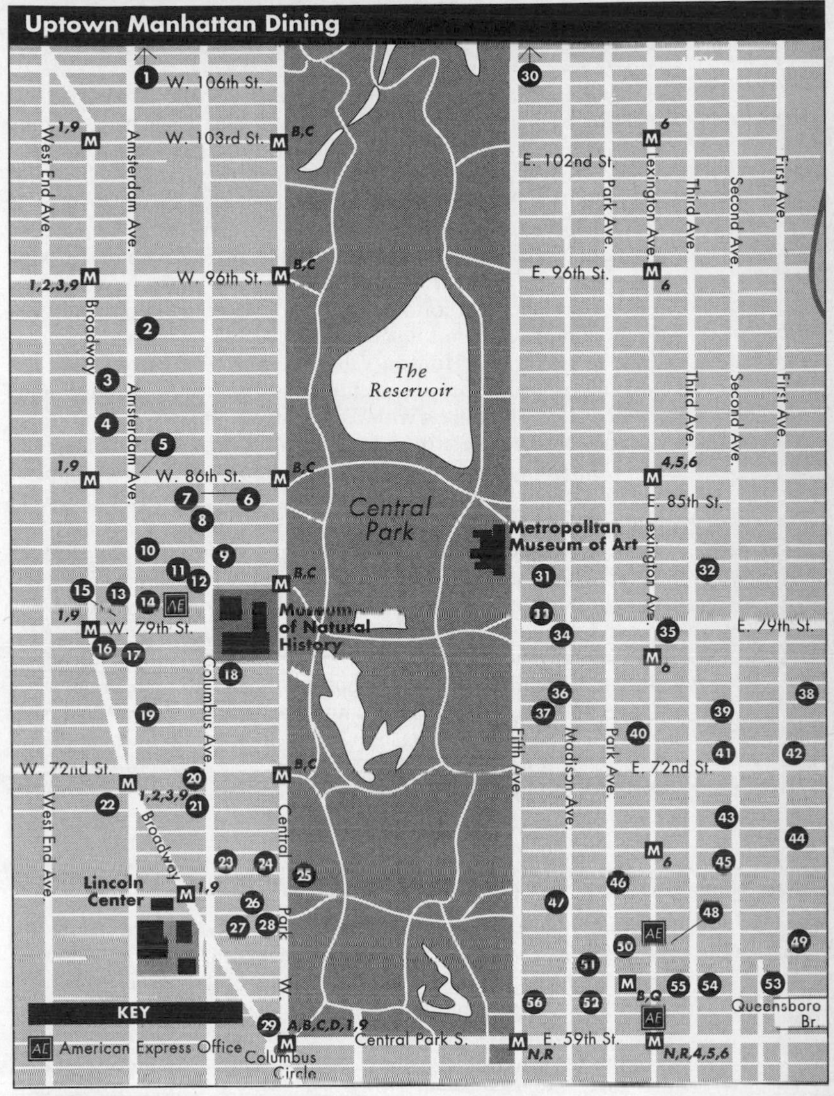

Afghan Kebab House #2, **43**
Aureole, **52**
Boonthai, **41**
Café des Artistes, **24**
Café Luxembourg, **22**
Café Pierre, **56**
Carmine's, **3**
China Fun, **20**
Coco Pazzo, **37**
Daniel, **36**
Decade, **53**
Emily's, **30**
Evergreen Cafe, **44**
Ferrier, **47**
Firehouse, **7**
Fujiyama Mama, **9**
Gabriela's, **2**
Hi-Life Restaurant and Lounge, **10**
Isabella's, **18**
Jean Georges, **29**
Jo Jo, **48**
Joe's Fish Shack, **6**
L'Absinthe, **45**
Lincoln Tavern, **27**
Lobster Club, **33**
Mad Fish, **17**
Main Street, **12**
Manhattan Grille, **49**
Matthew's, **55**
Nino's, **42**
Nola, **13**
Parioli Romanissimo, **31**
Park Avenue Cafe, **50**
Payard Pâtisserie & Bistro, **40**
Penang Columbus, **21**
Persepolis, **39**
Picholine, **28**
Popover Café, **5**
Post House, **51**
Rain, **11**
Red Tulip, **38**
Salt, **8**
Sarabeth's Kitchen, **14**
Savaan, **15**
Savannah Club, **4**
Serendipity 3, **54**
Seventh Regiment Mess and Bar, **46**
Shark Bar, **19**
Shun Lee West, **26**
Sofia Fabulous Pizza, **34**
Tavern on the Green, **25**
Terrace, **1**
Trois Jean, **35**
Two Two Two, **16**
Vince and Eddie's, **23**
Zócalo, **32**

without destroying. The small garden (seven to eight tables) is open in the summer. ✉ *34 E. 61st St., between Madison and Park Aves.,* ☎ *212/319–1660. Reservations essential. AE, DC, MC, V. Closed Sun. No lunch Sat.*

$$$–$$$$ ✕ **Decade.** Remember the swing and the hustle? Their newest home also offers fine dining in a sophisticated setting. The wine and spirits vault is one of the city's largest, and a walk-in humidor is stocked with more than 100 different cigars (you even get to smoke them in a NASA-engineered "smokeless" smoking environment). Behind the romantic upstairs dining room is a long table, perfect for small groups wanting privacy. The constantly changing tasting menu showcases the creative new American food, which is far better than you might expect, given the club-cum-lounge venue. The à la carte menu includes an appetizer of seared Hudson Valley foie gras with berry coulis, *vin santo,* and toasted brioche, and entrée stars such as horseradish-and-potato-crusted wild salmon with vegetable capellini in a citrus and sorrel sauce. Desserts are strong points: An assortment of homemade biscotti and smooth, intense ice creams and sorbets are showstoppers. ✉ *1117 1st Ave., between 61st and 62nd Sts.,* ☎ *212/835–5979. Jacket required. AE, DC, MC, V.*

$$$–$$$$ ✕ **Park Avenue Cafe.** American folk art, antique toys, and sheaves of dried wheat decorate this unpretentious pacesetter. The Flag Room, to the left of the bar, is more sedate. David Burke's presentations are imaginative and often whimsical: Salmon is cured like pastrami and arrives on a marble slab, with warm corn blini (pancakes), while the signature swordfish "chop" comes dressed with a numbered tag (save the tag, sign the book, and you may win an all-inclusive holiday). The pastry chef's masterpieces include a milk chocolate crème brûlée. ✉ *100 E. 63rd St., between Park and Lexington Aves.,* ☎ *212/644–1900. Reservations essential. AE, DC, MC, V. No lunch Sat.*

Eastern European

$$ ✕ **Red Tulip.** With the gypsy violins and high-back wooden booths, the atmosphere is early Budapest (via MGM), heavy on the gemütlichkeit. The food is a bit more contemporary; try the celebrated chicken paprika with egg dumplings, the crispy roast goose, the stuffed cabbage, or the sausage with onions, green peppers, and tomato sauce. *Palacsinta* (crepes) with assorted fillings are a graceful example of this time-honored dessert. ✉ *439 E. 75th St., between 1st and York Aves.,* ☎ *212/734–4893. AE, DC, MC, V. Closed Mon.–Tues. No lunch.*

French

$$$$ ✕ **Café Pierre.** The long room is a jewel, with its ornate mirrors, overhead cloud murals, and tables with gold lamé skirts under white cloths. The contemporary French cuisine gets high marks as does the selection of wines by the glass. You can have coffee or an after-dinner drink at the piano bar, where there's dancing Thursday, Friday, and Saturday nights. ✉ *2 E. 61st St., between 5th and Madison Aves.,* ☎ *212/940–8195. Reservations essential. Jacket and tie. AE, DC, MC, V.*

$$$$ ★ ✕ **Daniel.** At Daniel Boulud's $1.9 million restaurant, lavish flower arrangements, antique mirrors, and wall-to-wall celebrities adorn the main dining room, with its exquisite table settings by Limoges, gold-tinted walls, and red-checked banquettes. The cuisine, at once contemporary and classic, is among the best in New York. Note the uncommon tuna tartare, with a touch of curry, and the signature black sea bass, wrapped in a crispy potato shell. Spoil yourself with

the all-chocolate or all-fruit dessert menu. At press time the restaurant announced that it would change its format and open as a more informal place, Café Boulud, in the same location. A new Restaurant Daniel is planned for 60 East 65th Street; opening date is early 1999. ✉ *20 E. 76th St., between 5th and Madison Aves.,* ☎ *212/288–0033. Reservations essential. Jacket required. AE, D, DC, MC, V. Closed Sun. No lunch Mon.*

$$$ ★ ✕ **Jo Jo.** New York's most fashionable bistro has an upstairs dining area with burgundy banquettes, a black-and-white tile floor, and the obligatory etched-glass and gilt-edge mirrors. Jean-Georges Vongerichten (☞ Jean Georges, *in* Upper West Side, *below,* and Vong, *in* Midtown, *above*) follows a culinary approach that is personal (French with Asian accents), healthy (infused oils, juices, and reductions rather than heavy sauces), and classic (hardy bistro dishes freely updated). Goat-cheese-and-potato terrine is typical of Vongerichten's culinary range, as are the signature shrimp in spiced-carrot juice and Thai lime leaves, and the simple chicken roasted with ginger, green olives, and ginger juice, accompanied by chickpea-tahini fritters. ✉ *160 E. 64th St., between Lexington and 3rd Aves.,* ☎ *212/223–5656. Reservations essential. AE, MC, V. Closed Sun. No lunch Sat.*

$$$ ★ ✕ **L'Absinthe.** The wonderful Art Nouveau bistro decor features etched glass, huge gilt-framed mirrors, tile floors, and a few sidewalk tables. Chef-owner Jean-Michel Bergougnoux takes shellfish and cheese seriously, and they are both beautifully presented. Highlights on the menu include a fine foie gras terrine, slow-braised beef with carrots, poached free-range chicken in truffle broth, and a thin, crisp apple tart or warm chocolate cake. ✉ *227 E. 67th St., between 2nd and 3rd Aves.,* ☎ *212/794–4950. Reservations essential. AE, MC, V.*

$$$ ✕ **Trois Jean.** What makes Trois Jean one of the city's most exciting bistros is its special *plat du jour*: Monday, it's couscous (an exotic stew of lamb, chicken, vegetables and spices, served over the national cereal of North Africa); Tuesday, *choucroute* (Alsatian sauerkraut with smoked meats); Wednesday, pot-au-feu; Thursday, *blanquette de veau* (veal in white wine and cream); Friday, lobster bouillabaisse; Saturday, *boeuf bourguignon* (beef stewed in red wine); and Sunday, *gigot d'agneau* (roast leg of lamb). From late fall through early December, there is a special white and black truffle menu. Desserts are all wonderful—especially the signature chocolate pyramid. The captivating two-level restaurant offers a charming Parisian café atmosphere downstairs and an open kitchen in back. Upstairs is an a more formal bistro room with eye-catching paintings. ✉ *154 E. 79th St., between Lexington and 3rd Aves.,* ☎ *212/988–4858. Reservations essential. AE, MC, V.*

$$–$$$ ✕ **Ferrïer.** There are a few tables at its sidewalk café in the summer, but any time of the year, this very popular bistro will give you some idea of how tinned sardines must feel. The service and reception are so friendly and the food so delicious and copious you won't even mind the relatively high prices. Savor steak au poivre, grilled tuna Ferrier, and profiteroles. Alas, the wine list is not up to par. ✉ *29 E. 65th St., between Madison and Park Aves.,* ☎ *212/772–9000. Reservations essential. AE, DC, MC, V.*

$$–$$$ ★ ✕ **Payard Pâtisïserie & Bistro.** Pastry chef François Payard and Daniel Boulud (☞ Daniel, *above*) have created a knockout combination bistro and pastry shop (☞ Coffee Bars and Cafés, *below*). Mahogany paneling, gilt-frame mirrors, and, up front, a Roman-style mosaic floor (it depicts pastries) are a fresh, regal updating of a European café aesthetic.

Appetizers on the bistro menu include an adventurous salad of pig's-feet fritters and baby French-style green beans, and fresh terrine of homemade foie gras. Among the entrées are melt-in-your-mouth lamb shank with baby artichokes and eggplant and delicious caramelized sweetbreads with orange, rosemary, carrot, and turnip confit. Payard's desserts—tarts, soufflés, and cakes—are extraordinary. ✉ *1032 Lexington Ave., between 73rd and 74th Sts.,* ☎ *212/717–5252. Reservations essential. AE, MC, V. Closed Sun.*

Italian

$$$$ ✕ **Parioli Romanissimo.** One of New York's most astounding selections of imported cheese beckons at the entrance to the exquisite main dining area of this formal Italian restaurant, in a splendid Upper East Side town house. A marble fireplace, original plaster-molded ceiling, and spacious tables are the perfect setting for such graceful offerings as sautéed sea scallops seared in peppercorns, in a discreet watercress sauce, and roasted rack of young lamb, marinated in spicy oil, herbs, and garlic. The wine list showcases jewels from Italy, France, and California, and 12 kinds of teas are available, presented in apothecary jars. ✉ *24 E. 81st St., between 5th and Madison Aves.,* ☎ *212/288–2391. Reservations essential. Jacket required. AE, DC, MC, V. Closed Sun. No lunch.*

$$$ ✕ **Coco Pazzo.** The main dining room glows with ecru walls, yellow tablecloths, colorful murals, and huge urns of flowers—a setting that helps make this one of New York's best restaurants for celebrity spotting. All pastas and risottos are splendid; it's hard to resist the *maccheroncini al pepolino* (rectangles of fresh egg pasta in a rich tomato sauce with thyme and grated aged pecorino cheese). The roasted whole fish of the day is always a standout entrée. Though the *crosta di fruta fresca* (open-faced fruit tart) changes its face often, it never disappoints. Owner Pino Luongo has opened two clones: Coco Opera (✉ 58 W. 65th St., between Columbus Ave. and Central Park W, ☎ 212/873–3700), near Lincoln Center, and Coco Pazzo Teatro (✉ 235 W. 46th St., between Broadway and 8th Ave., in the Paramount Hotel, ☎ 212/827–4222). ✉ *23 E. 74th St., between 5th and Madison Aves.,* ☎ *212/794–0205. Reservations essential. AE, MC, V.*

$$$ ✕ **Nino's.** Lobster *fra diablo,* finished in a chafing dish and served on a bed of perfect linguine, is a specialty at this popular Italian restaurant, with its lively piano bar, sienna walls hung with large framed paintings, and breathtaking floral arrangements. Even fresh fruit becomes an uncommon dessert when it's artistically arranged on an ice sculpture, preceding a beautiful espresso *macchiato.* ✉ *1354 1st Ave., between 72nd and 73rd Sts.,* ☎ *212/988–0002. Reservations essential. AE, MC, V. No lunch.*

Mediterranean

$$–$$$ ✕ **Matthew's.** White shutters, ceiling fans, rattan chairs, jumbo potted plants, and warm colors give this café an airy, attractive setting. Chef Matthew Kenney's eclectic, contemporary style imparts a fresh touch to all the dishes. The tuna tartare, more coarsely chopped here than in most other new American restaurants, is served with a Mediterranean green-olive condiment. Terrific Moroccan-spiced lamb shank comes with dried fruits and couscous. A soft-center chocolate hazelnut cake makes life worth living. ✉ *1030 3rd Ave., at 61st St.,* ☎ *212/838–4343. Reservations essential. AE, DC, MC, V.*

Mexican

$$–$$$ ✕ **Zócalo.** Come here for the best margaritas in New York and for the lovely dips: warm *tomatillo* (green tomato), tomato *chipotle* (smoked chili), *pico de gallo* (raw onion-tomato salsa), and chunky guacamole, beautifully presented in the traditional *molcajete* (lava-rock utensil). Among the inventive dishes are grilled clams in a banana-leaf wrapping with a peanut-tomato sauce and chocolate sorbet laced with jalapeño peppers. Burnt orange and blue walls add zest to the attractive long main dining room. ✉ *174 82nd St., between Lexington and 3rd Aves.,* ☎ *212/717–7772. AE, DC, MC, V.*

Middle Eastern

$$ ✕ **Persepolis.** Smoked-glass mirrors, huge globe light fixtures, and carpeted banquettes decorate Manhattan's only authentic Persian restaurant. Order as many appetizers as you can handle, including *baba ghanoush* (eggplant and tahini puree), *torshi* (pickled carrots, eggplant, celery, garlic, and parsley), and the olive salad. The Persepolis kebab (filet mignon, chopped steak, and chicken) on skewers is a fine example of this delicate and choice cuisine. ✉ *1423 2nd Ave., between 74th and 75th Sts.,* ☎ *212/535–1100. AE, DC, MC, V.*

Pizza

$–$$ ★ ✕ **Sofia Fabulous Pizza.** Mediterranean-color friezes, an inviting upstairs terrace, and hordes of models and celebrities grace this very Italian café adorned with wine racks and wall sconces made of Japanese paper. Sofia serves some of Manhattan's best pizza and variations on focaccia (one secret: the menu claims the water used in the dough is filtered to resemble the waters of Naples). Mozzarella on the breathtaking thin-crust pizza is made daily with fresh milk. For a singular treat try the mashed potatoes slathered with homemade tomato sauce and Parmesan cheese and then baked in the oven. ✉ *1022 Madison Ave., near 79th St.,* ☎ *212/734–2676. AE, DC, MC, V.*

Steak

$$$–$$$$ ✕ **Post House.** Superior grilling and first-rate ingredients are only half the appeal. Good service, inventive daily specials, and the inordinately comfortable main dining room, with leather armchairs, capacious tables, and parquet floor, complete the picture. Triple lamb chops, Caesar salad, and the signature chocolate-box dessert—Belgian chocolate filled with white and dark chocolate mousse—are all perfectly prepared. The vast, beautifully organized wine list includes the "Wine Library" (wines at least 10 years old) and "California Cache" (California wines unavailable elsewhere). ✉ *28 E. 63rd St., between Madison and Park Aves., in the Lowell Hotel,* ☎ *212/935–2888. Reservations essential. Jacket required. AE, DC, MC, V. No lunch weekends.*

$$$ ★ ✕ **Manhattan Grille.** A bronze doorway that once graced the old Biltmore hotel is the appropriately grand portal of this steak house, where, inside, cut flowers, Art Deco chandeliers, Persian carpets, a glass-enclosed cafe, and deep hunter green upholstery are a far cry from the rush-and-crush atmosphere of most competitors. There's no better double sirloin or Porterhouse in town: huge, juicy, well-marbled and -aged—and perfectly grilled. Precede it with a terrific baby lobster cocktail, or stone crab (in season). The menu offers a noteworthy beef short rib, baked in a luscious honey-mustard sauce. Sunday brunch is a pleasure, and if you want one of the best lunch deals in town, go for the fabulous homemade roast beef hash or a super salad Nicoise (with fresh tuna). Manhattan Grille's wine list is easy to negotiate and offers lots of good choices under $30. ✉ *1161 1st Ave., between 63rd and 64th Sts.,* ☎ *212/888–6556. AE, DC, MC, V. No lunch Sat.*

Thai

$–$$ ✕ **Boonthai.** A warm greeting awaits at this mirrored, softly lighted charmer full of pretty paintings and crisply set tables. The service is accommodating—the heat of the food can be tempered to your taste. If you like it hot, sample the deep-fried whole fish with chili sauce. Or order the chicken in not-so-spicy *masman* (red Muslim curry) sauce, the pad thai, or the obliging deep-fried duck. ✉ *1393A 2nd Ave., be-*

tween 72nd and 73rd Sts., ☎ *212/249–8484. Reservations essential. AE, MC, V. No lunch weekends.*

Lincoln Center

Considering that Lincoln Center's theaters can accommodate more than 18,000 spectators at one time, you'd think the area would be chockablock with restaurants catering to all tastes and budgets. Alas, perhaps it's precisely because of its captive audience and its many diners eating under time constraints that keep this area from becoming one of the city's more distinguished culinary-wise. To increase your choices, consider restaurants in the northern reaches of Clinton and the Carnegie Hall areas, as well as those on and around Central Park South.

American/Casual

$$–$$$ ✕ **Vince and Eddie's.** Realistic prices, generous portions, and friendly service are the order of the day in this bucolic restaurant occupying a series of small rooms and a seasonal garden patterned on a country inn. Executive chef Scott Campbell's contemporary American fare is always a pleasure. Lamb shank with dried cherries and mashed turnips has deservedly become a classic. Save room for the magnificent desserts: Sorbets, ice creams, and even humble cobblers take on a new dimension. ✉ *70 W. 68th St., between Columbus Ave. and Central Park W,* ☎ *212/721–0068. Reservations essential. AE, DC, MC, V.*

$–$$ ✕ **Lincoln Tavern.** At this classic pub with wood walls, leather banquettes, and vintage black-and-white photographs, you have a good choice of classic and regional American entrées, typified by chicken quesadilla with fresh roasted corn and jalapeño Jack cheese, braised lamb shank with seasonal vegetables, and for dessert, a chocolate macadamia-nut brownie. ✉ *51 W. 64th St., between Broadway and Central Park W,* ☎ *212/721–8271. AE, DC, MC, V.*

Chinese

$$–$$$ ✕ **Shun Lee West.** This dramatically lighted study in black, accented by white dragons and monkeys, is a good choice when visiting Lincoln Center. The adjacent cafés is a bit less expensive and serves credible dim sum. Service is attentive, and considering the number of people the restaurant serves, the food can be excellent. Shanghai steamed dumplings and giant prawns make stellar starters. Then try the Peking duck, sweetbreads with hot peppers and scallions, or rack of lamb Szechuan style. Fresh fruit makes an ideal dessert. The food at **Shun Lee Palace** (✉ 155 E. 55th St., between Lexington and 3rd Aves., ☎ 212/371–8844), under the same management, is equally good. ✉ *43 W. 65th St., between Columbus Ave. and Central Park W,* ☎ *212/595–8895. Reservations essential. AE, DC, MC, V.*

Contemporary

$$$ ✕ **Tavern on the Green.** Impresario Warner LeRoy's lavish restaurant is a visual fantasy, and careful selection can yield a surprisingly satisfying meal. The simplest dishes are the best bet: Shrimp cocktail, southern American specialties like barbecued ribs or pork chops, and any of the above-average desserts, such as fruit cobbler or a decadent ice cream sundae. There's also jazz in the Chestnut Room, and cabaret. If you want drama, request the brilliant Crystal Room, for its view of the twinkle-lighted trees and fantastic mélange of chandeliers, or opt for alfresco dining in the engaging garden. Prix-fixe menus lower the tab. The wine list is well chosen if expensive. ✉ *In Central Park at 67th St.,* ☎ *212/873–3200. Reservations essential. AE, DC, MC, V.*

Continental

$$$–$$$$ ★ ✕ **Café des Artistes.** Restaurant consultant, entrepreneur, and writer, George Lang has created New York's most European café-restaurant. Polished-oak woodwork and rosy Howard Chandler Christy murals of nymphs at play contribute to the snug, beautiful ambience. The cuisine is as refined as the setting. Four-way salmon, with tidbits of the fish that are smoked, poached, dill-marinated, or raw, is a perfect introduction, and it would be hard to find a better pot-au-feu, the French variation on pot roast, here presented with bone marrow and traditional accompaniments. Desserts are appealing: Request the mocha *dacquoise* (layers of hazelnut meringue, sandwiched together with French butter cream). For wines go with the George Lang selections, *Gundel* wines from Hungary, or the special basket wines. Brunch is especially festive. ✉ *1 W. 67th St., at Central Park W,* ☎ *212/877–3500. Reservations essential. Jacket required. AE, DC, MC, V.*

French

$$–$$$ ✕ **Café Luxembourg.** This bustling, sophisticated bistro with airy arched windows, a zinc-top bar, and racks of newspapers brings a bit of SoHo to the Upper West Side. The well-heeled clientele comes for steak frîtes, soothing roasted free-range chicken with mashed potatoes, and a robust cassoulet. Desserts are mostly fine, especially the mouth-watering profiteroles. Several prix-fixe menus lower the tab. There is a very good selection of wines. ✉ *200 W. 70th St., between Amsterdam and West End Aves.,* ☎ *212/873–7411. Reservations essential. AE, DC, MC, V. No lunch Mon.*

Mediterranean

$$$–$$$$ ★ ✕ **Picholine.** Named for the small green Mediterranean olive of the same name (and the house olive, brought to your table at the start of your meal), this mellow restaurant is patterned on a Provençal farmhouse, with soft colors, wood floors, and dried flowers. Chef-proprietor Terrance Brennan's food is among the finest in Manhattan. Top dishes include the signature grilled octopus with fennel, potato, and lemon-pepper dressing; Moroccan-spiced loin of lamb with vegetable couscous and mint-yogurt sauce; and tournedos of salmon with horseradish crust, cucumbers, and salmon caviar. A cheese selection of some 30 varieties (the restaurant has its own cave in which they ripen it), in prime condition and served at room temperature, is indicative of Brennan's commitment to quality. The wine list offers outstanding wines by the glass; there's also a small wine area seating up to eight that offers special tasting menus. ✉ *35 W. 64th St., off Broadway,* ☎ *212/724–8585. Reservations essential. AE, DC, MC, V. Closed Sun. No lunch Mon.*

Upper West Side

The adventurous will find some interesting new ethnic options in this area, including American soul food, Dominican, and Latin coffee-shops-cum-diners, plus some moderately successful attempts at transferring a downtown spirit uptown.

American/Casual

$$ ✕ **Main Street.** Bring kids, friends, and an appetite, as everything at this American-as-apple-pie restaurant is served family style, from the whole roasted chicken to the terrific meat loaf. Since every order comes large enough to split four ways, don't let the prices turn you off (just divide by four). The lighting is a bit uncharitable, and the decibel level can be unfortunate, but the terrific puddings and pies will send you out on an high note. ✉ *446 Columbus Ave., between 81st and 82nd Sts.,* ☎ *212/873–5025. AE, DC, MC, V. No lunch weekdays.*

$–$$ ✕ **Popover Café.** There's a certain captivating, innocent quality to the honest American food in this vintage West Side tearoom-cum-restaurant full of teddy bears. Besides the superb popover, you'll admire the soups and the delectable sandwiches. Sunday brunch packs them in. ✉ *551 Amsterdam Ave., between 86th and 87th Sts.,* ☎ *212/595–8555. Reservations essential. AE, MC, V.*

$–$$ ✕ **Sarabeth's Kitchen.** Don't let the bric-a-brac and homespun charm deceive you: Sarabeth's, an Upper West Side legend, is more than a mere tearoom. The eclectic menu embraces such appetizers as crispy popcorn shrimp and piña colada slaw with cilantro dipping sauce, homespun American entrées like chicken potpie, and inventive takeoffs like a bow-tie pasta version of a BLT. The affordable wine list includes some unexpected bottles from small producers; such desserts as cranberry-pear bread pudding and homemade ice creams and sorbets are also noteworthy. This is a fine place for breakfast (served daily until 3:30) and brunch, and there are two branches with similar fare at 1295 Madison Avenue (✉ Between 92nd and 93rd Sts., ☎ 212/410–7335) and in the Whitney Museum of American Art (✉ 945 Madison Ave., at 75th St., ☎ 212/570–3670). ✉ *423 Amsterdam Ave., between 80th and 81st Sts.,* ☎ *212/496–6280. AE, DC, MC, V.*

$ ✕ **Firehouse.** There's a reason this find calls itself a firehouse: The sauce they use on the jerk-chicken pizza has enough kick to get you to Jamaica without an airplane (you can get tamer varieties of pizza, too). You'll also find good Buffalo wings, chili, and burgers. Be sure to check out the microbrewery beers. It's open until 4 AM. ✉ *522 Columbus Ave., between 85th and 86th Sts.,* ☎ *212/595–3139. AE, MC, V.*

Chinese

$ ✕ **China Fun.** Captivating swirls of color brighten the clean white walls in this cheerful eatery. The cooked ducks hanging in the steaming kitchen, visible as you enter, are just one entry on an extensive menu that features several regional cuisines and encompasses a savory array of barbecued food, 18 kinds of noodle soup, dumplings with all sorts of fillings, and a number of Chinese standards. The taro-shrimp cakes and pineapple-curry fried rice are both highly recommended. Save room for the terrific sesame-peanut-butter pancake for dessert. The **East Side branch** is at 1239 2nd Avenue, at 65th Street (☎ 212/752–0810). ✉ *246 Columbus Ave., at 71st St.,* ☎ *212/580–1516. AE, DC, MC, V.*

Contemporary

$$$$ ★ ✕ **Jean Georges.** All New York buzzed when celebrated chef Jean-Georges Vongerichten opened his eponymous restaurant in the Trump International Hotel and Towers (☞ Upper West Side, *in* Chapter 7). Taupe, ecru, and silver colors create warmth in the high-ceiling main dining room. Floor-to-ceiling windows, leather banquettes, white marble and terrazzo mosaics, china plates in geometric patterns of silver and gray, and three silver-leaf screens that frame the exhibition kitchen all contribute to the understated luxury. Still, Vongerichten's food garners center stage—it is dramatically plated table-side, appropriately amplifying aromas, especially of the lovingly used herbs. Few chefs serve dishes as evolved as sea scallops in caper-raisin emulsion with caramelized cauliflower, and the spring garlic soup perfumed with thyme and chunky with nuggets of boned, sautéed frogs' legs. For dessert try the breathtakingly simple strawberry "water" or a thin rhubarb tart with brown sugar and rhubarb *crème glaceé.* Personalized service and a beautifully selected wine list that includes wonderful Alsatian finds add to the singular dining experience. There's also an appealing terrace restaurant (Le Mistral) and a more casual à la carte room in the bar area (Nougatine) with a view of the open kitchen. Each has its own lighter

(and less expensive) menu. ✉ *1 Central Park W., at 59th St.,* ☎ *212/299–3900. Reservations essential. Jacket and tie. AE, DC, MC, V. Closed Sun.*

$$$ ✕ **Terrace.** Convenient to Columbia University, this elegant 16th-floor charmer offers staggering city views from its two large dining rooms and wraparound balcony. The Terrace's staid Continental food has long taken a back seat to the views, but with the arrival in 1997 of executive chef Kenneth Johnson (Picholine and Bouley), the jazzy eclectic cuisine now holds its own; try the risotto of Scottish brown hare with butternut squash, followed by the whole grilled Mediterranean white snapper, and for dessert, the pumpkin ice cream sundae, molded inside an edible chocolate case and embellished with candied walnuts, maple cream, and gingersnap cookies. ✉ *400 W. 119th St.,* ☎ *212/666–9490. Jacket required. AE, D, DC, MC, V. Closed Sun. No lunch Sat. and Mon.*

$$$ ✕ **Two Two Two.** This oak-paneled brownstone dining room, with its skylight, polished-wood floor, and massive chandelier, would be classy in any neighborhood—and the garden is a pleasure. The spicy salmon tartare with red caviar, lobster risotto with black truffles, filet mignon with wild mushrooms in red wine sauce, and baked apple in phyllo with raspberry coulis are representative of the offerings. ✉ *222 W. 79th St., between Broadway and Amsterdam Ave.,* ☎ *212/799–0400. Reservations essential. AE, DC, MC, V. No lunch.*

$$ ✕ **Salt.** In this bustling bistro, classic dishes such as steak frîtes share the menu with innovative American fare like roasted rosemary chicken and fluffy mashed potatoes. The daily dessert special is usually a pleasant surprise—melt-in-your-mouth chocolate cake will blow you socks off. Ceiling fans, exposed brick walls, bare wood floors, and changing photo exhibits set the scene. ✉ *507 Columbus Ave., between 84th and 85th Sts.,* ☎ *212/875–1993. AE, MC, V.*

French

$$ ★ ✕ **Savann.** Executive chef Danforth Houle, formerly of Bouley, performs culinary magic at what is possibly the best small restaurant on the West Side. Among the superb entrées are cornmeal-crusted oysters on creamy celery-root puree and pan-roasted medallions of salmon with spaghetti squash in roasted tomato vinaigrette. Apple *tarte Tatin* with cinnamon ice cream makes a wonderful finale. The dining area is all exposed brick, with brass ceiling fans and track lighting. **Savann Est** is at 181 East 78th Street (☎ 212/396–9300). ✉ *414 Amsterdam Ave., at 80th St.,* ☎ *212/580–0202. AE, MC, V. No lunch.*

Italian

$$ ★ ✕ **Carmine's.** Savvy West Siders and theater district goers are only too glad to line up at this busy spot with its dark woodwork and old-fashioned black-and-white tiles for its home-style Italian cooking, served family style. Kick off a meal with fried calamari or stuffed artichoke, then move on to the pastas or lobster *fra diabolo* (in a spicy tomato sauce). The huge portions make this a perfect place for groups and folks who like to share. ✉ *2450 Broadway, between 90th and 91st Sts.,* ☎ *212/362–2200;* ✉ *200 W. 44th St., between Broadway and 8th Ave.,* ☎ *212/221–3800. AE. No lunch.*

Japanese

$$ ✕ **Fujiyama Mama.** White-slipcovered side chairs line up like the statues in a vitrine in this creative restaurant with a high-tech design. In the startling spirit of the place, dishes have names like "Poseidon Adventure" and "Bermuda Triangle." Tell the waiter it's your birthday, and your tempura deep-fried ice cream comes with sparklers while the DJ lays on a "Happy Birthday to You" from his collection of weird

recordings of the. ✉ *467 Columbus Ave., between 82nd and 83rd Sts.,* ☎ *212/769–1144. Reservations essential. AE. No lunch.*

Malaysian

$–$$ ✕ **Penang Columbus.** Although it isn't as dramatic as its SoHo counterpart, this often crowded eatery with exposed brick walls and lacquered columns serves Malaysian food that is more assertively spiced (and more authentic) than the one downtown. A good place to start is with the house drink, "Coconut Scream," made with light and dark rum, coconut milk, lotus jelly, and coconut shavings. Follow this with *roti canai* (a flaky flat bread) to dip in chicken curry. For the main entrée, sample the whole steamed striped bass or one of the many noodle dishes. Ice *kacang,* made with ice cream, shaved ice, red beans and corn, is a refreshing dessert. ✉ *240 Columbus Ave., at 71st St.,* ☎ *212/769–3988. AE, MC, V.*

Mediterranean

$$ ✕ **Isabella's.** French doors lead to a pleasant sidewalk café, while, inside, the charming dining area has Mediterranean-yellow walls, French café chairs, and potted palms. Proprietor Steven Hanson also owns Coconut Grill, Blue Water Grill, Park Avalon, and the Honest Baker, all of which are sources of the house's pasta, bread, and desserts, which are practically guilt-free; try the reduced-fat chocolate decadence, a flourless chocolate cake with raspberry sauce, fresh berries, and yogurt. The grilled meat, seafood, and pasta dishes are all tasty; try the three-peppercorn Black Angus steak with garlic mashed potatoes or penne with eggplant and mushrooms. ✉ *359 Columbus Ave., at 77th St.,* ☎ *212/724–2100. AE, DC, MC, V.*

Mexican

$ ★ ✕ **Gabriela's.** This modest cantina with ceramic parrots hanging from the ceiling and a desert wall mural rewards all who love authentic Mexican cuisine. The menu has wonderful tacos, stuffed with beef tongue and *chicharron* (deep-fried pork skins) in a memorable bath of tomatillo and serrano sauce. The house specialty is a whole rotisserie chicken, Yucatán style, with rice, beans, and plantains. ✉ *685 Amsterdam Ave., at 93rd St.,* ☎ *212/961–0574. AE, DC, MC, V.*

Pan-Asian

$$ ✕ **Rain.** Conjuring up memories of the writings of Somerset Maugham, who wrote a short story "Rain," this pleasant restaurant has a friendly bar, rattan chairs with pillows in chintz, and wooden floors covered with Oriental runners. The first-rate Thai- and Vietnamese-inspired food includes *bahn cuon* (steamed ravioli with lump crab, bean sprouts, and chili sauce), crispy whole fish in three-flavor sauce, and tantalizing charred-beef salad. ✉ *100 W. 82nd St., between Amsterdam and Columbus Aves.,* ☎ *212/501–0776. Reservations essential. AE, DC, MC, V. No lunch.*

Seafood

$$–$$$ ✕ **Mad Fish.** Amusing murals depict cocktail parties with fish as the guests at this packed-to-the-gills seafood spot. You can sample boiled periwinkles, steamed lobster, seasonal oysters, and more at the long mahogany bar, but the kitchen also turns out such stylish fare as barbecued bluefish and fish-and-chips-cured fresh cod, gently coated with tempura and quickly deep-fried. Be sure to sample the warm flourless chocolate cake. ✉ *2182 Broadway, between 77th and 78th Sts.,* ☎ *212/787–0202. AE, DC, MC, V. No lunch.*

$$ ✕ **Nola.** Mottled gold walls, a copper-color tin ceiling, and comfortably upholstered redwood chairs decorate this comfortable restaurant. The eclectic food runs the gamut from a knockout presentation

of raw and steamed seafood, dramatically served in several tiers of plates know as "the plateau," to sandwiches and standard bistro fare, including well-prepared daily seafood specials. The ice cream sundae in an edible chocolate sundae glass is fun; the wine and beer list is also noteworthy. ✉ *428 Amsterdam Ave., between 80th and 81st Sts.,* ☎ *212/501–7515. AE, DC, MC, V. No lunch.*

$ ✕ **Joe's Fish Shack.** After you're seated in this rustic dining room with sawdust on the floor and an old rowboat hanging from the ceiling, the menu arrives attached to a clipboard, and a free small paper cup of corn bread and fried calamari is set before you on the table, which is covered with lacquered newspapers. Then try digging into creamy oyster stew, delicious fried belly clams, and shrimp steamed in beer and Old Bay Spice. ✉ *520 Columbus Ave., between 85th and 86th Sts.,* ☎ *212/873–0341. AE, DC, MC, V. No lunch.*

Southern

$$ ✕ **Savannah Club.** An attractive crowd tucks into lightened-up soul food at this airy restaurant with ceiling fans, French doors, and a bar flanked by columns rimmed with colored neon. Homemade corn bread and biscuits are giveaways, served with onion jam and sweet-potato butter. But leave room for the house specialty: a bowl of tender chicken and puffy dumplings. For dessert the dark chocolate pie is a must. ✉ *2420 Broadway, at 89th St.,* ☎ *212/496–1066. AE, DC, MC, V. No lunch.*

$$ ✕ **Shark Bar.** This popular Upper West Sider has three dining areas, including a friendly bar, a middle room with portraits of southern farmworkers, and an intimate room with red velvet drapes and velvet striped banquettes. The not-to-be-missed chicken wings come in three styles: jerked, Harlem-style (floured and deep-fried), and barbecued. Also check out the soul roll, a playful variation on an egg roll, made with chicken, collard greens, and black-eyed peas. ✉ *307 Amsterdam Ave., between 74th and 75th Sts.,* ☎ *212/874–8500. AE, DC, MC, V. No lunch Fri.–Tues.*

Harlem

Soul

$ ✕ **Emily's.** The bare Formica tables, paper napkins, and minimalist decor are clearly not the reasons to seek out this bargain-price Harlem discovery. The food is the reason: some of the best chopped barbecue sandwiches, deep-fried chicken livers (dunk them into the zesty house sauce), corn-bread stuffing (spiked with hot peppers and spices), and homemade potato salad this side of the Mason-Dixon Line. It's also a good bet for breakfast and brunch. ✉ *1325 5th Ave., at 111th St.,* ☎ *212/996–1212. AE, DC, MC, V.*

BROOKLYN AND QUEENS RESTAURANTS

With the exception of the River Café and Rasputin, the restaurants included here aren't in and of themselves destinations. Rather, they are small (and mostly inexpensively priced) ethnic haunts and neighborhood places—great choices when you want to try authentic ethnic food in a neighborhood into which you've already ventured to take in its cultural and historical sites (☞ Chapter 3), or you'd like to experience the pace and feel of a restaurant outside Manhattan.

Brooklyn

American

$–$$ ✕ **Henry's End.** Quarters may be tight, but this simple local hangout in chic Brooklyn Heights offers some of the borough's most interesting food. During fall's wild-game festival, you might sample barbecued rattlesnake or elk chops with honey-mustard glaze. Otherwise, go with raspberry duck, pumpkin ravioli, or blackened salmon or tuna. Desserts like fresh apple cobbler or black-bottom pie taste of home; beer and wine selections are superb. ✉ *44 Henry St., Brooklyn Heights,* ☎ *718/834–1776. AE, DC, MC, V. No lunch.*

Contemporary

$$$$ ★ ✕ **River Café.** Sipping a perfect cocktail or a glass of wine from the extensive list while watching the sun set over lower Manhattan, just across the East River: This is the incomparable experience offered by River Café, one of the city's most romantic and dazzlingly situated restaurants, just under the Brooklyn Bridge. Rick Laakkonen's food is a perfect match—favorite dishes include fruitwood-smoked salmon and grilled jumbo quail on white hominy puree. The "Brooklyn Bridge," sculpted out of a chocolate-mousse cake, is a typically dramatic dessert. Although prices are high—there's a three-course dinner or a more elaborate six-course tasting—the service is stellar. Sunday brunch is a joy, lunch less hectic. ✉ *1 Water St., at the East River, Brooklyn Heights,* ☎ *718/522–5200. Reservations essential. Jacket required. AE, DC, MC, V.*

Russian

$$$ ✕ **Rasputin.** Etched glass, hand-painted murals, crystal chandeliers, and carved doors are only a prelude to the two-story dining salon at the heart of this restaurant-nightclub extravaganza in Brighton Beach, Brooklyn's predominantly Russian stronghold. A magnificent inlaid dance floor and multilevel stage with a state-of-the-art sound system and laser lights is the setting for the lavish Rasputin Follies revue (nine dancers, seven singers, and an eight-piece orchestra); it starts at 10 PM Friday, Saturday, and Sunday. The mostly Russian clientele arrives dressed to the nines and stays until the wee hours, consuming a fabulous traditional Russian banquet. It begins with *zakuska,* hot and cold Russian appetizers ranging from smoked salmon to blini and caviar; entrées that include a perfect chicken Kiev follow. A full bottle of Absolut vodka (for four people) is included in the affordable price. ✉ *2670 Coney Island Ave., Brighton Beach,* ☎ *718/332–8111. Reservations essential. AE, DC, MC, V. No lunch.*

Southern

$–$$ ✕ **Harvest.** In Brooklyn's thriving Cobble Hill, this unpretentious neighborhood spot serves terrific southern food, with a nod to New Orleans. Gumbo excels, above-average crab cakes are lightly breaded and not overburdened with filler, and the shredded pork platter in molasses marinade is mighty impressive. Homemade apple pie offers a comforting conclusion. The settings are just right for this food: Downstairs is an open kitchen, zinc-top wine and beer bar, and brick walls from which hangs a red neon sign reading EATS. Upstairs, blue and white checked cloths, hand-stenciled sheaths of wheat, and antique fruit labels adorn a more sedate dining room. ✉ *218 Court St., Cobble Hill,* ☎ *718/624–9267. AE, DC, MC, V.*

Queens

Brazilian

$ ✕ **Green Field Churrascaria.** This sprawling Corona restaurant, which looks like an indoor parking garage, features a fixed-price, all-you-can-eat *rodizio* (meaning "going around"), the Brazilian orgy of grilled foods. Waiters parade skewers of grilled sirloin, chicken hearts, turkey nuggets, skirt steak, shoulder steak, chicken, duck, sausage, and roasted pork. Let them know when to stop by using the stop/go paddle on your table. Begin with a trip to the copious salad bar and hot buffet. ✉ *108–01 Northern Blvd., Corona,* ☎ *718/672–5202. AE.*

Colombian

$ ✕ **Tierras Colombianas.** Standout stick-to-the-ribs food at bargain prices is the reason to travel to this Queens Colombian restaurant with coffee-shop decor. "He-man" bowls of soup arrive bursting with beef ribs, corn on the cob, vegetables, and rice, accompanied by the delicious corn cake known as *arepa.* The combination plate—a variety of meats, plantains, and cassava—is also mammoth. Try the parchment-crisp hunk of pork called *chicharron* (served rind and all). The original is in colorful Jackson Heights, a block from the 82nd Street stop on the No. 7 subway—about 20 minutes from Manhattan; a fancier branch with a bar is in Astoria. ✉ *82–16 Roosevelt Ave., Jackson Heights, Queens,* ☎ *718/426–8868;* ✉ *3301 Broadway, Astoria,* ☎ *718/426–8868. No credit cards. BYOB.*

Greek

$$ ✕ **Karyatis.** One of the oldest and most elegant of Astoria's Greek restaurants, airy, multilevel Karyatis, with its live music and professional service, is perfect for a festive evening. Whole grilled fish of the day, wonderful vegetables, and skillfully executed sauces (especially the traditional *avgolemono,* or egg-lemon) lead the list of good choices. Greek wines are the appropriate accompaniment; also try a glass of ouzo, the sweet licorice-flavor liqueur, followed by baklava and a cup of thick Greek coffee. ✉ *35–03 Broadway, Astoria, Queens,* ☎ *718/204–0666. AE, DC, MC, V.*

$ ★ ✕ **Akroyiali.** One of the best bets in predominantly Greek Astoria, Akroyiali, with its walls entwined with grape vines and the blue and white colors typical of the *tavernas* of Athens, has the feel of Greek islands, yet it's only a quick subway ride from Manhattan. Hot and cold appetizers such as grilled octopus, fried cheese, and *taramasalata* (fish-roe spread) are standouts. There are also appetizing Greek salads and such delicious entrées as moussaka, grilled quail, souvlaki, whole grilled fish, and (surprisingly) a knockout double tenderloin. The Greek red wines offer good value. ✉ *33–04 Broadway, Astoria, Queens,* ☎ *718/932–7772. AE.*

$ ✕ **Elia's Corner.** There's no written menu in this once-diminutive storefront, now expanded, so start with the melt-in-your-mouth fried smelts or the amazingly tender grilled octopus. Then follow with whole red snapper, St. Pierre fish, or shrimp. Order a side of the incredible potatoes, mashed with garlic or fried with cheese. Wines are limited to some pleasant Greek selections; try the clean, grassy Kouras from the island of Patras. Weather permitting, head for the charming garden. ✉ *24–02 31st St., Astoria,,* ☎ *718/932–1510. Reservations not accepted. No credit cards. No lunch.*

COFFEE BARS AND CAFÉS

By Jennifer Paull

Cafés have been a New York institution since beat days, but only in the past few years has café culture, à la Seattle, taken off. Today Manhattan boasts as many cafés as once caffeine-addicted cities like Budapest and Vienna supported in their heyday. Dozens of independent coffeehouses compete with such upscale coffee-bar chains as Starbuck's, Timothy's, and New World Coffee. Plain and decaffeinated drip coffee and espresso are standard. (Note: "Regular coffee" in upscale spots comes with milk or cream; you must add your own sugar if you want your brew sweetened; in delis and old-fashioned coffee shops, however, "regular" still means with milk and sugar.) Among the more frequently offered café beverages are: *ristretto,* a highly refined espresso; *macchiato,* espresso with just a dab of foam; caffe latte, espresso with steamed milk; cappuccino, half espresso and half steamed milk, with foam; caffe mocha or *mochaccino,* espresso with steamed milk and chocolate syrup. Most of these concoctions come in a decaf variant; often you can request skim, low-fat, or soy milk instead of whole milk. Most coffee bars offer snacks, desserts, and accommodate tea drinkers. Although prices can top more than $2 for an espresso, all offer a bit of civilized sipping.

Greenwich Village

✕ **Caffè Dante.** A longtime Village haunt, this convivial spot has superlative espresso and knockout tiramisu. With good timing, you can exchange glances with indie-film star Lili Taylor. ✉ *79–81 MacDougal St., between Houston and Bleecker Sts.,* ☎ *212/982–5275.*

✕ **Caffè Dell'Artista.** This West Village Italian café has dark, romantic back rooms, delirium-inducing desserts, and mismatched wooden writing desks doubling as tables, complete with past patron's poems discarded in the drawers. ✉ *46 Greenwich Ave.,* ☎ *212/645–4431.*

✕ **Caffe Rafaella.** Parchment-paper lamp shades adorned with twittering red fringe, variously hued marble-top tables, and an antiques-store assortment of chairs make this one of the homiest old-world cafés anywhere in the city. ✉ *134 7th Ave. S, between 10th and Charles Sts.,* ☎ *212/929–7247.*

✕ **Caffè Reggio.** In the neighborhood's oldest coffeehouse, where a huge antique espresso machine gleams in the gloom, the tiny tables are *really* close together, perfect for eavesdropping. One of the paintings is an original of the school of Caravaggio. ✉ *119 MacDougal St., between 3rd and Bleecker Sts.,* ☎ *212/475–9557.*

✕ **Le Figaro Cafe.** A major beat hangout long ago, today Le Figaro attracts herds of tourists and students, but during off-hours it can be quiet enough to read Kerouac. There's live jazz a few nights a week. ✉ *184 Bleecker St., at MacDougal St.,* ☎ *212/677–1100.*

East Village, Little Italy, SoHo

✕ **Caffè Roma.** Manhattan's most authentic Italian coffeehouse has worn walls, marble tables, and strong, bracing, and foamy cappuccino. ✉ *385 Broome St., at Mulberry St.,* ☎ *212/226–8413.*

✕ **Cyber Café.** Cyber projects a healthier image than most of its computers-and-caffeine brethren—metal café chairs and squeaky-clean surfaces shine under its bright lights. Alas, wired night owls must head home by 10 PM (by 8 on Sunday!). The wraparound lineup of computer stations (all PCs, plus a scanner-equipped Mac) has comfortable chairs for hours of Web-crawling. ✉ *273 Lafayette, at Prince St.,* ☎ *212/334–5140.*

✕ **Dean & DeLuca.** Like the gourmet market nearby, the Prince Street Dean & DeLuca is a gracious, high-ceiling white space, the better to display its sweet-tooth tempters. Snake in line past the gingerbread, muffins, and cookies, then head toward the back for the banquettes and skylights. Though other branches have less floor space, their culinary lineup is just as toothsome. ✉ *121 Prince St., between Greene and Wooster Sts.,* ☎ *212/254–8776;* ✉ *75 University Pl., at 11th St.,* ☎ *212/473–1908;* ✉ *1 Rockefeller Plaza, at 49th St.,* ☎ *212/664–1363;* ✉ *235 W. 46th St., between Broadway and 8th Ave., in the Paramount Hotel,* ☎ *212/869–6890.*

✕ **Le Gamin.** It's easy to confuse SoHo for Paris at this hip little haven, where the menu includes all the French café standards: *croque monsieur,* quiche Lorraine, *salade Niçoise,* crepes (both sweet and savory), and big bowls of café au lait. Service can be desultory, but the upside is that you're free to lounge for hours. ✉ *50 MacDougal St., between Houston and Prince Sts.,* ☎ *212/254–4678.*

✕ **Marquet Patisserie.** At this friendly café, you can savor a French pastry and a café au lait; the menu also includes inventive salads, thick sandwiches, soups, and *croque monsieur.* ✉ *15 E. 12th St., between 5th Ave. and University Pl.,* ☎ *212/229–9313.*

✕ **Veniero's Pasticceria.** More than a century old, this bustling bakery-café sells every kind of Italian *dulce,* plus irresistible cheesecakes and pies. ✉ *342 E. 11th St., near 1st Ave.,* ☎ *212/674–7264.*

Chelsea

✕ **Milan Café and Coffee Bar.** A serious chef makes knockout sandwiches, salads, and desserts in this striking eatery with knotty pine tables and a ceiling of flags. ✉ *120 W. 23rd St., at 6th Ave.,* ☎ *212/807–1801.*

✕ **Newsbar.** This ultracasual resting place with four other Manhattan locations has good coffee and tea, a generous offering of magazines, and Cable News Network. ✉ *2 W. 19th St., between 5th and 6th Aves.,* ☎ *212/255–3996.*

✕ **Petite Abeille.** In this sunny stretch of a café, you can catch up on your Tintin reading while munching a warm *gaufre* (waffle). Euro treats like packages of Prince cookies are on sale. ✉ *107 W. 18th St., between 6th and 7th Aves.,* ☎ *212/604–9350.*

East Side

✕ **Café Bianco.** White tables fill this popular meeting place with excellent coffee, sinful desserts, and small meals; in warm weather, try the back garden with its pint-size pond. ✉ *1486 2nd Ave., between 77th and 78th Sts.,* ☎ *212/988–2655.*

✕ **Columbus Bakery.** In an airy space with chandeliers that look like loaves of bread, you can enjoy delicious bread, muffins, and pastries. Fans of almond bark have come to the right place. ✉ *957 1st Ave., between 52nd and 53rd Sts.,* ☎ *212/421–0334;* ✉ *474 Columbus Ave., between 82nd and 83rd Sts.,* ☎ *212/724–6880.*

✕ **Corrado Café.** A branch of a successful West Side restaurant, this convenient spot near several movie theaters (not to mention Bloomie's) has pastries, cookies, and cakes that outshine the coffee. ✉ *1013 3rd Ave., between 60th and 61st Sts.,* ☎ *212/753–5100.*

✕ **Fleur de Jour.** Lace curtains, patterned wallpaper, wonderful wicker baskets full of cookies, and an owner who seems to be everybody's best friend make this New York's most welcoming café; only about a dozen patrons can squeeze in. ✉ *348 E. 62nd St., between 1st and 2nd Aves.,* ☎ *212/355–2020.*

✕ **Le Pain Quotidien.** This place is Belgian to the bone—they use Belgian jams, Belgian flour for the crusty breads, even Belgian chocolate for their café mochas and hot chocolates. For a more substantial meal, take a seat at the long, wooden communal table. ✉ *1131 Madison Ave., between 84th and 85th Sts.,* ☎ *212/327–4900.*

✕ **Manhattan Espresso.** Romance languages are heard as often as English here; it's a favorite with international businesspeople, who hone in on the Illy espresso. Weekend hours are limited to a half day on Saturday. ✉ *146 E. 49th St., between 3rd and Lexington Aves.,* ☎ *212/832–3010.*

✕ **Payard Pâtisserie.** Petite quiches, baguette sandwiches, caviar-topped canapés, and impossibly perfect pastries beckon from the shining cases up-front at François Payard's patisserie and bistro. Snagging a marble-top café table can be tricky since you won't be alone in your adulation. ✉ *1032 Lexington Ave., between 73rd and 74th Sts.,* ☎ *212/717–5252.*

✕ **Sant Ambroeus.** You'll swear you're in Milan at this very Italian café with red leather banquettes and Murano chandeliers, where you can enjoy magnificent coffee and desserts, including intense gelato. ✉ *1000 Madison Ave., between 77th and 78th Sts.,* ☎ *212/570–2211.*

West Side

✕ **Café La Fortuna.** Weary Columbus Avenue strollers have long flocked to this comforting refuge offering Italian pastries, serious coffee, and opera music. ✉ *69 W. 71st St., between Columbus Ave. and Central Park W,* ☎ *212/724–5846.*

✕ **Café Lalo.** Linger over cappuccino, liqueurs, and crossword puzzles at this flashy, Lautrec-themed spot just off Broadway. Alas, some cakes fall short of their menu descriptions. ✉ *201 W. 83rd St., between Broadway. and Amsterdam Ave.,* ☎ *212/496–6031.*

✕ **Café Mozart.** Images of Mozart cover the walls at this spot, perfect after a night at Lincoln Center. Creamy desserts are the specialty; a pianist or classical duo often perform. On Friday and Saturday nights it's open until 3 AM, on other night until 1. ✉ *154 W. 70th St., between Broadway and Columbus Ave.,* ☎ *212/595–9797.*

✕ **Coffee Pot.** Overstuffed sofas and chairs, mirrors, brass chandeliers, good deals on coffee of the day, and pleasant service make this one of the theater district's most pleasant options. ✉ *350 9th Ave., at 49th St.,* ☎ *212/265–3566.*

✕ **Cupcake Café.** Intensely buttery old-fashioned cupcakes, doughnuts, coffee cake, and hearty soup are worth the trek to this funky spot on the western flank of the Port Authority. ✉ *522 9th Ave., at 39th St.,* ☎ *212/465–1530.*

✕ **Drip.** Blind-date notebooks have earned this café a notoriety its kitschy atmosphere and vintage '70s couches wouldn't alone garner. Still, the Toll House cookies excel. ✉ *489 Amsterdam Ave., between 83rd and 84th Sts.,* ☎ *212/875–1032.*

✕ **French Roast Café** (☞ Manhattan Restaurants, *above*).

7 Lodging

Though Manhattan hotels prices are at an all-time high, few other cities have such a wide range of remarkable accommodations—from elegant grand old hotels and bustling modern giants to stylish boutique hotels by star designers. Where else can you lie in bed while gazing out at the Empire State and Chrysler buildings, dine in the room where Dorothy Parker and the Algonquin Round Table once held court, have drinks in a bar whose walls were illustrated by Ludwig Bemelmans before he became famous for his Madeline children's books, or work out with a view of St. Patrick's Cathedral?

By Amy McConnell

IF ANY SINGLE ELEMENT OF YOUR TRIP to New York City will cost you dearly, it will be your hotel room. Thanks to a sustained boom in tourism, hoteliers have raised their rates into the stratosphere, to all-time highs: $200 per night is the average rate predicted by the end of 1998. Premium hotels such as the Four Seasons and the St. Regis are able to charge as much as $450 for standard rooms, and up to $7,000 for suites. Amazingly, enough of the city's roughly 32½ million visitors are willing and able to support such competition at the premium end of the spectrum. Given the city's perennially high occupancy rate (in 1997 it was 84%), market forces are unlikely to drive current prices down. Fleabags and flophouses aside, there's precious little here for less than $100 a night. (To add insult to injury, there's a 13¼% hotel tax, plus a $2 per room, per night city occupancy charge added onto room rates.) The good news is that hoteliers are engaged in a head-to-head battle to outdo each other's services and amenities in order to justify their soaring price tags—so once you've shelled out the big bucks, you're in for a treat. We have scoured the city for good-value hotels and budget properties, but even our $ category includes hotels that run as high as $135 for one night's stay in a double-occupancy room.

Our price categories are based on the "rack rate," or the standard room cost that hotels print in their brochures and quote over the phone. You almost never need to pay this much. If you book directly with the hotel, ask about corporate rates, seasonal special offers, or weekend deals. The last typically includes such extras as complimentary meals, drinks, or tickets to events. Ask your travel agent for brochures, search the Web, and look for advertisements in travel magazines or the Sunday travel sections of major newspapers such as the *New York Times,* the *Washington Post,* or the *Los Angeles Times.* Of course, booking any all-inclusive package, weekend or longer, will reduce the hotel rate.

If you should be unfortunate enough to arrive in New York City without a hotel reservation, you can also try the most direct method of lowering the room rate: asking. In periods (alas, increasingly rare) of low occupancy, hotels—especially at the expensive end of the market—will often reduce the price on rooms that would otherwise remain empty.

In general, Manhattan hotels don't measure up to those in other U.S. cities in terms of room size, parking, or outside landscaping. Many compensate with fastidious service, sprucely maintained properties, and restaurants that more than hold their own in a city of knowledgeable diners.

Common sense should tell you not to anticipate the same kind of personal service from even a top-flight convention hotel, such as the New York Hilton, as you would from a smaller, sedate property like the Shoreham, even though both have rooms in the same price range. Know your own taste and choose accordingly.

Note: Even the most exclusive hotels have security gaps. Be discreet with valuables everywhere, and stay alert in public areas.

CATEGORY	COST*
$$$$	over $260
$$$	$190–$260
$$	$135–$190
$	under $135

**All prices are for a standard double room, excluding 13¼% city and state taxes.*

Reservations

New York is constantly full of vacationers, conventioneers, and business travelers, all requiring hotel space. Try to book your room as far in advance as possible, using a major credit card to guarantee the reservation. Because this is a tight market, overbooking can be a problem, and "lost" reservations are not unheard of. When signing in, take a pleasant but firm attitude; if there is a mix-up, chances are the outcome will be an upgrade or a free night.

Hotels with famous restaurants appreciate it when guests who want to use those facilities book tables when they make their room reservations. All chefs mentioned were in charge at press time. Call to confirm the name under the toque. It can make *all* the difference.

Services

Unless otherwise noted in the individual descriptions, all the hotels listed have the following features and services: private baths, central heating, air-conditioning, private telephones, no-smoking rooms or floors, on-premises dining, room service (though not necessarily 24-hour or short-notice), TV (including cable and pay-per-view films), and a routine concierge staff. Almost all hotels now have dataports and phones with voice mail, as well as valet service. Most large hotels have video or high-speed checkout capability, and many can arrange baby-sitting.

Pools are a rarity, but most properties have exercise rooms or health clubs, and sometimes full-scale spas; hotels without on-site facilities usually have arrangements for guests at nearby facilities, for which a fee is sometimes charged.

Bringing a car to Manhattan can significantly add to your lodging expenses. Many properties in all price ranges *do* have parking facilities, but they are often at independent garages that charge as much as $20 or more per day. A handful of hotels have free parking; they are noted in the following reviews.

HOTELS

Midtown East

$$$$ 🏨 **Beekman Tower.** The jazziest of the nine Manhattan East Suite hotels, the Beekman Place is steps from the U.N. Its swanky Top of the Towers lounge, a rooftop bar with live piano, is a superb place to take in the view of the East River and beyond; downstairs, the Zephyr Grill looks out on First Avenue. Suites, which range from studios to one-bedrooms, are all very spacious, and all have kitchens. Moss-green carpets, black bedspreads with big floral prints, and framed botanical paintings give guest rooms a handsome, masculine look. ✉ *3 Mitchell Pl., 10017,* ☎ *212/355–7300 or 800/637–8483,* FAX *212/753–9366. 173 suites. Restaurant, 2 bars, in-room modem lines, in-room safes, kitchens, room service, exercise room, laundry service and dry cleaning, concierge, business services, meeting rooms, parking (fee). AE, D, DC, MC, V.*

$$$$ 🏨 **Crowne Plaza at the United Nations.** This 20-story building, built in 1931, is in historic Tudor City and a stone's throw from the U.N. and Grand Central Terminal. Interior spaces are classic and unassuming, with marble floors, handmade carpets, and hardwood reproduction furniture upholstered in brocades and velvets. The traditional, well-kept rooms all come with irons, ironing boards, and coffeemakers. For $30 extra per night, guests have access to the new Crowne Club Lounge, where complimentary breakfast and evening cocktails are served. ✉ *304 E. 42nd St., 10017,* ☎ *212/986–8800 or 800/879–8836,* FAX *212/986–1758. 278 rooms, 18 suites. Restaurant, bar, in-room*

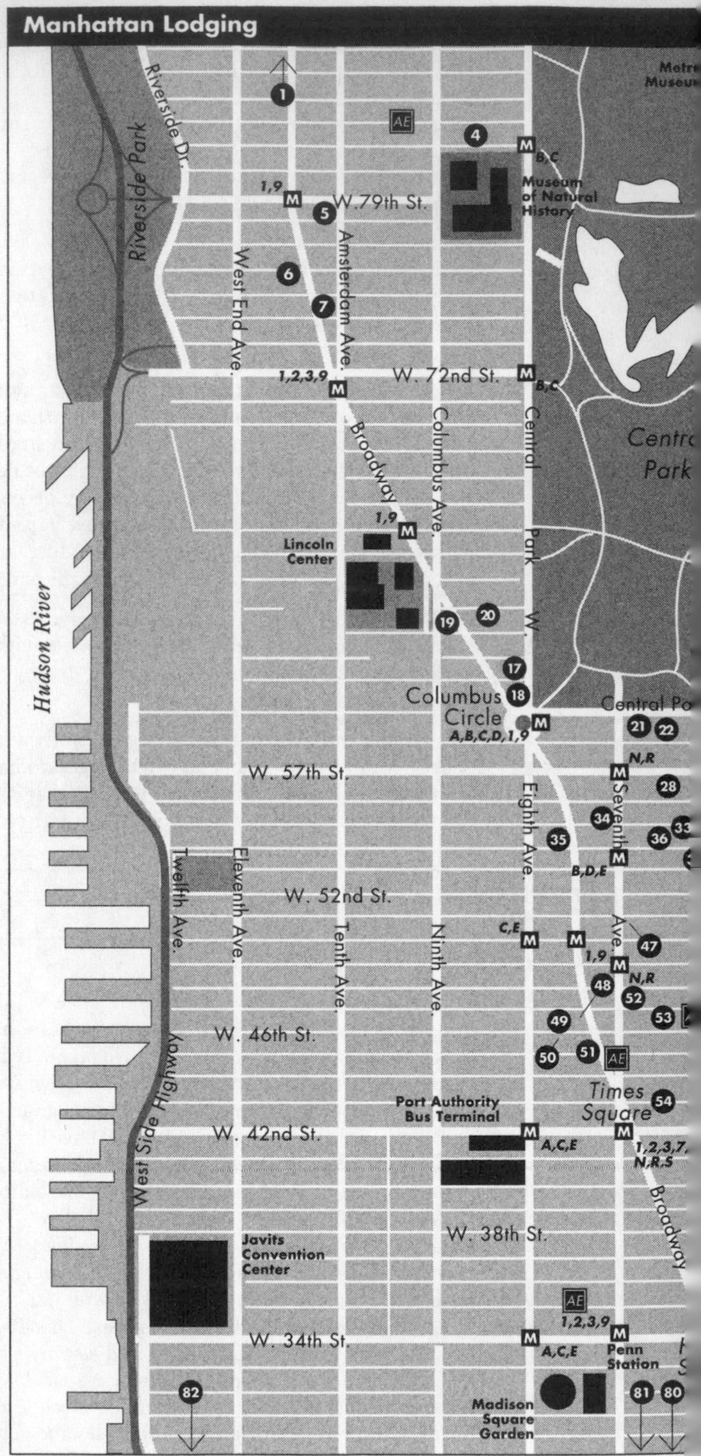

Manhattan Lodging
Riverside Park
Riverside Dr.
W. 79th St.
Museum of Natural History
West End Ave.
Amsterdam Ave.
W. 72nd St.
Broadway
Columbus Ave.
Central Park W.
Central Park
Lincoln Center
Hudson River
Columbus Circle
A,B,C,D,1,9
W. 57th St.
Eighth Ave.
Seventh Ave.
Twelfth Ave.
Eleventh Ave.
W. 52nd St.
Tenth Ave.
Ninth Ave.
W. 46th St.
West Side Highway
Times Square
Port Authority Bus Terminal
W. 42nd St.
W. 38th St.
Javits Convention Center
W. 34th St.
Penn Station
Madison Square Garden

Pierre, **10**
Plaza, **24**
Plaza Athénée, **11**
Plaza Fifty, **41**
Portland Square, **53**
Quality Hotel and Suites, **46**
Quality Hotel East Side, **71**
Radisson Empire, **19**
Regal U.N. Plaza, **56**
The Regency, **14**
Renaissance, **52**
Rihga Royal, **36**
Roger Smith, **44**
Roger Williams, **72**
Royalton, **59**
St. Regis, **25**
San Carlos, **43**
The Sherry-Netherland, **16**
Shoreham, **32**
SoHo Grand, **80**
Trump International Hotel and Towers, **18**
Vanderbilt YMCA, **55**
Waldorf-Astoria, **45**
Warwick, **38**
Washington Square, **77**
Wellington, **34**
Westin Central Park South, **22**
The Wyndham, **23**
YMCA West Side, **20**

modems, in-room safes, minibars, room service, sauna, exercise room, business services, meeting rooms, concierge, parking (fee). AE, D, DC, MC, V.

$$$$ 🏨 **The Drake.** Just off Park Avenue in the heart of corporate Manhattan, this Swissôtel property caters to business travelers with fax machines in every room and an extensive business center, complete with private office rooms. The modern, deco-style rooms are a welcome alternative to the traditional decor of many hotels in this price category; oversized desks and overstuffed chairs and couches may tempt you to stay for awhile. Schnitzel, bratwurst, rösti, and other Swiss specialties, as well as hard-to-find Swiss wines, are served in the convivial Drake Bar. ✉ *440 Park Ave., 10022,* ☎ *212/421–0900 or 800/372–5369,* FAX *212/371–4190. 385 rooms, 100 suites. Restaurant, bar, in-room faxes, in-room modem lines, in-room safes, refrigerators, room service, spa, baby-sitting, laundry service and dry cleaning, concierge, business services, meeting rooms, parking (fee). AE, D, DC, MC, V.*

$$$$ 🏨 **The Fitzpatrick.** This cozy hotel just south of Bloomingdale's, the first American venture for an established Irish company, is as friendly as any good Irish inn, which might explain why Gregory Peck, Liam Neeson, various Kennedys, Sinead O'Connor, and the Chieftains have all been guests. More than half of the units are suites, and all have emerald carpets and traditional dark-wood furniture. The publike bar is the heart of the hotel is as welcoming as any in Dublin. ✉ *687 Lexington Ave., 10022,* ☎ *212/355–0100 or 800/367–7701,* FAX *212/355–1371. 42 rooms, 50 suites. Restaurant, bar, room service, in-room modem lines, minibars, massage, health club, laundry service and dry cleaning, business services, meeting rooms, parking (fee). AE, D, DC, MC, V.*

$$$$ 🏨 **Four Seasons.** Architect I. M. Pei designed this limestone-clad stepped spire amid the prime shops of 57th Street. Everything here comes in epic proportions—from the prices (rooms *start* at $525); to the guest rooms, which average 600 square ft; to the aptly named sky-high Grand Foyer, with its French limestone pillars, marble, onyx, and acre upon acre of blond wood. The palatial, soundproof guest rooms have 10-ft-high ceilings, enormous English sycamore walk-in closets, and blond-marble bathrooms with tubs that fill in 60 seconds. ✉ *57 E. 57th St., 10022,* ☎ *212/758–5700 or 800/332–3442,* FAX *212/758–5711. 310 rooms, 62 suites. Restaurant, bar, in-room modem lines, in-room safes, minibars, room service, spa, health club, piano, baby-sitting, laundry service and dry cleaning, concierge, business services, meeting room, car rental, parking (fee). AE, DC, MC, V.*

$$$$ ★ 🏨 **Hotel Elysée.** Better known as the site of the trendy Monkey Bar (☞ Chapter 8), where the young and beautiful meet for drinks, this intimate boutique hotel has relatively affordable rates, given its high-style look, personalized service, and top-flight amenities. All guests have access to the Club Room, which feels like a personal living room, with complimentary coffee, tea, and snacks all day long, plus free wine and hors d'oeuvres on weeknights. A few of the elegant guest rooms have terraces at no extra charge; request one far in advance. ✉ *60 E. 54th St., 10022,* ☎ *212/753–1066 or 800/535–9733,* FAX *212/980–9278. 87 rooms, 12 suites. Restaurant, bar, in-room modem lines, in-room VCRs, refrigerators, room service, massage, piano, laundry service and dry cleaning, concierge, business services, meeting room, parking (fee). AE, DC, MC, V.*

$$$$ ★ 🏨 **New York Palace.** Over the past two years the Palace has reinvented its image with a string of new tricks, the most remarkable being the opening of the ultramodern, five-star restaurant Le Cirque 2000 (☞ Chapter 5) inside the landmark 1882 Villard Houses. Other recent developments: a snazzy lobby lounge, a Spanish restaurant (Istaña) with

an olive bar and a Mediterranean-style tapas tea service, and a new tier of glamorous deco-style guest rooms on various floors of the plush Tower level—a nice alternative to the more traditional, Empire-style rooms. The 7,000-square-ft health club has TVs with videos and headphones at every treadmill, and terrific views of St. Patrick's Cathedral. ✉ *455 Madison Ave., 10022,* ☎ *212/888–7000 or 800/697–2522,* FAX *212/303–6000. 800 rooms, 100 suites. 2 restaurants, 2 bars, in-room fax machine, in-room modem lines, in-room safes, minibars, room service, spa, health club, baby-sitting, laundry service and dry cleaning, concierge, concierge floors, business services, meeting room, parking (fee). AE, D, DC, MC, V.*

$$$$ **Omni Berkshire Place.** Omni Berkshire's flagship hotel brings sophistication to the Omni name. Though the cavernous reception area is less than inviting, there's a dramatic, two-story atrium lounge with a fireplace, an elaborately stained dark-wood floor, and bowls of Siamese fighter fish on every table. The spacious guest rooms (all 375 square ft) have a contemporary, Asian-influenced simplicity and plenty of modern amenities. ✉ *21 E. 52nd St., 10022,* ☎ *212/753–5800 or 800/843–6664,* FAX *212/754–5020. 396 rooms, 44 suites. Restaurant, bar, in-room faxes, in-room modem lines, in-room safes, minibars, room service, massage, health club, laundry service and dry cleaning, concierge, business services, meeting rooms, parking (fee). AE, D, DC, MC, V.*

$$$$ **The Peninsula.** Step into the marble Art Nouveau lobby off 55th Street and you'll be transported back to the 1940s, when bell captains wore sailor suits and afternoon tea was an institution. A major renovation has given guest rooms a more contemporary feel, though they still have the same sweeping views down 5th Avenue. Sumptuous marble bathrooms have separate shower stalls. The rooftop health club and pool both have dazzling views of midtown. ✉ *700 5th Ave., 10019,* ☎ *212/247–2200 or 800/262–9467,* FAX *212/903–3943. 200 rooms, 42 suites. 2 restaurants, 2 bars, in-room faxes, in-room modem lines, in-room safes, minibars, room service, pool, spa, health club, laundry service and dry cleaning, concierge, business services, meeting rooms, parking (fee). AE, D, DC, MC, V.*

$$$$ **Regal U.N. Plaza.** It's easy to miss the entrance to this favorite among the business and diplomatic set—it's on a quiet side street near (naturally) the U.N. Rooms, which begin on the 28th floor, have breathtaking views and framed tapestries donated by various missions. The views also dazzle from the 27th-floor pool, and the rooftop tennis courts attract top players. Service throughout the hotel is first-rate, and the business center is open 24 hours a day. If you plan to use the fitness facilities, ask to stay in the east tower, where they are located. ✉ *1 United Nations Plaza, 10017,* ☎ *212/758–1234 or 800/223–1234,* FAX *212/702–5051. 393 rooms, 33 suites. Restaurant, bar, in-room fax machine, in-room modem lines, in-room safes, minibars, room service, pool, massage, tennis court, health club, baby-sitting, laundry service and dry cleaning, concierge, business services, meeting rooms, parking (fee). AE, D, DC, MC, V.*

$$$$ **The Regency.** The travertine lobby, resplendent with gilded cherubs, hanging tapestries, and a crystal chandelier, does justice to the name of this Park Avenue monarch. Top execs meet to discuss the market over power breakfasts at the restaurant, 540 Park. More inviting is the Library, a cozy, wood-paneled lounge full of bookcases and comfortable seating arrangements. The traditional guest rooms have celadon carpets and salmon bedspreads. ✉ *540 Park Ave., at 61st St., 10021,* ☎ *212/759–4100 or 800/235–6397,* FAX *212/826–5674. 260 rooms, 100 suites. 2 restaurants, bar, lobby lounge, in-room faxes, in-room modem lines, in-room safes, minibars, room service, beauty salon, massage, exercise room, baby-sitting, laundry service and dry clean-*

ing, concierge, business services, meeting rooms, parking (fee). AE, D, DC, MC, V.

$$$$ ★ **St. Regis.** When Sheraton restored this 5th Avenue Beaux Arts landmark in the early 1990s at a cost of $150 million, architects and designers set the highest standard, with prices to match. Public spaces are ultrachic—from the celebrated restaurant, Lespinasse (☞ Chapter 6); to the Astor Court tea lounge, with its trompe-l'oeil cloud ceiling; to the King Cole Bar, an institution in itself, with its famous Maxfield Parrish mural. Guest rooms, all serviced by butlers, are straight out of a period film, with high ceilings, crystal chandeliers, silk wall coverings, Louis XV antiques, and expensive amenities such as Tiffany silver services. Marble bathrooms, with tubs, stall showers, and double sinks, are outstanding. ✉ *2 E. 55th St., 10022,* ☎ *212/753–4500 or 800/759–7550,* FAX *212/787–3447. 221 rooms, 92 suites. Restaurant, bar, in-room fax machine, in-room modem lines, in-room safes, minibars, room service, beauty salon, massage, sauna, health club, baby-sitting, laundry service and dry cleaning, concierge, business services, meeting rooms, parking (fee). AE, D, DC, MC, V.*

$$$$ **Sherry-Netherland.** Because this 5th Avenue grande dame is a co-operative apartment hotel with a three-to-one ratio of permanent residents to hotel guests, in-room amenities are somewhat hit-and-miss, depending on the whims of the individual owners. Still, the marble-lined lobby wows, with its fine, hand-loomed carpets, crystal chandeliers, and wall friezes from the Vanderbilt mansion. The enormous, utterly luxurious suites have separate living and dining areas, serving pantries, decorative fireplaces, fine antiques, and glorious marble baths. The dastardly expensive Harry Cipriani's provides room service (a liter of water costs about $20, no joke). ✉ *781 5th Ave., at 59th St., 10022,* ☎ *212/355–2800,* FAX *212/319–4306. 40 rooms, 35 suites. Restaurant, bar, refrigerators, room service, in-room VCRs, barbershop, beauty salon, exercise room, laundry service and dry cleaning, concierge, business services, meeting rooms, parking (fee). AE, D, DC, MC, V.*

$$$$ **Waldorf-Astoria.** This landmark Art Deco masterpiece built in 1931 is a hub of city life; the lobby, with its original murals and mosaics and elaborate plaster ornamentation, is a meeting place for the rich and powerful. Guest rooms, each individually decorated, are all traditional and elegant; Astoria-level rooms have the added advantages of great views, fax machines, and access to the Astoria lounge, where a lovely, free afternoon tea is served. The Tower section, well known to heads of state and discerning business travelers, is ultraexclusive—and expensive. ✉ *301 Park Ave., between 50th and 51st Sts., 10022,* ☎ *212/355–3000 or 800/925–3673,* FAX *212/872–7272. 1,176 rooms, 276 suites. 4 restaurants, 2 bars, in-room modem lines, minibars, room service, massage, health club, baby-sitting, laundry service and dry cleaning, concierge, concierge floors, business services, meeting rooms, parking (fee). AE, D, DC, MC, V.*

$$$–$$$$ **Plaza Fifty.** This Manhattan East Suite hotel has a distinctly businesslike mood—witness the granite-walled lobby, with its mirrors, stainless steel, and leather furniture—but it's also supremely comfortable. The spacious rooms and suites have a clean, modern design: royal-blue carpets, abstract art, oversize chairs and couches upholstered in beige or blue. Rooms have kitchenettes; suites have full-size kitchens. ✉ *155 E. 50th St., 10022,* ☎ *212/751–5710,* FAX *212/753–1468. 74 rooms, 138 suites. In-room modem lines, in-room faxes, in-room safes, kitchen or kitchenette, room service, exercise room, coin laundry, concierge, business services, meeting rooms, parking (fee). AE, D, DC, MC, V.*

$$$ **Barbizon.** Grace Kelly, Joan Crawford, and Liza Minelli all lived here at various times, back when the hotel was an exclusive women's residence club (from 1927 to 1981). Now you can sleep in their former rooms, thanks to a major renovation, completed in 1997, that has restored the building's once-tarnished elegance. The chic lobby has a marble-and-limestone floor and gold-leaf chairs with mohair upholstery. Guest rooms glow in soft tones of shell-pink or celadon fabrics and blond woods; zig-zag wrought-iron floor lamps and bedsteads recall the hotel's deco days. The three-floor spa facility, operated by the Equinox gym chain, includes a 55-ft lap pool. ✉ *140 E. 63rd St., 10021,* ☎ *212/838–5700 or 800/223–1020,* FAX *212/888–4271. 310 rooms, 13 suites. Breakfast room, in-room modem lines, in-room safes, minibars, room service, indoor lap pool, spa, health club, baby-sitting, laundry service and dry cleaning, business services, parking (fee). AE, D, DC, MC, V.*

$$$ ★ **The Roger Smith.** Roger Smith runs not only his eponymous boutique hotel, but also an adjacent art gallery (where he can often be found), so it's no wonder this hotel is an art lover's dream. Riotous murals cover the walls in Lily's, the café, and the circular lobby is almost as zany, with bronze busts and miniature sculptures set into recessed walls. Individually decorated bedrooms (with still more art) are homey and comfortable; some have stocked bookshelves and fireplaces. ✉ *501 Lexington Ave., between 47th and 48th Sts., 10017,* ☎ *212/755–1400 or 800/445–0277,* FAX *212/758–4061. 104 rooms, 32 suites. Restaurant, bar, refrigerators, room service, laundry service, meeting room, parking (fee). AE, D, DC, MC, V.*

$$ **San Carlos.** Comfortable and plain, this small residential-style property has friendly service and a safe, convenient location. The rooms are clean, modern, and spacious, and all have a kitchenette, a walk-in closet, and two phones. ✉ *150 E. 50th St., 10022,* ☎ *212/755–1800 or 800/722–2012,* FAX *212/688–9778. 70 rooms, 80 suites. Kitchenettes. AE, DC, MC, V.*

$ **Pickwick Arms Hotel.** This convenient East Side establishment charges $110 a night for standard doubles and has older singles with shared baths for as little as $65; as a result, it's routinely booked solid by bargain hunters. Privations you endure to save a buck start and end with the lilliputian size of some rooms, all of which have cheap-looking furnishings. However, some rooms look over the Manhattan skyline, and there's an excellent Middle Eastern lunchtime buffet for less than $7 in the adjoining café. ✉ *230 E. 51st St., 10022,* ☎ *212/355–0300 or 800/742–5945,* FAX *212/755–5029. 350 rooms, 175 with bath. Café, airport shuttle. AE, DC, MC, V.*

$ **Vanderbilt YMCA.** Of the various Manhattan Ys with accommodations, this one has the best facilities, including a full-scale fitness center. Rooms are little more than dormitory-style cells, each with a bed (bunks in doubles), dresser drawer, and TV; singles have desks. Only five rooms have private baths (these cost $110), but communal showers and toilets are clean. The Turtle Bay neighborhood is safe and convenient; Grand Central Terminal and the U.N. are both a few blocks away. ✉ *224 E. 47th St., 10017,* ☎ *212/756–9600,* FAX *212/752–0210. 370 rooms, 5 with bath. Restaurant, 2 indoor pools, sauna, steam room, basketball, health club, volleyball, coin laundry, meeting rooms, airport shuttle. MC, V.*

Midtown West

$$$$ **The Algonquin.** This beloved landmark hotel, where the Round Table group of writers and wits once met for lunch, still shelters celebrities, particularly literary types visiting nearby publishing houses or the

New Yorker magazine offices. The heartbeat of the hotel is the lobby, with its grandfather clock, overstuffed chairs, and house cat, Hamlet. Specialty suites are dedicated to Dorothy Parker, James Thurber, and *Vanity Fair.* A new cultural events series, which includes literary readings and opera dinners, round out the schedule in the hotel's famed Oak Room, still a leading cabaret venue (☞ Chapters 5 and 8). ✉ *59 W. 44th St., 10036,* ☎ *212/840–6800 or 800/548–0345,* FAX *212/944–1618. 142 rooms, 23 suites. 2 restaurants, bar, in-room modem lines, in-room safes, room service, exercise room, cabaret, library, laundry service and dry cleaning, concierge, business services, meeting rooms. AE, D, DC, MC, V.*

$$$$ **Le Parker Meridien.** This dramatic, modern French hotel has one of the city's more striking entryways: A long atrium with an elaborate painted-mosaic ceiling and massive Doric columns leads into a cavernous lobby, where a sheer cliff of blond wood backs the registration desk. Equally impressive are the hotel's rooftop swimming pool and 15,000-square-ft Club La Raquette fitness facility. Upstairs, the well-kept rooms have an elegant neoclassic motif in soothing tans and browns; most rooms face Central Park. ✉ *118 W. 57th St., 10019,* ☎ *212/245–5000 or 800/543–4300,* FAX *212/708–7477. 449 rooms, 249 suites. Restaurant, 2 bars, breakfast room, in-room faxes, in-room modem lines, in-room safes, minibars, room service, indoor pool, spa, health club, racquetball, baby-sitting, laundry service and dry cleaning, concierge, business services, meeting rooms, parking (fee). AE, D, DC, MC, V.*

$$$$ **Marriott Marquis.** This giant in the heart of the theater district is a place New Yorkers love to hate. It's obvious, brash, and bright, with a virtual minicity of restaurants, shops, meeting rooms, ballrooms, and even a large Broadway theater within its vast confines. As at other Marriotts, every room looks alike, but all are clean, pleasant, and functional, with desks, swivel chairs, and soothing framed prints. Some rooms have dramatic urban views. ✉ *1535 Broadway, at 45th St., 10036,* ☎ *212/398–1900 or 800/843–4898,* FAX *212/704–8966. 1,911 rooms, 95 suites. 3 restaurants, 3 bars, café, coffee shop, in-room modem lines, in-room safes, room service, beauty salon, massage, health club, theater, baby-sitting, laundry service and dry cleaning, concierge, business services, meeting rooms, parking (fee). AE, D, DC, MC, V.*

$$$$ **The Michelangelo.** Italophiles will feel right at home at this deluxe hotel, with its very long, wide lobby lounge full of multihued marble and Veronese-style oil paintings. Upstairs, the spacious rooms (averaging 475 square ft) have varying decorative motifs, from neoclassic (cherrywood furnishings with black accents) to Oriental—but all have marble foyers, sitting areas, king-size beds, and marble bathrooms equipped with bidets, TVs, phones, and 55 gallon tubs. Complimentary cappuccino, pastries, and other Italian treats are served each morning in the Baroque lobby lounge. ✉ *152 W. 51st St., 10019,* ☎ *212/765–1900 or 800/237–0990,* FAX *212/581–7618. 128 rooms, 50 suites. Restaurant, bar, in-room fax machine, in-room modem lines, minibars, room service, exercise room, baby-sitting, laundry service and dry cleaning, concierge, business services, meeting rooms, parking (fee). AE, DC, MC, V.*

$$$$ **New York Hilton.** New York City's largest hotel and the epicenter of the city's hotel-based conventions, the Hilton has myriad business facilities, eating establishments, and shops, all designed for convenience. Hilton spends vast sums to keep the hotel trim, and it shows: There's a distinctive landscaped driveway and a sprawling, brassy lobby—more businesslike than beautiful but always buzzing. Considering the size of this property, guest rooms are surprisingly well maintained, and all have coffeemakers, hair dryers, and ironing boards. ✉

1335 6th Ave., 10019, ☎ 212/586–7000 or 800/445–8667, FAX 212/261–5902. 2,041 rooms, 20 suites. 2 restaurants, café, sports bar, in-room modem lines, in-room safes, minibars, room service, barbershop, beauty salon, hot tub, massage, health club, baby-sitting, laundry service and dry cleaning, concierge, concierge floors, business services, meeting rooms, parking (fee). AE, D, DC, MC, V.

$$$$ **Renaissance.** The Renaissance markets itself as a business hotel, though vacationers often take advantage of its low off-season rates and its proximity to Broadway. Elevators lead from street level to the third-floor art deco reception area. On the second floor are two bars and Foley's Fish House, a restaurant with up-close views of Times Square. Rooms are warm and inviting, with dark cherrywood and a tan-and-black color scheme. The marble bathrooms have deep soaking tubs. ✉ *714 7th Ave., between 47th and 48th Sts., 10036, ☎ 212/765–7676 or 800/628–5222, FAX 212/765–1962. 295 rooms, 10 suites. Restaurant, bar, in-room modem lines, in-room safes, room service, minibars, in-room VCRs, massage, exercise room, baby-sitting, laundry service and dry cleaning, business services, meeting rooms, parking (fee). AE, D, DC, MC, V.*

$$$$ **Rihga Royal.** The Rihga Royal Hotel group has long been recognized for its luxury properties in Japan, and its New York property is a low-profile favorite among celebrities and business travelers. Each of its luxurious, contemporary-style suites has a spacious living room with bay windows and a bedroom enclosed by French doors; the large marble bathrooms have glass-enclosed showers and separate tubs. Every suite has a fax machine; pricier Pinnacle Suites also have CD players, cellular phones, and "miniature business center" machines that print and copy. ✉ *151 W. 54th St., 10019, ☎ 212/307–5000 or 800/937–5454, FAX 212/765–6530. 500 suites. Restaurant, bar, in-room fax machine, in-room modem lines, in-room safes, in-room VCRs, minibars, room service, massage, exercise room, baby-sitting, laundry service and dry cleaning, concierge, business services, meeting rooms, parking (fee). AE, D, DC, MC, V.*

$$$$ **The Royalton.** Ian Schrager and the late Steve Rubell's second Manhattan hotel (Morgans came first; ☞ *below*) is a second home to the world's media, music, and fashion-biz folk, who often meet for martinis in the all-white lobby lounge or the inconspicuous, unadvertised Vodka Bar. The centerpiece of each Philippe Starck–designed guest room is a low-lying, custom-made bed with built-in pin lights; there are also geometrically challenged but comfy blue velvet chairs, and window banquettes. The staff here does a good job catering to people who feel it's their lot in life to be waited on. ✉ *44 W. 44th St., 10036, ☎ 212/869–4400 or 800/635–9013, FAX 212/575–0012. 145 rooms, 23 suites. Restaurant, bar, in-room modem lines, minibars, room service, massage, exercise room, baby-sitting, laundry service and dry cleaning, business services, meeting rooms, parking (fee). AE, DC, MC, V.*

$$$$ **The Shoreham.** This is a miniature, low-attitude version of the Royalton—and it's comfortable to boot. Almost everything is metal or metal colored, from perforated steel bed headboards (lit from behind) to the steel sink in the shiny, tiny bathrooms to the silver-gray carpets. Other pleasant touches include black oval night tables with digital gadgetry and a single red rose, and in-room VCRs and CD players. Cedar-lined closets are icing on the cake. ✉ *33 W. 55th St., 10019, ☎ 212/247–6700 or 800/553–3347, FAX 212/765–9741. 47 rooms, 37 suites. In-room modem lines, in-room safes, in-room VCRs, massage, baby-sitting, laundry service and dry cleaning, business services, parking (fee). AE, DC, MC, V.*

$$$–$$$$ **Ameritania Hotel.** This busy crash pad just off Broadway has raised its standards (and its prices) and is now one of the area's trendiest hotels. Settle into one of the oversize chairs in the cavernous, terrazzo-floored lobby, the better to size up the young, hip crowd, many of whom choose the Ameritania for its proximity to the Letterman Show's Ed Sullivan Theater. Dimly lit hallways create a feeling of perpetual nighttime—an impression that lingers in the bedrooms, where black metal furniture dominates. Bar 54 jams with hit tunes until 2 AM. ✉ *1701 Broadway, at 54th St., 10019,* ☏ *212/247–5000 or 800/922–0330,* FAX *212/247–3316. 195 rooms, 12 suites. Restaurant, bar, room service, exercise room, laundry service and dry cleaning, concierge, parking (fee). AE, D, DC, MC, V.*

$$$ ★ **Casablanca.** Morocco meets the Mediterranean in every nook and cranny of this fanciful midtown hotel: Moorish mosaic tiles, framed antique Berber scarves and rugs, and a mural of a northern African city drenched in sunlight conjure up an exotic desert oasis. In Rick's Café—a spacious lounge with a fireplace, piano, 41-inch movie screen, and bookshelves stocked with Bogart-abilia—look for complimentary breakfast and evening wine and cheese on weeknights, in addition to 24-hour cappuccino and cookies. Rattan furniture, ceiling fans, and Moroccan-style wood shutters dress up the smallish rooms, which adjoin elaborately tiled bathrooms with wicker tables. A plant-filled greenhouse garden with a skylight roof and a rooftop wet bar (in the works at press time) add to the allure. ✉ *147 W. 43rd St., 10036,* ☏ *212/869–1212,* FAX *212/391–7585. 44 rooms, 4 suites. Bar, breakfast room, in-room modems, refrigerators, in-room VCRs, piano, business services, meeting room, parking (fee). AE, DC, MC, V.*

$$$ **The Gorham.** An inviting lobby with paneled maple walls, marble floors, Persian rugs, and potted plants sets the cosmopolitan mood for this little midtown gem, which prides itself on its cozy breakfast room and sunny, meticulously maintained exercise room. Fully equipped kitchenettes make the spacious rooms a bargain, whether or not you like the Euro-modern decor of red-lacquer furniture and marbleized countertops. Bathrooms have plenty of shelf space and nifty digital water-temperature settings. The quietest rooms are in the front of the hotel, on 55th Street. ✉ *136 W. 55th St., 10019,* ☏ *212/245–1800 or 800/735–0710,* FAX *212/582–8332. 70 rooms, 45 suites. Breakfast room, in-room safes, kitchenettes. AE, D, DC, MC, V.*

$$$ **The Mansfield.** Built in 1904 as lodging for well-heeled bachelors, this small hotel is Victorian and clublike. Turn-of-the-century details abound, from the lobby's coffered ceiling, warm ivory walls, and yellow limestone floor, to the black-marble bathrooms, dark-wood venetian blinds, and sleigh beds in the guest rooms. Movies are shown on a big screen in the audiovisual lounge, where a high-tech machine dispenses cappuccino 24 hours a day; and nightly piano and harp recitals take place in the intimate drawing room, where breakfast, afternoon tea and after-theater dessert are served. Best of all, there's free parking, a rarity in New York. ✉ *12 W. 44th St., 10036,* ☏ *212/944–6050 or 800/255–5167,* FAX *212/764–4477. 123 rooms, 25 suites. Room service, in-room VCRs, cinema, concert hall, library, meeting room, business services, free parking. AE, MC, V.*

$$$ **The Paramount.** The work of the team responsible for the Royalton (☞ *above*) and Morgans (☞ *below*), the fashionable Paramount caters to a somewhat more bohemian and cost-conscious clientele than either of its cousins. The rooms, though diminutive, all bear the Philippe Starck stamp: framed headboards (some bearing the image of Vermeer's *The Lacemaker,*), conical steel sinks in the bathrooms. In the lobby a sheer platinum wall and a glamorous sweep of staircase lead to a mezzanine gallery of squashy seating, tiny nightclub-style table lamps, and a so-so restaurant—the perfect place to spy on the glitterati below. Three establishments—Whiskey Bar, a trendy late-night spot; Coco Pazzo Teatro, a Pino Luongo–run Italian restaurant; and a small Dean & DeLuca—are a boon to what is otherwise a staid block. ✉ *235 W. 46th St., 10036,* ☎ *212/764–5500 or 800/225–7474,* FAX *212/575–4892. 590 rooms, 10 suites. 2 restaurants, bar, café, in-room modem lines, room service, in-room VCRs, exercise room, nursery, laundry service and dry cleaning, concierge, business services, meeting rooms. AE, D, DC, MC, V.*

$$$ ★ **The Warwick.** Built by William Randolph Hearst in 1927, the Warwick remains a midtown favorite, catercorner from the New York Hilton (☞ *above*) and well placed for theater and points west. Its handsome, Regency-style rooms have soft pastel color schemes, mahogany armoires, and marble bathrooms. The elegant, marble-floored lobby buzzes with activity; the Warwick Bar adjoins it on one side, Ciao Europa, an Italian restaurant, on the other. ✉ *65 W. 54th St., 10019,* ☎ *212/247–2700,* FAX *212/489–3926. 346 rooms, 70 suites. Restaurant, bar, minibars, room service, laundry service and dry cleaning, business services, meeting rooms, parking (fee). AE, DC, MC, V.*

$$ **Quality Hotel and Suites.** This relatively small prewar hotel is near many theaters, Rockefeller Center, and some of the city's best-known Brazilian restaurants. The peculiar lobby has a narrow corridor that snakes off around a corner, photo-realist cityscape murals, and some rather handsome Art Deco Bakelite lights. The rooms are very plain, but most are well maintained and clean. This is a popular stop for South Americans, although you'll see a few U.S. business travelers, too. This block is one of midtown's most deserted at night, so lone travelers should use caution coming and going. ✉ *59 W. 46th St., 10036,* ☎ *212/719–2300 or 800/848–0020. 193 rooms, 21 suites. In-room modem lines, barber shop, beauty salon, business services. AE, D, DC, MC, V.*

$$ **Wellington Hotel.** This large, old-fashioned property's main advantages are reasonable prices and a location near Carnegie Hall (both are draws for many budget-conscious Europeans). Rooms are small but clean; baths are serviceable. ✉ *871 7th Ave., at 55th St., 10019,* ☎ *212/247–3900 or 800/652–1212,* FAX *212/581–1719. 550 rooms, 150 suites. Restaurant, bar, coffee shop, beauty salon, parking (fee). AE, DC, MC, V.*

$$ ★ **The Wyndham.** This bargain sleeper has three major trump cards: a plum location catercorner to Central Park South; enormous rooms and suites; and a brilliant collection of art, all of it framed and dramatically lit, filling all the rooms and public areas. Each well-worn room is unique, but count on a walk-in closet, a few choice paintings, and a handful of books stacked in shelves. The breezy, summer-house mood is enhanced by pastel wall coverings and fresh flowers. ✉ *42 W. 58th St., 10019,* ☎ *212/753–3500 or 800/257–1111,* FAX *212/754–5638. 142 rooms, 70 suites. Restaurant, bar. AE, D, MC, V.*

$ ★ **Broadway Inn Bed & Breakfast.** In the heart of the theater district, this friendly, comfortable, reasonably priced B&B has spartan but cheerful rooms, with black-lacquer beds and folding chairs. Breakfast is served in the Victorian-style lobby, whose brick walls, stocked bookshelves, and framed photos of old New York encourage lingering. An extra $70 or $80 gets you a suite with an additional fold-out sofabed and kitchenette, separated from the main room by closet doors. ✉ *264 W. 46th St., 10036,* ☎ *212/997–9200 or 800/826–6300,* FAX *212/768–2807. 40 rooms. AE, D, DC, MC, V.*

$ **Herald Square Hotel.** Sculpted cherubs on its facade and vintage magazine covers adorning the hallways inside lend character to this historic hotel, housed in the former headquarters of the original *Life*, a humor magazine that preceded Henry Luce's *Life*. Rooms are basic and clean, with deep-green carpets and floral-print bedspreads; all have TVs, phones with voice mail, and in-room safes. There's no concierge and no room service, but what does it matter when rooms cost as little as $75. ✉ *19 W. 31st St., 10001,* ☎ *212/279–4017 or 800/727–1888,* FAX *212/643–9208. 120 rooms. In-room safes. AE, D, MC, V.*

$ **Hotel Edison.** This offbeat old hotel is a popular budget stop for tour groups from here and abroad. The loan-shark murder scene in *The Godfather* was shot in what is now Sophia's restaurant, and the pink-plaster coffee shop is a hot place to eavesdrop on show-business gossip. Guest rooms are clean and fresh; bathrooms are minuscule. There's no room service, but this part of the theater district has many restaurants and delis. ✉ *228 W. 47th St., 10036,* ☎ *212/840–5000 or 800/637–7070,* FAX *212/596–6850. 800 rooms. Restaurant, bar, coffee shop, beauty salon, airport shuttle. AE, D, DC, MC, V.*

$ **Portland Square Hotel.** You can't beat this theater district old-timer for value, with its clean, simple rooms, exercise facility (albeit tiny), coin laundry, and business services. James Cagney lived in the building, and—as the story goes—a few of his Radio City Rockette acquaintances lived upstairs. Rooms have green carpets and floral-print bedspreads; those on the east wing have oversize bathrooms. ✉ *132 W. 47th St., 10036,* ☎ *212/382–0600 or 800/388–8988,* FAX *212/382–0684. 142 rooms, 112 with bath. In-room safes, exercise room, coin laundry. AE, MC, V.*

Central Park South/59th Street

$$$$ ★ **Essex House.** The lobby of this stately Central Park South property is an Art Deco masterpiece fit for Fred and Ginger. The talented Christian Delouvrier oversees the cuisine, both in the informal Café Botanica (which faces Central Park and resembles a lush prewar English greenhouse) and in the acclaimed Les Célébrités, where art painted by celebrities like James Dean covers the walls (for both ☞ Chapter 6). British Chippendale or French Louis XIV antiques decorate the guest rooms; all have large, marble bathrooms, many have breathtaking views of the park. The staff is discreet, efficient, and friendly. ✉ *160 Central Park S, 10019,* ☎ *212/247–0300,* FAX *212/315–1839. 516 rooms, 81 suites. 2 restaurants, bar, in-room modem lines, in-room safes, minibars, room service, in-room VCRs, spa, health club, baby-sitting, laundry service and dry cleaning, concierge, business services, meeting rooms, parking (fee). AE, D, DC, MC, V.*

$$$$ **The Plaza.** With its unsurpassed 5th Avenue address, opposite Central Park and F.A.O. Schwarz, the Plaza is one of the New York's highest-profile hotels (☞ Chapter 2). Donald Trump bought it (in 1988), the fictional Eloise ran riot in it, and film upon film has featured it. Its legendary reputation is well deserved: Even the smallest guest rooms have crystal chandeliers and 14-ft-high ceilings. A stroll by the fin-de-siècle Palm Court will give you a sense of what makes the city tick. A brand-new spa was scheduled to open in April, 1998. ✉ *5th Ave. at 59th St., 10019,* ☎ *212/759–3000 or 800/759–3000,* FAX *212/546–5324. 670 rooms, 135 suites. 4 restaurants, 2 bars, in-room modem lines, in-room safes, minibars, room service, spa, health club, baby-sitting, laundry service and dry cleaning, concierge, business services, meeting room, parking (fee). AE, D, DC, MC, V.*

$$$$ **Westin Central Park South** Despite the sudden, much-publicized loss of its prestigious Ritz-Carlton name in late 1997, this Central Park South classic still ranks among the city's top hotels. From the swank address to the very polished service to the fine art that adorns virtually every wall, everything about the hotel is first-class. Guest rooms are graced with rich brocades, polished woods, and marble bathrooms; some have breathtaking Central Park views. The restaurant, Fantino, serves contemporary cuisine on china designed by Gianni Versace. The friendly bartender, Norman, has been entertaining guests and local barflies for the past 18 years. ✉ *112 Central Park S, 10019,* ☎ *212/757–1900 or 800/937–8461,* FAX *212/757–9620. 193 rooms, 15 suites. Restaurant, bar, in-room modem lines, minibars, room service, steam room, health club, baby-sitting, dry cleaning, laundry service, concierge, business services, meeting room, parking (fee). AE, D, DC, MC, V.*

Upper East Side

$$$$ ★ **The Carlyle.** European tradition and Manhattan swank come together at New York's most lovable grand hotel. Everything about this Madison Avenue landmark suggests refinement, from the Mark Hampton–designed rooms, with their fine antique furniture and artfully framed Audubons and botanicals, to the first-rate service. Many guests head straight to the Bemelmans Bar, named after Ludwig Bemelmans, illustrator of the beloved children's book character Madeline and the "twelve little girls in two straight lines"; he created the murals here. Others come just to hear Barbara Cook or Bobby Short perform at the clubby Café Carlyle, the quintessential cabaret venue. ✉ *35 E. 76th St., 10021,* ☎ *212/744–1600 or 800/227–5737,* FAX *212/717–4682. 145 rooms, 45 suites. Restaurant, bar, café, kitchenettes, in-room faxes, in-room modem lines, minibars, room service, spa, health club, laundry service and dry cleaning, concierge, business services, meeting rooms, parking (fee). AE, DC, MC, V.*

$$$$ ★ **The Lowell.** You may be tempted to check in long term at this elegant, pied-à-terre–style landmark on a tree-lined street between Madison and Park avenues. Guest rooms, more than half of which are suites, have all the comforts of home—kitchenettes (or minibars), stocked bookshelves, and even umbrellas; 33 of the suites have working fireplaces, and 10 have private terraces. A gym suite has its own private fitness center, a Hollywood suite has an entertainment center and framed photos of Hollywood stars, and a garden suite has two beautifully planted terraces. The Pembroke Room serves a fine high tea, and the Post House is renowned for its steaks. ✉ *28 E. 63rd St., 10021,* ☎ *212/838–1400 or 800/221–4444,* FAX *212/319–4230. 21 rooms, 44 suites. Restaurant, breakfast room, in-room fax machine, in-room modem lines, kitchenettes, minibars, room service, in-room VCRs, massage, health club, baby-sitting, laundry service and dry cleaning, concierge, parking (fee). AE, D, DC, MC, V.*

$$$$ ★ **The Mark.** A block north of the Carlyle and steps from Central Park, the Mark is a haven of tranquility among more rambunctious and showy hotels. The feeling of calm that pervades the cool, Biedermeier-furnished marble lobby follows you into the clubby, deep-green and burgundy bar, where even lone women travelers feel comfortable. The serenity continues at Mark's Restaurant, where afternoon tea is served. Bedrooms are understated and elegant, with cream-color walls, muted gold and olive fabrics, museum-quality prints, plump armchairs, a potted palm or two, and Frette bed linens. ✉ *25 E. 77th St., 10021,* ☎ *212/744–4300 or 800/843–6275,* FAX *212/744–2749. 120 rooms, 60 suites. Restaurant, bar, in-room fax machine, in-room modem lines, in-room safes, kitchenettes, minibars, room service, in-room VCRs, massage, health club, baby-sitting, laundry service and dry cleaning, concierge, business services, meeting rooms, parking (fee). AE, D, DC, MC, V.*

$$$$ **The Pierre.** Before Canada's Four Seasons hotel group opened its eponymous flagship on 57th Street (☞ Midtown East, *above*), the Pierre was its pride and joy, and it remains a high-profile presence. Quite the

opposite of the understated Four Seasons, the Pierre owes a lot to the Palace of Versailles, with its chandeliers and handmade carpets, murals depicting putti, and Corinthian columns in the Rotunda lounge, where afternoon tea is an institution. Chintz and dark wood adorn the grand and traditional guest rooms, whose gleaming Art Deco bathrooms are spacious for New York. ✉ *5th Ave. at 61st St., 10021,* ☎ *212/838–8000 or 800/332–3442,* FAX *212/758–1615. 149 rooms, 54 suites. Restaurant, bar, in-room modem lines, in-room safes, room service, beauty salon, massage, health club, concierge, business services, meeting rooms, parking (fee). AE, D, DC, MC, V.*

$$$$ **Plaza Athénée.** This Parisian-style boutique hotel is worthy of Marie Antoinette—indeed, it feels more like an apartment in the 16th arrondissement than a hotel in New York City. Quietly elegant rooms are done in soothing hues of beige and coral, with French Directoire–style mahogany furniture and hand-painted silk drapery and bedspreads; marble baths are fittingly luxurious. The crowd here is trés soignée; if you prefer a casual atmosphere, you may want to stay elsewhere. ✉ *37 E. 64th St., 10021,* ☎ *212/734–9100 or 800/447–8800,* FAX *212/772–0958. 117 rooms, 36 suites. Restaurant, bar, in-room modem lines, in-room safes, minibars, room service, massage, exercise room, baby-sitting, laundry service and dry cleaning, concierge, business services, meeting rooms, parking (fee). AE, D, DC, MC, V.*

$$$ **Hotel Wales.** In tony Carnegie Hill, this relatively modestly priced hotel is a pleasant surprise. Every effort has been made to retain the turn-of-the-century mood of this 1901 landmark—from the cavernous lobby done in deep burgundies and greens to the Pied Piper parlor, where vintage children's illustrations cover the walls. Fireplaces, fine oak woodwork, fresh flowers, and in-room VCRs and CDs make up for minuscule bathrooms and slightly gloomy color schemes. A generous European-style breakfast and nightly dessert buffet are served in the parlor, along with 24-hour cappuccino. ✉ *1295 Madison Ave., at 92nd St., 10128,* ☎ *212/876–6000 or 800/528–5252,* FAX *212/860–7000. 87 rooms, 40 suites. Restaurant, bar, room service, in-room VCRs, laundry service and dry cleaning, parking (fee). AE, MC, V.*

$$ **The Franklin.** The Gotham Hospitality Group, which also owns the Hotel Wales (☞ *above*), the Shoreham (☞ Midtown West, *above*), and the Roger Williams (☞ Murray Hill, *below*), transformed this formerly seedy, low-rent property into its current incarnation as a ravishing uptown version of the Paramount (☞ Midtown West, *above*). The tiny lobby—constructed of black granite, brushed steel, and cherrywood—looks like an art installation. Most rooms are also tiny (some measure 100 square ft), but what they lack in size they make up for in style: All have funky, custom-built steel furniture, gauzy white canopies over the beds, and cedar closets. Added bonuses are the daily breakfast and dessert buffets, 24-hour cappuccino, and free parking. ✉ *164 E. 87th St., 10128,* ☎ *212/369–1000 or 800/428–5252,* FAX *212/369–8000. 47 rooms. In-room safes, in-room VCRs, library, free parking. AE, MC, V.*

Upper West Side

$$$$ **Trump International Hotel and Towers.** A large unisphere gleams outside the Donald's staggeringly expensive, showy namesake hotel, which occupies the first 17 floors of the well-situated, black-glass-clad tower. The hotel's restaurant, Jean Georges (☞ Chapter 6), is one of the city's finest; if you want to dine in, a Jean Georges chef is on hand to prepare meals in your suite. Rooms and suites resemble mini-apartments: All have fully equipped kitchens with black-granite countertops, entertainment centers with stereos and VCRs, and mini-telescopes, which you can use to gaze through the floor-to-ceiling windows. Creamy-beige marble bathrooms are stocked with bath salts and loofahs. Complimentary cellular phones and personalized stationery and business cards are offered—but why anyone staying here wouldn't have cards of his or her own is a mystery. ✉ *1 Central Park W, 10023,* ☎ *212/299–1000 or 888/448–7867,* FAX *212/299–1150. 38 rooms, 129 suites. Restaurant, bar, café, in-room fax machine, in-room modem lines, in-room safes, kitchenettes, minibars, in-room VCRs, indoor pool, spa, baby-sitting, laundry service and dry cleaning, concierge, business services, meeting room, parking (fee). AE, D, DC, MC, V.*

$$$ **Mayflower.** Inside the Mayflower's long, low, wood-paneled lobby, with its gilt-framed oils of tall ships and flowers, you can serve yourself a cup of coffee and a cookie from the 24-hour side tray after a walk through Central Park, which lies just across the street. The large, comfortable rooms, though not quite high-style, have thick, sea-green carpeting, fruit-and-flower-print drapes, dark wood colonial-style furniture, and walk-in closets; most also have walk-in pantries with a fridge and sink. An extra $20 buys a spectacular park view. Service has been shaky at times, but most of the staff is friendly and helpful. ✉ *15 Central Park W, 10023,* ☎ *212/265–0060 or 800/223–4164,* FAX *212/265–2026. 117 rooms, 160 suites. Restaurant, bar, in-room modem lines, refrigerators, room service, exercise room, meeting rooms, parking (fee). AE, DC, MC, V.*

$$$ **Radisson Empire Hotel.** This Empire is one of the city's better buys, and it has an unbeatable location across from Lincoln Center. Crimson carpet and hanging tapestry adorn its warm, inviting English country–style lobby. Rooms and suites are small but appealing; all have textured teal carpets, dark-wood furnishings, and high-tech electronics. A nearby health club is accessible for a small fee. ✉ *Broadway at 63rd St., 10023,* ☎ *212/265–7400 or 800/333–3333,* FAX *212/244–3382. 355 rooms, 20 suites. Restaurant, bar, in-room modem lines, minibars, in-room VCRs, meeting rooms, parking (fee). AE, D, DC, MC, V.*

$$ **The Excelsior.** Directly across the street from the American Museum of Natural History, this atmospheric old hotel rubs shoulders with fine prewar doorman buildings. An old-fashioned coffee shop with bar-stool seating is off the warm, wood-paneled, coffered-ceiling lobby. The French country–style rooms have emerald-green carpets, hardwood bedsteads and desks, and tiny closets; flower-pattern tiles and pastel shower curtains give the sparkling bathrooms a feminine flair. ✉ *45 W. 81st St., 10024,* ☎ *212/362–9200 or 800/368–4575,* FAX *212/721–2994. 130 rooms, 60 suites. Coffee shop. AE, D, DC, MC, V.*

$$ **The Lucerne.** In a handsome brownstone building on a quiet, Upper West Side side street, this bargain newcomer enjoys a constant buzz of activity, thanks to the publike Wilson's Bar & Grill next door. The multihued-marble lobby, with its earth-tone walls and columns and comfortable olive-green couches, has more pizzazz than the predictable guest rooms, with their requisite dark-wood reproduction furniture and chintz bedspreads. A sunny exercise room on the top floor has an excellent view of the city. ✉ *201 W. 79th St., 10024,* ☎ *212/875–1000,* FAX *212/362–7251. 140 rooms, 40 suites. Restaurant, bar, in-room modems, room service, exercise room, meeting rooms, concierge. AE, D, DC, MC, V.*

$ ★ **Hotel Beacon.** The Upper West Side's best budget buy is three blocks from both Central Park and Lincoln Center, and just footsteps from Zabar's gourmet bazaar. All rooms and suites have kitchenettes with coffeemakers, full-size refrigerators, and stoves; some have microwaves. Closets are huge; the bathrooms have Hollywood dressing room–style mirrors. The Beacon has neither a restaurant nor a bar, but with so many in the neighborhood, it's not a serious liability. ✉ *2130 Broadway, at 75th St., 10023,* ☎ *212/787–1100 or 800/572–4969,* FAX *212/*

724–0839. 110 rooms, 100 suites. Kitchenettes, business services, meeting room, parking (fee). AE, D, DC, MC, V.

$ **Malibu Studios.** This hip, youth-oriented, budget crash pad could almost pass for a college dorm, especially given its proximity to Columbia University. Though it's farther north than you may care to venture, it's in a lively, safe neighborhood, with the Cathedral of St. John the Divine, inexpensive ethnic restaurants, and the Nos. 1/9 subway station all nearby. It's well worth the effort for the money you'll save: Clean, modern double-occupancy rooms with private bath start at $79; those with shared bath start at $45. Every room has a TV, a desk with a writing lamp, and black-and-white prints of New York. ✉ *2688 Broadway, at 103rd St., 10025,* ☎ *212/222–2954 or 800/647–2227,* FAX *212/678–6842. 150 rooms, 100 with bath. No credit cards.*

$ **The Milburn.** Convenient to Lincoln Center, Central Park, and Zabar's, this small bohemian hotel has a lobby that resembles a Bavarian castle, with salmon-pink walls, black-and-white marble floor, heraldic doodads, and abundant gilt. The homey, spacious rooms are a chaotic but cozy assemblage of, say, burgundy carpet and blue drapes, a glass-top brass table, and framed posters on pink floral walls. All have kitchenettes equipped with a microwave and coffeemaker. ✉ *242 W. 76th St., 10023,* ☎ *212/362–1006 or 800/833–9622,* FAX *212/721–5476. 50 rooms, 50 suites. In-room safes, kitchenettes, coin laundry. AE, DC, MC, V.*

$ **YMCA West Side.** Though the fitness center here is not quite as polished as the one at the Vanderbilt YMCA (☞ *above*), you can't beat this YMCA for value, location, and atmosphere: Two blocks from Lincoln Plaza and a short jaunt from Central Park, it's housed in what looks like a Spanish cloister, with gargoyles adorning its arched neo-Byzantine entrance. Rooms are as tiny as jail cells, but red carpeting and spreads make them a little more cheerful. Those with private bath cost $95. ✉ *5 W. 63rd St., 10023,* ☎ *212/787–4400,* FAX *212/875–1334. 533 rooms, 25 with bath. Restaurant, 2 indoor pools, sauna, health club, racquetball, coin laundry, meeting room, airport shuttle. AE, MC, V.*

Chelsea and Gramercy Park

$$$$ ★ **The Inn at Irving Place.** New York City's most charming small inn occupies two grand 1830s town houses steps from Gramercy Park. With its cozy tea salon (complete with a working fireplace and antique tea pots), its antiques-filled living room scattered with fine Oriental and needlepoint rugs, and details such as an original 1834 curving stair banister, the inn vividly evokes a more genteel era. Each guest room has an ornamental fireplace, four-poster bed with embroidered linens, wood shutters, and glossy cherrywood floors; Madame Olenska's room has a bay window with a sitting nook. In the morning, steaming pots of tea and coffee are served in the tea salon, along with homemade pastries and breads. ✉ *56 Irving Place, 10003,* ☎ *212/533–4600 or 800/685–1447,* FAX *212/533–4611. 12 rooms. Bar, in-room faxes, in-room modems, minibars, room service, massage, laundry service and dry cleaning, parking (fee). AE, D, DC, MC, V.*

$$ **Chelsea Savoy Hotel.** Affordable rates and a friendly though often harried young staff make this Chelsea newcomer a sensible choice. Jade-green carpets, butterscotch-colored wood furniture, and perhaps a framed van Gogh print enliven the small, basic rooms. Off the bland lobby, a huge, salmon-pink sitting room with mismatched chairs and sofas is a nice place to meet and greet. A café is in the works at press time. ✉ *204 W. 23rd St., 10011,* ☎ *212/929–9353,* FAX *212/741–6309. 90 rooms. Café. AE, MC, V.*

$ ★ **Chelsea Inn.** The eclectic, country ambience here is a refreshing change from the characterless hotels that dominate this price category. Housed in an old brownstone on a chic Chelsea street, it's a favorite of young budget travelers, who appreciate the in-room cooking facilities (some have full kitchenettes; others have just a refrigerator and sink). Rooms are a cozy hodgepodge of country quilts and thrift-shop antiques, with a basket or two of dried flowers in most. A few rooms in back overlook a little courtyard with an ivy-draped fence. ✉ *46 W. 17th St., 10011,* ☎ *212/645–8989,* FAX *212/645–1903. 27 rooms, 4 with bath. Kitchenettes. AE, D, V.*

Murray Hill

$$$$ **The Kitano.** The first Japanese-owned hotel in New York City when it opened in 1973, the Kitano brings austere grandeur to an otherwise low-key stretch of Park Avenue South. A large Botero bronze of a stylized dog presides over the chic mahogany and marble lobby. Handsome cherry and mahogany furnishings, luxurious beds with duvet comforters, and watercolor still lifes impart an air of serenity to the rooms and suites; soundproof windows make them among Manhattan's quietest. There's a self-service tea room, and individual Japanese tea makers in every room. The Japanese restaurant is known for its high-priced but authentic cuisine; and the swank, second-floor lounge has a Japanese jazz band on weekend nights. For business meetings, the Kitano is hard to beat: Two of the top-floor banquet rooms have floor-to-celing glass doors leading to expansive balconies with dazzling city views. ✉ *66 Park Ave., at 38th St., 10016,* ☎ *212/885–7000,* FAX *212/885–7100. 131 rooms, 19 suites. 2 restaurants, 2 bars, in-room faxes, in-room modem lines, in-room safes, minibars, room service, spa, baby-sitting, laundry service and dry cleaning, concierge, business services, meeting rooms, parking (fee). AE, D, DC, MC, V.*

$$$–$$$$ **Doral Court and Doral Tuscany.** These sister hotels are not only neighbors in the off-the-tourist-map, peaceful Murray Hill, but they allow guests to sign up for food and drinks at one another's facilities. Which to choose? The Tuscany is a bit smaller and more intimate, but the Court has more one-bedroom suites. In both hotels, however, rooms and suites are unusually spacious and uncluttered, with walk-in closets and contemporary, high-style trappings: oversize dark-wood desks; a gigantic, silk-covered chaise longue; a full-size framed mirror leaning casually against a wall. Linen drapes let in natural light, and brushed-chrome lamps and candlesticks set a romantic evening mood. Homey touches—chenille throw-blankets, potted orchids, perhaps a swivel chair, and refrigerators stocked with milk and cereal in addition to the usual minibar snacks—make these feel like mini-apartments rather than hotel rooms. ✉ *Court: 130 E. 39th St., 10016,* ☎ *212/685–1100 or 800/223–6725 reservations,* FAX *212/889–0287.* ✉ *Tuscany: 120 E. 39th St., 10016,* ☎ *212/779–7822 or 800/223–6725 reservations,* FAX *212/696–2095. Court: 150 rooms, 48 suites; Tuscany: 110 rooms, 12 suites. 2 restaurants, 2 bars, in-room modem lines, minibars, room service, exercise room, baby-sitting, concierge, business services, meeting rooms. AE, D, DC, MC, V.*

$$$ ★ **Doral Park Avenue.** The lobby rotunda of this stately Park Avenue hotel is neoclassic with a twist: A giant painting of an ancient Greek city is offset by palm trees and art deco details. Neoclassic headboards and throw pillows in muted colors of gold, celadon, and cranberry grace the warm, inviting guest rooms. The swanky lounge off the lobby has big windows facing Park Avenue, and the restaurant, Saturnia, has garden-theme murals that give the illusion of dining in a greenhouse conservatory. ✉ *70 Park Ave., at 38th St., 10016,* ☎ *212/687–7050 or*

800/223–6725, FAX *212/973–2497. 185 rooms, 3 suites. Restaurant, bar, in-room modem lines, minibars, room service, massage, baby-sitting, laundry service and dry-cleaning, concierge, business services, meeting rooms, parking (fee). AE, D, DC, MC, V.*

$$$ **Jolly Madison Towers.** The Italian Jolly Hotels chain brings a European flair to this friendly hotel on a residential Murray Hill corner. The tasteful and traditional rooms have dark-wood furnishings. Suites are downright luxurious, with huge bathrooms with glass shower stalls, bidets, and make-up mirrors. Cinque Terre serves good northern Italian cuisine, and the cozy Whaler Bar has a fireplace and a wood-beamed ceiling. A separate concession on the premises offers shiatsu massage and Japanese sauna. ✉ *22 E. 38th St., 10016,* ☎ *212/802–0600 or 800/225–4340,* FAX *212/447–0747. 245 rooms, 6 suites. Restaurant, bar, in-room modem lines, minibars, massage, sauna, laundry service and dry cleaning, concierge. AE, DC, MC, V.*

$$$ **Morgans.** The first hotel in nightclub mavens Ian Schrager and the late Steve Rubell's triumphant triumvirate (☞ Paramount *and* Royalton *in* Midtown West, *above*) is a magnet for celebrities (there's no sign outside). A minimalist, high-tech look prevails in the stunning rooms, with low-lying, futonlike beds and 27-inch Sony TVs on wheels; the tiny bathrooms have crystal shower doors, steel surgical sinks, and poured-granite floors. Asia de Cuba, the scene-making restaurant (☞ Chapter 6), is booked solid by the young and the trendy—the same crowd that frequents the cavelike, candlelit Morgans Bar, downstairs from the hotel. ✉ *237 Madison Ave., between 37th and 38th Sts., 10016,* ☎ *212/686–0300 or 800/334–3408,* FAX *212/779–8352. 113 rooms, 26 suites. Restaurant, 2 bars, in-room modem lines, minibars, room service, baby-sitting, laundry service and dry cleaning, concierge, business services, meeting rooms, parking (fee). AE, D, DC, MC, V.*

$$$ ★ **Roger Williams Hotel.** The vintage-1928 Roger Williams charged $40 a night—and even gave over some of its floors to housing homeless families—until the Gotham Hospitality Group bought and transformed the hotel into a masterpiece of industrial chic in 1997. Sleek, maple walls, zinc-fluted pillars, and a Steinway grand piano distinguish the cavernous lobby. Bedrooms make up for their diminutive size with high-style, custom-made blond-birch furnishings—including sliding shoji screens behind the beds—and dramatic downlighting; each is equipped with a 27-inch Sony TV, VCR, and CD player. Some baths have a cedarwood-floor shower stall. There's a nightly dessert buffet as well as 24-hour cappuccino. ✉ *131 Madison Ave., at 31st St., 10016,* ☎ *212/448–7000,* FAX *212/448–7007. 181 rooms, 1 suite. In-room modem lines, in-room VCRs, piano, free parking. AE, D, MC, V.*

$–$$ **Quality Hotel East Side.** The least antiseptic of Manhattan's three Apple Core hotels (☞ Midtown West, *above*), this East-sider on a pleasant residential block has sunny, simple rooms done in primary colors, with framed Americana prints. A small exercise room and a tiny business center with a credit card–operated fax, photocopier, and computer are in the basement. ✉ *161 Lexington Ave., at 30th St., 10016,* ☎ *532–2255 or 800/567–7720,* FAX *212/481–7270. 176 rooms. Café, exercise room, business services, airport shuttle. AE, D, DC, MC, V.*

$ **Carlton Arms.** Every wall, ceiling, and other surface here is engulfed by murals, commissioned over the years by the hip, free-spirited managers. Each room has a theme: The Versailles Room (5A) by Fabian Compton is an outré symphony of trompe l'oeil trellises and classical urns; the Cow Spot Room (3C) by Heinz Burkhardt has a Holstein motif of cow-spotted rugs, bedspreads, and walls. All rooms have double-glazed windows but are phoneless, TV-less, almost free of furniture, and sometimes bathless—but who needs amenities with art like this? ✉ *160 E. 25th St., 10010,* ☎ *212/684–8337 or 212/679–0680 for reservations. 34 rooms, 20 with bath. MC, V.*

$ ★ **The Gershwin.** Young, foreign travelers flock to this hip budget hotel-cum-hostel, housed in a converted 13-story Greek Revival building. A giant primary-color cartoony sculpture, one of many works by house artist Brad Howe, visually assaults from the lobby. (A gallery next door showcases other avant-garde creations.) Rooms are all painted in custard yellow and kelly green and are somewhat crumbly in places, with no air-conditioning. Dormitories have four or eight beds and a remarkable $22 rate. You won't be spending much time in your room, however, because of all the activities here: band appearances, film series, and summer rooftop barbecues in summer. ✉ *7 E. 27th St., 10016,* ☎ *212/545–8000,* FAX *212/684–5546. 120 rooms; 15 dorm rooms. Restaurant, bar. MC, V.*

Greenwich Village, SoHo, Chinatown

$$$$ **Mercer Hotel.** After years of delays (signs in the windows read "coming soonish" for months on end), SoHo's second hotel has arrived. Was it worth the wait? Yes, if you like hotels that feel more like lofts. Owner Andre Balazs, known for his Château Marmont in Hollywood, has a knack for adapting the aesthetic to the neighborhood. Here, it's SoHo industrial all the way. So minimalist is the sprawling 100-seat lobby with its vintage book library and casual bar, that you may not even realize it's a hotel until you notice the unmarked reception desk toward the back wall. Guest rooms are enormous, with long entryways, high ceilings, and walk-in closets. No chintz or framed Monet prints here. Instead, dark African woods and high-tech light fixtures make a subtle statement. But the bathrooms steal the show with their decadent two-person tubs, some of them surrounded by mirrors. Downstairs is the Mercer Kitchen, Jean-Georges Vongerichten's newest venture. ✉ *99 Prince St., 10012,* ☎ *212/966–6060,* FAX *212/965–3838. 67 rooms, 8 suites. Restaurant, 2 bars, in-room modem lines, in-room safes, minibars, room service, in-room VCRs, concierge, business services. AE, D, DC, MC, V.*

$$$$ ★ **SoHo Grand.** SoHo's first and until recently, only hotel has an appropriately modernist industrial aesthetic. Starting from the first floor, the grand, self-suspended staircase of translucent bottle glass and iron recalls the vast, columned interiors and fanciful cast-iron embellishments of the neighborhood's 19th-century buildings. Upstairs in the Grand Salon, 16 ft high windows and overscaled furniture complement the immense stone pillars that rise from below. Guest rooms have custom-designed furnishings, including drafting table–style desks, nightstands that mimic sculptors' stands, and minibars made of old campaign chests. The tavern-style Canal House serves the best macaroni and cheese east of Sheboygan. ✉ *310 W. Broadway, 10013,* ☎ *212/965–3000 or 800/965–3000,* FAX *212/965–3244. 365 rooms, 4 suites. Restaurant, bar, in-room modem lines, in-room safes, minibars, room service, massage, exercise room, baby-sitting, laundry service and dry cleaning, concierge, business services, meeting room, parking (fee). AE, D, DC, MC, V.*

$$ **Holiday Inn Downtown.** In the heart of Chinatown and just a few steps from Little Italy and SoHo, this is one of the few hotels between midtown and the financial district. Though the Asian-decorated lobby and the excellent dim sum at Pacifica Restaurant attract a healthy sampling of Asian business travelers, many foreigners and young budget travelers also stay here. Rooms and suites have high ceilings, pastel walls and carpets, black-framed furniture, and framed watercolors with an

Asian motif. ✉ *138 Lafayette St., 10013,* ☎ *212/966–8898 or 800/465–4329,* FAX *212/966–3933. 213 rooms, 12 suites. Restaurant, bar, room service, laundry service and dry cleaning, concierge, parking (fee). AE, D, DC, MC, V.*

$ ★ **Larchmont Hotel.** You might miss the entrance to this Beaux Arts brownstone, whose geranium boxes and lanterns blend right in with the old New York feel of West 11th Street. If you don't mind shared bathrooms and no room service (though there is a communal kitchen for guest use), the residential-style accommodations are all anyone could ask for the price. Rooms have a tasteful safari theme, with rattan furniture, ceiling fans, and framed animal or botanical prints; your own private sink and stocked bookshelf will make you feel right at home. ✉ *27 W. 11th St., 10011,* ☎ *212/989–9333,* FAX *212/989–9496. 77 rooms, none with bath. AE, D, DC, MC, V.*

$ ★ **Washington Square Hotel.** Quietly situated at the northwest corner of Washington Square Park, this cozy hotel has a true European feel and style, from the wrought iron and gleaming brass in the small, elegant lobby to the personal attention given by the staff. Rooms are simple but pleasant and well maintained; request one with a window. There's also a good, reasonably priced restaurant, C3, and a low-key lounge of the same name; the Blue Note jazz club is just down the street. ✉ *103 Waverly Pl., 10011,* ☎ *212/777–9515 or 800/222–0418,* FAX *212/979–8373. 150 rooms. Restaurant, bar, exercise room. AE, MC, V.*

Lower Manhattan

$$$$ **Millenium Hilton.** The class act of downtown, this sleek black monolith is across the street from the World Trade Center. The modern, beige-and-wood rooms have a streamlined look, with contoured built-in desks and night tables; almost all have expansive views of landmark buildings and both the Hudson and the East rivers. The health club has an Olympic-size pool with windows that look out on St. Paul's Church. Live piano music adds sparkle to the smart lobby lounge. ✉ *55 Church St., 10007,* ☎ *212/693–2001,* FAX *212/571–2317. 458 rooms, 103 suites. 2 restaurants, 3 bars, in-room modem lines, in-room safes, minibars, room service, indoor pool, massage, health club, piano, baby-sitting, laundry service and dry cleaning, concierge, business services, meeting room, parking (fee). AE, D, DC, MC, V.*

$$$ **New York Marriott World Trade Center.** This downtown giant, nestled between the World Trade Center's twin towers, became Marriott's flagship New York hotel in 1996. The fabulous skylit lobby has a contemporary green-granite and marble entrance, a grand curved staircase, and a fountain. Rooms are sleek, modern, and spacious by Manhattan standards. The 22nd-floor health club has phenomenal views of Lower Manhattan. ✉ *3 World Trade Center, 10048,* ☎ *212/938–9100 or 800/550–2344,* FAX *212/321–2107. 788 rooms, 29 suites. Restaurant, bar, in-room modem lines, minibars, room service, indoor pool, health club, laundry service and dry cleaning, concierge, business services, meeting room, travel service, car rental, parking (fee). AE, D, DC, MC, V.*

$$ **Best Western Seaport Inn.** This thoroughly pleasant, restored 19th-century building is one block from the waterfront—close to South Street Seaport. With its cozy, library-like lobby, it has the feel of a Colonial sea captain's house, though the reasonably priced rooms are clearly those of a chain hotel—with dark wood, white walls, and floral nylon bedcovers. For $25–$35 extra you can have a room with a whirlpool tub and/or an outdoor terrace with a view of the Brooklyn Bridge. ✉ *33 Peck Slip, 10038,* ☎ *212/766–6600 or 800/468–3569,* FAX *212/766–*

6615. 71 rooms. In-room safes, refrigerators, in-room VCRs. AE, D, DC, MC, V.

BED-AND-BREAKFASTS

For value-conscious travelers who prefer a lived-in, low-key style and are willing to bypass luxuries like room service and personal voice mail, hundreds of bed-and-breakfasts can be found in residential neighborhoods of Manhattan and the other boroughs—especially Brooklyn. These are not the gingerbread-house B&Bs of smaller towns and cities: In Manhattan, the term simply refers to a private apartment you may rent for a few nights' stay. Though amenities, service, and privacy may fall short of what you get in hotels (often you don't even get breakfast, despite the B&B name) you may pay as little as $100 for this type of accommodation; and depending on the apartment you choose, it may even be more comfortable than a hotel. Be sure to ask your booking service for details on decor, location, and amenities: Predictably, you'll pay more for a central location, a doorman building, and special features such as balconies and gardens.

B&B's booked through a service may either be hosted (you are the guest in someone's occupied apartment) or unhosted (you have full use of someone's vacated apartment, including kitchen privileges—though you may not get maid service). Most B&B services represent both kinds. Make reservations as far in advance as possible; refunds (minus a $25 service charge) are given up to 10 days before arrival. A minimum three-night stay is the norm.

A Hospitality Co. (✉ 580 Broadway, 10012, ☎ 212/965–1102 or 800/987–1235, FAX 212/965–1149). **Abode Bed and Breakfasts Ltd.** (✉ Box 20022, 10021, ☎ 212/472–2000 or 800/835–8880). **Bed & Breakfast (& Books)** (✉ Box 20022, 10021, ☎ 212/865–8740 or 800/835–8880 [outside New York]). **Bed and Breakfast Network of New York** (✉ 134 W. 32nd St., Suite 602, 10001, ☎ 212/645–8134 or 800/900–8134). **City Lights Bed and Breakfast** (✉ Box 20355, Cherokee Station,10021, ☎ 212/737–7049, FAX 212/535–2755). **Manhattan Getaways** (☎ 212/265–7915, FAX 212/265–3561). **New World Bed and Breakfast** (✉ 150 5th Ave., Suite 711, 10011, ☎ 212/675–5600 or 800/443–3800 in the U.S., FAX 212/675–6366). **New York Habitat** (✉ 307 7th Ave., Suite 306, 10001, ☎ 212/647–9365, FAX 212/627–1416). **Urban Ventures** (✉ Box 426, 10024; ✉ 38 W. 32nd St., 10001; ☎ 212/594–5650 for both locations, FAX 212/947–9320).

8 Nightlife

The city that never sleeps has enough diversions to keep even the most gung-ho night owls occupied for weeks. In the same evening you can head for a classic West Village jazz haunt, a sleek TriBeCa bar, a sophisticated uptown cabaret, a grungy East Village club, or a raucous comedy club. Whether you're in the mood for loud rock, Broadway ballads, a Brazilian beat, blues, or bluegrass, you're sure to find it in Manhattan.

Updated by Paula S. Bernstein

NEW YORK NIGHTLIFE REALLY STARTED TO SWING in 1914, when a pair of ballroom dancers, Florence and Maurice Walton, took over management of the Parisian Room, in what is today's theater district. At Chez Maurice, as their new club was called, the city's café society learned a sensual dance at Tango Teas. Then came the Harlem Renaissance of the 1920s and '30s, and the New York jazz scene shifted north of 110th Street. In the 1950s nightspots mushroomed in Greenwich Village and the East 50s. Along 52nd Street in those years, recalls journalist Pete Hamill, "you could walk down a single block and hear Art Tatum, Billie Holiday, and Charlie Parker. And you could go to the Latin Quarter and see girls running around with bananas on their heads."

Well, fruit as headgear is out, but night-owling while wearing the look of the moment never will be. The nightclub scene is now downtown—in drab-by-day East Village dives, classic jazz joints in the West Village, and trendy TriBeCa see-and-be-seen boîtes. Preppy hangouts are also still alive and well on the Upper East and Upper West sides.

There are enough dedicated club hoppers in Manhattan to support nightspots for almost every idiosyncratic taste. But keep in mind that *when* you go is just as important as where you go in club land. These days night prowlers are more loyal to floating parties, DJs, even party promoters, than they are to addresses. A spot is only hot when it's hopping, and you may find the same club or bar that raged last night completely empty tonight.

Style can be a tricky issue. An appropriate costume for a night on the town could include a rubber mini, a Balenciaga gown, or chains and leather. Fortunately, "velvet-rope syndrome"—that is, gimlet-eyed bouncers arbitrarily picking and choosing the "right" clientele at the door—has largely gone the way of the big-money '80s. The atmosphere now is looser and more accepting. So even if you do wind up wearing the wrong shoes, you probably won't be left standing out in the cold in them. Two quick fashion tips to help you blend: wear black and leave your sneakers at home.

For the tattooed and pierced, *Paper* magazine's "P.M. 'Til Dawn" and bar sections have as good a listing as exists of the roving clubs and the best of the fashionable crowd's hangouts. *Time Out New York* offers a comprehensive weekly listing of amusements by category. The more staid Friday *New York Times*'s "Weekend/Movies and Performing Arts" section runs "Pop and Jazz" and "Cabaret" columns that can clue you in to what's in the air, as can the *Village Voice,* a weekly newspaper that probably has more nightclub ads than any other rag in the world. The *Village Voice* is now free and disappears from its red kiosks on street corners all over the city often by the afternoon it arrives there (Wednesday). Some newsstands and bookstores also stock it. Flyers about coming events and club passes are stacked in the entry at Tower Records (⊠ Broadway and E. 4th St., ☎ 212/505–1500; ⊠ Broadway and W. 66th St., ☎ 212/799–2500). You may also get good tips from a suitably au courant hotel concierge. Keep in mind that events change almost weekly, and clubs have the life span of the tsetse fly, so phone ahead to make sure your target nightspot hasn't closed or turned into a polka hall. Most charge a cover, which can range from $2 to $25 or more depending on the club and the night. And take cash, because many places don't accept plastic.

CLUBS AND ENTERTAINMENT

Quintessential New York

These are the crème de la crème of New York's nightlife venues—distinguished by locale (sometimes sky-high), age (you'd think even the newest of these has been there for years), style (elegance prevails), or a peerless combination of the three. Reservations are essential.

The Carlyle. Bobby Short plays the hotel's discreetly sophisticated Café Carlyle when he's in town, and Barbara Cook and Eartha Kitt also often purr by the piano here. Bemelmans Bar, with murals by the author of the Madeline books, regularly stars pianist-singers Barbara Carroll and Peter Mintun. ✉ *35 E. 76th St.,* ☎ *212/744–1600.*

The Greatest Bar on Earth. Although it doesn't live up to its name (what bar could?), this glittering, oversize bar—actually three bars—at Windows on the World does afford one of the greatest views on earth. A multiethnic bar menu, dancing after 10 PM, and the adjacent Skybox, an oasis for cigar smokers, are additional draws. ✉ *1 World Trade Center, 107th fl.,* ☎ *212/524–7000.*

Oak Room. This fabled room in one of New York's most famous hotels still offers yesteryear's charms. You might find the hopelessly romantic singer Andrea Marcovicci crooning here. ✉ *Algonquin Hotel, 59 W. 44th St.,* ☎ *212/840–6800.*

Rainbow Room and Rainbow & Stars. Rockefeller Center's 65th floor offers two kinds of heaven: The Rainbow Room serves dinner (☞ Chapter 6) and dancing to the strains of the Rainbow Orchestra big band and occupies a floor right out of an Astaire-Rogers musical. At the intimate Rainbow & Stars, classy singers such as Maureen McGovern and Rosemary Clooney entertain, backlighted by twinkling city lights. At press time there were plans to change the format of these rooms; call ahead. ✉ *30 Rockefeller Plaza,* ☎ *212/632–5000.*

Supper Club. The last four digits of the telephone number give it all away: This huge prix fixe dinner-and-dancing club specializes in cheek-to-cheek big-band sounds with a full orchestra on Friday and Saturday nights followed by swing dancing from midnight until early morning. You wouldn't recognize it the rest of the week, when touring alternative and rock-and-roll acts like Mazzy Star and the Black Crows take the stage. ✉ *240 W. 47th St.,* ☎ *212/921–1940.*

Tatou. This pleasing addition to the supper-club scene, with red-velvet decor, offers dinner, dancing, jazz, and cabaret under one stylish roof. ✉ *151 E. 50th St.,* ☎ *212/753–1144.*

Dance Clubs

The city's busiest clubs are as much places to bump and grind as to see and be seen. Revelers come to socialize, to find romance, to scream business deals over the music, to show off their glad rags, or to be photographed rubbing shoulders with stars. Some are cavernous spaces filled with throbbing music and writhing bodies. Others are clubs in a different sense, like parties thrown by a mutual friend for people who don't know one another; comers are drawn by a common interest, a likeness of spirit, which can be created almost anyplace. The venues mentioned below are dance clubs, but parties—with or without dancing—with DJs and themes ranging from '60s bossa nova nights to soul-and-drag galas have been known to crop up at places like **Circa** (☞ Watering Holes, *below*) and **Irving Plaza** and **Coney Island High** (☞ Rock Clubs, *below*). So read some rags of the paper variety and make some calls.

Close-up

DANCE WITH ME!

STRICTLY BALLROOM AND *Shall We Dance?* brought the ballroom to the big screen, but for the inimitable real-life experience—from salsa and mambo to tango, waltz, and swing—you can't beat New York's dance halls and clubs, where couples dancing to live music is all the rage.

Swing

The Big Apple swings from Wall Street to Harlem: At **Windows on the World** (☞ Chapter 6), you can swing before the spectacular 107th-floor views. Swing out to the Flying Nutrenos or get down with zydeco bands at **Louisiana Community Bar & Grill** (✉ 622 Broadway, ☎ 212/460–9633). The Roy Gerson Orchestra fills the dance floor on Savoy Sundays at ☞ **Irving Plaza.** Neoswing bands play the elegant, retro ☞ **Supper Club,** in the theater district. You can shimmy to the Flipped Fedoras at **Swing 46** (✉ 349 W. 46th St., ☎ 212/262–9554). For an evening of sexy West Coast swing, try ☞ **Denim and Diamonds** or the relaxed **North River Bar** (✉ 145 Hudson St., ☎ 212/226 9411). The 16-piece Harlem Renaissance Orchestra accompanies the fried chicken, collard greens, and waffles at the cozy **Wells Restaurant** (✉ 2247 Adam Clayton Powell Blvd., ☎ 212/234–0700).

Salsa

Lights glitter in giant champagne glasses suspended from the ceiling of ☞ **SOB's,** where couples sway to the Latin rhythms of Pasión, a hot all-female salsa band. Or try the **Copacabana** (✉ 617 W. 57th St., ☎ 212/582–1672)—the later the better, especially on weekends. The **Latin Quarter** (✉ 2551 Broadway, ☎ 212/864–7600) and **El Flamingo** (✉ 547 W. 21st St., ☎ 212/243–2121) are also good bets; more casual is the cavernous restaurant **Gonzalez y Gonzalez** (✉ 625 Broadway, ☎ 212/473–8787), or **Bayamo** (✉ 704 Broadway, ☎ 212/475–5151).

Tango

Tango to an Argentine band between courses at **Il Campanello** (✉ 136 W. 31st St., ☎ 212/695–6111), and brush up on your technique with a lesson, then practice all night at **Bistro Latino** (✉ 1711 Broadway, ☎ 212/956–1000). Or try **La Belle Epoque** (✉ 827 Broadway, ☎ 212/254–6436).

Ballroom

For latter-day Fred and Gingers, the ne plus ultra ☞ **Rainbow Room,** with its revolving dance floor, is the plus ultra. The bloom may be off the rose at the historic ☞ **Roseland Ballroom,** but it's still Manhattan's most spacious place to waltz, fox-trot, and rumba with a crowd that remembers when. In summer there's dancing under the stars at **Midsummer Night Swing** at Lincoln Center's Fountain Plaza (☎ 212/875–5766), and at **Wollman Rink** in Central Park.

Know Before You Go

Expect a cover charge ($5–$25) and, at many places, a two-drink minimum. Latin clubs can be cheaper for women and more expensive after 10 PM. Heels and skirts for women and suits for men are required at upscale and Latin places. Swing parties attract couples in retro costume; ballroom dancing is done in everything from gowns to slacks. Going solo is common; both men and women can expect to find willing partners in most venues. Many clubs offer lessons. Schedules change often, so call to confirm before heading out, or hit www.nycdc.com.

Chaos. This flashy SoHo club is a great place to people-watch—or rather, model-watch, as the case may be. Alas, they have no cabaret license, so dancing is verboten. ✉ *23 Watts St.,* ☎ *212/925–8966.*

Cheetah. One of *the* hot places (the 20th anniversary party for Studio 54 was held here), Cheetah pays homage to the '70s with disco in a faux-leopard setting. ✉ *12 W. 21st St.,* ☎ *212/206–7770.*

China Club. Further proof that the '80s are back with a vengeance, this symbol of high-living excess has relocated from its original Upper West Side home to an 8,000-square-ft bi-level space in Hell's Kitchen. The exclusionary velvet ropes are again in place, but there's also a mass-market gift shop. ✉ *268 W. 47th St.,* ☎ *212/398–3800.*

Den of Thieves. They spin everything from new wave to reggae to acid jazz at this tiny club, which caters to a young and energetic clientele. If you're over 30 or tend to get claustrophobic, think twice before paying the cover. ✉ *145 E. Houston St.,* ☎ *212/477–5005.*

Denim and Diamonds. Break out your boots for country line dancing every night of the week. Lessons are given at 7 and 8. There are two pool tables and a DJ spinning country-and-western on the main floor; upstairs in the Roadhouse there's live music Friday and Saturday. Southwestern food is served here, too. ✉ *511 Lexington Ave.,* ☎ *212/371–1600.*

Le Bar Bat. This bamboo-encrusted, multitiered monster of a club fits right in with the Planet Hollywood–type places on 57th Street's Theme Restaurant Row, but you can have a flashy good time here among the Euro and prepster poseurs. ✉ *311 W. 57th St.,* ☎ *212/307–7228.*

Life. Club kids and drag queens don't mind waiting on line or paying a high cover to get into this late-night club, which recalls the excesses of '80s-era New York. VIP regulars include Billy Corgan, Lenny Kravitz, and Marilyn Manson. Check for special parties and to see if go-go dancers will be performing. ✉ *158 Bleecker St.,* ☎ *212/420–1999.*

Nell's. Back in vogue, Nell Campbell (of *Rocky Horror* fame) reintroduced sophistication to nightlife with her club. The tone in the upstairs live-music jazz salon is Victorian; downstairs you can dance to a DJ. The boîte opens at 10 PM and closes at 4 AM nightly. ✉ *246 W. 14th St.,* ☎ *212/675–1567.*

Roseland. This famous old ballroom dance floor is still open for ballroom dancing on Sunday (music by a live orchestra and a DJ). ✉ *239 W. 52nd St.,* ☎ *212/247–0200.*

Roxy. Most nights this huge hall is a standard bridge-and-tunnel dance club, mostly attracting those who live in other New York boroughs and in New Jersey and occasionally drawing a mixed rave crowd. Wednesday is roller disco night. Call ahead for special events. ✉ *515 W. 18th St.,* ☎ *212/645–5156.*

Sapphire. This small Lower East Side club gets started late, but the DJ keeps the lively, diverse crowd going with every kind of music from ska to disco. Ultrafriendly patrons might drag you onto the floor to strut your stuff. ✉ *249 Eldrige St.,* ☎ *212/777–5153.*

Webster Hall. This fave among New York University students and similar species boasts 40,000 square ft, four floors, and five eras of music. Go for the live bands on Thursday and Friday, the dance DJs on Friday and Saturday—or the trapeze artists any night. ✉ *125 E. 11th St.,* ☎ *212/353–1600.*

Jazz Clubs

Greenwich Village is still New York's jazz mecca, with more than 10 jazz nightclubs, although many others are strewn around town.

Birdland. From 5 PM until 2 AM you'll find up-and-coming groups here—plus dinner. ✉ *315 W. 44th St.,* ☎ *212/581–3080.*

Blue Note. Considered by many to be the jazz capital of the world, the Blue Note could see on an average week Spyro Gyra, the Modern Jazz Quartet, and Jon Hendricks. Expect a steep music charge, except on Monday, when record labels promote their artists' new releases for an average ticket price of $7.50. ✉ *131 W. 3rd St.,* ☎ *212/475–8592.*

Cajun. This landlocked Chelsea restaurant with a French Quarter feel dishes New Orleans–style jazz alongside Cajun-Creole grub. Live music from the likes of former Louis Armstrong clarinetist Joe Muranyi will make you feel like you've ducked in off Bourbon Street. Dixieland, bebop, and swing are on tap every night save Monday, when modern swing takes over. ✉ *129 8th Ave.,* ☎ *212/691–6174.*

Knitting Factory. This eclectic gem of a cross-genre music café in TriBeCa features avant-garde jazz in a homey, funky setting. ✉ *74 Leonard St.,* ☎ *212/219–3055.*

Michael's Pub. Woody Allen sometimes moonlights on the clarinet here on Monday nights when he performs with his New Orleans Jazz Band for a very monied, very uptown crowd. ✉ *57 E. 54th St.,* ☎ *212/758–2272.*

Red Blazer Too. Roaring '20s, Dixieland, and swing are served with a smile here. It heats up when the post-theater crowd pours in, and you can sup then as well. ✉ *32 W. 37th St.,* ☎ *212/262–3112.*

Smalls. Where can you find jazz till dawn and beyond? After the Village Vanguard closes, poke your head around the corner into this pocket-size club, where the music keeps coming until 8 AM. ✉ *183 W. 10th St.,* ☎ *212/929–7565.*

Sweet Basil. A little ritzy, though reliable, this nightspot features a 15-piece jazz ensemble nearly every night. Sunday brunch (2–6) with pianist Chuck Folds is truly a religious experience. ✉ *88 7th Ave. S,* ☎ *212/242–1785.*

Village Vanguard. This former Thelonious Monk haunt, the prototype of the old-world jazz club, lives on in a smoky cellar, in which you might hear jams from the likes of Wynton Marsalis and James Carter, among others. ✉ *178 7th Ave. S,* ☎ *212/255–4037.*

Zinno. The food (northern Italian) is as good as the jazz (usually duos and trios) at this mellow village club, which boasts a stellar wine list. ✉ *126 W. 13th St.,* ☎ *212/924–5182.*

Rock Clubs

The roots of rock may lie in America's heartland, but New York has added its own spin. Crowds at the Big Apple's rocketerias are young, enthusiastic, and hungry; the noise is often deafening, but you can catch many a rising star in this lively scene. In summer you can also find live music when **Central Park SummerStage** (✉ Rumsey Playfield, Central Park at E. 72nd St., ☎ 212/360–2777) presents everything from alternative to rap to world music.

Arlene Grocery. This relative newcomer to the rock club scene on the Lower East Side is known for spotting new bands with promising futures. No cover charge and a welcoming atmosphere also set it apart. ✉ *95 Stanton St.,* ☎ *212/358–1633.*

Bitter End. This old Village standby still serves up its share of new talent; Lisa Loeb, Joan Armatrading, and Warren Zevon have played here. Check before arriving; blues, country, rock, and jazz all make appearances here. ✉ *147 Bleecker St.,* ☎ *212/673–7030.*

Brownie's. It's catch-as-catch-can at this East Village dive, but the hard thrashing sounds occasionally pull people in off the street to join the pierced and tattooed throngs. ✉ *169 Ave. A,* ☎ *212/420–8392.*

CBGB & OMFUG. American punk rock (the Ramones, Blondie, the Talking Heads) was born in this long, black tunnel of a club. Today expect Shirley Temple of Doom, Trick Babies, Xanax 25, and other inventively named bands. **CB's 313 Gallery,** next door at 313 Bowery, attracts a quieter (and older) crowd with mostly acoustic music. ✉ *315 Bowery,* ☎ *212/982–4052.*

Coney Island High. Murals of Coney Island amusement-park sideshow acts don't add much cheer to this hard-core rock haven, which is not nearly as old as its state of decrepitude suggests. ✉ *15 St. Marks Pl.,* ☎ *212/674–7959.*

Continental. This knockdown version of CBGB appeals to thrifty college kids on their last nickel. ✉ *25 3rd Ave.,* ☎ *212/529–6924.*

The Cooler. A trendy bar, live-music dive, and DJ dance party are all in one at this former meat cooler in the shady yet up-and-coming meatpacking district. Come here for a mix of rap, reggae, techno, and jazz. ✉ *416 W. 14th St.,* ☎ *212/229–0785.*

Don Hill's. At this TriBeCa favorite, you'll find bands both popular and not yet signed. Friday nights is Squeeze Box, a riotous party usually hosted by drag impresarios. ✉ *511 Greenwich St.,* ☎ *212/334–1390.*

Irving Plaza. Looking for Marilyn Manson, the Jesus Lizard, or Better Than Ezra? You'll find them in this perfect-size place for general-admission live music. There's a small balcony with a bar and a tiny lounge area. ✉ *17 Irving Pl.,* ☎ *212/777–6800 or 212/777–1224 for concert hot line.*

Mercury Lounge. With one of the best sound systems in the city, this East Village club holds a quiet cachet with bands and industry insiders. ✉ *217 E. Houston St.,* ☎ *212/260–4700.*

Rock 'n' Roll Café. Nostalgic for the Doors, Led Zep, Hendrix, or Clapton? Choose a night and the appropriate concert T-shirt and rock out. ✉ *149 Bleecker St.,* ☎ *212/677–7630.*

Wetlands. If you can ignore the environmental murals and the hokey broken-down VW bus–cum–gift shop, this hard-to-find club rules, mostly because it draws great, often danceable, often psychedelic bands. Dave Matthews, Soul Coughing, and Hootie and the Blowfish "developed" here. ✉ *161 Hudson St.,* ☎ *212/966–4225.*

World Music Venues

A former mayor once called New York a "gorgeous mosaic" for the rich ethnic mix of its inhabitants, and the music in some of its clubs reflects that. Brazilian, Celtic, and of course Latin—salsa, samba, merengue—integrate with the ever-present urban energy of the streets.

Copacabana. Music and passion were always in fashion at this legendary nightclub, but now it's in the form of Latin music by such performers as the three Titos: Ruiz, Riojas, and Nieves. Women often pay less on special promotional nights. ✉ *617 W. 57th St.,* ☎ *212/582–2672.*

Knitting Factory. This cross-genre music café (☞ Jazz Clubs, *above*) regularly features performers from far and wide. ✉ *74 Leonard St.,* ☎ *212/219–3055.*

Paddy Reilly's Music Bar. Irish rock-and-roots hybrid Black 47 (named for the year of the great famine) make this cramped but congenial club their home when in New York. Thursday there's a traditional Irish jam session. ✉ *519 2nd Ave.,* ☎ *212/686–1210.*

SOB's. Since 1982 SOB's (the initials stand for Sounds of Brazil) has been *the* place for reggae, Trinidadian carnival, zydeco, African, and especially Latin tunes and salsa rhythms. The decor is à la Tropicana; the favored drink, a Brazilian *caipirinha.* ✉ *200 Varick St.,* ☎ *212/243–4940.*

Blues, Acoustic, and R&B Venues

For something acoustic, folksy, or bluesy, the West Village has many options.

Bottom Line. Clubs come and go, but this granddaddy prevails. Its reputation is for showcasing talents on their way up, as it did for both Stevie Wonder and Bruce Springsteen. Recent visitors include Buster Poindexter and Jane Siberry. When a name pulls in a crowd, patrons are packed like sardines at mostly long, thin tables. ✉ *15 W. 4th St.,* ☎ *212/228–7880.*

Chicago Blues. Big Time Sarah, Jimmy Dawkins, the Holmes Brothers, and others have cozied into this nothing-fancy, just-plain-folksy West Village blues club. ✉ *73 8th Ave.,* ☎ *212/924–9755.*

Louisiana Community Bar & Grill. It's not exactly the Big Easy, but there's swing on Monday and live music every night at this restaurant. ✉ *622 Broadway,* ☎ *212/460–9633.*

Manny's Car Wash. Powerhouse blues jams on Manhattan's soul-free Upper East Side? Sounds shocking, but such is the scene at Manny's. Jams are only on Sunday, but live bands dish up the blues seven nights. ✉ *1558 3rd Ave.,* ☎ *212/369–2583.*

Rodeo Bar. There's never a cover at this full-scale Texas roadhouse, complete with barn-wood siding and a barbecue and Tex-Mex menu and featuring "music with American roots" country, rock, rockabilly, swing, bluegrass, and blues. ✉ *375 3rd Ave.,* ☎ *212/683–6500.*

Sidewalk Bar–Restaurant. Depending on who's playing, this salon will be packed with bikers, slackers, finger-snapping neo-beatniks, or other fans of the mix of poetry and acoustic blues, rock, and folk, which goes under the label *antifolk.* ✉ *94 Ave. A,* ☎ *212/473–7373.*

Tramps. Since 1975 Tramps has delivered bands like the Dixie Dregs and NRBQ, Ray Charles, Bruce Springsteen, and George Jones. It's home to roots music, major country acts, and just about every other kind of music around. ✉ *45 W. 21st St.,* ☎ *212/727–7788.*

Comedy Clubs

Neurotic New York comedy is known the world over, and a few minutes watching these hilarious Woody Allen types might just make your own problems seem laughable. Comedy isn't pretty here, nor is it especially cheap. Expect to pay around $15 per person on a weekend, sometimes on top of a drink minimum, and reservations are usually necessary. One warning: Only those skilled in the art of repartee should sit in the front. The rest are advised to hide in a corner or risk being relentlessly heckled. The *Village Voice* and *Time Out New York* cover the comedy scene well; it's worth checking listings because some music clubs book comedians for periods between sets. The clubs below are devoted exclusively to comedy.

Boston Comedy Club. It's so named because the owner's from Beantown, but comedians come here from all over the country to test their stuff. Monday is open-mike night for amateurs. ✉ *82 W. 3rd St.,* ☎ *212/477–1000.*

Caroline's Comedy Club. This high-gloss club features established names as well as comedians on the edge of stardom. Joy Behar, Sandra Bernhard, and Gilbert Gottfried have appeared. ✉ *1626 Broadway,* ☎ *212/757–4100.*

Catch a Rising Star. You may indeed catch a rising comedy star at this local link of a chain, but you might also catch established headliners such as Janeane Garafalo, Denis Leary, or *Saturday Night Live* cast members. The restaurant serves contemporary American cuisine from Tuesday through Saturday. ✉ *253 W. 28th St.,* ☎ *212/462–2824.*

Chicago City Limits. This troupe's been doing improvisational comedy for a long time, and it seldom fails to whip its audiences into a laughing frenzy. Chicago City Limits performs in a renovated movie theater and is very strong on audience participation. ✉ *1105 1st Ave.,* ☎ *212/888–5233.*

Comedy Cellar. This spot has been running for nearly 20 years now beneath the Olive Tree Café, with a bill that's a good barometer of who's hot. ✉ *117 MacDougal St.,* ☎ *212/254–3480.*

Comic Strip Live. The atmosphere here is strictly corner bar ("More comfortable than a nice pair of corduroys," says daytime manager J. R.). The stage is brilliantly lighted but minuscule; the bill is unpredictable but worth checking out. ✉ *1568 2nd Ave.,* ☎ *212/861–9386.*

Dangerfield's. Since 1969 this has been an important showcase for prime comic talent. It's owned by comedian Rodney Dangerfield. ✉ *1118 1st Ave.,* ☎ *212/593–1650.*

Freestyle Repertory Theater. On "Spontaneous Broadway" nights, an audience member shouts out a song title, the troupe will improvise a show tune—and then a whole musical—around it; on other evenings teams compete to outperform one another in head-to-head "theater sports" matches. ✉ *Various theaters,* ☎ *212/642–8202 to find locations.*

Gotham Comedy Club. Housed in a landmark historic building in the Flatiron district, this classy venue—complete with a turn-of-the-century chandelier and custom copper bars—attracts an upscale crowd that enjoys such popular headliners as Chris Rock and David Brenner. Once a month there's a Latino comedy show. ✉ *34 W. 22nd St.,* ☎ *212/367–9000.*

New York Comedy Club. This intimate club, chock-full of comedy memorabilia and talent such as Brett Butler, Colin Quinn, and Damon Wayans, has been referred to as "the Wal-Mart of comedy" because covers are the lowest in town. ✉ *241 E. 24th St.,* ☎ *212/696–5233.*

Original Improvisation. The Improv is to comedy what the Blue Note is to jazz. Lots of now-famous comedians got their first laughs here, among them Richard Pryor. ✉ *433 W. 34th St.,* ☎ *212/279–3446.*

Stand-Up NY. The Upper West Side option for comedy devotees, this club books bright faces off recent TV gigs. Robin Williams has stopped in. ✉ *236 W. 78th St.,* ☎ *212/595–0850.*

Cabaret and Performance Spaces

Cabaret takes many forms in New York City, from a lone crooner at the piano to a full-fledged song-and-dance revue. Various nightspots have stages; almost all have a cover and a minimum food-and/or-drink charge (☞ Quintessential New York, *above*).

Danny's Skylight Room. Housed in Danny's Grand Sea Palace, a fixture on Restaurant Row, this venue offers a little bit of everything: jazz performers, crooners, and ivory ticklers. ✉ *346 W. 46th St.,* ☎ *212/265–8133.*

Don't Tell Mama. Composer-lyricist hopefuls and established talents show their stuff until 4 AM at this convivial theater district spot. Extroverts will be tempted by the piano bar's open-mike policy. In the two cabaret rooms you might find singers, comedians, or female impersonators. ✉ *343 W. 46th St.,* ☎ *212/757–0788.*

Downstairs at the West Bank Café. Below an attractive bistro-type restaurant across from Theater Row, moonlighting musical-comedy triple threats (actor-singer-dancers) show off; on occasion, new plays are read. ✉ *407 W. 42nd St.,* ☎ *212/695–6909.*

The Duplex. New York's oldest continuous cabaret (opened in 1951), on Greenwich Village's busy Sheridan Square, hosts young singers on the rise, drop-ins fresh from Broadway at the open mike, and comediennes polishing their acts. Plays and rock bands round out the scope of entertainment offerings. ✉ *61 Christopher St.*, ☎ *212/255–5438.*

Eighty Eight's. Come here for songs by the best of Broadway's tunesmiths and inventively assembled programs. A piano bar is downstairs; the cabaret space is upstairs. ✉ *228 W. 10th St.*, ☎ *212/924–0088.*

55 Grove Street. On top of Rose's bar, this landmark cabaret offers a piano bar, singers, and sketch comedy (a Judy Garland impersonator sparring with an Ann Miller impersonator, for instance). ✉ *Near Bleecker and 7th Ave. S*, ☎ *212/366–5438.*

Firebird Cafe. The city's newest cabaret venue, on Restaurant Row beside the restaurant of the same name (☞ Chapter 6), is a swank spot to hear leading crooners and sample rare vodkas from the vast selection. ✉ *367 W. 46th St.*, ☎ *212/586–0244.*

Judy's Restaurant and Cabaret. This cabaret and piano bar next to the Hotel Iroquois is known for singing pianists in the Michael Feinstein mold. ✉ *49 W. 44th St.*, ☎ *212/764–8930.*

BARS

Although the health-club craze may have hit New York hard, there's little danger that Manhattanites will abandon their bars. Drinking establishments thrive and multiply, particularly in TriBeCa, where it appears bar design has become a minor art. The city's liquor law allows bars to stay open until 4 AM, so it's easy to add on a watering stop at the end of an evening's merriment.

Vintage Classics

Algonquin Hotel Lounge. This is a venerable spot, not only because it was the site of the fabled literary Algonquin Roundtable but also because it has an elegant tone. (☞ Oak Room *in* Quintessential New York, *above.*) ✉ *59 W. 44th St.*, ☎ *212/840–6800.*

Café des Artistes. George Lang's restaurant, as well known for its glorious Art Nouveau murals as for its food (☞ Chapter 6), has a small, warm bar where interesting strangers tell their life stories and the house drink is pear champagne. ✉ *1 W. 67th St.*, ☎ *212/877–3500.*

Elaine's. The food's nothing special, and you will be relegated to an inferior table, but go to gawk; try going late at night, when the stars rise in Elaine's firmament. Woody Allen's favorite table is by the cappuccino machine. ✉ *1703 2nd Ave.*, ☎ *212/534–8103.*

Fantino. In the former Ritz-Carlton, now the Westin Central Park South, this restaurant bar is dressy and traditional—a very double-martini place. ✉ *112 Central Park S*, ☎ *212/757–1900.*

Four Seasons. Miró tapestries in the lobby greet you as you enter this power bar in the Grill Room (☞ Chapter 6). Watch for Kissingers and Trumps. ✉ *99 E. 52nd St.*, ☎ *212/754–9494.*

King Cole Bar. The famed Maxfield Parrish mural is a welcome sight at this gorgeous midtown rendezvous spot. ✉ *St. Regis Hotel, 2 E. 55th St.*, ☎ *212/753–4500.*

Oak Bar. Bedecked with plush leather chairs and oak walls, this old favorite continues to age well. Its great location draws sophisticates, shoppers, businesspeople, tourists in the know, and stars. ✉ *Plaza Hotel, 5th Ave. and 59th St.*, ☎ *212/759–3000.*

Pen Top Bar and Lounge. Take a break from 5th Avenue shopping at this glass-lined penthouse hotel bar on the 22nd floor. Drinks are pricey, but the views are impressive. Especially nice is the open-air rooftop seating area. ✉ *Peninsula Hotel, 700 5th Ave.,* ☎ *212/247–2200.*

River Café. An eminently romantic spot hidden at the foot of the Brooklyn Bridge, this restaurant offers smashing views of Wall Street and the East River. ✉ *1 Water St., Brooklyn,* ☎ *718/522–5200.*

Top of the Tower. There are higher hotel-top lounges, but this one on the 26th floor still feels halfway to heaven. The atmosphere is elegant and subdued. ✉ *Beekman Tower, 3 Mitchell Pl., near 1st Ave. at 49th St.,* ☎ *212/355–7300.*

"21" Club Famous for its old-time club atmosphere even before it became a setting in *All About Eve,* "21"'s conservative environs evoke a sense of connections, power, and prestige. ✉ *21 W. 52nd St.,* ☎ *212/582–7200.*

Watering Holes

Exploring neighborhood by neighborhood, you'll find a glut of mahogany-encrusted historic old-town taverns in the West Village; chichi wine bars in SoHo and TriBeCa; yuppie and collegiate minifrats on the Upper West and Upper East sides; and terribly trendy and kitschy bars in the East Village, including Alphabet City.

Lower Manhattan, SoHo, and TriBeCa

Bridge Café. This busy little restaurant flanks the Brooklyn Bridge, a hop, skip, and a jump from the South Street Seaport. The bar is small, but its inventory is huge: you can choose from a list of 80 domestic-only wines and about 50 single-malt scotches. ✉ *279 Water St., at Dover St.,* ☎ *212/227–3344.*

Broome Street Bar. A classic hangout, this SoHo standard attracts artsy types from Manhattan on weekdays and from the other boroughs on weekends. ✉ *363 W. Broadway, at Broome St.,* ☎ *212/925–2086.*

Ear Inn. There's nothing fancy in this 1817 Federal house. It's the artsy crowd that makes the place, along with Saturday-afternoon poetry readings—"lunch for the ear." ✉ *326 Spring St.,* ☎ *212/226–9060.*

El Teddy's. You can't miss the gigantic Lady Liberty crown out front, and the Judy Jetson Goes to Art Camp decor at this former mob haunt. The margaritas (on the rocks, *por favor*) at this enduring TriBeCa bar are phenomenal. ✉ *219 W. Broadway,* ☎ *212/941–7070.*

Fanelli's. This is a casual SoHo neighborhood bar where many come on Sunday with the fat *New York Times* under their arms. The food's good, too. ✉ *94 Prince St.,* ☎ *212/226–9412.*

I Tre Merli. Happy drinkers spill out of the massive doors of this wide, inviting restaurant-bar. ✉ *463 W. Broadway,* ☎ *212/254–8699.*

Lucky Strike. Now that the supermodels party elsewhere, this über-cool SoHo bistro has quieted down. Young Euro types lounge at the cozy back tables; DJs play funky tunes at crowded weekend dance parties. ✉ *59 Grand St.,* ☎ *212/941–0479.*

Max Fish. This crowded, grungy, kitschy palace on an artsy Lower East Side strip boasts a twisted image of a grimacing Julio Iglesias over the bar and a pool table in back. Downtown mainstays like the Ramones have been spotted here. ✉ *178 Ludlow St.,* ☎ *212/529–3959.*

MercBar. A chic European crowd and New Yorkers in the know come to this dark, rather nondescript bar for the wonderful martinis. Its street number is barely visible—look for the French doors, which stay open in summer. ✉ *151 Mercer St.,* ☎ *212/966–2727.*

Naked Lunch. Dazzlingly successful, this William Burroughs–inspired, earth-tone SoHo haunt is said to be often graced by Robert De Niro, among others. ✉ *17 Thompson St.,* ☎ *212/343–0828.*

North Star Pub. This snug London-style pub is one of the only places at the South Street Seaport not completely overrun with tourists. Have an imperial (20-ounce) pint of Guinness, but skip the greasy, expensive bar food. ✉ *93 South St.,* ☎ *212/509–6757.*

Pravda. Martinis are the rule at this Russian-theme trendy bar and lounge, where there are more than 70 brands of vodka and nearly as many types of martinis. ✉ *281 Lafayette St.,* ☎ *212/226–4696.*

Screening Room. As people often have dinner and/or drinks on a night out at the movies, it makes sense to hold that audience captive as is often done in Britain. The movie theater here is small but inviting, and this spot has made a splash with the TriBeCa crowd since its 1996 opening. Think well-worn velvet, and you'll get the picture. ✉ *54 Varick St., at Canal St.,* ☎ *212/334–2100.*

SoHo Kitchen and Bar. Pass on the food but sidle up to the long bar, where you can get "flights" of wine (for example, a tasting of three South American reds), 110 wines by the glass, and myriad beers and scotches. ✉ *103 Greene St.,* ☎ *212/925–1866.*

Sporting Club. The six 10-ft screens and 11 TV monitors here stay tuned to the evening's major sports event. Aficionados come in after punching out on Wall Street. ✉ *99 Hudson St.,* ☎ *212/219–0900.*

Spy. The Artist Formerly Known as Prince, as well as aspiring starlets and models, have been known to visit this ever-trendy spot. Settle into a plush couch and enjoy the baroque parlor setting and pretty people. ✉ *101 Greene St.,* ☎ *212/343–9000.*

Walker's. First-precinct NYPD detectives, TriBeCa artists, Wall Street types, and the odd celeb somehow all manage to call this cozy restaurant-bar home. ✉ *16 N. Moore St.,* ☎ *212/941–0142.*

Wax. One of the trendiest hangouts in Manhattan's trendy heart, this doorman-guarded lounge has bare wooden floors and rather uncomfortable settees, but the legions of good-looking patrons don't seem to mind. ✉ *113 Mercer St.,* ☎ *212/226–6082.*

Chelsea and the Village

For perhaps the most bizarre bar crawl Manhattan has to offer, consider a mug-hoisting stroll along the West Village's esoteric and enchanting Washington Street, which is one street east of the West Side Highway. Begin while it's light out at the dingy corner of Washington and West 13th streets with a visit to **Hogs & Heifers** (✉ 859 Washington St., ☎ 212/929–0655). This seems to be Gotham's homage to the movie *Deliverance,* but it still manages to attract star power like Drew Barrymore, Julia Roberts, and Harrison Ford. Next, walk a block south through the big cobblestone plaza to **Rio-Mar** (✉ 7 9th Ave., ☎ 212/243–9015), a throwback to Spain that serves tapas until about 6 PM (there's an adjoining dining room for later dining). Next stop is **Braque** (✉ 775 Washington St., ☎ 212/255–0709), where the outdoor café is frequented by the likes of RuPaul; leather club chairs adorn the adjoining indoor restaurant. Across the street, pop into **Tortilla Flats** (✉ 767 Washington St., ☎ 212/243–1053) and check out the backroom "Vegas Lounge," a tribute to the stars of Vegas, from Lewis and Martin to Siegfried and Roy. Proceed next to the French bistro–inspired **Black Sheep** (✉ 344 W. 11th St., ☎ 212/242–1010). Then stumble in to the always-hopping **Automatic Slim's** (✉ 733 Washington St., ☎ 212/645–8660), a gritty bar that gets patrons dancing on bars to loud music and eating surprisingly sophisticated food. From here you can finish off an A1 evening by hailing a cab.

Bar Six. An idyllic stop for a soft, summer night, with French doors opening onto the street, this elegant bar and restaurant has all the trappings of a New York hot spot without the attitude. ✉ *502 6th Ave.,* ☎ *212/691–1363.*

Chelsea Commons. With an old-fashioned pub in front and a small tree-shaded, lamplit courtyard in back, this west Chelsea bar draws a disparate but friendly crowd of bookworms, sports fans, and slackers. ✉ *242 10th Ave.,* ☎ *212/929–9424.*

Chumley's. There's no sign to help you find this place—they took it down during Chumley's speakeasy days—but when you reach the corner of Barrow Street, you're very close. A fireplace warms this relaxed spot, where the burgers are hearty and the clientele collegiate. ✉ *86 Bedford St.,* ☎ *212/675–4449.*

Cornelia Street Café. A street-side table on this quaint West Village lane is a romantic spot to share a bottle of Merlot. Inside you can groove to live jazz from Wednesday through Saturday. ✉ *29 Cornelia St.,* ☎ *212/989–9319.*

Corner Bistro. Founded in 1966, this pub-and-grub-style bar has finally come into its own. The cozy place is so inviting and the young, professional crowd so friendly, you might think you ducked into a small-town place. ✉ *331 W. 4th St.,* ☎ *212/242–9502.*

Dix et Sept. They say they're "*comme à* Paris—without the attitude," but what they mean is they've substituted a New York attitude, which suits this lively spot just fine. ✉ *181 W. 10th St.,* ☎ *212/645–8023.*

Flight 151. This popular, unpretentious neighborhood hangout serves lunch, dinner, and a bargain all-you-can-eat brunch on weekends. The polished wood bar, candlelighted booths, and friendly staff create a welcoming atmosphere. Don't miss Tuesday's Flip Night or Thursday's Trivia Night, when you can get your drink on the house if you play along. ✉ *151 8th Ave.,* ☎ *212/229–1868.*

Flowers. In this ultratrendy models' hangout, you, too, can escape your fans by taking to the roof, which overlooks the hip photo district and the flower district. ✉ *21 W. 17th St.,* ☎ *212/691–8888.*

Heartland Brewery. Considered by some beer aficionados to be among the East Coast's best breweries, this restaurant-bar is also a fun—and packed—after-work joint. ✉ *35 Union Sq. W,* ☎ *212/645–3400.*

McSorley's Old Ale House. One of New York's oldest saloons (opened in 1854), immortalized by *New Yorker* writer Joseph Mitchell, this is a must-see for first-timers to Gotham. ✉ *15 E. 7th St.,* ☎ *212/473–9148.*

Peculier Pub. From Abbaye de Brooklyn to Zywiec—the nearly 500 beers, representing 43 countries, including Peru, Vietnam, and Zimbabwe, are the draw at this heart-of-the-Village pub. ✉ *145 Bleecker St.,* ☎ *212/353–1327.*

Slaughtered Lamb. This themed restaurant-pub is decorated with werewolves and skeletons as well as electrocution and guillotine scenes. If you like, you can dine in the dungeon. ✉ *182 W. 4th St.,* ☎ *212/727–3350.*

White Horse Tavern. Dylan Thomas drank himself to death in 1953 at this historic 110-year-old tavern. From April through October there's outdoor café drinking. ✉ *567 Hudson St.,* ☎ *212/989–3956.*

Lower East Side and East Village through East 20s

B Bar. Long lines peer through venetian blinds at the fabulous crowd within this trendy bar formerly known as the Bowery Bar. If the bouncer says there's a private party going on, more likely than not, it's his way of turning you away nicely. ✉ *358 Bowery,* ☎ *212/475–2220.*

Barmacy. Appealing to club kids and Upper East Side collegiate types, this East Village bar looks like a small-town old-fashioned pharmacy. But don't expect to have your prescription filled—unless it's in the form of a martini. ✉ *538 E. 14th St.,* ☎ *212/228–2240.*

Beauty Bar. If you've ever wanted to try out the beauty parlor in *Steel Magnolias,* this is your chance. Come during happy hour to get your nails done. ✉ *231 E. 14th St.,* ☎ *212/539–1389.*

Belmont Lounge. Top-notch DJs spin great music Wednesday–Sunday 10 PM–4 AM at this velvet-rope protected hot spot. Better-than-usual snacks and excellent but overpriced drinks are a plus. ✉ *117 E. 15th St.,* ☎ *212/533–0009.*

Café Tabac. Practice your glare before entering the lounge of this pretentious salon, known to have been frequented by Madonna, Drew Barrymore, Christian Slater, and Ethan Hawke. Good luck trying to get in a game at the pool table. ✉ *232 E. 9th St.,* ☎ *212/674–7072.*

Circa. Blond and tony, with C-shape velvet banquettes and high ceilings, Circa supplies a surprising slice of the Upper East Side on ever-gentrifying 2nd Avenue. ✉ *103 2nd Ave.,* ☎ *212/777–4120.*

Cloister Café. With one of Manhattan's largest and leafiest outdoor gardens, the Cloister is a perfect perch for stargazing and elbow bending. ✉ *238 E. 9th St.,* ☎ *212/777–9128.*

Coffee Shop. The moonlighting models bringing your food and drinks may not be the fastest waitstaff in the city, but a flashy, gorgeous crowd makes for a never-ending spectacle. ✉ *29 Union Sq. W,* ☎ *212/243–7969.*

Coyote Ugly. The name is appropriate for this dive, where the raucous regulars can be heard across the 'hood singing along with the Skynyrd wailing from the jukebox. ✉ *153 1st Ave.,* ☎ *212/477–4431.*

Fez. Tucked away in the trendy Time Café, this Moroccan-theme Casbah offers nightly events, including drag and comedy shows, readings, jazz (make reservations in advance for big-name bands), and the monthly "Loser's Lounge" show (homages to kitschy pop-culture figures such as Burt Bacharach) amid a polished young crowd. ✉ *380 Lafayette St.,* ☎ *212/533–2680.*

Flamingo East. Kidney-shape sofas, style-mad patrons, and moody lighting make this haute downtown restaurant and bar a cool good time. Upstairs starts late and is only sporadically open to the public, but the balcony overlooking 2nd Avenue is a treat, and the food is delicious. ✉ *219 2nd Ave.,* ☎ *212/533–2860.*

Jules. A *très français, très romantique* wine bar with a perfect people-watching patio out front. ✉ *65 St. Marks Pl.,* ☎ *212/477–5560.*

Lucky Cheng's. Have a bite beside the goldfish pond downstairs, or mingle amid the gilt and leopard and be served by lovely waiters and bartenders in drag at this Pacific Rim restaurant–cum–cross-dressing cabaret. ✉ *24 1st Ave.,* ☎ *212/473–0516.*

Ludlow Bar. The Lower East Side is the latest off-the-beaten path Manhattan neighborhood being trendified, and this low-key bar is one of its main draws. There's a pool table in back, but the young crowd also finds enough room to shake their fashionable booties. ✉ *165 Ludlow St.,* ☎ *212/353–0536.*

Old Town Bar and Restaurant. Proudly unpretentious, this watering hole is heavy on the mahogany and redolent of "old New York." True to its name, the Old Town has been around since 1892. ✉ *45 E. 18th St.,* ☎ *212/529–6732.*

Pete's Tavern. This saloon is famous as the place where O. Henry is alleged to have written "The Gift of the Magi" (at the second booth to the right as you come in). These days it's still crowded with noisy, friendly souls. ✉ *129 E. 18th St.,* ☎ *212/473–7676.*

Republic. This trendy noodle shop right on Union Square has an elegant and active bar up front. The concept took on so well that another opened on the Upper West Side (✉ 2290 Broadway, ☎ 212/579–5959) and another is slated for Grand Central Terminal. ✉ *37 Union Sq. W,* ☎ *212/627–7172.*

Telephone Bar. Imported English telephone booths and a polite, handsome crowd mark this pub. ✉ *149 2nd Ave.,* ☎ *212/529–5000.*

Temple Bar. Romantic and upscale, this unmarked haunt is famous for its martinis and is a treat at any price. ✉ *332 Lafayette St.,* ☎ *212/925–4242.*

WCOU Radio Bar. Also known as Tile Bar or the Radio Bar, this no-nonsense neighborhood spot has one of the best happy hours in the city, when all drinks go for half price. The jukebox plays everything from Dire Straits to Tom Waits. ✉ *115 1st Ave.,* ☎ *212/254–4317.*

Midtown and the Theater District

Barrymore's. The requisite show posters hang on the wall at this pleasantly downscale theater-district spot. ✉ *267 W. 45th St.,* ☎ *212/391–8400.*

Café Un Deux Trois. This old hotel lobby, charmingly converted, is chicly peopled. The bar itself is small, but it's a hot spot before and after the theater. ✉ *123 W. 44th St.,* ☎ *212/354–4148.*

Halcyon Bar. A big, airy restaurant and bar, Halcyon has large and well-spaced tables and is great for a private chat. ✉ *Rihga Royal Hotel, 151 W. 54th St.,* ☎ *212/307–5000.*

Howard Johnson's. A little anachronistic, perhaps, the local HoJo's has a quaintly charming (albeit sleazy and cramped) cocktail lounge. The daily happy hour is 4–7. ✉ *1551 Broadway,* ☎ *212/354–1445.*

Joe Allen. At this old reliable on Restaurant Row, celebrated in the musical version of *All About Eve,* everybody's en route to or from a show. The posters that adorn the "flop wall" are from Broadway musicals that bombed. ✉ *326 W. 46th St.,* ☎ *212/581–6464.*

Monkey Bar. A big, hairless ape greets patrons at the door of this posh '90s creation, though neither it nor the jungle murals bring out much barbarism in the mannered banker-types who shoot back Scotch here. ✉ *60 E. 54th St.,* ☎ *212/838–2600.*

Morgans Bar. Supermodels and their kin tuck themselves into this little bar, all gilt mirrors and candles, housed in the basement of the Morgans hotel (☞ Murray Hill, *in* Chapter 7). ✉ *237 Madison Ave.,* ☎ *212/686–0300.*

Landmark Tavern. This aged redbrick pub (opened in 1868) is warmed by the glow of potbellied stoves on each of its three floors. The original mahogany bar and hand-press tin ceilings and walls give the tavern a 19th-century feel. The waiters insist the place is haunted. ✉ *626 11th Ave.,* ☎ *212/757–8595.*

The Royalton. Phillipe Starck's modernistic midtown hotel has two places to drink—the open seating area in the lobby-restaurant and the tiny Vodka Bar. ✉ *44 W. 44th St.,* ☎ *212/768–5000 or 212/869–4400.*

Sardi's. "The theater is certainly not what it was," croons a cat in *Cats*—and he could be referring to this venerable spot as well. Still, if you care for the theater, make time for a drink in one of the red-leather booths, which are surrounded by caricatures of stars past and present. ✉ *234 W. 44th St.,* ☎ *212/221–8440.*

Whiskey. Small, dark, and crowded, the Whiskey is a favorite Times Square area bar among hipsters. The Paramount Hotel's facade isn't identified, so look for the voile curtains and potted plants outside. ✉ *Paramount Hotel, 235 W. 46th St.,* ☎ *212/764–5500.*

East Side

American Trash. The name refers to the decor, not necessarily to the clientele—old pipes, bike wheels, and golf clubs line the walls and ceilings. ✉ *1471 1st Ave.,* ☎ *212/988–9008.*

Dakota Southwestern Bar & Grill. A mix of yuppies fresh out of college and neighborhood lifers congregate around the 52-ft, 4-inch bar, one of the longest in Manhattan. ✉ *1576 3rd Ave.,* ☎ *212/427–8889.*

Divine Bar. You may think you're in SoHo when you see this bar's zebra-stripe bar chairs, cigar area, and cozy velvet couches upstairs. There's a gourmand's selection of tapas, wines, and beers, but no hard liquor is served. ✉ *244 E. 51st St.,* ☎ *212/319–9463.*

Harglo's. The spicy Cajun food and bright neon sign attract white collars who just can't seem to go straight home after a long day at the office. ✉ *974 2nd Ave.,* ☎ *212/759–9820.*

P. J. Clarke's. Mirrors and polished wood adorn New York's most famous Irish bar, which recalls the days of Tammany Hall. Lots of afterwork types unwind here. ✉ *915 3rd Ave.,* ☎ *212/759–1650.*

Polo Lounge and Restaurant. This place is, in a word, classy; it's frequented by European royalty and Knickerbocker New York. ✉ *Westbury Hotel, 840 Madison Ave.,* ☎ *212/439–4835.*

Subway Inn. A block from Bloomingdale's, this old-time bar appeals to both cigar-smoking white-collar patrons and kitsch-loving college kids. ✉ *143 E. 60th St.,* ☎ *212/223–8929.*

Twins. Owned by twin sisters Debbie and Lisa Ganz and actor Tom Berenger, this restaurant employs 37 additional pairs of twins and often sees as many as 15 sets of twins as customers a night. Enjoy the double-chocolate fondue—as well as some singular food delights—and cigars. ✉ *Broadway and 54th St.,* ☎ *212/289–1777.*

Water Club. Right on the East River, with a pleasing outside deck (you're not on a boat, but you'll somehow feel you are), this is a special-occasion kind of place—especially for those who've already been to all the special landlocked spots in town. ✉ *500 E. 30th St.,* ☎ *212/683–3333.*

Upper West Side

On the Yupper West Side, as it's sometimes referred to, Amsterdam Avenue between 79th and 86th streets is a promenade for young revelers, many still wearing their college sweatshirts. Weave up and down the avenue, and be sure to make a detour down to the classy, racially mixed **Shark Bar** (✉ 307 Amsterdam Ave., between 75th and 76th Sts., ☎ 212/874–8500). Then try **Hi-Life** (✉ 477 Amsterdam Ave., ☎ 212/787–7199), big with the neighborhood's bon vivants.

Iridium. The owners spent untold sums to make this lavish restaurant and jazz club near Lincoln Center stand out, which it does. If nothing else, take a look inside for an eyeful of Gaudí-esque construction. ✉ *48 W. 63rd St.,* ☎ *212/582–2121.*

Museum Café. Trendy, overdesigned joints on Columbus Avenue come and go, but this oasis across from the American Museum of Natural History endures thanks to nice street-side windows and high, airy ceilings. ✉ *366 Columbus Ave.,* ☎ *212/799–0150.*

O'Neal's. Mike O'Neal, the owner of the beloved but now defunct Ginger Man, has moved the bar from that establishment down the street and created a series of rooms (one with a fireplace) serving good pub food. ✉ *49 W. 64th St.,* ☎ *212/787–4663.*

The Saloon. The menu goes on and on, the bar is large and informal, and the waitresses and waiters are mostly aspiring entertainers. It may be crowded, but the spirit of fun is infectious, and the people-watching is second to none. ✉ *1920 Broadway,* ☎ *212/874–1500.*

Wilson's. There must be a reason for the line out the door of this otherwise unremarkable but enduringly popular bar. Perhaps it's the live music (R&B and disco) Wednesday and Friday or the possibility of forging a formidable connection. ✉ *201 W. 79th St.,* ☎ *212/769–0100.*

Theme Dreams

Fashion Café. Backed by supermodels Elle MacPherson, Claudia Schiffer, Naomi Campbell, and Christy Turlington, this joint tries hard to be glamorous with its catwalk and displays of couture clothes. ✉ *51 Rockefeller Plaza,* ☎ *212/765–3131.*

Hard Rock Cafe. This spot was formerly embraced by the kids of stars—now, in fact, its clientele seems to be eternally prepubescent kids accompanied by muttering parents who find it big, crowded, and far too noisy for talk. ✉ *221 W. 57th St.,* ☎ *212/459–9320.*

Harley-Davidson Cafe. Motorcycles are not allowed to park outside, which should give you an idea of the authenticity of this upholstered showroom-size restaurant. Still, rock stars and other biker fans do drop in on occasion. ✉ *1370 6th Ave.,* ☎ *212/245–6000.*

Jekyll & Hyde Club. The self-billed "restaurant and social club for eccentric explorers and mad scientists," this multiple-story eating and ogling extravaganza features 250 varieties of beer and actors dressed as horror meisters. ✉ *1409 6th Ave.,* ☎ *212/541–9505.*

Motown Café. The food is actually quite tasty in this dining homage to the music that puts a smile on everyone's face. ✉ *104 W. 57th St.,* ☎ *212/581–8030.*

Planet Hollywood. It's touristy, it doesn't take reservations, and waiting lines are long. Still, the place has cachet, an undeniable star quality, and such movie memorabilia as the original Chewbacca. ✉ *140 W. 57th St.,* ☎ *212/333–7827.*

Gay and Lesbian Bars

For advice on the bar scene, health issues, and other assorted quandaries, call the **Gay and Lesbian Switchboard** (☎ 212/777–1800) or stop by the **Lesbian and Gay Community Services Center** (✉ 208 W. 13th St., ☎ 212/620–7310). Check out *HomoExtra, Next* magazine, the *New York Blade, Time Out New York, Sappho's Isle, Metro Source,* the *Village Voice,* or *Paper* for what's what.

Dance Clubs and Parties

Clit Club. Leather-vested and well-pierced Harley dykes as well as "lipstick" lesbians dance Friday night away. Call first, because this club roves. ✉ *Mother, 432 W. 14th St.,* ☎ *212/529–3300.*

Jackie 60. This super-hip, gay-friendly house dance party on Tuesday has weekly glam, fetish, and other far-side-of-the-fringe special events; call for details and dress-code guidelines. ✉ *Mother, 432 W. 14th St.,* ☎ *212/929–6060.*

1984. On Friday relive the '80s here in all its new-wave syntho-trash glory. ✉ *Pyramid, 101 Ave. A,* ☎ *212/802–9502.*

Twilo. Saturday is the gay night at this super-modern club. ✉ *530 W. 27th St.,* ☎ *212/268–1600.*

Men's Bars

Barracuda. The comfy couches in back are the big draw at this Chelsea hangout, where the pool table also helps draw a crowd. ✉ *275 W. 22nd St.,* ☎ *212/645–8613.*

The Break. The scene is usually quite young and swells according to the number and generosity of the night's drink specials. ✉ *232 8th Ave.,* ☎ *212/627–0072.*

Cleo's 9th Avenue Saloon. Near the theater district, this small, narrow neighborhood bar draws a convivial, laid-back older crowd. ✉ *656 9th Ave.,* ☎ *212/307–1503.*

Dakota. This 20-year-old Murray Hill neighborhood spot now attracts a diverse midtown crowd as well as interlopers from the East Village, the Upper East Side, and beyond. ✉ *405 3rd Ave.,* ☎ *212/684–8376.*

The Eagle. This leather-and-Levi's bar is serious about three things: drinking, glaring, and shooting pool. ✉ *142 11th Ave.,* ☎ *212/691–8451.*

g. This new, up-to-the-minute Chelsea favorite draws an upscale, mostly male crowd to its huge circular bar and two airy, relaxed rooms lined with leather settees. ✉ *223 W. 19th St.*, ☎ *212/929–1085.*

hell. Tucked away on a quiet street in the up-and-coming meatpacking district, this swanky lounge, with crystal chandeliers and red drapes, attracts a hip, attractive crowd of Chelsea men and downtowners. ✉ *59 Gansevoort St.*, ☎ *212/727–1666.*

The Monster. A longstanding West Village contender, the Monster has piano bar upstairs and a pitch-black disco downstairs that continue to draw a busy mix of ages, races, and genders. ✉ *80 Grove St.*, ☎ *212/924–3558.*

Rawhide. The older Wild West crowd of this Chelsea nook is mostly local and usually leathered up. ✉ *212 8th Ave.*, ☎ *212/242–9332.*

The Spike. Here, at the ultimate parade of black leather, chains, and Levi's, the bark is always bigger than the bite. ✉ *120 11th Ave.*, ☎ *212/243–9688.*

Splash Bar. Most nights go-go dancers writhe in translucent shower cubicles at this large, perenially crowded Chelsea hangout. ✉ *50 W. 17th St.*, ☎ *212/691–0073.*

Stonewall. With its odd mix of tourists chasing down gay history and down-to-earth locals, the scene is everything but trendy. ✉ *53 Christopher St.*, ☎ *212/463–0950.*

The Townhouse. On good nights it's like stepping into a Brooks Brothers catalog—cashmere sweaters, Rolex watches, distinguished-looking gentlemen—and it's surprisingly festive. ✉ *236 E. 58th St.*, ☎ *212/754–4649.*

Ty's. Though its clientele is close-knit and fiercely loyal, this small, jeans-and-flannel neighborhood saloon never turns away friendly strangers. ✉ *114 Christopher St.*, ☎ *212/741–9641.*

The Works. Whether it's Thursday's $1 margarita party or just a regular Upper West Side afternoon, the crowd is usually J. Crew–style or disco hangover at this bar, which has been around for nearly two decades. ✉ *428 Columbus Ave.*, ☎ *212/799–7365.*

Women's Bars

Crazy Nanny's. The crowd is wide-ranging—from urban chic to shaved head—and tends toward the young and the wild. Wednesday and Friday find the crowd grooving to a house DJ while Thursday is C&W line-dancing night. ✉ *21 7th Ave. S*, ☎ *212/366–6312.*

Henrietta Hudson. A little more upscale than Crazy Nanny's, this place has two huge rooms and a pool table. ✉ *438 Hudson St.*, ☎ *212/924–3347.*

Julie's. Popular with the sophisticated-lady, upper-crust crowd, this brownstone basement has a piano bar—and dancing on Sunday and Wednesday nights. ✉ *204 E. 58th St.*, ☎ *212/688–1294.*

9 Outdoor Activities and Sports

The Dodgers may have long since abandoned Brooklyn's Ebbets Field for Los Angeles, but New York's die-hard sports fans still bemoan the loss, and devote themselves wholeheartedly to the city's half dozen major-league sports teams. But this isn't just a city of fans. From boccie to rock climbing, no matter how fringe the sport, there's a place to pursue it, and adherents galore. Head to Central Park at dawn and join the metropolis's earliest-rising, most energetic denizens: cyclists zooming by on thousand-dollar bikes, blissed-out runners plugged into portable stereos, bird-watchers admiring the latest avian arrivals, rollerbladers literally dancing in the streets.

By Karen Cure

Updated by Hannah Borgeson

YOU'LL FIND OASES OF GREENERY you'd never imagine here (13% of the city, or approximately 27,000 acres, is, in fact, parkland). And if you strike up a conversation while waiting to rent a boat or a bike at the Loeb Boathouse, while stretching before a jog around the reservoir in Central Park, or before sliding your kayak into the Hudson, you'll discover a friendly, relaxed side of New Yorkers that you might not otherwise get the chance to see. Just one word before you set out: Weekends are very busy. If you need to rent equipment or secure specific space—for instance, a tennis court—go very early or be prepared to wait.

BEACHES

Fine weather brings sun-worshiping New Yorkers out in force. Early in the season the nearest park or even a rooftop (what some New Yorkers call Tar Beach) is just fine for catching rays, but later on everyone heads for New York City and Long Island beaches. Before you go, call to check on swimming conditions.

City Beaches

The tame waves of **Coney Island** (☎ 718/946–1350) are the closest many New Yorkers get to a surf all year. The last stop in Brooklyn on the B, D, F, and N lines, the beach here, which has the boardwalk and the famous amusement-park skyline of the Cyclone and the Wonder Wheel as its backdrop, is busy every day the sun shines. If you want to see surfers riding the waves in wet suits, venture out on the A train to the beaches in the **Rockaways** (☎ 718/318–4000) section of Queens—at 9th Street, 23rd Street, or between 80th and 118th streets.

Long Island

New Yorkers' favorite strand may be **Jones Beach** (☎ 516/785–1600), one of the great man-made beaches of the world, built during the late 1920s under the reign of former parks commissioner Robert Moses. In summer the Long Island Railroad (☎ 718/217–5477) runs regular trains from Penn Station to Freeport, where you transfer to a bus to the beach. On the west end of Fire Island, there's a good beach at **Robert Moses State Park** (☎ 516/669–0449), which can be reached in summer via the Long Island Railroad and a bus (☎ 718/217–5477).

PARTICIPANT SPORTS

For information about athletic facilities in Manhattan as well as a calendar of sporting events, pick up a complimentary copy of the monthly *MetroSports* newspaper at sporting goods stores and health clubs.

Bicycling

Although space comes at a premium in Manhattan apartments, many locals keep a bicycle around for transportation—they'll swear it's the best (and fastest) way to get around—and for occasional rides on glorious days. A sleek pack of dedicated racers zooms around Central Park at dawn and at dusk daily, and on weekends parks swarm with recreational cyclists. **Central Park** has a 6-mi circular drive with a couple of decent climbs that is closed to traffic from 10 AM to 3 PM (except the southeast portion between 6th Avenue and East 72nd Street) and from 7 AM to 10 PM on weekdays, and from 7 PM Friday to 6 AM Monday. On holidays it's closed from 7 PM the night before until 6 AM the day after. In **Riverside Park** the promenade between 72nd and 110th streets, with its Hudson River view, gets an easygoing crowd of slow-pedaling cyclists. The **Hudson River Park's esplanade,** which has a bike lane, runs along the waterfront from 14th Street down to Battery Park. From there it's a quick ride to the Wall Street area, which is deserted on weekends. The 3.3-mi circular drive in Brooklyn's beautiful **Prospect Park** (☞ Chapter 3) is closed to cars on weekends year-round and from 10 to 3 and 7 to 10 on weekdays April–November.

Bike Rentals

Expect to leave a deposit or a credit card when renting a bike. **AAA Bikes in Central Park** (✉ Loeb Boathouse, midpark, near E. 74th St., ☎ 212/861–4137) provides cycles for the whole family. **Larry & Jeff's Bicycles Plus** (✉ 1690 2nd Ave., at 87th St., ☎ 212/722–2201) features 10-speeds, mountain bikes, and hybrids. **Toga Bike Shop** (✉ 110 West End Ave., at 64th St., ☎ 212/799–9625) offers all kinds of bikes. **Pedal Pusher** (✉ 1306 2nd Ave., between 68th and 69th Sts., ☎ 212/288–5592) has everything from clunky three-speeds to racing bikes to hybrids in its rental fleet.

Group Trips

For organized rides with other cyclists, call or write before you come to New York. **Transportation Alternatives** (✉ 115 W. 30th St., Suite 1207, 10001-4010, ☎ 212/629–8080) can provide an ongoing update of group rides throughout the metropolitan area. **Hosteling International–American Youth Hostels** (✉ 891 Amsterdam Ave., at 103rd St., ☎ 212/932–2300) runs the Five-Borough Bicycling Club, which organizes day and weekend trips on a regular basis. The **New York Cycle Club** (✉ Box 1354 Midtown Station, 10018, ☎ 212/886–4545) sponsors weekend rides around Central Park and the metropolitan region for every level of fitness. **Time's Up!** (☎ 212/802–8222) leads free recreational rides at least twice a month for cyclists as well as skaters; the Central Park Moonlight Ride (10 PM the last Friday of the month year-round; meet at Columbus Circle) is a favorite. The **Staten Island Bicycling Association** (☎ 718/815–9290) sponsors trips in New York's most countrified borough, as well as other pretty spots.

Billiards

It used to be that pool halls were dusty, grimy, sticky places—and there are still a few of those around. But they've been joined by a group of oh-so-chic spots with deluxe decor, high prices, and even classical music or jazz in the background. Most halls are open late.

Amsterdam Billiard Club (✉ 344 Amsterdam Ave., between 76th and 77th Sts., ☎ 212/496–8180) is particularly fashionable and part-owned by comedian David Brenner. **Amsterdam Billiard Club East** (✉ 210 E. 86th St., between 2nd and 3rd Aves., ☎ 212/570–4545) has 32 tables, a café, and an international beer bar. **Billiard Club** (✉ 220 W. 19th St., between 7th and 8th Aves., ☎ 212/206–7665), in Chelsea, has a classy look and loud rock music. **Chelsea Billiards** (✉ 54 W. 21st St., between 5th and 6th Aves., ☎ 212/989–0096) has 50 pool tables and eight for snooker on two floors. **Corner Billiards** (✉ 85 4th Ave., at 11th St., ☎ 212/995–1314) draws many yuppies to its 28 tables. **East Side Billiard Club** (✉ 163 E. 86th St., between 3rd and Lexington Aves., ☎ 212/831–7665) serves up pizza and beer. **Soho Billiards** (✉ 56 E. Houston St., between Mott and Mulberry Sts., ☎ 212/925–3573) has a great location to attract weary bar hoppers. **West Side Billiard Club** (✉ 601 W. 50th St., at 11th Ave., ☎ 212/246–1060) has 12 pool tables and eight Ping-Pong tables.

Bird-Watching

Manhattan's green parks and woodlands provide habitats for thousands of birds, everything from fork-tailed flycatchers to common nighthawks. Because the city is on the Atlantic flyway, a major migratory route, you can see birds that nest as far north as the high Arctic. May is the best season, since the songbirds are in their freshest colors—so many sing at once that you can hardly distinguish their songs. To find out what's been seen where, call the **Rare Bird Alert** (☎ 212/979–3070). For information on the best bird-watching spots in city parks, call the **Urban Park Rangers,** a uniformed division of the Parks Department: Citywide (☎ 800/201–7275), Manhattan (☎ 212/427–4040), the Bronx (☎ 718/430–1832), Brooklyn (☎ 718/438–0100), Queens (☎ 718/699–4294), and Staten Island (☎ 718/667–6042).

Birders will like 1,146-acre **Van Cortlandt Park** (☎ 718/430–1890), in the Bronx, with its varied habitats, including freshwater marshes and upland woods. In Brooklyn, **Green-Wood Cemetery** (☎ 718/768–7300 for permission to enter grounds) features Victorian-era headstones, as well as a nice woodland that attracts hawks and songbirds. The Ramble in Manhattan's **Central Park** is full of warblers in springtime and may attract as many birders as it does birds. In recent years a pair of red-tailed hawks that set up home on the 12th-floor ledge of a 5th Avenue apartment building (at East 74th Street, across the street from Woody Allen's penthouse) has also attracted legions of birders to the park (the hawks have even been the subject of a book, Marie Winn's *Red-tails in Love*). In Queens try **Jamaica Bay Wildlife Refuge,** where birds are drawn to the 9,155 acres of salt marshes, fresh and brackish ponds, and open water; stop by the visitor center (✉ Crossbay Blvd., Broad Channel, Queens, ☎ 718/318–4340) to get a permit. In Staten Island head for the mostly undeveloped 312-acre **Wolfe's Pond Park** (☎ 718/984–8266), where the pond and the nearby shore can be dense with geese and ducks during the annual migrations.

Guided Walks

The **New York City Audubon Society** (✉ 71 W. 23rd St., between 5th and 6th Aves., ☎ 212/691–7483) has occasional bird-watching outings; call Monday–Thursday 10–4 for information. Also check with the Urban Park Rangers at the numbers listed above.

Boating and Kayaking

The boating available on New York City's ponds and lakes conjures up 19th-century images of a parasol-twirling lady rowed by her swain. The Hudson River attracts more intrepid sorts.

In **Central Park** the boats are rowboats (plus one Venetian gondola for nighttime glides in the moonlight), and the rowing terrain is the 18-acre Central Park Lake. Rent your boat at Loeb Boathouse (☎ 212/517–2233), near East 74th Street, from spring through fall. **Floating the Apple** (✉ W. 44th St. and Hudson River, ☎ 212/564–5412) has free rows and sails in community group–made boats from Pier 84.

In **Prospect Park** pedal boats can be rented at the Wollman Memorial Rink (☎ 718/282–7789) weekends and holidays from April through the end of October; the cost is $10 per hour, and it's well worth it, as 60-acre Prospect Lake is one of the city's largest bodies of water.

Try kayaking at the **Downtown Boathouse** (✉ Pier 26, N. Moore St. and Hudson River, ☎ no phone), which gives lessons and lets you take a kayak out for a paddle, all for free on summer weekends. **Manhat-**

tan Kayak Company (✉ Pier 60, Chelsea Piers, near 23rd St., ☎ 212/336–6068) runs individual trips and gives lessons for all levels.

Boccie

This pinless Italian version of bowling thrives in New York, with close to 100 city courts. The easiest courts to reach from midtown are at 96th Street and 1st Avenue; at East River Drive and 42nd Street; and at the Thompson Street Playground (at Houston Street), in Greenwich Village. There's also a boccie court at **Il Vagabondo** (✉ 351 E. 62nd St., between 1st and 2nd Aves., ☎ 212/832–9221), a vintage Italian restaurant east of Bloomingdale's.

Bowling

AMF Chelsea Piers Bowl (✉ Between Piers 59 and 60, Chelsea Piers, near 18th St., ☎ 212/835–2695) has 40 spanking new lanes and all the latest bowling trends—glow-in-the-dark and "extreme" bowling—and fine finger foods. The **Leisure Time Bowling & Recreation Center** (✉ Port Authority Bus Terminal, south bldg., 2nd level, at 42nd St., ☎ 212/268–6909) offers 30 lanes and New York's most traditional bowling-alley atmosphere. Newly renovated **Bowlmor** (✉ 110 University Pl., between 12th and 13th Sts., ☎ 212/255–8188), as funky as ever, is a 42-lane bi-level operation frequented by a colorful Village crowd; many stay until closing time: 4 AM on weekends.

Boxing

Chelsea Piers Sports Center (✉ 23rd St. and the Hudson River, ☎ 212/336–6000) has a boxing ring and equipment circuit run by Gleason's (☞ *see below*). **Crunch Fitness** (✉ 404 Lafayette St. at E. 4th St., ☎ 212/614–0120; ✉ 54 E. 13th St., ☎ 212/475–2018) has a boxing ring at its Lafayette Street location and kickboxing classes at its gym on East 13th Street. Brooklyn's venerable **Gleason's** (✉ 75 Front St., ☎ 718/797–2872), home of more than 100 world champs, including Muhammad Ali, instructs visitors and allows spectators for a small fee.

Chess and Checkers

In **Central Park,** the Chess & Checkers House is picturesquely situated atop a massive stone outcrop. Twenty-four outdoor tables are available during all daylight hours. Bring your own or pick up playing pieces at the Dairy (✉ Midpark at 64th St., ☎ 212/794–6564) Tuesday–Sunday 11–5; there is no charge, but a photo ID is required.

Downtown in Greenwich Village, the **Village Chess Shop** (✉ 230 Thompson St., between Bleecker and W. 3rd Sts., ☎ 212/475–9580) has 20 boards that it rents by the hour for play in the store, along with timers for those who play speed chess. The **Manhattan Chess Club** (✉ 353 W. 46th St., between 8th and 9th Aves., ☎ 212/333–5888) sponsors tournaments and exhibitions and has a bookstore.

Dance and Aerobics

Crunch Fitness (✉ 404 Lafayette St., at E. 4th St., ☎ 212/614–0120; ✉ 54 E. 13th St., ☎ 212/475–2018; ✉ 162 W. 83rd St., ☎ 212/875–1902) offers everything from straight-up aerobics to African dance and body sculpting. **New York Sports Clubs** (✉ 30 Wall St., ☎ 212/482–4800; ✉ 1601 Broadway, at 49th St., ☎ 212/977–8880; ✉ 200 Madison Ave., at 36th St., ☎ 212/686–1144; ✉ 125 7th Ave. S, at W. 10th St., ☎ 212/206–1500 and numerous other locations throughout New York City) cram in every kind of conditioning and strength-training class imaginable at a time and location likely to suit even the oddest travel schedule. The **Vanderbilt YMCA** (✉ 224 E. 47th St., between 2nd and 3rd Aves., ☎ 212/756–9600) schedules more than 100 different drop-in aerobics and exercise classes every week. None requires membership for classes.

Golf

Bethpage State Park (☎ 516/249–0700; 516/249–0707 reservation hot line), on the outskirts of the Long Island town of Farmingdale, about 1¼ hours from Manhattan, is home to five well-groomed golf courses, including its 7,065-yard par-71 Black, generally ranked among the nation's top 25 public courses. All five courses are busy seven days a week; reservations can be made up to two days in advance.

Of the 13 city courses, the 6,281-yard Split Rock, in **Pelham Bay Park,** the Bronx, is the most challenging (☎ 718/885–1258). Slightly easier is its sister course, the 6,405-yard Pelham, which has fewer trees with which to contend. **Van Cortlandt Park,** in the Bronx, has the nation's first public golf course, established in 1895—the hilly 6,102-yard Van Cortlandt (☎ 718/543–4595). Queens has a 6,300-yard newly renovated course at **Forest Park,** in Woodhaven (✉ Park La. S and Forest Pkwy., ☎ 718/296–0999). Staten Island has the links-style 6,050-yard **Silver Lake** golf course (✉ 915 Victory Blvd., 1 block south of Forest Ave., ☎ 718/447–5686).

Driving Ranges

In midtown you can take lessons or practice your swing in netted cages with bull's-eye backdrops at the **Richard Metz Golf Studio** (✉ 425 Madison Ave., at 49th St., 3rd floor, ☎ 212/759–6940). Jutting out into the Hudson, the **Golf Club at Chelsea Piers** (✉ 23rd St. and the Hudson River, ☎ 212/336–6400) has a 200-yard artificial-turf fairway, a computerized tee-up system, and heated hitting stalls—so you can keep right on swinging even in winter.

Miniature Golf

At **Hackers, Hitters & Hoops** (✉ 123 W. 18th St., ☎ 212/929–7482), you can outsmart the obstacles on nine holes. The 18-hole outdoor course at **Pier 25** (✉ Hudson River at Reade St., ☎ 212/732–7467), open seasonally, has a great riverside location.

Horseback Riding

A trot on the bridle path around Central Park's reservoir provides a pleasant look at New York. The **Claremont Riding Academy** (✉ 175 W. 89th St., ☎ 212/724–5100) is the city's oldest riding academy (established in 1892) and the only public riding stable in Manhattan. Experienced English riders can rent horses, at $33 per hour, for an unescorted walk, trot, or canter in nearby Central Park; call ahead to reserve.

Hotel Health Clubs

Although space is tight in Manhattan hotels, most offer some kind of fitness facility, even if it's just an arrangement enabling guests to use a nearby health club.

Doral Fitness Center (✉ 90 Park Ave., ☎ 212/370–9692), available to guests of the **Doral Park Avenue, Doral Court,** and **Doral Tuscany,** is a serious health club with a number of workout programs. The **Four Seasons** (✉ 57 E. 57th St., ☎ 212/758–5700) has a spacious and high-tech facility, including an aerobics room with video, free weights, Stair-

Master, and Cybex machines. **Holiday Inn Manhattan** (✉ 440 W. 57th St., ☎ 212/581–8100) guests can use the facilities at New York Underground Fitness, which include cardiovascular workout machines, circuit training equipment, and full locker rooms. The hotel's outdoor rooftop pool, open in summer, also allows outside visitors for a fee ($15 weekdays, $25 weekends). **Holiday Inn Crowne Plaza** (✉ 1605 Broadway, at 49th St., ☎ 212/977–4000) has a fitness center operated by the New York Sports Club, with a pool, weights and cardiovascular equipment, and an aerobics studio. The **Peninsula** (✉ 700 5th Ave., ☎ 212/247–2200) reserves Floors 21–22 for its 35,000-square-ft health club and spa, with a pool on the 22nd floor, plus exercise machines, free weights, a poolside dining terrace, and a full range of bodywork. The **Sheraton Manhattan** (✉ 790 7th Ave., at 51st St., ☎ 212/581–3300) has a health club including a large, glass-enclosed pool, cardiovascular and aquatic exercise equipment, swimming lessons, and a sundeck. Nonguests can use the facilities for $20. The **Millennium Broadway** (✉ 145 W. 44th St., ☎ 212/768–4400) and the **Millenium Hilton** (✉ 55 Church St., ☎ 212/693–2001) each offer a fitness center with Lifecycles, treadmills, StairMasters, and free weights. The Broadway location has a steam room, and there's a heated pool and sauna downtown.

Ice-Skating

Each of the city's rinks has its own character, but all have scheduled skating sessions. Lockers, skate rentals, music, and snack bars complete the picture. Major rinks include the outdoor one in **Rockefeller Center** (✉ 50th St. at 5th Ave., lower plaza, ☎ 212/332–7654), which is fairly small yet utterly romantic, especially when the enormous Christmas tree towers above it. Central Park's beautifully situated **Wollman Memorial Rink** (✉ 6th Ave. at 59th St., ☎ 212/396–1010) offers skating in the open air beneath the lights of the city. Be prepared for crowds on weekends. **Lasker Rink** (✉ 106th St., ☎ 212/534–7639), at the north end of Central Park, is usually less crowded than Wollman Rink. Chelsea Piers' **Sky Rink** (✉ Pier 61, near 23rd St., ☎ 212/336–6100) has two year-round indoor rinks jutting out over the Hudson; one is almost always open for general skating, and the other hosts leagues, lessons, and special events.

In-Line Skating

New York is wild over in-line skating. **Peck & Goodie** (✉ 917 8th Ave., at 54th St., ☎ 212/246–6123) sells and rents skates. **Blades** has several Manhattan stores, including East (✉ 160 E. 86th St., between 3rd and Lexington Aves., ☎ 212/996–1644), 2nd Avenue (✉ 1414 2nd Ave., between 73rd and 74th Sts., ☎ 212/249–3178), West (✉ 120 W. 72nd St., between Amsterdam and Columbus Aves., ☎ 212/787–3911), and TriBeCa (✉ 128 Chambers St., ☎ 212/964–1944); they sell and rent skates along with all the appropriate protection. **Empire Skate Club** (☎ 212/592–3674) runs recreational trips and fields skating questions.

Central Park is headquarters for city skaters. Most skaters seem to prefer circling the park, though not everyone is strong enough to make it up the hill at the park's northwest corner; to skip it, take the cutoff at 103rd Street. On weekends, between the Mall and Bethesda Fountain, disco-dancing skaters whirl and twirl to music blasting from speakers. Block-long cone slalom courses are often set up on the loop road south of West 67th Street. On weekends from April through October the **Central Park Skate Patrol** (☎ 212/439–1234) holds free stopping clinics at both 72nd Street entrances (west and east). The **Hudson River Park Esplanade,** from West 14th Street down to Battery Park, is packed with skaters on warm days. For other route ideas *see* Bicycling, *above.*

The two outdoor roller rinks at the **Chelsea Piers** complex (✉ Pier 62, 23rd St. and the Hudson River, ☎ 212/336–6200) have free-skates, classes, Rollaerobics, and hip-hop dance parties. There's also a skate park, with ramps, half-pipes, rails, and other in-line challenges. The **Roxy** (✉ 515 W. 18th St., ☎ 212/645–5156), a downtown dance club, goes roller-disco on Tuesday and Wednesday nights.

Jogging and Racewalking

Jogging

In New York, dog walkers jog, librarians jog, rock stars jog, and parents jog (sometimes pushing their toddlers ahead of them in speedy three-wheel strollers). Publicity notwithstanding, crime is not a problem as long as you jog when and where everybody else does. On Manhattan streets, figure 20 north–south blocks per mile.

In Manhattan, **Central Park** is the busiest spot, specifically along the 1.6-mi track circling the **Jacqueline Kennedy Onassis Reservoir.** A runners' lane has been designated along the park roads (for closing times, *see* Bicycling, *above*). A good 1¾-mi route starts at Tavern on the Green along the West Drive, heads south around the bottom of the park to the East Drive, and circles back west on the 72nd Street park road to your starting point; the entire loop road is a hilly 6 mi. **Riverside Park,** along the Hudson River bank in Manhattan, is glorious at sunset. You can cover 4½ mi by running from 72nd to 116th streets and back.

Other favorite Manhattan circuits are around **Gramercy Park** (⅓ mi), **Washington Square Park** (½ mi), the **East River Esplanade** (just over 3 mi), the **Battery Park City Esplanade** (about 2 mi), and the **Hudson River Esplanade** (about 1½ mi). In Brooklyn try the **Brooklyn Heights Promenade** (⅓ mi), which faces the Manhattan skyline, or the loop in **Prospect Park** (3⅓ mi).

The **New York Road Runners Club** (✉ 9 E. 89th St., ☎ 212/860–4455) organizes a year-round schedule of races and group runs; the latter begin at 6:30 PM on weekdays and at 10 AM Saturday, starting at the club headquarters. The 5-km Runners' World Midnight Run, held on New Year's Eve in Central Park, is popular—many runners show up wearing inventive costumes, and the night culminates with fireworks. The New York City Marathon (☞ Spectator Sports, *below*) is the club's best-known event.

Racewalking

Elbows pumping vigorously at their sides, racewalkers can move as fast as some joggers, the great difference that their heels are planted firmly with every stride. A number of competitive racewalking events are held regularly; for information contact the **Park Race Walkers' Club** (✉ 320 E. 83rd St., Box 18, 10028, ☎ 212/628–1317).

Parasailing

The new **Parasail New York** (✉ North Cove Yacht Harbor at World Financial Center, ☎ 212/691–0055) can give you one of the most exhilarating views of the downtown skyline, as you're suspended in air by a parachute towed by a motorboat. Wall Streeters have been seen parasailing in suits on their lunch hour—air time is about 10 minutes, and participants stay dry. The season is mid-May–October, Thursday–Sunday; a ride costs about $50.

Rock Climbing

Indoor rock climbing has grown popular in New York, thanks to the opening of several walls in Manhattan. Lessons and equipment rentals (harness and climbing shoes) are available, and experienced climbers should expect to take a belay test before they're free to climb. You can usually find a belay partner if you're solo. **Chelsea Piers** (✉ 23rd St. and the Hudson River, ☎ 212/336–6000) has two climbing areas: a 30-ft wall in the field house, which is used primarily by children and nonmembers, and a 46-footer plus a separate bouldering wall in the Sports Center. Both allow nonmembers, though the day rate is higher in the Sports Center. Newest on the Manhattan scene is the **Extra Vertical Climbing Center** (✉ Broadway between 62nd St. and 63rd Sts., ☎ 212/586–5718), which has an indoor/outdoor (covered) wall ranging from 30 to 50 ft high in the public Harmony Atrium; even if you're not a climber, you might enjoy watching for a few minutes if you're in the neighborhood. The wall at **Manhattan Plaza Health Club** (✉ 482 W. 43rd St., ☎ 212/563–7001) is 20 ft.

Swimming

Asphalt Green (✉ York Ave. between 90th and 92nd Sts., ☎ 212/369–8890) has a breathtaking 50-meter (54-yard) pool (known as AquaCenter) and a full fitness center; the daily drop-in fee is $15. The **Carmine Street Recreation Center** (✉ 7th Ave. S and Clarkson St., ☎ 212/242–5228) has a 23-yard indoor pool and a 105-yard outdoor pool (only one is open at a time). For the $25 membership fee, you can use the pool and take advantage of fitness facilities and classes, but you have to bring your own padlock and towel. **Chelsea Piers Sports Center** (✉ Pier 60, 23rd St. and the Hudson River, ☎ 212/336–6000) has a six-lane, 25-yard lap pool overlooking the Hudson, with an adjacent whirlpool and sundeck. Day passes for the exercise club, of which the pool is a part, are $31. The **U.N. Plaza–Park Hyatt** (✉ 1 United Nations Plaza, ☎ 212/702–5016) has a lovely 27th-floor swimming pool that can be used by nonguests for a $25-a-day fee. The **YWCA** (✉ 610 Lexington Ave., at 53rd St., ☎ 212/755–4500) has a sparkling 75-ft lap pool available at $6 to members of all YWCAs and $8 to nonmembers for a single swim; after 5 the price is higher. The **YMCA** (Vanderbilt Y, ✉ 224 E. 47th St., ☎ 212/756–9600; West Side Y, ✉ 5 W. 63rd St., ☎ 212/787–4400) has clean, brightly lighted lap pools open to nonmembers (fee varies).

Tennis

The New York City Parks Department maintains scores of tennis courts. Some of the most scenic are the 26 clay courts and four hard courts in **Central Park** (✉ Midpark, near 94th St., ☎ 212/280–0206), set in a thicket of trees with the skyline beyond. Same-day admission is available for $5 an hour per person.

The newly renovated and expanded **USTA National Tennis Center** (✉ Flushing Meadows–Corona Park, Queens, ☎ 718/760–6200), site of the U.S. Open Tournament, has 45 courts (36 outdoor and 9 indoor, all Deco Turf II), most of which are open to the public 300 days a year. Reservations are accepted up to two days in advance, and prices range from $28 to $40, depending on when you play.

Several local clubs will book courts to nonmembers: **Crosstown Tennis** (✉ 14 W. 31st St., ☎ 212/947–5780) has four indoor hard courts that are air-conditioned in summer. **HRC Tennis** (✉ Piers 13 and 14, East River at Wall St., ☎ 212/422–9300) has eight Har-Tru courts under two bubbles, which are air-conditioned in summer. HRC Tennis also owns **Village Tennis Courts** (✉ 110 University Pl., between 12th and 13th Sts., ☎ 212/989–2300), with two hard rubber courts that are air-conditioned in summer. Hourly fees can be up to $100 for nonmembers. **Manhattan Plaza Racquet Club** (✉ 450 W. 43rd St., ☎ 212/594–0554) offers five hard surface courts on which WTA and U.S. Open players have been known to practice—not to mention a soap opera star or two, since many actors live in special housing near the club. At **Midtown Tennis Club** (✉ 341 8th Ave., at 27th St., ☎ 212/989–8572) it's best to make reservations for one of their eight courts (some outdoor in summer, bubbled in winter) a couple of days in advance.

SPECTATOR SPORTS

Many sporting events—ranging from boxing to figure skating—take place at **Madison Square Garden** (✉ 7th Ave. between 31st and 33rd Sts.); tickets can be ordered by phone through the box office (☎ 212/465–6000) or Ticketmaster (☎ 212/307–7171). Several New York pro teams, including its two football teams and one of its basketball teams, perform across the Hudson River at the **Meadowlands Sports Complex** (✉ Rte. 3 and New Jersey Turnpike Exit 16W, East Rutherford, NJ, ☎ 201/935–3900 for box office and information), which includes the **Continental Airlines Arena** and **Giants Stadium.** Whenever there's a game (or even a concert), buses run directly from the Port Authority in Manhattan. When events are sold out, you can sometimes pick up a ticket outside the venue on the day of the game from a fellow sports fan whose guests couldn't make it at the last minute. Meadowlands officials have designated Gate D (for both venues) as a resale area, although professional scalpers now mostly work the perimeter roadways outside the complex proper. Ticket agencies, listed in the Manhattan Yellow Pages phone directory and the sports pages of the *Daily News* can be helpful—for a price.

Baseball

The **New York Mets** play at Shea Stadium (✉ Roosevelt Ave. off Grand Central Pkwy., ☎ 718/507–8499), at the penultimate stop on the No. 7 train, in Flushing, Queens. Although owner George Steinbrenner keeps threatening to move the team out of town, the **New York Yankees** still have their home at Yankee Stadium (✉ Yankee Stadium, 161st St. and River Ave., ☎ 718/293–6000), accessible by the No. 4, D, or C train to the 161st Street station in the Bronx. Ferries also run from Manhattan's east side on game nights (☎ 800/533–3779). The baseball season runs from April through October.

Basketball

Currently, the **New York Knickerbockers** (the Knicks) arouse intense hometown passions, which means tickets for home games at Madison Square Garden (✉ 7th Ave. between 31st and 33rd Sts.) are *extremely* hard to come by. For up-to-date game roundups, phone the New York Knickerbockers Fan Line (☎ 212/465–5867). The **New Jersey Nets,** New York's second NBA team, play at the Meadowlands in the Continental Airlines Arena (✉ Rte. 3, East Rutherford, NJ). For tickets—which are remarkably easy to obtain—call the Meadowlands box office (☎ 201/935–3900) or Ticketmaster (☎ 201/507–8900). The basketball season goes from late October through April. The **Liberty,** New York's Women's National Basketball Association team, played a very respectable opening season in 1997 and attracted spirited fans, including more women and girls than usually attend pro sports games. The season, mid-June–August, fills a traditionally slow time for Madison Square Garden (⊠ 7th Ave. between 31st and 33rd Sts., ☎ 212/564–9622 for tickets).

Boxing and Wrestling

Major and minor **boxing** bouts are staged in Madison Square Garden (⊠ 7th Ave. between 31st and 33rd Sts., ☎ 212/465–6000). **Wrestling,** a more frequent presence at Madison Square Garden (⊠ 7th Ave. between 31st and 33rd Sts., ☎ 212/465–6000) since the days of "Gorgeous" George and "Haystack" Calhoun in the late '50s, is stagy and outrageous, drawing a rowdy but enthusiastic crowd.

Football

The enormously popular **New York Giants** play at Giants Stadium in the Meadowlands Sports Complex (⊠ Rte. 3, East Rutherford, NJ, ☎ 201/935–8111). Most seats for Giants games are sold on a season-ticket basis—and there's a very long waiting list for those. However, single tickets are occasionally available at the stadium box office. The hapless **New York Jets** play at Giants Stadium (⊠ Rte. 3, East Rutherford, NJ, ☎ 516/560–8100 fan club, ☎ 516/560–8200 tickets). Although they're nowhere near as scarce as Giants tickets, most Jets tickets are snapped up by hopeful fans before the season opener. The football season runs from September through December.

Arena Football

A kind of cross between indoor soccer and football, this chaotic sport is played April–July. Teams play in a padded indoor arena. The scoring is similar to football, and the ball is identical, but passes are allowed to rebound off the walls. The **New Jersey Red Dogs** play at the Continental Airlines Arena (⊠ Rte. 3, East Rutherford, NJ, ☎ 201/935–3900). The **New York CityHawks** got off to a questionable start in 1997; as a result, tickets are easier to come by. They play at Madison Square Garden (⊠ 7th Ave. between 31st and 33rd Sts., ☎ 212/465–6741).

Hockey

The **New York Rangers** play at Madison Square Garden (⊠ 7th Ave. between 31st and 33rd Sts., ☎ 212/465–6741; 212/308–6977 for Rangers hot line). The **New York Islanders** skate at Nassau Veterans Memorial Coliseum in Uniondale, Long Island (☎ 516/888–9000 for tickets). The area's third hockey team, the **New Jersey Devils,** fights for the puck at the Continental Airlines Arena at the Meadowlands (⊠ Rte. 3, East Rutherford, NJ, ☎ 201/935–3900). Tickets for the Islanders and Devils are usually available at game time; Rangers tickets are more difficult to find. The hockey season runs from October through April.

Horse Racing

Modern **Aqueduct Racetrack** (⊠ 110th St. and Rockaway Blvd., Ozone Park, Queens, ☎ 718/641–4700), with its spate of lawns and gardens, holds Thoroughbred races late October–early May from Wednesday to Sunday. In May the action moves from Aqueduct Racetrack to **Belmont Park** (⊠ Hempstead Turnpike, Elmont, Long Island, ☎ 718/641–

4700), home of the third jewel in horse racing's triple crown, the Belmont Stakes. The horses run here May–June from Wednesday to Sunday. Then after a few weeks upstate at Saratoga, they return to Belmont from late August through October. On weekends a package that includes breakfast and tram tour, as well as races, is available—ask about Breakfast at Belmont. The **Meadowlands** (✉ Rte. 3, East Rutherford, NJ, ☎ 201/935–8500) has Thoroughbred racing from September to mid-December and harness racing the rest of the year (late December–mid-August). **Yonkers Raceway** (✉ Yonkers Ave., Yonkers, ☎ 718/562–9500) features harness racing every evening except Wednesday and Sunday year-round.

Running

The **New York City Marathon** has taken place annually on a Sunday in early November since it was started by New Yorker Fred Lebow in 1970, and it's grown to involve some 2 million spectators cheering on the pack of more than 30,000 international participants (some 95% of them finish). Racewalkers, "jogglers," oldsters, youngsters, and competitors with disabilities help to make this what former Olympic Organizing Committee president Peter V. Ueberroth called "the best sporting event in the country." Spectators line rooftops and sidewalks, promenades, and terraces all along the route, which begins on the Staten Island side of the Verrazano-Narrows Bridge and covers ground in all five boroughs—but don't go near the finish line in Central Park around 2 PM unless you relish mob scenes. Contact the **New York Road Runners Club** (✉ 9 E. 89th St., ☎ 212/860–4455).

Soccer

Since 1996 the tristate area has had a national major-league soccer team, the **MetroStars.** Games take place at Giants Stadium (✉ Rte. 3, East Rutherford, NJ, ☎ 201/935–3900), and perhaps because of the team's unspectacular record, tickets are easy to get.

Tennis

The annual **U.S. Open Tournament,** held from late August through early September at the USTA National Tennis Center (✉ Flushing Meadows–Corona Park, Queens, ☎ 718/760–6200), is one of the high points of the tennis buff's year, and tickets to watch the late rounds are some of the hottest in town. Early round matches are entertaining, too, and with a stadium-court ticket you can also view matches in outlying courts, where the bleachers are so close you can almost count the sweat beads on the players' foreheads, and in the grandstand, where bleacher seating is first-come, first-served. Wherever you sit (and from some seats the players look like ants), the eclectic mix of casual visitors, tennis groupies, and celebrities makes for terrific people-watching. A $254 million expansion project, which saw the 1997 completion of the new 23,000-seat Arthur Ashe Stadium, where the championships are played, means the Open can accommodate even more fans. Tickets go on sale in May through Tele-charge (☎ 800/524–8440).

The tennis year winds up with the **WTA Tournament,** a major women's pro event held at Madison Square Garden (✉ 7th Ave. between 31st and 33rd Sts., ☎ 465–6000) in mid-November. Tickets go on sale in September.

10 Shopping

Is it any surprise that New York has five of the world's costliest retail destinations? Elegant 5th Avenue, monumental Rockefeller Plaza, knock-your-socks-off Times Square and 57th Street, and devastatingly chic Madison Avenue—along these streets are the world's finest department stores, glossy couture houses, and renowned art galleries. But as the buzzing in SoHo, Nolita, and Chelsea attest, no one neighborhood has a monopoly on style, upstart clothing lines, and tiny exotic home-design stores. No matter which threshold you cross, shopping is, more than ever, an event.

By Jennifer Paull

THERE'S SOMETHING FOR EVERYONE in every price range in New York. Do you have a sudden yearning for Japanese stress-busting gum? Head to Daily 235. Want a selection of skulls? Either Evolution or Danse Macabre can outfit you nicely. Or if you favor high-end designers (especially Italian), the couture houses along Madison Avenue will sharpen your acquisitive appetite.

One of Manhattan's biggest shopping lures is the bargain—a temptation fueled in recent years by the opening of Loehmann's and other discount divas. Hawkers of not-so-real Gucci watches are stationed at street intersections (even on Madison Avenue), and Canal Street is lined with faux Prada backpacks. There are thrift shops where well-known socialites send their castoffs and movie stars snap up antique lace. Although resale prices are definitely higher than in smaller cities, the sheer selection can make up for it. Designers' showroom sales allow you to buy cheap at the source; auctions promise good prices as well.

Sales

Sales take place late June and July (for summer merchandise) and late December and January (for winter wares); these sales are announced in the papers. Be sure to check out *New York* magazine's "Sales and Bargains" column, which often lists sales in manufacturers' showrooms that are otherwise never promoted publicly, and *Time Out New York*'s "Shoptalk" page, which includes sales. The *Village Voice* is also a good source for tip-off sale ads. If your visit is planned for April or October, when many manufacturers' sales take place, you might phone your favorite designer and ask whether one is in the offing. Find out before you go if you can try on the clothes and whether the seller requires cash or accepts credit cards and checks (local or out-of-state).

Shopping Neighborhoods

New York shops are, for the most part, collected in neighborhoods rather than in malls, so take advantage of good weather to prowl the stores—not only are the odds good that you'll find an irresistible something, but you'll get a strong sense of an area's personality as well. The following sections single out shopping highlights in each neighborhood. Addresses for shops, if not included here, can be found in store listings below. Cross streets are provided only for stores not bulleted on a map.

South Street Seaport

The past few years at the Seaport have been choppy; the Fulton Market Building, once a linchpin, is almost empty. Developers plan to add new stores, but for now most shops are located along the cobbled, pedestrians-only extension to Fulton Street and on the three levels of Pier 17. Stores in this area tend toward the conservative upscale; for dependable women's clothing try **Ann Taylor** and **Liz Claiborne** (✉ 133 Beekman St., ☎ 212/346–9190). The big catalog house **J. Crew** is in one of the Seaport's old waterfront hotels. Pier 17 has few surprises, but there are some few-of-a-kind shops, including **Mariposa** (☎ 212/233–3221), for rare butterflies mounted under Lucite.

World Financial Center

The World Financial Center, due west across the West Side Highway from the World Trade Center, may yet emerge as a shopping and cultural destination in its own right. Beyond the elevator banks of financial giants like Merrill Lynch and clustered around the huge marble-cloaked Winter Garden, which is the architectural centerpiece here, are such suitably chichi stores as **Barneys New York,** for clothing, and **Rizzoli**'s, for books and magazines. There are also some good travel resources: a large American Express Travel Services branch and the **Civilized Traveller** (☏ 212/786–3301) bookstore.

Lower East Side and the East Village

Once home to millions of Jewish immigrants from Russia and Eastern Europe, the Lower East Side is New Yorkers' bargain beat. The center of it all is narrow, unprepossessing Orchard Street, which is crammed with tiny, no-nonsense clothing stores and open stalls ranging from kitschy to relatively elegant (you can even buy a tux). Don't expect to schmooze with salespeople, especially on Sunday, the busiest day of the week (on Saturday shops in the Orchard Street area are closed). Essential stops include **Fine & Klein,** for handbags; **Forman's,** for women's clothing; the colorful, cartooned clothing in **Marcoart** (⊠ 186 Orchard St.); and the lovely **Klein's of Monticello,** for deals on dressy clothes. Grand Street off Orchard Street and south of Delancey Street is chockablock with linens, towels, and other items for the home; the Bowery between Grand and Delancey streets, with lamps and lighting fixtures. Ludlow Street, one block east of Orchard Street, is starting to buzz with little storefronts selling, as one puts it, "20th-century pop culture." (Some of these shops are open on Saturday.) There are still plenty of Jewish stores scattered about; many sell candy, nuts, dried fruit, and Israeli sweets. The East Village offers diverse, offbeat specialty stops, including **Little Rickie,** for collectible kitsch, and some great vintage-clothing boutiques, especially along East 7th Street.

Nolita

This Nabokovian nickname, shorthand for "*No*rth of *Li*ttle *It*aly," describes an up-and-coming neighborhood that is, in effect, an expansion of SoHo's eastern flank. Nolita's parallel spines are Elizabeth, Mott, and Mulberry streets, between Houston and Spring streets. Tiny boutiques (as well as similarly diminutive but generally good eateries) are sprouting like mushrooms after rain. Among the small, funky housewares and design shops are **Shì** and **Michael Anchin glass co.** (⊠ 250 Elizabeth St.), with its shelves full of rainbow-color long-neck vases. The clothing stores are equally stylish—a trio of shops, **Jade, Calypso,** and **Tracy Feith** (⊠ 280 Mulberry St.), is rife with exotic glamour. There are swank shoes at **Sigerson Morrison** and even a delicious cashmere store, **Lucien Pellat-Finet.** Super-premium ice-cream maker **Ciao Bella** (⊠ 262 Mott St.) sells ice cream and sorbet at a window (open seasonally) in its world headquarters here.

SoHo

The mall-ification of SoHo continues. Chain stores such as **Victoria's Secret** and **Eddie Bauer** have Broadway addresses, and **J. Crew** has an outpost on Prince Street. However, there are still many unique shops, especially for housewares and fashion. Recent additions such as **Helmut Lang** for double-take-worthy clothes hone the creative edge. Some well-known stops include **Wolfman-Gold & Good Company,** for decorative items; **Dean & DeLuca,** a gourmet food emporium; **Zona** and **Moss,** full of well-designed home furnishings and gifts; and the remarkable **Enchanted Forest** toy store. On Lafayette Street below Houston, a hip new strip includes shops outside the mainstream, mainly dealing in home furnishings. Many SoHo stores are open seven days a week.

Chelsea and the Flatiron District

Fifth Avenue south of 23rd Street, along with the streets fanning east and west, is home to a lively downtown crowd. Many locals sport clothes from the neighborhood—a mix of the hip such as **Emporio Armani, Paul**

SoHo Shopping

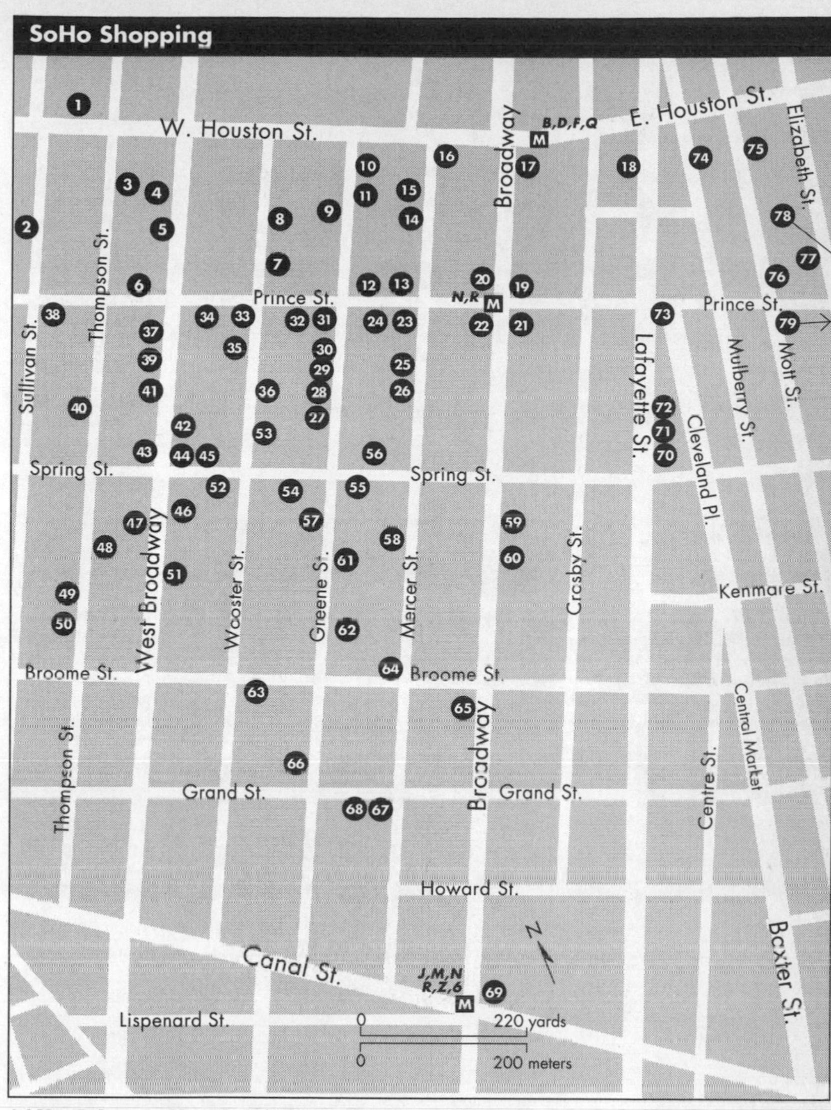

Ad Hoc Softwares, **43**
Agnès B., **32**
Agnès B. Homme, **57**
Alice Underground, **65**
Alicia Mugetti, **38**
Anna Sui, **30**
Aveda, **4**
A/X: Armani Exchange, **19**
Back Pages Antiques, **9**
Betsey Johnson, **8**
Broadway Panhandler, **63**
Calypso, **75**
Canal Jean, **60**
Caswell-Massey, **44**
Chuckies, **46**
City Barn Antiques, **73**
Comme des Garçons, **36**
Costume National, **53**
D&G, **39**
David Zwirner, **66**
Dean & DeLuca, **21**
Enchanted Forest, **58**
Face Stockholm, **31**
First Peoples Gallery, **55**
Gagosian, **7**
Gates of Marrakesh, **79**
Guggenheim Museum SoHo, **20**
Helmut Lang, **61**
Holly Solomon, **16**
J. Crew, **13**
Jade, **74**
Jekyll & Hyde, **27, 68**
John Fleuvog, **24**
Joovay, **37**
Kate Spade, **50, 64**
Kate's Paperie, **22**
Keiko New York, **62**
Label, **72**
Le Corset, **48**
Leo Castelli, **41**
Lilliput, **70**
L'Occitane, **52**
Lucien Pellat-Finet, **78**
MAC, **56**
Marc Jacobs, **15**
Metropolitan Museum of Art Shop, **12**
Miu Miu, **23**
Morgane le Fay, **45**
Moss, **10**
Multiple Impressions, **54**
New York Firefighter's Friend, **71**
Nicole Miller, **34**
The 1909 Company, **49**
O.K. Harris, **51**
Otto Tootsi Plohound, **42**
Pageant Book and Print Shop, **1**
Pearl River Mart, **69**
Peter Fox, **40**
Pop Shop, **18**
Pottery Barn, **17**
Rizzoli, **5**
Robert Lee Morris, **47**
Rugby North America, **26**
Sean, **3**
Shì, **77**
Sigerson Morrison, **76**
SoHo Provisions, **59**
Stork Club, **2**
Stuart Moore, **33**
Tocca, **14**
Todd Oldham, **35**
Troy, **11**
Untitled, **6**
Vivienne Tam, **29**
Wolfman-Gold & Good Company, **25**
Yohji Yamamoto, **67**
Zona, **28**

Agnès B., **9**
Alicia Mugetti, **14**
Ann Taylor, **90**
Archivia, **26**
Baccarat, **94**
Bang & Olufsen, **24**
Barneys New York, **88**
Barry Friedman, **62**
Betsey Johnson, **8**
Billy Martin's, **59**
Bonpoint, **55**
Bottega Veneta, **91**
Bulgari, **67**
Calvin Klein, **89**
Cerruti, **63**
Chocolate Soup, **25**
Coach, **75,101**
Cole-Haan, **86**
Cozy's Cuts for Kids, **1**
Crate and Barrel, **93**
Crawford Doyle Booksellers, **6**
D. Porthault, **52**
David A. Schorsch, **22**
David Findlay, **18**
DeLorenzo, **21**
Didier Aaron, **62**
Dolce & Gabbana, **49**
Dooney & Burke, **65**
E. A. T. Gifts, **7**
Emanuel Ungaro, **61**
Emporio Armani, **99**
Etro, **74**
Exclusive Oilily Store, **36**
Florian Papp, **19**
Floris, **77**
Frette, **57**
Gagosian, **17**
G.C. Williams, **2**
Gianfranco Ferre, **41**
Gianni Versace, **48**
Giorgio Armani, **69**
Givenchy, **23**
Hirschl & Adler, **39**
Hoya Crystal Gallery, **81**
Infinity, **5**
Issey Miyake, **15**
Jacadi, **66**
James Danziger Gallery, **34**
James Robinson, **98**
Jane Kahan Gallery, **29**

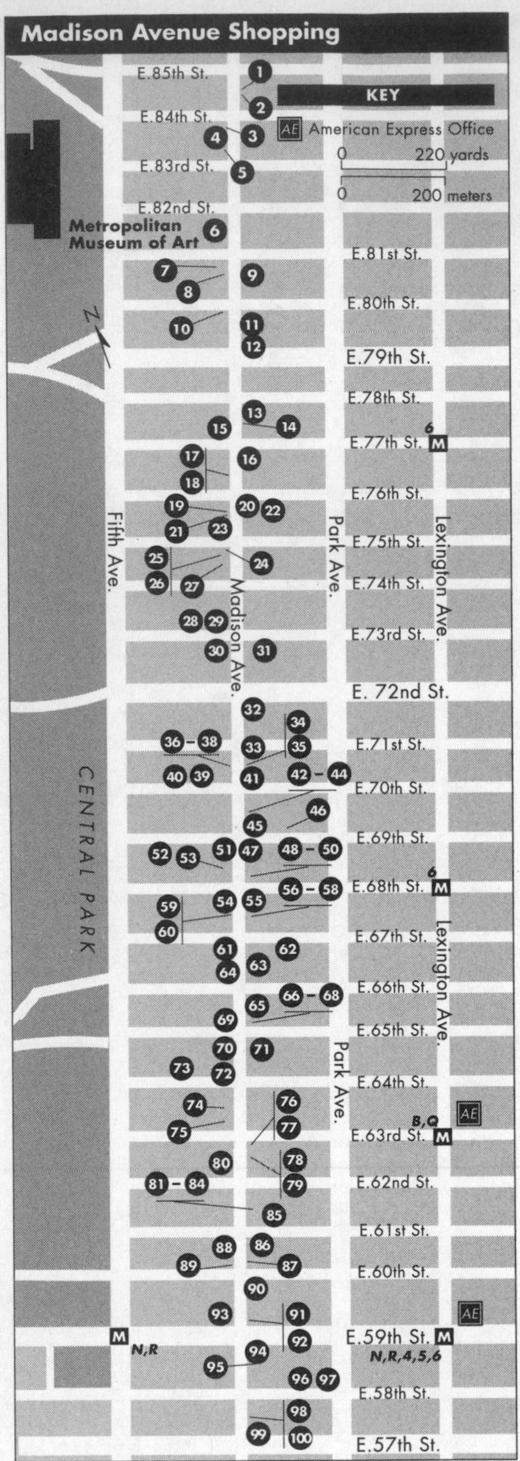

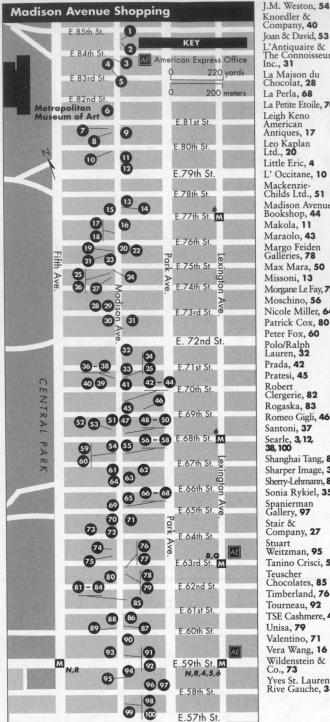

J.M. Weston, **54**
Knoedler & Company, **40**
Joan & David, **53**
L'Antiquaire & The Connoisseur Inc., **31**
La Maison du Chocolat, **28**
La Perla, **68**
La Petite Etoile, **70**
Leigh Keno American Antiques, **17**
Leo Kaplan Ltd., **20**
Little Eric, **4**
L' Occitane, **10**
Mackenzie-Childs Ltd., **51**
Madison Avenue Bookshop, **44**
Makola, **11**
Maraolo, **43**
Margo Feiden Galleries, **78**
Max Mara, **50**
Missoni, **13**
Morgane Le Fay, **72**
Moschino, **56**
Nicole Miller, **64**
Patrick Cox, **80**
Peter Fox, **60**
Polo/Ralph Lauren, **32**
Prada, **42**
Pratesi, **45**
Robert Clergerie, **82**
Rogaska, **83**
Romeo Gigli, **46**
Santoni, **37**
Searle, **3,12, 38,100**
Shanghai Tang, **87**
Sharper Image, **30**
Sherry-Lehmann, **84**
Sonia Rykiel, **35**
Spanierman Gallery, **97**
Stair & Company, **27**
Stuart Weitzman, **95**
Tanino Crisci, **58**
Teuscher Chocolates, **85**
Timberland, **76**
Tourneau, **92**
TSE Cashmere, **47**
Unisa, **79**
Valentino, **71**
Vera Wang, **16**
Wildenstein & Co., **73**
Yves St. Laurent Rive Gauche, **33**

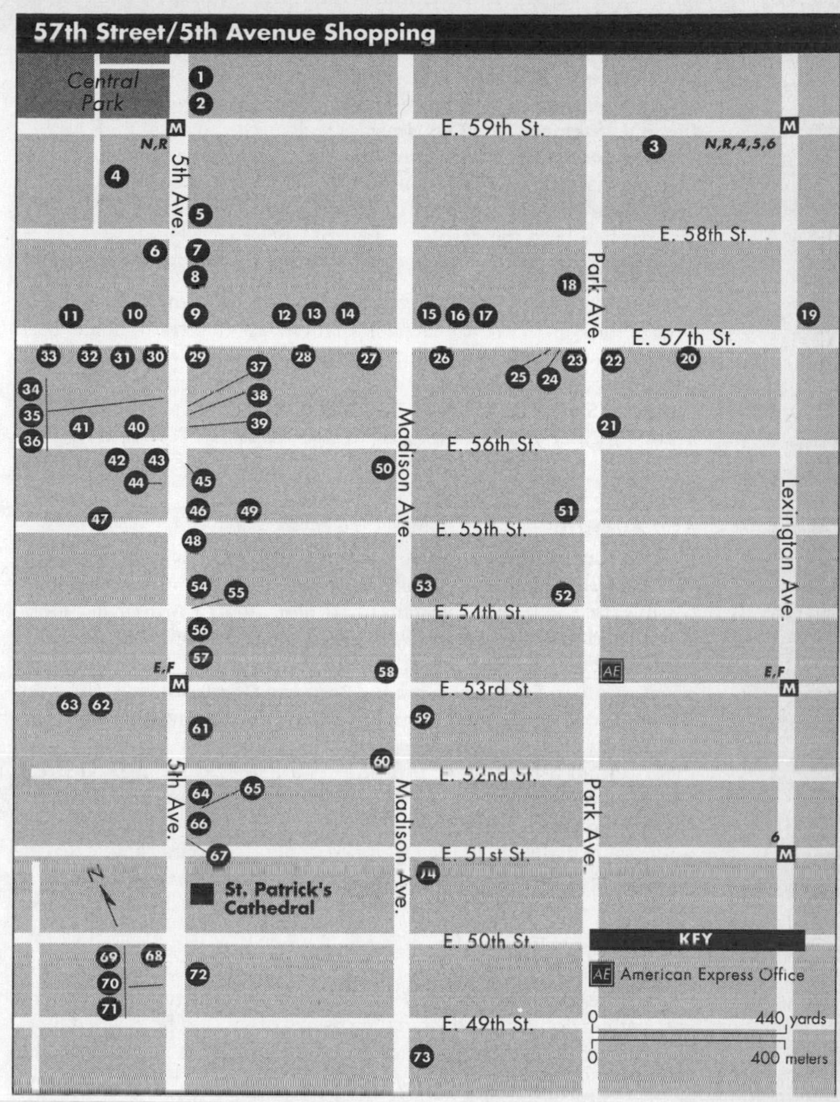

A La Vieille Russie, **2**
Alfred Dunhill of London, **23**
American Craft Museum, **62**
André Emmerich Gallery, **15**
Argosy Bookstore, **3**
Asprey, **39**
Aveda, **59**
A/X: Armani Exchange, **67**
Bergdorf Goodman, **6, 7**
Bulgari, **30**
Burberrys, **12**
Cartier, **64**
Chanel, **14**
Charivari 57, **32**
Cole-Haan, **68**
Christian Dior, **48**
Church's English Shoes, **73**
David Findlay Jr. Fine Art, **15**
David Webb, **22**
Dempsey & Carroll, **20**
The Disney Store, **46**
Edwynn Houk Gallery, **8**
F.A.O. Schwarz, **5**
Façonnable, **55**
Felissimo, **42**
Fortunoff, **57**
Galleri Orrefors Kosta Boda, **24**
Geoffrey Beene, **1**
Gianni Versace, **65**
Gucci, **56**
H. Stern, **66**
Hammacher Schlemmer, **19**
Harry Winston, **43**
Hélène Arpels, **18**
Henri Bendel, **44**
Hermès, **13**
Holland & Holland, **25**
Israel Sack, **34**
J.N. Bartfield, **33**
Joseph Helman, **31**
Lederer, **74**
Librairie de France/Libraria Hispanica, **69**
Louis Féraud, **40**
Louis Vuitton, **17**
Manolo Blahnik, **47**
Mary Boone Gallery, **8**
Mikimoto, **35**
Metropolitan Museum of Art Shop, **70**
Morrell & Company, **53**
Neuchatel Chocolates, **4**
Niketown, **28**
Norma Kamali O.M.O., **41**
Museum of Modern Art Design Store, **63**
O'Hara Gallery, **15**
Pace Wildenstein, **26**
Peter Findlay Gallery, **15**
Prada, **16, 36**
Richart Design et Chocolat, **49**
Rizzoli, **11**
Saks Fifth Avenue, **72**
Salvatore Ferragamo, **38, 61**
Sony Style, **50**
Steuben, **45**
Sulka, **51**
Syms, **52**
T. Anthony, **21**
Takashimaya, **54**
Teuscher Choclolates, **71**
Thomas Pink, **58**
Tibor de Nagy Gallery, **36**
Tiffany & Co., **29**
Tourneau, **27, 60**
Trump Tower, **37**
Van Cleef & Arpels, **10**
Warner Bros. Studio Store, **9**

Smith, and **Matsuda** and discounters like **Moe Ginsburg.** Broadway has a smattering of stores dear to New Yorkers' hearts, including **ABC Carpet & Home** and **Paragon Sporting Goods.** In the low 20s on 6th Avenue are a cluster of superstores, including **Barnes & Noble, T. J. Maxx, Filene's Basement,** and **Old Navy,** as well as the colossal **Bed, Bath & Beyond. Loehmann's, Williams-Sonoma,** and **Pottery Barn** are within walking distance on 7th Avenue. Farther west, between 10th and 11th avenues, an expanding array of art galleries is increasing foot traffic in what had been the desolate fringe of Chelsea.

Herald Square

Reasonable prices prevail at this intersection of 34th Street and Avenue of the Americas (6th Avenue). Giant **Macy's** has traditionally been the linchpin. Opposite is **Toys "R" Us** (⊠ 1293 Broadway, at 34th St.). Next door on 6th Avenue, the seven-story Manhattan Mall is anchored by **Stern's** department store (⊠ 899 6th Ave., at 33rd St.), which is good for bargain browsing, as are **Lechter's** (⊠ 10 W. 34th St., between 5th and 6th Aves., and other locations) for housewares, and **HMV,** for its large music selection.

5th Avenue

Fifth Avenue from Central Park South to Rockefeller Center still wavers between the money-no-object crowd and an influx of more accessible stores. Designer big guns like **Prada** and **A/X Armani Exchange** shouldered their way in, in 1998, as did the über-chain **Gap** and a retail newcomer, the **NBA Store.** The perennial favorites will eat up a lot of shoe leather: **F.A.O. Schwarz** and **Bergdorf Goodman,** at 58th Street; **Tiffany** and **Bulgari** jewelers, at 57th Street; **Ferragamo** and other various luxury stores in **Trump Tower,** at 56th Street; **Henri Bendel,** across the street; **Takashimaya,** at 54th Street; **Cartier** jewelers, at 52nd Street; and so on down to the flag-bedecked **Saks Fifth Avenue,** at 50th Street. **Rockefeller Center** harbors smaller specialty shops, both along the outdoor promenade and in the revamped underground marketplace. Perhaps the splashiest opening was that of **Tuscan Square,** a restaurant-and-retail evocation of Tuscany. To the south, at 39th Street is the venerable **Lord & Taylor** department store.

57th Street

The short section of 57th Street between 5th and Madison Avenues is still settling down after the building frenzy of 1997. The coveted block is no longer limited to top-echelon fashion houses, as more affordable (and sizable) stores have set up shop. **NikeTown** and the **Tourneau TimeMachine** are now birds of a feather: Nike hawks high-tech sports equipment and Tourneau deals in glittering watches, but both lure customers in with video screens and batteries of gleaming display cases. Exclusive stores such as **Chanel, Burberrys, Escada,** and **Hermès** have closed ranks on the north side of the street, near Madison Avenue; an **Original Levi's Store** is just a few doors away. Above many of these jostling stores perch top art galleries such as **André Emmerich** and **Pace Wildenstein.** To the west of 5th Avenue are more humanly scaled shops, such as the **Compleat Strategist** game store (between 8th and 9th avenues), **Coliseum Books,** a very oak-paneled branch of **Rizzoli**'s bookstores, and **Paron Fabrics.**

Columbus Avenue

Between 66th and 86th streets, this former tenement district is now home to a decent shopping strip. Stores are mostly modern in design, upscale but not top-of-the-line; many are branches of familiar chain stores like Banana Republic. Still, you can find some not-too-prevalent places, like **Nautica** (⊠ 216 Columbus, at 70th St.) for sport and prepster menswear and the **Maraolo** factory store for discounted office-worthy shoes. If you venture west to Broadway between 80th and 81st streets, you'll find the wonderful **Gryphon** used bookstore.

Madison Avenue

Madison Avenue, roughly between 57th and 79th streets, can satisfy almost any couture craving. A deluge of international designer stores arrived in 1996–97—including Giorgio Armani, Dolce & Gabbana, and Prada—but newcomers are continuing to open. At press time, New York's hometown designer Donna Karan had started construction on the world's first DKNY store at the corner of 60th and Madison, while Cerruti readied its flagship between 66th and 67th streets. The majority of these flagships engulf much larger spaces than traditional, one-level Madison boutiques; still, some smaller boutiques such as Agnona (for wool and cashmere) were able to squeeze in. Madison isn't just a fashion funnel, however; there are several outstanding antiques and art dealers as well.

Blitz Tours

Get your MetroCard ready and save enough cash for cab fare to lug all your packages home from these shopping itineraries. They're arranged by special interest; addresses, if not included here, can be found in the store listings below.

Antiques

Spend two hours at the **Manhattan Art & Antiques Center,** on 2nd Avenue at 55th Street; then swing over to 57th Street for an even posher array of European, American, and Asian treasures. Stroll westward across 57th Street, stopping at **Lillian Nassau,** of Tiffany lamp and Art Nouveau furniture fame, and **Israel Sack,** nearby on 5th Avenue, with superb American antique furniture. Then head up Madison to **Didier Aaron** (on 67th Street), **Stair & Company** (near 74th Street), **DeLorenzo** and **Leo Kaplan** (near 75th Street), **Florian Papp** (at 76th Street), **Leigh Keno** (near 76th Street), and **Barry Friedman** (at 83rd Street).

Bargains

Start early at **Century 21** and **Syms** in lower Manhattan. Take a cab to Hester and Orchard streets and shop along Orchard Street to Houston Street; be sure to stop in at **Klein's of Monticello.** (Prowl along Grand Street if you're more interested in goods for your home than in clothing.) By mid-afternoon take a cab to Chelsea; shop the Chelsea discounters—**Old Navy, Bed, Bath & Beyond, Moe Ginsburg,** and others, for everything from clothes to housewares; then tackle **Loehmann's,** which has men's clothes as well as women's. A reminder: On Saturday, most Lower East Side shops are closed.

Home Furnishings

For a French accent, start at the luscious, two-story **La Maison Moderne** (☒ 144 W. 19th St.), which has gorgeous bibelots. Walk east on 19th Street to **ABC Carpet & Home** on Broadway; this phenomenal emporium could eat up hours on end, so keep an eye on the time and move on to Greenwich Village to **William-Wayne & Co.** for elegant decorative items, often with a whiff of the exotic. If your bags aren't too heavy yet, head down to SoHo, making sure not to miss an irresistible trio: **Wolfman-Gold & Good, Moss,** and **Zona.** For cross-cultural finds, walk east and poke around the pocket-size boutiques on Elizabeth Street between Houston and Spring streets. Cab it back uptown to **Crate & Barrel** for great lower-priced selections and finally head over to **Bloomingdale's,** open late on Thursday, or to **Macy's,** open late Monday, Thursday, and Friday.

Close-up

THE FOOD LOVERS' NONPAREIL MANHATTAN BLITZ TOUR

ATTENTION FOODIES! There's no time to waste, as Manhattan has more destinations for food lovers than ever before. Start early to cover downtown by lunchtime. Begin in Chinatown, at **Kam-Man** (⊠ 200 Canal St., ☎ 212/571–0330), packed with dried squid, steamed bread, edible birds' nests, and dried shark fins. Next stop: **Mott Street** (below Grand Street), where markets and stalls sell ginger root, vegetables, meat, and live fish. Egyptian mint leaves, sun-dried Japanese *kombu* (seaweed), and Jamaican jerk seasoning perfume **SoHo Provisions** (⊠ 518 Broadway, ☎ 212/334–4311). Up the street, brilliantly white **Dean & DeLuca** (⊠ 560 Broadway, ☎ 212/431–1691) artfully displays intriguing produce and prepared food like horned melons and stuffed quail; gleaming racks of cookware are in back. For more affordable kitchen gear, try **Broadway Panhandler** (⊠ 477 Broome St., ☎ 212/966–3434), where Calphalon, Le Creuset, and other professional-level makers are priced lower than retail.

Monday, Wednesday, Friday, and Saturday mornings, farmers and other food producers arrive at dawn at the **Union Square Greenmarket** bearing organic produce, flowers, homemade bread, preserves, fish, and seasonal fare. A few blocks away in the West Village, the ceilings of **Balducci's** (⊠ 424 6th Ave., ☎ 212/673–2600) are hung with strings of garlic, onions, and woven baskets, while below, pasta, dark green frills of herbs, and hearty prepared dishes beckon. A square block of foodie heaven, **Chelsea Market** (☎ 75 9th Ave., ☎ 212/243–6005) is home to butchers, bakers, and a dozen other specialty food purveyors. For professional-kitchen-quality equipment, visit nearby **Lamalle Kitchenwares** (⊠ 36 W. 25th St., ☎ 212/242–0750).

The next two destinations require a subway or taxi ride. **Macy's Cellar** (⊠ Herald Sq., 34th St. and 6th Ave., ☎ 212/695–4400) is a great place to rummage through gadgets. Farther uptown, at **Zabar's** (⊠ 2245 Broadway, ☎ 212/787–2000), grab a loaf of the fabled bread, examine the smoked fish and cheeses, and head upstairs to the well-priced kitchenware section.

IF YOU'VE STILL GOT TIME, head over to the East Side; these stores also make a fine minitour. On weekdays order an enchanting fruit basket from **Manhattan Fruitier** (⊠ 105 E. 29th St., ☎ 212/686–0404). At **Bridge Kitchenware** (⊠ 214 E. 52nd St., ☎ 212/688–4220), a dusty, unpretentious hideaway, you can scoop up tiny ramekins and countless doodads. Farther uptown, the **Vinegar Factory** (⊠ 431 E. 91st St., ☎ 212/987–0885) carries bread from the *other* Zabar brother, Eli, who sells a great selection of vinegar and oils, plus fresh produce, cheese, kitchenware, and has a loft space for weekend brunch. At press time, a second branch was underway at 80th Street and Third Avenue. Nearby, the **Kitchen Arts & Letters** bookstore (⊠ 1435 Lexington Ave., ☎ 212/876–5550) has thousands of cookbooks and other titles on food and wine. For a fitting conclusion, head back down to **Payard** (⊠ 1032 Lexington Ave., ☎ 212/717–5252), a glossy, Parisian-perfect pâtisserie where you can sample impeccable pastries and pick up elegant chocolates or hard-to-find *pâtes de fruits* (fruit jellies).

–Jennifer Paull

Department Stores

Most of these stores keep regular hours on weekdays and are open late (until 8 or 9) at least one night a week. Many have personal shoppers who can walk you through the store at no charge.

Barneys New York. Like a true gentleman, Barneys does not betray its financial woes (the bankrupt, formerly family-owned company was bought out in 1997). The original Chelsea space may have closed, but the Madison Avenue branch continues to spin cocoons of couture. The extensive menswear selection has introduced a handful of edgier designers such as Alexander McQueen. (Made-to-measure is always available.) The women's department is a showcase of cachet names like Armani, Jil Sander, and Helmut Lang. ✉ *660 Madison Ave.,* ☎ *212/826–8900; World Financial Center,* ☎ *212/945–1600.*

Bergdorf Goodman. Good taste reigns in an elegant and understated setting; you can visit the salon in the former Goodman family penthouse apartment. Remember that elegant doesn't necessarily mean sedate—Bergdorf's carries some brilliant, exclusive (or almost) lines such as Philip Treacy's dramatic hats and accessories or the ultracolorful clothes by Voyage. The home department has rooms full of wonderful linens, tableware, and gifts. The expanded men's store, across the street, is the perfect companion. ✉ *754 5th Ave.; men's store:* ✉ *745 5th Ave.,* ☎ *212/753–7300.*

Bloomingdale's. Only a handful of department stores occupy an entire city block; Macy's is one, and this New York institution is another. The main floor is a stupefying maze of cosmetic counters, mirrors, and black walls. Get past this, and you'll find some good buys on dependable designers, bedding, and housewares. Don't mind the harried salespeople or none-too-subtle promotions—chalk it up to the Bloomie's experience. ✉ *1000 3rd Ave.,* ☎ *212/355–5900.*

Henri Bendel. In 1997 Bendel's introduced a surprising new clothing design team—its own. Although most department stores focus on dozens of high-profile labels, Bendel's now showcases its luxurious in-house lines. (Other designers, such as Michael Kors and Jean-Paul Gaultier, are still available.) Shoe lovers should be forewarned that there is no footwear department. To console yourself, visit the wonderful tearoom on the second floor; try to get a table near the Lalique windows. ✉ *712 5th Ave.,* ☎ *212/247–1100.*

Lord & Taylor. Though a bit faded, Lord & Taylor is a stronghold of classic American-designer clothes. Instead of unpronounceable labels, you'll find Dana Buchman, Jones New York, and a lot of casual wear; there are also lines by Donna Karan (though nothing too revealing). It's refined, comfortably conservative, and never overwhelming. ✉ *424 5th Ave., between 38th and 39th Sts.,* ☎ *212/391–3344.*

Macy's. Macy's main store claims to be the largest retail store in America. Its ongoing renovation is sprucing up departments one by one—expect to be rerouted at least once and totally lose your bearings at least twice. Fashion-wise, there's a concentration on the mainstream rather than the luxe; there's no couture, but there are some extravagant doodads like Mont Blanc pens. For cooking gear and housewares, the Cellar nearly outdoes Zabar's. ✉ *Herald Sq., Broadway at 34th St.,* ☎ *212/695–4400.*

Pearl River Mart. From the street, the entrance to this sizeable Asian department store looks like a typical Canal Street faux-handbag shop. Upstairs, however, are three floors packed with everything from tatami slippers to sacks of rice, parasols, lanterns, masks, videos, and Western drugstore-type goods—and it's all pretty cheap. Rows of noodles, dried seaweed, and sugarcane juice fill the food section. This is definitely the place to get faux-silk brocade clothes; a long Mandarin-style dress will run $70–$100. ✉ *277 Canal St.,* ☎ *212/431–4770.*

Saks Fifth Avenue. A fashion-only department store, Saks sells an astonishing array of apparel. Although the stock is not absolutely cutting edge, the roster of American and European designers is impressive—the women's selection includes Issey Miyake, Richard Tyler, and Marc Jacobs, plus devastating ball gowns galore. The men's department is strongest in conservative styles: Oxford Clothes, Alan Flusser, and the like. ✉ *611 5th Ave.,* ☎ *212/753–4000.*

Shanghai Tang. Redefining the idea of "Made in China," flashy entrepreneur David Tang has created a store filled with electric colors and irreverent takes on Chinese cultural symbols. The clothing's Asian styling is equally inventive: Cotton sweaters come with frogging, silk or cashmere jackets are done in egg-yolk yellow or hot pink (as well as black). Although it offers everything from children's clothes to custom tailoring, the store's intimate scale keeps it from being overwhelming. ✉ *667 Madison Ave.,* ☎ *212/888–0111.*

Takashimaya New York. This pristine branch of Japan's largest department store carries stylish clothes and fine household items, all of which reflect a combination of Eastern and Western designs. In the Tea Box downstairs, you can have a *bento* box lunch in the serene, softly lighted tearoom or stock up on green tea. The gardening-section–cum–front-window-display is one of 5th Avenue's most refreshing sights. ✉ *693 5th Ave.,* ☎ *212/350–0100.*

Discount

Century 21. For many New Yorkers, this is the mother lode of discount shopping. Three large floors are crammed with everything from Helmut Lang T-shirts to Ralph Lauren bedding—on a good day it may seem to lack nothing but a nice, private dressing room. Men's merchandise is less pawed-over than the women's; Moschino shirts, Katharine Hamnet denim pants, and Calvin Klein sport coats are typical goods and often half price. An unharmed Martine Sitbon jacket for $100 (down from $1,150) is a typical terrific deal for women. Don't pass up lingerie, where you can find Valentino silks. The basement linens department has choice buys on pure cotton sheets, wool blankets, even satin sheets, but watch for IRREGULAR stickers. Cosmetics are the only goods not directly discounted, but a purchase elicits coupons good for deductions on other store merchandise. ✉ *22 Cortlandt St., between Broadway and Church St.,* ☎ *212/227–9092.*

Specialty Shops

Many specialty stores have several branches in the city; in those cases, we have listed the locations in the busier shopping neighborhoods.

Antiques

Antiquing is fine sport in Manhattan. Goods run the gamut from rarefied museum-quality to wacky and eminently affordable. Premier shopping areas are on Madison Avenue north of 57th Street, 57th Street east of 5th Avenue, and 60th Street between 2nd and 3rd avenues, where more than 20 shops, dealing in everything from 18th-century French furniture to Art Deco lighting fixtures, cluster on one block. Around 11th and 12th streets between University Place and Broadway a tantalizing array of settees, bedsteads, and rocking chairs can be seen in the windows of about two dozen dealers, many of whom have TO THE TRADE signs on their doors; a card from your architect or decorator, however, may get you inside. Most dealers are open on Saturday.

Many small dealers cluster in three antiques "malls."

Chelsea Antiques Building. With a full 12 floors of antiques and collectibles, the options run the gamut from antique books to vintage Georg Jensen silver to lunch boxes. ✉ *110 W. 25th St., between 6th and 7th Aves.,* ☎ *212/929–0909.*

Manhattan Art & Antiques Center. Art Nouveau perfume bottles and samovars, samurai swords, pewter pitchers, and much more fill 100-plus galleries. The level of quality is not, as a rule, up to that of Madison Avenue, but then neither are the prices. ✉ *1050 2nd Ave., between 55th and 56th Sts.,* ☎ *212/355–4400.*

Metropolitan Arts and Antiques Pavilion. Good for costume jewelry, offbeat bric-a-brac, and '50s kitsch, this antiques mall holds regularly scheduled auctions and specialty shows featuring rare books, photography, tribal art, Victoriana, and other lots. ✉ *110 W. 19th St., between 6th Ave. and 7th Aves.,* ☎ *212/463–0200.*

AMERICAN AND ENGLISH

Beshar's. Among the English and American antiques here are a sprinkling of Asian pieces—as well as a good Asian rug selection. ✉ *1513 1st Ave., at 79th St.,* ☎ *212/288–1998.*

City Barn Antiques. Come for your fill of Heywood-Wakefield originals (many refinished) and streamlined pieces from the '30s to the '50s. ✉ *269 Lafayette St.,* ☎ *212/941–5757.*

Florian Papp. The shine of gilt—on ormolu clocks, chaise longues, and marble top tables—lures customers in, but this store has an unassailed reputation among knowledgeable collectors. ✉ *962 Madison Ave.,* ☎ *212/288–6770.*

Hyde Park Antiques. This store features English decorative arts from the 18th and 19th centuries. ✉ *836 Broadway, between 12th and 13th Sts.,* ☎ *212/477–0033.*

Israel Sack. This is widely considered one of the very best places in the country for 18th-century American furniture. ✉ *730 5th Ave.,* ☎ *212/399–6562.*

Kentshire Galleries. Elegant furniture in room settings is displayed on eight floors, with an emphasis on formal English pieces from the early 18th and 19th centuries, particularly the Georgian and Regency periods. ✉ *37 E. 12th St., between University Pl. and Broadway,* ☎ *212/673–6644.*

Leigh Keno American Antiques. Before he was 30, Leigh Keno set an auction record in the American antiques field by paying $2.75 million for a hairy-paw-foot Philadelphia wing chair. He has a good eye and an interesting inventory. ✉ *980 Madison Ave.,* ☎ *212/734–2381.*

Stair & Company. Period rooms stylishly show off fine 18th- and 19th-century English mahogany and other pieces. ✉ *942 Madison Ave.,* ☎ *212/517–4400.*

Steve Miller American Folk Art. This gallery is run by one of the country's premier folk-art dealers, the author of ✉ *The Art of the Weathervane.* ✉ *17 E. 96th St., between Madison and 5th Aves.,* ☎ *212/348–5219.*

Thomas K. Woodard. Americana and antique quilts are among the specialties of this prestigious dealer. ✉ *506 E. 74th St., between York Ave. and FDR Dr.,* ☎ *212/794–9404.*

ECLECTIC

Newel Art Galleries. Near the East Side's interior-design district, this is the city's biggest antiques store, with a huge collection that roams from the Renaissance to the 20th century. ✉ *425 E. 53rd St., between 1st Ave. and Sutton Pl.,* ☎ *212/758–1970.*

EUROPEAN

Barry Friedman. Wiener Werkstätte, Bauhaus, De Stijl, Russian Constructivist, and other European avant-garde movements star. ✉ *32 E. 67th St., between Park and Madison Aves.,* ☎ *212/794–8950.*

DeLorenzo. Come here for the sinuous curves and highly polished surfaces of French Art Deco furniture and accessories. ✉ *958 Madison Ave., between 75th and 76th Sts.,* ☎ *212/249–7575.*

Didier Aaron. This highly esteemed gallery specializes in superb 18th- and 19th-century French furniture and paintings. ✉ *32 E. 67th St.,* ☎ *212/988–5248.*

L'Antiquaire & The Connoisseur, Inc. Proprietress Helen Fioratti has written a guide to French antiques, but she is equally knowledgeable about the Italian and Spanish furniture and decorative objects from the 15th through the 18th centuries, as well as the medieval arts, that compose her stock. ✉ *36 E. 73rd St.,* ☎ *212/517–9176.*

Leo Kaplan Ltd. The impeccable items here include Art Nouveau glass and pottery, porcelain from 18th-century England, stunning antique and modern paperweights, and Russian artwork. ✉ *967 Madison Ave.,* ☎ *212/249–6766.*

Malmaison Antiques. The country's largest selection of Empire furniture and decorative arts is sold at this gallery. ✉ *253 E. 74th St., between 2nd and 3rd Aves.,* ☎ *212/288–7569.*

Pierre Deux Antiques. The company that brought French provincial to a provincial America still offers an excellent selection. ✉ *369 Bleecker St., at Charles St.,* ☎ *212/243–7740.*

FUN STUFF

Back Pages Antiques. To acquire a restored antique jukebox or slot machine, just drop in—or rather, down, since this is on the basement level. ✉ *125 Greene St.,* ☎ *212/460–5998.*

Darrow's Fun Antiques. The first of the city's nostalgia shops, the store is full of whimsy: antique toys, animation art, and other collectibles. ✉ *1101 1st Ave., between 60th and 61st Sts.,* ☎ *212/838–0730.*

Art Galleries

America's art capital, New York has thousands of wealthy collectors, so many galleries are essentially minimuseums that welcome browsing. Some midtown buildings along 5th Avenue and 57th Street offer floor after floor of galleries; in the Fuller Building, at 57th Street and Madison Avenue, for example, you can let the golden Deco elevators whisk you from Calder mobiles to contemporary Latin American art. Be sure to delve into Chelsea's thriving art scene (in the low '20s between 10th and 11th avenues), where former warehouses and storage facilities allow for striking large-scale installations; there are now 20 galleries and counting. Call ahead for hours since some galleries run on "SoHo time" (Tuesday–Saturday) and some on "Chelsea time" (Wednesday–Sunday). A helpful resource is the Art Now *Gallery Guide,* available in most galleries.

CHELSEA

See also Chelsea *in* Chapter 2.

Bonakdor Jancou Gallery. Part of the Soho-to-Chelsea shift, this gallery continues to show intriguing artists such as Uta Barth. ✉ *521 W. 21st St., between 10th and 11th Aves.,* ☎ *212/414–4144.*

Matthew Marks Gallery. Marks shows prominent modern artists such as Ellsworth Kelly. On 24th Street a two-story former garage is newly divided among three noteworthy dealers collectively nicknamed MGM: Matthew Marks, Barbara Gladstone, and Metro Pictures. ✉ *522 W. 22nd St., between 10th and 11th Aves.,* ☎ *212/243–0200;* ✉ *523 W. 24th St., between 10th and 11th Aves.,* ☎ *212/243–0200.*

Pat Hearn Gallery. Emerging and established artists are showcased here. A recent exhibit showed the collaborative paintings of William S. Burroughs and George Condo. ✉ *530 W. 22nd St., between 10th and 11th Aves.,* ☎ *212/727–7366.*

Paula Cooper Gallery. A SoHo groundbreaker, Cooper has moved to a grand new space in Chelsea, complete with skylights, wood-beamed ceilings, a bookstore—and a vast main gallery room big enough for installations like Sol LeWitt's *Four-Sided Pyramid.* ✉ *534 W. 21st St., between 10th and 11th Aves.,* ☎ *212/255–1105.*

57TH STREET/MIDTOWN

André Emmerich Gallery. This gallery in the Art Deco Fuller Building displays first-rate works by major modern artists such as Man Ray. ✉ *41 E. 57th St.,* ☎ *212/752–0124.*

David Findlay Jr. Fine Art. Although the uptown gallery handles mostly European painters (☞ Upper East Side, *below*), this branch concentrates on American 19th- and 20th-century artists from John Singer Sargent to Arthur Dove to Andrew Wyeth. ✉ *41 E. 57th St.,* ☎ *212/486–7660.*

Edwynn Houk Gallery. Houk's impressive stable of 20th-century photographers includes such artists as Sally Mann, Lynn Davis, and Brassaï; it also shows prints by masters like Edward Weston and Alfred Steiglitz. ✉ *745 5th Ave.,* ☎ *212/750–7070.*

Joseph Helman. Contemporary art by Brian Hunt, Robert Moskowitz, Joe Andoe, and Ellsworth Kelly, among others, is displayed here. ✉ *20 W. 57th St.,* ☎ *212/245–2888.*

Mary Boone Gallery. A hot gallery from the '80s, this venue is now uptown and still intriguing, with such artists as Barbara Kruger. ✉ *745 5th Ave.,* ☎ *212/752–2929.*

O'Hara Gallery. Another of the Fuller Building crowd, this space has works by Andy Warhol, Jean Michel Basquiat, Picasso, and Boris Zaborov. ✉ *41 E. 57th St.,* ☎ *212/355–3330.*

Pace Wildenstein. This large white display space focuses on such modern and contemporary artists as Piet Mondrian, Julian Schnabel, and New York School painter Ad Reinhardt. Upstairs is Pace Prints (☎ 212/421–3237), where you can rifle through open racks of prints and multiples by artists like Richard Diebenkorn, David Hockney, and Kiki Smith. Pace Master Prints (☎ 212/421–3688), also here, has works by Tiepolo, Goya, and Matisse. ✉ *32 E. 57th St.,* ☎ *212/421–3292.*

Peter Findlay Gallery. Covering 19th- and 20th-century works by American and European artists, this gallery shows pieces by Mary Cassatt, Paul Klee, and Alberto Giacometti. ✉ *41 E. 57th St.,* ☎ *212/644–4433.*

Spanierman Gallery. More than a half century old and now in handsome quarters, this gallery deals in 19th- and early 20th-century American painting and sculpture. ✉ *45 E. 58th St.,* ☎ *212/832–0208.*

Tibor de Nagy Gallery. The contemporary shows here include work by Arthur Dove, Georgia O'Keeffe, Allen Ginsberg, and Trevor Winkfield. ✉ *724 5th Ave.,* ☎ *212/262–5050.*

SOHO/TRIBECA

Art in General. Works in a variety of media by emerging contemporary artists are brokered through this nonprofit organization (it puts you in touch with the artist rather than selling directly from the exhibitions). ✉ *79 Walker St., between Broadway and Lafayette St.,* ☎ *212/219–0473.*

A Clean, Well-Lighted Place. Drop in here for prints by well-known artists, including Sean Scully, Susan Rothenberg, Robert Motherwell, and David Hockney. ✉ *363 Bleecker St., at Charles St.,* ☎ *212/255–3656.*

David Zwirner. Strong proof that SoHo's art scene still has some lifeblood, this gallery has very high-caliber contemporary shows. ✉ *43 Greene St.,* ☎ *212/966–9074.*

First Peoples Gallery. Paintings, sculpture, and magnificent pottery by many of the country's top Native American artists are showcased here. ✉ *114 Spring St.,* ☎ *212/343–0166.*

Holly Solomon Gallery. Solomon's foresight is legendary—she was an early champion of photographer Robert Mapplethorpe. Now artists such as William Wegman and Nick Waplington are represented. ✉ *172 Mercer St.,* ☎ *212/941–5777.*

Leo Castelli. The man who put pop in the national consciousness continues to represent Jasper Johns, Roy Lichtenstein, Ed Ruscha, and Ed Rosenquist. ✉ *420 W. Broadway,* ☎ *212/431–5160.*

Multiple Impressions. Twentieth-century American, European, Asian, and South American paintings and prints are offered here at reasonable prices. ✉ *128 Spring St.,* ☎ *212/925–1313.*

O. K. Harris. The oldest gallery in SoHo, opened in 1969, O. K. Harris showcases paintings, sculpture, and photography by contemporary artists. ✉ *383 W. Broadway,* ☎ *212/431–3600.*

UPPER EAST SIDE

David Findlay. Descend into a warren of rooms to view contemporary, color-soaked paintings. Represented artists include Pierre Lesieur, Roger Mühl, and (for a striking slice of the New York streets) Tom Christopher. ✉ *984 Madison Ave.,* ☎ *212/249–2909.*

Gagosian. Works on display are by such established artists as Richard Serra, Willem de Kooning, and Jasper Johns. ✉ *980 Madison Ave., 6th floor,* ☎ *212/744–2313;* ✉ *136 Wooster St.,* ☎ *212/228–2828.*

Hirschl & Adler. Although this gallery has a selection of European works, it is best known for its American paintings, prints, and decorative arts. Among the celebrated artists whose works are featured: Thomas Cole, Frederick Childe Hassam, John Storrs, and William Merritt Chase. ✉ *21 E. 70th St.,* ☎ *212/535–8810.*

Isselbacher. This gallery offers prints by late-19th- and 20th-century masters such as Henri Matisse, Marc Chagall, Joan Miró, Pablo Picasso, and Edvard Munch. Call ahead for an appointment. ✉ *64 E. 86th St.,* ☎ *212/472–1766.*

James Danziger Gallery. Having moved to this second-story space in early 1998, Danziger continues to show the work of *très* high profile photographers; they're the exclusive representative for Annie Leibovitz and the Cecil Beaton estate. Prints by Ansel Adams, Richard Avedon, and Edward Weston are also available. ✉ *851 Madison Ave.,* ☎ *212/734–5300.*

Jane Kahan Gallery. Besides ceramics by Picasso (this gallery's specialty), you'll see works by 19th- and 20th-century artists like Henri de Toulouse-Lautrec, Jean Arp, and Jean Dubuffet. ✉ *922 Madison Ave.,* ☎ *212/744–1490.*

Knoedler & Company. Knoedler helped many great American collectors, including Henry Clay Frick, start their collections. Now their represented artists include Helen Frankenthaler, Robert Motherwell, and Frank Stella. ✉ *19 E. 70th St.,* ☎ *212/794–0550.*

Margo Feiden Galleries. Illustrations by theatrical caricaturist Al Hirschfeld, who has been delighting readers of the *New York Times* for more than 60 years, are the draw here. ✉ *699 Madison Ave.,* ☎ *212/677–5330.*

Wildenstein & Co. This branch of the Wildenstein art empire was the first to take root in New York; its reputation for brilliant holdings was cemented by the acquisition of significant private collections. Look for Old Master and Impressionist exhibitions. ✉ *19 E. 64th St.,* ☎ *212/879–0500.*

Beauty

Aveda Aromatherapy Esthetique (✉ 509 Madison Ave., ☎ 212/832–2416; 456 W. Broadway, ☎ 212/473–0280); **Aveda Environmental Lifestyle Store** (✉ 140 5th Ave., at 19th St., ☎ 212/645–4797). Natural ingredients and plant extracts are the hallmarks of Aveda's shampoos and hair treatments. You can concoct your own perfumes from the impressive selection of essential oils.

Caswell-Massey. The original displays its toiletries in polished old cases; branches are in the World Financial Center and at South Street Seaport. All stores sell headily scented scrubs, soaps, creams, and other bath supplies. ✉ *518 Lexington Ave., at 48th St.,* ☎ *212/755–2254;* ✉ *155 Spring St.,* ☎ *212/219–3661.*

Face Stockholm. Besides the pretty pastels and neutrals, Face carries some brazenly colored nail polish (emerald green, sky blue) and little pots of jewel-tone glitter. ✉ *110 Prince St.,* ☎ *212/966–9110;* ✉ *224 Columbus Ave., at 70th St.,* ☎ *212/769–1420.*

Floris. Floral English toiletries beloved of the British royals fill this re-creation of the cozy London original. There's also a nice selection of shaving sets. ✉ *703 Madison Ave.,* ☎ *212/935–9100.*

Kiehl's. At this favored haunt of top models and stylists, white-smocked assistants can advise you on the relative merits of the skin lotions and hair potions, all packaged in disarmingly simple bottles (prices are on a list distributed near the doorway). ✉ *109 3rd Ave., between 13th and 14th Sts.,* ☎ *212/677–3171.*

L'Occitane. Extra mild soaps, shampoos, and creams here pack an olfactory punch with Provençal scents (think sage, thyme, and the ever-present lavender). ✉ *1046 Madison Ave.,* ☎ *212/639–9185;* ✉ *146 Spring St.,* ☎ *212/343–0109;* ✉ *198 Columbus Ave.,* ☎ *212/362–5146.*

MAC. Fashion hounds pack this angularly designed boutique, where the latest color or gloss can sell out fast (try department store counters instead). ✉ *113 Spring St.,* ☎ *212/334–4641.*

Books

Manhattan is the epicenter of the nation's book and magazine publishing industries and supports dozens of bookstores, small and large. All the big national chains—**Barnes & Noble, Borders,** and **Waldenbooks**—are here, with branches all over town.

Biography Bookshop. Published diaries, letters, biographies, and autobiographies fill this neighborly store. ✉ *400 Bleecker St., at W. 11th St.,* ☎ *212/807–8655.*

Coliseum Books. This supermarket of a bookstore has a huge, quirky selection of remainders, best-sellers, and scholarly works. ✉ *1771 Broadway, at 57th St.,* ☎ *212/757–8381.*

Crawford Doyle Booksellers. You're as likely to see the Riverside Shakespeare or an old edition of Czech fairy tales as a best-seller in the window of this shop. There's a thoughtful selection of fiction, nonfiction, biographies, etc., plus some rare books on the tight-fit upstairs balcony. Salespeople proffer their opinions *and* ask for yours. ✉ *1082 Madison Ave.,* ☎ *212/288–6300.*

Gotham Book Mart. The late Frances Steloff opened this store in 1920 with just $200 in her pocket, half of it on loan. But she helped launch James Joyce's *Ulysses,* D. H. Lawrence, and Henry Miller and is now legendary among bibliophiles—as is her bookstore. ✉ *41 W. 47th St., between 5th and 6th Aves.,* ☎ *212/719–4448.*

Librairie de France/Libraria Hispanica. These collections of foreign-language books, videos, and periodicals, some in exotic tongues, are among the country's largest. Books in French and Spanish predominate. ✉ *610 5th Ave., in Rockefeller Center,* ☎ *212/581–8810.*

Madison Avenue Bookshop. This bona fide neighborhood store bursts with books, which are stacked everywhere—on the floor, on top of bookcases, even on the narrow winding staircase. You can find everything from coffee-table photo books to the latest biographies to a good pulper. ✉ *833 Madison Ave.,* ☎ *212/535–6130.*

Rizzoli. Uptown, an elegant marble entrance, oak paneling, chandeliers, and classical music accompany books and magazines on art, architecture, dance, design, photography, and travel; the downtown stores come with fewer frills, though the SoHo location has a quirky gift shop. The latest branch is in the Sotheby's building. ✉ *31 W. 57th St.,* ☎ *212/759–2424;* ✉ *454 W. Broadway,* ☎ *212/674–1616;* ✉ *World Financial Center,* ☎ *212/385–1400; 1334 York Ave., at 72nd St.,* ☎ *212/606–7434.*

Shakespeare & Co. The stock here represents what's happening in publishing today in just about every field. Late hours at the downtown location (till midnight on Saturday, 11 PM the rest of the week) are a plus. ✉ *939 Lexington Ave., between 68th and 69th Sts.,* ☎ *212/570–0201;* ✉ *716 Broadway, at Washington Pl.,* ☎ *212/529–1330.*

Three Lives & Co. At a picture-perfect West Village corner, Three Lives has one of the city's most impeccable selection of books. The display tables and counters highlight the latest literary fiction and serious nonfiction, classics, quirky gift books, and gorgeously illustrated tomes. ✉ *154 W. 10th St., at Waverly Pl.,* ☎ *212/741–2069.*

GAY AND LESBIAN

A Different Light. The city's preeminent gay and lesbian store is one of the nation's largest, with a huge selection of fiction, nonfiction, periodicals, calendars, and posters. Free local periodicals and fliers by the door are a great source of information about gay life and happenings citywide. A café and a downstairs gallery (where readings and other events are held nightly—the Sunday-night movie series is popular) are other pluses, and it's open daily until midnight. ✉ *151 W. 19th St., between 6th and 7th Aves.,* ☎ *212/989–4850.*

Oscar Wilde Memorial Bookshop. Opened in 1967, this was the first gay and lesbian bookstore in the city. It's just steps from the site of the Stonewall riots. ✉ *15 Christopher St., between 6th and 7th Aves.,* ☎ *212/255–8097.*

MUSIC

Carl Fischer. The landmark East Village store is famous for its excellent selection of sheet music for all instruments, including music for choir and band. ✉ *62 Cooper Sq., between 7th and 8th Sts.,* ☎ *212/777–0900.*

Joseph Patelson Music House. A huge collection of scores has long made this the heart of the music lover's New York. ✉ *160 W. 56th St., between 6th and 7th Aves.,* ☎ *212/582–5840.*

MYSTERY AND SUSPENSE

Murder Ink. Mystery lovers have relied on this Upper West Side institution for years; ask the knowledgeable staff for recommendations. ✉ *2486 Broadway, between 92nd and 93rd Sts.,* ☎ *212/362–8905.*

Mysterious Bookshop. Come to this atmospheric shop to uncover one of the largest selections of mystery, suspense and detective fiction in the city—new, used, and out-of-print volumes, as well as first editions. ✉ *129 W. 56th St., between 6th and 7th Aves.,* ☎ *212/765–0900.*

Partners & Crime. Imported British paperbacks, helpful staff, a rental library, and whodunits galore—new, out-of-print, and first editions—make this a must-browse for fans. Revered mystery writers give readings here. Check out the "radio mystery hour" on Saturday evenings. ✉ *44 Greenwich Ave., between 10th and 11th Sts.,* ☎ *212/243–0440.*

RARE AND USED BOOKS

Academy Book Store. Out-of-print, used, antiquarian, scholarly, and art books overflow here. Academy also deals with autographs and carries a selection of classical and jazz records and CDs. ✉ *10 W. 18th St., between 5th and 6th Aves.,* ☎ *212/242–4848.*

Archivia. The shop stocks new, used, and out-of-print books on all sorts of design and decorative arts. ✉ *944 Madison Ave.,* ☎ *212/439–9194.*

Argosy Bookstore. This sedate landmark, established in 1921, keeps a scholarly stock of books and autographs. It's also a great place to look for low-priced maps and prints. ✉ *116 E. 59th St.,* ☎ *212/753–4455.*

Bauman Rare Books. This successful Philadelphia firm now offers New Yorkers the most impossible-to-get titles, first editions, and fine leather sets. ✉ *Waldorf-Astoria, lobby level, 301 Park Ave., at 50th St.,* ☎ *212/759–8300.*

Gryphon. This narrow, wonderfully crammed space is a book lover's lifesaver in the otherwise sparse Upper West Side. Squeeze in among the stacks of art books and fiction; clamber up the steep stairway, and you'll find all sorts of rare books, including the Oz series. ✉ *2246 Broadway, between 80th and 81st Sts.,* ☎ *212/362–0706.*

J. N. Bartfield. A legend in the field offers old and antiquarian books distinguished by binding, author, edition, or content. ✉ *30 W. 57th St., 3rd floor,* ☎ *212/245–8890.*

Pageant Book and Print Shop. This old, reliable shop carries a broad selection of used books, prints, and maps. ✉ *114 W. Houston St.,* ☎ *212/674–5296.*

Skyline Books & Records, Inc. Come here for out-of-print and unusual books in all fields. The store handles literary first editions, as well as jazz and rock records. ✉ *13 W. 18th St., between 5th and 6th Aves.,* ☎ *212/675–4773.*

The Strand. The Broadway branch proudly claims to have 8 mi of books; craning your neck among the tall-as-trees stacks will likely net you something. Rare books are next door, at 826 Broadway, on the third floor. The Fulton Street branch is close to the South Street Seaport. ✉ *828 Broadway, at 12th St.,* ☎ *212/473–1452; 95 Fulton St.,* ☎ *212/732–6070.*

Cameras and Electronics

Bang & Olufsen. Bang & Olufsen stereos are unmistakable—slim, flat cases, with transparent doors that open when you reach toward them, displaying the whirling CDs inside. Loudspeakers and telephones share the ultramodern design. In the back of the store is a mock living room, where you can test the impressive surround sound. ✉ *952 Madison Ave.,* ☎ *212/879–6161.*

Harvey Electronics. A well-informed staff offers top-of-the-line audio equipment. ✉ *2 W. 45th St., between 5th and 6th Aves.,* ☎ *212/575–5000;* ✉ *888 Broadway, at 19th St., inside ABC Carpet & Home,* ☎ *212/982–7191.*

J&R Music and Computer World. J&R has emerged as the city's most competitively priced one-stop electronics outlet, with computers, video equipment, stereos, cameras, and small appliances; ☞ CDs, Tapes, and Records, *below.* ✉ *23 Park Row, between Beekman and Ann Sts.,* ☎ *212/238–9000.*

SONY Style. This audio and video equipment store comes in a glossy package—window displays are designed by artists like Kenneth Scharf and Maurice Sendak. Plunge into the blue-velvet-swathed downstairs area for a demonstration. ✉ *550 Madison Ave.,* ☎ *212/833–8800.*

Willoughby's. Calling itself the world's largest camera store, Willoughby's rates high among amateurs and pros for selection and service. ✉ *136 W. 32nd St., between 6th and 7th Aves.,* ☏ *212/564–1600.*

CDs, Tapes, and Records

The city's best record stores provide browsers with a window to New York's hipper subcultures. The East Village is especially good for dance tracks and used music.

Academy. You can walk into Academy with just $10 and walk out happy. The CDs, tapes, and records are well organized, low-price, and in good condition; sometimes they've never even been opened. ✉ *12 W. 18th St., between 5th and 6th Aves.,* ☏ *212/242–3000.*

Bleecker Bob's Golden Oldies. The staff sells punk, new wave, progressive rock, and reggae, plus good old rock on vinyl, until the wee hours. ✉ *118 W. 3rd St., at MacDougal St.,* ☏ *212/475–9677.*

Downstairs Records. This gold mine of old 45s is a good place to unearth original and reissued vinyl from the past four decades. ✉ *1026 6th Ave., between 38th and 39th Sts.,* ☏ *212/354–4684.*

Footlight Records. Stop here to browse through New York's largest selection of old and new musicals and movie soundtracks, as well as a good choice of jazz and American popular standards. ✉ *113 E. 12th St., between 3rd and 4th Aves.,* ☏ *212/533–1572.*

Gryphon Record Shop. One of the city's best rare-record stores, it stocks some 90,000 out-of-print and rare LPs. ✉ *233 W. 72nd St., between Broadway and West End Aves.,* ☏ *212/874–1588.*

HMV. These state-of-the-art record superstores stock hundreds of thousands of discs, tapes, and videos. ✉ *57 W. 34th St., at 6th Ave.,* ☏ *212/629–0900; 2081 Broadway, at 72nd St.,* ☏ *212/721–5900;* ✉ *1280 Lexington Ave., at 86th St.,* ☏ *212/348–0800;* ✉ *565 E. 46th St., at 5th Ave.,* ☏ *212/681–6700.*

House of Oldies. The specialty here is records made between 1950 and the late 1980s—45s and 78s, as well as LPs; there are more than a million titles. ✉ *35 Carmine St., between Bleecker St. and 6th Ave.,* ☏ *212/243–0500.*

Jazz Record Center. The city's only jazz-record specialist also stocks collectibles. ✉ *236 W. 26th St., 8th floor, between 7th and 8th Aves.,* ☏ *212/675–4480.*

J&R Music World. This store offers a huge selection, with good prices on major releases. Jazz recordings are sold at 25 Park Row, classical at No. 33. You can even buy music by telephone. ✉ *23 Park Row, between Beekman and Ann Sts.,* ☏ *212/732–8600.*

Kim's Video & Music. Scruffy and eclectic, Kim's is a compact crystallization of the downtown music scene. Their top-20 list is a long, long way from the Top 40; instead, there's a mix of electronica, jazz, lounge, and experimental. ✉ *6 St. Marks Pl., between 2nd and 3rd Aves.,* ☏ *212/598–9985;* ✉ *144 Bleecker St., between Thompson St. and La Guardia Pl.,* ☏ *212/260–1010;* ✉ *350 Bleecker St., at W. 10th St.,* ☏ *212/675–8996.*

Midnight Records. This rock specialist stocks obscure artists from the '50s onward. ✉ *263 W. 23rd St., between 7th and 8th Aves.,* ☏ *212/675–2768.*

Tower Records and Videos. The scene in each branch is pure New York: At the Village location, many customers are in head-to-toe black, while at the Lincoln Center branch patrons discuss jazz in the store café. The East 4th Street location is a clearance center for music, books, videos, and music. ✉ *692 Broadway, at E. 4th St.,* ☏ *212/505–1500;* ✉ *1961 Broadway, at 66th St.,* ☏ *212/799–2500;* ✉ *725 5th Ave., basement level of Trump Tower,* ☏ *212/838–8110;* ✉ *20 E. 4th St., at Lafayette St.,* ☏ *212/228–7317.*

Virgin Megastore Times Square. Touted as the largest music-entertainment complex in the world (big enough to hold 938 taxis), this glitzy emporium encompasses a café, a travel shop, a wide-ranging book selection, an interactive game wall, and even a special section on New York–theme movies. A 50-ft DJ tower cuts through the three levels of consumer frenzy. At press time, construction was underway for a new Megastore on Union Square. ✉ *1540 Broadway, between 45th and 46th Sts.,* ☎ *212/921–1020.*

Children's Clothing

Children's stores are listed in Shopping *in* Chapter 4; they are, however, bulleted on the maps in this chapter.

Chocolate and Candy

Black Hound. More Upper East Side than East Village, Black Hound has exquisite truffles and unusual sweets. Swing by after an earlyish dinner; they're open weekdays until 8. ✉ *149 1st Ave., at 9th St.,* ☎ *212/979–9505.*

Elk Candy Co. This slice of old Yorkville carries European treats like Mozartkugen and Bahlsen spice cookies, along with specialty chocolates and wonderful marzipan. ✉ *1628 2nd Ave., between 84th and 85th Sts.,* ☎ *212/650–1177.*

La Maison du Chocolat. This is the New York branch of the famous Parisian chocolatier, whose bonbons have been described in *Vogue* as "the most refined and subtle in the world." Look for the thick-as-mud bottled hot chocolate. ✉ *25 E. 73rd St.,* ☎ *212/744–7117.*

Li-Lac Chocolates. This charming nook has been feeding the Village's sweet tooth with homemade selections in the French tradition since 1923. ✉ *120 Christopher St., between Bleecker and Hudson Sts.,* ☎ *212/242–7374.*

Neuchatel Chocolates. Neuchatel's velvety chocolates, which come in five dozen varieties, are all made in New York to approximate the Swiss chocolates. ✉ *Plaza Hotel, 2 W. 59th St.,* ☎ *212/751–7742.*

Perugina. This Italian confectionery is most famous for its Baci, hazelnut chocolates wrapped in a multilingual love note—a tradition begun during a secret love affair of an heir to the company. ✉ *520 Madison Ave.,* ☎ *212/688–2490.*

Richart Design et Chocolat. For dark chocolate lovers, this French shop is worth its weight in cacao beans. Many of the sophisticated chocolates use high percentages of cacao; couturier Sonia Rykiel designed some of the images imprinted on the flat tablets. ✉ *7 E. 55th St.,* ☎ *212/371–9369.*

Teuscher Chocolates. Fabulous chocolates made in Switzerland are flown in weekly for sale in these jewel-box shops, newly decorated each season. ✉ *620 5th Ave., in Rockefeller Center,* ☎ *212/246–4416; 25 E. 61st St.,* ☎ *212/751–8482.*

Crystal

Baccarat. "Life is worth Baccarat," say the ads—in other words, the quality of crystal shown here is priceless. ✉ *625 Madison Ave.,* ☎ *212/826–4100.*

Galleri Orrefors Kosta Boda. Stop here for striking Swedish crystal, including work from the imaginative and often brightly colored Kosta Boda line. ✉ *58 E. 57th St.,* ☎ *212/752–1095.*

Hoya Crystal Gallery. The stunningly designed vases beg for an exotic bloom or two. ✉ *689 Madison Ave.,* ☎ *212/223–6335.*

Rogaska. The understated wares made in Slovenia carried here are sold at relatively modest prices. ✉ *685 Madison Ave.,* ☎ *212/980–6200.*

Steuben. The stunning and adventurous designs on display often go beyond the basic vase. ✉ *715 5th Ave.,* ☎ *212/752–1441.*

Fun and Games

These are stores by adults, for adults, but with such humor and whimsy that kids will like them, too.

Darts Shoppe Ltd. Exquisitely crafted English darts and boards are sold here. ✉ *30 E. 20th St., between Broadway and Park Ave. S,* ☎ *212/533–8684.*

Flosso Hornmann. This modest magic shop offers museum-class memorabilia, including a hand-painted crate used by Harry Houdini. ✉ *45 W. 34th St., Room 607, between 5th and 6th Aves.,* ☎ *212/279–6079.*

Little Rickie. Wacky novelties and vintage treasures pack this fun spot. (Some may look eerily familiar, like those TV-show lunch boxes.) ✉ *49½ 1st Ave., at 3rd St.,* ☎ *212/505–6467.*

Tannen Magic Co. This magicians' supply house stocks sword chests, dove-a-matics, magic wands, and crystal balls, not to mention the all-important top hats with rabbits. ✉ *24 W. 25th St., between 5th and 6th Aves.,* ☎ *212/929–4500.*

Uncle Futz. This delicious toy shop is crammed with supercool puzzles, board games, and souped-up yo-yos. ✉ *408 Amsterdam Ave., at 79th St.,* ☎ *212/799–6723.*

Gadgets

Hammacher Schlemmer. The store that offered America its first pop-up toaster still ferrets out the outrageous, the unusual, and the best-of-kind in-home electronics. ✉ *147 E. 57th St.,* ☎ *212/421–9000.*

Sharper Image. This retail outlet of the catalog company stocks gifts for the pampered executive who has everything. ✉ *Pier 17, South Street Seaport,* ☎ *212/693–0477;* ✉ *4 W. 57th St., at 5th Ave.,* ☎ *212/265–2550;* ✉ *900 Madison Ave.,* ☎ *212/794–4974.*

Home Decor and Gifts

ABC Carpet & Home. Resembling a lifelong hoarder's attic, this immense, crammed emporium sells everything from ornate furniture and rugs to vintage tea sets, linens, and meditation cushions. The in-house Parlour Café serves a bottomless stack of pancakes and other fare. ✉ *888 Broadway, at 19th St.,* ☎ *212/473–3000.*

Avventura. Glory in Italian design in all its streamlined beauty here. Tabletop items and handblown glass accessories are all stunning. ✉ *463 Amsterdam Ave., at 82nd St.,* ☎ *212/769–2510.*

Be Seated. Manhattan's source for new and vintage African and Asian baskets also stocks cotton fabrics from India and Indonesia. ✉ *66 Greenwich Ave., near 11th St.,* ☎ *212/924–8444.*

Bed, Bath & Beyond. This huge Chelsea emporium has some 80,000 different household items at reasonable prices. Weekends are mob scenes. ✉ *620 6th Ave., between 18th and 19th Sts.,* ☎ *212/255–3550.*

Crate & Barrel. A terrific selection of practically everything imaginable for the home and kitchen, including glassware, kitchen and bath items, and stylish furniture, is the hallmark of this bright blond-wood-lined store. ✉ *650 Madison Ave.,* ☎ *212/308–0011.*

Eclectic Home. The first contemporary home-design store in Chelsea has an especially grand range of decorative (and sometimes downright silly) lighting. ✉ *224 8th Ave., between 21st and 22nd Sts.,* ☎ *212/255–2373.*

Felissimo. Spread over four stories of a Beaux Arts town house are unusual objets d'art and accessories, many handcrafted, which marry classic European and modern Asian sensibilities. Some items (Japanese incense, aromatherapy and *feng shui* sets) whisper elegant New Age-iness, while others (Moroccan tagines, beautiful glassware, antique silver) are unabashedly material. Scones *and* tarot card readings are offered in the tearoom. ✉ *10 W. 56th St.,* ☎ *212/247–5656.*

Gates of Marrakesh. Sharpen your acquisitive streak in this small Moroccan shop, where light filters through henna-painted sheepskin lamps. ✉ *8 Prince St.,* ☎ *212/925–4104.*

La Maison Moderne. Home accessories with a Gallic flair are a specialty here—for example, to cheer up your mornings, check out the sunny yellow Banania breakfast dishes. ✉ *144 W. 19th St., between 6th and 7th Aves.,* ☎ *212/691–9603.*

Let There Be Neon. Browse among the terrific collection of new and antique neon signs, clocks, and tabletop accessories. ✉ *38 White St., between Broadway and Church St.,* ☎ *212/226–4883.*

MacKenzie-Childs Ltd. Fantastical windows and a palatial birdcage, home to elegant live chickens, make this a store unlike any other. Handmade majolica ware, table settings, and trimmings are done with a Victorian exuberance for detail. ✉ *824 Madison Ave.,* ☎ *212/570–6050.*

Miya Shoji Interiors. This shop offers a superb selection of beautifully crafted Japanese folding screens. ✉ *109 W. 17th St., between 6th and 7th Aves.,* ☎ *212/243–6774.*

Moss. Who knew citrus juicers and toilet brushes could be so beautiful? Philippe Starck, for one; he and the other designers represented in this sleek boutique put a fantastic spin on even the most utilitarian objects. ✉ *146 Greene St.,* ☎ *212/226–2190.*

The Pillowry. The selection of one-of-a-kind decorative pillows is vast. It opens weekdays at 11:30, Saturday by appointment. ✉ *132 E. 61st St., between Park and Lexington Aves.,* ☎ *212/308–1630.*

Pottery Barn. With its all-occasions glassware, artsy knickknacks, and relatively grounded prices, Pottery Barn has become one of the most influential style mongers of the interiors world. The Broadway at 67th Street and SoHo locations do double time as concept stores, with large home-design studios. Overstocks are discounted at the 10th Avenue location. ✉ *600 Broadway, at Houston St.,* ☎ *212/219–2420;* ✉ *117 E. 59th St., between 5th and Madison Aves.,* ☎ *212/753–5424;* ✉ *1965 Broadway, at 67th St.,* ☎ *212/579–8477;* ✉ *250 W. 57th St., between 7th and 8th Aves.,* ☎ *212/315–1855;* ✉ *231 10th Ave., between 23rd and 24th Sts.,* ☎ *212/206–8118; and other locations.*

Scully & Scully. Leather footstools in animal shapes and small pieces of reproduction antique furniture exemplify this store's high-WASP style. ✉ *504 Park Ave., between 59th and 60th Sts.,* ☎ *212/755–2590.*

Shi. Good design prevails here—whether it be a triangular Ricard ashtray, burnished wooden chopsticks, or a bumpy glass carafe. ✉ *233 Elizabeth St.,* ☎ *212/334–4330.*

Troy. In this spare space, the clean lines of wicker, leather, and wooden furniture and home accessories may well wreak havoc with your credit card. ✉ *138 Greene St.,* ☎ *212/941–4777.*

William-Wayne & Co. Ostrich eggs, Viennese playing cards, butler's trays: These whimsical, mildly exotic decorative items are hard to resist. A low-key monkey theme puts smiling simians on dishes, candleholders, wall sconces and tea towels. ✉ *40 University Pl., at 9th St.,* ☎ *212/533–4711;* ✉ *846 Lexington Ave., at 64th St.,* ☎ *212/737–8934;* ✉ *850 Lexington Ave., at 64th St.,* ☎ *212/288–9243.*

Wolfman-Gold & Good Company. Half antique and half contemporary in spirit, this chic SoHo shop focusing on tableware is a major New York trendsetter. Check in the back, where there's always a sofa on sale (sometimes with a fat cat asleep on it). ✉ *117 Mercer St.,* ☎ *212/431–1888.*

Zona. One of the first stores to have drawn shoppers to SoHo has proved to be much more than a flash in the pan. Homey good-living accoutrements dominate—quilts, sturdy wooden furniture, coasters made out of LPs. ✉ *97 Greene St.,* ☎ *212/925–6750.*

LINENS

Madison Avenue has an inviting handful of high-end linen shops; move downtown for less expensive—and less conventional—lines. Grand Street on the Lower East Side has a spate of dry-goods merchants.

Ad Hoc Softwares. You'll feel very SoHo as you browse here—natural fibers and nubby textures abound. The merchandise continues to expand into the home accessory arena. ✉ *410 W. Broadway*, ☏ *212/925–2652.*

D. Porthault. Porthault's showcase beds are virtual cocoons of pale, crisp linens and pillows. ✉ *18 E. 69th St.*, ☏ *212/688–1660.*

Frette. Thread counts rise well above 250 here. ✉ *799 Madison Ave.*, ☏ *212/988–5221.*

Pratesi. To complement its pristine bedding, Pratesi has layettes, fragrances, and home gift lines, including damask table linens so fine they could almost stand in for the bedding. ✉ *825 Madison Ave.*, ☏ *212/288–2315.*

Jewelry, Watches, and Silver

Most of the world's premier jewelers have retail outlets in New York, and the nation's wholesale jewelry center is on 47th Street.

A La Vieille Russie. Stop here to behold bibelots by Fabergé and others, enameled or encrusted with jewels. ✉ *781 5th Ave., at 59th St.*, ☏ *212/752–1727.*

Asprey. The only branch of the distinguished London jeweler, which holds three royal warrants, this store is just the place for crystal, silver, leather goods, or, perhaps, a brooch fit for a queen. ✉ *725 5th Ave.*, ☏ *212/688–1811.*

Beads of Paradise. Enjoy a startlingly rich selection of African bead necklaces, earrings, and rare artifacts. Also, you can create your own designs. ✉ *16 E. 17th St., between 5th Ave. and Broadway*, ☏ *212/620–0642.*

Bulgari. This Italian company is certainly not shy about its name, which encircles gems, watch faces, even lighters. There are beautiful, weighty rings, pieces mixing gold with stainless steel or porcelain, and Venetian-theme silk neckties and scarves. ✉ *730 5th Ave.*, ☏ *212/315–9000;* ✉ *783 Madison Ave.*, ☏ *212/717–2300;* ✉ *2 E. 61st St. , in the Hotel Pierre*, ☏ *212/486–0326.*

Cartier. Legend has it that Pierre Cartier obtained this stately mansion by trading it with Mrs. Morton Plant for two rows of natural pearls. Having passed the 150-year mark, Cartier's work continues on in its classically designed way—the dazzling gems do the talking. ✉ *653 5th Ave.*, ☏ *212/446–3400.*

David Webb. Featured here are gem-studded pieces, often enameled and in animal forms. ✉ *445 Park Ave.*, ☏ *212/421–3030.*

Fortunoff. Good prices on jewelry, flatware, and hollowware draw crowds to this large store. ✉ *681 5th Ave.*, ☏ *212/758–6660.*

Harry Winston. Oversize stones of impeccable quality glitter in Harry Winston's inner sanctum—this is where the Hollywood stars come to borrow diamonds for Oscar night. No wonder the jeweler was immortalized in the song "Diamonds Are a Girl's Best Friend." ✉ *718 5th Ave.*, ☏ *212/245–2000.*

H. Stern. This revamped store puts its sleek designs in an equally modern setting; smooth cabochon-cut stones (most from South America) glow in pale wooden display cases, while *objets* like moccasins or glossy feathers evoke the company's Brazilian origins. There's a notable use of semiprecious stones such as citrine, smoky quartz, and topaz. ✉ *645 5th Ave.*, ☏ *212/688–0300.*

James Robinson. This family-owned business sells handmade flatware, antique silver, fine estate jewelry, and 18th- and 19th-century china. ✉ *480 Park Ave., at 58th St.,* ☎ *212/752–6166.*

Jean's Silversmiths. Where to replace the butter knife that's missing from your great-aunt's set? Try this dusty, crowded shop. ✉ *16 W. 45th St., between 5th and 6th Aves.,* ☎ *212/575–0723.*

Mikimoto. As the originator of the cultured pearl, Mikimoto has a stunning display of perfectly formed pearls. Besides the creamy strands from their own pearl farms, there are whopping colored South Sea pearls and some freshwater varieties. ✉ *730 5th Ave.,* ☎ *212/664–1800.*

Robert Lee Morris. Striking originals in silver, gold, and gold plate can be discovered at this SoHo jewelry and accessory mecca. ✉ *400 W. Broadway,* ☎ *212/431–9405.*

Stuart Moore. Many designs here are minimalist or understated—but stunning: the sparkle of a small diamond offset by matte, brushed platinum, or gold. Pieces tend to be smaller in scale. ✉ *128 Prince St.,* ☎ *212/941–1023.*

Tiffany & Co. The display windows can be elegant, funny, or just plain breathtaking. Along with the $80,000 platinum-and-diamond bracelets, a lot is affordable on a whim—and everything comes wrapped in that unmistakable Tiffany blue. ✉ *727 5th Ave.,* ☎ *212/755–8000.*

Tourneau. Each of this trio of stores stocks a wide range of watches, but the three-level 57th Street TimeMachine, apparently taking a cue from its neighbor, NikeTown, is the scene-stealer: More than a dozen clock faces encircle the facade, time-related quotes line the walls (NO TIME LIKE THE PRESENT), and video monitors add high-tech inspiration. A museum downstairs has timepiece exhibits, both temporary and permanent. They carry more than 70 brands, from status symbols like Patek Philippe, Cartier, and Rolex, to more casual styles by Swatch, Seiko, and Swiss Army. ✉ *500 Madison Ave.,* ☎ *212/758–6098;* ✉ *12 E. 57th St.,* ☎ *212/758–7300;* ✉ *200 W. 34th St., at 7th Ave.,* ☎ *212/563–6880.*

Van Cleef & Arpels. The jewelry here is sheer perfection. ✉ *744 5th Ave.,* ☎ *212/644–9500.*

Luggage and Leather Goods

Altman Luggage. Great bargains (a Samsonite Pullman for a little over $100) are the thing at this discount store, which also stocks tough Timberland and Jansport backpacks. ✉ *135 Orchard St., between Delancey and Rivington Sts.,* ☎ *212/254–7275.*

Bottega Veneta. Bottega Veneta's signature crosshatch weave graces stunning handbags, satchels, and shoes, both in leather and satin. There's also a small selection of leather coats and accessories. ✉ *635 Madison Ave.,* ☎ *212/371–5511.*

Coach. Coach's classic glove-tanned leather goes into handbags, briefcases, wallets, and dozens of other accessories. ✉ *710 Madison Ave.,* ☎ *212/319–1772;* ✉ *595 Madison Ave.,* ☎ *212/754–0041;* ✉ *725 5th Ave., in Trump Tower,* ☎ *212/355–2427;* ✉ *342 Madison Ave., at 44th St.,* ☎ *212/599–4777; and other locations.*

Crouch & Fitzgerald. Since 1839 this store has offered a terrific selection in hard- and soft-sided luggage, as well as handbags. ✉ *400 Madison Ave., at 48th St.,* ☎ *212/755–5888.*

Dooney & Bourke. Besides the traditional pebbly-textured leather satchels, handbags, and duffels (often with tan trim), Dooney & Bourke has a line of Cabriolet bags—leather-trimmed but made of the same tough cloth used for cars' convertible tops. ✉ *759 Madison Ave.,* ☎ *212/439–1657;* ✉ *725 5th Ave., Trump Tower,* ☎ *212/308–0520.*

Fine & Klein. Among the deals at this discounter are woven Sak bags ($30–$55, 30% less the usual price) and bags by Laura, a close-enough Coach knockoff. ✉ *119 Orchard St., between Delancey and Rivington Sts.,* ☎ *212/674–6720.*

Lederer Leather Goods. The excellent selection here includes exotic skins. ✉ *457 Madison Ave., no phone at press time.*

Louis Vuitton. Vuitton's famous monogrammed pieces range from purses to extravagant steamer trunks. A new (and larger) store, on 57th Street between 5th and Madison Avenues, was under construction at press time. ✉ *49 E. 57th St.,* ☎ *212/371–6111.*

Rugby North America. This Canadian-based store specializes in ultra-simple, unisex calfskin postman's bags, tough backpacks, and sturdy belts, plus unfussy men's and women's jackets. To get into the spirit, cozy into a leather chair. ✉ *115 Mercer St.,* ☎ *212/431–3069.*

T. Anthony. This store's hard- and soft-sided luggage of coated fabric with leather trim has brass fasteners that look like precision machines. ✉ *445 Park Ave.,* ☎ *212/750–9797.*

Men's Clothing

Agnès b. Homme. This French designer's love for the movies makes it easy to come out looking a little Godard around the edges. Trench coats, lean black suits, and black leather porkpie hats demand the sangfroid of Belmondo. ✉ *79 Greene St.,* ☎ *212/431–4339.*

Alfred Dunhill of London. Corporate brass comes here for finely tailored clothing, both ready-made and custom-ordered, and smoking accessories; the walk-in humidor stores top-quality tobacco and cigars. ✉ *450 Park Ave.,* ☎ *212/753–9292.*

Façonnable. This French company has a lock on the Euro-conservative look. Their sport coats (about $800) and Italian-made suits may be expensive, but the tailoring and canvas-fronting will make them withstand years of dry cleaning. ✉ *689 5th Ave.,* ☎ *212/319–0111.*

Holland & Holland. This is no Ralph-Lauren-does-country-squire; Holland & Holland provides the Prince of Wales (and wealthy colonials) with country clothing and accessories such as leather falcon hoods. There's a special safari tailoring section and a gun room on the fifth floor. ✉ *50 E. 57th St.,* ☎ *212/752–7755.*

J. Press. Oxford-cloth shirts, natural-shoulder suits, madras-patch Bermuda shorts, and amusing club ties are the emphasis here. ✉ *7 E. 44th St.,* ☎ *212/687–7642.*

Jekyll & Hyde. The quietly hip, not-too-expensive European threads here include many British labels, including Ted Baker shirts. Accessories are even more tempting, from the plain-knot Duchamp silk ties to cool cuff links and flasks, though the vests can be a little outré. ✉ *107 Grand St.,* ☎ *212/966–9535; 93 Greene St.,* ☎ *212/966–8503.*

Paul Smith. Dark mahogany Victorian cases set off British-made suits with excellent (if sometimes too dandyish) styling. Impeccably produced shirts, sweaters, ties, shoes, and other accessories scream the very latest from london. ✉ *108 5th Ave., at 16th St.,* ☎ *212/627–9770.*

Paul Stuart Inc. The fabric selection is interesting, the tailoring superb, and the look traditional but not stodgy. ✉ *Madison Ave. at 45th St.,* ☎ *212/682–0320.*

Sean. A welcome antidote to the omnipresent minimalist boxes, this snug shop carries low-key, well-priced, and comfortable apparel from France—soft cardigans, very-narrow-wale corduroy pants, and a respectable collection of suits and dress shirts. ✉ *132 Thompson St.,* ☎ *212/598–5980.*

Sulka. Most of the elegant clothes here are Italian—and the silk robes are so swank they've shown up on Broadway in a Noël Coward play. ✉ *430 Park Ave.,* ☎ *212/980–5200.*

Thomas Pink. London's Jermyn Street shirtmaker has crossed the water with its traditional, impeccably tailored shirts, which come in several styles; besides the British-favored spread collars and French cuffs, there are buttoned collars and cuffs. The eponymous color crops up often (and sometimes in brighter shades than Americans are used to). Silk ties, cuff links, and two lines of women's shirts round out the selection. ✉ *520 Madison Ave.,* ☎ *212/838–1928.*

Worth & Worth. This classy shop stocks stylish handmade hats. ✉ *331 Madison Ave., at 43rd St.,* ☎ *212/867–6058.*

DISCOUNTS

Eisenberg and Eisenberg. Bargain hunters have relied on this store for decades. ✉ *85 5th Ave., at 16th St., 6th floor,* ☎ *212/627–1290.*

Moe Ginsburg. Come here for a large selection of discounted American and European suits and outerwear. There's an even-deeper-discount floor, where prices are dirt cheap. ✉ *162 5th Ave., at 21st St.,* ☎ *212/242–3482.*

MEN'S SHOES

Billy Martin's. Quality hand-tooled and custom-made boots are carried here. ✉ *810 Madison Ave.,* ☎ *212/861–3100.*

Church's English Shoes. Church's has been selling traditionally styled, beautifully made English shoes since 1873. For the conservative dresser, its especially well located, since it's just a few blocks from Brooks Brothers and Paul Stuart. ✉ *428 Madison Ave., at 49th St.,* ☎ *212/755–4313.*

Cole-Haan. Cole-Haan endlessly varies the basic elements of its woven, moccasin, and loafer styles in brown and black, for a look that's both classic and casual. ✉ *620 5th Ave., at Rockefeller Center,* ☎ *212/765–9747;* ✉ *667 Madison Ave.,* ☎ *212/421–8440.*

J. M. Weston. Specially treated calfskin for the soles and careful handcrafting have made these a French favorite; they could also double the price of your outfit. The few women's shoes are made exactly like the men's. ✉ *812 Madison Ave.,* ☎ *212/535–2100.*

John Fluevog Shoes. The inventor of the Angelic sole (protects against water, acid. . . "and Satan"), Fluevog designs chunky shoes and boots that are much more than mere Doc Marten copies. ✉ *104 Prince St.,* ☎ *212/431–4484.*

Otto Tootsi Plohound. Downtown New Yorkers swear by Tootsi Plohound's large selection of super-cool shoes; many are thickset and almost all, needless to say, are black. Shoes run $200-plus, though sales can reduce them to about $80. ✉ *137 5th Ave., between 20th and 21st Sts.,* ☎ *212/460–8650;* ✉ *413 W. Broadway,* ☎ *212/925–8931.*

Salvatore Ferragamo. This branch has traditional, classy men's shoes, plus a limited line of compatible clothes and accessories. ✉ *725 5th Ave., at Trump Tower,* ☎ *212/759–7990.*

Santoni. Those who equate Italian with slightly flashy haven't seen these discreet, meticulously finished handmade shoes. ✉ *864 Madison Ave.,* ☎ *212/794–3820.*

Stuart Weitzman. The specialty here is hard-to-find sizes and widths. This store carries the designer's entire line. ✉ *625 Madison Ave.,* ☎ *212/750–2555.*

To Boot. To Boot's stylish shoes and boots have a fashionable business look. ✉ *256 Columbus Ave., between 71st and 72nd Sts.,* ☎ *212/724–8249.*

Men's and Women's Clothing

A/X: Armani Exchange. A/X's down-home basics make it possible for most people to own an Armani . . . something. T-shirts and dark-washed jeans abound, but there are also sharp zip-front jackets, pea coats, and stretchy knits. ✉ *568 Broadway,* ☎ *212/431–6000.*

Brooks Brothers. The clothes at this classic American haberdasher are, as ever, traditional, comfortable, and fairly priced. Seersucker (in summer), navy blue blazers, and the peerless oxford shirts have been staples for generations. The women's selection has variations thereof. ✉

346 ✉ Madison Ave., at 44th St., ☎ 212/682–8800; ✉ 1 Church St., Liberty Plaza, ☎ 212/267–2400.

Calvin Klein. Calvin Klein's huge, stark flagship store emphasizes the luxe end of the designer's clothing line. Men's suits tend to be soft around the edges; women's evening gowns are often a fluid pouring of silk. There are also shoes, accessories, housewares, and, yes, underwear. ✉ *654 Madison Ave., ☎ 212/292–9000.*

Canal Jean. A riotous mix of discounted new and funky old clothes fills this yawning space. Alongside the predictable CK jeans are items from French Connection and other youth-focused lines. Hawaiian shirts, tux shirts, flannels, housedresses, and seasonal apparel fill the vintage racks. ✉ *504 Broadway, ☎ 212/226–1130.*

Comme des Garçons. Japanese designer Rei Kawakubo challenges basic assumptions about clothes: Evening gowns, for instance, have come equipped with a padded hump; women's clothes in general can be voluminous. Men's suits are tamer, though some are the fabric equivalent of mixed-media. ✉ *116 Wooster St., ☎ 212/219–0660.*

Costume National. Men's and women's clothes are done in the same dark, hip styles here. Black velvet, sheer shirts, and techno-fabrics slink down the rack regardless of gender. The blunt, black shoes are in the back. The store is apparently lighted for those who rarely see the light of day. ✉ *108 Wooster St., between Prince and Spring Sts., ☎ 212/431–1530.*

D&G. The first U.S. store for the secondary Dolce & Gabbana line, D&G aims for younger customers addicted to luxe. The striped sweaters and skinny pants for men and crocheted dresses and embroidered fabrics for women are all somewhat akin to the clothes at the uptown store (☞ *below*). ✉ *434 W. Broadway, ☎ 212/965–8000.*

Diesel Superstore. The display windows styled like washing machines will tip you off as to Diesel's industrial edge; men's and women's clothes sizes tend to be generous (but they don't all shrink). ✉ *770 Lexington Ave., at 60th St., ☎ 212/308–0055.*

Dolce & Gabbana. It's easy to feel like an Italian movie star amid the extravagant (in every sense) clothes here. Pinstripes are a favorite; for women, they could be paired with something sheer and leopard-print, while for men they elongate the sharp suits. The wine-color, velvet-cloaked dressing rooms make trying on brocades, bustiers, and exaggerated hats a dream, but leave time to peek at the small terrace garden. ✉ *825 Madison Ave., ☎ 212/249–4100.*

Emporio Armani. At this "middle child" of the Madison Avenue Armani trio, the clothes are dressy without quite being formal, often in the ever-cool shades of soot. ✉ *601 Madison Ave., ☎ 212/317–0800; ✉ 110 5th Ave., at 16th St., ☎ 212/727–3240.*

Etro. There are echoes of 19th-century luxury in Etro's clothing; vest dandies will be particularly happy. The rich fabrics are sometimes saturated with strong color: russet, indigo, or ruby. ✉ *720 Madison Ave., ☎ 212/317–9096.*

Gianni Versace. The five-story flagship store, in a restored turn-of-the-century landmark building, hums with colored neon lights. Although the exuberant designs and colors of Versace clothes might not be to everyone's taste, they're never boring. A second five-story store (✉ 647 5th Ave., ☎ 212/317–0224. ✉ 815 Madison Ave., ☎ 212/744–6868) has a steely, modern take; it focuses on the higher-end women's and men's clothes and accessories. ✉ 647 5th Ave., ☎ 212/317–0224.

Giorgio Armani. Armani managed to beat out Calvin Klein on the exterior-minimalism front; inside, the space has a museumlike quality, reinforced by the stunning cuts of the clothes. ✉ *760 Madison Ave., ☎ 212/988–9191.*

Gucci. Designer Tom Ford's revamp campaign shows no signs of slowing down—the venerable name has an increasingly svelte edge. The most hyped items are overtly sexy, like the stilettos, but there are still some beautiful (and respectable) suits. ✉ *685 5th Ave.,* ☎ *212/826–2600.*

Helmut Lang. Lang's men's and women's clothes—mostly in black, white, and blue, plus the denim line—are tough distillations of his white-shirt, skinny-pants aesthetic, with off-kilter stripes, straps, and beltings tacked on. Black, mirror-ended walls slice up the space; it helps to have some sharp edges yourself. ✉ *80 Greene St.,* ☎ *212/925–7214.*

Hermès. Patterned silk scarves, neckties, and the sacred "Kelly" handbags are hallmarks. ✉ *11 E. 57th St.,* ☎ *212/751 3181.*

Issey Miyake. Tightly pleated fabrics have become the Miyake signature—some in ultra-high-tech textiles. ✉ *992 Madison Ave.,* ☎ *212/439–7822.*

J. Crew. At these pristine showcases for East Coast chic, the 14 labels for men and women range from flannels to the Collection, an exclusive, Calvin Klein–ish women's line. ✉ *99 Prince St.,* ☎ *212/966–2739;* ✉ *203 Front St., at Fulton St.,* ☎ *212/385–3500;* ✉ *91 5th Ave., between 16th and 17th Sts.,* ☎ *212/255–4848.*

Lucien Pellat-Finet. Cashmere and nothing but—not what you'd expect in Nolita, but these slim-cut, phenomenally soft sweaters are worthy of Madison Avenue or a Hollywood opening (just ask Tom Cruise, who was snapped wearing one). ✉ *226 Elizabeth St.,* ☎ *212/343–7033.*

Marc Jacobs. Next door to a garage lie multi-thousands worth of elegant cashmere, silk, and wool separates. Jacobs's muted palette is occasionally interrupted, as by a shocking orange men's sweater. ✉ *163 Mercer St.,* ☎ *212/343–1490.*

Matsuda. Matsuda's clothes have a cool sense of humor, a sophisticated cut, and a not insignificant price tag. ✉ *156 5th Ave., between 20th and 21st Sts.,* ☎ *212/645–5151.*

Old Navy. The Gap's kissing cousin has quickly garnered legions of fans with its kick-around clothes at terrific prices. ✉ *610 6th Ave., at 18th St.,* ☎ *212/645–0663;* ✉ *Pier 17, South Street Seaport,* ☎ *212/571–6159.*

Polo/Ralph Lauren. One of New York's most distinctive shopping experiences, Lauren's flagship store is in the turn-of-the-century Rhinelander mansion. Clothes range from summer-in-the-Hamptons madras to exquisite silk gowns and Purple Label men's suits. Across the street **Polo Sport** (✉ 888 Madison Ave., ☎ 212/434–8000) carries casual clothes and sports gear. ✉ *867 Madison Ave.,* ☎ *212/606–2100.*

Prada. Prada's gossamer silks, slick black techno-fabric suits, and ultraluxe shoes and leather goods are one of the last great Italian fashion coups of the millennium. Its high profile has led it onto Fifth Avenue, where the newest store opened in fall 1998. The Madison Avenue store pulses with pale "verdolino" green walls (remember this if you start questioning your skin tone). ✉ *724 Fifth Ave., phone not available at press time.* ✉ *841 Madison Ave.,* ☎ *212/327–4200;* ✉ *45 E. 57th St.,* ☎ *212/308–2332.*

Spazio Romeo Gigli. More gorgeous Italian design reigns here, this time with decadently rich fabrics and a hint of Renaissance about the cut. ✉ *21 E. 69th St.,* ☎ *212/744–9121.*

Valentino. The mix here is at once audacious and beautifully cut; the fur or feather trimmings, low necklines, and opulent fabrics are about as close as you can get to celluloid glamour. ✉ *747 Madison Ave.,* ☎ *212/772–6969.*

Yohji Yamamoto. Though almost entirely in black and white, these clothes aren't as severe as they seem. Wool sweaters can be so fine they're translucent; necklines, hems, and waists are tweaked imaginatively. ✉ *103 Grand St.,* ☎ *212/966–9066.*

DISCOUNT

Klein's of Monticello. One of the most genteel stores in the Lower East Side (no fluorescent lighting!), Klein's has authentic labels—Malo cashmere sweaters, Les Copains separates—normally for 20% to 30% off. ✉ *105 Orchard St., at Delancey St.,* ☎ *212/966–1453.*

Loehmann's. After 75 years of selling exclusively women's clothes, Loehmann's added a men's department, where label searchers can turn up $40 Polo/Ralph Lauren chinos and Donna Karan and Dolce & Gabbana suits. The women's designer section also carries American and European designers, though you may need to make a repeat visit or two before emerging victorious. ✉ *101 7th Ave., at 16th St.,* ☎ *212/352–0856.*

Syms. There are some excellent buys to be had for designer suits and separates. Men can flip through racks of Bill Blass and Cerruti, while women can turn up Calvin Klein and Christian Dior without even trying. Nondesigner racks can be uninspiring. ✉ *400 Park Ave.,* ☎ *212/317–8200;* ✉ *42 Trinity Pl., at Rector St.,* ☎ *212/797–1199.*

Museum Stores

Virtually every museum now has a gift shop with postcards and posters of its most popular works. The largest museums, however, have taken merchandising to new levels: Their gift shops have become excellent resources for art books, reproductions, and unique souvenirs. Following are a few of the best.

American Craft Museum. The tie-ins to ongoing exhibits can yield beautiful handmade glassware, unusual jewelry, or enticing textiles. ✉ *40 W. 53rd St.,* ☎ *212/956–3535.*

Guggenheim Museum SoHo. Among the spin-offs are Lichtenstein calendars, lamps covered in strips of film, and mugs shaped like the uptown Guggenheim building. Children's art activity books fill several shelves. ✉ *575 Broadway,* ☎ *212/423–3500.*

Metropolitan Museum of Art Shop. The store in the museum itself has a phenomenal book selection, as well as posters, art videos, and computer programs. Repros of jewelry from famous paintings, statuettes, and models of William (the plump little Egyptian hippo, which has become the museum's mascot) fill the gleaming cases in every branch. ✉ *5th Ave. at 82nd St.,* ☎ *212/879–5500;* ✉ *113 Prince St.,* ☎ *212/614–3000;* ✉ *15 W. 49th St., Rockefeller Center,* ☎ *212/332–1360.*

Museum of Modern Art Design Store. Diagonally across the street from the museum is a hoard of good, eye-catching design: Frank Lloyd Wright furniture reproductions, vases designed by Alvar Aalto, and lots of clever trinkets. Posters (from Mondrian to van Gogh's *Starry Night*) and a wide-ranging selection of books are across the street at the museum's bookstore (✉ 11 W. 53rd St., ☎ 212/708–9700). ✉ *44 W. 53rd St.,* ☎ *212/767–1050.*

Odds and Ends

Danse Macabre. You could have an interest in radiology. Or you could be morbid enough to want an interesting skull or two. This ossiferous collection also includes Mexican Day of the Dead folk art, African death masks, and the like. ✉ *263½ Lafayette St., between Prince and Spring Sts.,* ☎ *212/219–3907.*

Forbidden Planet. The sci-fi stash here is considerable—action figures, videos, and rows and rows of books and magazines (not all of which are for younger children). ✉ *840 Broadway, at 13th St.,* ☎ *212/473–1576.*

Kate Spade. Kate Spade's only boutique doesn't exactly stock leather goods—instead, the eminently desirable (and oft-copied) handbags come in various fabrics, from velvet to tweed to her trademark black, satin-finish microfiber. Specialty bags include a dog carrier. At press time, the old storefront at 59 Thompson Street was being primed to carry new Spade lines. ✉ *454 Broome St.*, ☎ *212/274–1991.*

Keiko New York. End bathing-suit trauma once and for all by getting your swimsuit customized here—or pick out one of the ready-made, brightly colored numbers (both men's and women's). ✉ *62 Greene St.*, ☎ *212/226–6051.*

New York Firefighter's Friend. Appropriately enough, this store is right near a fire station. On sale are firefighter-themed toys, books, and some authentic firefighters' gear, like the apparently indestructible reflective-stripe jackets. ✉ *263 Lafayette St.*, ☎ *212/226–3142.*

Tender Buttons. Squeeze into this stronghold of clothes fasteners and riffle through the boxes of buttons—mother-of-pearl, novelty-shape plastic, or big, crested bronze numbers. ✉ *143 E. 62nd St., between Lexington and 3rd Aves.*, ☎ *212/758–7004.*

Uncle Sam Umbrella Shop. The only store of its kind in the whole country sells umbrellas of all sorts and also does repairs. Cases of antique walking sticks are in the back. ✉ *161 W. 57th St., between 6th and 7th Aves.*, ☎ *212/582–1976.*

Paper, Greeting Cards, Stationery

Dempsey & Carroll. Supplying New York's high society for a century, this firm is always correct but seldom straitlaced. ✉ *110 E. 57th St.*, ☎ *212/486–7526.*

Kate's Paperie. Heaven for paper lovers, Kate's features fabulous wrapping papers, bound blank books, writing implements of all kinds, paper lamp shades, and more. ✉ *561 Broadway*, ☎ *212/941–9816;* ✉ *8 W. 13th St., between 5th and 6th Aves.*, ☎ *212/633–0570.*

Ordning & Reda. This Swedish store is practically guaranteed to start your organizational synapses buzzing. The handmade, recycled-product notebooks, stationery, folders, and other paper goods are snappily arranged floor to ceiling, color by bright color. ✉ *253 Columbus Ave., between 71st and 72nd Sts.*, ☎ *212/799–0828.*

Untitled. The stock here includes thousands of tasteful greeting cards and art postcards. ✉ *159 Prince St.*, ☎ *212/982–2088.*

Performing Arts Memorabilia

Drama Book Shop. The comprehensive stock here includes scripts, scores, and librettos. ✉ *723 7th Ave., between 48th and 49th Sts.*, ☎ *212/944–0595.*

Motion Picture Arts Gallery. Vintage posters enchant collectors here. ✉ *133 E. 58th St., 10th floor*, ☎ *212/223–1009.*

Movie Star News. It's hard to doubt their claim to have the world's largest variety of movie photos and posters when scanning the walls, which are entirely covered by signed pictures of such stars as Billy Crystal, Lauren Bacall, Anjelica Houston, and even Elvira. Posters in the outer garage area run $10–$25. ✉ *134 W. 18th St., between 6th and 7th Aves.*, ☎ *212/620–8160.*

One Shubert Alley. Souvenirs from past and present Broadway hits reign at this theater district shop. ✉ *Shubert Alley between 44th and 45th Sts.*, ☎ *212/944–4133.*

Richard Stoddard Performing Arts Books. This veteran dealer, who offers out-of-print books, also has the largest stock of old Broadway *Playbills* in the world. ✉ *18 E. 16th St., Room 305*, ☎ *212/645–9576.*

Triton Gallery. Theatrical posters large and small can be found here for hits and flops. ✉ *323 W. 45th St., between 8th and 9th Aves.*, ☎ *212/765–2472.*

Souvenirs of New York City

Ordinary Big Apple souvenirs can be found in and around major tourist attractions. More unusual items can be found at:

City Books. Discover all kinds of books and pamphlets that have to do with New York City's government and its various departments (building, sanitation, etc.), as well as pocket maps, Big Apple lapel pins, and sweatshirts featuring subway-token motifs. It's closed on weekends. ✉ *61 Chambers St., at Centre St.,* ☎ *212/669–8246.*

New York City Transit Museum Gift Shop. This museum shop was built mostly by transit employees. All the merchandise is somehow linked to the MTA, from "straphanger" ties to old subway tokens. ✉ *Boerum Pl. and Schermerhorn St., Brooklyn Heights,* ☎ *718/243–5068.*

The Pop Shop. Images from the late artist Keith Haring's unmistakable pop art cover a wealth of paraphernalia, from backpacks to key chains. ✉ *292 Lafayette St.,* ☎ *212/219–2784.*

Sporting Goods

Chain stores such as **Eastern Mountain Sports** (✉ 611 Broadway, near Houston St., ☎ 212/505–9860; ✉ 20 W. 61st St., between Central Park W and Columbus Ave., ☎ 212/397–4860), **Speedo Authentic Fitness** (✉ 1 World Trade Center, ☎ 212/775–0977; ✉ 150 Columbus Ave., between 66th and 67th Sts., ☎ 212/501–8140; ✉ 40 E. 57th St., between Madison and Park Aves., ☎ 212/838–5988; ✉ 90 Park Ave., at 39th St., ☎ 212/682–3830; ✉ 721 Lexington Ave., at 58th St., ☎ 212/688–4595) and the **Sports Authority** (✉ 401 7th Ave., at 33rd St., ☎ 212/563–7195; ✉ 845 3rd Ave., at 51st St., ☎ 212/355–9725; ✉ 57 W. 57th St., between 5th and 6th Aves., ☎ 212/355–6430) are reliable, but here are a couple of unique spots to try.

NikeTown. A fusion of high-tech and school gym, Nike's "motivational retail environment" is its largest sports-gear emporium. Inspirational quotes in the floor, computer-driven NGAGE foot sizers, and a heart-pumping movie shown on an enormous screen in the entry atrium make it hard to leave without something in the latest high-tech wick-away fabric or footwear design. ✉ *6 E. 57th St.,* ☎ *212/891–6453.*

Paragon Sporting Goods. Tennis rackets, Ping-Pong paddles, kayaks, swim goggles, hockey sticks, croquet mallets: Paragon stocks virtually everything any athlete needs, no matter what the sport. They keep up with the trends (snow blades) and don't neglect the old-fashioned (horseshoes). Camping gear includes a wide selection of sleeping bags and tents; Polo sweats and Armani golf shirts attract the label-conscious. ✉ *867 Broadway, at 18th St.,* ☎ *212/255–8036.*

Tent & Trails. New Yorkers who climb Everest outfit themselves at this family-owned survivor from an earlier retail era. Even if you don't need crampons, climbing ropes, or wilderness survival kits, come for the huge selection of outerwear and backpacks and the informed advice. ✉ *21 Park Pl., between Broadway and Church St.,* ☎ *212/227–1760.*

Toys

During February's Toy Week, when out-of-town buyers come to place orders for the next Christmas season, the windows of the Toy Center at 23rd Street and 5th Avenue display the latest thing (☞ Fun and Games, *above* and Shopping *in* Chapter 4).

B. Shackman & Co. In 1998 B. Shackman's marked its 100th year in business; small wonder that its dollhouse miniatures, paper dolls, and reproduction tin toys have a timeless quality. At press time, a move was imminent. ✉ *85 5th Ave., at 16th St.,* ☎ *212/989–5162.*

Classic Toys. Collectors and kids scrutinize the rows of miniature soldiers, toy cars, and other figures. It's a prime source for toy soldiers from Britain's Ltd., the United Kingdom's top manufacturer. ✉ *218 Sullivan St., between Bleecker and W. 3rd Sts.,* ☎ *212/674–4434.*

Compleat Strategist. These stores have a great spread—from board games and classic soldier sets to mah-jongg and even sock monkey kits. ✉

11 E. 33rd St., between 5th and Madison Aves., ☏ *212/685–3880;* ✉ *342 W. 57th St., between 8th and 9th Aves.,* ☏ *212/582–1272;* ✉ *630 5th Ave., Rockefeller Center,* ☏ *212/265–7449.*

Disney Store. All branches carry merchandise relating to Disney films and characters. The flagship 5th Avenue store has the largest collection of Disney animation art in the country. ✉ *711 5th Ave.,* ☏ *212/702–0702; 210 W. 42nd St., at 7th Ave.,* ☏ *212/221–0430;* ✉ *39 W. 34th St., between 5th and 6th Aves.,* ☏ *212/279–9890;* ✉ *141 Columbus Ave., at W. 66th St.,* ☏ *212/362–2386.*

E.A.T. Gifts. Piñatas hang from the ceiling, and the shelves are full of toys, gizmos, and knickknacks. Tintin and Babar fans will have a field day. ✉ *1062 Madison Ave.,* ☏ *212/861–2544.*

Enchanted Forest. Stuffed animals peer out from almost every corner of this fantastic shop, packed with all manner of curiosity-provoking gizmos, plus old-fashioned tin toys and a small but choice selection of children's books. ✉ *85 Mercer St.,* ☏ *212/925–6677.*

F.A.O. Schwarz. The constant tinkle of "Welcome to Our World of Toys" fills this sprawling toy fantasyland. Beyond the large mechanical clock are two floors of stuffed animals, dolls (including an inordinate number of Barbies), things with which to build (including blocks by the pound), computer games, and much, much more (☞ Shopping *in* Chapter 4). ✉ *767 5th Ave.,* ☏ *212/644–9400.*

Geppetto's Toy Box. Most toys here are handmade, ranging from extravagant costumed dolls to tried-and-true rubber duckies. ✉ *161 7th Ave. S, between Perry St. and Waverly Pl.,* ☏ *212/620–7511.*

Kidding Around. This unpretentiously smart shop emphasizes old-fashioned wooden toys, fun gadgets, craft and science kits, and a small selection of infant clothes. ✉ *60 W. 15th St., between 5th and 6th Aves.,* ☏ *212/645–6337;* ✉ *68 Bleecker St., between Broadway and Lafayette St.,* ☏ *212/598–0228.*

Warner Bros. Studio Store. Bugs Bunny has a very high 5th Avenue profile. Besides seemingly endless amounts of entertainment-related merchandise and current movie tie-ins, there's a 3-D movie theater. ✉ *1 E. 57th St.,* ☏ *212/754–0300.*

Wine

Acker Merrall & Condit. Known for its selection of red burgundies, this store has knowledgeable, helpful personnel. ✉ *160 W. 72nd St., between Amsterdam and Columbus Aves.,* ☏ *212/787–1700.*

Best Cellars. In a novel move, the stock here is organized by the wine's characteristics (sweet, fruity) rather than region—and not only that, the prices are amazingly low. ✉ *1291 Lexington Ave., between 86th and 87th Sts.,* ☏ *212/426–4200.*

Garnet Wines & Liquors. Its fine selection includes champagne at prices that one wine writer called "almost charitable." ✉ *929 Lexington Ave., between 68th and 69th Sts.,* ☏ *212/772–3211.*

Morrell & Company. Peter Morrell is a well-regarded and very colorful figure in the wine business; his store reflects his expertise. ✉ *535 Madison Ave.,* ☏ *212/688–9370.*

Sherry-Lehmann. This New York institution is a great place to go for good advice and to browse through sales on intriguing vintages. ✉ *679 Madison Ave.,* ☏ *212/838–7500.*

Union Square Wine & Spirits. The store stocks a great selection and has a regular schedule of wine seminars and special tasting events. ✉ *33 Union Sq. W, near 16th St.,* ☏ *212/675–8100.*

Women's Clothing

CLASSICS

Ann Taylor. This chain has nearly cornered the market for moderately priced, office-appropriate clothing and shoes. The Madison Avenue store has a whole floor of petites. ✉ *2015–2017 Broadway, near 69th St.,* ☎ *212/873–7344; 2380 Broadway, at 87th St.,* ☎ *212/721–3130;* ✉ *4 Fulton St., between Water and Front Sts.,* ☎ *212/480–4100;* ✉ *645 Madison Ave.,* ☎ *212/832–2010; and other locations.*

Burberrys. The look is classic and conservative, especially in the Burberrys signature plaid, which lines raincoats and covers umbrellas. ✉ *9 E. 57th St.,* ☎ *212/371–5010.*

Laura Ashley. Laura Ashley's last Manhattan holdout still purveys the hyperfloral look, although some flower prints are nearly abstract, and there are simple linen sundresses. ✉ *398 Columbus Ave., at 79th St.,* ☎ *212/496–5110.*

DESIGNER SHOWCASES

Chanel. The flagship Chanel store has often been compared to a classic Chanel suit—slim, elegant, and timeless. The building includes fashion and jewelry boutiques, as well as a five-story, Provence-saturated Frédéric Fekkai salon. ✉ *15 E. 57th St.,* ☎ *212/355–5050.*

Christian Dior. An elegant, two-level, dove-gray-hued outpost of one of France's most venerable fashion houses, this shop offers both daytime and evening clothes, plus its signature accessories and perfumes. ✉ *703 5th Ave.,* ☎ *212/223–4646.*

Emanuel Ungaro. The style here is body-conscious, but it's never flashy. ✉ *792 Madison Ave.,* ☎ *212/249–4090.*

Geoffrey Beene. This small but splendid boutique has some curvaceous day and evening wear, which often makes much of the waist. ✉ *783 5th Ave.,* ☎ *212/935–0470.*

Gianfranco Ferre. This Italian designer throws a strong dash of old-style Hollywood extravagance into his women's pret-a-porter line. ✉ *845 Madison Ave.,* ☎ *212/717–5430.*

Givenchy. Crisp suits and crisper white blouses may make you want to don gloves. Shimmering long evening gowns are tucked in back. ✉ *954 Madison Ave.,* ☎ *212/772–1040.*

Louis Féraud. The couturier's deft hand is seen in the superb cuts and colorations at his only freestanding North American boutique. ✉ *3 W. 56th St.,* ☎ *212/956–7010.*

Max Mara. Think subtle colors and enticing fabrics—photo exhibits lend to the genteel atmosphere. ✉ *813 Madison Ave.,* ☎ *212/879–6100.*

Morgane Le Fay. The clothes here borrow from centuries past (swaddlings of silk, high waists); you almost have to be either tall and willowy or French to carry it off. ✉ *746 Madison Ave.,* ☎ *212/879–9700;* ✉ *151 Spring St.,* ☎ *212/925–0144.*

Moschino. IT'S BETTER TO DRESS AS YOU WISH THAN AS YOU SHOULD! proclaims one of the walls of the multistory Moschino flagship. People with a penchant for comedic couture won't have any trouble finding their wardrobe soul mate in this whirligig store. ✉ *803 Madison Ave.,* ☎ *212/639–9600.*

Norma Kamali O.M.O. Dim corners and dislocated stairs characterize this bunkerlike store—an odd setting for evening gowns, long tunics, and resort-ready bathing suits. ✉ *11 W. 56th St.,* ☎ *212/957–9797.*

Sonia Rykiel. Paris's "queen of knitwear" sets off strong colors like fuchsia or orange with, *naturellement,* black. ✉ *849 Madison Ave.,* ☎ *212/396–3060.*

TSE Cashmere. Soft delicacy doesn't stop at the fabric; TSE's sweaters are hopelessly refined. ✉ *827 Madison Ave.,* ☎ *212/472–7790.*

Vera Wang. Sumptuous made-to-order bridal and evening wear is shown here by appointment only. Periodic pret-a-porter sales offer designer dresses for a (relative) song. ✉ *991 Madison Ave.,* ☎ *212/628–3400.*

Yves Saint Laurent Rive Gauche. Yves Saint Laurent is still riding his theatrical black, orange, and fuchsia wave; you can find something in black velvet year round. The men's store is next door, at 859 Madison Avenue (☎ 212/517–7400). ✉ *855 Madison Ave.*, ☎ *212/988–3821.*

DISCOUNT

Forman's. The discounts on designer sportswear have made this one of the city's biggest budget draws. The Orchard Street store is particularly good—plenty of conservative clothes by Lauren by Ralph Lauren, Jones New York, and Liz Claiborne, and lots of merchandise for both petite and plus sizes. ✉ *82 Orchard St., between Broome and Grand Sts.*, ☎ *212/228–2500;* ✉ *145 E. 42nd St., between Lexington and 3rd Aves.*, ☎ *212/681–9800;* ✉ *59 John St.*, ☎ *212/791–4100.*

S&W. Prices here are good to great on coats, suits, shoes, handbags, and other accessories. ✉ *165 W. 26th St., between 6th and 7th Aves.*, ☎ *212/924–6656.*

HIP STYLES

Agnès B. With this quintessentially French line you can approximate a Parisienne—in gauzy scarves, snap-front tops, slender pants, and delicately tinted makeup. ✉ *116 Prince St.*, ☎ *212/925–4649;* ✉ *13 E. 16th St., between 5th Ave. and Union Sq. W*, ☎ *212/741–2585;* ✉ *1063 Madison Ave.*, ☎ *212/570–9333.*

Alicia Mugetti. Silks and velvets are layered, softly shaped, and sometimes hand-painted, giving the designs a times-past richness. ✉ *999 Madison Ave.*, ☎ *212/794–6186;* ✉ *186 Prince St.*, ☎ *212/226–5064.*

Anna Sui. The violet-and-black salon, hung with Beardsley prints and neon alterna-rock posters, is the perfect setting for Sui's flapper- and rocker-influenced designs. ✉ *113 Greene St.*, ☎ *212/941–8406.*

Betsey Johnson. The latest SoHo store departs from the traditional (if such a word can be applied) hot pink interior; instead its walls are sunny yellow with painted roses; and there's a bordello-red lounge area in back. Besides the quirkily printed dresses, available in all stores, there's a slinky upscale line. This is not the place for natural fibers—it's ruled by rayon, stretch, and the occasional faux-fur. ✉ *138 Wooster St.*, ☎ *212/995–5048;* ✉ *251 E. 60th St., between 2nd and 3rd Aves.*, ☎ *212/319–7699;* ✉ *248 Columbus Ave., between 71st and 72nd Sts.*, ☎ *212/362–3364;* ✉ *1060 Madison Ave.*, ☎ *212/734–1257.*

Calypso. With feathers, fringe, sequins, and appliqués, Calypso adds a measure of decadence to its flippant clothes. ✉ *280 Mott St.*, ☎ *212/965–0990.*

Charivari 57. Charivari maintains an intriguing selection, including Nicole Farhi, Dries van Noten, and Martin Margiela, though only one location remains of this high-flying-in-the-'80s, era-defining store. ✉ *18 W. 57th St.*, ☎ *212/333–4040.*

Daryl K. One of Daryl K's early, no-nonsense design goals was to make her derriere look good in a pair of jeans, and she now doles out the favor with short-rise, skinny-legged styles (about $120–$130). Long coats, asymmetrically hemmed skirts, and other downtown-chic items go beyond denim. ✉ *208 E. 6th St., between 2nd and 3rd Aves.*, ☎ *212/475–1255;* ✉ *21 Bond St., between the Bowery and Lafayette St.*, ☎ *212/777–0713.*

Jade. Aglow with silk and brocade, this little store turns jewel-toned rough silk into shirtdresses and mandarin jackets. There are brocade skirts and dresses, jade pendants, and even purses in the shape of Chinese-food cartons. ✉ *284 Mulberry St.*, ☎ *212/965–8910.*

Label. Familiar logos get an extra dose of irony from designer Laura Whitcomb—images of Che Guevera or 007 can show up on stretchy dresses. ✉ *265 Lafayette St.*, ☎ *212/966–7736.*

Makola. Neither splashy nor minimalist, this Italian designer makes bell-shaped skirts (sometimes held by a crinoline) that make your waist look like two hands could span it. ✉ *1045 Madison Ave.*, ☎ *212/772–2272.*

Miu Miu. Responding to the huge appetite for the designs of Miuccia Prada, the company opened its first North American Miu Miu boutique here. You can get the same filmy-fabrics-and-chunky-shoes aesthetic here for a little less money. ✉ *100 Prince St.*, ☎ *212/334–5156.*

Nicole Miller. Known for her silk prints spoofing almost any topic imaginable (French wine, Dalmatians, sports), Nicole Miller also sells some simple dresses. ✉ *780 Madison Ave.*, ☎ *212/288–9779;* ✉ *134 Prince St.*, ☎ *212/343–1362.*

Patricia Field. This store collects the essence of the downtown look—lots of marabou, techno-fabrics, and humor. A hair salon does specialty dye jobs; animal prints are popular. ✉ *10 E. 8th St., between 5th Ave. and University Pl.*, ☎ *212/254–1699.*

Searle. Strung along the East Side, these stores have a devoted following for their coats: pea coats, long wool coats, shearlings, leather, or even fluffy Mongolian lamb. ✉ *1051 3rd Ave., at 62nd St.*, ☎ *212/838–5990;* ✉ *860 Madison Ave., at 70th St.*, ☎ *212/772–2225;* ✉ *1035 Madison Ave., at 79th St.*, ☎ *212/717–4022;* ✉ *605 Madison Ave., at 58th St.*, ☎ *212/753–9021;* ✉ *1124 Madison Ave., at 84th St.*, ☎ *212/988–7318.*

Tocca. This deliciously girly store has soft pastel dresses, often embroidered and/or sweetly A-line. ✉ *161 Mercer St.*, ☎ *212/343–3912.*

Todd Oldham. The cutting-edge designer's SoHo shop is the perfect antidote to too much beige. Compared to the tie-dyed velvet dressing room curtains and crazily tiled floor, the brightly colored clothes can look positively mellow. ✉ *123 Wooster St.*, ☎ *212/219–3531.*

Trash and Vaudeville. Black, white, and electric colors are the focus here—and you never know when you might see Lou Reed buying jeans. ✉ *4 St. Marks Pl., between 2nd and 3rd Aves.*, ☎ *212/982–3590.*

United Colors of Benetton. Benetton's three-level flagship store is in the old Scribner building on 5th Avenue; they periodically host readings in the espresso bar. Besides the colorful, casual clothes, you'll find an extensive sporting goods section. ✉ *597 5th Ave., at 48th St.*, ☎ *212/317–2501;* ✉ *805 Lexington Ave., at 62nd St.*, ☎ *212/752–5283.*

Vivienne Tam. Tam's playful touch with familiar Asian images is everywhere: Chinese dragons crawl across T-shirts, embroidered flowers and koi fish spill down shifts, and the Buddha smiles unperturbably from gauzy dresses. ✉ *99 Greene St.*, ☎ *212/966–2398.*

LINGERIE

Joovay. This tiny store has underwear from floor to ceiling: bras by Rigby & Peller, Mystère, and Natori, chemises, and bathrobes. ✉ *436 W. Broadway*, ☎ *212/431–6386.*

La Perla. The sizing is a little unusual—using 1, 2, 3, and so on instead of cup sizes—but they'll be happy to measure you. The silk and lace underwear, shapers, and nightwear are so sophisticated they've inspired a book. ✉ *777 Madison Ave.*, ☎ *212/570–0050.*

La Petite Coquette. Among the signed photos on the walls is one of ultimate authority—from Frederique, longtime Victoria's Secret model. The store's own line of silk slips, camisoles, and other underpinnings comes in a rainbow of colors. ✉ *52 University Pl., between 9th and 10th Sts.*, ☎ *212/473–2478.*

Le Corset. This lovely boutique naturally stocks its namesake. ✉ *80 Thompson St.*, ☎ *212/334–4936.*

Women's Shoes

For dressy, expensive footwear, Madison Avenue is always a good bet. But 8th Street between 5th and 6th avenues is what most New Yorkers mean when they refer to Shoe Street; it's crammed with small shoe-storefronts, hawking funky styles from steel-toe boots to outrageous platforms.

Chuckies. The name may be aw-shucks, but the shoes certainly aren't. Designer pumps by Dolce & Gabbana, Sonia Rykiel, and Fendi are uptown, while the downtown store stocks more of Chuckies' own cool, slightly lower-price line (check out the knee-high boots). ✉ *1073 3rd Ave., between 63rd and 64th Sts.,* ☎ *212/593–9898;* ✉ *399 W. Broadway,* ☎ *212/343–1717.*

Joan & David. Somewhat conservative but never dull, these shoes can complement a man-tailored suit (the fall wingtips) or a curvy sundress (the strappy-but-not-too-high-heeled sandals). ✉ *816 Madison Ave.,* ☎ *212/772–3970;* ✉ *104 5th Ave., at 16th St.,* ☎ *212/627–1780.*

Manolo Blahnik. These are, notoriously, some of the most expensive shoes money can buy. They're also devastatingly sexy, with pointed toes, low-cut vamps, and the "spindly heel," which is even narrower than a regular stiletto but supposedly easier to walk in. ✉ *15 W. 55th St.,* ☎ *212/582–3007.*

Maraolo. These mid-price shoes are perfect for business meetings; small wonder midtown is full of them. The West 72nd Street location is a factory outlet, where tidy pumps go for less than the cost of a client lunch. ✉ *782 Lexington Ave., between 60th and 61st Sts.,* ☎ *212/832–8182;* ✉ *551 Madison Ave., at 55th St.,* ☎ *212/308–8793;* ✉ *835 Madison Ave.,* ☎ *212/628–5080;* ✉ *131 W. 72nd St., between Columbus and Amsterdam Aves.,* ☎ *212/787–6550.*

Patrick Cox. With their slightly retro feel, these shoes have become regulars on the club circuit. ✉ *702 Madison Ave.,* ☎ *212/759–3910.*

Peter Fox. Combining old-fashioned lines, such as Louis heels, and modern touches like thin platforms, these shoes defy categorization. The Thompson Street store has an extensive bridal section. ✉ *105 Thompson St.,* ☎ *212/431–7426;* ✉ *806 Madison Ave.,* ☎ *212/744–8340.*

Robert Clergerie. High-price and polished, these shoes are not without their sense of fun. Pick up a pump and you may find an oval or triangular heel. ✉ *681 Madison Ave.,* ☎ *212/207–8600.*

Rockport. After a day of pounding the sidewalk, a stop here may be just what you need. The comfort-first shoes run from athletic to dressy, and you can be fitted for a customized footbed—after a complimentary reflexology foot massage. ✉ *160 Columbus Ave., between 67th and 68th Sts.,* ☎ *212/579–1301.*

Salvatore Ferragamo. Join the ranks of Sophia Loren and the late Audrey Hepburn as a Ferragamo customer. Sometimes you'll find reinventions of the designer's most distinctive styles, such as his scalloped heel. ✉ *661 5th Ave.,* ☎ *212/759–3822.*

Sigerson Morrison. The details make these shoes—like the just-right T-straps, small buckles, or interesting two-tones. Prices hover around $200. ✉ *242 Mott St.,*☎ *212/219–3893.*

Unisa. Unisa is quick to pick up a trend and price it reasonably; most pumps, loafers, slides, and sandals are less than $60. ✉ *701 Madison Ave.,* ☎ *212/753–7474.*

Secondhand Shops

Thrift Shops

The thrift shops listed below are run for charity; the closet-cleanings of affluent New Yorkers often result in high-quality donations. Hours are limited, so call ahead.

Council Thrift Shop. ✉ *246 E. 84th St.,* ☎ *212/439–8373.*

Everybody's Thrift Shop. ✉ *261 Park Ave. S, between 20th and 21st Sts.,* ☎ *212/674–4298.*

Housing Works Thrift Shop. These shops benefit housing services for people with AIDS. ✉ *143 W. 17th St., between 6th and 7th Aves.,* ☎ *212/366–0820;* ✉ *202 E. 77th St., at 3rd Ave.,* ☎ *212/772–8461;* ✉ *307 Columbus Ave., between 74th and 75th Sts.,* ☎ *212/579–7566.*

Irvington Institute for Medical Research Thrift Shop. ✉ *1534 2nd Ave., at 80th St.,* ☎ *212/879–4555.*

Memorial Sloan-Kettering Cancer Center Thrift Shop. ✉ *1440 3rd Ave., between 81st and 82nd Sts.,* ☎ *212/535–1250.*

Vintage and Consignment Clothing

Alice Underground. Subterranean no longer, Alice now has what almost all vintage-clothing stores lack—elbow room. Staples include cashmere sweaters ($45–$85), jeans, and the store's own line of bowling shirts. ✉ *481 Broadway,* ☎ *212/431–9067.*

Cheap Jack's. Three floors are jammed with almost everything you could wish for: track suits, bomber jackets, early '80s madras shirts, beaded sweaters, and fur-trimmed wool ladies' suits with the eau-de-mothball stamp of authenticity. Sometimes, though, Jack's not so cheap. ✉ *841 Broadway, between 13th and 14th Sts.,* ☎ *212/777–9564.*

The 1909 Company. There are excellent picks here, all for women—a special display case holds the Gucci and Pucci, while the racks have '60s suits in great condition. ✉ *63 Thompson St.,* ☎ *212/343–1658.*

Out of Our Closet. A godsend for couture seekers, this consignment shop is a sure source for real finds: last season's Dolce & Gabbana, Jil Sander suits, Missoni pants (about $250), or a Matsuda men's jacket (around $300), plus a small assortment of shoes, accessories, and jewelry. ✉ *136 W. 18th St. between 6th and 7th Aves.,* ☎ *212/633–6965.*

Screaming Mimi's. Vintage '60s and '70s clothes and retro-wear include everything from lingerie to soccer shirts to prom dresses. ✉ *382 Lafayette St., between 4th and Great Jones Sts.,* ☎ *212/677–6464.*

Auctions

New York is one of the world's major auctioning centers, where royal accoutrements, ancient art, and pop-culture memorabilia all have their moment on the block. Look for announcements in the *New York Times,* or in the weekly magazines *Time Out New York* and *New York.* If you plan to raise a paddle, be sure to attend the sale preview and review the catalog for price estimates.

MAJOR HOUSES

Christie's (✉ 502 Park Ave., at 59th St., ☎ 212/546–1000) has more than 200 years of formidable history behind it. British born-and-bred Christie has presided over the high-profile auctions of the late Princess Diana's gowns and the phenomenal Ganz Collection of 20th-century art. Special departments are devoted to such non-fine-art valuables as wine, cars, and cameras. **Christie's East** (✉ 219 E. 67th St., ☎ 212/606–0400) is a less extravagant branch.

Sotheby's. Established in London more than 250 years ago, Sotheby's is now American-run, and has a slightly sleeker aura than its arch-competitor, Christie's. It has recently sold off the effects of the Duke and Duchess of Windsor, the collection of Leonard Bernstein, and "Sue," the largest and most complete *Tyrannosaurus rex* skeleton ever unearthed. Collectibles such as wine, vintage cars, and animation art have their own departments. Their **Arcade,** at the same address, handles more affordable selections. ✉ *1334 York Ave., at 72nd St.,* ☎ *212/606–7000.*

SMALLER HOUSES

Guernsey's. This is a great source for modern memorabilia and collections; one recent auction put up hundreds of items that belonged to

JFK. ✉ *108 E. 73rd St., between Park and Lexington Aves.,* ☎ *212/794–2280.*

Swann Galleries. Swann specializes in works on paper—letters, photographs, antiquarian books, and the like. ✉ *104 E. 25th St., between Park and Lexington Aves., 6th floor,* ☎ *212/254–4710.*

Tepper Galleries. General estate collections are sold here every other Saturday, with previews given the Friday before. ✉ *110 E. 25th St., between Park and Lexington Aves.,* ☎ *212/677–5300.*

William Doyle Galleries. Having built its reputation on furniture and decorative arts, William Doyle has reached into celebrity estates (Bette Davis, James Cagney) and on-site auctions (items from the Russian Tea Room). In 1998 the house allied itself with Bonhams, London. ✉ *175 E. 87th St., between Lexington and 3rd Aves.,* ☎ *212/427–2730.*

Flea Markets

The season runs from March or April through November or December at most of these markets in school playgrounds and parking lots.

Annex Antiques Fair and Flea Market. It can be more miss than hit, but it's open weekends year-round. ✉ *6th Ave. at 26th St.,* ☎ *212/243–5343.*

The Garage. The newest flea market in town, this one is indoors in a 23,000-square-ft, two-story former parking garage and is open weekends year-round. ✉ *112 W. 25th St., between 6th and 7th Aves.,* ☎ *212/647–0707.*

Green Flea. Green Flea runs the P.S. 183 market on Saturday, and the I.S. 44 market on Sunday. ✉ *I.S. 44 Market: Columbus Ave. at 77th St.,* ☎ *212/721–0900 evenings;* ✉ *P.S. 183 Market: E. 67th St. and York Ave.*

11 Portrait of New York City

Books and Videos

BOOKS AND VIDEOS

Memoirs

Some of the best full-length accounts are *Christopher Morley's New York,* a mid-1920s reminiscence; *Walker in the City,* by Alfred Kazin; and *Apple of My Eye,* a 1978 recollection of writing a New York guidebook, by Helene Hanff. Dan Wakefield recalls his early literary days in *New York in the 50s. Back Where I Came From* brings together essays on the city that A. J. Liebling wrote for the *New Yorker. Up in the Old Hotel* is a collection of stories by another *New Yorker* writer, Joseph Mitchell, who etches memorable portraits of several colorful city characters. Other literary memoirs include *New York Days,* by Willie Morris, and *Manhattan When I Was Young,* by Mary Cantwell. And don't forget E. B. White's excellent 1949 essay "Here Is New York," which can be found in many New York anthologies.

History and Current Affairs

For a witty early history of New York, turn to the classic *Knickerbocker's History of New York,* by Washington Irving. The heavily illustrated *Columbia Historical Portrait of New York,* by John Kouwenhoven, provides a good introduction to the city. Another profusely illustrated history of the metropolis is Eric Homberger's *The Historical Atlas of New York City. You Must Remember This,* by Jeff Kisseloff, is an oral history of ordinary New Yorkers early in this century.

Fiorello H. La Guardia and the Making of Modern New York, by Thomas Kessner, is a biography of the depression-era mayor. Robert Caro's Pulitzer Prize–winning *The Power Broker* relates the story of parks commissioner Robert Moses. In *Prince of the City,* Robert Daley covers New York police corruption. Highly critical accounts of city politics of the '70s and '80s can be found in *The Streets Were Paved with Gold,* by New Yorker writer Ken Auletta; *The Rise and Fall of New York City,* by Roger Star; *Imperial City,* by Geoffrey Moorhouse; and *City for Sale,* by Jack Newfield and Wayne Barrett. *A License to Steal,* by Benjamin J. Stein, concerns Wall Street's Michael Milken, as does *Den of Thieves,* by James B. Stewart.

For Theater Lovers

Theater lovers will want to look at *Act One,* the autobiography of playwright Moss Hart; *The Season,* by William Goldman; David Mamet's *The Cabin;* and Neil Simon's *Rewrites. From Manet to Manhattan,* by Peter Watson, explores the city's art world. *Literary New York,* by Susan Edmiston and Linda D. Cirino, traces the haunts of famous writers. Shaun O'Connell's *Remarkable, Unspeakable New York, A Literary History* discusses writers who wrote about the city. *The Heart of the World,* by Nik Cohn, is a vivid block-by-block account of the high- and lowlife of Broadway.

Architecture

AIA Guide to New York City, by Elliot Willensky and Norval White, is the definitive guide to the city's architectural styles; Paul Goldberger's *The City Observed* describes Manhattan building by building.

Fiction

Many writers have set their fiction here. Jack Finney's *Time and Again* is a delightful time-travel story illustrated with 19th-century photos; *Winter's Tale,* by Mark Helprin, uses surreal fantasy to create a portrait of New York's past. Novels set in 19th-century New York include Henry James's *Washington Square,* Edith Wharton's *The Age of Innocence* (also available as an audio book), Stephen Crane's *Maggie, A Girl of the Streets,* and two more recent works, *The Alienist,* by Caleb Carr, and *The Waterworks,* by E. L. Doctorow (both available as audio books). O. Henry's short stories depict the early years of this century, while Damon Runyon's are set in the raffish underworld of the 1930s and 1940s. F. Scott Fitzgerald (*The Beautiful and the Damned*), John Dos Passos (*Manhattan Transfer*), John O'Hara (*Butterfield 8*), and Mary McCarthy (*The Group*) all wrote about this city. J. D. Salinger's *Catcher in the Rye* partly takes place here, as does Thomas Pynchon's *V.* Truman Capote's 1958 novella

Breakfast at Tiffany's is a favorite of many New Yorkers.

John Cheever, Bernard Malamud, Grace Paley, and Isaac Bashevis Singer have written many short stories celebrating New York and its inhabitants. More current New York novels include *Bonfire of the Vanities,* by Tom Wolfe (also available as an audio book); *The Mambo Kings Play Songs of Love,* by Oscar Hijuelos; *The New York Trilogy,* by Paul Auster; and *People Like Us,* by Dominick Dunne.

African-American and Jewish Interest

The black experience in Harlem and New York City has been chronicled in Ralph Ellison's *Invisible Man,* James Baldwin's *Go Tell It on the Mountain,* and Claude Brown's *Manchild in the Promised Land.* For a portrait of 1920s Harlem, try *When Harlem Was in Vogue,* by David Levering Lewis. The history of New York's Jewish population can be traced in such books as *World of Our Fathers,* by Irving Howe; *Call It Sleep,* by Henry Roth; *The Promise,* by Chaim Potok; and *Our Crowd,* by Stephen Birmingham.

Mysteries

Mysteries set in New York City range from Dashiell Hammett's urbane 1933 novel *The Thin Man* to Rex Stout's series of Nero Wolfe mysteries. More recent picks include *While My Pretty One Sleeps,* by Mary Higgins Clark; *Greenwich Killing Time,* by Kinky Friedman; *Dead Air,* by Mike Lupica; and *Unorthodox Practices,* by Marissa Piesman.

Suggested Videos

Perhaps the quintessential New York City movie is *Breakfast at Tiffany's* (1961), directed by Blake Edwards and based on Truman Capote's novella. *On the Town* (1949) stars Gene Kelly and Frank Sinatra as sailors on a 24-hour leave.

Filmmaker Woody Allen has filmed almost all his movies in Manhattan. *Annie Hall* (1977), *Manhattan* (1979), *Broadway Danny Rose* (1985), *Hannah and Her Sisters* (1987), *Another Woman* (1988), *Crimes and Misdemeanors* (1989), *Alice* (1990), *Manhattan Murder Mystery* (1993), *Bullets over Broadway* (1994), *Mighty Aphrodite* (1995), and *Everyone Says I Love You* (1996) are a few.

Director Martin Scorsese has made some of his best films in New York. *Mean Streets* (1973) and *Taxi Driver* (1976), both starring Robert De Niro and Harvey Keitel, show a darker side of the city.

Sidney Lumet's films often deal with misfits and police corruption. Look for *Serpico* (1973) and *Dog Day Afternoon* (1975), both starring Al Pacino, *Prince of the City* (1981), *Q&A* (1990), and *Night Falls on Manhattan* (1997).

Some of director Paul Mazursky's most entertaining films have New York settings: *Next Stop, Greenwich Village* (1976), *An Unmarried Woman* (1978), *Moscow on the Hudson* (1984), and *Enemies, A Love Story* (1989), based on the novel by Isaac Bashevis Singer.

Neil Simon films with city locations include *Barefoot in the Park* (1967), *The Odd Couple* (1968), *The Sunshine Boys* (1975), *The Goodbye Girl* (1977), and *Brighton Beach Memoirs* (1986).

Joan Micklin Silver portrays the Lower East Side in different eras in *Hester Street* (1975) and *Crossing Delancey* (1988). For a look at the African-American experience in Manhattan and Brooklyn, try the films of Spike Lee, including: *She's Gotta Have It* (1988), *Do the Right Thing* (1990), *Jungle Fever* (1991), and *Crooklyn* (1994). *I Like It Like That* (1994), directed by Darnell Martin, deals with a Latino woman in the Bronx.

Other New York City–set movies include *Sweet Smell of Success* (1957), *Love with the Proper Stranger* (1963), *A Thousand Clowns* (1965), *Up the Down Staircase* (1967), *Wait Until Dark* (1967), *Midnight Cowboy* (1969), *Kramer vs. Kramer* (1979), *Fame* (1980), *Tootsie* (1982), *Moonstruck* (1987), *New York Stories* (1989), *True Believer* (1989), *Sea of Love* (1989), *Metropolitan* (1990), *Night and the City* (1992), *Household Saints* (1993), *A Bronx Tale* (1993), *Little Odessa* (1994), *City Hall* (1996), *Smoke* (1996), *Walking and Talking* (1996), *Ransom* (1996), *Basquiat* (1996), *The First Wives Club* (1996), *Sleepers* (1996), *The Mirror Has Two Faces* (1996), *One Fine Day* (1996), *Donnie Brasco* (1997), and *The Devil's Own* (1997).

INDEX

✕ = restaurant, 🏨 = hotel